THE ENCYCLOPEDIA OF
WEAPONS
FROM WORLD WAR II TO THE PRESENT DAY

GENERAL EDITOR:
CHRIS BISHOP

THUNDER BAY
P·R·E·S·S
San Diego, California

Thunder Bay Press
An imprint of the Advantage Publishers Group
5880 Oberlin Drive, San Diego, CA 92121-4794
www.thunderbaybooks.com

All notations of errors or omissions should be addressed to Thunder Bay Press,
Editorial Department, at the above address. All other correspondence (author inquiries,
permissions) concerning the content of this book should be addressed to
Amber Books Ltd., Bradley's Close, 74–77 White Lion Street, London N1 9PF,
United Kingdom. www.amberbooks.co.uk.

ISBN-13: 978-1-59223-629-9
ISBN-10: 1-59223-629-4

Library of Congress Cataloging-in-Publication Data available upon request.

Printed in Singapore

1 2 3 4 5 10 09 08 07 06

PICTURE CREDITS
All photographs and illustrations provided by Art-Tech/Aerospace Publishing,
except the following:
8–9: U.S. Department of Defense

CONTENTS

The MLRS (Multiple Launch Rocket System) has become an integral part of modern warfare. The MLRS can operate with only two crew, and it is possible for one man to fire and load the system alone.

Introduction

There have been few advances in military technology which changed history, but the development of gunpowder and the weapons to use it is definitely at the top of the list. Gunpowder was invented in China, but its first application in weapons came in Europe in the 14th Century.

INITIALLY THERE WAS NO DIFFERENCE other than size between what would now be called artillery and weapons that could be described as small arms. Artillery pieces were large and heavy, while small arms could be carried and fired by one or two men.

Full-power battle rifles have been superseded by assault rifles, but their long range makes them ideal for snipers. The M21 rifle still in service with the US Army is a more accurate version of the M14 rifle.

For much of their existence, most guns were simple tubes into which gunpowder and a projectile was placed, usually loaded through the muzzle. The other essential requirement was some means of igniting the powder and so firing the shot. The earliest guns were fired by applying a slow-match to a small hole drilled into the weapon, and for five hundred years artillery continued to be fired in this way. More sophisticated firing locks were developed for small

arms, however, culminating in the flintlock and the percussion cap.

Small Arms

In the 19th Century, however, the effects of the industrial revolution began to be felt, initially with small arms. The development of the metal cartridge case and more efficient metallurgy meant that in the middle of the century the first effective breech-loading, magazine-fed rifles appeared, and in the shape of rifles like the

Spencer and Henry, and pistols like the Colt revolver, they played their part in the American Civil War. However, most of the mass of infantry employed on each side were still equipped with smoothbore, muzzle-loading muskets little different than those that had been used at Lützen in the 30 Years War or at Blenheim in 1704.

The first true modern military rifles were the Dreyse Needle Gun and the Chassepot rifle used in the Franco-Prussian War. These

set the pattern for the bolt-action, magazine-fed infantry rifles for the next 80 years. Soon these characteristics were combined with the new, smokeless nitro-cellulose propellant in place of the old black powder, and by the beginning of the 20th Century most infantrymen were carrying weapons capable of shooting accurately out to 1000 metres or more.

Handguns divided into two main types. The revolver matured early, and improvements were largely a matter of better ammunition and manufacture. However, in the 1890s the first practical magazine-fed self-loading pistols entered service. These used a variety of methods to harness the explosive force of firing a round to re-cock the pistol. Not as strong as the revolver, the self-loading or semi-automatic pistol could be fired much more quickly.

The second half of the 19th Century also saw the development of the first true rapid-fire weapons. Early experiments with hand-cranked multi-barrel guns like the Gatling were followed by the true machine gun, developed by innovators like Hiram Maxim. These used either recoil or the gas generated in firing a cartridge to cock a weapon automatically, giving a single machine gunner the firepower of an entire infantry platoon.

Artillery Pieces
Technology also revolutionised the world of artillery. Although simple muzzle loaders continued to have a limited place on the battlefield, in the shape of the infantry mortar, artillery pieces had changed out of all recognition by 1900. The simple muzzle-loader had been dominant until the American Civil War in the 1860s, but in the following years new guns were developed with hydraulic recoil absorbing systems which made the weapons far easier to control on firing. Powerful new smokeless propellants had as marked an effect on artillery as they had on rifles, and improved metallurgy meant that gun barrels could sustain much higher pressures. As a result, the range of standard artillery pieces increased dramatically.

Ammunition also improved. The adoption of single-piece rounds combining projectile and propellant into a single metallic cartridge case made loading much easier, and combined with the interrupted screw system for locking the breech they greatly increased the rate of fire for guns.

Artillery began to fall into two main categories. The word gun was applied specifically to high-velocity pieces firing unitary ammunition at relatively low elevations. These were

Although most front-line artillery is now based on self-propelled chassis, there is still a place for towed artillery. The US Army's M119 howitzer is based on the British 105-mm Light Gun. It provides direct and indirect fire support to light infantry units, and provides a maximum of firepower with a minimum of combat weight.

complemented by the howitzer, which used separate loading projectiles and propellants. Howitzers were designed to fire at high elevations, bringing plunging fire down on enemy strongpoints and fortifications. Range was adjusted by varying the amount of propellant charge used.

In the first decade of the 20th Century the change from weapons developed from Renaissance models to fully modern equipment was complete. They were soon put to the test in the Great War.

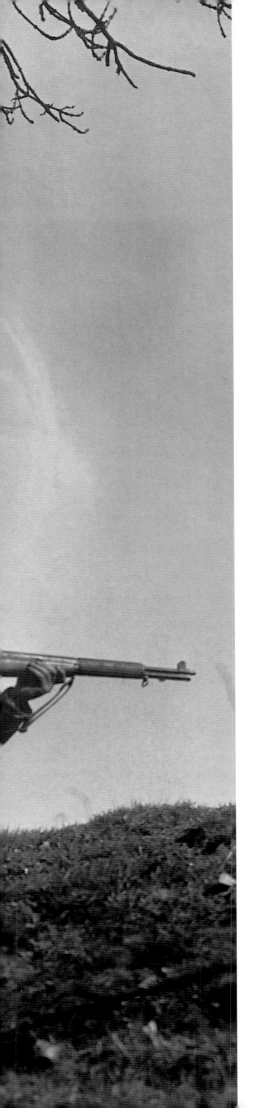

World War II Small Arms

The majority of the armies that entered World War II were equipped with personal weapons that dated back to the Great War or before. However, infantry firearms were about to undergo a significant evolution.

The sub-machine gun, born out of the need for easily handled firepower in the trenches, had grown in importance in the interwar years. Practical self-loading rifles were also entering service. Combat experience would show that most rifles were overpowered, and by the end of the war the first true assault rifles had made their combat debuts.

Possibly the most important innovation was the German development of the general purpose machine gun. Light enough to be carried by one man in an infantry squad, it could be used in the direct support role as well as from a tripod to provide indirect supporting fire, combining the capabilities of the light and heavy machine gun in a single weapon.

Left: Infantrymen of the 3rd US Army engage German positions across the Rhine near Mannheim in March 1945. They are armed with the M1 Garand rifle, which although not the first self-loading infantry weapon was the first to be standard issue with any army.

Enfield No. 2 Mk 1 and Webley Mk 4 Pistols

During World War I the standard British service pistol was the 0.455-in (11.56-mm) Webley revolver in one or other of its forms. These were very effective weapons for the type of close-quarter fighting that typified the trench combat of that war. However, their weight and bulk made the pistols notably difficult to handle correctly and effectively, unless a great deal of training had been provided and then followed by constant practice, both of them commodities that were in short supply at the time.

After 1919 the British army decided that a smaller pistol firing a heavy 0.38-in (9.65-mm) round would be just as effective as the larger-calibre weapon but would offer the advantages of being easier to handle and of requiring less training. As a result Webley and Scott, which up to that time had been pistol manufacturer of a virtually official status for the British armed forces, took its 0.455-in (11.56-mm) revolver, scaled it down and offered the result to the military.

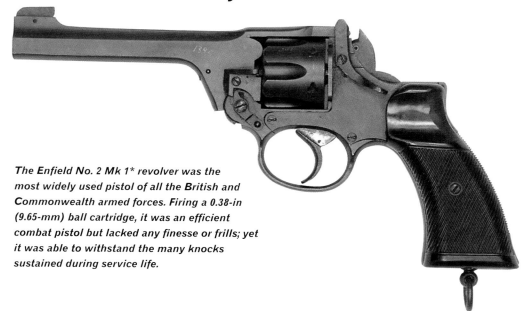

The Enfield No. 2 Mk 1* revolver was the most widely used pistol of all the British and Commonwealth armed forces. Firing a 0.38-in (9.65-mm) ball cartridge, it was an efficient combat pistol but lacked any finesse or frills; yet it was able to withstand the many knocks sustained during service life.

Double-action Enfield

To the company's chagrin, the military simply took the design, made a few minor alterations and placed the result in production as an 'official' government design produced at the Royal Small Arms Factory at Enfield Lock in Middlesex. This procedure took time, for Webley and Scott offered its design in 1923 and Enfield Lock took over the design in 1926. Webley and

Scott was somewhat nonplussed at the course of events but proceeded to market its 0.38-in (9.65-mm) revolver, known as the **Webley Mk 4**, all over the world with limited success.

The Enfield product became the **Pistol, Revolver, No. 2 Mk 1.** In service the pistol proved to be sound and effective. However,

the increasing degree of mechanisation in this period meant that large numbers of these pistols were issued to the crews of tanks and other mechanised equipments, who rapidly made the unfortunate discovery that the long hammer spur had a tendency to catch on the many internal fittings of tanks and other vehicles with

what could be nasty results. This led to a redesign in which the Enfield pistol had its hammer spur removed altogether and its trigger mechanism lightened to enable the weapon to be fired only as a double-action pistol. This became the **Pistol, Revolver, No. 2 Mk 1***, and existing Mk 1 weapons were modified to the new standard.

An airborne soldier stands guard on a house in Holland during Operation Market Garden. The pistol is an Enfield No. 2 Mk 1* with the hammer spur removed to prevent snagging on clothing or within the close confines of vehicles or aircraft. These pistols were issued to airborne soldiers such as glider pilots.

The double action made the pistol very difficult to use accurately at all except minimal range, but that was a matter of little consequence.

World War II service

Webley and Scott re-entered the scene during World War II, when delivery of the Enfield pistol was too slow to meet ever-expanding demand. Thus the Webley Mk 4 was ordered to eke out supplies, and Webley and Scott went on to supply thousands of its design to the British army after all. The two pistols were virtually identical in appearance, but unfortunately there were enough minor differences between the two types to prevent interchangeability of parts.

Wartime service

Both pistols saw extensive use between 1939–45, and although the Enfield revolvers (there was also a **Pistol, Revolver, No. 2 Mk 1**** embodying wartime production expedients such as

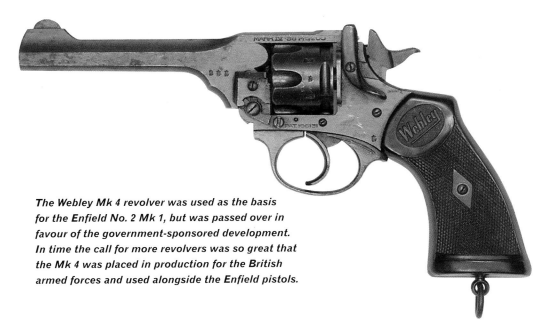

The Webley Mk 4 revolver was used as the basis for the Enfield No. 2 Mk 1, but was passed over in favour of the government-sponsored development. In time the call for more revolvers was so great that the Mk 4 was placed in production for the British armed forces and used alongside the Enfield pistols.

the elimination of the hammer safety stop) were the official standard pistols, the Webley Mk 4 was just as widely used among British and Commonwealth armed forces. Both remained in service until the 1960s, and were still encountered as service pistols up until the 1980s.

SPECIFICATION	
Pistol, Revolver, No. 2 Mk 1	**Webley Mk 4**
Cartridge: 0.38-in (9.65-mm) SAA ball	**Cartridge:** 0.38-in (9.65-mm) SAA ball
Length overall: 260 mm (10.25 in)	**Length overall:** 267 mm (10.5 in)
Length of barrel: 127 mm (5 in)	**Length of barrel:** 127 mm (5 in)
Weight: 0.767 kg (1.7 lb)	**Weight:** 0.767 kg (1.7 lb)
Muzzle velocity: 183 m (600 ft) per second	**Muzzle velocity:** 183 m (600 ft) per second
Chamber capacity: 6 rounds	**Chamber capacity:** 6 rounds

Tokarev TT-33 Pistol

The standard pistol of the Russian forces at the beginning of the 20th century and therefore inherited by the Soviet forces after the revolution of 1917, was the Nagant Model 1895G. This was a perfectly orthodox 7.62-mm (0.3-in) revolver with a seven-round cylinder. The weapon was of Belgian design, and although initially manufactured at Liège, was later made by the arsenal at Tula after its adoption for service with the Tsarist forces.

Standard model

The first automatic pistol adopted for major employment by the Soviet forces was designed by Fyedor V. Tokarev and manufactured at Tula, which explains the use of the TT prefix in this weapon's designation. Standardised in 1930, as suggested by the numerical part of its designation, this weapon was the **TT-30**, but not many examples of this early weapon

had been produced before a modified design known as the **TT-33** succeeded it in production during 1933. This TT-33 pistol was then adopted as the standard pistol in succession to the Nagant. In the event the TT-33 did not wholly replace the reliable Nagant until after the 1945 end of the 'Great Patriotic War', as the Soviets called their involvement in World War II. This was largely as a result of the fact that the revolver, which had been produced in very large numbers, was still a completely reliable and sturdy weapon under the rough active service conditions of the various fronts on which the Soviet forces fought from the time of the Russian Civil War onward.

Soviet copy

Like the preceding TT-30, the TT-33 semi-automatic pistol was created as basically a Soviet version of the Colt-Browning

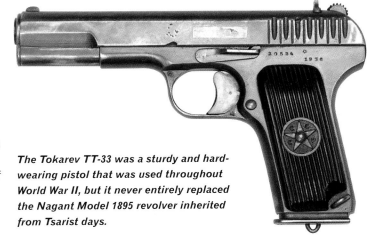

The Tokarev TT-33 was a sturdy and hard-wearing pistol that was used throughout World War II, but it never entirely replaced the Nagant Model 1895 revolver inherited from Tsarist days.

SPECIFICATION	
TT-33	**Weight:** 0.83 kg (1.83 lb)
Cartridge: 7.62-mm (0.3-in) Type P (M30)	**Muzzle velocity:** 420 m (1,380 ft) per second
Length overall: 196 mm (7.68 in)	**Magazine:** 8-round box
Length of barrel: 116 mm (4.57 in)	

pistols with a recoil-operated action, and used the swinging-link system of operation employed in the Americans' M1911 pistol designed as a 'man-stopper' for service with the US Army. The TT-33 was somewhat unusual, however, in having the

hammer and its spring and other components combined as a single removable module fitting into the rear edge of the butt. However, the ever-practical Soviet designers introduced several other slight alterations (including locking lugs all round the barrel

rather than just above it) that made the mechanism easier to produce and easier to maintain under field conditions, and production even went to the length of machining the vulnerable magazine feed lips into the main receiver to prevent damage and subsequent misfeeds if and when a slightly distorted magazine was loaded into the weapon. The result was a practical and sturdy weapon that, like all the best items of Soviet equipment, consistently proved itself able to absorb a surprising amount of hard use and still remain functional.

Captured weaponry

The Germans made extensive use of captured weapons in World War II, and among this source of supply was a vast quantity of small arms seized during the initially successful days of Germany's advance into the Soviet Union as far to the east as Moscow. Examples of

the TT-30 and TT-33 were issued to German army units, and also to field formations of the German air force, with the designation **Pistole 615(r)**. This German use was facilitated by the fact that the Soviet 7.62-mm Model 1930 Type P cartridge was in all essentials identical to the German 7.63-mm Mauser cartridge, which could therefore be used in the two Soviet pistols.

By 1945 the TT-33 had virtually replaced the Nagant revolver in service, and as Soviet influence spread over Europe and elsewhere, so did production and employment of the TT-33. Thus the TT-33 may be found in a variety of basically similar forms, one of which is the Chinese **Type 51**. Poland also produced the TT-33 for their own use and for export to East Germany and to Czechoslovakia. Yugoslavia manufactured the TT-33 for local and export service as the **M65**, while North Korea had its own variant in the form of the **M68**.

The Soviet Tokarev TT-33 in action in a well-posed propaganda photograph dating from about 1944. The officer is leading a section of assault infantry and has his pistol on the end of the usual lanyard. Snipers on all sides came to recognise such 'pistol wavers' as prime targets.

The most prolific producer of the TT-33 was Hungary, which rejigged the design in several respects and recalibred it for the 9-mm Parabellum cartridge. The result was known as the **Model 48** or, in its export form for Egypt, the **Tikagypt** that was issued widely to the local police forces.

Enter the Makarov

The TT-33 was replaced in first-line Soviet service by the Makarov PM blowback-operated semi-automatic pistol. Entering service in 1952 with a weight of 0.73 kg (1.61 lb) and ammunition feed from an eight-round detachable box magazine in the butt, the PM is chambered for the 9-mm Makarov cartridge created specifically to yield

the maximum performance from a pistol firing from an unlocked breech.

The numbers of TT-33 pistols made and the type's ready availability to Soviet satellites and clients ensured that the type enjoyed a long period of service: the weapon was crudely finished by Western standards, but this proved to be of little significance to third world countries who prefered reliability and low cost to the 'flash factor' of more modern Western weapons.

Despite the introduction of the Makarov, many second-line and militia units within the Warsaw Pact organisation retained the TT-33 for many years after its offical replacement in first-line service.

P 08 (Luger) Pistol

The pistol that is now generally, but misleadingly, known just as the **Luger** has its design origins in an automatic pistol design first produced in 1893 by one Hugo Borchardt. Georg Luger further developed this design to create the weapon that bears his name. The first Luger semi-automatic pistols were manufactured to fire a 7.65-mm (0.301-in) bottle-necked cartridge, and were first adopted by the Swiss army in 1900. Eventually, well over two million examples were produced by various manufacturers in at least 35 main variants.

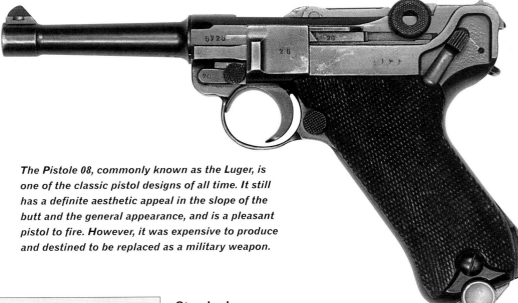

The Pistole 08, commonly known as the Luger, is one of the classic pistol designs of all time. It still has a definite aesthetic appeal in the slope of the butt and the general appearance, and is a pleasant pistol to fire. However, it was expensive to produce and destined to be replaced as a military weapon.

Standard weapon

The **Pistole 08** (or **P 08**) was one of the main variants. After the German navy had adopted a Luger pistol in 1904, the German army adopted a Luger pistol in 1908, and the weapon remained the standard German service pistol into the late 1930s. The Luger was produced in a number of calibres, but the primary calibre of the P 08 is 9 mm (0.354 in), and the 9-mm Parabellum cartridge was developed specifically for the Luger pistol in 1902. It should be noted, however, that versions were also made in 7.65-mm calibre.

The operating cycle of the P 08 is as follows. When the trigger is pulled, a connecting piece forces back a pin that drives out a spring-retaining lock, which allows the striker to move forward and fire the chambered cartridge. As the bullet passes down the barrel, the barrel and the recoiling mechanism, locked together, move back about 12.5 mm (0.49 in). Behind the breech block is a toggle joint with its rear fixed by a sturdy pin to the barrel extension. As the breech pressure drops to a safe level, the toggle joint's central element reaches a sloping section of the frame, breaking the toggle joint's straight line upward in exactly the same way that a knee bends, but still drawing the breech block straight back in the barrel extension's guide.

Coil spring

As the action is opened, a short coil spring, which is located inside the breech block and whose function it is to drive the firing pin, is compressed and caught by the sear. The extractor in the upper part of the breech block's face pulls back the spent cartridge case to strike an ejector piece and be ejected out of the weapon, whereupon a small coil spring pushes the extractor back into place.

As the toggle joint buckles upward, a hook lever (hanging from its pin and hooked under claws that are connected to the recoil spring in the grip) compresses the recoil spring. The magazine spring lifts a fresh cartridge into alignment with the breech block. The compressed recoil spring can now pull down

The P 08 in service with a section of house-clearing infantry during the early stages of the advance into the USSR during 1941. The soldier with the pistol is armed with Stielgranate 35 grenades and is festooned with ammunition belts for the section MG 34 machine gun.

A StuG III assault gun with a short 75-mm (2.95-in) weapon supports advancing infantry during an attack on the Voronezh front during January 1943. Although the pistol carried by the soldier on the right is blurred, it appears to be a P 08.

against the hook lever, driving down the bent toggle and pushing forward its front lever in a motion that drives the attached breech block straight ahead in its guide and strips the top cartridge from the magazine into the chamber.

The breech block and two toggle levers are now in a straight line with the toggle axis slightly lower than the other axes, locking the action. The sear now connects with the trigger mechanism, the trigger spring driving the trigger into position, and the pistol is ready to fire once more.

Good 'pointability'

The P 08 handles well, is easy to 'point', is usually very well made, and relies on a rather complicated action. In fact it is arguable that this toggle action is basically undesirable in a service pistol. However, the P 08 was replaced in production and service by the P 38 only because it was too demanding in terms of production resources. It was late 1942 before the last 'German' examples came off the production lines, and the P 08 was never wholly replaced by the P 38 in German service. After 1945 the Luger was manufactured for the commercial market.

A truly classic pistol

The standard P 08 had a barrel 103 mm (4.055 in) long, although some variants such as the **P 17 Artillerie** model had a 203-mm (8-in) or longer barrel and a snail-shaped magazine holding 32 rounds rather than the standard eight rounds. However, the P 17 Artillerie was no longer a service weapon by the beginning of World War II in 1939. Luger pistols were among the most prized of all World War I and II trophies, and many still survive today as collector's pieces. The type continues to attract the eye and attention of all pistol buffs throughout the world.

SPECIFICATION	
Pistole 08	(4.055 in)
Cartridge: 9-mm (0.34-in) Parabellum	**Weight:** 0.877 kg (1.92 lb)
	Muzzle velocity: 381 m (1,250 ft) per second
Length overall: 222 mm (8.75 in)	
Length of barrel: 103 mm	**Magazine:** 8-round detachable box

Walther PP & PPK Pistols

The **Walther PP** (Polizei Pistole) was first produced in 1929 and marketed as a semi-automatic police weapon. In the 1930s it was adopted by many uniformed police forces. The PP is a light and handy design with few frills, but it is characterised by a clean overall shaping suiting it for holster carriage. The needs of plain clothes police units led to another model, the **PPK**, in which the designation's final letter indicated Kurz (short) or, according to other sources, Kriminal. The PPK was basically the PP reduced in overall size to enable it to be carried conveniently in a pocket. This reduction process trimmed overall length to 148 mm (5.83 in) and the weight to 0.568 kg (1.25 lb). The magazine had a capacity of six 9-mm (0.354-in) or seven 7.65-mm (0.301-in) rounds.

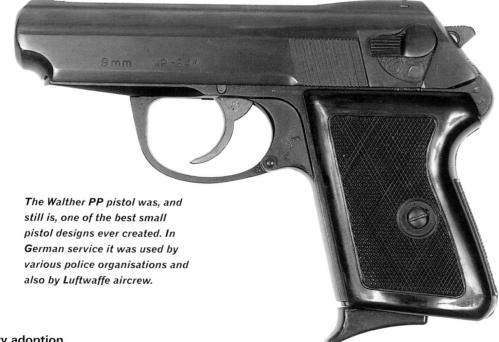

The Walther PP pistol was, and still is, one of the best small pistol designs ever created. In German service it was used by various police organisations and also by Luftwaffe aircrew.

Military adoption

Although intended as weapons for the use of civilian police forces, the PP and the PPK were adopted as military police weapons and, after 1939, were both kept in production for service use. Each model was widely used by the Luftwaffe, was often carried by the men of the many German police organisations, and was used by staff officers as a personal weapon. Both types could also

SPECIFICATION

Walther PP	Walther PPK
Cartridge: 9-mm short (0.354-in ACP), 7.65-mm (0.301-in ACP), 6.35-mm (0.25-in ACP) & 5.58-mm (0.22-in) LR	**Cartridge:** 9-mm short (0.38-in ACP), 7.65-mm (0.32-in ACP), 6.35-mm (0.25-in ACP) & 5.58-mm (0.22-in) LR
Length overall: 173 mm (6.8 in)	**Length overall:** 155 mm (6.1 in)
Length of barrel: 99 mm (3.9 in)	**Length of barrel:** 86 mm (3.39 in)
Weight: 0.682 kg (1.5 lb)	**Weight:** 0.568 kg (1.25 lb)
Muzzle velocity: 290 m (950 ft) per second	**Muzzle velocity:** 280 m (920 ft) per second
Magazine: 8-round box	**Magazine:** 7-round box

be encountered in a range of calibres, the two main calibres being 9-mm Short and 7.65-mm, but versions were produced in the 5.56-mm (0.22-in LR) and 6.35-mm (0.25-in) calibres.

All these variants operated on a straightforward blowback principle, and more than adequate safety arrangements were incorporated. One of these safeties was later widely copied: a block was placed in the way of the firing pin when it moved forward, and was removed only when the trigger was given a definite pull. Another innovation was the provision of a signal pin above the hammer, which protruded when a round was actually in the chamber to provide a positive 'loaded' indication. This feature was omitted from wartime production, in which the general standard of finish was lower. Production resumed soon after 1945 in such countries as France and Turkey. Hungary also adopted the type for a while but production was then resumed once more at Ulm by the parent Walther company.

Manufacture is still mainly for police duties but purely commercial sales are common to pistol shooters who appreciate the many fine points of the basic design.

British use

One small item of interest regarding the PP is that it is now a rarely seen pistol used by the British armed forces as the **XL47E1**. This weapon has been used for the type of undercover operation in which civilian clothing is worn. The weapon was often issued to soldiers of the Ulster Defence Regiment for personal protection.

Walther P 38 Pistol

The **Walther P 38** was developed primarily to replace the P 08, which was an excellent weapon but expensive to produce. After the National Socialist party came to power in Germany in 1933, it decided upon a deliberate programme of military expansion of the type in which the P 08 was only poorly suited. What was wanted at this stage was a pistol that could be produced both quickly and easily, but which nonetheless embodied all the many and various design features (such as a hand-cocked trigger and improved safeties) that were then becoming more common. Walther eventually received the contract for this new pistol in 1938, but only after a long programme of development.

Walther Waffenfabrik had produced its first original automatic pistol design back in 1908 and there followed a string of designs that led to the PP of 1929. The PP had many novel features, but had been created specifically as a police weapon and not a service pistol. Walther

Even today one of the best service pistols available, the Walther P 38 was developed to replace the Luger P 08, but by 1945 had only supplemented it. The pistol had many advanced features including a double-action trigger mechanism.

therefore developed a new semi-automatic weapon known as the AP (Armée Pistole, or army pistol), which did not have the protruding hammer of the PP but was chambered for the 9-mm (0.354-in) Parabellum cartridge. From this came the **HP (Heeres Pistole,** or Army Pistol), which had the overall appearance of the weapon that would become the P 38. But the German army requested the implementation of some small changes to facilitate rapid

production, Walther obliged, and the P 38 was taken into German service use, the HP being kept in production for commercial sales. In the event, Walther was never able to meet demand for the P 38 and the bulk of the HP production also went to the German armed forces.

Excellent pistol

From the beginning, the P 38 was an excellent service pistol which was robust, accurate and hard-wearing. Walther production versions, which were later supplemented by P 38 pistols produced by Mauser and Spreewerke, were always very well finished with shiny black plastic grips and an overall matt black plating. The weapon could

be stripped easily and was well equipped with safety devices, including the hammer safety carried over from the PP along with the 'chamber loaded' indicator pin. It was a well-liked pistol and became a trophy only slightly less prized than the P 08.

In 1957 the P 38 was put back into production for the West German army, this time as the **Pistole 1 (P 1)** with a Dural slide in place of the original steel component. This pistol has enjoyed a long run, and has been adopted by many nations.

SPECIFICATION

Walther P 38	
Cartridge: 9-mm (0.354-in) Parabellum	**Weight:** 0.96 kg (2.12 lb)
Length overall: 219 mm (8.58 in)	**Muzzle velocity:** 350 m (1,150 ft) per second
Length of barrel: 124 mm (4.88 in)	**Magazine:** 8-round box

Pistole Automatique Browning modèle 1910

Automatic pistol

The **Pistole Automatique Browning modèle 1910** is something of an oddity among pistol designs, for although it remained in production virtually non-stop since 1910, it has never been officially adopted as a service weapon. Despite this it has been used widely by many armed forces at one time or another and the basic design has been widely copied and/or plagiarised by other designers.

Pistol design

As the name implies, this blowback-operated automatic pistol was yet another product of the fertile mind of John Moses Browning. Nearly all the modèle 1910 weapons have been produced at the Fabrique Nationale d'Armes de Guerre (commonly known simply as FN) near Liège in Belgium. The reason why this particular pistol should have achieved such

longevity is now not easy to determine, but the overall design is clean enough, with the forward part of the receiver slide around the barrel possessing a tubular appearance. This results from the fact that the recoil spring is wrapped around the barrel itself instead of being situated under or over the barrel as in most other designs of comparable type. This spring is held in place by a bayonet lug around the muzzle, providing the modèle 1910 with another recognition point. Grip and applied safeties are provided.

Variants

The modèle 1910 may be encountered in one of two calibres, either 7.65 mm (0.32 ACP) or 9 mm (0.380 ACP) short. Externally the two variants are identical, and each uses a

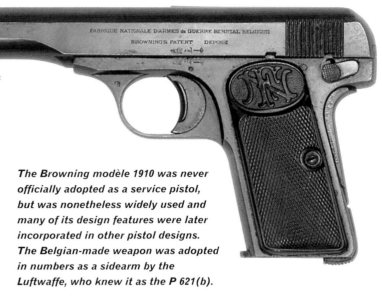

The Browning modèle 1910 was never officially adopted as a service pistol, but was nonetheless widely used and many of its design features were later incorporated in other pistol designs. The Belgian-made weapon was adopted in numbers as a sidearm by the Luftwaffe, who knew it as the P 621(b).

detachable seven-round inline box magazine. As is the case with all other FN products, the standard of manufacture and the finish are excellent, but copies made in such places as Spain lack this quality of finish. The excellent finish was continued with one of the few large-scale production runs for the modèle 1910. This occurred after 1940, when the German forces occupying Belgium required large numbers of pistols.

The modèle 1910 was kept in production to meet this demand, the bulk of this new output being allocated to Luftwaffe aircrew who knew the type as the **Pistole P 621(b)**. Before that the modèle 1910 had been issued in small numbers to the Belgian armed forces, and many other nations obtained the type for limited use. The numbers of modèle 1910s produced must have run into the hundreds of thousands.

SPECIFICATION	
Browning modèle 1910	**Weight:** 0.562 kg (1.24 lb)
Cartridge: 7.65-mm (0.32 ACP) or 9-mm short (0.380 ACP)	**Muzzle velocity:** 299 m (980 ft) per second
Length overall: 152 mm (6 in)	**Magazine:** 7-round box
Length of barrel: 89 mm (3.5 in)	

Pistole Automatique Browning, modèle à Grande Puissance (Browning HP)

9-mm automatic pistol

The **Browning HP** may be regarded as one of the most successful pistol designs ever produced. Not only is it still in widespread service, in numbers that must surely exceed those of all other types combined, but it has also been produced at many locations in many countries.

Into production

It was one of the last weapon designs produced by John Browning before he died in 1925, but it was not until 1935

that the HP was placed in production by FN at Herstal near Liège. From this derives the name which is generally given as the **HP** (High Power) or **Pistole Automatique Browning GP 35 (Grand Puissance modèle 1935)**. Numerous versions may be encountered, but they all fire the standard 9-mm (0.354-in) Parabellum cartridge. Versions exist with both fixed and adjustable rear sights, and some models were produced with a lug on the butt to enable a stock (usually the wooden holster)

to be fitted, allowing the pistol to be fired as a form of carbine. Other versions exist with light alloy receiver slides to reduce the weight.

Two factors that are common to all the numerous Browning HP variants are strength and reliability. Another desirable

feature that has often proved invaluable is the large-capacity box magazine in the butt, which can hold a useful 13 rounds. Despite the width resulting from this, the grip is not too much of a handful, although training and general familiarisation are necessary to enable a firer to

SPECIFICATION	
Browning GP 35	**Weight:** 1.01 kg (2.23 lb)
Cartridge: 9-mm (0.354-in) Parabellum	**Muzzle velocity:** 354 m (1,160 ft) per second
Length overall: 196 mm (7.75 in)	**Magazine:** 13-round box
Length of barrel: 112 mm (4.41 in)	

get the best out of the weapon. The weapon uses a recoil-operated mechanism powered by the blowback forces produced on firing and has an external hammer. In many ways the action can be regarded as the same as that of the Colt M1911 (also a Browning design), but it was adapted to suit production and to take advantage of the experience gained in the design.

Service pistol

Within a few years of the start of production the Browning HP had been adopted as the service pistol of several nations including Belgium, Denmark, Lithuania and Romania. After 1940 production continued, but this time it was for the Germans, who adopted the type as the standard pistol of the Waffen SS, although other arms of the German forces also used the weapon. To the Germans the Browning HP was known as the **Pistole P 620(b)**. The Germans did not have the HP all to themselves, however, for a new production line was opened in Canada by the John Inglis Company of Toronto, and from there the HP was distributed to nearly all the Allied nations as the **Pistol, Browning, FN, 9-mm HP No. 1**, large numbers being sent to China to equip the nationalist forces. After 1945 the type was put back in production at Herstal, and many nations now use the weapon as

The Browning GP 35 has been adopted by so many nations since its first appearance in 1935 that it must now be the most widely used of all pistols. It is remarkably robust, hard-hitting and reliable in use.

their standard pistol. Various commercial models have been developed, and the type has even been adapted to produce a target-shooting model. The British

Army still uses the Browning HP as the **Pistol, Automatic L9Al**. In 2001 the UK MoD announced orders for a further 2,000 L9A1s to add to those already in service.

Liberator M1942 Assassination gun

This very odd little pistol had its origins in the committee rooms of the US Army Joint Psychological Committee, which sold to the Office of Strategic Services the idea of a simple assassination weapon that could be used by anyone in occupied territory without the need for training or familiarisation. The OSS took up the idea and the US Army Ordnance Department then set to and produced drawings. The Guide Lamp Division of the General Motors Corporation was given the task of producing the weapon, and the division took the credit for churning out no less than one million between June and August 1942.

Flare pistol

The 0.45-in (11.43-mm) **Pistol M1942** was provided with the cover name **Flare Pistol M1942**, but it was also known as the

Liberator or the **OSS Pistol**. It was a very simple, even crude device that could fire only a single shot. It was constructed almost entirely of metal stampings and the barrel was a smooth-bore unit. The action was just as simple as the rest of the design: a cocking piece was grasped and pulled to the rear; once back a turn locked it in place as a single M1911 automatic cartridge was loaded, and the cocking piece was then swung back for release as the trigger was pulled. To clear the spent cartridge the cocking piece was once more moved out of the way, and the case was pushed out from the chamber by poking something suitable down the barrel from the muzzle.

One-shot weapon

Each pistol was packed into a clear plastic bag together with 10 rounds, and a set of

instructions in comic strip form provided, without words, enough information for any person finding the package to use the pistol. There was space in the butt to carry five of the rounds provided, but the pistol was virtually a one-shot weapon and had to be used at a minimal range to be effective. Each Liberator pistol cost the American government just $2.40. Exactly how effective it was is now difficult to say, for there seems to be no record of how these numerous pistols were ever employed or where they were distributed. It is known that some were parachuted into occupied Europe, but many more were used in the Far East and in China. The concept was certainly deemed good enough to be revived in 1964 when a much modernised equivalent to the

The diminutive M1942 Liberator was purely and simply an assassination weapon and was produced as cheaply and easily as possible. The barrel was unrifled, there was no spent case ejector, and the mechanism was crude to a degree. However, the weapon proved effective and during World War II was used mainly in the Far East and China.

Liberator, known as the 'Deer Gun', was produced for possible use in Vietnam. Several thousands were made but never issued, maybe because assassination weapons have a tendency to be double-edged.

SPECIFICATION	
M1942 Liberator	**Weight:** 0.454 kg (1 lb)
Cartridge: 0.45-in (11.43-mm) ball M1911	**Muzzle velocity:** 336 m (1,100 ft) per second
Length overall: 140 mm (5.55 in)	**Magazine:** none, but space in butt for five rounds
Length of barrel: 102 mm (4 in)	

Colt M1911 and M1911A1 Automatic pistols

The **Colt M1911** vies with the Browning HP as one of the most successful pistol designs ever produced, for it has been manufactured in millions and is in widespread service all over the world some 90 years after it was first standardised for service in 1911.

Colt-based design

The design had its origins well before then, however, for the weapon was based on a Colt Browning Model 1900 design. This weapon was taken as the basis for a new service pistol required by the US Army to fire a new 0.45-in (11.43-mm) cartridge deemed necessary as the then-standard calibre of 0.38 in (9.65 mm) was considered by many to be too light to stop a charging enemy. The result was a series of trials in 1907, and in 1911 the **Pistol, Automatic, Caliber .45, M1911** was accepted. Production was at first slow, but by 1917 was well

enough under way to equip in part the rapid expansion of the US Army for its new role in France.

Production changes

As the result of that battle experience it was decided to make some production changes to the basic design, and this led to the **M1911A1**. The changes were not extensive, being confined to items such as the grip safety configuration, the hammer spur outline and the mainspring housing.

Overall the design and operation changed only little. The basic method of operation remained the same, and this mechanism is one of the

This pistol is the M1911 (the M1911A1 had several detail changes), and with its later variant was the standard US Army service pistol for more than 80 years. Firing a 0.45-in (11.43) ball round, it is still a powerful man-stopper, but is a bit of a handful to fire and requires training to use to its full potential. In US Army service, the weapons have since been replaced by the licence-built Beretta 9-mm Pistol M9.

strongest ever made. Whereas many contemporary pistol designs employed a receiver stop to arrest the backwards progress of the receiver slide, the M1911 had a locking system that also produced a more positive stop. The barrel had lugs machined into its outer surface that fitted into corresponding lugs on the slide. When the pistol was fired the barrel and slide moved

backwards a short distance with these lugs still engaged. At the end of this distance the barrel progress was arrested by a swinging link which swung round to pull the barrel lugs out of the receiver slide, which was then free to move farther and so eject the spent case and restart the loading cycle.

This robust system, allied with a positive applied safety and a grip safety, make the M1911 and M1911A1 very safe weapons under service conditions. But the pistol is a bit of a handful to handle and fire correctly, and a good deal of training is required to use it to full effect.

The M1911 and M1911A1 were both been manufactured by numerous companies other than Colt Firearms, and have been widely copied direct in many parts of the world, not always to very high levels of manufacture. Modified 'fine tuned' variants continue to serve with the US Marine Corps and with special forces units.

SPECIFICATION	
Colt M1911A1	
Cartridge: 0.45-in (11.43-mm) ball M1911	**Weight:** 1.36 kg (3 lb)
Length overall: 219 mm (8.6 in)	**Muzzle velocity:** 252 m (825 ft) per second
Length of barrel: 128 mm (5.03 in)	**Magazine:** 7-round box

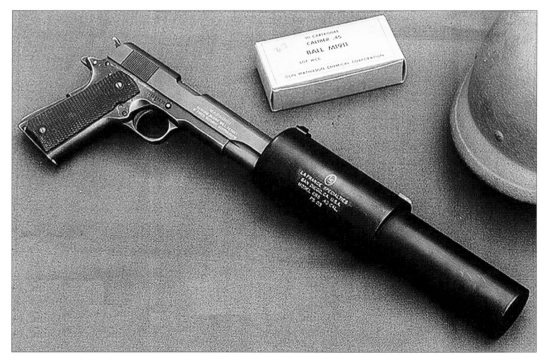

A suppressed US Army M1911A1 from World War II is shown together with its boxed 0.45-in ammunition.

Smith & Wesson 0.38/200 Pistol

In 1940 the British army was in a desperate plight after the disaster of the French campaign and the evacuation from Dunkirk, with few combat-trained formations and even fewer weapons with which to equip them. Fortunately the USA, although not yet actually involved in World War II as a combatant, was at least sympathetic to the point where that nation would produce weapons for the British and to British designs. The British planned very substantial increases in military manpower

The Smith & Wesson 0.38/200 revolver was an alliance of American workmanship and British combat experience that produced a robust and reliable pistol with no frills. Made from the best materials, the pistol was sometimes not finished to the highest possible standard in an effort to speed production, but manufacturing standards were never lowered.

A New Zealand officer armed with a Smith & Wesson 0.38/200 revolver during one of the campaigns in the desert. The revolver is being worn with the lanyard in the 'correct' position around the neck, but many preferred to wear it around the waist to prevent strangulation by an enemy in close-quarter combat.

levels, and was also faced with the problems of obtaining the weapons with which to equip them. Among the required weapons were pistols. Smith & Wesson was willing to produce revolvers to a British specification, however, and the result was the pistol known either as the **Revolver 0.38/200** or the **Pistol, Revolver, 0.38-in, Smith & Wesson No. 2.**

Orthodox and sound

Whatever its designation, the pistol was a strictly orthodox concept that was conventional in every respect. It was straightforward in design and operation, and embodied not only Smith & Wesson craftsmanship but also British requirements, the resulting weapon being robust to an extreme. This was just as well, for the British pistol production lines were never able to catch up with demand and the British/American design more than filled the gap. The pistol

was issued to all arms of the British forces, went to many Commonwealth forces as well, and was even handed out to various European resistance movements. Between 1940 and the time production ended in 1946 over 890,000 had been produced and issued. Many are still to be found in service, and it was well into the 1960s before the weapon was replaced in some British units by the Browning HP.

Simple mechanism

The Revolver 0.38/200 fires a 200-grain bullet and uses the classic Smith & Wesson chamber release to the left. Once the weapon has been opened, fired cartridge cases can be cleared with a sprung plunger rod. The trigger action can be either single- or double-action. The finish of the pistols is plain, and at times was neglected in order that the numbers required could be churned out without production-line delay.

SPECIFICATION	
0.38/200 Revolver	**Weight:** 0.88 kg (1.94 lb)
Cartridge: 0.38-in (9.65-mm) SAA ball	**Muzzle velocity:** 198 m (650 ft) per second
Length overall: 257 mm (10.125 in)	**Chamber capacity:** 6 rounds
Length of barrel: 127 mm (5 in)	

But the standard of manufacture never wavered from a basic excellence, and only the finest materials were used.

Normally the pistol was carried in a closed leather or webbing holster that masked the hammer, so the snagging problem encountered with the Enfield revolver was not so acute, but a typical British touch was that the revolver was usually fitted to a waist or neck lanyard to prevent an enemy taking the pistol away from the firer at close quarters. The weapon appears never to have gone wrong, even when sub-jected to the worst treatment.

A Canadian sergeant loads his Smith & Wesson 0.38/200 revolver. Empty cartridge cases were ejected by moving out the cylinder to the left and pressing a plunger normally under the barrel. All six spent cases were ejected together to allow each chamber to be reloaded one at a time, as seen here.

Smith & Wesson M1917 Pistol

During World War I the UK placed sizeable orders in the USA for weapons of all types. One of these contracts was placed with Smith & Wesson of Springfield, Illinois, for the supply of military revolvers with a calibre of 0.455 in (11.56 mm), which was then standard for British military pistols. Many of the requested revolvers were supplied, however, only after the USA had entered the war in 1917. It was at this time that it was realised that large numbers of pistols would be needed to arm the rapidly expanding US Army, and that the output from Colt's production facilities of the M1911 pistol would fall

When the United States of America entered World War I in 1917, there were not enough pistols to arm the gathering throngs of recruits. The Smith & Wesson M1917 was rushed into production after being adapted to fire the standard 0.45-in (11.43-mm) cartridge and was produced in large numbers.

considerably short of the numbers necessary to meet the growing requirement. As a direct result, Smith & Wesson's British contract was taken over for the American forces, only for a new

problem to crop up once the pistol had been adapted to create a weapon chambered for the American 0.45-in (11.43-mm) cartridge.

'Half moon' clip

Nearly all pistol ammunition produced in 1917 was for the M1911 semi-automatic pistol and was thus of the rimless type. The use of rimless ammunition

in the cylinder of a revolver posed several problems, however, as revolver cartridges are normally rimmed. This led to the adoption of a compromise solution, in the form of three M1911 cartridges held in a 'half moon' clip to keep the cartridges from slipping too far into the revolver chambers when loaded. After firing, the spent cartridges could be ejected in the normal

SPECIFICATION	
Smith & Wesson M1917	**Weight:** 1.02 kg (2.25 lb)
Cartridge: 0.45-in ball M1911	**Muzzle velocity:** 253 m (830 ft) per second
Length overall: 274 mm (10.8 in)	
Length of barrel: 140 mm (5.5 in)	**Chamber capacity:** 6 rounds

way together with their clips, and the clips could be reused if necessary. This solved the problem and the revolver was taken into US Army service and subsequently saw service in France and elsewhere.

The **Revolver, Caliber .45, Smith & Wesson Hand Ejector, M1917**, as the pistol was designated in US service, is a large and notably robust weapon that is completely orthodox in design, operation and construction with the exception of the three-round 'half moon' clips. The revolving cylinder swings out to the left for loading and spent case ejection, and the action is of the single- or double-action type. Like many other pistols of its type, the M1917 is extremely robust and had already been well accepted by the British army before the US Army took over the type. The British used the weapon again in 1940, when large numbers of M1917 revolvers were sent over from the USA for issue to Home Guard units and for service with the Royal Navy.

Colt Firearms also produced a revolver very similar to the Smith & Wesson weapon as the **Revolver, Caliber .45, Colt New Service, M1917**. The weapon was also produced in 0.455-in calibre for British use, used a three-round 'half moon' clip, and included in its data a length of 274 mm (10.8 in), barrel length of 140 mm (5.5 in), weight of 1.135 kg (2.5 lb), and muzzle velocity of 253 m (830 ft) per second. Total production of both weapons was over 300,000, and in 1938 Brazil purchased some 25,000 Smith & Wesson revolvers, which many US military police units were still using as late as 1945.

Pistolet Radom wz.35 Pistol

By the early 1930s the Polish army, which had come into being only in the aftermath of World War I, was still trying to rationalize its equipment, much of it supplied as war-surplus items by a number of countries. The army currently had several pistol types in service, and sensibly wished to standardise on one weapon. An all-Polish design was created by P. Wilniewczyc and I. Skrzypinski, and this was put into production at the Fabryka Broni w Radomiu, initially under the supervision of Belgian engineers from the Fabrique Nationale organisation. The new 9-mm (0.354-in) weapon was selected in 1935 as the standard Polish service pistol with the name **Pistolet Radom wz.35** or, in recognition of the designers, **Pistolet ViS wz.35,** with 'wz' standing for wzor (model).

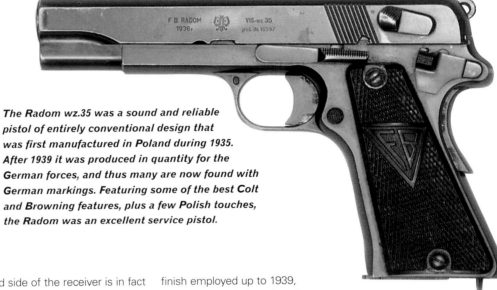

The Radom wz.35 was a sound and reliable pistol of entirely conventional design that was first manufactured in Poland during 1935. After 1939 it was produced in quantity for the German forces, and thus many are now found with German markings. Featuring some of the best Colt and Browning features, plus a few Polish touches, the Radom was an excellent service pistol.

Mixed parentage

In overall concept, the wz.35 was a combination of Browning and Colt design features, adapted and finalised with a few Polish touches. The recoil-operated semi-automatic weapon is entirely conventional, but lacks an applied safety catch and therefore relies only a grip safety: the feature that appears to be the applied safety catch on the left-hand side of the receiver is in fact only a catch used when stripping the pistol. The weapon is chambered for the 9-mm Parabellum cartridge, but the discharge of this powerful round from the wz.35 is no great problem, for the size and mass of the pistol are such that the firing stresses are absorbed to a remarkable degree by the weapon without being passed on to the firer. This combination or size and mass also make the wz.35 a somewhat better-than-average pistol for the rigours of service life. The weapon's reliability and safety were also enhanced by the high standards of manufacture, materials and finish employed up to 1939, when Germany's invasion of Poland marked the beginning of World War II.

German production

When the Germans overran Poland in September 1939, they took the Radom arsenal, complete with its pistol production line, essentially undamaged. Finding that the wz.35 was a thoroughly serviceable weapon firing a cartridge that was already standard in their own service, the Germans adopted the type as a service pistol and kept it in production for their own use under the formal designation **Pistole 645(p)** that for some reason was often rendered as **P 35(p)**. The Germans' requirement for pistols was so great, however, that in an effort to speed production they eliminated some small features and reduced the overall standard of finish to the extent that the P 645(p) is readily distinguishable from the earlier wz.35 by its appearance alone. The Germans kept the pistol in full-scale production into 1944, when the surging westward advance of the Soviet forces destroyed the factory.

Collector's item

When the new Polish army was re-established after 1945 it adopted the Soviet TT33 as its standard pistol. Many wz.35 pistols are still around as collectors' items, for the bulk of the German production went to the Waffen-SS and was marked appropriately. Thus these pistols have an added collection value.

SPECIFICATION	
Radom wz.35	**Weight:** 1.022 kg (2.25 lb)
Cartridge: 9-mm Parabellum	**Muzzle velocity:** 351 m (1,150 ft) per second
Length overall: 197 mm (7.76 in)	
Length of barrel: 121 mm (4.76 in)	**Magazine:** 8-round box

Automaticky Pistole vz.38 (CZ 38) 9-mm automatic pistol

By the time that the German army marched into Czechoslovakia in 1938 and 1939 the Czechs had developed one of the most industrious and innovative armaments industries in all Europe. They were even supplying armour plate to the British for the Royal Navy's new battleships. Pistols were one of the many weapon types produced, mainly at the Ceska Zbrojovka (CZ) in Prague, and from there emanated a string of excellent designs that included the vz.22, 24, 27 and 30 (vz, stands for vzor, or model). These pistols all fired the 9-mm (0.354-in) short cartridge and had many features in common with the Walther pistols of the period, but in 1938 came a pistol that bore no relation to anything that had been produced before.

The new pistol was the **CZ 38** (otherwise known as the **Automaticky Pistole vz. 38**), and by all accounts this was not one of the better service pistols of the time. It was a large automatic weapon using a

Generally regarded as a less than successful design, the Czech CZ 38 (or vz.38) was a large and somewhat cumbersome pistol firing a 9-mm (0.354-in) short round. The weapon could be stripped down very easily but the stiff and slow double-action made accurate shooting difficult.

simple blowback mechanism, but it fired the 9-mm (0.354-in) short cartridge even though its size and weight could have accommodated a more powerful round. One feature that was unusual and outdated even at that time was that the trigger mechanism was double-action only. In other words, when you pulled the trigger you were

cocking and releasing the hammer all in one motion – something that requires a much heavier pull than merely releasing the hammer. Because of the amount of force required to pull the trigger it is very difficult to shoot with any accuracy. Most other automatics carried an external hammer, so the weapon could be cocked prior to shooting. One redeeming feature was that the pistol could be stripped very easily by releasing a catch to allow the barrel to be cleaned once the slide was clear.

Under occupation

Not many of these pistols were produced for the Czech army before the Germans moved in, but the type was kept in production for some time. To the Germans the CZ 38 was known as the **Pistole P 39(t)**, but most of the production went to police forces and some second-line army and paramilitary units. Few survived after 1945. It is one of the few pistol designs that has not contributed some points to later designs.

SPECIFICATION	
CZ 38 (vz.38)	
Cartridge: 9-mm short (0.380 ACP)	**Weight:** 0.909 kg (2 lb)
Length overall: 198 mm (7.8 in)	**Muzzle velocity:** 296 m (970 ft) per second
Length of barrel: 119 mm (4.69 in)	**Magazine:** 8-round box

94 Shiki Kenju 8-mm automatic pistol

In the 1930s the Japanese armed forces had in service a sound design of automatic pistol known to most Westerners as the 'Nambu' (8-mm Pistol Type 14), but following the large-scale Japanese incursions into China in the mid 1930s the demand for more pistols for the expanding Japanese forces could not be met. An easy solution appeared on the scene in the shape of an 8-mm (0.315-in) automatic pistol

that had been commercially produced in 1934, but sales of this pistol had been few, as a result mainly of the odd and clumsy appearance of the weapon. The armed forces were then able to purchase existing stocks of these pistols and took over the production of more. The resultant weapons were initially issued to tank and air force personnel, but by the time production ended in 1945 (after more than

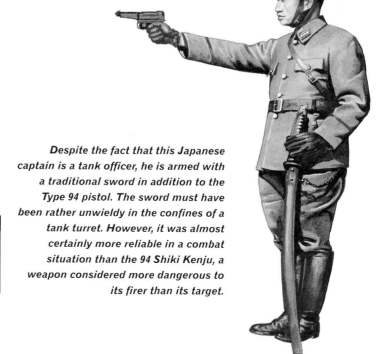

Despite the fact that this Japanese captain is a tank officer, he is armed with a traditional sword in addition to the Type 94 pistol. The sword must have been rather unwieldy in the confines of a tank turret. However, it was almost certainly more reliable in a combat situation than the 94 Shiki Kenju, a weapon considered more dangerous to its firer than its target.

SPECIFICATION	
Pistol Type 94	
Cartridge: 8-mm Taisho 14	**Weight:** 0.688 kg (1.52 lb)
Length overall: 183 mm (7.2 in)	**Muzzle velocity:** 305 mm (1,000 ft) per second
Length of barrel: 96 mm (3.78 in)	**Magazine:** 6-round box

70,000 had been made) its use had spread to other arms.

Inferior pistol

By all accounts this pistol, known as the **94 Shiki Kenju** (or Pistol type 94), was one of the worst service pistols ever produced. The basic design was unsound in several respects, the overall appearance was wrong and the weapon handled badly, but allied to this was the fact that it was often unsafe. Part of the trigger mechanism protruded from the left side of the frame, and if this was pushed when a round was in the chamber the pistol would fire. Another bad feature was the device to ensure that only single shots would be fired each time the trigger was pulled.

Unfortunately this also made it possible to fire a cartridge

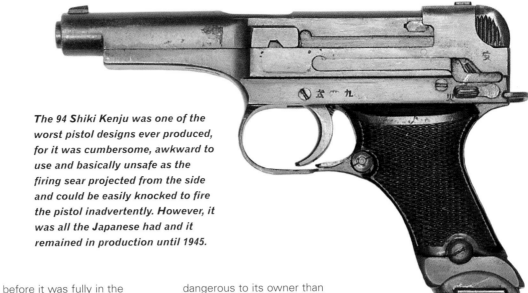

The 94 Shiki Kenju was one of the worst pistol designs ever produced, for it was cumbersome, awkward to use and basically unsafe as the firing sear projected from the side and could be easily knocked to fire the pistol inadvertently. However, it was all the Japanese had and it remained in production until 1945.

before it was fully in the chamber. When these faults were combined with poor manufacture and low quality materials the result was a weapon that was probably more dangerous to its owner than the intended target.

Examples have been found that still bear file or other machine tool marks on the outside, and the degree of 'slop'

in the mechanisms of some should signify that the Type 94 is a pistol that should not be carried or fired.

Pistola Automatica Glisenti modello 1910 9-mm pistol

The pistol that is now generally known as the **Pistola Automatica Glisenti modello 1910** was originally known as the **Brizia**, but the production and other patents were taken over by the Societa Siderugica Glisenti in the first decade of the 20th century. In 1910 this pistol was adopted by the Italian army as its standard service pistol, but for many years it managed only to supplement the earlier 10.35-mm (0.41-in) modello 1889 revolver, and in fact this ancient pistol remained in production until the 1930s.

Unorthodox design

The Glisenti had several unusual features, and its mechanism was of a type little encountered in other designs. It used an operating system loosely described as a delayed blowback, in which the barrel and the receiver recoiled to the rear on firing. As it recoiled the action caused a rotary bolt to start to turn, and this rotation continued once the barrel had stopped moving after a distance of about 7 mm (0.276 in). The barrel was held in place by a rising wedge

The Glisenti modello 1910 was an unusual mixture of design innovations allied with a weak frame design. The pistol was chambered to fire a unique cartridge, the 9-mm (0.354-in) Glisenti, which was similar to the 9-mm Parabellum with a reduced propellant load. In service, the pistol supplemented the modello 1889 revolver.

which was freed as the receiver moved forward again to chamber a fresh cartridge. All this movement had several effects: one was that while everything was moving the action was open and thus exposed to the ingress of debris such as sand (as in the

North African deserts), and another was that the trigger pull was long and 'creepy', which made accurate fire that much more difficult. The action itself was made no more reliable by being constructed in such a way that the entire left side had no

supporting frame and was held in place by a screwed-on cover plate. In prolonged use this plate could come separated from the pistol, causing it to jam. Even in place the action was 'sloppy' and the moving parts had an unpleasant amount of movement.

To overcome the worst of this action the Italians introduced a special cartridge for this pistol known as the 9-mm Glisenti. In appearance and dimensions it resembled the standard 9-mm Parabellum, but the propellant load was reduced to produce less recoil and thus lower internal stress. However, the cartridge was unique to the Glisenti, and if normal 9-mm ammunition was inadvertently loaded and fired the results could be disastrous to pistol and firer! The Glisenti remained in production until the late 1920s but it was still in use in the ranks of the Italian army until 1945. It is now a collector's piece only.

SPECIFICATION	
Glisenti modello 1910	**Weight:** 0.909 kg (2 lb)
Cartridge: 9-mm Glisenti	**Muzzle velocity:** 320 m (1,050 ft) per second
Length overall: 210 mm 8.27 in)	
Length of barrel: 102 mm (4.02 in)	**Magazine:** 7-round box

Pistola Automatica Beretta modello 1934 9-mm pistol

The diminutive **Pistola Automatica Beretta modello 1934** is today highly regarded by pistol collectors. It was adopted as the standard Italian army service pistol in 1934, but it was then only the latest step in a long series of automatic pistols that could be traced back as far as 1915. In that year numbers of a new pistol design were produced to meet the requirements of the expanding Italian army, and although the Pistola Automatica Beretta modello 1915 was widely used it was never officially accepted as a service model. These original Beretta had a calibre of 7.65 mm (0.301 in) although a few were made in 9-mm (0.354-in) short, the cartridge that was to be the ammunition for the later modello 1934.

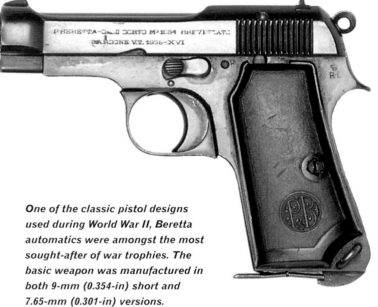

One of the classic pistol designs used during World War II, Beretta automatics were amongst the most sought-after of war trophies. The basic weapon was manufactured in both 9-mm (0.354-in) short and 7.65-mm (0.301-in) versions.

Classic appearance

After 1919 other Beretta pistols appeared, all of them following the basic Beretta design. By the time the modello 1934 appeared the 'classic' appearance had been well established with the snub outline and the front of the cutaway receiver wrapped around the forward part of the barrel to carry the fixed foresight. The short pistol grip held only seven rounds and thus to ensure a better grip the characteristic 'spur' was carried over from a design introduced back in 1919. In operation it was a conventional blowback design without frills or anything unusual, but although the receiver was held open once the magazine was empty it moved forward again as soon as the magazine was removed for reloading. (Most pistols of this type were designed to keep the receiver slide open until the magazine had been replaced). The modello 1934 did have an exposed hammer which was not affected by the safety once applied, so although the trigger was locked when the safety was applied the hammer could be cocked either by hand or by accident, which was an unfortunate feature in an otherwise sound design.

Trophy of War

The modello 1934 was almost always produced to an excellent standard of manufacture and finish, and the type became a sought-after trophy of war.

British and American soldiers fighting at the front line in Italy in 1943–45 did a thriving trade in captured pistols to rear echelon personnel who wanted something to show for their war. Virtually the entire production run was taken for use by the Italian army, but there was a modello 1935 in 7.65 mm which was issued to the Italian air force and navy. Apart from its calibre this variant was identical to the modello 1934. The Germans used the type as the **Pistole P671(i).** Despite its overall success the modello 1934 was technically underpowered, but it is still one of the most famous of all the pistols used during World War II.

Beretta automatics were too light to be effective service pistols, but as personal weapons to officers such as the colonel depicted, they were highly prized.

SPECIFICATION	
Beretta modello 1934	**Weight:** 0.568 kg (1.25 lb)
Cartridge: 9-mm short (0.380 ACP)	**Muzzle velocity:** 290 m (950 ft) per second
Length overall: 152 mm (6 in)	
Length of barrel: 90 mm (3.4 in)	**Magazine:** 7-round box

Owen Gun

It took some time before Lieutenant Evelyn Owen was able to persuade the Australian military to adopt his design of sub-machine gun in 1940. At the time the Australian army had little or no interest in the sub-machine gun, and by the time it realised the weapon's importance it expected to receive all the Sten guns it required from the UK. It took some time for the army to appreciate that it was going to receive no Sten guns as the British army wanted all that could be produced. So finally the Australians adopted the **Owen** gun, but even then they were not sure in what calibre. Thus the first trials batches were produced in four

The Owen sub-machine gun was a sturdy and reliable weapon that soon gained itself a high reputation. The example has a camouflage paint scheme.

calibres before the universal 9-mm (0.354-in) was adopted.

Overhead magazine

The Owen can be easily recognised by its magazine, which points vertically upward. This arrangement was apparently chosen for no other

SPECIFICATION	
Owen Gun	**Rate of fire, cyclic:** 700 rounds per
Calibre: 9-mm (0.354-in)	minute
Length overall: 813 mm (32 in)	**Muzzle velocity:** 420 m (1,380 ft) per
Length of barrel: 250 mm (9.84 in)	second
Weight loaded: 4.815 kg (10.6 lb)	**Magazine:** 33-round vertical box

reason than that it worked, and it must be said that it worked very well. The Owen was kept in service until well into the 1960s and its successor retains the overhead magazine. The rest of the gun was fairly conventional and very robust under all conditions. As production increased, changes were introduced to the design. The early fins around the barrel were removed and some changes were made to the butt, which could be found in versions with just a wire skeleton, an all-wood design, and one version that was half outline and half wood.

Another feature unique to the Owen was its quick-change barrel. Why this feature was incorporated is uncertain, for it

The Australian Owen sub-machine gun's most prominent recognition feature was the vertically-mounted box magazine. The example shown here is one of the early production models.

would have taken a long period of firing for the barrel to become unusably hot. Another odd point regarding the Owen was that once in service it was often painted in camouflage schemes to suit the terrain in New Guinea, where Australian soldiers found the Owen ideal for the close-quarter combat that the jungles enforced. It was true that the Owen was rather heavier than most comparable models but the forward-mounted grip and the pistol grip made it easy to handle. The top-mounted magazine meant that the sights had to be offset to the right side of the body, but this was of little consequence as the Owen was almost always fired from the hip.

Production of the Owen ceased in 1945 but in 1952 many were virtually rebuilt and provision was made for a long bayonet to be fitted to the muzzle; some versions which were made in 1943 used a much shorter bayonet.

ZK 383 Gun

The Czechoslovak **ZK 383** is a sub-machine guns that is virtually unknown in the West as it was little used outside Eastern Europe and its combat use was limited mainly to the war against the USSR. The ZK 383 was a very important weapon type for its time, however, and remained in production from the late 1930s until 1948.

Designed during the early 1930s, the ZK 383 went into

The Czechoslovak ZK 383 was very well made from machined parts and had such luxuries as a bipod and a variable rate of fire mechanism. There was even a quick-change barrel. The bulk of these weapons was later produced for the German Waffen SS, whose men found it a heavy but reliable weapon.

production at the famous Brno arms plant, known for the later introduction of what was to be the Bren gun. The ZK 383 was a

relatively large and heavy weapon for the sub-machine gun class, a feature emphasised by uncommon application of a

bipod under the barrel on some models. This bipod was the result of the Czech army's tactical philosophy, for it regarded the weapon as a form of light machine gun, in direct contradiction of the usually accepted role of a close-quarter combat weapon. This odd approach was further emphasised by the use of what was one of the ZK 383's oddest features, namely a capability for two rates of fire (500 or 700 rounds per minute) provided by the addition or subtraction of a small 0.17-kg (0.37-lb) weight to the breech block – with the weight removed, the breech block could move faster and thus the rate of fire could be increased. The slower rate of fire was used when the ZK 383 was used with its bipod as a light machine gun, and the faster fire rate when the ZK was carried as an assault weapon.

Limited export

But that was only the Czechoslovak army's point of view, and the feature does not appear to have been used much by the other customers for the weapon. The Bulgarian army adopted the type as its standard sub-machine gun (it used the ZK 383 until at least the early 1960s), but by far the largest number of ZK 383s were produced after 1939 for the German army. When they took over Czechoslovakia in 1939 the Germans found the ZK 383 production line still intact, and it was a sensible move as far as they were concerned to keep it intact for their own uses. The Brno factory was taken over for SS weapon production and thus the ZK 383 output was diverted to the Waffen SS, which used the weapon only on the Eastern Front. The Waffen SS examples were all known as the **vz 9** (vz for vzor, the Czech for model) and the Waffen SS found it effective enough for it to become one of their standard weapons. Numbers were kept in Czechoslovakia for use by the civil police who had their own version, the **ZK 383P**, which was produced without the bipod. The only nations other than Czechoslovakia, Bulgaria and Germany that purchased the ZK 383 were Brazil and Venezuela, and even then the numbers involved were not large. Apart from its use in Eastern Europe, the ZK 383 had few points to attract attention and in many ways it was too complicated for the role it was called upon to play. The Czechoslovak army's predilection for the design as a light machine gun led to all manner of detail extras that the weapon did not need.

The dual rate of fire feature has already been mentioned, as has the bipod, but the sub-machine gun does not really need a complex barrel-change mechanism, an all-machined mechanism made from the finest steels available or an angled breech block return spring angled into the butt. The ZK 383 had all these, making it a very reliable, sound weapon but one that was really too complex for its role.

SPECIFICATION	
ZK 383	
Calibre: 9-mm (0.354)	**Muzzle velocity:** 365 m (1,200 ft) per second
Length overall: 875 mm (34.45 in)	**Rate of fire, cyclic:** 500 or 700 rounds per minute
Length of barrel: 325 mm (12.8 in)	
Weight loaded: 4.83 kg (10.65 lb)	**Magazine:** 30-round straight box

Suomi m/1931 Gun

The **Suomi m/1931** resulted from German-inspired designs from the early 1920s. As sub-machine gun designs go, there was little remarkable about the m/1931, for it used a conventional blowback action and an orthodox layout. Where it did score over many existing designs was that it was extremely well made (to the point of lavishness in the quality of material used and the excellence of the machining) and used very good feed systems that were later copied widely. There were two main versions,

The Suomi m/1931 was one of the highest-quality sub-machine guns ever manufactured, for practically every part was machined from solid metal.

one a 50-round vertical box and the other a 71-round drum. In the box magazine the normal lengthy bulk of 50 rounds of ammunition was overcome by having the magazine split into two vertical columns, rounds being fed from one column and then the other. In action this feed system was much favoured as it enabled a soldier to carry into action far more ready rounds than would be possible with a conventional magazine. Despite this, there was also a normal 30-round box magazine.

Proved in service

The m/1931 was produced for the Finnish army in numbers and proved itself in action during the 'Winter War' of 1939–40 with the Soviets. There were several export models, some of

The Suomi m/1931 in action, fitted with the 71-round magazine. Unlike many other sub-machine guns, the m/1931 had a long barrel that was accurate enough for aimed fire at most combat ranges.

them with small bipods under the barrel or body, and these were purchased by Sweden and Switzerland, which set up their own production lines, as did a company in Denmark. The type was adopted by the Polish police before 1939, and examples popped up during the Spanish Civil War on both sides. It was still in limited Scandinavian service until recent times, and this longevity can be explained by one factor other than its excellent construction: this is the weapon's reliability under any conditions without ever seeming to go wrong. These factors alone explain the high regard shown for the m/1931 in the past, but there was also another factor. When the m/1931 was produced, no pains were spared on detail machining; the whole of the gun, the body and bolt included, were machined from solid metal.

Consequently the gun was very accurate for its type. Most sub-machine gun types are accurate only to a few yards and most are almost useless at ranges over 50 m (55 yards). The m/1931 can be used accurately at ranges up to 300 m (330 yards). In relative terms, few were used in World War II but the influence of the design can be detected in many wartime models. The design was also made under licence in Switzerland.

SPECIFICATION	
Suomi m/1931	**Muzzle velocity:** 400 m (1,310 ft) per second
Calibre: 9-mm (0.354-in)	
Length overall: 870 mm (34.25 in) with the butt extended	**Rate of fire, cyclic:** 900 rounds per minute
Length of barrel: 314 mm (12.36 in)	**Magazine:** 30- or 50-round box, or 71-round drum
Weight loaded: 7.04 kg (15.52 lb) with drum magazine	

MAS Modèle 1938 Gun

Often quoted as the **MAS 38**, this French sub-machine gun was first produced at St Etienne in 1938, hence the model number. The MAS 38 was the outcome of a long period of development, and was the follow-on from a weapon produced in 1935. But it must be stated that the development period was well spent, for the MAS 38 proved to be a sound enough weapon well in advance of its period.

There were some rather odd features about the MAS 38, however. It was quite compli-cated and also fired a cartridge produced only in France. Both these features can be explained by the period when it was designed. At that time there appeared to be no reason to make the weapon as simple as possible, for existing production methods seemed adequate to churn out the limited numbers then required. The calibre can be explained by the fact that it was available at the time and so the MAS 38 had a calibre of 7.65 mm (0.301 in) and used a cartridge available only in France, the 7.65-mm Long. While this cartridge was accurate, it was not very powerful, and had the disadvantage that no one else was likely to adopt it once the 9-mm calibre had been universally adopted.

The MAS 1938 was a sound, advanced weapon. Unfortunately for its future prospects, it fired an underpowered cartridge available only in France, and was complicated and therefore slow and expensive to manufacture.

Complex mechanism

The MAS 38 has a complex mechanism with a long bolt travel that was partially offset by having the gun body sloping down into the solid wooden butt. The cocking handle was separate from the bolt once firing started, a good but complex feature. Another good point was a flap over the magazine housing that closed as the magazine was withdrawn to keep out dust and dirt. Very few other designs had this feature and most of them managed to work perfectly well without it.

In fact the MAS 38 turned out to be rather too good for the customer, who at first decided that it did not want a sub-machine gun after all. The French army turned down the weapon when it was first offered, and the initial production examples went to some of the more para-military members of one of the French police forces. When hostilities did start in 1939, the French army soon changed its mind and ordered large quantities, but the complex machining that went into the MAS 38 resulted in a slow rate of introduction into service, and the French army was driven to ordering numbers of Thompson sub-machine guns from the USA. These arrived too late to make any difference to the events of May and June 1940, and France capitulated. When the French forces rearmed under the Vichy regime the MAS 38 was kept in production: in fact the weapon was kept in production until 1949, and it was used in the Indo-China War.

The MAS 38 never got the recognition it deserved. It was rather too complicated, fired an odd cartridge and it was never possible to produce it in quantity when it was required. It is therefore now little known outside France and few, if any, modern weapon designs owe anything to its influence. The only armies to use the MAS 38, other than some of the ex-French colonies, were the Germans who captured enough in 1940 to issue them as **Maschinenpistole 722(f)**.

SPECIFICATION	
MAS 38	**Muzzle velocity:** 350 m (1,150 ft) per second
Calibre: 7.65-mm (0.301-in)	
Length overall: 623 mm (24.53 in)	**Rate of fire, cyclic:** 600 rounds per minute
Length of barrel: 224 mm (8.82 in)	
Weight loaded: 3.356 kg (7.4 lb)	**Magazine:** 32-round straight box

MP 38, MP 38/40 & MP 40 Sub-machine guns

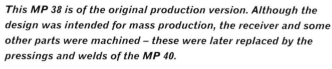

When the **MP 38** was first produced in 1938 it revolutionised weapon design, not by any particular feature of the design but as a result of the method of manufacture employed. Gone was the accurate machine tooling of yesteryear, along with the finely produced wooden fittings, and the standard of finish upon which gunsmiths so prided themselves. With the introduction of the MP 38 came rough and simple metal stampings, die-cast parts, plastic instead of wood and a finish that lacked any finesse or even plating of any kind. The MP 38 looked what it was: a weapon mass-produced to meet a precise military need, namely a simple and cheap weapon that would work when called upon to fire, and nothing more. On the MP 38 there was no wooden butt, just a bare folding heavy wire frame-work that folded under the body for use in close confines such as the back of a vehicle.

Stamped metal parts

The body was produced from simple sheet metal stampings that could be churned out in any metal workshop, and the breech block was provided with only a minimum of machining. Most of the outer surfaces were left in their bare metal state and at best were just painted. Despite all these cost-cutting measures the MP38 had an immediate impact out of all proportion to its design attributes, for in the years after 1938 more and more weapons adopted similar mass-production techniques first introduced on the MP 38.

The MP 38 was quite orthodox so far as operation went. It had a conventionally functioning blowback bolt, and the vertical

magazine under the body fed 9-mm (0.354-in) Parabellum rounds into a conventional feed system. A cocking handle along the left-hand side of the body operated in an open slot, but although dust and dirt could enter the internal workings the weapon could absorb an appreciable amount of foreign bodies before it jammed. Under the muzzle there was an odd projection that was designed to catch on the edge of vehicles to act as a firing rest but the same item also acted as a muzzle cover to keep out dirt.

Once in action in 1939, one rather nasty habit of the MP 38 came to light. The gun operated from the openbreech position (the bolt was cocked to the rear before the trigger could release it to fire) but if the gun was jarred the bolt could jump forward and start the firing cycle by itself. This nasty fault caused many casualties before it was modified out by the machining of a slot over the breech block's 'home' position, through which a pin could engage and lock after being pushed through a hole on the other side of the body. This modification turned the MP 38 into the **MP 38/40**.

Further simplification

During 1940 the simple manufacture of the MP 38 was taken one stage further with the

This MP 38 is of the original production version. Although the design was intended for mass production, the receiver and some other parts were machined – these were later replaced by the pressings and welds of the MP 40.

introduction of even more metal stampings and even simpler manufacturing methods. The new version was called the **MP 40**. To the soldier in the field it was little different from the MP 38/40, but for the German economy it meant that the MP 40 could be easily manufactured anywhere, with subassemblies produced in simple workshops and assembled at central workshops. The weapon was churned out in tens of thousands, and in the field proved a most popular and handy weapon, with Allied troops using any examples they could find or capture. The MP 38/40 was often used by resistance forces and partisans as well.

The only major change to the MP 40 after 1940 was the introduction of a twin-magazine feature with the **MP 40/2**. This was not a success and was little used.

One odd word about this weapon: it is often known as the 'Schmeisser'. Exactly where this name came from is unknown, but it is incorrect as Hugo Schmeisser had nothing to do with the design, which originated with the Erma concern.

The MP 40, as used by this corporal during the invasion of the USSR, was almost identical to the MP 38 except that it was much simpler to manufacture.

SPECIFICATION	
MP 40	
Calibre: 9-mm (0.354-in) Parabellum	**Weight loaded:** 4.7 kg (10.36 lb)
Length overall: 833 mm (32.8 in) with the stock extended and 630 mm (24.8 in) with the stock folded	**Muzzle velocity:** 365 m (1,200 ft) per second
	Rate of fire, cyclic: 500 rounds per minute
Length of barrel: 251 mm (9.88 in)	**Magazine:** 32-round straight box

MP 38

The MP 38 presaged a major shift in the world's thinking about the sub-machine gun. From this time onward, this type of close attack weapon was seen as semi-expendable and fit for manufacture by the cheapest possible process. Although this thinking found its first expression in the MP 38, this important German weapon was in fact a half-way stage in the process, for its still incorporated a relatively high proportion of high-quality machined elements.

The MP 38's barrel was a unit 9.9 in (250 mm) long with six grooves disposed in a right-hand twist.

The barrel of the MP 38 was secured to the body of the weapon under a large collar which provided access to the large threaded barrel nut, so that the barrel unit could be removed.

The muzzle end of the MP 38's barrel was fitted on its upper surface with a hooded barley corn fore sight and on its lower surface with a device designed to allow the firer to hook his weapon over the side of a vehicle such as a half-track carrier.

The MP 38 was a blowback-operated weapon capable only of automatic fire, and the trigger mechanism was very simple. There was no applied safety. The cocking handle could be lodged in the small upper extension of the handle's operating slot to hold the bolt in the rear position.

Above: The MP 38 and its successors in the line-up of German sub-machine guns were appreciated by Allied soldiers for exactly the same reasons that the Germans liked the weapons. It was not uncommon for captured weapons to be turned against their former owners, especially as the ammunition was readily available.

Right: An MP 40 in action during the Stalingrad fighting. Although many German propaganda photographs tend to give the impression that the MP 40 was in widespread use, its issue was restricted mainly to front-line divisions and Panzergrenadier units in particular.

The butt comprised a butt plate and two arms, and by operation of the catch at the rear of the weapon's body could be freed to hinge down and then forward into its folded position under the weapon's body. The firer held the weapon with his right hand on the pistol grip and left hand on the magazine housing just below and behind the breech section.

MP 18, MP 28, MP 34, & MP 35
Sub-machine guns

The MP 28 was a revised version of the original MP 18, retaining the general outline of its predecessor but able to deliver either single-shot or full automatic fire.

Although it was preceded by the Italian Villar Perosa, the **MP 18** can be considered as the father of the modern sub-machine gun. In general concept, operating principle and all-round appearance, the MP 18 had all the features that became standard for such weapons.

The design of the MP18 began on a low priority in 1916 to provide front-line troops with a short-range rapid-fire weapon. The designer was Hugo Schmeisser, the man whose name later came to be synonymous with the sub-machine gun. It was not until 1918 that the new weapon, known to the Germans as a Maschinen-Pistole (hence MP, machine pistol), was issued to the troops on the Western Front. The MP 18 had little more than local impact at the time.

Blowback operation
The MP 18 was a simple blowback weapon firing the classic 9-mm (0.354-in) Parabellum round. The MP 18 was well made, with a solid wooden stock and a 32-round 'snail' magazine mounted in a housing on the left of the body. The barrel was covered by a perforated jacket to aid barrel cooling after firing, and the weapon fired on full automatic only.

When Germany was largely disarmed after 1919, the MP 18 was passed to the police in an attempt to keep the concept alive. In police service the weapons were modified during the 1920s to replace the Luger 'snail' magazine with a simple inline box magazine that again became the virtual prototype of what was to follow. In 1928

the MP 18 was placed back into limited production in Germany, this time as the **MP 28**, with new sights, a single-shot fire capability, some small internal changes on the breech block, and extras such as the mounting for a bayonet. The MP 28 had the new box magazine as standard and the type was produced in Belgium, Spain and elsewhere for export all over the world.

Pattern established
Perhaps the greatest importance of the MP 18 and MP 28 was not in their use as weapons but in their example for other designers to follow.

At first sight the **MP 34** and **MP 35** appeared to be direct copies of the MP 18 and MP 28, but there were in reality many differences. Easily missed at first glance was that on the MP 34 and MP 35 the magazine protrudes from the right- rather than left-hand side of the gun body. The trigger mechanism used double-pressure system to control the rate of fire: a light pull produced single shots, while full pressure provided automatic fire.

The MP 34 was designed by the Bergmann brothers, and improvements led to the MP 35. This was produced in long- and short- barrel versions, and niceties such as bayonet attachments and even light bipods were introduced.

Reliability
It was reliability, largely due to the use of a rear-mounted rather than side-located cocking bolt to keep the weapon's body much clearer of dirt and debris, that brought the MP 35 to the attention of what was to be the biggest customer for the weapon. This was the Waffen SS, which was planning its own procurement arrangements separate from those of the German army.

From late 1940 all MP 35 production went to the Waffen SS, continuing until World War II ended in 1945. Many of the weapons can still be found in use with South American police forces. The reason for this longevity is quite simply that the MP 34 and MP 35 were very well manufactured, with nearly all parts machined from the solid metal.

These truck-borne troops carry MP 28 sub-machine guns with bayonets fixed. The MP 28 was an excellent weapon in qualitative terms, but was too expensive for manufacture on a very large scale.

SPECIFICATION	
MP 18	**MP 35**
Calibre: 9-mm (0.354-in) Parabellum	**Calibre:** 9-mm (0.354-in) Parabellum
Length overall: 815 mm (32.09 in)	**Length overall:** 840 mm (33.07 in)
Length of barrel: 200 mm (7.87 in)	for the standard model
Weight loaded: 5.245 kg (11.56 lb)	**Length of barrel:** 200 mm (7.87 in)
Muzzle velocity: 365 m (1,200 ft) per second	**Weight loaded:** 4.73 kg (10.43 lb)
Rate of fire, cyclic: 350–450 rpm	**Muzzle velocity:** 365 m (1,200 ft) per second
Magazine: 32-round 'snail', later 20- or 32-round box	**Rate of fire, cyclic:** 650 rpm
	Magazine: 24- or 32-round box

Beretta Sub-machine guns

The first of the Beretta series of sub-machine guns, designed by the company's highly talented chief designer, Tullio Marengoli, was the **Beretta Moschetto Automatico Modello 38A**, which was produced at the company's headquarters in the northern Italian city of Brescia. The first examples were produced in 1935, but it was not until 1938 that the first mass-produced examples appeared for issue to the Italian armed forces. The term 'mass production' is perhaps rather misleading for the Beretta sub-machine guns; although the weapons were produced on normal production lines, the care and attention that went into each example was so considerable that they can almost be regarded as hand-made. In fact the Beretta weapons are still regarded as some of the finest examples of the sub-machine gun that it is possible to obtain, and the early Modello 38A weapons were destined to become among the most prized of all.

Simple but well made

In design terms the Beretta guns had little enough of note. They

Above: The Modello 38A was a sound and well-balanced weapon that was a joy to handle and use. No expense was spared in its manufacture, and consequently it was very reliable and accurate. This example is fitted with a 10-round magazine. Note the double-trigger arrangement and the well-finished wooden stock.

Below: The demands of war production meant that Beretta was unable to maintain its pre-war standards of excellence. Even so, the Modello 38/42 was a weapon of much better design than many of its contemporaries and retained many of the features of the pre-war model.

had a well finished wooden stock, a tubular body, a ownward-pointing box magazine and a perforated barrel jacket (sometimes with provision for a folding bayonet at the muzzle). There was nothing really remarkable in these points, but what was very noticeable and indeed notable was the way in which the weapon was balanced and the way it handled in action. The Modello 38A turned out to be a truly remarkable sub-machine gun. The superb finish endeared it to all who used the type, and one result of the painstaking

assembly and finishing was the emergence of a weapon that was highly reliable and very accurate under all combat conditions.

The ammunition feed proved to be exceptional, but only when the proper magazines were used. There were several sizes of magazines (holding 10, 20, 30 or 40 rounds), and these were issued together with a loading device. The round used on the early Beretta sub-machine guns was a special high-velocity 9-mm (0.354-in) cartridge, but this was later changed to the 9-mm

Parabellum cartridge that was more readily obtainable as it was employed in large numbers of other weapons.

There were several variations on the Modello 38A theme. One of these lacked the bayonet and some of the refinements as it was intended as a special lightweight model for use in desert regions.

After Italy had entered World War II in June 1940, a small revision of manufacturing practices was made in an effort to streamline production and speed deliveries of the weapon, but the soldier at the front would be hard put to recognise the implementation of these changes, for the overall finish remained beautiful. Close examination revealed that the

Italian troops in Tunisia, their Beretta Modello 38As ready to hand. The weapon on the left is equipped with a 10-round magazine, which was often employed when single-shot fire was required. The Modello 38A was very accurate and could be used in the manner of a rifle at combat ranges up to 300 m (330 yards).

barrel jacket was altered into a stamped and welded component, but that was about the only concession to mass-production technology, and the Modello 38A retained its high reputation.

German use

By 1944 the war situation had changed radically, with Italy divided since the September 1943 armistice with the Allies between pro-Allied and pro-German portions in the south and north respectively, as one of the results of this division was the manufacture of Beretta sub-machine guns for the German army. By this time the basic design of the Modello 38A had been revised by the addition of simpler assembly and manufacturing methods to the point that it had become the **Modello 38/42**, while an even later version was the **Modello 1.** Relatively few of these two versions were produced, the bulk of them being produced after 1945. Both were easily recognisable as Berettas, and while they retained the overall excellence they were generally simpler and lacked some of the finesse of the Modello 1938A.

As mentioned above, by 1944 Berettas were being produced for the Germans, who used the Modello 38A and Modello 38/42 as the **MP 739(i)** and **MP 738(i)** respectively. Romania also used the Modello 38A and Modello 38/42.

Allied troops greatly prized the Berettas and used them in place of their own weapons whenever they could capture sufficient numbers, but their use by the Allies was restricted to a great extent by a shortage of Beretta magazines. Apparently the sub-machine guns were often captured without their vital magazines, which was perhaps just as well for the Italians.

The nature of the Italian Fascist state was such that by the time he entered the army, any youth was already well trained in the use of most of the service's standard weapons. This included the Beretta Modello 38A, seen here carried by a Young Fascist being decorated by General Bastico.

SPECIFICATION	
Moschetto Automatico Modello 38A	**Muzzle velocity:** 420 m (1,380 ft) per second
Calibre: 9-mm (0.354-in)	**Rate of fire, cyclic:** 600 rounds per minute
Length overall: 946 mm (37.24 in)	**Magazine:** 10, 20, 30- or 40-round box
Length of barrel: 315 mm (12.4 in)	
Weight loaded: 4.97 kg (10.96 lb)	

Type 100 Sub-machine gun

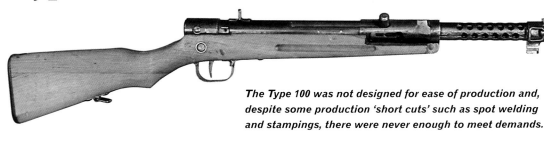

The Type 100 was not designed for ease of production and, despite some production 'short cuts' such as spot welding and stampings, there were never enough to meet demands.

The Japanese were surprisingly late entrants into the field of sub-machine gun design, a fact made all the more remarkable considering the combat experience their troops had gained in their protracted campaigns in China before 1941, and the number of different sub-machine gun designs that had been imported for service use or for evaluation. It was not until 1942, indeed, that the first example of what had already progressed through several years of low-priority development left the Nambu production lines in the form of the **Type 100** sub-machine gun, or **100 Shiki Kikanshoju.** This was a sound but unremarkable design that was destined to be the only sub-machine gun that the Japanese produced in any numbers.

Complex devices

The Type 100 was moderately well made but had several rather odd features. One of these was a complex ammunition feed device that ensured that the round was fully chambered before the firing pin could be released. Other than the safety of the firer, the exact purpose of this feature is rather uncertain, for the cartridge used by the Type 100 sub-machine gun was the 8-mm (0.315-in) pistol round, a rather weak and ineffective cartridge that was also hampered by its bottle-necked layout, which added further problems to the creation of the feed mechanism. The Type 100's barrel was chrome-plated to aid cleaning and reduce wear, and to add to such niceties the design had complex sights and a curved magazine. Other oddities were the use of a complicated muzzle brake on some models and the fitting of a large bayonet-

SPECIFICATION	
Type 100 (1944 version)	**Magazine:** 30-round curved box
Calibre: 8-mm (0.315-in)	**Rate of fire, cyclic:** 800 rounds per minute
Length overall: 900 mm (35.43 in)	**Muzzle velocity:** 335 m (1,100 ft) per second
Length of barrel: 230 mm (9.06 in)	
Weight loaded: 4.4 kg (9.70 lb)	

This Japanese private first class is armed with the Type 100 sub-machine gun. He is equipped for jungle fighting, and is typical of the 1942 period.

mounting lug under the barrel. Some versions also had a bipod for enhanced firing accuracy when the firer was lying down.

There were three different versions of the Type 100. The first had an overall length of 867 mm (2 ft 10 in) and a barrel length of 228 mm (9 in). The second had a folding butt stock and was intended for service with the Japanese paratroop force: the stock was hinged just behind the gun body to fold forward along the side of the weapon, reducing length to 464 mm (22.2 in) but also weakening the weapon in combat situations, and relatively few examples were made. The third version of the Type 100 appeared in 1944 when demand for sub-machine guns was coming from all fronts. In order to speed manufacture, the basic Type 100 was greatly simplified and, in the redesign that created this variant, also lengthened slightly. The wooden stock was often left roughly finished and the rate of fire was increased from the early weapons' 450 rpm to 800 rpm. The sights were reduced to little more than aiming posts and the large muzzle lug for a bayonet was replaced by a simpler fitting. At the muzzle, the barrel protruded more from the perforated jacket and had a simple muzzle brake formed by two ports drilled in the barrel. Welding, often rough, was used wherever possible. The result was a weapon that was much cruder than the earlier version, but one that was sound enough for its purpose.

The main problem for the Japanese by 1944 lay not so much in the fact that the Type 100 was not good enough for its intended task, but that the Japanese lacked the industrial capacity to turn out the huge numbers of these weapons now needed. Thus the Japanese troops had to fight their last-ditch defensive campaigns at a permanent disadvantage against the better-armed Allied troops.

Steyr-Solothurn S1-100 Sub-machine gun

Although the Steyr-Solothurn sub-machine gun is often designated as a Swiss weapon, for it was manufactured mainly in Switzerland, it was in fact designed in Austria. The complicated process whereby an Austrian sub-machine gun became a Swiss weapon had its origins in the end of World War I and the defeat of the Central Powers (Germany and Austria-Hungary). By the treaties that finalised their defeats, both Germany and Austria were severely restricted in the design and manufacture of automatic weapons. The German company

The Steyr-Solothurn S1-100 was an Austrian version of the German MP18 produced during the 1920s and 1930s mainly for commercial sale on the export market. The type was well made and could be supplied with a range of accessories including tripods, bayonets and oversize magazines.

Rheinmetall successfully sought to circumvent these restrictions by the purchase of Solothurn, a Swiss company, as its manufacturing arm in a neutral country. Under the supervision of its new German owner, Solothurn then acquired an interest in a major Austrian armaments manufacturer, the Österreichische Waffenfabrikk-Gesellschaft based in Steyr. It was this last company, which developed several sub-machine gun designs, that in the 1920s actually created the final design of the weapon that became known as the **Steyr-Solothurn S1-100**.

Intended for export

In its full production form as the

The Steyr-Solothurn S1-100 is seen here in a drill-book position, mainly because the picture has been taken from a German manual produced for the type after the Germans had taken over Austria and its arsenal during 1938.

Steyr-Solothurn S1-100, this sub-machine gun was by 1930 in full production mainly for the export market. As with so many other designs of the period, the S1-100 was based on the general outlines and operating method of the MP18, a pioneering German sub-machine gun introduced late in World War I. However, by the time the Swiss manufacturer had finished its development of the design, the weapon had reached a high point of refinement and detail manufacture. The blowback-operated S1-100 was an excellent product that was very well designed and engineered, made from the finest materials and excellently finished, robust, reliable and adaptable. This last was notably important, for the nature and demands of the export market meant that the sub-machine gun had to be capable of production in a whole host of calibres and with a seemingly endless string of extra and accessories, the latter including a magazine filling slot on the magazine housing on the left-hand side of the weapon at the forward end of the weapon's wooden furniture.

The S1-100 was produced in no less than three separate variations of the 9-mm (0.354-in) calibre. Apart from the usual 9-mm Parabellum, the weapon was thus produced in 9-mm Mauser and 9-mm Steyr, the latter specially produced for the S1-100. Models for export to China, Japan and South America were produced in 7.63-mm (0.3-in) Mauser calibre, and the Portuguese purchased a large batch chambered for the 7.65-mm (0.301-in) Parabellum cartridge. The extras were many and varied, the most outlandish perhaps being a tripod to convert the weapon into what must have been a rather ineffective light machine-gun: even so, a number of these tripod mountings were sold to China during the mid-1930s. There were also various forms of bayonet-securing devices, and several barrel lengths were available, some of them very long indeed for what were only pistol cartridges. Another Steyr-Solothurn selling ploy was to present the S1-100 to a customer packed in individually fitted chests containing not only the weapon but all manner of special magazines, special cleaning tools, spare parts, etc.

German use

By the mid-1930s the S1-100 was the standard sub-machine gun of the Austrian army and police force, and after they had peacefully annexed Austria after the Anschluss of 1938 the Germans also took over the armoury of the Austrian armed forces. Thus the S1-100 became the German **Maschinenpistole 34(ö),** a designation which must have caused at least some confusion with another MP 34 weapon, the Bergmann sub-machine gun. After a short period of front-line German service the confusion of no less than three types of 9-mm ammunition to be supplied for the type was too much even for the adaptable German army supply network, and the MP 34(ö) was therefore relegated to service with the German military police; it was also retained by what was left of the Austrian police forces. Until recent times the S1-100 was still to be found in odd corners of the world, but only in very small numbers. Perhaps the most combat seen by the type was in China, where at one point the S1-100 was in use by the Chinese and Japanese armies. The latter even made a copy and used some of the design's features in their own 8-mm Type 100.

SPECIFICATION	
S1-100 (9-mm Parabellum)	**Magazine:** 32-round box
Calibre: 9-mm (0.354-in)	**Rate of fire, cyclic:** 500 rounds per
Length overall: 850 mm (33.46 in)	minute
Length of barrel: 200 mm (7.87 in)	**Muzzle velocity:** 418 m (1,370 ft) per
Weight loaded: 4.48 kg (9.88 kg)	second

Lanchester Sub-machine gun

In 1940, with the Dunkirk evacuation completed and invasion apparently imminent, the Royal Air Force decided to adopt a sub-machine gun for airfield defence. With no time to spare for the development of a new weapon it decided to adopt a direct copy of the German MP 28. The period was so desperate that the Admiralty decided to join the RAF in adopting the new weapon, but in the event it was only the Admiralty which adopted the resultant weapon.

The British copy of the German MP 28 was called the Lanchester after George H. Lanchester, who was charged with producing the weapon at the Sterling Armament Company at Dagenham. The Lanchester emerged from its British development as a sound, sturdy weapon in many ways ideal for use by boarding and raiding parties. It was a very solid, soundly engineered piece of

Obviously based on the German MP 28, the Lanchester was ideally suited to the rough-and-tumble of shipboard life. It had a one-piece wooden stock based on the outline of the Lee-Enfield No. 1 Mk 3 rifle, and there was a bayonet lug under the muzzle. The brass magazine housing can be seen.

weaponry with all the trimmings of a former era. Nothing was left off from the gunsmith's art. The Lanchester had a well-machined wooden butt and stock, the blowback mechanism was very well made of the finest materials, the breech block well machined and, to cap it all, the magazine housing was fabricated from solid brass.

A few typical British design details were added, such as a mounting on the muzzle for a long-blade British bayonet (very useful in boarding party situations), and the rifling differed from that of the German original in details to accommodate the different type of ammunition fired by the Lanchester.

Large magazine

The box magazine for the Lanchester was straight and carried a useful load of 50 rounds. Stripping was aided by a catch on top of the receiver, and the first model was the **Machine Carbine, 9-mm Lanchester, Mk I** capable of single-shot or automatic fire. On the **Lanchester Mk I*** this was changed to automatic fire mode only, and many Mk Is were converted to Mk I* standard at the Royal Navy workshops.

The Lanchester was an unashamed copy of a German design, but gave good service to the Royal Navy throughout and after World War II. Many old sailors still speak of the Lanchester with respect but not with affection, for it was a heavy weapon. The Lanchester did, however, have one rather off-putting feature: if the butt was given a hard knock or jar while the gun was cocked and loaded it would fire. The last example left Royal Navy use during the 1960s, and the Lanchester is now a collector's item.

SPECIFICATION	
Lanchester Mk I*	**Magazine:** 50-round box
Calibre: 9-mm (0.354-in)	**Rate of fire, cyclic:** 600 rounds per
Length overall: 851 mm (33.50 in)	minute
Length of barrel: 203 mm (8.00 in)	**Muzzle velocity:** about 380 m (1,245
Weight empty: 4.34 kg (9.57 lb)	ft) per second

Lanchesters in a typical naval environment as captured U-boat personnel are escorted ashore in a Canadian port – the blindfolds were a normal procedure. The Lanchesters are carried using Lee-Enfield rifle slings.

Sten Sub-machine gun

After the Dunkirk evacuation of mid-1940, the British army had few weapons left. In an attempt to launch rapid rearmament, the military authorities put out an urgent request for simple sub-machine guns that could be produced in quantity. Using the concept of the MP 38 as an example, the designers went to work. Within weeks the result was adopted. It was the product of two designers, Major R. V. Shepherd and H. J. Turpin who worked at the Enfield Lock Small Arms Factory, and from these three names came the universally accepted name **Sten** for the new weapon.

The first variant was the **Sten Mk I**, which must be regarded as one of the unloveliest weapon designs of all time. It was schemed for production as quickly and cheaply as possible using simple tools and a minimum of time-consuming machining, and so was made from steel tubes, sheet stampings and easily produced parts all held together with welds, pins and bolts. The main body was a steel tube and the butt a steel framework. The barrel was a drawn steel tube with either two or six rifling grooves, roughly carved. The magazine was again sheet steel and on the Sten Mk I the trigger mechanism was shrouded in a wooden stock. There was a small wooden foregrip and a rudimentary flash hider. It looked horrible and occasioned some very caustic comments when it was first issued, but it worked and troops soon learned to accept it for what it was, a basic killing device.

Primitive yet effective

The Sten Mk I was produced to the tune of about 100,000

By the time the Sten Mk V entered production there had been time for some finesse to be added to the basic design. While the original outline was retained, a wooden butt and pistol grip and a No. 4 rifle foresight had been added.

examples, all delivered within months. By 1941 the **Sten Mk II** was on the scene and this was even simpler than the Mk I. In time the Sten Mk II became regarded as the 'classic' Sten gun, and it was an all-metal version. Gone was the wooden stock over the trigger mechanism, replaced by a simple sheet-metal box. The butt became a single tube with a flat buttplate at its end. The barrel was redesigned to be unscrewed for changing, and the magazine housing (the box magazine protruded to the left) was designed as a simple unit that could be rotated downward, once the magazine had been removed, to keep out dust and dirt. The butt could be removed easily to provide access for the removal of the breech block and spring for cleaning.

By the time the weapon had been disassembled it occupied very little space, and this turned out to be one of the Sten's great advantages. When the initial needs of the armed forces had been met from several production lines, including those set up in Canada and New Zealand, the Sten was still produced in tens of thousands for paradrop into occupied Europe for resistance forces.

The very simplicity of the Sten and the ease with which it could be broken proved a major asset.

A silenced version of the Sten Mk II was produced in small numbers as the **Sten Mk IIS** for commando and raiding forces. Then came the **Sten Mk III**. This was basically an even simpler version of the original Mk I as its barrel could not be removed and it was encased in a simple steel-tube barrel jacket. Again, tens of thousands were produced.

Definitive model

The **Sten Mk IV** was a model intended for parachute troops but not placed in production. By the time the **Sten Mk V** was on the scene things were going better for the Allies and the Mk V could be produced with rather more finesse. The Mk V was easily the best of the Stens, for it was pro-duced to much higher standards and had extras such as a wooden butt, forestock and a fitting for a

small bayonet. It had the foresight of the Lee-Enfield No. 4 rifle. The Mk V was issued to the airborne troops in 1944, and after World War II became the standard British SMG.

The Sten was a crude weapon in nearly every way, but it worked and it could be produced in large numbers at a time when it was desperately needed. In occupied Europe it was revealed as an ideal resistance weapon and all over the world underground forces have copied the design almost direct. The Germans even produced their own copies in 1944 and 1945 to complement captured Mk III and Mk IIS weapons, designated MP 749(e) and MP 751(e) respectively.

The Sten was one of the first weapons issued to the newly formed airborne troops of the British army, and this example is unusual in being fitted with a small spike bayonet.

SPECIFICATION	
Sten Mk II	
Calibre: 9-mm (0.354-in) Parabellum	**Muzzle velocity:** 365 m (1,200 ft) per second
Length overall: 762 mm (30 in)	**Rate of fire, cyclic:** 550 rpm
Length of barrel: 197 mm (7.75 in)	**Magazine:** 32-round straight box
Weight loaded: 3.7 kg (8.16 lb)	

Sten Mk II

Quickly designed, easy and very cheap to manufacture, and effective in use, the Sten sub-machine was an ideal weapon with which to begin the re-equipment of the British army in the dark days after its retirement from Europe in the Dunkirk evacuation of mid-1940. The weapon was extremely reliable, largely as a result of its simple design, and was steadily upgraded in features and basic finish as and when the time and manufacturing facilities became available later in World War II.

The barrel of the Sten sub-machine gun was a simple drawn steel tube with two or six rifling grooves with a right-hand twist. The barrel was 197 mm (7.75 in) long

The straight box magazine was a simple steel unit loaded with the aid of a special hand loader provided with the weapon. This tool was very useful in overcoming the strength of the magazine spring.

The magazine housing, located just to the rear of the chamber on the left-hand side of the weapon's body, accepted and locked the 32-round box magazine. When not being used, the housing could be rotated downward to block the feed slot and so prevent dirt and debris entering the weapon

The bolt and firing pin were driven forward from the cocked position when the trigger was pulled, the force for this action being provided by the compressed return spring in the rear of the cylindrical body.

The Sten gun was cocked by pulling back the handle in the long slot on the right-hand side of the body, and until the weapon was needed the handle was then dropped into a small safety slot.

Under the safety slot on the right-hand of the Sten gun's body was a button which, when pushed through the weapon from the left and right, provided single-shot or automatic fire respectively.

Maquis in the Haute Loire conducting a weapon training session using the Sten Mk II as the subject. This Sten has the steel 'outline' butt in place of the more usual 'T-shape'. Both types could be easily removed.

The trigger group of the Sten gun was very simple, with a large and angular trigger guard.

The Sten gun appeared with a number of different and detachable butt units, this Sten Mk II having the simplest of them — a buttplate with two lightening holes supported by a single tube.

Left: This is likely to be a posed picture (1944) of the French Resistance in action. It shows two Stens and a shotgun, a fairly typical Resistance weapon combination.

Left: Street fighting in the Mediterranean theatre. This example of the Sten has had a non-standard foregrip added to enhance its handling qualities.

M1 Thompson Sub-machine gun

One of the most famous weapons in history, the **Thompson sub-machine gun** is one of the few firearms whose nickname has become a generic term. Known universally, thanks to Hollywood, as the **'Tommy Gun'** the Thompson's origins date back to 1918 and the trenches of World War I.

The vicious close-quarters nature of trench fighting called for a short-range automatic weapon to 'sweep' the trenches clear of enemies. Since such a 'trench broom' needed to operate only at short ranges, a powerful long-range cartridge was not necessary.

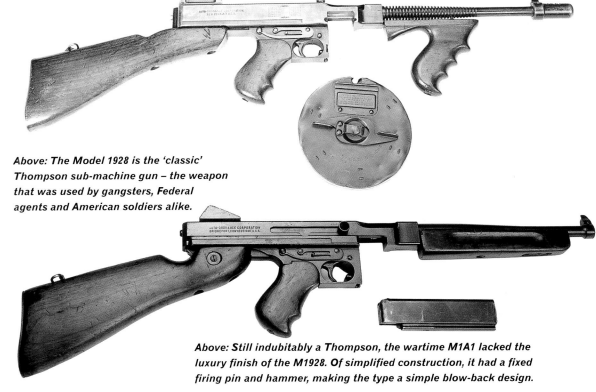

Above: The Model 1928 is the 'classic' Thompson sub-machine gun – the weapon that was used by gangsters, Federal agents and American soldiers alike.

The first SMGs

The German army had drawn the same conclusions and produced the MP 18. On the American side, a former ordnance officer, General John Thompson, initiated the development of an automatic weapon using the standard 0.45-in (11.43-mm) pistol cartridge. It became known as a sub-machine gun. **The Thompson Gun**, as it was soon labelled, was produced in a variety of models. Military sales were limited with the end of the war, but the Thompson became notorious during the prohibition era. Gangsters and government agents both used the Thompson

Above: Still indubitably a Thompson, the wartime M1A1 lacked the luxury finish of the M1928. Of simplified construction, it had a fixed firing pin and hammer, making the type a simple blow-back design.

as their weapon of choice. When Hollywood started to make gangster films the gun became famous overnight.

The US Marines used a few Thompsons in Nicaragua in 1927, and the Navy adopted the type as the **Model 1928** a year later.

In 1940 several European nations were clamouring for Thompson guns. The unexpected employment by the Germans of sub-machine guns on a large scale in 1939 and 1940 produced requests for similar weapons from Britain and France, and the Thompson was the only example on offer. Large-scale production commenced for France, the UK and Yugoslavia, but the orders were overtaken by events.

The French and other orders were diverted to the United Kingdom, where the M1928 was used until the Sten became available. Even then Thompsons were issued for Commando raids and were used later in jungle fighting in Burma. When the USA entered the war the US

SPECIFICATION	
M1 Thompson	**Muzzle velocity:** 280 m (920 ft) per second
Calibre: 0.45-in (11.43-mm)	**Rate of fire:** 700 rpm cyclic
Weight: loaded 4.74 kg (10.45 lb)	**Magazine:** 20- or 30-round box
Length: 813 mm (32 in); length of barrel 267 mm (10.5 in)	

army also decided that it wanted sub-machine guns but the Thompson had to be redesigned for mass production. The Thompson was an awkward weapon to mass-produce because of the large number of complex machining processes involved.

The M1 Thompson, type-classified in April 1942, was a simpler weapon with a straightforward blowback action. The awkward drum magazine, was replaced by a vertical box magazine. The even simpler **M1A1** which appeared in October 1942 did away with the foregrip and barrel ribbing, but it was still largely made from machined parts.

Although costs came down from over $200 per gun in 1939

to under $70 in 1944, the Thompson could not compete with the ugly but functional M3 Grease gun, which had a unit cost of $10 or less!

In spite of the fact that the M1 was heavy, difficult to strip and a problem to maintain in the field, its toughness made it a firm favourite with the troops. Total production, after the last US Army order was delivered at the end of 1944, had reached 1,750,000, most being made by the Savage Firearms Company between 1940 and 1944.

Winston Churchill strikes a famous pose with a 'Tommy Gun'. The weapon has a 50-round drum magazine, a device that proved to be too complex for service use.

A Thompson gunner in action on Okinawa in 1945. He is using an M1A1, fitted with a horizontal foregrip in place of the original forward pistol grip.

Thompson M1928

Compensator
The Cutt's compensator was intended to divert some muzzle gases upwards to keep the muzzle down when firing. Being of limited value and complex to manufacture, it was simplified and eventually omitted from later models.

Foregrip
The fore pistol grip is characteristic of early Thompson guns. However, the Marines found it unnecessary when they used the weapon in Nicaragua in the 1920s, and on military versions it was soon replaced by a simple horizontal foregrip.

Firing pin
The original Thompson guns used a separate firing pin struck by a hammer, but this was really too complex for the task and later models used a fixed firing pin – which was much cheaper to make.

Magazine
The M1928 originally utilised a 20-round box magazine and the 50-round drum magazine made famous by Hollywood. However, during World War II a 30-round box magazine was most commonly fitted.

Sight
Thompsons of the 1920s had a finely machined Lyman rear gun sight calibrated to 50 m (165 ft) and (optimistically) to 550 m (1,800 ft). This was later replaced by a simple 'L'-shaped battle sight.

Fire selector
The fire selector was on the left of the trigger group and could be set for semi-automatic (single shot) or full automatic at a cyclic rate of 725 rounds per minute for early guns. This was reduced to 600 rpm on the first military models of 1928 and on later weapons.

Fixed stock
Wartime variants of the Thompson did away with the removable butt, the heavy wooden stock remaining fixed. Other changes included the removal of the foregrip, the elimination of the machined cooling fins on the barrel and the fitting of a simplified firing mechanism which allowed the removal of the cocking handle from the top of the receiver, as seen here, to the right side.

Stock
If required, the butt could be easily removed by unscrewing the two screws shown. This was rarely utilised in action, as the butt stabilised the aim and reduced firing vibrations. The butt contained an oiling bottle behind a butt trap.

Although its pistol cartridge meant that the Thompson had very little range, and its solid, heavy construction meant that it was something of a burden on the march, it was more popular with individual soldiers than its lighter, cheaper replacements.

Below: A Gurkha keeps watch on the upper floor of a ruined house in Cassino, during the fierce fighting for the strategically positioned Benedictine Abbey overlooking the town. Designed for action in trenches, the Thompson's compact size and close-range firepower made it equally suitable for fighting in built-up areas.

Above: The Thompson was very popular because of its solid reliability. After extensive service in World War II, it continued to be used by US troops in Korea and Vietnam, and can still be found in use in out-of-the-way wars.

M3 and M3A1

The American M3 'Grease Gun' was the equivalent of the British Sten and the German MP40, for it was designed for mass production. It was a sound enough weapon but the American troops never really took to the type, preferring the Thompson.

By the beginning of 1941, although the United States was not yet directly involved in World War II, the American military authorities had acknowledged that the sub-machine gun had a definite role to perform on the modern battlefield. They already had to hand numbers of Thompson guns and more were on their way, but the appearance of the German MP38 and the British Sten indicated the production methods that could be employed in future mass-produced designs. Using an imported Sten, the US Army Ordnance Board initiated a design study to produce an American Sten-type weapon.

The study was handed over to a team of specialists who included the same George Hyde who had developed the Hyde M2 and to executives from General Motors, to whom the mass-production aspects were entrusted. In a very short time they had designed a weapon and development models were produced for trials.

Sense of urgency

The first of these models was handed over for trials just before Pearl Harbor brought the United States into World War II. As a result the project got a higher priority and it was not long before the design

Unpopular with its users in Europe, the 'Grease Gun' gained acceptance in the Pacific, where there was no alternative weapon.

was issued with the designation **M3**. The M3 was just as unpleasant looking as the Sten. Construction was all-metal with most parts simple steel stampings welded into place. Only the barrel, breech block and parts of the trigger mechanism required any machining. A telescopic wire butt was fitted and the design was simple to the point that there was no safety system fitted and the gun could fire fully-automatic only.

The main gun body was tubular and below it hung a long 30-round box magazine. An awkwardly placed and flimsy cocking handle was placed just forward of the trigger on the right-hand side, and the cartridge election port was under a hinged cover. The barrel screwed into the tubular body. Sights were very rudimentary and there were no luxuries such as sling swivels.

Early problems

The M3 was rushed into production and once issued to the troops it soon ran into acceptance troubles. The very appearance of the weapon soon provided it with the nickname of 'Grease Gun' and it was regarded with about as much affection. Once in action though, it soon showed itself to be effective, but the rush into production on lines that were more used to producing motor car and lorry components led to all manner of in-service problems. The cocking handles broke off, the wire stocks bent in

use, some important parts of the mechanism broke because they were made of too soft a metal, and so on. Consequently the M3 received more than its fair share of in-service development and modification, but what was more important at the time was that it rolled off the production lines in huge numbers for issue to the troops at the front.

Unpopular model

The M3 never overcame the initial reception its appearance engendered. Whenever possible the troops in the front line opted for the Thompson M1 or used captured German MP38s and MP40s, but in the Pacific there was often no choice other than to use the M3 and when this happened the design often gained grudging acceptance. For some arms of the US forces the M3 became a virtual blanket issue. These arms included the drivers in the many transport units and tank crews, as for both the M3 was easy to stow and easy to handle in close confines.

From the outset the M3 had been designed to have the capability of being rapidly converted to 9-mm calibre by simply changing the barrel, magazine and breech block. This facility was sometimes employed in Europe when the M3 was dropped to resistance forces.

Design modifications

Simple as the M3 was to produce it was decided in 1944

to make it even simpler. The result of combat experience allied with production know-how resulted in the **M3AI**, which followed the same general lines as the M3 but with some quite substantial changes. For the soldier the most important item was that the ejection cover was enlarged to the point where the full breech block travel was exposed. This enabled the firer to place his finger into a recess in the block to pull the block to the rear for cocking, thus doing away with the awkward and flimsy cocking handle. A flash hider was added to the muzzle and some other minor changes were incorporated. The M3A1 was still in production when the war ended, by which time it had been decided to phase out the Thompson guns in favour of the M3 and M3AI.

Poor production

Apart from the appearance problem, the M3 guns were not perfect weapons. They were rather prone to breakages, the ammunition feed was often far from perfect and the lack of a safety often gave rise to alarm. But it worked and it was available – those two factors are more important than hankering after something better. Thus the M3 and M3A1 were used wherever the US Military went.

SPECIFICATION	
M3	(22.44 in)
Calibre: 0.45-in (11.43-mm) or 9-mm	**Weight loaded:** 4.65 kg (10.25 lb)
Length, butt extended: 745 mm (29.33 in)	**Magazine:** 30-round box
	Rate of fire: 350–450 rpm
Length, butt retracted: 570 mm	**Muzzle velocity:** 280 m (920 ft) per second

Reising Model 50 and Model 55

The **Reising Model 50** and the later **Model 55** are two more examples of how things can go wrong when the basic blow-back action used on the sub-machine gun is ignored and replaced with something that seems to offer a better action. On the Reising Model 50, which was first produced in 1940, the basic action was altered so that instead of the breech block moving forward to the chamber when the trigger was pulled, the action operated when the bolt was forward with a round in the chamber. This action can work quite well but it needs a system of levers to operate the firing pin in the breech block and these levers have to disconnect once the breech block moves. This all adds complexity and cost and adds something to the system which can break.

Commercial venture

Thus it was with the Reising Model 50. The design was the result of a commercial venture and was thus not so influenced by military considerations as would have been the case a few years later, but the Model 50 was a well-made design with an unusual system of cocking the weapon by means of a small

Above: The Reising Model 50 was one of the least successful of all American sub-machine guns to see service, for it employed a complex mechanism that added to the cost, performance and reliability of the weapon.

Below: The Reising Model 55 differed from the Model 50 in that it dispensed with the wooden stock in favour of a folding wire butt for use by airborne troops. Like the Model 50, the weapon was not popular and was prone to malfunctioning due to the ingress of dirt.

catch sliding in a slot under the fore-stock. This left the top of the gun body free of many of the usual hazards such as the cocking slot that usually provides an ingress for dirt to clog the system. But on the Model 50 all that happened was that the dirt got into the slot underneath and was difficult to clean out, thus providing one source of potential bother. From the outside the Model 50 looked a fairly simple weapon but the internal arrangements were complex to the point where there was too much to go wrong, hence there were more stoppages and general unreliability.

When the Reising Model 50 was first offered to the US forces the US Marine Corps was some way down the list of priorities, a position it was later dramatically to reverse, so in the absence of any other source of sub-machine guns it obtained numbers of the Model 50. Once the USMC had the Model 50 it soon found the weapon wanting and obtained other weapon types. Some Model 50s were obtained by a British Purchasing Commission but few were involved and some others went to Canada. Yet more were sent to the Soviet Union and by 1945 the Model 50 was still in production and over 100, 000 had been made, a modest enough total but well worthwhile as far as the manufacturers were concerned. Some of this total was made up by the Model 55 which was the same as the Model 50 other than that the all-wood stock of the Model 50 was replaced by a folding wire butt for use by airborne and other such units. The Model 55 was no more successful than the Model 50.

SPECIFICATION	
Model 50	**Magazine:** 12- or 20-round box
Calibre: 0.45-in (11.43-mm)	**Rate of fire, cyclic:** 550 rpm
Length: 857 mm (33.75 in)	**Muzzle velocity:** 280 m (920 ft) per second
Length of barrel: 279 mm (11.00 in)	
Weight loaded: 3.7 kg (8.16 lb)	

UD M42

In accounts of the American submachine gun scene between 1939 and 1945 one weapon is often not mentioned at all, and that is the submachine gun known under a number of names but usually called the **UD M42**. This weapon was designed in the days just prior to World War II as a commercial venture in 9-mm calibre. It was ordered under rather odd circumstances by an organisation known as the United Defense Supply Corporation, a US government body that ordered all manner of item for use overseas, but the main point of its existence was that it was an American secret service 'front' for all forms of underground activities. Exactly why the United Defense (hence UD) concern ordered the

The UD M42 was not accepted as an official US service weapon, but numbers were purchased for issue to some odd undercover and special mission units.

design that was produced by the Marlin Firearms Company is now not known, but the name 'Marlin' was subsequently often given to the weapon that became the UD M42. The general impression given at the time was that the weapons were to be shipped to Europe for use by some underground organisations working for the US interest, but events in Europe overtook the scheme. Some UD M42s were certainly sent to the

Dutch East Indies before the Japanese invasion of the area, but they vanished without trace.

Most of the UD M42s did find their way to Europe but in some very odd hands. Most were handed out to some of the numerous resistance and partisan groups that sprang up in and around the German- and Italian-occupied areas of the Mediterranean Sea. There they took part in some very odd actions, the most famous of which was when British agents kidnapped a German general on Crete. Other actions often took place so far from the public gaze that today these actions and the part the UD M42 took in them are virtually forgotten.

This is perhaps a pity for many weapon authorities now regard the UD LT42 as one of the finest sub-machine gun types used in World War II. Being made on a commercial and not a military basis it was well machined and very strong. The action was smooth and the gun very accurate, and by all accounts it was a joy to handle. It could withstand all manner of ill-treatment (including immersion in mud and water) and it would still work.

After all these years it now seems very unlikely that the full service record of the UD M42 will ever be told, but at least the very existence of the weapon should be better known.

SPECIFICATION	
UD M42	
Calibre: 9-mm	**Magazine:** 20-round box
Length: 807 mm (31.75 in)	**Rate of fire:** 700 rpm
Length of barrel: 279 mm (11.00 in)	**Muzzle velocity:** 400 m (1,310 ft) per second
Weight loaded: 4.54 kg (10.00 lb)	

PPSh-41 Sub-machine gun

In many ways the **Pistolet-Pulyemet Shpagina obrazets 1941g**, generally known as the **PPSh-41**, was to the Red Army what the Sten was to the British and the MP 40 to the Germans: in short, it was the Soviet equivalent of the mass-produced sub-machine gun making the maximum possible use in its concept of ways of simplifying the weapon, and in its construction of reducing to the lowest possible figure the number of costly and time-consuming machining operations. Unlike the Sten and the MP 40, however, the PPSh-41 was the result of a more measured and involved development process, and as a consequence the Soviet firearm was a much better all-round weapon.

The PPSh-41 was one of the 'classic' Red Army weapons of World War II, and was produced in its millions. It was an emergency design born out of the disruption following the German invasion of June 1941.

Huge production total

The PPSh-41 was designed and developed from 1940 by Georgi S. Shpagin, but it was not until a time early in 1942, in the wake of the upheavals of the German invasion from June of the previous year, that the first examples were issued to the Red Army on a large scale. As it had been designed from the outset for the very maximum ease of production, the PPSh-41 was churned out in the tens of thousands in all manner of workshops ranging from

properly equipped arsenals to shed workshops in rural areas.

It has been estimated that by the end of the 'Great Patriotic War' in 1945 that more than five million examples of the PPSh-41 had been produced. Considering that it was a mass-produced

weapon, the PPSh-41 was a well-made design with a heavy solid wooden butt. It used the conventional blowback operating system, but it had a high rate of fire and in order to absorb the shock of the recoiling breech block a buffer of laminated

SPECIFICATION	
PPSh-41	
Calibre: 7.62-mm (0.3-in)	**Magazine:** 71-round drum or 35-round box
Length overall: 828 mm (32.60 in)	**Rate of fire, cyclic:** 900 rounds per minute
Length of barrel: 265 mm (10.43 in)	**Muzzle velocity:** 488 m (1,600 ft) per minute
Weight loaded: 5.4 kg (11.90 lb)	

Involvement in the fighting extended throughout the population, for during some of the many sieges, such as those at Leningrad, Sevastopol and Stalingrad, even women and children took up weapons.

leather or felt blocks was provided at the rear of the breech block's travel. The gun body and the barrel jacket were simple shaped steel stampings, and the muzzle had a downward sloping shape that doubled as a rudimentary muzzle brake. The muzzle was also fitted with a device termed a compensator, and this was intended to reduce the amount of muzzle climb produced by the recoil forces when the gun was fired. The barrel was chrome-plated, a standard Soviet practice to ease cleaning and reduce barrel wear, but at one time the need for weapons was so great that the barrels were simply old Mosin-Nagant rifle barrels cut down to the appropriate length for use in the sub-machine gun.

The weapon was supplied with ammunition from a 35- or 71-round drum magazine, and this was of exactly the same type as that used on the earlier

Soviet sub-machine guns. Fire selection (single shot or full automatic) was made by a simple lever located just forward of the trigger. In construction the PPSh-41 was wholly reliant on welding, pins and seam stampings. The overall result was a tough, reliable and highly effective weapon.

The PPSh-41 had to be tough, for once the Red Army started to receive the type in appreciable numbers it adopted the weapon in a way that no other army even attempted to consider. Quite simply the PPSh-41 was issued to entire infantry battalions and regiments, to the almost virtual exclusion of any type of weapon other than hand grenades. These units formed the vanguard of the shock assault units that were carried into the attack on the backs of T-34 medium tanks, from which these shock assault units descended only for an attack or for food and rest. These personnel of these units carried enough ammunition only for their immediate needs, their general life standards were low, and their combat lives were very short. But in their tens of thousands these hordes armed

with the PPSh-41 sub-machine swept across eastern Russia and across Europe, carrying all before them. They were a fearful force and the PPSh-41 with which they were equipped became a virtual combat symbol of the Red Army.

German service

Under such circumstances the PPSh-41 (known to its users as the 'Pah-Pah-Shah') received virtually no maintenance or even any cleaning. Under Eastern Front conditions it soon became apparent that the best way to keep the weapon going under summer dust or winter ice conditions was to keep it completely dry and free from any sort of oil, otherwise its action clogged or froze.

So many PPSh-41 sub-machine guns were produced that the type became a virtual standard weapon for the German army as well as the Red Army, the Germans even going to the extent of recalibring some of their captured hoard to their own 9-mm (0.354-in) Parabellum cartridge: this process required the replacement of the Soviet barrel and magazine housing by a new barrel and a housing able to accept the magazine of the MP 40. Unaltered weapons in German service received the official inventory designation **Maschinenpistole 717(r)**, but the designation of recalibred weapons remains unknown. Partisan forces operating behind the German lines found the PPSh-41 an ideal weapon for their purposes, and after the war the type was used by virtually every nation that came within the Soviet sphere of influence. It still turns up in the hands of 'freedom fighters' all over the world.

The German army was much impressed with the Soviet PPSh-41, and when supplies of their own MP 40 sub-machine guns were lacking they took to using large numbers of captured PPSh-41s. If Soviet 7.62-mm (0.3-in) ammunition was in short supply the weapon could fire the German 7.63-mm Mauser pistol round, and by 1945 numbers of PPSh-41s were being adapted to fire German 9-mm (0.354-in) ammunition.

PPD-1934/38 Sub-machine gun

The USSR had sufficient troubles during the 1920s and 1930s without worrying too much about the design of modern weapons for its armed forces, but after matters had settled down enough for re-equipment of the Red Army to be contemplated, the creation of a sub-machine gun design was not very high on the list of Soviet military priorities. Rather than make any innovations in sub-machine gun design, Vasili A. Degtyarev opted to design a weapon combining features that had already appeared in other countries' weapons. The result was the **Pistolet-Pulyemet Degtyareva obrazets 1934g**, or **PPD-1934**.

Derivative design

First produced in 1934, the blowback-operated weapon combined Finnish Suomi m/1931 and German MP 18 and MP 28 features. It remained in production until 1940, by which time the introduction of modifications justified the **PPD-1934/38** designation. There was nothing very remarkable about the PPD-1934/38. The mechanism was almost the same as that of the German weapons and the magazine was

a direct copy of the Suomi unit. This was a 71-round drum that was to become the virtual norm for subsequent Soviet sub-machine guns, but a smaller 25-round box magazine was also issued on occasion. This box magazine had to be curved as the cartridge used for all the Soviet sub-machine guns was the 7.62-mm (0.3-in) Tokarev (Type P) rimless cartridge, which had a bottle-necked shape and would not therefore lie completely flat for feeding from the magazine lips into the gun body.

General improvement

There was one variant of the PPD-1934/38, and this was placed in production during 1940 as the **PPD-1940**. The new variant offered a general all-round improvement over the earlier design. It did have one very noticeable recognition feature in that the drum magazine fitted up into the gun through a large slot in the stock.

Very few other sub-machine gun designs used this magazine fixing system.

When the Germans and their allies invaded the USSR in 1941 the PPD guns were still in relatively short supply among Red Army units, and for this reason had little real effect on the outcome of events as the Axis forces drove east. The success of this initial phase of the Axis campaign meant that the Germans captured useful but not very large numbers of PPD sub-machine guns, which they issued to their own second-line units. In

The Soviet PPD-1934 introduced one feature later used on all Soviet sub-machine gun designs: the chromed barrel to reduce wear and ease cleaning.

German service the PPD was known as the **Maschinenpistole** 716(r), and the Germans used either captured Soviet ammunition or alternatively the 7.63-mm (0.3-in) Mauser cartridge, which was virtually identical to the Soviet round. By the end of 1941 even the PPD-40 had ceased production as the Germans had overrun the arsenals at Tula and Sestroretsk, and there was no time to set up the extensive machine shops elsewhere. The Red Army therefore had to resort to more easily produced SMGs.

SPECIFICATION	
PPD-1934/38	**Magazine:** 71-round drum or
Calibre: 7.62-mm (0.3-in)	25-round box
Length overall: 780 mm (30.71 in)	**Rate of fire, cyclic:** 800 rounds per
Length of barrel: 269 mm (10.60 in)	minute
Weight loaded: 5.69 kg (12.54 lb)	**Muzzle velocity:** 488 m (1,600 ft) per
	second

PPS-42 and PPS-43 Sub-machine guns

Few weapons can have been designed and produced under conditions as desperate as those that surrounded the advent of the **Soviet Pistolet-Pulyemet Sudareva obrazets 1942g** (or **PPS-42**) sub-machine gun. In 1942 the city of Leningrad (now St Petersburg) was under siege from the south and north by the German and Finnish armies respectively, and the trapped Red Army units were short of every war-making necessity including weapons. Leningrad contained a large number of manufacturing facilities and machine shops, so

when it came to local production of weapons the fighting troops were relatively well off, but they needed these weapons as quickly as possible. Under such conditions the sub-machine gun provides an obvious basis on which to work, so it was a weapon of this type that the small arms designer A. I. Sudarev created.

Crude yet effective

Sudarev was limited in the design he could create by the materials to hand and the type of machines that would be available to work these materials. By sheer pragmatic trial and error, Sudarev developed a sub-machine gun that embodied all the features to be found in other emergency designs such as the

The Soviet PPS-43 was the full production version of the emergency-produced PPS-42 designed during the siege of Leningrad. The PPS-43 introduced a measure of finesse, but it was essentially a simple weapon.

British Sten and American M3. The result was a simple and very robust gun manufactured from sheet metal stampings, most of them heavy as that was the only material to hand. The gun was held together by welds, rivets and pins, and a simple metal butt, capable of being folded, was provided. The 35-round magazine used on earlier Soviet sub-machine guns was adopted almost unchanged, for the simple reason that production of a drum magazine would have proved too difficult.

The firing trials were carried out quite simply by handing examples straight from the production shops to front-line soldiers. Their comments and results were fed straight back to the assembly shops where any changes were made on the spot. One of these changes involved the use of a curved steel plate, pierced by a central hole through which the bullet passed, over the muzzle to act as a partial compensator and muzzle brake, and this crude and simple device was retained when the weapon

entered production. In time the new sub-machine gun received an official designation.

Massive production

In action around Leningrad the PPS-42 proved to be a thoroughly sound design and one that could be produced quickly and cheaply. Thus it was not long after the 900-day siege of Leningrad had been lifted that the weapon was adopted for general Red Army service. When this took place there was opportunity to remove some of the more rushed and crude features of the weapon. The folding butt was revised so that it could be hinged upward to clear the ejection port, and the original rough wooden pistol grip was replaced by a hard rubber type. The overall finish was generally

improved, and in this form the weapon became the **PPS-43**. In time the PPS-43 took its place in service with the units of the Red Army alongside the PPSh-41, but never in quite the same numbers. Considering the inauspicious beginnings of the design it proved to be an excellent weapon in service wherever it was taken, and in 1944 it was adopted by the Finns as their standard sub-machine gun once they came into the Soviet sphere of influence. The Germans also used captured PPS-43s as **Maschinenpistole 709(r)** weapons. The PPS-43 has long been out of service with its parent country but remains in limited service elsewhere and, like the British Sten, has the distinction of being copied in many backyard workshops.

SPECIFICATION	
PPS-43	
Calibre: 7.62-mm (0.3-in)	**Weight loaded:** 3.9 kg (8.60 lb)
Length: 808 mm (31.81 in) with butt extended and 606 mm (23.86 in) with butt retracted	**Magazine:** 35-round curved box
	Rate of fire, cyclic: 700 rounds per minute
Length of barrel: 254 mm (10.0 in)	**Muzzle velocity:** 488 m (1,600 ft) per second

Lebel and Berthier Rifles

Some of the rifles in French reserve use in 1939 were obsolete 1886 models, unaltered from their introduction to service. They were outmoded within 10 years.

In 1939 the French army was equipped with an almost bewildering array of rifles, for the French appear to have adopted a policy of never throwing anything away. Some of the personal weapons could trace their origins back to the mle 1866 Chassepot rifle. One of them, the **Fusil Gras mle 1874**, was a single-shot weapon but still in use with some French second-line and colonial units at the time of the German invasion of 1940.

The original Lebel rifle, the **Fusil d'infanterie mle 1886**, was updated in 1893 to produce the **Fusil mle 1886/93**. It was with this Lebel rifle that the French army fought World War I, but another weapon also in use at that time was a Berthier carbine, the **Mousqueton mle 1890** (and similar **mle 1892**), a

version of the original mle 1886 revised with the Mannlicher magazine system. On the Berthier the magazine was of the orthodox box type loaded from a clip, but on the Lebel it was a tubular magazine holding more rounds loaded singly.

Berthier rifle

The first Berthier rifle was the **Fusil mle 1907**, but in 1915 this weapon for colonial troops was largely replaced by the **Fusil d'infanterie mle 07/15**. With the introduction of the mle 07/15 the older Lebel rifles gradually faded in importance as production concentrated on the Berthiers, but the Lebels were never replaced in service. They were still used in 1939.

The original Berthier magazine system held only three rounds,

but it was soon realised that this was not enough and the **Fusil d'infanterie mle 1916** had a 5-round magazine. To complicate matters further there were carbine or other short versions of all the models mentioned above, and to complicate matters still more the French sold or gave away masses of all of these weapons in the inter-war years to many nations who promptly applied their own designations.

Thus Lebel and Berthier rifles turned up not only in all the French colonies

This Moslem Spahi of the 1st Moroccan Spahi Regiment of the Vichy colonial army is armed with the old Lebel rifle. Note the long bayonet in the man's belt.

but in nations such as Greece, Yugoslavia, Romania and other Balkan states.

In 1934 the French decided to attempt to make some sense out of their varied rifle and carbine arsenal by adopting a new calibre. Up to this time the normal French calibre had been 8-mm (0.315-in), but in 1934 the 7.5-mm (0.295-in) calibre was adopted.

That same year the French started to modify the old Berthier rifles to the new calibre and at the same time introduced a new magazine (still holding only five rounds) and several other changes along with the new barrel. This 'new' version was the **Fusil d'infanterie mle 07/15 M34**, but the change went so slowly that in 1939 only a small proportion of the available stocks had been converted, ensuring that all the other models were still in use.

German service

After the French capitulation of June 1940, the Germans found themselves with masses of all the various French rifles. Some they could use as they were, and many of these were issued to garrison and second-line formations. Others were stockpiled only to be dragged out in 1945 to arm Volkssturm and other such units. No doubt the Germans found that the variety of French rifle and carbine types was too much, even for their assorted stocks, but as they never had enough rifles to arm their ever-growing forces the French weapons were no doubt handy. Few of the old French rifles are seen today except in museums and collections.

SPECIFICATION	
Fusil mle 1886/93	**Fusil mle 1907/15 M34**
Calibre: 8-mm (0.315-in)	**Calibre:** 7.5-mm (0.295-in)
Length overall: 1303 mm (51.3 in)	**Length overall:** 1084 mm (42.7 in)
Length of barrel: 798 mm (31.4 in)	**Length of barrel:** 579 mm (22.8 in)
Weight: 4.245 kg (9.35 lb)	**Weight:** 3.56 kg (7.85 lb)
Muzzle velocity: 725 m (2,380 ft) per second	**Muzzle velocity:** 823 m (2,700 ft) per second
Feed: 8-round tubular magazine	**Feed:** 5-round box magazine

Fusil MAS36 Rifle

The MAS36 was the last bolt-action rifle adopted by a major army anywhere in the world. It was a fair weapon with some anachronistic features, but few of the weapons saw service before 1939.

In the period following World War I the French army decided to adopt a new standard service cartridge in 7.5-mm (0.295-in) calibre. The new cartridge was adopted in 1924, but following some low-priority and therefore lengthy trials, it was found that the new cartridge was unsafe under certain circumstances and thus had to be modified in 1929. In that year the French decided to adopt a new rifle to fire the new round, but it was not until 1932 that a prototype was ready. Then followed a series of further trials that went on at a slow pace until 1936, when the new rifle was accepted for service.

The new rifle was the **Fusil MAS36** (MAS for Manufacture d'Armes de Saint Etienne). This used a much-modified Mauser action which was so arranged that the bolt handle had to be angled forward quite sharply.

The box magazine held only five rounds. The MAS36 had the odd distinction of being the last bolt-action service rifle to be adopted for military service anywhere (all later new weapons using some form of self-loading action) and in some other ways the MAS36 was anachronistic. In typical French style the weapon had no safety catch, and the overall appearance of the design belied its year of introduction, for it looked a much older design than it was.

Very slow progress

Production of the new rifle was so slow that a modification programme to convert some of the old rifles for the new cartridge had to be undertaken. This lack of urgency was typical of the period for the nation seemed to suffer from an internal lethargy that could be traced back to the nation's exertions of World War I. Thus by 1939 only a relatively few French army units were equipped with the MAS36, and these were mainly front-line troops. The MAS36 could have had little effect on the events of May and June 1940, but many of the troops who left France at that time took their MAS36s with them and for a while it remained the favoured weapon of the Free French forces in exile. The Germans also took over numbers of MAS36s for service, with the designation **Gewehr 242(f),** by their own garrison units based in occupied France.

One odd variation of the basic MAS36 was a version known as the **MAS36 CR39**. This was a short-barrel version intended for paratroop use, and had an aluminium butt that could be folded forward alongside the body to save stowage space. Only a relative few were ever made, and even fewer appear to have been issued for service use.

When World War II ended, the new French army once more took the MAS36 into use and retained it for many years, using it in North Africa and Indo-China. Many are still retained for use as ceremonial parade weapons and the type is still used by the forces and police of many colonial or ex-colonial states.

SPECIFICATION	
Fusil MAS36	**Muzzle velocity:** 823 m (2,700 ft) per second
Calibre: 7.5-mm (0.295-in)	**Feed:** 5-round box magazine
Length overall: 1019 mm (40.1 in)	
Length of barrel: 574 mm (22.6 in)	
Weight: 3.67 kg (8.09 lb)	

Rifle Types 38 & 99

The Type 99 rifle was a monopod-fitted version of the Type 38 employing the new 7.7-mm (0.303-in) calibre cartridge. The Japanese design drew on current Mauser and Mannlicher features, and first appeared in 1905.

The **Rifle Type 38** was adopted for Imperial Japanese service in 1905, and was a development of two earlier rifles selected by a commission headed by one Colonel Arisaka, who gave his name to a whole family of Japanese service rifles. The Type 38 used a mixture of design points and principles taken from contemporary Mauser and Mannlicher designs, mixed with a few Japanese innovations. The result was a sound enough rifle in 6.5-mm (0.256-in) calibre. This relatively small calibre, coupled with a cartridge of modest power, produced a rifle with a small recoil that exactly suited the slight Japanese.

This fact was further aided by the Type 38 rifle being rather long: when the rifle was used with a bayonet, as it usually was in action, this gave the Japanese soldier a considerable reach advantage for close-in warfare, but it also made the Type 38 a rather awkward rifle to handle. As well as being used by all the Japanese armed forces, the Type 38 was exported to nations such as Thailand, and was also used by several of the warring factions then prevalent in China. At one point during WWI the Type 38 was even purchased as a training weapon by the British army.

A shorter version, the **Carbine Type 38**, was widely used, and there was a version with a folding butt for use by airborne troops. There was also a version of the Type 38 known as the **Sniper's Rifle Type 97** which, apart from provision for a telescopic sight, had a revised bolt handle.

New calibre

During the 1930s the Japanese gradually adopted a new service cartridge of 7.7-mm (0.303-in) calibre, and the Type 38 was revised as the **Rifle Type 99**. The Type 99 had several new features, including a sight that was supposed to be effective for firing at aircraft, and a folding monopod to assist accuracy. A special paratroop model that could be broken down into two halves was devised, but proved to be unreliable and was replaced by a 'take-down' version known as the **Parachutist's Rifle Type 2**. Not many were made.

Once the Pacific war was under way, from 1942 the production standards of Japanese rifles and carbines deteriorated rapidly; any items that could be left off were deleted, and simplifications were introduced onto the production lines. But overall standards went down to the point where some of the late production examples were virtually lethal to the user, many of them being constructed from very low-quality materials, for the simple reason that the Allied air and sea blockade denied the Japanese the use of anything better.

Dire straits

By the end the arsenals were reduced to producing primitive single-shot weapons firing 8-mm (0.315-in) pistol cartridges, and even black-powder weapons. There was even a proposal to use bows firing explosive arrows. It was all a long way from when the Type 38 was one of the most widely used service rifles.

Japanese infantry during the assault on the Yenanyaung oilfields in Burma. The great length of the Arisaka type rifle, especially with bayonet attached, is obvious. This made the weapon awkward to handle, but also gave the generally short-statured Japanese soldier an effective reach in close combat.

SPECIFICATION	
Rifle Type 38	
Calibre: 6.5-mm (0.256-in)	**Weight:** 4.2 kg (9.25 lb)
Length overall: 1275 mm (50.2 in)	**Muzzle velocity:** 731 m (2,400 ft) per second
Length of barrel: 797.5 mm (31.4 in)	**Feed:** 5-round box magazine

Gewehr 98 and Karabiner 98k Rifles

The 7.92-mm (0.312-in) **Gewehr 98** was the rifle with which the German army fought through World War I. It was a Mauser rifle first produced in 1898, but based on a design dating back to 1888.

In service the Mauser action proved sturdy and reliable, but in the years following 1918 the German army carried out a great deal of operational analysis that revealed, among other things, that the Gew 98 was too long and bulky for front-line use. As an immediate result the surviving Gew 98s were modified to Karabiner 98b standard. Karabiner is the German for carbine, but there was nothing of the carbine in the **Karabiner 98b** with a length unchanged from that of the Gew 98. The only changes were to the bolt handle, the sling swivels and the ability to use improved ammunition. To confuse matters further the original Gew 98 markings were retained.

Shortened model

The Kar 98b was still in service with the German army in 1939 (and remained so throughout World War II), but by then the standard rifle was a slightly

Above: The Karabiner 98k was a slightly shortened version of the Gewehr 98, which served Germany in World War I and, although supposedly a carbine, it was as long as many rifles of the period.

shorter version of the basic Mauser known as the **Karabiner 98k**. This was slightly shorter than the original Gew 98 but was still long for a carbine, despite the letter suffix 'k' standing for kurz (short). This rifle was based on a commercial Mauser model known as the **Standard** and widely produced throughout the inter-war years in countries such as Czechoslovakia, Belgium and China. The German version was placed in production in 1935 and thereafter made in very large numbers.

Worsening standards

At first the standard of production was excellent, but once World War II had started the overall finish and standards fell to the extent that by the end of the war the wooden furniture was often laminated or of an inferior material, and items such as bayonet lugs were omitted. All manner of extras were evolved by the gadget-minded

Germans for the Kar 98k, including grenade-launching devices, periscopic sights and folding butts for weapons used by airborne troops. There were also variations for sniper use, some with small telescopic sights mounted half way along the forestock and others with larger telescopes mounted over the bolt action.

Despite all the innovations by the Germans during World War II, the Kar 98k was still in production as the war ended, looking not all that different overall from the original Gew 98 except for the rough finish resulting from wartime shortages of labour and materials. By this time the Germans had to hand a whole array of Mauser rifles drawn from nearly all the armies of Europe, and most of them were used to equip one arm or another of the services by 1945. Some of these Mausers, most of which were very similar to the Gew 98 or Kar 98k, and were kept in

production on Belgian and Czechoslovak lines for German use after 1939–40. Away to the east the Chinese armies were mainly equipped with the Mauser Standard rifles virtually identical to the Kar 98k.

There will always be arguments as to whether or not the Mauser rifles were better service rifles than the Lee-Enfield, M1903 Springfield and M1 Garand, but although the Mausers lacked some of the

German soldiers train for combat, armed with Kar 98k rifles. The photograph was probably taken between the wars, as indicated by the mix of old and new pattern helmets being worn at the same time.

overall appeal of the Allied rifles they provided the German forces with long and reliable service. Very few remain in use, but many are still prized as collector's pieces and match rifles.

Digging in during the early stages of the war. The length of the Mauser-designed Kar 98k is obvious, making it difficult to handle in confined spaces. Given the short combat ranges typical of World War II, the Kar 98k's long-range capability was largely superfluous.

SPECIFICATION	
Gewehr 98	**Karabiner 98k**
Calibre: 7.92-mm (0.312-in)	**Calibre:** 7.92-mm (0.312-in)
Length overall: 1250 mm (49.2 in)	**Length overall:** 1107 mm (43.6 in)
Length of barrel: 740 mm (29.1 in)	**Length of barrel:** 600 mm (23.6 in)
Weight: 4.2 kg (9.26 lb)	**Weight:** 3.9 kg (8.6 lb)
Muzzle velocity: 640 m (2,100 ft) per second	**Muzzle velocity:** 755 m (2,477 ft) per second
Feed: 5-round box magazine	**Feed:** 5-round box magazine

Maschinenpistole 43 and Sturmgewehr 44 Rifles

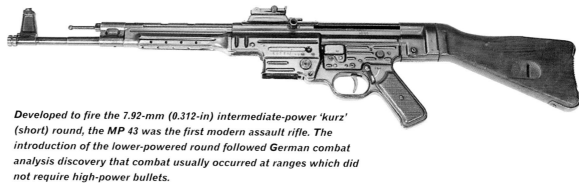

Despite the orders of Adolf Hitler, the German army was so determined to develop and use the gas-operated assault rifle that had been developed by Louis Schmeisser to fire the new 7.92-mm (0.312-in) Polte *kurz* (short) cartridge that it hid the experimental work under a new name. Originally the new rifle/cartridge combination was the **Maschinenkarabiner 42(H)** (the H was for Haenel, the developer and manufacturer), but to distract attention once Hitler had issued his ill-advised order it was changed to **Maschinenpistole 43**, or **MP 43**.

With the weapon in this form, the army went ahead from the development to the production stage, and the first examples were rushed to the Eastern Front, where they soon proved to be invaluable.

Earliest assault rifle

The MP 43 was the first of what are today termed assault rifles. It could fire single shots for selective fire in defence, and yet was capable of producing automatic fire for shock effect in the attack or for close-quarter combat. It was able to do this by firing a relatively low-powered round that was adequate for most combat ranges but which could still be handled comfortably when the weapon was producing automatic fire. Tactically this had a tremendous effect on the way the infantryman could fight, as he was no longer dependent on supporting fire from machine-

Developed to fire the 7.92-mm (0.312-in) intermediate-power 'kurz' (short) round, the MP 43 was the first modern assault rifle. The introduction of the lower-powered round followed German combat analysis discovery that combat usually occurred at ranges which did not require high-power bullets.

guns, being able to take his own personal support fire with him. This made German infantry units far more powerful because of the quantum increase in firepower that they could produce by comparison with that of units equipped with bolt-action rifles.

Once the importance of this increase in firepower had been fully realised, the MP 43 became a priority weapon and urgent requests were made for more and still more for the front-line troops. Initial supplies went mainly to elite units, but most went to the Eastern Front where they were most needed.

Unusually for wartime Germany, priority was given to production rather than development, and the only major change to the design was the **MP 43/1**, which had fittings for a grenade-launching cup on the muzzle. In 1944, for a reason undiscovered, the designation of the weapon was changed to **MP 44**, and late in the same year, after Hitler lifted his opposition to the weapon, a more forceful but also more accurate designation was bestowed on the weapon, which thereupon became known as the

German troops seen late in the war on the Eastern Front illustrate the superb quality of German military equipment. In addition to the revolutionary Sturmgewehr being carried by the soldier third from the left, they are also equipped with the MG42 and the Panther tank.

Sturmgewehr 44, which was generally abbreviated as **StG 44**. There were few if any production alterations to the design. Final production of the StG 44 was undertaken by Erma and Mauser as well as Haenel, and these major companies drew on the efforts of at least seven subcontractors producing parts and assemblies.

Irrelevant accessories

Some accessories were produced for the MP 43 series. One was an infra-red night sight known as *Vampir*, but one of the oddest items ever to be produced for any weapon was the *Krummlauf* curved barrel that could direct bullets around corners. Apparently this device was developed for the clearing of tank-killing infantry squads from armoured vehicles, but it was a bizarre device that never worked properly and yet managed to absorb a great deal of development potential at a time when this could have been directed towards more rewarding things. The curved barrels were intended to direct fire at angles of between 30° and 45°, and special periscopic mirror sights were devised to aim their fire. Few were actually produced and even fewer were used operationally.

After the war large numbers of MP 43s were used by several nations such as Czechoslovakia.

The Waffen SS were among the first troops to acquire the MP 43, and many were used in the battle of the Ardennes. The first combat use was probably on the Eastern Front, however, where the weapon was an immediate success.

SPECIFICATION	
StG 44	
Calibre: 7.92-mm (0.312-in)	**Muzzle velocity:** 650 m (2,132 ft) per second
Length overall: 940 mm (37 in)	**Rate of fire, cyclic:** 500 rounds per minute
Length of barrel: 419 mm (16.5 in)	**Feed:** 30-round box magazine
Weight: 5.22 kg (11.5 lb)	

Gewehr 41(W) & Gewehr 43 Rifles

The German army maintained an overall 'quality control' section that constantly sought ways to increase efficiency, and by 1940 this section had discovered the need for a self-loading rifle.

A specification was duly issued to industry, and Walther and Mauser each put forward designs that proved to be remarkably similar. Both used a method of operation known as the Bang system after its Danish designer, in which gases trapped around the muzzle are used to drive back a piston to carry out the reloading cycle. Troop trials soon proved that the Mauser design was unsuitable for service use and it was withdrawn, leaving the field free for the Walther design which became the 7.92-mm (0.312-in) **Gewehr 41(W)**.

Unfortunately for the Germans, once the Gewehr 41(W) reached front-line service, mainly on the Eastern Front, it proved to be somewhat less than a success. The Bang system proved to be too complex for reliable operation under service conditions, and the weapon was also too heavy for comfortable use as it was generally unhandy. The Gewehr 41(W) also proved to be difficult to manufacture and, as if all this was not enough, in action the

Developed from the Gewehr 41(W) with the Tokarev gas operating system, the Gewehr 43 was fitted with a telescopic sight mount and was a good sniper's rifle.

weapon proved to be difficult and time-consuming to load. But for a while it was the only self-loading rifle the Germans had and it was kept in production to the extent of tens of thousands.

Most of the Gewehr 41(W)s were used on the Eastern Front, and it was there that the Germans encountered the Soviet Tokarev automatic rifle. This used a gas-operated system that tapped off gases from the barrel to operate the mechanism, and once they had investigated this system the Germans realised that they could adapt it to suit the Gewehr 41(W). The result was the **Gewehr 43**, which used the Tokarev system virtually unchanged.

Swift production exit

Once the Gewehr 43 was in production, manufacture of the Gewehr 41(W) promptly ceased.

The Gewehr 43 was much easier to make, and it was soon being churned out in large numbers. Front-line troops greatly appreciated the ease with which it could be loaded compared with the earlier rifle, and it became a popular weapon. All manner of production short-cuts were introduced into the design, including the use of wood laminates and even plastics for the furniture, and in 1944 an even simpler design known as the **Karabiner 43** was introduced, the Karabiner designation being adopted although the overall

length was reduced by only some 50 mm (2 in).

Both the Gewehr 41(W) and the later Gewehr 43 used the standard German 7.92-mm cartridge, and were in no way related to the assault rifle programme that involved the 7.92-mm *kurz* cartridge. The retention of the rifle cartridge enabled the Gewehr 43 to be used as a very effective sniper rifle with a telescopic sight. The Gewehr 43 was so good in the sniper role that many were retained in service with the Czechoslovak army after WWII.

SPECIFICATION	
Gewehr 41(W)	**Gewehr 43**
Calibre: 7.92-mm (0.312-in)	**Calibre:** 7.92-mm (0.312-in)
Length overall: 1124 mm (44.25 in)	**Length overall:** 1117 mm (44 in)
Length of barrel: 546 mm (21.5 in)	**Length of barrel:** 549 mm (21.61 in)
Weight: 5.03 kg (11.09 lb)	**Weight:** 4.4 kg (9.7 lb)
Muzzle velocity: 776 m (2,546 ft) per second	**Muzzle velocity:** 776 m (2,546 ft) per second
Magazine: 10-round box	**Magazine:** 10-round box

Fallschirmjägergewehr 42 Rifle

By 1942 the Luftwaffe was encroaching on the preserves of the German army to an alarming extent for no other reason than petty wrangling, and when the army decided to adopt a self-loading rifle, the Luftwaffe decided that it too had to have such a weapon. Instead of following the path followed by the army with its adoption of the *kurz* round, the Luftwaffe decided instead to retain the standard 7.92-mm (0.312-in) rifle cartridge and asked Rheinmetall to design a weapon to arm the Luftwaffe's parachute troops, the *Fallschirmjäger*.

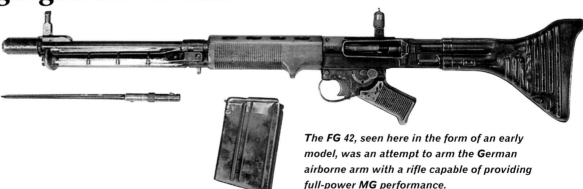

The FG 42, seen here in the form of an early model, was an attempt to arm the German airborne arm with a rifle capable of providing full-power MG performance.

Rheinmetall accordingly designed and produced one of the more remarkable small arms designs of World War II. This was the **Fallschirmjägergewehr 42** or **FG 42**, a weapon that somehow managed to compress the action

required to produce automatic fire into a volume little larger than that of a conventional bolt action.

The FG 42 was certainly an eye-catching weapon, for the

first examples had a sloping pistol grip, an oddly shaped plastic butt and a prominent bipod on the forestock. To cap it all there was a large muzzle attachment and provision for mounting a spike bayonet. The ammunition feed was from a side-mounted box magazine on the left, and the mechanism was gas-operated. All in all, the FG 42 was a complex weapon, but was not innovative as it was an amalgam of several existing systems.

Difficult manufacture

Needless to say the Luftwaffe took to the FG 42 avidly and asked for more. It did not get them, for it soon transpired that the novelties of the FG 42 had to be paid for in a very complex and costly manufacturing process. In an attempt to speed production, some simplification

was introduced. A simpler wooden butt was used and the pistol grip was replaced by a more orthodox component. The bipod was moved forward to the muzzle, and other shortcuts were introduced. Even so, by the end of the war only about 7,000 had been made.

It was after the war that the FG 42 made its biggest mark, for many of its design features were incorporated into later designs. Perhaps the most important of these was the compact gas-operated

mechanism which could fire from a closed bolt position for single-shot fire and from an open bolt for automatic fire.

The FG 42 was a highly advanced design for its day, and its other advanced features included the 'straight line' layout from butt to muzzle. But for all this the FG 42 was too difficult to produce, and even by 1945 there were still some bugs to be ironed out. For all that, the FG 42 was a truly remarkable design achievement in overall terms.

A drill book photograph of the FG 42 being fired in the prone position with its bipod folded. The FG 42 was a precursor of the modern-concept assault rifle.

SPECIFICATION	
FG 42	**Muzzle velocity:** 761 m (2,500 ft) per second
Calibre: 7.92-mm (0.312-in)	
Length overall: 940 mm (37 in)	**Rate of fire, cyclic:** 750–800 rpm
Length of barrel: 502 mm (19.76 in)	**Magazine:** 20-round box
Weight: 4.53 kg (9.99 lb)	

Tokarev Rifle

Over the years the Soviets revealed a considerable talent for innovatory small arms design, and thus they were early in the move toward self-loading rifles. The first of these was the **Avtomaticheskaya Vintovka Simonova** designed by S. G. Simonov for introduction in 1936 (and thus known also as the **AVS36**). Although many were made and issued, the AVS was not a great success for it produced a prodigious muzzle blast and recoil, and it was all too easy for dust and dirt to get into the complex mechanism. The AVS thus had only a short service life.

The **Samozariadnyia Vintovka Tokareva** (**SVT38**) that replaced the AVS in 1938 was designed by F. V. Tokarev, and

The SVT40 was an early Soviet self-loading rifle, usually issued to NCOs and marksmen. A most influential weapon, it lent features to the German MP 43, and was the start of a chain leading to the modern AK range.

was initially not much of an improvement on the AVS. It was a gas-operated weapon, like the AVS, but in order to keep the rifle light the mechanism was far too flimsy for the stresses and strains of prolonged use. While the combination of a gas-operated system and a locking block cammed downwards into a recess in the receiver base proved basically sound, it gave rise to frequent troubles, mainly

because parts broke. Thus the SVT38 was removed from production during 1940 and replaced by the much better **SVT40** in which the basic mechanism was retained but everything made more robust.

Continued problems

Even so, the SVT40 had a fierce recoil and considerable muzzle blast. To offset these effects, the SVT40 was fitted with a muzzle brake, initially with six ports but eventually with two. Theses muzzle brakes were of doubtful efficiency.

In order to get the best from the SVT40 the weapon was usually issued only to NCOs or

carefully trained soldiers who could use their rapid fire potential to good effect. Some were fitted with telescopic sights for sniper use. A few weapons were converted to produce fully automatic fire as the **AVT40**, but this conversion was not a great success. There was also a carbine version, but this probably suffered excessively from the heavy recoil problem and only a few were made.

Germans impressed

When the Germans invaded the USSR in 1941 they soon encountered the SVT38 and the SVT40. Any they could capture

Marines of the Soviet Northern Fleet in defensive positions, probably on exercise near Murmansk. The nearest man has a PPSh-41 sub-machine gun, and the others have Tokarev SVT40 rifles.

they promptly used under the designation **Selbstlade-gewehr 258(r)** and **Selbstladegewehr 259(r)**, but once the basic mechanism had been examined it was incorporated into the Gewehr 43.

Soviet production of the SVT40 continued almost until the end of the war. Although there were never enough produced to meet demand, the SVT40 had a considerable influence on future Soviet small arms development leading to the AK-47 series. It also made a

considerable impact on Soviet infantry tactics for the SVT40 demonstrated the importance of increased firepower for the infantry in its attempt to increase kill ratios, a factor later emphasized by the introduction of the German MP 43 on the Eastern Front.

SPECIFICATION	
Tokarev SVT40	**Weight:** 3.89 kg (8.58 lb)
Calibre: 7.62-mm (0.3-in)	**Muzzle velocity:** 830 m (2,723 ft) per
Length overall: 1222 mm (48.1 in)	second
Length of barrel: 625 mm (24.6 in)	**Magazine:** 10-round box

Mosin-Nagant Rifle

When the Russian army decided to adopt a magazine rifle to replace its Berdan rifles during the late 1880s, it opted for a weapon combining the best features of two designs, one by the Belgian Nagant brothers and the other a Russian design by a Captain Mosin. The result was the **Mosin-Nagant Model 1891** (otherwise **Vintovka obrazets 1891g**) with which the Tsarist army fought its last battles up to 1917. The Model 1891 was then adopted by the new Red Army, and the rifle remained in use for many years.

The Model 1891 fired a 7.62-mm (0.3-in) cartridge and was a sound but generally unremarkable design. The bolt action was rather complicated and the ammunition feed used a holding device that offered only one round under spring tension to the bolt for reloading. But for all this it was a sound enough weapon, although rather long. This was mainly to increase the reach of the rifle when fitted with the long socket bayonet, which was almost a permanent fixture in action. The bayonet had a cruciform point that was used to dismantle the weapon.

Metric updating

The original Model 1891s had their sights marked in

A Model 1938 Mosin-Nagant carbine. This variant, like the Model 1930, was simplified for ease of manufacture and was issued to the cavalry. Many were captured by Germany in the early war years.

arshins, an archaic Russian measurement equivalent to 0.71 m (27.95 in), but after 1918 these sights were metricated. In 1930 there began a modernisation programme, and all new rifles were produced to the new **Model 1891/30** standard, which was slightly shorter than the original and had several design alterations. It was the Model 1891/30 that was the main Red Army service rifle of World War II.

Carbine variants

The Mosin-Nagant weapons were also produced in carbine form. The first of these was the **Model 1910**, followed much later by the **Model 1938** equivalent to the Model 1891/30. In 1944 there appeared the **Model 1944**, but this was only a Model 1938 with a permanently fixed folding bayonet.

The Mosin-Nagant rifles were also used by the Finns

(**m/27** shortened Model 1891, **m/28/30** with altered sights, and re-stocked **m/39**), the Poles (**karabin wz 91/98/25**) and also by the Germans, who issued captured weapons to their own second-line garrison and militia units. Most of these were Model 1891/30s redesignated **Gewehr 254(r)**, but by 1945 even Model 1891s were being issued under the designation **Gewehr 252(r)**.

With the introduction of the automatic rifle in the years after World War II, the surviving Mosin-Nagant rifle soon disappeared from Red Army service.

A Red Army private at about the time of the 'Winter War' with Finland in the winter of 1940. He is armed with the Model 1930 variant of the Mosin-Nagant, a dragoon- length version of the rifle.

SPECIFICATION	
Model 1891/30 rifle	**Model 1938 carbine**
Calibre: 7.62-mm (0.3-in)	**Calibre:** 7.62-mm (0.3-in)
Length overall: 1232 mm (48.5 in)	**Length overall:** 1016 mm (40 in)
Length of barrel: 729 mm (28.7 in)	**Length of barrel:** 508 mm (20 in)
Weight: 4 kg (8.8 lb)	**Weight:** 3.47 kg (7.6 lb)
Muzzle velocity: 811 m (2,660 ft) per second	**Muzzle velocity:** 766 m (2,514 ft) per second
Magazine: 5-round box	**Magazine:** 5-round box

Rifle No. 4 Mk I

Although the Lee-Enfield No. 1 Mk III rifle performed sterling service throughout World War I, it was an expensive and time-consuming weapon to produce as every example had to be made virtually by hand. In the years after 1919, consideration was therefore given to a version of the basic design that could be mass-produced, and in 1931 a trial series of a rifle known as the No. 1 Mk VI was produced. This was accepted as suitable for service, but at the time there were no funds to launch production, so it was not until November 1939 that the go-ahead was given for what was then redesignated the **Rifle No. 4 Mk I**.

The No. 4 Mk I was designed from the outset for mass production, and differed from the original No. 1 Mk III in several respects: the No. 4 Mk I had a much heavier barrel that improved overall accuracy; the muzzle protruded from the forestock by an easily discernible amount and provided the No. 4 Mk I with a definite recognition point; and the sights

A No. 4 Mk I rifle dating from 1941 (top). The No. 4 was a simplified version of the No. 1, or SMLE (bottom). Major differences include deletion of the nose cap, relocation of the rear sight and redesign of the foresight.

were moved back to a position over the receiver, which made them easier to use and also provided a longer sighting base, again an aid to accuracy.

Unpopular bayonet

There were numerous other small changes, most of them introduced to assist production, but for the soldier the biggest change was to the muzzle. Here, a different fitting was introduced for a new bayonet, which was a light and simple spike with no grip or anything

like it, so depriving the soldier of one of his favourite front-line tools. The spike bayonet was not liked but, being simple and easy to produce, it was retained in use for many years.

Alongside the No. 1

The first No. 4 Mk Is were issued late in 1940, and thereafter the type supplemented the No. 1 Mk III. But during World War II the No. 1 Mk III was never entirely replaced. This was not for lack of production effort, for the No. 4 Mk I was churned out in very

Carrying No. 1 rifles with bayonets fixed, New Zealand infantry fight their way into a building during the battle of Cassino in 1943-44.

large numbers by numerous small arms production facilities all over the UK and even in the USA. These 'American' rifles were made at the Stevens-Savage plant in Long Branch and were known as the **No. 4 Mk I*** as they differed in the manner in which the bolt could be removed for cleaning. These

Men of a Gurkha regiment are briefed by an officer before a foray in the jungles of Burma. The men have No. 4 rifles, which were on the large side for the comparatively small stature of the Gurkhas, and also relatively unwieldy for jungle fighting.

American examples also differed in other small details, introduced mostly to assist production on US tooling and by American methods.

In service the No. 4 Mk I proved itself an excellent weapon, to the extent that many now regard the design as one of the finest of all service rifles of the bolt-action era. It was capable of withstanding even the roughest handling, and could deliver accurate fire for prolonged periods. It was relatively easy to strip and keep clean using the 'pull-through' carried inside the butt trap along with an oil bottle and a few pieces of the famous 'four by two' cleaning rag.

Special sniper's versions of the No. 4 were also produced. These used various types of telescopic sight over the receiver, as well as a special butt plate. The rifles were usually selected from production examples and were virtually rebuilt and restocked before issue with the revised designation **Rifle No. 4 Mark I(T)**.

The No. 4 Mk I is still in limited service around the world. Many examples have been revised with new 7.62-mm (0.3-in) barrels, and others have been converted to match or hunting rifles.

In the ruins of the Norman city of Caen, British infantry had to be especially careful as the debris made excellent sniper cover. This man carries a No. 4 rifle.

SPECIFICATION	
Rifle No. 4 Mk I	**Weight:** 4.14 kg (9.125 lb)
Calibre: 0.303-in (7.7-mm)	**Muzzle velocity:** 751 m (2,465 ft) per
Length overall: 1129 mm (44.4 in)	second
Length of barrel: 640 mm (25.2 in)	**Magazine:** 10-round box

Rifle No. 5 Mk I

By 1943 the British and Commonwealth armies fighting in the jungles of Burma and other Far Eastern areas began to question the suitability of the No. 1 and No. 4 Lee-Enfield rifles, which were too long and awkward. A shortened No. 4 was requested, and by September 1944 approval had been given for the **Rifle No. 5 Mk I**. This was virtually the No. 4 Mk I with a much shortened barrel, the forestock modified to accommodate the new barrel, and the sights changed to reflect the decreased-range performance of the shorter barrel.

Flash hider

Two other modifications were also introduced, both of them associated with the short barrel: these were a conical muzzle attachment that was meant to act as a flash hider, and a rubber pad on the butt. Both had to be introduced as the shortening of the barrel gave rise to two unwanted side effects: the prodigious muzzle flash produced by firing a normal rifle cartridge in a short barrel, and the ferocious recoil resulting from the same unfortunate factor.

In a normal long rifle barrel most of the flash produced on firing is contained within the barrel and so are some of the recoil forces. In a shortened barrel a good proportion of the propellant gases are still 'unused' as the bullet leaves the muzzle, hence the added recoil.

Developed specifically for jungle operations, the No. 5 rifle was not an unqualified success as it had a vicious recoil. It saw action in Kenya and Malaya (shown here), as well as at the end of World War II.

Lack of enthusiasm

The soldiers did not like the new weapon one bit, but they had to admit that in jungle warfare the No. 5 Mk I was a much handier weapon to carry and use. They also welcomed the reintroduction of a blade-type bayonet that fitted onto a lug under the muzzle attachment. In fact, following on from the first production order for 100,000 rifles made in 1944 it was thought that the No. 5 Mk I would become the standard service rifle of the years following World War II, despite the recoil and flash factors. But this did not happen.

The No. 5 Mk I had one built-in problem, quite apart from the flash and recoil, and that problem was never eradicated. For a reason that was never discovered the weapon was inaccurate. Even after a long period of 'zeroing', the accuracy would gradually 'wander' and be lost. All manner of modifications to the stocking of the weapon were tried, but the inaccuracy was never eliminated and the true cause was never discovered. Thus the No. 5 was not accepted as the standard service rifle, the No. 4 Mk I being retained until the Belgian FN was adopted in the 1950s. Most of the No. 5 rifles were retained for use by specialist units such as those operating in the Far East and Africa, and some are still there today.

SPECIFICATION	
Rifle No. 5 Mk I	**Weight:** 3.25 kg (7.15 lb)
Calibre: 0.303-in (7.7-mm)	**Muzzle velocity:** about 730 m (2,400
Length overall: 1003 mm (39.5 in)	ft) per second
Length of barrel: 476 mm (18.75 in)	**Magazine:** 10-round box

Rifle, Caliber .30, Model 1903

In 1903 the US Army decided to replace its existing Krag-Jorgensen rifles and adopted a rifle based on the Mauser system. This rifle, officially known as the **US Magazine Rifle, Caliber .30, Model of 1903** (or **M1903**) was first produced at the famous Springfield Arsenal and has thus become almost exclusively known as the **Springfield**. It was produced as a weapon for use by infantry and cavalry, and was thus much shorter than most contemporary rifles, but it was a well-balanced and attractive rifle that soon proved itself to be a fine service weapon.

Updated ammunition

Soon after the M1903 had entered production the original blunt-nosed ammunition was replaced by newer 'pointed' ammunition that is now generally known as the .30-06 (thirty-ought six) as

A Mauser patterned rifle, the M1903 Springfield proved a fine weapon, serving into the Korean war. The sniper version had a Weaver telescopic sight, and the conventional 'iron' sights have been removed entirely.

it was a 0.3-in (7.62-mm) round introduced in 1906. This remained the standard US service cartridge for many years. The M1903 served throughout World War I, and in 1929 the design was modified to **M1903A1** standard by the introduction of a form of pistol grip to assist aiming. The **M1903A2** was produced as a sub-calibre weapon inserted into the barrels of coastal guns for low-cost training purposes.

When the USA entered World War II in 1941 the new M1 Garand rifle was not available in the numbers required, so the M1903 was placed back into large-scale production, this time as the **M1903A3**. This version was modified to suit modern mass-production methods, but it was still a well-made rifle. Some parts were stampings rather than machined units, but the main change was movement of the sights from over the barrel to a position over the bolt action.

Sniper's model

The only other service version was the **M1903A4**. This was a sniper's version fitted with a Weaver telescopic sight without conventional 'iron' sights. The M1903A4 was still in service during the Korean War of the 1950s. It was used by several Allied armies during World War II. Many of the US troops who landed in Normandy on D-Day in June 1944 were still equipped with the Springfield. In 1940 some were sent to the UK to equip Home Guard units, and the type was even placed back into production to a British order, only for the order to be taken over for the use of US forces.

The M1903 and its variants may still be met today with a few smaller armed forces. But many are also retained as target or hunting rifles, for the M1903 Springfield is still regarded as one of the classic rifles of all time. It is even now a rifle that is a delight to handle and fire, and many are now owned by weapon collectors.

SPECIFICATION	
M1903A1	**Weight:** 4.1 kg (9 lb)
Calibre: 7.62-mm (0.3-in)	**Muzzle velocity:** 855 m (2,805 ft) per
Length overall: 1105 mm (43.5 in)	second
Length of barrel: 610 mm (24 in)	**Magazine:** 5-round box

The accuracy of the M1903 made it a popular weapon with sharpshooters, and in positions where a single well-aimed shot can be decisive, the small box magazine of five rounds was no handicap.

Rifle, Caliber .30, M1 (Garand)

The Garand was the first self-loading rifle accepted as a standard military weapon. Strong and sturdy, the gas-operated M1 was rather heavier than its predecessor, the M1903 Springfield bolt-action rifle.

One of the main distinctions of the **Rifle, Caliber .30, M1**, almost universally known as the **Garand**, is that it was the first self-loading rifle to be accepted for military service. That acceptance happened during 1932, but there followed a distinct gap before the rifle entered service. This interval resulted from the fact that it took some time for the production facilities to tool up for the complex manufacturing processes demanded by the design. The rifle was created by John C. Garand, who spent a great deal of time developing the design. This had the useful benefit that once the weapon had entered production, it was found to require very few alterations. As a result, the last M1 to be completed looked very much like the first weapon of the series.

A sturdy rifle

As already mentioned, the M1 was a complicated and expensive weapon to manufacture, largely as a result of the numerous machining operations that were needed on many of the weapon's components. But in overall terms the Garand was a strong weapon, and in action proved to be sturdy. On the other hand, however, the Garand was somewhat heavier than comparable bolt-action rifles.

The M1 was a gas-operated weapon. Thus gases were tapped off from the barrel near the muzzle to drive back a piston that in turn worked the operating system through the cycle of unlocking and driving back the bolt. The spent cartridge case was extracted and ejected as the bolt mechanism moved to the rear until checked and driven forward once more by the main spring to lift and chamber a fresh round before reaching its forward position and being locked once more, allowing the firer to pull the trigger once again.

When the USA entered World War II at the beginning of December 1941, most of the American regular forces were equipped with the M1. However, the rapid increase of numbers of men in uniform meant that the old M1903 Springfield rifle had to be placed back into production as a quick increase in the flow of M1s from the lines was virtually impossible for reason largely of the tooling problems. But gradually the manufacturing rate was built up, and some 5.5

A GI runs for cover as he comes under fire on Okinawa. The self-loading Garand gave US infantrymen a rate of fire advantage over opponents armed with bolt-action weapons.

million of these rifles had been made by the end of the war. Even so, production of the M1 was resumed during the Korean War of the early 1950s.

Genuine war winner

For the American forces the M1 Garand was a war-winning weapon whose strong construction earned the gratitude of many. But the rifle did possess one significant operational fault, namely its ammunition feed. Firstly, ammunition was fed into the rifle in eight-round clips, and the loading system was so arranged that it was possible to load only the full eight rounds or nothing. Secondly, after the last round had been fired, the empty clip was ejected from the receiver with a definite and pronounced sound that advertised to any nearby enemy that the firer's

rifle was empty. This problem was not eliminated from the M1 until 1957, when the US Army introduced the M14 rifle which was virtually a reworked M1 Garand with an increased ammunition capacity.

Many sub-variants of the M1 were produced but few actually saw service as the basic M1 proved adequate. There were two special sniper versions. the **M1C** and the **M1D**, both produced in modest numbers during 1944. Each had extras such as a muzzle flash cone and butt plates.

German service

The Germans used as many M1 rifles as they could capture with the designation **Selbstladegewehr 251(a)**, and the Japanese produced their own copy, the 7.7-mm (0.303-in) **Rifle Type 5**, of which only prototypes had been completed

by the time the war ended.

Post-war the M1 went on for many years as the standard US service rifle, and some were to be found in the hands of National Guard and other such units until recent times. Several nations continue to use the M1, and many designers have used the basic action: many Beretta rifles from Italy use the Garand system, as does the US 5.56-mm (0.22-in) Ruger Mini-14.

Garand-armed infantrymen of the US 4th Armored Division are seen in action in the Ardennes during the drive to relieve Bastogne and the trapped 101st Airborne Division at the end of 1944 and start of 1945.

SPECIFICATION	
Rifle M1	
Calibre: 7.62-mm (0.3-in)	**Weight:** 4.313 kg (9.5 lb)
Length overall: 1.107 m (43.6 in)	**Muzzle velocity:** 855 m (2,805 ft) per second
Length of barrel: 609 mm (24 in)	**Magazine:** 8-round box

Carbine, Caliber .30, M1, M1A1, M2 and M3

Above: Originally produced by Winchester, the lightweight M1 carbine was eventually manufactured by more than 10 companies in numbers exceeding six million.

The traditional personal weapon of second-line troops and specialists such as machine-gunners has generally been the pistol. However, when the US Army considered the equipment of such soldiers during 1940 it made a request for some form of carbine that could be easily handled and also readily stowed in the vehicles that were often used by such troops.

The result was a competition in which several manufacturers submitted proposals for a

weapon that was likely to be ordered in large and therefore lucrative numbers. The winning design was that offered by the Winchester company, and this was standardised for service as the **Carbine, Caliber .30, M1**.

Intermediate power

The M1 carbine was based on the use of an unusual gas-operated system and was designed round a special cartridge that was intermediate in power between a pistol cartridge and rifle cartridge.

The system works by tapping propellant gases from the underside of the barrel through a very small hole to pass into a sealed cylinder and so impinge on the head of a piston-like operating slide that moves back and thus starts the process of unlocking the bolt, extracting the spent case, compressing the return spring, chambering a fresh round and finally locking the bolt once more.

From the start the M1 carbine was an immediate success with

the troops to whom it was issued. It was light and easy to handle, and this led to the situation in which the employment of the new weapon soon spread from the second-echelon troops who were supposed to be issued with the carbine, to front-line troops such as officers and weapon teams.

In order to speed its introduction into service the M1 had been created as a single-shot weapon, and there was also a special variant with a folding stock known as the **M1A1**. This was produced for use by airborne units.

Later during World War II, a capability for automatic fire was added to create the variant known as the **M2**, which had a cyclic rate of about 750 to 775 rounds per minute; the weapon used a curved box magazine holding 30 rounds that could also be used on the M1.

The **M3** was a special night-fighting version with a large infra-red night sight, but only about 2,100 of these weapons were made. The M3 proved to be the one version of the M1 carbine series that was not produced in quantity, for by the time the war ended the production total had reached

Left: Front-line troops soon found that the easily handled M1 carbine was much less of a burden than a rifle when slogging through the surf or the jungle, and it began appearing with front-line US Marine Corps units.

Above: A US Marine, member of a machine-gun crew in the Pacific, clutches his M1 carbine and also the ammunition belt for a Browning 7.62-mm (0.3-in) machine-gun while waiting for his partner to hurl a hand grenade.

6,332 million examples of all versions, making the series the most prolific personal weapon family of the World War II period.

For all its handiness, the M1 carbine series had one major drawback, and that was the cartridge round which it had been designed. Being an intermediate-power type, the cartridge was characterised by a general lack of stopping power, even at close ranges. Being a carbine the M1 also lacked range, and was effective only to 100 m (110 yards) or so. But these drawbacks were more than offset by the overall handiness of the weapon. The M1 and its derivatives were easy to stow in vehicles or aircraft, and the M1A1 with its folding butt was even smaller. The weapon handled well in action and, after enough had been captured in the later stages of the European war, was deemed good enough for German use as the **Selbstladekarabiner 455(a)**.

Rapid disappearance

But for all its mass production and wartime success, the M1 is now little used by armed forces anywhere. Many police forces retain the type, mainly because the low-powered cartridge offers a lower possibility of causing 'collateral damage' to bystanders and others, than more powerful cartridges, especially in operations in urban areas. Typical of these police operators was the Royal Ulster Constabulary, which used the Carbine M1 as a counter to the far more powerful Armalites typically used by the nationalist terrorists of the Irish Republican Army and their rival loyalist terrorists.

Another part of the M1 story is the current lack of adoption of the M1's intermediate-power cartridge. During the war years these cartridges were churned out in millions but now the cartridge is little used.

SPECIFICATION	
Carbine M1	**Weight:** 2.36 kg (5.2 lb)
Calibre: 7.62-mm (0.3-in)	**Muzzle velocity:** 600 m (1,970 ft) per second
Length overall: 904 mm (35.6 in)	
Length of barrel: 457 mm (18 in)	**Magazine:** 15- or 30-round box

Lehky Kulomet ZB vz 26 and vz 30
Light machine guns

This is the Czechoslovak ZB vz 26, one of the most influential designs of its day and the forerunner of the British Bren gun; this example lacks its 20- or 30-round box magazine.

When Czechoslovakia was established as a state after 1919 it contained within its borders a wide range of skills and talents, and among them was small arms expertise. In the early 1920s a company was established at Brno as Ceskoslovenska Zbrojovka for the design and production of all types of small arms. An early product was a machine gun known as the **Lehky Kulomet ZB vz 24** using a box magazine feed, but it remained a prototype only for an even better design was on the stocks. Using some details from the vz 24 the new design was designated the **Lehky Kulomet ZB vz 26**.

This light machine gun was an immediate success and has remained one of the most inspirational of all such weapons ever since. The vz 26 was a gas-operated weapon with, under its barrel, a long gas piston operated by propellant gas tapped from the barrel via an adjustable gas vent about half-way down the finned barrel. Gas operating on the piston pushed it to the rear and a simple arrangement of a hinged breech block on a ramp formed the locking and firing basis. Ammunition was fed downward

from a simple inclined box magazine, and the overall design emphasised the virtues of ease in stripping, maintaining and using the weapon. Barrel cooling was assisted by the use of prominent fins all along the barrel, but a simple and rapid barrel change method was also incorporated.

The vz 26 was adopted by the Czechoslovak army and soon became a great export success, being used by a whole string of nations that included China, Yugoslavia and Spain. The vz 26 was followed in production by a slightly improved model, the **Lehky Kulomet ZB vz 30**, but to the layman the two models were identical, the vz 30 differing only in the way it was manufactured and in some of the internal details. Like the vz 26, the vz 30 was also an export success, being sold to such countries as Persia and Romania.

Many nations set up their own licensed production lines, and by 1939 the two were among the world's most numerous light machine gun types.

German use

When Germany started to seize most of Europe, starting with Czechoslovakia, the vz 26 and vz 30 became German weapons as the **MG 26(t)** and **MG 30(t)** respectively, and even remained in production at Brno for a while to satisfy the demands of the German forces. They were used all over the world and

were even issued as standard German civil and military police machine guns.

Of all the nations involved in World War II, none took to the type more avidly than China where production facilities were established. Perhaps the most lasting influence the vz 26 and vz 30 had was on other designs. The Japanese copied them, and so did the Spanish who produced a machine gun known as the FAO. The vz 26 was also the starting point for the British Bren, and the Yugoslavs produced their own variants.

SPECIFICATION	
ZB vz 26	**ZB vz 30**
Calibre: 7.92-mm (0.312-in)	**Calibre:** 7.92-mm (0.312-in)
Length overall: 1161 mm (45.7 in)	**Length overall:** 1161 mm (45.7 in)
Length of barrel: 672 mm (26.46 in)	**Length of barrel:** 672 mm (26.46 in)
Weight: 9.65 kg (21.3 lb)	**Weight:** 10.04 kg (22.13 lb)
Muzzle velocity: 762 m (2,500 ft) per second	**Muzzle velocity:** 762 m (2,500 ft) per second
Rate of fire, cyclic: 500 rpm	**Rate of fire, cyclic:** 500 rpm
Feed: 20- or 30-round inclined box	**Feed:** 30-round inclined box

Fusil Mitrailleur mle 1924/29 and Mitrailleuse mle 1931
Machine-guns

France's effort after World War I to develop an effective light machine gun led to a weapon whose action was based on that of the BAR but altered to suit the new French 7.5-mm (0.295-in) cartridge. The first model was the **Fusil Mitrailleur modèle 1924** (Automatic Rifle M1924). The design was modern and used an overhead 25- or 26-round box magazine. Separate triggers provided single-shot or automatic fire.

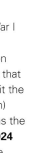

The Chatellerault modèle 1924/29 was the standard French light machine gun of 1940; it had a calibre of 7.5-mm (0.295-in) and used two triggers, one for automatic fire and the other for single shots.

Teething problems

Neither the gun nor the cartridge was fully developed before

introduction to service, resulting in barrel explosions. The solution was found in reducing the power

of the cartridge and beefing up some of the weapon's parts to create the **Fusil Mitrailleur**

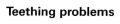

modèle 1924/29. A special variant of the mle 1924/29 was produced, initially for use in the Maginot Line defences but then also for tanks and other AFVs, as the **Mitrailleuse modèle 1931**. The mle 1931 had a peculiarly shaped butt and a side-mounted 150-round drum magazine. The internal arrangements were the same as the mle 1924/29, even if the overall length and barrel length were increased. In static defences the increased weight was of no handicap and the mle 1931 was produced in large numbers.

German service

France's defeat in June 1940 yielded large numbers of mle 1924/29 and mle 1931 weapons that the Germans used as the **leichte MG 116(f)** and **Kpfw MG 331(f)** respectively. Only a relatively few remained in French hands in the Middle East and North Africa. After 1945 the mle 1924/29 was returned to production and remained in service for many years.

The German booty of 1940 meant that many mle 1924/29s and mle 1931 machine guns were later incorporated into the defences of the Atlantic Wall, and the mle 1931 was especially favoured by the Germans as an anti-aircraft weapon. But for all this widespread use the mle 1924/29 and mle 1931 were never entirely trouble-free, and their cartridge was generally underpowered and lacking in range: maximum useful range was only 500 to 550 m (550 to 600 yards) instead of the 600 m (655 yards) or more of many contemporary designs.

SPECIFICATION	
Fusil Mitrailleur mle 1924/29	**Mitrailleuse mle 1931**
Calibre: 7.5-mm (0.295-in)	**Calibre:** 7.5-mm (0.295-in)
Length overall: 1007 mm (39.6 in)	**Length overall:** 1030 mm (40.55 in)
Length of barrel: 500 mm (19.69 in)	**Length of barrel:** 600 mm (23.6 in)
Weight: 8.93 kg (19.7 lb)	**Weight:** 11.8 kg (26.0 lb)
Muzzle velocity: 820 m (2,690 ft) per second	**Muzzle velocity:** 850 m (2,790 ft) per second
Rate of fire, cyclic: 450-600 rpm	**Rate of fire, cyclic:** 750 rpm
Feed: 25-round box	**Feed:** 150-round drum

Breda Machine guns

During World War I the standard Italian machine gun was the water-cooled Fiat modello 1914, and after the war this was modernised as the air-cooled Mitriaglice Fiat modello 1914/35. It was heavy, even in its new air-cooled form, and the design of a new light machine gun was initiated. This was produced by Breda, which used the experience gained by the production of earlier models in 1924, 1928 and 1929 to produce the **Fucile Mitriagliatori Breda modello 30** that became the Italians' standard light machine gun.

A 6.5-mm (0.256-in) Breda modello 30 light machine gun, one of the least successful machine guns ever designed. Despite a litany of faults, the gun served the Italians throughout World War II.

Many design failings

The modello 30 was one of those machine gun designs that could at best be deemed unsatisfactory. In appearance it looked to be all odd shapes and projections, and this was no doubt a hindrance to anyone who had to carry it as these projections snagged on clothing and other equipment. But this was not all, for the designers introduced a feed system using 20-round chargers which were rather flimsy and gave frequent trouble. These chargers were fed into a folding magazine that had a delicate hinge, and if this magazine or the fitting was damaged the gun could not be used.

To compound this problem, the extraction of the used cartridge cases was the weakest part of the whole gas-operated mechanism, and to make the gun work an internal oil pump was used to lubricate the spent cases and so aid extraction. While this system worked in theory, the added oil soon picked up dust and other debris to clog the mechanism, and in North Africa sand was an ever-present threat. As if this were not enough, the barrel-change method, although operable, was rendered awkward by the fact that there was no barrel handle (and thus no carrying handle), so the operator had to use gloves. With no other type in production the modello 30 had to be tolerated, and there was even a later **modello 38** version in 7.35-mm (0.29-in) calibre.

The other two Breda machine guns were better than the modello 30. One was the **Mitrigliera Breda RM modello 31**, produced for mounting on the light tanks operated by the Italian army. This had a 12.7-mm (0.5-in) calibre and used a large curved vertical box magazine that must have restricted the weapon's use in AFV interiors.

Heavy machine gun

As a heavy machine gun the company produced the **Mitragliace Breda modello 37**. In overall terms this was a satisfactory weapon, but was tactically hampered by its unusual feed arrangement: a flat 20-round feed tray which worked its way through the receiver to accept the spent cartridge cases. Exactly why this complex and quite unnecessary system was adopted is now impossible to ascertain, for the spent cases had to be removed from the tray before it could be reloaded with fresh rounds. The oil-pump extraction method was retained, thereby rendering the modello 37 prone to the same debris clogging as the lighter modello 30. Thus the modello 37 was no more than adequate, even though the type became the Italian army's standard heavy machine gun. A version of the modello 37 for tank mountings was produced as the **Mitriaglice Breda modello 38**.

SPECIFICATION	
modello 30	**modello 37**
Calibre: 6.5-mm (0.256-in)	**Calibre:** 8-mm (0.315-in)
Length overall: 1232 mm (48.5 in)	**Length overall:** 1270 mm (50 in)
Length of barrel: 520 mm (20.47 in)	**Length of barrel:** 740 mm (29.13 in)
Weight: 10.32 kg (22.75 lb)	**Weights:** gun 19.4 kg (42.8 lb) and tripod 18.7 kg (41.2 lb)
Muzzle velocity: 629 m (2,065 ft) per second	**Muzzle velocity:** 790 m (2,590 ft) per second
Rate of fire, cyclic: 450–500 rpm	**Rate of fire, cyclic:** 450–500 rpm
Feed: 20-round charger	**Feed:** 20-round tray

Type 11 & Type 96 Light machine guns

The heavy machine guns the Japanese used between 1941 and 1945 were both derivatives of the French Hotchkiss machine gun. When it came to lighter machine guns, the Japanese designed their own, the first of which was based on the same operating principles as the Hotchkiss but with the usual local variations.

The first of these was the 6.5-mm (0.256-in) **Light Machine Gun Type 11** that entered service in 1922 and remained in service until 1945. Its Hotchkiss origins were readily apparent in the heavily ribbed barrel and less obviously in the internal mechanisms. The design was credited to General Kijiro Nambu and it was as the 'Nambu' that the type was known to the Allies.

It was in its ammunition feed system that the Type 11 was unique, for it used a hopper system employed by no other machine gun. The idea was that a small hopper on the left of the receiver could be kept filled with the rounds fired by the rest of the Japanese infantry squad. The rounds could be fed into the hopper still in their five-round clips, thus rendering special magazines or ammunition belts

The Japanese 6.5-mm (0.256-in) Type 96 light machine gun was one of the few machine guns ever equipped with a bayonet, and was a combination of Czechoslovak and French designs.

unnecessary. But in practice this advantage was negated by the fact that the internal mechanism was so delicate and complex that firing the standard rifle round caused problems. Thus a special low-powered round had to be used, and matters were exacerbated by having to use a cartridge lubrication system that attracted the usual dust and other action-clogging debris.

Automatic fire only

The Type 11 was capable only of automatic fire, and when the weapon was fired the ammunition hopper tended to make the whole system unbalanced and awkward to fire. A special version, the **Tank Machine Gun Type 91**, was produced for use in tanks, with a 50-round hopper. The bad points of the Type 11 became very

apparent after early combat experience in China during the 1930s, and in 1936 there appeared a new **Light Machine Gun Type 96**. While the Type 96 was a definite improvement on the Type 11, it did not replace the earlier model in service as Japanese industry could never produce enough weapons of any type to meet demand.

The Type 96 used a mix of features from Hotchkiss and Czechoslovak ZB vz 26 weapons. One of the latter was the

overhead box magazine that replaced the hopper of the Type 11, but internally the cartridge-oiling system had to be retained. But the Type 96 did have a quick-change barrel system and there was a choice of drum or telescopic rear sights. The telescopic sights soon became the exception, but a handy magazine-filling device was kept. One accessory that was unique to the Type 96 among all other machine gun designs was a bayonet mounting.

SPECIFICATION	
Light Machine Gun Type 11	**Light Machine Gun Type 96**
Calibre: 6.5-mm (0.256-in)	**Calibre:** 6.5-mm (0.256-in)
Length overall: 1105 mm (43.5 in)	**Length overall:** 1054 mm (41.5 in)
Length of barrel: 483 mm (19.0 in)	**Length of barrel:** 552 mm (21.75 in)
Weight: 10.2 kg (22.5 lb)	**Weight:** 9.07 kg (20 lb)
Muzzle velocity: 700 m (2,295 ft) per second	**Muzzle velocity:** 730 m (2,395 ft) per second
Rate of fire, cyclic: 500 rpm	**Rate of fire, cyclic:** 550 rpm
Feed: 30-round hopper	**Feed:** 30-round box

Browning Automatic Rifle

The Browning Automatic Rifle M1918A2. This last production variant of the BAR light machine gun and/or automatic assault rifle used a 20-round box magazine and lacked the rapid-change barrel of other more modern light machine guns.

The **Browning Automatic Rifle**, or **BAR** as it is usually known, is one of those odd weapons that falls into no precise category. It may be regarded as a rather light machine-gun or as a rather heavy assault rifle, but in practice it was generally used as

a light machine gun.

As its name implies, the BAR was a product of John M. Browning's inventive mind, and Browning produced the first prototypes in 1917. When demonstrated they were immediately adopted for US

Army service and were thus taken to France for active use during 1918. But the numbers involved at that time were not large, and the few used were employed as heavy rifles. This was not surprising as the first variant was the **BAR M1918** that

had no bipod and could be fired only from the hip or shoulder. A bipod was not introduced until 1937 with the **BAR M1918A1**, and the BAR **M1918A2** final production version had a revised bipod and the facility for a monopod stock rest to be added

Combining assault rifle and light machine gun capabilities, the Browning Automatic Rifle was popular with its users in two world wars. Its weakest point was a magazine holding only 20 rounds.

SPECIFICATION	
BAR M1918A2	**Muzzle velocity:** 808 m (2,650 ft) per second
Calibre: 0.3-in (7.62-mm)	**Rate of fire, cyclic:** 500–600 rpm (fast rate) or 300–450 rpm (slow rate)
Length overall: 1214 mm (47.8 in)	
Length of barrel: 610 mm (24.0 in)	
Weight: 8.8 kg (19.4 lb)	**Feed:** 20-round straight box

for added stability. It was the M1918A1 and M1918A2 that were to become the main

The Browning Automatic Rifle is shown being carried by a US soldier in 1944.

American operational models, and they were issued to bolster squad fire power rather than as a squad support weapon.

The original M1918 did have a role to play in World War II, for the type was delivered to the UK in 1940 to provide additional firepower for the British Home Guard, and some found their way into other second-line use. The later models were produced in considerable numbers and, once in service in large numbers, they became a weapon upon which soldiers came to rely.

Not enough rounds

This is not to say that the BAR did not have faults, for the box magazine had a capacity of only 20 rounds, which was far too limited for most infantry

operations. Created as something of an interim weapon, the BAR had few tactical adherents in the theoretical field, but soldiers swore by the BAR and always wanted more. The BAR was used again in Korea in the early 1950s and was not replaced in US Army service until 1957.

Belgian manufacture

One little-known facet of BAR production is the pre-1939 output of a Belgian **modèle 30** variant by Fabrique Nationale. From this source there emerged a string of BAR

models in various calibres for many armies. Poland set up an assembly line for the BAR in 7.92-mm (0.312-in) calibre rather than the 7.65 mm (0.301 in) typical of Belgian production.

Many Polish BARs ended in Soviet hands after 1939, and even the German army used BARs captured from a variety of sources.

The Poles thought extremely highly of the BAR and even mounted the weapon on a specially produced, very complex and heavy tripod; there was also a special anti-aircraft version.

Browning M1919 Machine gun

The **Browning M1919** machine gun differed from the M1917 weapon in that the original water-cooled barrel was replaced by an air-cooled barrel. The M1919 weapon was originally intended for use in the many tanks the United States was planning to produce at that time, but the end of World War I led to the cancellation of the tank contracts, along with those for the original M1919. But the air-cooled Browning was developed into the **M1919A1**, **M1919A2** (for use by the US Cavalry) and then **M1919A3**. The production totals for these early models were never very high, but with the

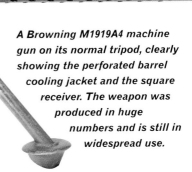

A Browning M1919A4 machine gun on its normal tripod, clearly showing the perforated barrel cooling jacket and the square receiver. The weapon was produced in huge numbers and is still in widespread use.

M1919A4 the totals soared. By 1945 the production total stood at 438,971, and more have been produced after that.

The M1919A4 was produced

mainly for infantry use, and proved to be a first-class heavy machine gun capable of pouring out masses of fire and absorbing all manner of abuse

and punishment. As a partner for this infantry version, a special model for use on tanks was produced as the **M1919A5**. There was also a US Army Air

Corps model, the **M2**, for use in both fixed and trainable installations, and the US Navy had its own range based on the M1919A4 and known as the **AN-M2**.

Among all these types, and in such a long production run, there were numerous minor and major modifications and production alterations, but the basic M1919 design was retained throughout. The M1919 used a fabric or metal-link belt feed. The normal mount was a tripod, and of these there were many designs ranging from normal infantry tripods to large and complex anti-aircraft mountings. There were ring- and gallows-type mountings for use on all sorts of trucks from jeeps to fuel tankers, and there were numerous special mountings for all manner of small craft.

Light machine gun

Perhaps the strangest of the M1919 variants was the **M1919A6**. This was produced as a form of light machine gun to bolster infantry squad power, which until the introduction of the M1919A6 had to depend on the firepower of the BAR and the rifle. The M1919A6 was a 1943 innovation: it was basically the M1919A4 fitted with an awkward-looking shoulder stock, a bipod, a carrying handle and a lighter barrel. The result was a light machine gun that was rather heavy but at least had the advantage that it could be produced quickly on existing production lines. Disadvantages were the general awkwardness of the weapon and the need to wear a mitten to change the barrel after it had become hot. Despite these factors, the M1919A6 was churned out in large numbers (43,479 by the time production ended), and troops had to endure it as it was better in its role than the BAR.

If there was one overall asset that was enjoyed by all the versions of the M1919 series of machine guns it was reliability, for the types would carry on working even in conditions in which other designs (other than perhaps the Vickers) would have given up. They all used the same recoil method of operation: muzzle gases push back the entire barrel and breech mechanism until a bolt accelerator continues the rearward movement to a point at which springs return the whole mechanism to restart the process.

The M1919 series is still in widespread use, the M1919A6 is now being used by only a few South American states.

Despite the fact that it was an air- rather than water-cooled weapon, the Browning M1919A4 was a capable machine gun for the sustained-fire role. Ammunition was delivered in boxed fabric or metal-link belts.

SPECIFICATION	
Browning M1919A4	**Browning M1919A6**
Calibre: 0.3-in (7.62-mm)	**Calibre:** 0.3-in (7.62-mm)
Length overall: 1041 mm (41 in)	**Length overall:** 1346 mm (53 in)
Length of barrel: 610 mm (24 in)	**Length of barrel:** 610 mm (24 in)
Weight: 14.06 kg (31 lb)	**Weight:** 14.74 kg (32.5 lb)
Muzzle velocity: 854 m (2,800 ft) per second	**Muzzle velocity:** 854 m (2,800 ft) per second
Rate of fire, cyclic: 400–500 rpm	**Rate of fire, cyclic:** 400–500 rpm
Feed: 250-round fabric or metal-link belt	**Feed:** 250-round fabric or metal-link belt

Browning 0.5-in Heavy machine gun

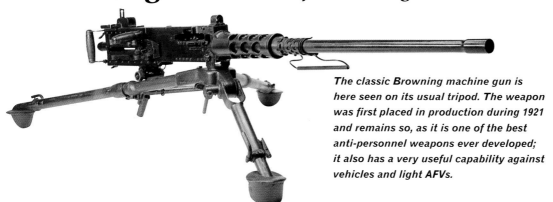

The classic Browning machine gun is here seen on its usual tripod. The weapon was first placed in production during 1921 and remains so, as it is one of the best anti-personnel weapons ever developed; it also has a very useful capability against vehicles and light AFVs.

Ever since the first examples of this weapon were produced in 1921, the 0.5-in (12.7-mm) Browning heavy machine gun has been one of the most feared anti-personnel weapons likely to be encountered. The projectile fired by the type is a prodigious man-stopper, and the machine gun can also be used to defeat vehicles and light armour, especially when firing armour-piercing rounds. The round is really the heart of the gun and early attempts by Browning to produce a heavy machine gun all foundered on the lack of a suitable cartridge.

German round

It was not until the examination of a captured German round, the 13-mm (0.51-in) type fired by the Mauser T-Gewehr anti-tank rifle, that the solution was found, and thereafter all was well. The basic cartridge has remained essentially unchanged, although there have been numerous alternative propellants and projectile types.

From the original **Browning M1921** heavy machine gun evolved a whole string of variants based on what was to become known as the **M2**. On all these variants the gun mechanism remained the same, being very similar to that used on the smaller M1917 machine gun. Where the variants differed from each other was in the type of barrel fitted and the fixtures used to mount the gun.

One of the most numerous of the M2s has been the **M2HB**, the suffix denoting the Heavy Barrel. The HB version can be used in all manner of installations, and in the past has been employed as an infantry gun, as an anti-aircraft gun and also as a fixed and trainable aircraft gun. For infantry use the M2HB is usually mounted on a heavy tripod, but it can also be used mounted on vehicle pintles, ring mountings and pivots. Other M2s have included versions with water-cooled barrels, usually employed as anti-aircraft weapons, especially on US Navy

vessels on which in World War II they were often fixed in multiple mountings for use against low-flying attack aircraft. Single water-cooled mountings were often used to provide anti-aircraft defence for shore installations.

Barrel lengths

The main change between ground and air versions is that the aircraft model has a barrel 914 mm (36 in) long whereas the ground version had a barrel 1143 mm (45 in) long. Apart from the barrel and some mounting fixtures, any part of the M1921 and M2 machine guns are interchangeable.

More 0.5-in Browning machine guns have been produced in the USA than any other design. The figure runs into millions, and during the late 1970s two US companies found it worth putting the type back into production. The same was true of the Belgian FN concern.

There are many companies throughout the world Keit find it profitable to provide spares and other such backing for the M2, and ammunition producers frequently introduce new types of cartridge. Many dealers find it profitable just to sell or purchase such weapons alone. The M2 will be around for decades to come, and there is no sign of any replacement entering the lists. The M2 must rank as one of the most successful machine gun designs ever produced.

SPECIFICATION	
Browning M2HB	tripod 19.96 kg (44 lb) for M3 type
Calibre: 0.5-in (12.7-mm)	**Muzzle velocity:** 884 m (2,900 ft) per
Length overall: 1654 mm (65.1 in)	second
Length of barrel: 1143 mm (45 in)	**Rate of fire, cyclic:** 450–575 rpm
Weights: gun 38.1 kg (84 lb) and	**Feed:** 110-round metal-link belt

Bren Light machine gun

The **Bren Gun** was evolved from the Czechoslovak ZB vz 26 light machine gun, but the development path was one that involved as much British as Czechoslovak expertise. During the 1920s the British army sought far and wide for a new light machine gun to replace the generally unsatisfactory Lewis Gun, trying all manner of designs of which most were found wanting in some way or other. In 1930 there began a series of trials involving several designs, among them the vz 26 in the form of a slightly revised model, the vz 27. The vz 27 emerged as a clear winner from these trials. It was made only in 7.92-mm (0.312-in) calibre, though, and the British army wanted to retain the 0.303-in (7.7-mm) cartridge with its outdated cordite propellant and its awkward rimmed case.

Thus started a series of development models that involved the vz 27, the later vz 30 and eventually an interim model, the vz 32. Then came the vz 33, and it was from this that the Royal Small Arms Factory at Enfield Lock evolved the prototype of what became the Bren Gun (Bren from the 'Br' of Brno, the place of origin,

The Bren gun is seen here in its original production form with a drum rear sight and adjustable bipod legs – on later versions these were replaced by simpler components that were easier to make and simpler to service.

and the 'en' of Enfield Lock). Tooling up at Enfield Lock resulted in the completion in 1937 of the first production **Bren Gun Mk 1**, and thereafter the type remained in production at Enfield and elsewhere until well after 1945. By 1940 well over 30,000 Bren Guns had been produced and the type was firmly established in service, but the result of Dunkirk gave the Germans a useful stock of Bren Guns, for service with the revised designation **leichte MG 138(e)**, and ammunition, and also led to a great demand for new Bren Guns to re-equip the British army.

Simplified design

The original design was thus much modified to speed production, and new lines were established. The original gas-operated mechanism of the ZB design was retained, as were the the breech locking system and general appearance, but out went the rather complicated drum sights and extras such as the under-butt handle in the **Bren Gun Mk 2**. The bipod became much simpler but the curved box magazine of the 0.303-in Bren was carried over. In time more simplifications were made (**Bren Gun Mk 3** with a shorter barrel and **Bren Gun Mk 4** with a

modified butt assembly), and there was even a reversion to the 7.92-mm calibre when Bren Guns were manufactured in Canada for China.

Classic of its type

The Bren Gun was a superb light machine gun. It was robust, reliable, easy to handle and to maintain, and it was not too heavy for its role. It was also very accurate. In time a whole range of mountings and accessories was introduced, including some rather complex anti-aircraft mountings that included the Motley and the Gallows mountings.

A 200-round drum was developed but little used, and various vehicle mountings were designed and introduced. The Bren Gun outlived all of these accessories, for after 1945 the type remained in service and the wartime 'extras' were phased out as being irrelevant to the increasingly 'hi-tech' modern battlefield, and they were also costly to maintain.

The Bren Gun on its basic bipod did linger on, however, and is still in limited service with some armies as the Bren Gun L4 series. It has revisions to fire the NATO standard 7.62-mm (0.3-in) cartridge through a barrel chrome-plated to reduce wear.

Against a backdrop of palms and a Stuart light tank, Australians attack a Japanese strongpoint in New Guinea. The men in the foreground have Bren light machine guns.

SPECIFICATION	
Bren Light Machine Gun Mk 1	**Muzzle velocity:** 744 m (2,440 ft) per
Calibre: 0.303-in (7.7-mm)	second
Length overall: 1156 mm (45.5 in)	**Rate of fire, cyclic:** 500 rpm
Length of barrel: 635 mm (25 in)	**Feed:** 20-round curved box
Weight: 10.03 kg (22.12 lb)	magazine

Vickers Machine guns

A 0.303-in (7.7-mm) Vickers machine gun in its late production form with no corrugations on the barrel jacket, the final form of the muzzle attachment and the indirect-fire sight in position.

The series of Vickers machine guns had its origins in the Maxim gun of the late 19th century, and was little changed from the original other than that the Maxim locking toggle design was inverted in the Vickers product. The **Vickers Machine Gun Mk 1** had done magnificently in World War I, out-performing nearly all of its contemporaries in many respects. After 1918, therefore, the Vickers remained the standard heavy machine gun of both the British army and many of the Commonwealth forces. Many were exported all over the world but much of these were ex-stock weapons as production was kept at a very low ebb at Vickers' main production plant at Crayford in Kent.

However, some innovations were introduced before 1939; the introduction of the tank had led to the design of Vickers machine guns to arm the new fighting machines, and by 1939 Vickers had in production two types of tank machine gun.

Two calibres

These were produced in two calibres: the **Vickers Machine Gun Mks 4B, 6, 6*** and **7** were of 0.303-in (7.7-mm) calibre and the **Vickers Machine Gun Mks 4** and **5** of 0.5-in (12.7-mm) calibre to fire a special cartridge. Both were produced for all types of tank initially, but the introduction of the Besa air-cooled machine guns for use in most heavier tanks meant that the majority of the Vickers tank machine guns ended either in light tanks, or infantry tank types such as the Matilda 1 and 2. The 0.5-in machine guns were also produced in a variety of forms for the Royal Navy as the **Vickers Machine Gun Mk 3** for installation on several types of mounting for the anti-aircraft defence of ships and shore installations. The ship installations included quadruple mountings, but the cartridge produced for this weapon was underpowered and therefore not a success. Nevertheless, in the absence of any alternative, the weapon

SPECIFICATION	
Vickers Machine Gun Mk 1	water, and tripod 22 kg (48.5 lb)
Calibre: 0.303-in (7.7-mm)	**Muzzle velocity:** 744 m (2,440 ft) per
Length overall: 1156 mm (45.5 in)	second
Length of barrel: 721 mm (28.4 in)	**Rate of fire, cyclic:** 450–500 rpm
Weight: gun 18.1 kg (40 lb) with	**Feed:** 250-round fabric belt

Men of the Cheshire Regiment using their Vickers machine guns on a range, circa 1940; note the water cans to condense steam from the barrel jacket back into cooling water.

was produced in considerable numbers, only later being replaced by 20-mm cannon and other such weapons.

Thus 1939 found the Vickers machine gun still in large-scale service. By 1940 stockpiled older weapons were being used in a host of roles including emergency anti-aircraft mountings to bolster home defences, and large-scale manufacture was soon under way once more.

Production shortcuts

Demand was so heavy, most of the British army's machine gun stocks having been before or during the Dunkirk episode, that production shortcuts were introduced. The most obvious of these was the replacement of the corrugated water jacket round the barrel by a simpler smooth jacket. Later a new muzzle booster design was introduced and by 1943 the new Mk 8Z boat-tailed bullet was in widespread use to provide a useful effective range of 4115 m (4,500 yards), enabling the Vickers machine gun to be used for the indirect fire role once a mortar sight had been adapted for the role.

After World War II the Vickers served on (and still does) with armies such as those of India and Pakistan. The British army ceased to use the type in 1968 but the Royal Marines continued to use theirs effectively until well into the 1970s.

Vickers-Berthier Light machine guns

The Vickers-Berthier series of light machine guns was evolved from a French design of just before World War I. Despite some promising features, the design was not adopted in numbers by any nation, but in 1925 the British Vickers company purchased rights to the type, mainly to give its Crayford factory a new model to replace the Vickers machine gun. After a series of British army trials the type was adopted by the Indian Army as its standard light machine gun, and eventually a production line for this **Vickers-Berthier Light Machine Gun Mk 3** was established at Ishapore in India.

The Vickers-Berthier Mk 3B produced for the Indian Army, showing the overall clean lines and general resemblance to the Bren Gun. The 30-round box magazine is not fitted.

Bren similarities

In appearance and design the Vickers-Berthier light machine gun was similar to the Bren Gun, but internally and in detail there were many differences. Thus at times observers thought that the Vickers-Berthier weapon was a Bren Gun.

Apart from the large Indian Army contract the only other sales were to a few Baltic and South American states, and today the Vickers-Berthier is one of the least known of all World War II machine guns. This is not because there was anything wrong with the type, which was a sound and reliable design, but because it had poor 'press' coverage and numerically was well outnumbered by the Bren Gun. But even today it remains in reserve use in India.

There was one Vickers-Berthier gun derivative that did, however, obtain a much better showing. This was a much modified version with a large drum magazine mounted above the receiver, and a spade grip at the rear where

SPECIFICATION	
Vickers-Berthier Light Machine Gun Mk 3	**Vickers G.O. Gun**
Calibre: 0.303-in (7.7-mm)	**Calibre:** 0.303-in (7.7-mm)
Length overall: 1156 mm (45.5 in)	**Length overall:** 1016 mm (40 in)
Length of barrel: 600 mm (23.6 in)	**Length of barrel:** 529 mm (20.83 in)
Weight: 11.1 kg (24.4 lb)	**Weight:** 9.5 kg (21 lb)
Muzzle velocity: 745 m (2,450 ft) per second	**Muzzle velocity:** 745 m (2,450 ft) per second
Rate of fire, cyclic: 450–600 rpm	**Rate of fire, cyclic:** 1,000 rpm
Feed: 30-round box magazine	**Feed:** 96-round drum magazine

the butt would normally have been fitted. The weapon was a special design for installation on a Scarff ring mounting on open-cockpit aircraft, in which it would be used by the observer/gunner.

Aircraft use

Large numbers of this design were produced for the Royal Air Force, by which it was known as the Vickers G.O (G.O. for gas operated) or **Vickers K** gun, but almost as soon as the type had been introduced to service the era of the open cockpit came to a sudden close with the introduction of higher-speed aircraft. The G.O. proved difficult to use in the close confines of aircraft turrets and impossible to use in wing installations, so almost immediately it was placed in store; some were used by the Fleet Air arm on aircraft such as the Fairey Swordfish and thus remained in use until 1945, but their numbers were relatively few.

In 1940 many G.O. guns were taken out of store for extensive use in the airfield defence and related roles. In North Africa the G.O. was widely used by the irregular forces that sprang up for behind-the-lines operations, such as 'Popski's Private Army', on heavily armed jeeps and trucks. The weapon proved ideal in the role and gave a good indication of how the original Vickers-Berthier machine guns would have performed given a greater opportunity. The G.O. guns were used until the end of the war in Italy and a few other theatres, and then passed right out of use.

This sepoy, carrying a Vickers-Berthier Mk 3, is dressed in standard issue khaki drill, with two large pouches for spare magazines. The Indian Army was the major user of the Vickers-Berthier gun.

Maschinengewehr MG 34 General-purpose machine gun

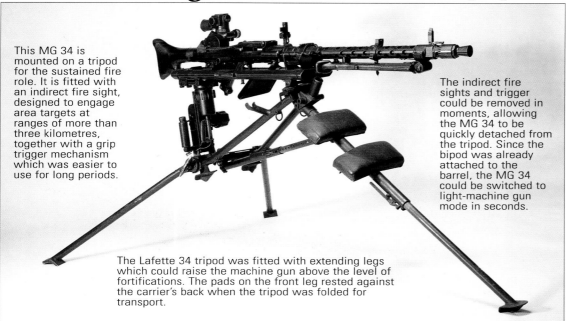

This MG 34 is mounted on a tripod for the sustained fire role. It is fitted with an indirect fire sight, designed to engage area targets at ranges of more than three kilometres, together with a grip trigger mechanism which was easier to use for long periods.

The indirect fire sights and trigger could be removed in moments, allowing the MG 34 to be quickly detached from the tripod. Since the bipod was already attached to the barrel, the MG 34 could be switched to light-machine gun mode in seconds.

The Lafette 34 tripod was fitted with extending legs which could raise the machine gun above the level of fortifications. The pads on the front leg rested against the carrier's back when the tripod was folded for transport.

The terms of the Versailles Treaty of 1919 specifically prohibited the development of any form of sustained-fire weapon by Germany. However, this provision was circumvented by the Rheinmetall-Borsig arms concern during the early 1920s by the simple expedient of setting up a 'shadow' company under its control over the border at Solothurn in Switzerland.

Research carried out into air-cooled machine gun designs led to a weapon that evolved into the Solothurn Modell 1930, an advanced design that introduced many of the features that were incorporated in later weapons. A few production orders were received, but it was felt by the Germans that something better was required and thus the Modell 1929 had only a short production run before being used as the starting point for an aircraft machine gun, the Rheinmetall MG 15. This long remained in production for the Luftwaffe.

First GPMG

From the Rheinmetall designs came what remains viewed as one of the finest machine guns ever made, the **Maschinengewehr 34** or **MG 34**. Mauser designers at the Obendorff plant used the Modell 1929 and the MG 15 as starting points for what was to be a new breed of weapon, the general-purpose machine gun (GPMG). Fired from a bipod, it could be carried and used by an infantry squad. Mounted on a heavier tripod it could be equally effective in providing long periods of sustained fire.

Selective fire

The mechanism was of the all-in-line type, with a quick-change barrel for use in sustained fire. The ammunition could be fed either from a saddle-drum magazine holding 75 rounds inherited from the MG 15, or a belt feed. To add to all this technical innovation, the

MG 34 had a high rate of fire and could thus be effective against low-flying aircraft.

The MG 34 was also one of the first selective-fire weapons. The trigger mechanism was hinged in the centre: pressure on the top half of the trigger gave the firer single shots, while pressure on the lower half provided fully automatic fire.

The MG 34 was an immediate success, and went straight into production for the German armed forces and police. Demand for the MG 34 remained high through to 1945,

and consistently outstripped supply. The supply situation was not aided by the number of mounts and gadgets that were introduced.

These varied from heavy tripods and twin mountings to expensive and complex fortress and tank mountings. There was even a periscopic sight to enable the weapon to be fired from trenches. These accessories consumed a great deal of production potential to the detriment of gun production proper, but production of the MG 34 was in any case not aided by the fact that the design was really too good for military use.

The MG 34 took too long to manufacture, and involved too many complex and expensive machining processes. The result was a weapon without peer, but actually using it was rather like using a Rolls-Royce as a taxi – it did the job superbly, but at much too high a cost.

Variants of the basic machine gun included the **MG 34m** with a heavier barrel jacket for use in AFVs, and the shorter **MG 34s** and **MG 34/41** intended for use in the AA role and capable of automatic fire only. The overall length and barrel length of the latter two were about 1170 mm (46 in) and 560 mm (22 in).

SPECIFICATION	
MG 34	**Rate of fire, cyclic:** 800–900 rounds per minute
Calibre: 7.92-mm (0.31-in)	**Feed:** 250 round belt (comprising five linked 50-round belt lengths), or 75-round saddle drum
Length overall: 1219 mm (48 in)	
Length of barrel: 627 mm (24.5 in)	
Weight: 11.5 kg (25.3 lb) with bipod	**Effective range:** 700 m (2,296 ft) direct fire, 3500 m (11,483 ft) indirect fire
Muzzle velocity: 755 m (2,475 ft) per second	

Mounted on a tripod, the MG 34 was a steady and effective weapon, but its relatively light weight and high rate of fire meant that on a bipod it was less steady and could not achieve the accuracy of which it was capable.

Maschinengewehr MG 42 General-purpose machine gun

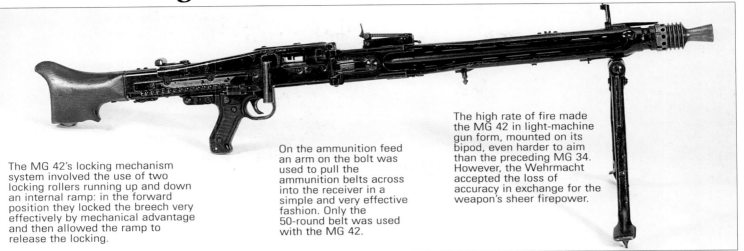

The MG 42's locking mechanism system involved the use of two locking rollers running up and down an internal ramp: in the forward position they locked the breech very effectively by mechanical advantage and then allowed the ramp to release the locking.

On the ammunition feed an arm on the bolt was used to pull the ammunition belts across into the receiver in a simple and very effective fashion. Only the 50-round belt was used with the MG 42.

The high rate of fire made the MG 42 in light-machine gun form, mounted on its bipod, even harder to aim than the preceding MG 34. However, the Wehrmacht accepted the loss of accuracy in exchange for the weapon's sheer firepower.

The MG 34 was an excellent weapon but was really too good for its task in terms of cost and production requirements. Despite the setting up of a full production facility and constant demand, by 1940 the Mauser designers were examining simpler options. The manufacturers of the 9-mm MP 40 sub-machine gun had showed what could be done to introduce production simplicity and reduce cost. Following this example the Mauser designers decided to adopt new production methods using as few expensive machining processes as possible allied with new operating mechanisms.

Hybrid design

The new mechanisms came from a number of sources.

Experience with the MG 34 had indicated how the feed could be revised. Polish designs from arms factories over-run in 1939 promised a new and radical breech locking system, and other ideas came from Czechoslovakia. From this wealth of innovation came a new design, the **MG 39/41**, and out of a series of trials carried out with this design emerged the **Maschinengewehr 42** or **MG 42,** one of the most effective and influential fireams in history.

The MG 42 introduced mass production techniques to the machine gun on a large scale. Earlier designs had used some simple sheet metal stampings and production short-cuts, but the harsh environment that the

machine gun has to endure meant that few had any success.

Unlike earlier guns made on the cheap, the MG 42 was an immediate success. Sheet metal stampings were extensively used for the receiver and for the barrel housing, which incorporated an ingenious barrel-change system. The ability to change barrels quickly was vital, for the MG 42 had a prodigious rate of fire of up to 1400 rounds per minute, twice as fast as any Allied weapon.

Rate of fire

This was a result of the new locking mechanism, which the designers had borrowed from several sources and was both simple and reliable.

These design details merged to form a very effective general-purpose machine gun,

which could be attached to a wide range of mounts and accessories.

The MG 42's operational debut came in 1942, appearing simultaneously in both the USSR and North Africa. Thereafter it was used on every front. In general, issue was made to front-line troops only, for though intended to supplant the MG 34, in fact the MG 42 only supplemented it.

Not content with producing one of the finest machine gun designs ever produced, the Mauser design team tried to go one better and came up with the MG 45 with an even higher rate of fire. The end of the war put paid to that design for the time being, but the MG 42 and its descendants will continue to serve armies all over the world.

SPECIFICATION	
MG 42	second
Calibre: 7.92 mm (0.303 in)	**Rate of fire:** up to 1,550 rounds per
Length overall: 1220 mm (48 in)	minute cyclic
Length of barrel: 533 mm (21 in)	**Feed:** 50-round belt
Weight: 11.5 kg (25 lb 6 oz) with bipod	**Effective range:** 3000 m (9,842 ft)
Muzzle velocity: 755 m (2,475 ft) per	indirect, 600 m (1,968 ft) direct fire

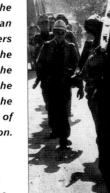

Right: The MG 42 was the primary weapon of the German infantry squad. All members carried a part of the load on the move. The gunner carried the gun, a second man carried the tripod, and everyone in the squad carried spare links of ammunition.

Left: German mountain troops with an MG 42. The Allies came to fear the distinctive 'ripping linoleum' sound produced by the sheer number of rounds the machine gun could put out.

DShK1938, SG43 & others
Heavy machine guns

The SG43 was designed by P. M. Goryunov in 1942 to provide a wartime replacement for the elderly Maxim Model 1910, and even used the old Maxim's wheeled carriage.

If there has ever been a single factor differentiating machine guns of Russian and Soviet design from those created in other nations it has been the simple factor of weight. For many years Russian and Soviet machine guns were built to such a standard of robustness that weight alone was used as a means of incorporating strength, the ultimate example being the old M1910 Maxim guns that almost resembled small artillery pieces with their wheeled and shielded carriages. Eventually this avoidable trait was recognised by the Red Army at the time that mobility began to make its importance felt within the context of long-term planning. By the mid-1930s, when there appeared the requirement for a new heavy machine gun, emphasis was finally placed more on strength as a factor that could be

created by design rather than as a by-product of mass.

The new heavy machine gun was intended to be in the same class as the 12.7-mm (0.5-in) Browning designed in the USA, but the Soviet equivalent turned out to be slightly lighter than its American counterpart. It used a 12.7-mm (0.5-in) cartridge and was intended for a variety of roles. To its long-lasting credit, the new **DShK1938** (in full the *Krasnoi Pulyemet Degtyereva-Shpagina obrazets 1938g*) has proved to be almost as successful as the Browning weapon, for it long remained in production, albeit in a modified form after World War II as the **DShK1938/46**, and is still in widespread service.

Massive carriage

If the DShK1938 was lighter as a gun than the Browning, the same could not be said of its

SPECIFICATION

DShK1938	**SG43**
Calibre: 12.7-mm (0.5-in)	**Calibre:** 7.62-mm (0.3-in)
Length overall: 1602 mm (63.1 in)	**Length overall:** 1120 mm (44.1 in)
Length of barrel: 1002 mm (39.45 in)	**Length of barrel:** 719 mm (28.3 in)
Weight: 33.3 kg (73.5 lb)	**Weight:** 13.8 kg (30.4 lb)
Muzzle velocity: 843 m (2,765 ft) per second	**Muzzle velocity:** 863 m (2,830 ft) per second
Rate of fire, cyclic: 550–600 rpm	**Rate of fire, cyclic:** 500–640 rpm
Feed: 50-round metal-link belt	**Feed:** 50-round metal-link belt

mount, for as an infantry gun the DShK1938 retained the old wheeled carriage of the M1910, although a special anti-aircraft tripod was also introduced and is still in use. The type became a virtual fixture on most Soviet tanks from the IS-2 heavy tanks onward, and Czechoslovakia produced a quadruple mounting with DShK1938s for anti-aircraft use. There was even a special version for use on armoured trains.

The smaller **SG43** was introduced during 1943 to replace earlier 7.62-mm (0.3-in) machine guns, including the venerable M1910. During the initial phases of the German invasion of the USSR the Soviet forces lost huge amounts of *materiel*, including machine

Similar in performance to the 12.7-mm (0.5-in) Browning M2, the DShK1938/46 is still in large-scale service.

guns, and if their new production facilities were to replace these losses they might as well be modern designs. Thus the *Stankovii Pulyemet Goryunova obrazets 1943g* came into being. It was a gas-operated and air-cooled design that combined several operating principles (including the well-established Browning principles), but the overall design was original and soon proved to be sound. The SG43 was issued in very large numbers and even today the basic weapon is still in widespread use in a modified and upgraded **SGM** form.

Both the SG43 and the larger DShK1938 have the same basic operational simplicity. Working parts have been kept to a minimum and very little routine maintenance, apart from simple cleaning, is required. Both designs can operate under extremes of temperature and they are most forgiving of dirt and dust in their works. In other words both weapons are exactly suited to the environment for which they were designed.

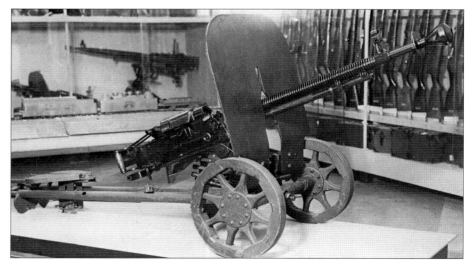

DP/DPM/DT/DTM
Light machine guns

Above: The salient features of this light machine gun are evident in this view of the DP: the gas cylinder under the barrel, main spring coiled round the under-barrel piston in an arrangement that led to loss of temper as a result of firing heat, forward-mounted bipod, and clockwork-driven drum magazine.

In 1921 Vasili Alekseivitch Degtyarev began work on the first all-Russian machine gun. This was trialled for two years before entering production in 1926 as the **Ruchnoi Pulyemet Degtyaryeva Pekhotnii** (automatic weapon, Degtyarev, infantry) or **DP**. The gun was of simple but reasonably robust construction and contained a mere 65 parts, only six of them moving. The weapon had some deficiencies, most especially excessive friction in the action, susceptibility to the ingress of dirt, and overheating because barrel removal was slow and tedious (and useless as there was no spare barrel). The first guns had finned barrels to help dissipate the heat, but the problem was never fully

overcome: thus the rate of fire had to be limited to the capacity of the barrel to disperse heat. The gun was used in the Spanish Civil War of 1936–39, and as a result improvements were made.

The gun is gas-operated, and the bolt-locking arrangement is relatively unusual. On each side of the bolt is a hinged lug lying in its own recess. When the bolt face is firm against the base of the round in the chamber the bolt halts, but the piston continues briefly, taking with it a slider to which the firing pin is attached. During this final movement the firing pin cams the locking lugs into recesses in the receiver's

The DPM overcame some of the DP's limitations, most notably by introducing a barrel-change capability that was somewhat cumbersome, and by the relocation of the main spring to a separate tube located under the receiver. Like the DP, the DPM was capable only of automatic fire.

side walls, thus locking the breech mechanism at the instant of firing.

Drum magazine

The feed arrangement is reasonably good: rimmed cartridges usually cause problems in light automatic weapons, but are generally worse in those using box magazines. The large flat single-deck drum of the

Degtyarev, driven by a clockwork mechanism rather than by the action of the gun, at least eliminates the problem of double feed. The magazine was originally 49 rounds, generally reduced in practice to 47 rounds to reduce the chance of jams.

In 1944 there appeared the **DPM** with a barrel that could be removed somewhat laboriously with the aid of a special spanner, and the main spring moved to a tube under the barrel to eliminate the heat-induced weakening to which it had previously been prone.

The versions of the DP and DPM for use in tanks were the **DT** and **DTM**, which are still found in some world regions.

Left: Like all successful tactical weapons of Soviet design and manufacture, the DP was notable for its ability to remain wholly functional under the most adverse terrain and climatic conditions.

Below: The DP was both cheap and easy to manufacture using indifferent equipment and semi-skilled labour, and despite its operational limitations was a weapon with which the Soviets were justifiably satisfied.

SPECIFICATION	
Degtyarev DP	**Degtyarev DTM**
Calibre: 7.62-mm (0.3-in)	**Calibre:** 7.62-mm (0.3-in)
Length overall: 1265 mm (49.8 in)	**Length overall:** 1181 mm (46.5 in)
Length of barrel: 605 mm (23.8 in)	**Length of barrel:** 597 mm (23.5 in)
Weight: 11.9 kg (26.13 lb)	**Weight:** 12.9 kg (28.4 lb)
Muzzle velocity: 845 m (2,772 ft) per second	**Muzzle velocity:** 840 m (2,756 ft) per second
Rate of fire, cyclic: 520–580 rounds per minute	**Rate of fire, cyclic:** 600 rounds per minute
Feed: 47-round drum magazine	**Feed:** 60-round drum magazine

Mortier Brandt de 81 mm modèle 27/31

Even though the Stokes Mortar of World War I established the overall design shape and form of the modern mortar, it was still a very rudimentary weapon. The Stokes Mortar was little more than a pipe supported on a simple frame and sitting on a base plate to take the recoil forces. The French Brandt company changed all that in the years after World War I by a careful redesign and drastic improvement in the type of bomb fired. At first sight the modifications inspired by Brandt were difficult to detect, for there remained the overall form of the Stokes design, but improvements were there nonetheless. The weapon's overall handiness was one of the first of these improvements, and was apparent on a new Brandt model, introduced as the **Mortier Brandt de 81 mm modèle 27** in 1927 and updated in 1931 as the **modèle 27/31** to take advantage of ammunition improvements.

Setting up the original Stokes Mortar often took time, but the redesign of the Brandt bipod was such that it could be set up on any piece of ground: the levelling of the sights was easily carried out by the bipod leg design, on which only one leg needed to be adjusted. The sights were clamped to a position close to the muzzle, one that was convenient for the layer to peer through without having to stand over the weapon, and slight changes of traverse were easily made using a screw mechanism on the sight bracket. But the main changes came with the ammunition. The early grenades of the Stokes Mortar were replaced by well-shaped bombs that not only carried more explosive payload but also offered a much greater range. In fact Brandt produced a wide range of mortar bombs for its mle 27/31, but they fell into three main brackets. First there was one with an HE payload, and this was used as the standard bomb. Then there was a bomb that was twice the weight of the standard, but which had a shorter range. The third type of bomb used was smoke. Within these three categories came numerous marks and sub-marks: various coloured smokes were available, for instance.

Influential design

The mle 27/31 greatly influenced mortar designs from the moment it was announced. Within a few years the mle 27/31 was being either produced under licence or simply plagiarised all over Europe and elsewhere. The mortar's calibre, 81.4 mm (3.2 in), became the virtual standard European calibre for infantry mortars, and nearly every infantry mortar in use during World War II had some feature or other derived from the mle 27/31, and many were indeed direct copies. This influence was wide enough to encompass the standard mortars of Germany, the USA, the Netherlands, China and even the USSR. All of these nations made their own alterations and innovations, but the resultant weapons were all basically the mle 27/31 at heart.

The Brandt influence survives today, although current 81-mm mortars outrange the mle 27/61 by a factor of nearly six. But the mle 27/31 was more than good enough for its time.

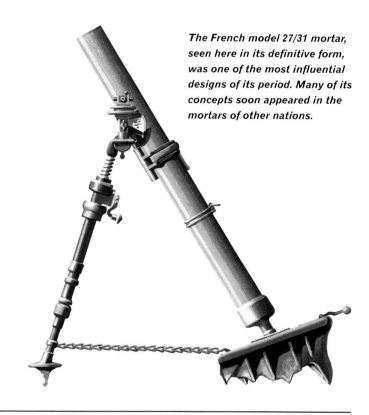

The French model 27/31 mortar, seen here in its definitive form, was one of the most influential designs of its period. Many of its concepts soon appeared in the mortars of other nations.

SPECIFICATION	
Mortier Brandt de 81 mm modèle 27/31	**Elevation:** +45 to +80 degrees
Calibre: 81.4-mm (3.2-in)	**Traverse:** 8 to 12 degrees variable
Lengths: barrel 1.2675 m (49.9 in);	with elevation
bore 1.167 m (45.94 in)	**Maximum range:** standard bomb
Weights: in action 59.7 kg	1900 m (2,078 yards); heavy bomb
(131.6 lb); barrel 20.7 kg (45.6 lb);	1000 m (1,094 yards)
bipod 18.5 kg (40.8 lb); base plate	**Bomb weight:** standard 3.25 kg
20.5 kg (45.2 lb)	(7.165 lb); heavy 6.9 kg (15.21 lb)

45/5 modello 35 'Brixia'

To the little **45/5 modello 35 'Brixia'** must go the prize for being the World War II mortar that offered a level of over-design and over-engineering unexcelled in any other weapon. Quite why the designers of the modello 35 went to such lengths, introducing wholly needless complexities, in a light support mortar with a very limited performance and a relatively ineffective projectile is now difficult to fathom. Nevertheless the result was issued to the Italian armed forces.

In this weapon's designation, 45/5 indicates the calibre of 45 mm (1.77 in) and the length of the barrel in calibres, i.e. 5 x 45 mm, although actually it was marginally longer. So small a calibre could fire only a very light bomb that turned the scales at a mere 0.465 kg (1.025 lb), with a correspondingly small explosive payload. The barrel was breech loaded: operating a lever opened the breech and closing it also fed a charge from a magazine holding 10 cartridges. A trigger was used to fire the bomb, and to vary the range a gas port was opened or closed to vent some of the propellant gases. There were also complex elevation and traverse controls.

SPECIFICATION	
45/5 modello 35 'Brixia'	**Elevation:** +10 to +90 degrees
Calibre: 45-mm (1.77-in)	**Traverse:** 20 degrees
Lengths: barrel 0.26 m (10.2 in);	**Maximum range:** 536 m (586 yards)
bore 0.241 m (9.49 in)	**Bomb weight:** 0.465 kg (1.025 lb)
Weight: in action 15.5 kg (34.17 lb)	

Man-portable

The barrel of the modello 35 was located in a folding frame arrangement that rested against a carrier's back using a cushion pad to ease the load against the body. In use this frame was unfolded in such a way that the firer could then sit astride the weapon if required. In action the modello 35 could manage a fire rate of up to about 10 rounds per minute, and in trained hands the weapon was quite accurate. But even when they landed right on target, the little bombs were relatively ineffective, mainly as a result of the small payload that often resulted in erratic and ineffective fragmentation.

The modello 35 was widely used by the Italian armed forces, mainly at platoon level. All Italian soldiers were trained in its use, some of them while still in one or other of the Italian youth movements, which were issued with an equally complex but

The Italian 45/5 modello 35 'Brixia' mortar was one of the most complicated mortar designs ever created. It was based on a lever-operated breech mechanism, and fired tiny 0.465-kg (1.025-lb) bombs of decidedly inadequate tactical utility.

even less effective version of the modello 35, this time in 35-mm (1.38-in) calibre. These weapons were meant only for training, usually firing inert bombs.

The Italians were not the only users of the modello 35. There were times during the North African campaigns when the Afrika Korps found itself using the things, usually for logistical reasons when serving alongside Italian formations. There was

even an instruction manual written in German for this very purpose, the German designation of the weapon being **4.5-cm Granatwerfer 176(i)**.

It seems almost certain that Italian soldiers found to their cost the limitations of the modello 35 and retained the weapon in service for the simple reason that there was little chance of Italian industry being able to produce anything

better in the then-foreseeable future. Having expended so much time and effort into getting the modello 35 into the hands of the troops, the limited ability of the Italian defence industries would have required too much time to design, develop and produce yet another weapon. So the Italian soldiers simply had to make do with what they were given, which was not much.

50-mm light mortars

There were two main types of 50-mm (1.97-in) mortar in service with the Imperial Japanese army in World War II. Both of them were grenade launchers rather than real mortars, for they used projectiles that were little more than finned hand grenades. The weapons were mainly used at squad level for purely local support.

The first version to enter service was the **Grenade Discharger Type 10**, which entered service in 1921. This was a simple weapon of the smooth-bore type, and fired its grenade by means of a trigger mechanism. An adjustable gas vent was provided to give variations in range. The Type 10 originally fired HE grenades, but with the introduction of the later model it was used more

and more to fire pyrotechnic grenades for target illumination and similar purposes. The main drawback of the Type 10 was its limited range, which was only some 160 m (175 yards), a fact that gave rise to development of the second weapon in this class, the **Type 89** discharger.

Universal service

By 1941 the Type 89 had all but replaced the Type 10 in service, and differed from the earlier weapon in several respects, one being that the barrel was rifled instead of smooth-bored. The other main change was the elimination of the previous gas vent system in favour of a firing pin that could be moved up and down the barrel: the higher the firing pin was up the barrel the shorter the resultant range. The Type 89 mortar fired

How not to do it: For some reasons the Americans decided quite wrongly that the small spade baseplate enabled the weapon to be fired from the thigh or knee (hence 'knee mortar').

a new series of grenades to an effective range of 650 m (710 yards), which was a substantial increase over that possible with the Type 10. Grenades developed for the Type 89 included the usual HE, smoke, signalling and flares. Development of this weapon reached the point where a special version for use by airborne troops was produced. Normally both the Type 10 and Type 89 could be dismantled for carrying in a special leather case.

'Knee' mortar

The main version encountered by the Allies was the Type 89. Somehow the word spread among the Allies that these little mortars were 'knee' mortars and the name stuck. Exactly how many fractured thighs this completely misleading nickname caused among untrained users is now impossible to determine, but attempting to fire either of these mortars with the baseplate resting against a leg would result in immediate injury. The recoil of these little weapons was considerable and the baseplate had to be held against the ground or something really substantial. Aiming was rudimentary, for there were no sights other than a line marked on the barrel, but in a short time almost any soldier could learn to use the weapon fairly effectively.

The mortar was readily man-portable and handy in action, but the grenade was somewhat on the light side for real effectiveness. What mattered, though, was that any soldier could carry one slung over a shoulder while still carrying a normal load, and the resultant increase in squad firepower was appreciable.

The Japanese 50-mm (1.97-in) Grenade Discharger Type 10 was first produced in 1921, and was later replaced by the improved Type 89 weapon. With a limited range of 160 m (175 yards), it was a light and handy weapon that could fire a range of HE, smoke and flare grenades.

SPECIFICATION	
Grenade Discharger Type 89	**Weight:** 4.65 kg (10.25 lb)
Calibre: 50-mm (1.97-in)	**Maximum range:** 650 m (711 yards)
Lengths: overall 0.61 m (24 in); barrel 0. 254 m (10 in)	**Grenade weight:** 0.79 kg (1.74 lb)

Soviet light mortars

The Red Army used great numbers of mortars throughout World War II. In general they were robust weapons usually much heavier than their counterparts elsewhere.

During the 1930s Soviet arms designers developed several light infantry mortars. The smallest of these was an odd little 37-mm (1.45-in) weapon that could be configured as a

Left: Used in very large numbers by first-line units, the 82-mm (3,228-in) mortars allowed infantry to lay down a barrage of anti-personnel fire before they moved forward.

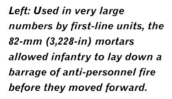

Below: A major advantage of the mortar over tube artillery is its ability to land bombs over a range that can be brought down to a very small figure if needed.

mortar with its barrel supported by a monopod, or as an entrenching tool with the baseplate attached to the rear of the barrel to create a spade blade and handle. The Germans accorded the type the reporting designation **3.7-cm Spatengranatwerfer 161(r)**.

The primary capable for light mortars was standardised as 50 mm (1.97 in). The main series began with the **50-PM 38**, captured examples of which were used by the Germans with the designation **5-cm Granatwerfer 205/1(r)**. This was a conventional design with range varied by gas vents at the base of the barrel, which was held in its bipod at either of two fixed angles. This model was difficult to produce and replaced by the **50-PM 39 (5-cm Granatwerfer 205/2(r)** to the Germans) without the gas vent feature but with standard bipod elevation methods. While effective, this model was still thought too difficult to produce and it was

SPECIFICATION	
50-PM 40	
Calibre: 50-mm (1.97-in)	**Traverse:** 5° to 10° variable
Lengths: barrel 630 mm (24.8 in); bore 533 mm (20.98 in)	**Maximum range:** 3100 m (3,390 yards)
Weight: in action 9.3 kg (20.5 lb)	**Bomb weight:** 3.4 kg (7.5 lb)
Elevation: 45° or 75° fixed	
Traverse: 9° or 16°	**107-PBHM 38**
Maximum range: 800 m (875 yards)	**Calibre:** 107-mm (4.21-in)
Bomb weight: 0.85 kg (1.874 lb)	**Lengths:** barrel 1570 mm (61.8 in); bore 1400 m (55.12 in)
	Weight: in action 170.7 kg (376 lb)
82-PM 41	**Elevation:** +45° to +80°
Calibre: 82-mm (3.228-in)	**Traverse:** 6°
Lengths: barrel 1320 mm (51.97 in); bore 1225 mm (48.23 in)	**Maximum range:** 6315 m (6,905 yards)
Weight: in action 45 kg (99.2 lb)	**Bomb weight:** 8 kg (17.64 lb)
Elevation: +45° to +85°	

The Soviet army found that the mortar, such as this 50-mm (1.97-in) weapon, was suited to urban warfare as its high trajectory allowed bombs to be lobbed over buildings.

therefore replaced by the **50-PM 40 (5-cm Granatwerfer 205/3(r)** to the Germans).

Mass production

This was designed for genuinely mass production, and the bipod legs and baseplate were simple pressed steel components. The 50-PM 40 proved reliable and useful, even though the range was somewhat limited. There

was one further model in this calibre, the **50-PM 41 (5-cm Granatwerfer 200(r)** to the Germans) on which the bipod was replaced by a barrel yoke attached to a large baseplate. A gas venting system was also used, but not many were made as production was concentrated on the 50-PM 40.

While the 50-mm mortars were used at company or squad level, battalion mortars had an 82-mm (3.228-in) calibre. There were three models in this family, the **82-PM 36** which was a direct copy of the Brandt mle 27/31 and known to the Germans as the **8.2-cm Granatwerfer 274/1(r)**, the revised **82-PM 37** with recoil springs to reduce firing loads on the bipod and designated **8.2-cmGranatwerfer 274/2(r)** by the Germans, and the much simplified **82-PM 41** making extensive use of stampings to ease production, and known as the **8.2-cm Granatwerfer 274/3(r)** to the Germans. Wheels could be

added to the ends of the short bipod for hand-towing, and this was taken further on the **82-PM 43** with an even simpler bipod to ease towing.

Mountain mortar

There remains one further 'light' mortar worthy of mention. This was the 107-mm (4.21-in) **107-PBHM 38**, a specialised mountain mortar that was

known to the Germans as the **10.7-cm Gebirgsgranatwerfer 328(r)**. This was an enlarged version of the 82-PM 37, and was used with a light limber for horse traction. Alternatively the mortar could be broken down into loads for pack transport. Firing could be by the normal 'drop' method or by means of a trigger. This mountain version saw extensive use during WWII.

The 82-PM 37 was derived closely from the French series of Brandt mortars in the same 82-mm (3.228-in) calibre. The Soviets introduced a circular baseplate and recoil springs between the barrel and bipod to reduce the effect of recoil forces on the laying and sighting arrangements.

120-HM 38 mortar

The Soviet 120-mm (4.72-in) **120-HM 38** is one of the great success stories in the history of mortars, for it was introduced to service during 1938 and it is still in relatively widespread service today. The primary reason for the weapon's longevity is the excellent combination of bomb weight, mobility and range it offers. When introduced, the weapon was regarded as a regimental mortar for the production of fire support in place of conventional tube artillery, and as WWII continued and production yielded more weapons, it was issued down to battalion level.

In design terms there was nothing really remarkable about

the 120-HM 38. One feature that proved to be very useful was the large circular baseplate, for this allowed rapid changes in traverse as there was none of the usual need to dig out the baseplate and align it to the new direction of fire, as would have been the case with the more conventional rectangular baseplate. The weapon was towed with the baseplate still attached and the weapon lying on a wheeled frame. A lunette was fitted into the muzzle as the towing ring, and this was attached to the same limber as used for the smaller 107-PBHM 38 mortar. This limber usually incorporated an ammunition box

The Soviet 120-HM 38 was one of the most successful mortars of World War II, and was even copied without significant modification by the Germans for their own use. The weapon offered a useful combination of firepower and mobility, and on occasion replaced support artillery.

Left: The 120-HM 38 is seen here in travelling order – the eye of the lunettte in the muzzle attachment is connected to the towing vehicle or draft animal.

Below: Part of a Red Army mortar battery equipped with the 120-HM 38, seen here in action during September 1942 in the foothills of the Caucasian range.

SPECIFICATION	
120-HM 38	
Calibre: 120-mm (4.72-in)	**Elevation:** +45° to +80°
Lengths: barrel 1862 mm (73.3 in); bore 1536 mm (60.47 in)	**Traverse:** 6°
Weight: in action 280.1 kg (617 lb)	**Maximum range:** 6000 m (6,560 yards)
	Bomb weight: HE 16 kg (35.3 lb)

holding 20 rounds, and the combination was towed by either a light vehicle or a team of horses.

High mobility
Getting the 120-HM 38 in to and out of action was therefore relatively rapid and easy, so after fire had been opened it was usually a simple matter to move off again before the Germans could begin retaliatory fire.

As the Germans moved across the USSR in 1941 and 1942 they were much impressed by the firepower and mobility combination offered by the 120-HM 38 mortar. As the recipients of the weapon's efficiency and overall capabilities on many occasions, they had good reason to note the power of the bomb's warhead, and therefore decided to adopt the design for their own manufacture and use. In the short term the Germans had recourse to the expedient of using as many captured examples as they could lay their hands on, under the designation **12-cm Granatwerfer 378(r)**. The Germans then went one stage further and copied the design exactly for production in Germany. This was known to them as the **12-cm Granatwerfer 42** and was widely issued, even taking the place of short-barrel support guns in some infantry formations. Thus what was essentially the same weapon was used by both sides during the fighting on the Eastern Front.

Effective bomb
The usual bomb fired by the 120-HM 38 on both sides was the HE round, but smoke and chemical rounds were produced (although the latter were never used). The rate of fire could be as high as 10 rounds per minute, so a battery of four of these mortars could lay down considerable amounts of fire in a very short period. Over a period of action the baseplates did have a tendency to 'bed in', making relaying necessary, but this was partially eliminated by introduction of the improved **120-HM 43**, which differed from its predecessor in its use of a spring-loaded shock absorber mechanism on the barrel/bipod mounting. It is this version, which was otherwise unchanged from the original, that is most likely to be encountered today. Over the years some changes have been made to the ammunition, which now has a longer range than the wartime equivalent, and another change is that many modern versions are now carried on various types of self-propelled carriage.

The Soviets also developed and used a scaled-up 160-mm (6.3-in) version of the 120-HM 38 under the designation **160-HM 43**. This was breech-loaded and trigger-fired, and was allocated to divisional artillery units as it could fire a 41.14-kg (90.17-lb) HE bomb from a minimum range of 750 m (820 yards) out to a maximum of 5150 m (5,630 yards) at the rate of three bombs per minute.

German infantry support weapons

German weapon designers between the world wars were presented with virtually a clean slate on which to work. Thus when a requirement was released for a light infantry mortar for issue at squad level, Rheinmetall-Borsig's design team opted not to follow the usual barrel/ baseplate/bipod

form but instead to create a design in which the barrel was permanently secured to the baseplate and the bipod was virtually eliminated in favour of a monopod device fixed to the baseplate. The result was a complex little 50-mm (1.97-in) weapon known as the **5-cm leichte Granatwerfer 36** or

leGrW 36 (light grenade-launcher model 1936) and first issued during 1936.

The leGrW 36 was a good example of the Germans' general love of gadgetry in their weapons, and ranged from the traverse controls built onto the baseplate to a very complicated but wholly superfluous

telescopic sight. This latter was very much the designers' attempt to make the weapon as perfect as possible and ensure accuracy. But the ranges at which the little leGrW 36 was used were such that a simple line painted on the barrel was all that was needed, and the sight was dropped during 1938.

The weapon could be carried by one man using a handle at the base of the barrel. For all it was small, at 14 kg (30.8 lb) the leGrW 36 was rather heavy. Thus one man had to carry the mortar and another the ammunition (only HE bombs were fired) in a steel box. In action the baseplate was placed on the ground and all barrel adjustments were made using coarse and fine control knobs. A trigger-actuated firing mechanism was used.

While the designers were rather proud of the leGrW 36, troops in the field were less enthusiastic. They felt that the leGrW 36, quite apart from its weight problem, was too complicated and the bomb not worth all the trouble involved. The bomb weighed only 0.9 kg (1.98 lb) and the maximum range was a mere 520 m (570 yards).

Expensive to make

Added to this, as far as higher authorities were concerned, was the fact that the weapon took too much time and money to manufacture in relation to its capabilities. Such a situation could not endure once war had started, of course, and by 1941 the leGrW 36 had been removed from production. Existing weapons were gradually

withdrawn from front-line service in favour of something better, and passed on to second-line and garrison units: many were allocated to units manning the Atlantic Wall as part of the beach defences. Some were passed on to the Italian army.

In overall terms, therefore, the leGrW 36 was not one of the German weapon designers' best efforts. They allowed a small weapon to become far too complex and costly to justify the result, and the German army was astute enough to realise the fact and so progressed to the use of more effective weapons.

Up the calibre ladder

The German army's **8-cm schwere Granatwerfer 34** or **8-cm sGrW 34** (heavy grenade-launcher model 1934) gained an enviable reputation among Allied front-line soldiers for its accuracy and rate of fire. The weapon was encountered wherever the German army fought, for the sGrW 34 was one of the Germans' standard weapons from 1939 right through to the last days of World War II in May 1945. The mortar was designed and made by Rheinmetall-Borsig once again,

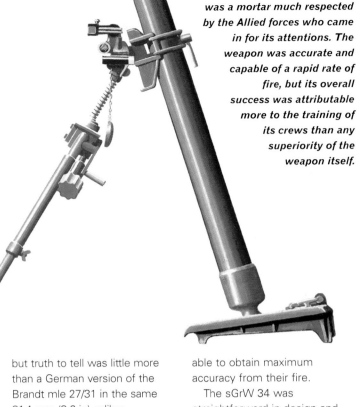

The schwere Granatwerfer 34 was a mortar much respected by the Allied forces who came in for its attentions. The weapon was accurate and capable of a rapid rate of fire, but its overall success was attributable more to the training of its crews than any superiority of the weapon itself.

but truth to tell was little more than a German version of the Brandt mle 27/31 in the same 81.4-mm (3.2-in) calibre.

Despite its reputation as a high-quality weapon, there was nothing remarkable in the design of the sGrW 34. So much of the respect it gained as a weapon should instead have gone to the thorough training and efficiency of the men who used it: throughout the war the German mortar crews seemed always to have an edge over their rivals. They became experts at getting their sGrW 34s in and out of action rapidly, and by careful use of plotting boards and other fire-control aids were

The 5-cm leGrW was the German army's standard light mortar in the first part of World War II, but it fired too small a bomb and was overly complex in its features. As a result it was phased out of first-line service from 1941.

able to obtain maximum accuracy from their fire.

The sGrW 34 was straightforward in design and very well made. It was consequently very robust and could be broken down into three loads for man-pack portability; more men were needed to carry the ammunition. There was also a special version for mounting in the rear of SdKfz 250/7 half-track vehicles.

Several centres were involved in production of the weapon, and more with the manufacture of the associated ammunition, for the types of bombs that could be fired from the sGrW 34 were numerous. There were the usual HE and smoke bombs, but also illuminating and target-marking bombs to aid ground-attack aircraft, and there was even a special 'bouncing bomb' known as the 8-cm Wurfgranate 39 that was driven back up into the air after it had struck the ground. This was achieved by the use of a tiny

SPECIFICATION	
leGrW 36	
Calibre: 50-mm (1.969-in)	**Elevation:** + 42° to + 90°
Lengths: barrel 0.465 m (18.3 in); bore 0.35 m (13.78 in)	**Traverse:** 34°
Weight: in action 14 kg (30.8 lb)	**Maximum range:** 520 m (570 yards)
	Bomb weight: 0.9 kg (1.98 lb)

rocket motor, and at a predetermined height the bomb exploded to scatter its fragments over a much wider area than would be the case with a conventional ground-detonated bomb.

Again, this was a typically German weapon innovation that was really too expensive and unreliable for general use, and the numbers produced were never large. One extra bonus for the sGrW 34 was that it could fire a wide range of captured ammunition, although usually with some loss in range performance.

For airborne use a special shortened version of the sGrW 34 was developed in 1940 as the **kurzer Granatwerfer 42**, known as the **Stummelwerfer** in general use. This was issued in quantity from about 1942 onward, but saw little service with airborne forces and instead became a replacement for the little 5-cm leGrW 36. It fired the same bombs as the sGrW 34 but to a maximum range reduced by more than half.

Infantry gun

One of the many tactical lessons learned by the German army in World War I was the desirability of providing each infantry battalion with a measure of organic artillery support. This led to the allocation of lightweight infantry guns to each battalion. During the 1920s one of the first priorities of the then severely restricted German weapons industry was the development of a new light infantry gun, or leichte Infantriegeschütz. A 75-mm (2.95-in) design was produced by Rheinmetall-Borsig as early as 1927 and was issued for service in 1932 as the **7.5-cm leIG 18**, or **7.5-cm leichte**

Infantriegeschütz 18.

The first examples had wooden spoked wheels, but later versions for service with motorised formations had metal disc wheels with rubber tyres. The leIG 18 had an unusual loading mechanism: operation of a lever opened not the breech but instead moved the entire barrel section upwards in a square slipper to expose the loading chamber. This system was yet another example of German design innovation simply for its own sake, and the mechanism offered no real advantage over conventional systems. The rest of the gun was orthodox, and in action it was sturdy and reliable. The range was limited as a result of the short barrel.

Two variants

There were two variants of the leIG 18. One was developed for mountain warfare units and known as the **leichte Gebirgs Infantriegeschütz 18** or **leGebIG 18** (light mountain infantry gun model 18). This was developed from 1935 as an leIG 18 that could be broken down into 10 loads for pack transport on mules or light vehicles. To save weight the ordinary box trail was replaced by tubular steel trail legs, and the shield became optional. The leGebIG 18 was heavier than the original but the pack load feature made it much more suitable for its intended role. It was meant as an interim weapon, but it served up to 1945. There was also an airborne forces' version.

SPECIFICATION	
sGrW 34	
Calibre: 81.4-mm (3.2-in)	**Traverse:** 9° to 15° variable with elevation
Lengths: barrel 1.143 m (45 in); bore 1.033 m (40.67 in)	**Maximum range:** 2400 m (2,625 yards)
Weight: in action 56.7 kg (125 lb)	**Bomb weight:** 3.5 kg (7.72 lb)
Elevation: +40° to +90°	

Left: The shape of the 8-cm sGrW 34 mortar's bomb can be clearly seen here as it is held ready for loading into the weapon's muzzle. The bomb weighed 3.5 kg (7.72 lb) and had a ring of multiple fins round its tail for stability in flight. The layer is making fine azimuth adjustments using the simple sight mounted on the bipod.

Right: An 8-cm sGrW 34 crew in action. The pear-shaped bomb is being introduced into the muzzle, from which it will fall down the barrel on to a fixed firing pin to initiate the propellant charge and propel the bomb out to a maximum range of 2400 m (2,625 yards).

SPECIFICATION	
leIG 18	
Calibre: 75-mm (2.95-in)	**Muzzle velocity:** 210 m (689 ft) per second
Lengths: gun overall 0.9 m (35.43 in); barrel 0.884 m (34.8 in)	**Maximum range:** 3550 m (3,882 yards)
Weight: in action 400 kg (882 lb)	**Bomb weight:** HE 5.45 or 6 kg (12 or 13.2 lb); hollow charge 3 kg (6.6 lb)
Elevation: 10° to +73°	
Traverse: 12°	

The crew of a 7.5-cm leIG 18 is captured by the camera in training during 1940. Note the relatively small size of the round being handed to the loader, and the way in which one crew member is kneeling on the end of the trail to stabilise it.

British mortars

The first British 2-in (50.8-mm) mortar made its appearance in 1918 toward the end of World War I, but this did not remain in service for long, being rendered obsolete in 1919. This was followed with a light mortar interregnum, for it was not until the 1930s that the notion of reintroducing a light mortar for use at platoon or squad level was put forward. There was no 'history' of the development of such small mortars in the UK at that time, so it was decided to run a selection competition between the offerings from various armaments manufacturers. The first result of this procurement process was a flood of models from a number of concerns, and after a series of trials one of these was selected for production and service.

Winning design

The winner was a design from the Spanish manufacturer ECIA. In its original form this weapon was thought needy of improvement, and the further work was carried out in the UK, leading to full production during 1938. The first production version was the **Ordnance, ML 2-inch Mortar Mk II** (ML for muzzle loading), but this was only the first of a long string of marks and sub-marks. In basic terms there were two types of 2-inch mortar. One was the pure infantry version, which was a simple barrel with a small baseplate and a trigger mechanism to fire the bomb after it had been loaded. The second was meant for use on Bren Gun or Universal Carrier light tracked vehicles and had a much larger baseplate and a more complicated aiming system. If required, the carrier version could be dismounted for ground use, and a handle was supplied for this purpose. However, between these two, there were at the least 14 different variants, with differences in barrel length, sighting arrangements and production variations. There were even

special versions for use by the Indian Army and by airborne divisions.

Bomb types

To go with this array of weapon variants there was an equally daunting range of ammunition types. The usual bomb fired by the 2-inch mortar was HE, but smoke and flare types were also fired, the latter being particularly useful for target illumination at night. Having a trigger firing mechanism, the weapon could be used at angles close to the horizontal, a factor that was especially useful in house-to-house combat.

The bombs were normally carried in tubes, each holding three, and arranged in handy packs of three tubes. The normal 2-inch Mortar team consisted of two men, one carrying the mortar and the other carrying the ammunition.

3-in mortar

The first 3-in (76.2-mm) mortar used by the British army was the original Stokes Mortar that saw its initial service during March 1917. This version remained in use for many years after World War I, and as funds for weapon development were sparse in the financially straitened times between the two world wars the Stokes Mortar remained in service virtually unchanged for some years.

However, a measure of development work was carried out on the basic design to the point at which it was decided during the early 1930s that the Ordnance, ML Mortar, 3-inch would remain in first-line service as the standard infantry support weapon: this resulted from the 1932 decision that the mortar would replace the 3.7-in (94-mm) howitzer as the British army's standard infantry support

Above: Soldiers of the 1st Battalion, the Hampshire Regiment, in action in Sicily with a 2-in mortar. The gunner is operating the trigger while his partner watches for the impact.

Left: A 2-in mortar team of the Royal Scots Fusiliers in action in Normandy, late June 1944. The mortar's small size made it a handy and portable weapon.

weapon. The weapon standardised for this task was not the original Ordnance, ML Mortar, 3-inch Mk I but rather the **Ordnance, ML Mortar 3-inch Mk II**, which was thus the weapon in service with the British when World War II broke out in September 1939.

This modernised Mk II weapon went through numerous changes from the original Mk I mortar of World War I, especially in the ammunition, which introduced many of the innovatory features of the mortar bombs created by the French Brandt armaments company.

SPECIFICATION	
2-inch Mortar Mk II	**Weight:** 4.1 kg (9 lb)
Calibre: 2-in (50.8-mm)	**Maximum range:** 455 m (500 yards)
Lengths: barrel 665 mm (26.2 in); bore 506.5 mm (19.94 in)	**Bomb weight:** HE 1.02 kg (2.25 lb)

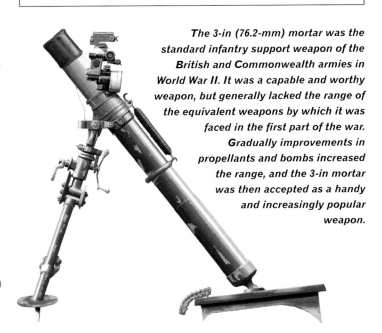

The 3-in (76.2-mm) mortar was the standard infantry support weapon of the British and Commonwealth armies in World War II. It was a capable and worthy weapon, but generally lacked the range of the equivalent weapons by which it was faced in the first part of the war. Gradually improvements in propellants and bombs increased the range, and the 3-in mortar was then accepted as a handy and increasingly popular weapon.

Right: A 3-in mortar attacks German positions across the Maas river in the bitter January of 1945. Judging by the pile of ready-use bombs, the team had a long mission.

Greater range needed

It was not long after the start of the war that it began to become apparent that although the Mk II was a sturdy and reliable weapon, it lacked the range of many of its contemporaries. The early versions had a range of only some 1465 m (1,600 yards), which compared badly with the 2400 m (2,625 yards) of its German equivalent, the 8-cm sGrW 34. A long series of experiments and trials using new propellants then succeeded in increasing this range to 2515 m (2,750 yards), which overcame many of the original drawbacks, but it took some time to get the new propellants into the hands of British front-line troops, so at times many captured German and Italian mortars were used by British troops, especially in the course of the North African campaigns.

Apart from the ammunition changes, other alterations were made to the basic design. Later developments, starting with the **Ordnance, ML Mortar, 3-inch Mk IV**, were equipped with a new and heavier baseplate design as well as improved sighting arrangements, and there was even a specially lightened version (the **Ordnance, Mortar, 3-inch Mk V**) developed for use in the Far East, but only 5,000 of these were made and, for obvious reasons, some were issued to the British airborne divisions.

Transport options

The usual method of getting the weapon into action was pack carriage in three loads by men, but the British army's mechanised battalions carried their weapons on specially equipped Universal Carriers. On these the mortar was carried on the back of the vehicle ready to be assembled for normal ground use; the mortar was not fired from the carrier itself, which also had stowage for the mortar's ammunition. When the mortar was para-dropped, the barrel and the bipod were dropped in one container, a second container carried the baseplate, and a third container held the ammunition.

Short minimum range

The ammunition for the family was largely confined to HE and smoke, although other payloads such as illuminants were developed. By juggling with the propelling charge increments and barrel elevation angles it was possible to drop a bomb as close as 115 m (125 yards) away, a useful feature in close-quarter combat.

Somehow the 3-in mortar never achieved the respect that was given to its opponents, but this should not be allowed to disguise the fact that once the weapon's original range shortcomings had been rectified, the 3-in mortar proved to be a sound enough weapon that remained in service with the British army until the 1960s, and indeed is used by some of the smaller ex-Commonwealth armies.

4.2-in mortar

By 1941 it had been noted by British army staff planners that there had appeared a pressing need for a mortar that could fire projectiles producing large amounts of tactical smoke for screening and other purposes: in this appreciation the planners had no doubt been impressed by reports from front-line formations of the capabilities of the 10-cm Nebelwerfer mortars used by German Nebeltruppen (smoke troops).

Accordingly a new design of 4.2-in (106.7-mm) heavy mortar was developed. But almost as soon as the first examples were ready for issue to Royal Engineer smoke production units, the requirement was changed to convert the new weapon into a heavy mortar firing conventional HE bombs for issue to Royal Artillery batteries. Thus the new mortar became the **Ordnance, SB 4.2-inch Mortar** (SB standing for smooth-bore).

The 4.2-in mortar was produced at a time when the British defence industry was fully stretched and production facilities of all kinds were in short supply. This was particularly noticeable in the production of the bombs to be fired by the new weapon. The designers wanted the bombs to have forged bodies to reduce weight and also produce a better ballistic shape. At that time the required forging facilities were not available, though, so the bomb bodies had to be cast. This resulted in a maximum range of only 3020 m (3,300 yards) as opposed to the required 4025 m (4,400 yards).

No option

These bombs had to be used, for they were all that could be made at the time pending the introduction of a new design with a streamlined body. Again, these had to be manufactured using cast iron but they did manage a range of 3660 m (4,000 yards). By that time HE bombs were the main projectile used, but the original smoke function had not been entirely forgotten and some smoke bombs were also produced.

Hefty equipment

The 4.2-in mortar was fairly hefty to move around, so the usual method of getting it into action was to tow it using a Jeep or other light vehicle. The baseplate and the barrel/bipod were so arranged that they could be lifted

SPECIFICATION	
Mortar, 3-inch Mk II	
Calibre: 3-in (76.2-mm)	**Elevation:** +45° to +80°
Length overall: 1295 mm (51 in)	**Traverse:** 11°
Length of barrel: 1190 mm (46.8 in)	**Maximum range:** 2515 m (2,750 yards)
Weight: in action 57.2 kg (126 lb)	**Bomb weight:** HE 4.54 kg (10 lb)

without undue difficulty onto a small wheeled mounting. Once on site they could be lowered from the mounting and the barrel and bipod quickly assembled. When carried on a Universal Carrier things were even simpler. The baseplate was simply dropped off the back, the barrel was inserted and the bipod shoved into place, and firing

could start almost at once. Getting out of action was just as rapid. This led to the 4.2-in mortar being viewed with some suspicion by the troops who relied upon its firepower support. While they valued its supporting fire they knew that as soon as a 4.2-in mortar battery was brought into action nearby it would be off again before the incoming

counter-battery fire from the enemy arrived. By that time the 4.2-in mortar battery would be some distance away, leaving the units close to their former position to receive the fire.

The 4.2-in mortar was widely used by the Royal Artillery.It was used wherever British troops served from late 1942 onwards, and was still in use during the Korean War.

SPECIFICATION	
4.2-inch Mortar	**Elevation:** +45° to +80°
Calibre: 4.2-in (106.7-mm)	**Traverse:** 10°
Lengths: barrel 1730 mm (68.1 in); bore 1565 mm (61.6 in)	**Maximum range:** 3750 m (4,100 yards)
Weight: in action 599 kg (1,320 lb)	**Bomb weight:** 9.07 kg (20 lb)

A 4.2-in mortar fires on German positions in the foot hills of Mt Etna during the Sicilian campaign of 1943, the crew protecting their ears against muzzle blast.

US mortars

The mortar teams of the US Army have always referred to their charges as 'cannon' and during World War II they had a lot of these cannons to hand. The smallest of these was not an American by origin, but rather a French weapon as this **60-mm Mortar M2** was a direct licence-produced copy of a Brandt design.

It was in 1938 that the US Army bought eight examples of the French mortar for evaluation as **60-mm Mortar M1** weapons in the USA, where the type's

capabilities were immediately realised and the weapon ordered into American production. The 60-mm Mortar M2 soon became the standard US Army mortar for use down to company level, and for it American industry produced a wide range of ammunition types, including the standard M49A2 HE bomb but also one odd projectile, the M83 bomb that was meant to illuminate low-flying aircraft at night so that light anti-aircraft weapons could deal with them.

Although the 60-mm mortar M2 was a capable weapon that

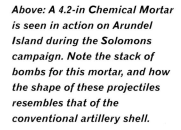

Above: A 4.2-in Chemical Mortar is seen in action on Arundel Island during the Solomons campaign. Note the stack of bombs for this mortar, and how the shape of these projectiles resembles that of the conventional artillery shell.

Left: This 81-mm Mortar M1 is seen in action in the type of terrain in which the mortar came into its own. Firing at a high angle of elevation, the mortar could lob its bombs over obstacles such as trees to deliver plunging fire into the enemy's lines.

Left: The American 60-mm (2.38-in) Mortar M19 was a much simplified version of the Mortar M2, and used a simpler baseplate but no bipod. The weapon lacked range and accuracy, and saw little service except with airborne units.

Right: The light weight of the 60-mm Mortar M2 made it an ideal weapon for front-line support right down to small unit level. The bomb left the tube with a velocity of 158 m (518 ft) per second.

SPECIFICATION	
60-mm Mortar M19	**Traverse:** 14 degrees
Calibre: 60-mm (2.38-in)	**Maximum range:** 1815 m
Length: barrel 0.726 m (28.6 in)	(1,985 yards)
Weight: in action 19.05 kg (42 lb)	**Bomb weight:** 1.36 kg (3 lb)
Elevation: +40 to +85 degrees	

offered the US Army a new level of battlefield support down to unit level, the planners of the US Army soon become conscious of the fact that American know-how could be used to effect major improvements on this pioneering mortar, largely with a view to reducing weight and enhancing mobility.

Poor performance

From the M2 the Americans therefore developed their **60-mm Mortar M19**, which can be regarded as the US equivalent of the British 2-in Mortar, which it closely resembled. By comparison with the 60-mm Mortar M2, the main changes were the elimination of

the bipod supporting the front of the barrel and the replacement of the large square baseplate, with rounded-off corners, by a smaller rectangular baseplate, again with rounded-off corners, that was curved downward to earth side of its longitudinal centreline so that the edges bedded themselves into the each as the weapon was fired.

Not many M19s were produced, for it was appreciated soon after the type entered service that it lacked both range and accuracy, and most of these went to airborne formations as these had great need for lightweight support weapons for their paratroop and gliderborne forces. The M19 fired the same range of bombs as the M2, but with only one charge rather than the M2's propellant arrangement of up to five charges. The data for the 60-mm mortar M19 included a calibre of 60.5-mm (2.38-in), overall length of 0.726 m (28.6 in), weight in action of 9 kg (19.8 lb), unlimited elevation and traverse angles as the weapon was installed on a universal joint, and range between minimum and maximum figures of 68 and 750 m (75 and 815 yards) with an HE bomb weighing 1.36 kg (3 lb) fired with a muzzle velocity of 89 m (292 ft) per second. The practical range was 320 m (350 yards).

Heavier firepower

The standard battalion mortar of the US Army was another Brandt licence-built product, yet one more variation of the mle 27/31 design. The Americans produced their version as the **81-mm Mortar M1**, and with some slight alterations to suit local production methods this

was manufactured throughout World War II and in every theatre where Americans forces fought. This M1 weapon was provided with a number of bomb types, including at least two HE and one smoke bombs, and its range bracket was made very flexible at the tactical level

by the use of a six-charge propellant arrangement.

One odd American piece of equipment used with this weapon was a small hand cart onto which the mortar and its ammunition could be loaded. Just two men were required to tow this handy little carrier, known as the Hand Cart M6A1. Other carriers included mules, for which a special harness set was devised, but perhaps the most universally used was the M21 halftrack carrier from which the M1 mortar could be fired without being dismounted.

The mortar was elevated by up/down movement of the tube supporting the upper end of the barrel, and traversed by a screw arrangement under the barrel attachment unit.

Little modification

Throughout its service life the M1 remained virtually unchanged. A special T1 barrel extension tube was devised to increase range but this was little used, and a shortened version, known as the **T27 'Universal'** and of which much was expected, was not accepted for service on a large scale.

Perhaps the best known of all World War II American mortars was the **4.2-in Chemical Mortar**, the main reason for its fame probably being that it remained in service with the US Army until comparatively recent times. As with its British counterpart, this was devised to be a mortar firing smoke projectiles (hence the Chemical Mortar designation), but it was not long before it was realised that HE bombs would be very effective as well. It was a large and cumbersome weapon with a massive and heavy baseplate that was later replaced by much lighter designs, and the barrel was rifled to fire bombs that closely resembled conventional artillery projectiles. The rifling made the 4.2-in Chemical Mortar very accurate, and the projectiles were much heavier than their smoothbore equivalents. In action they were often used as infantry support weapons, but many were issued to smoke screen units. The one major drawback to the 4.2-in Chemical Mortar was its weight and bulk. It was not an easy weapon to deploy and to overcome this various self-propelled carriages were devised for it.

Special-role mortars

The Americans also made very limited use of the **105-mm Mortar T13** in 4.13-in calibre, and the **155-mm Mortar T25** in 6.1-in calibre. The T13 was introduced in 1944 and was intended for the immediate support of forces that had just made an amphibious landing, pending the arrival of heavier weapons. This substantial weapon weighed only 86.4 kg (190.3 lb) and fired a 15.9-kg (35-lb) bomb to a maximum range of 3660 m (4,000 yards). However, the availability of the 4.2-in Chemical Mortar firing a wide range of ammunition types effectively made the T13 superfluous to requirement, and the few weapons completed and issued were withdrawn from service almost immediately after WWII's end.

The basically contemporary T25 was designed for heavier support of amphibious forces, and was used in small numbers in the South-West Pacific theatre, largely for evaluation purposes. The T25 weighed 259.2 kg (571 lb) and fired a 28.83-kg (63.5-lb) bomb to a range of 2285 m (2,500 yards).

SPECIFICATION	
81-mm Mortar M1	
Calibre: 81.4-mm (3.2-in)	**Traverse:** 14 degrees
Length: barrel 1.257 m (49.5 in)	**Maximum range:** 3008 m
Weight: in action 61.7 kg (136 lb)	(3,290 yards)
Elevation: +40 to +85 degrees	**Bomb weight:** 3.12 kg (6.87 lb)

SPECIFICATION	
4.2-in Chemical Mortar	
Calibre: 106.7-mm (4.2-in)	**Traverse:** 7 degrees
Length: barrel 1.019 m (40.1 in)	**Maximum range:** 4023 m
Weight: in action 149.7 kg (330 lb)	(4,400 yards)
Elevation: +45 to +59 degrees	**Bomb weight:** 14.5 kg (32 lb)

Above: This is a piece of equipment typical of those used by mortar crews, here that of an 81-mm Mortar M1 operating in mountain terrain. Such a weapon needed ammunition supply personnel in addition to its two-man crew if a high rate of fire was to be maintained.

Left: Weapons such as the 81-mm Mortar M1 were invaluable in the war of the infantryman as they could respond virtually instantly with great accuracy right down to very short battlefield ranges.

Panzerfaust

The excellence of Soviet tanks came as a nasty shock to the German army in 1941. German anti-tank guns could only knock out a Soviet tank at point-blank range. The race began in order to develop an infantry anti-tank system. Bigger guns were quickly produced, but they were bulky, needing large crews and a vehicle to tow them. The Germans first encountered the T-34 near Grodno in June 1941, and found it to be vastly superior to their own PzKpfw IV. At that time, German infantry relied on anti-tank rifles and small calibre guns (used in the attack, as opposed to British tactics which only used anti-tank guns in the defence); but they found to their horror that the only weapon effective against the T-34 was the 88-mm (3.46-in) flak gun. During late 1941 a Soviet KV-1

the tank and dropping a fused Teller mine under the tracks or turret overhang.

German response

The ultimate German response to the T-34 was the **Panzerfaust** (tank fist). A small bomb fired from a disposable launcher it went some way to redress the balance against the T-34. It was not just used against the T-34: after D-Day, entire Volkssturm units were armed with nothing else; and their capabilities are attested by the fact that on 29 March 1945 a small party of Volkssturm held up a squadron from the 1st Royal Tank Regiment for the best part of a day.

Monroe effect

The Panzerfaust project was initiated by Dr Langweiter of

plate at some 6000 m (19,685 ft) per second. In the case of a tank, this jet melted a hole in the armour allowing the ingress of hot gas and vaporised metal. This caused the tank's ammunition to explode, generally making life untenable for the crew. The problem was how to deliver the bomb. Artillery shells were too fast and too powerful to achieve this optimum distance: they either bounced off the tank or exploded too close to the armour, and although the difference could often be measured in millimetres – this was usually enough to make the warhead ineffective. Langweiter's solution was the disposable rocket launcher. This was manufactured by Volkswagen Werker at Fallersleben, and by 1943, over 200,000 missiles per month were being produced.

The original weapon was called the **Faustpatrone**, and was designed to be fired at arm's length and at right angles to the body. After it was found that this made aiming slightly difficult unless the operator

Desperate to halt the Allies, the Nazis set up the Volkssturm. Men previously considered unsuitable for front-line combat were armed with Panzerfausts and, with the minimum of training, were thrown into the battle.

was very close to the T-34, the first **Panzerfaust (Gretchen)** was developed.

Its official classification was the **Panzerfaust 30 (klein).** It was a 76.2-cm (30-in) long tube, firing a 1.5-kg (3.3-lb) bomb at 30 m (98 ft) per second and possessing a maximum effective range of 30 m (98 ft); the bomb's diameter was 100 mm (3.94 in), and the explosive charge could penetrate 140-mm (5.5-in) of armour sloped at 30°.

Propulsion was by a charge in the tube base, and a rocket-charge through later versions. The Panzerfaust 30 (klein) was superseded by the **Panzerfaust 30, 60** and **100** (the numbers indicating the range given in metres) which fired a 3-kg bomb (6.6-lb) at 30, 45 and 62 m (98, 148 and 203 ft) per second respectively.

The more complex sight indicates that this is a Panzerfaust 60. The fired bomb weighed 3 kg (6.6 lb) and the warhead could penetrate 200 mm (7.87 in) of armour.

tank held up an entire German division for 48 hours, dug in by a bridge, until an 88-mm gun was called in to destroy it. Even then it took seven rounds, of which only two actually penetrated! In the absence of an 88-mm gun, the standard defence against the T-34 entailed some brave but foolhardy soldier rushing up to

Hugo Schneider AG. What Langweiter required was a delivery system for a new type of bomb or projectile that he felt would be effective against well-armoured tanks. This bomb used the Monroe effect: the high explosive warhead was produced with a cone-shaped hollow interior, copper-lined and open end facing forward, so that when the head was detonated at the optimum distance away from armour plate, the explosive force went forward. At the same time, a thin, focused jet of molten metal and superheated gas was directed at the armour

SPECIFICATION	
Panzerfaust 60	**Projectile diameter:** 150 mm (6 in)
Range: 60 m (197 ft)	**Muzzle velocity:** 45 m (148 ft) per second
Weights: total 6.8 kg (15 lb); projectile 3 kg (6.6 lb)	**Armour penetration:** 200 mm (8 in)

SPECIFICATION	
Panzerfaust 30 (klein)	**Projectile diameter:** 10 cm (4 in)
Range: 30 m (98 ft 4.5 in)	**Muzzle velocity:** 30 m (98 ft) per second
Weights: total 1.475 kg (3.24 lb); projectile 0.68 kg (1.49 lb)	**Armour penetration:** 140 mm (6 in)

Panzerfaust

The Panzerfaust was the scourge of Red Army and Allied tanks alike. It proved to be an important weapon in the dying days of World War II in the European theatre. Hitler Youth and Volkssturm troops used them to great effect during the Battle of Berlin. As can be seen from the illustration, one of their great assets was their simplicity in operation.

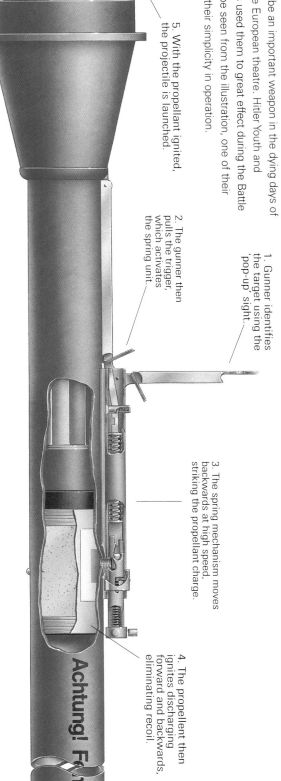

5. With the propellant ignited, the projectile is launched.

1. Gunner identifies the target using the 'pop-up' sight.

2. The gunner then pulls the trigger, which activates the spring unit.

3. The spring mechanism moves backwards at high speed, striking the propellant charge.

4. The propellent then ignites discharging forward and backwards, eliminating recoil.

Achtung! Feun! ——→

Left: By mid-1944 the Panzerfaust was widely issued to all front-line combat troops. This unfortunate German soldier was killed at Sept Vents, Normandy, on 30 July 1944, a Panzerfaust 30 (klein) at his side.

Below: Raising the simple leaf sights armed the trigger mechanism of the Panzerfaust 30, and the firer used the sight and a mark on the bomb to aim the weapon. After being fired the bomb was stabilised by folding fins.

Above: The Panzerfaust suited the German defensive tactics of 1943–45 exactly. Allied tank crews feared the weapon. It was available in huge numbers, and if aimed properly from the correct distance, every German could have at least one Allied tank to his credit.

Anti-tank Rifle Type 97 Japanese 20-mm rifle

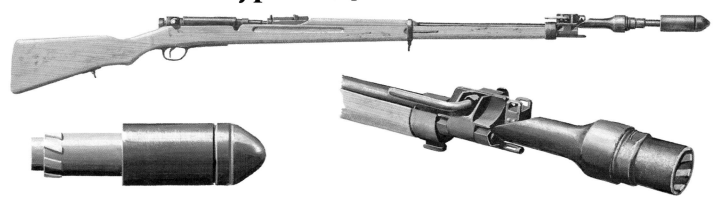

Above: The Japanese Type 2 anti-tank grenade launchers could be fitted to the muzzle of all Japanese service rifles. They were direct copies of the German Gewehr Panzergranate and the grenades had calibres of 30 or 40 mm (1.18 or 1.57 in).

When it came to anti-tank rifles, the Japanese general staff decided to go one better than most contemporary designs and produce a rifle firing a powerful 20-mm (0.79-in) cartridge, This emerged as the **Anti-tank Rifle Type 97**, and while it was certainly a powerful weapon by the standards of the day it was also extremely heavy, weighing no less than 67.5 kg (148.8 lb) when being carried and 51.75 kg (114.1 lb) once emplaced. Much of this weight resulted from the adoption of a gas-operated mechanism which was locked by a tilting breech block. Ammunition was fed from an overhead seven-round box magazine.

Bipod mounting

Once emplaced the Type 97 used a bipod mounted just forward of the body and a monopod under the butt. Despite the ferocious recoil the weapon was intended to be directed and fired from the shoulder, which cannot have endeared the weapon to its users. Normally the Type 97 was carried on two special poles by two men, but more often four men were used. It was possible to fit a small shield for added protection and to this shield could be added a carrying bar that resembled bicycle handlebars, though this component was often omitted to reduce the weight of the weapon. Another one of these carrying bars could be added under the butt. In action the Type 97 was often difficult to spot as it was a long, low weapon.

Limited penetration

During the early months of the Pacific campaign the Type 97 proved itself to be a useful weapon against the light tanks it was called upon to tackle but once larger and heavier tanks (such as the American M4 Sherman) appeared on the scene the Type 97 was no longer of much value. At best it could penetrate 30 mm (1.18 in) of case-hardened armour at 250 m (273 yards), and against anything heavier it was of little use. But the Japanese did not phase out the Type 97 as they were far too short of modern weapons to let any be discarded. The Type 97 was retained, but no longer primarily for anti-armour use: instead many of those available were emplaced as anti-invasion weapons on the Pacific islands, where they were sometimes able to cause damage to landing craft and light amphibious landing vehicles. Some measure of anti-armour capability was retained by the fitting of special grenade launcher cups to some Type 97s. These launcher cups could be secured to the muzzle by means of a locking bar once the circular muzzle brake had been unscrewed. The idea was a copy of the German Schiessbecker grenade-launchers, and used very similar grenades. But the principle, although of some effectiveness, was more suited to orthodox service rifles than to the large and complex Type 97 so it was not used extensively.

Production problems

Overall, the Type 97 was not used by the Japanese in any great numbers. The complexity of the weapon made it rather difficult and thus costly to produce, and after 1942 the operational requirement for it was limited.

Above: The 20-mm (0.79-in) Type 97 anti-tank rifle used a gas-operated mechanism, but the heavy recoil involved meant that a fully-automatic mode could be little used. Four men were needed to carry this rifle using special frames, and a shield was an optional extra. The box magazine held seven rounds.

The ammunition fired by the Type 97 was produced in several forms. Apart from the usual armour piercing round (with tracer) there was a high explosive projectile (with tracer and with an optional self-destruct), a high explosive incendiary and a practice round. The armour-piercing projectile had a solid steel body, and there was also an incendiary projectile complete with a tracer element.

SPECIFICATION	
Anti-tank Rifle Type 97	(148.8 lb); in action 51.75 kg
Calibre: 20 mm (0.79 in)	(114.1 lb)
Lengths: overall 2.095 m (6 ft	**Muzzle velocity:** 793 m (2,602 ft) per
10.5 in); barrel 1.063 m (3 ft 5.9 in)	second
Weights: travelling 67.5 kg	

Panzerwurfmine (L)
Anti-tank grenade

The **Panzerwurfmine (L)** was developed to provide special German tank-killer squads with a potent one-man stand-off weapon. It was a specialised form of anti-tank grenade with a hollow-charge warhead to defeat the target tank's armour, and to ensure that the warhead was facing the target armour when it struck the tank, the grenade was fitted with a finned tail for stabilisation and guidance.

The Panzerwurfmine was thrown at its target in a special manner. Behind the grenade warhead was a steel body attached to a wooden handle. The user gripped this handle and held it behind his back with the warhead pointing vertically upward. When ready, the user swung his arm forward and released the handle. As soon as the grenade was in flight, four canvas fins unfolded from the handle, and the drogue effect of these fins maintained the warhead in its correct forward position for maximum effect as it struck. In practice the Panzerwurfmine was not an easy weapon to use effectively. For a start the maximum possible

range was limited by the strength and ability of the thrower, and was usually no more than 30 m (32.8 yards) and frequently less. Accuracy could only be ensured by practice with an inert training version.

Despite these disadvantages, some German anti-tank personnel favoured the Panzerwurfmine. Compared with other German close-in anti-tank weapons, the Panzer-wurfmine was relatively small, light and handy. It was also potent, for the warhead was made up of RDX and TNT in equal measures and weighed 0.52 kg (1.146 lb). Combined with the hollow-charge principle, this usually ensured penetration of even the thickest armour. It also had the advantage of not requiring the user to approach the tank to place the grenade on the target. Further safety was provided in that the warhead was not fully fused until the grenade was in flight.

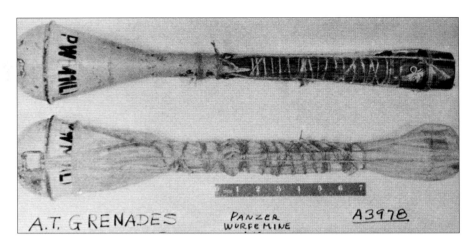

Two examples of the German Panzerwurfmine (L) are shown as they would have been issued, with their stabiliser tails wrapped in cord around the throwing handle. These grenades were not a general issue as they required some skill for use in an effective manner, and they were therefore issued mainly to specialist close-in tank killer squads.

Despite its success, the Panzerwurfmine was not copied closely by any of the Allies. Captured examples were used when they fell into Allied hands, especially by the Red Army, but the Americans often misused them for at first they thought that the weapon should be thrown as an oversized dart. After 1945 the

principle was used by various Warsaw Pact nations, and in the 1970s Egypt in effect copied the Panzerwurfmine as part of the output of their new indigenous arms industry. The Egyptians discovered that this type of hand-launched anti-tank weapon was exactly suited to their infantry anti-tank tactics.

SPECIFICATION	
Panzerwurfmine (L)	279.4 mm (11 in)
Body diameter: 114.3 mm (4.5 in)	**Weights:** overall 1.35 kg (2.98 lb);
Lengths: overall 533 mm (21 in);	warhead 0.52 kg (1.146 lb)
body 228.6 mm (9 in); fins	

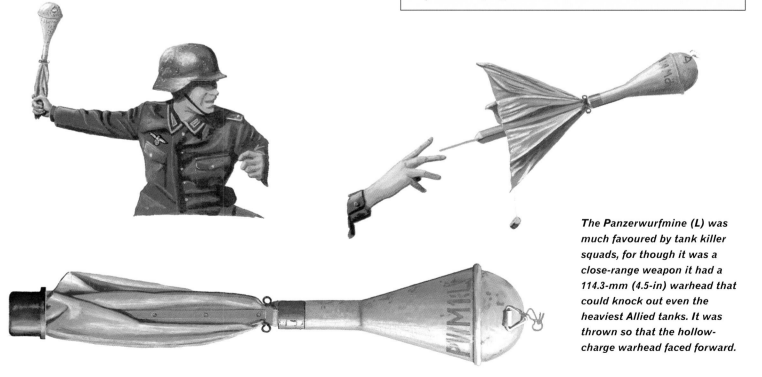

The Panzerwurfmine (L) was much favoured by tank killer squads, for though it was a close-range weapon it had a 114.3-mm (4.5-in) warhead that could knock out even the heaviest Allied tanks. It was thrown so that the hollow-charge warhead faced forward.

Püppchen
Rocket launcher

Once the Germans learned that the artillery projectile was not the most efficient way to deliver a hollow-charge warhead to an armoured target (it moved too fast for the hollow-charge to have full effect), they moved to the rocket as a delivery system. The result was a small 8.8-cm (3.46-in) rocket carrying a hollow-charge warhead able to penetrate the armour of any Allied tank.

The German designers appear to have had little experience of what a rocket-launcher should be, and in the end developed what was in effect a small artillery piece to 'fire' the rocket. This device was known as the **Püppchen** (dolly), or more formally as the **8.8-cm Raketenwerfer 43**, and it had all the appearances of a small gun. There was a shield, and the launcher was moved on wheels. Once in position the wheels could be removed to lower the silhouette of the weapon, which then rested on rockers. The rocket was even loaded using a conventional breech mechanism. Where the Püppchen differed from artillery pieces was that there was no recoil mechanism. The recoil forces produced by firing the rocket were absorbed by the mass of the carriage alone, and the aimer could point the launcher tube by using a twin-handled grip and looking along the barrel.

The Püppchen was introduced into service in 1943, and in use had a maximum range of about 700 m (765 yards), though for anti-tank use the maximum effective range was about 230 m (250 yards) as the sighting system was rather rudimentary and the time of flight of the

A British soldier demonstrates a Püppchen captured in Tunisia in 1943, clearly showing its low silhouette. This rocket launcher had no recoil mechanism and used a simple breech, but compared with the RP 43 series it was much more complex and expensive to produce. The wheels could be removed to lower the silhouette.

rocket could be measured in seconds. It was possible to fire up to 10 rockets per minute. Other design features of the Püppchen were that it could be broken down into seven loads for pack transport, and that skis could be used for movement over snow. There were even instructions printed on the inside of the shield for untrained personnel to use it on a battlefield.

Phased out

The Püppchen did not remain in production for long. Almost as soon at the first items had been issued, American bazookas were captured in Tunisia and examined by German technical personnel, who realised that the simple pipe was all that was needed to launch their 8.8-cm rocket without the complexity of the Püppchen. Production was then switched to the simple RPzB series. But those Püppchen equipments that had been made and issued were not wasted. They were retained in use until

the war ended, especially in Italy where a sizeable number were captured by the Allies and subjected to close investigation by intelligence and technical staffs. It seems that there were plans to mount modified Püppchen launchers on light armoured vehicles, but none of these came to anything.

The 8.8-cm (3.46-in) Raketenwerfer 43 or 'Püppchen' was a form of anti-tank rocket launcher that was superseded, almost as soon as it entered service in 1943, by the RP 43 series, firing a very similar rocket. The RP 43 could be produced far more cheaply and quickly than the Püppchen, seen here while being examined by American soldiers.

SPECIFICATION	
Püppchen	2.66 kg (5.86 lb)
Calibre: 88-mm (3.46-in)	**Elevation:** -18 to +15 degrees
Lengths: overall 2.87 m (9 ft 5 in); barrel 1.60 m (5 ft 3 in)	**Traverse:** 60 degrees
Weights: travelling 146 kg (322 lb); in action 100 kg (220 lb); rocket	**Ranges:** maximum 700 m (766 yards); practical 230 m (252 yards)

Raketenpanzerbüchse Rocket launcher

In 1943 examples of the US 60-mm (2.36-in) M1 bazooka were captured in Tunisia and soon examined by German technicians, who quickly appreciated the advantages of its simple and cheap construction. Before long the first German equivalent appeared. This German launcher fired a rocket very similar to that used on the Püppchen but modified for electrical firing. This first German launcher was known as the **8.8-cm Raketenpanzerbüchse 43** (**RPzB 43**) and was little more than a simple tube, open at both ends, from which the rocket could be launched. The firer rested the 'pip' on his shoulder and operated a lever to power a small electrical generator. Releasing a trigger allowed the power so produced to be passed via wires to the rocket motor for firing. The weapon was completed by a simple sight system.

Instant success

The RPzB 43 was an immediate success. Firing a large-calibre rocket, it had a better anti-armour capability than the bazooka, but the rocket was limited in range to about 150 m (165 yards). Another

disadvantage was that the rocket motor was still burning as it left the muzzle, so the user had to wear protective clothing and a gas mask to avoid being burnt. The rocket exhaust was dangerous for a distance up to 4 m (13.1 ft) to the rear of the tube on firing, and this exhaust could also kick up clouds of dust and debris to betray the firing position. This did little to endear the RPzB 43 to its users.

Further development produced the **RPzB 54**, which had a shield to protect the firer and so remove the need for

The German RP 43 was inspired by the American bazooka, but used a larger 8.8-cm (3.46-in) rocket. Sometimes known as Panzerschreck, this weapon had a range of 150 m (165 yards) and could knock out all Allied tanks.

SPECIFICATION	
RPzB 43	**RPzB 54**
Calibre: 88-mm (3.46-in)	**Calibre:** 88 mm (3.46 in)
Weights: launcher 9.2 kg (20.3 lb); rocket 3.27 kg (7.21 lb); warhead 0.65 kg (1.43 lb)	**Weights:** launcher 11 kg (24.25 lb); rocket 3.25 kg (7.165 lb)
Length: 1.638 m (5 ft 4.5 in)	**Length:** 1.638 m (5 ft 4.5 in)
Range: maximum 150 m (164 yards)	**Range:** maximum 150 m (164 yards)
	Rate of fire: 4–5 rpm

protective clothing, and the later **RPzB 54/1** fired a more advanced rocket needing a shorter launching tube but offering the increased range of 180 m (197 yards). The RPzB 54 and RPzB 54/1 replaced the RPzB 43 in production, and the

early models were passed to second- line and reserve units.

Major service

These weapons soon became very widely distributed and used. The later rockets could penetrate up to 160 mm (6.3 in) of armour, but they were close-range weapons that meant crews often had to 'stalk' a target. The usual crew was two men, one aiming and firing, and the other loading the rockets and connecting the ignition wires to the launcher contacts. The RPzB series had nicknames, including **Ofenrohr** (oven chimney) and **Panzerschreck** (tank terror).

British troops examine an RPzB 54 captured in Normandy, July 1944. The shield can be seen, as can the main lever for the electrical generator used for firing: this looks like a large trigger under the tube. The RPzB 54/1 was essentially similar but used a shorter launching tube.

Anti-tank rifles

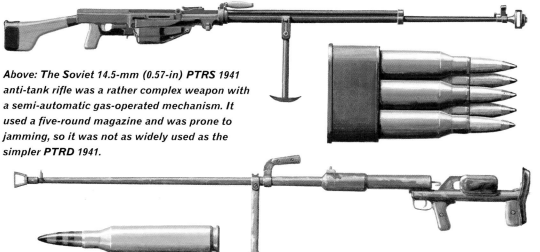

Above: The Soviet 14.5-mm (0.57-in) PTRS 1941 anti-tank rifle was a rather complex weapon with a semi-automatic gas-operated mechanism. It used a five-round magazine and was prone to jamming, so it was not as widely used as the simpler PTRD 1941.

Left: The Soviet PTRD 1941 fired the same steel-cored ammunition as the more complex PTRS 1941. It fired single shots only, but used a semi-automatic breech. It was widely used by the Red Army and partisans, and even the Germans used captured examples to arm garrison units. It was used for many years after 1945.

The Red Army used two anti-tank rifles during World War II, both of them very distinctive as they were long weapons firing the same 14.5-mm (0.57-in) round. The Soviets had neglected the anti-tank rifle when other nations were just adopting the type, and introduced it only at the time that others were discarding it. It must be said, though, that the Soviet rifles were more viable weapons than most in use.

This Soviet 14.5-mm (0.57-in) PTRD 1941 anti-tank rifle has had a round loaded into the breech with the loader's left hand, a subsequent tap on the firer's helmet then indicating that the rifle is ready to fire.

The more numerous of the Soviet rifles was the **PTRD 1941** (or **PTRD-41**) from the Degtyarov bureau and introduced in mid-1941 just in time for the German invasion. A very long weapon that was nearly all barrel, the PTRD-41 had a semi-automatic breech and its steel- or tungsten-cored projectile could penetrate up to 25 mm (0.98 in) of armour at 500 m (545 yards). A large muzzle brake and a bipod were fitted.

The second weapon was the **PTRS 1941** (or **PTRS-41**) from the Simonov bureau. Compared with the PTRD-41 it was a heavier and more complex weapon but had identical performance. The main change in the PTRS-41 was the use of a gas-operated mechanism and the addition of a five-round magazine, which combined to make the PTRS-41 a more trouble-prone weapon than the simpler and lighter PTRD-41. Further complexity was added by a feature that allowed the barrel to be removed for ease in carrying.

Despite the fact that these two anti-tank rifles reached the Red Army at a time when its anti-armour capability was being reduced by a rapid increase in German tank armour thicknesses, they remained in service until well after 1945. The Red Army found the PTRD-41 and PTRS-41 to be very useful all-round weapons: they were useful against soft-skin targets such as trucks, in house-to-

house fighting they were unhandy but very powerful weapons and, when the opportunity arose, the Red Army even used these rifles against low-flying aircraft. Some light armoured cars carried the rifles as their main armament, and Lend-Lease vehicles such as Universal Carriers often mounted one.

The Red Army was not the only World War II operator of these anti-tank rifles, for the Germans pressed into their own use captured weapons: in German service up to 1943 the PTRD-41 was the **14.5-mm Panzerab-wehrbüchse 783(r)** and the PTRS-41 was the **14.5-mm Pab 784(r)**.

The German army used two main types of anti-tank rifle but

attempted to develop many more models. The first in-service weapon was the **7.92-mm Panzerbüchse 38**, a 0.312-in rifle from Rheinmetall-Borsig. It was a complex and expensive weapon whose breech featured a small sliding breech block and an automatic ejector for the spent case. About 1,600 of the weapons were bought by the German army, but the type was not accepted as for full service although those that had been delivered were retained in service and were used during the early years of the war. Fired from a necked-down 13-mm (0.51-in) cartridge, the bullet could pierce 30 mm (118 in) of armour at 100 m (110 yards) at an impact angle of 60°.

The standard German anti-tank rifle was the **7.92-mm Panzerbüchse 39**. Created by the Gustloff-Werke of Suhl, this was a much simpler weapon than the Pzb 38 but with the same armour-penetration capability. Even though it still had a sliding breech block, this was operated by pulling down the pistol grip. Like the earlier rifle it was a single-shot weapon and the stock could be folded to make carriage more handy. Extra ammunition could be carried on the weapon in small boxes on the sides of the breech.

The two anti-tank rifles fired the same ammunition, which originally used a hard steel core. In 1939 Polish Marosczek anti-tank rifles were captured, and examination revealed that its

The Panzerbüchse 39 is shown in the travelling position (below) and with the bipod lowered and stock extended ready for action (above). German anti-tank rifles were rendered obsolete by the increasing thickness of tank armour.

bullets had a tungsten core that gave much better armour penetration. The Germans seized upon this principle as a means of extending the operational viability of their own anti-tank rifles, which would otherwise have been made obsolete by increases in tank armour thicknesses.

The Germans developed a surprising number of follow-on designs in an effort to replace the Pzb 39, and though several manufacturers produced a series of prototypes, all of them in 7.92-mm calibre, none of these got past the prototype stage. There was even a programme to develop an anti-tank machine gun, the MG 141, but again this did not proceed far.

One other anti-tank rifle used by the Germans was a Swiss product known as the **7.92-mm M SS 41**. This was produced by

the Waffenfabrik Solothurn to a German specification, but not many appear to have been made or delivered (some were used in North Africa). Solothurn also made a weapon more accurately described as an anti-tank cannon. This **2-cm Pab 785(s)**

was a bulky weapon towed on a two-wheeled mounting, and again only a few were procured by the Germans. Others went to Italy, where the type was known as the **Fucile anticarro**. It was an automatic weapon that used five- or 10-round magazines.

Above: The German Granatbüchse 39 was a converted Pzb 39 anti-tank rifle fitted with a 'Schiessbecker' grenade-launcher cup on the muzzle. The grenades fired by this weapon included small hollow-charge anti-tank grenades (see cross-section) that were effective only against the very lightest armour at ranges up to 125 m (135 yards).

A German soldier is seen in North Africa with a 7.92-mm (0.312-in) Panzerbüchse 39. This was a single-shot rifle firing a projectile (even when tungsten-cored) with only limited armour-piercing capability, denying the weapon the facility to tackle anything but the lightest tanks after 1940.

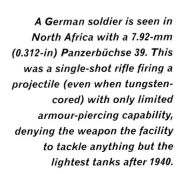

Improvised anti-tank weapons

Easy to make and use, the **Molotov cocktail** appears to have had its operational debut during the Spanish Civil War of 1936–39, when it was first used against Nationalist tanks by the Republican forces.

The basic weapon is simply a glass bottle containing petrol (or some other flammable substance) with an oil-soaked rag or something similar around the neck. This rag is ignited immediately before the weapon is thrown at a target, the breaking of the bottle as it hits its target allowing the contents to be ignited. It is very simple, easily understood and easily used, but the snag was that it was not very efficient. It was also discovered that petrol alone was not a very efficient anti-armour weapon as it simply runs off the sides of a tank even as it is burning. In order to make the flame-producing mixture 'stick', the petrol had to be mixed with a thickening agent such as diesel or oil or in

Left: The Molotov cocktail was an international weapon, and shown here from the left are examples from the Soviet Union, (the second an 'official' Red Army version), Britain (using a milk bottle), Japan and Finland. All use the same basic form, with petrol-soaked rags acting as fuses for ignition.

some cases various forms of latex were used.

Phosphorus grenade

An offshoot of the petrol bomb was the phosphorus grenade. Used by several nations, this was designed as a smoke grenade, but the white phosphorus, which started to burn as soon as it was exposed to the air, also made it a very useful anti-personnel and anti-armour weapon. There were several of these types of grenade but typical was the British

Grenade, Self-Igniting, Phosphorus, No. 76. This was a glass milk bottle filled with a mix of phosphorus, water and benzine, and was intended primarily for the anti-tank role. It could be thrown at its target or launched from the Northover Projector, and contained a piece of smoked rubber that gradually dissolved in the mixture to make it 'stick' better to its target. Each No. 76 grenade weighed about 0.535 kg (1.18 lb).

Boys anti-tank rifle

The **Rifle, Anti-tank, 0.55-in, Boys, Mk 1** was originally known as the **Stanchion Gun**, and was designed as the standard infantry anti-tank weapon of the British army. The first of the type entered service during the late 1930s and by 1942 the weapon was obsolete.

The Boys anti-tank rifle had a calibre of 13.97 mm (0.55-in) and fired a powerful cartridge whose projectile could pierce 21 mm (0.827 in) at 300 m (330 yards). The cartridge produced an equally powerful recoil, and to reduce this recoil somewhat the long slender barrel was fitted with a muzzle brake. Ammunition was fed into the bolt-action firing mechanism from a five-round overhead box magazine. The Boys was long and heavy, so it was often mounted as the main weapon on board Bren Gun or Universal Carriers, or as the main armament of light armoured cars.

The first production Boys anti-tank rifles used a forward-

British troops train with Molotov cocktails in 1940. The British Army referred to these weapons as 'bottle bombs' and even established production lines for them, often using milk bottles filled with petrol and phosphorus.

mounted monopod combined with a handgrip under the butt plate, After Dunkirk various modifications were made to speed production, and among the measures taken was replacement of the forward monopod by a Bren Gun bipod and of the circular muzzle brake attachment by a new Solothurn muzzle brake with holes drilled along the sides; this latter was easier to produce than the original. In this form the Boys saw out its short service life, as by late 1940 it was regarded as being of only limited use as an anti-armour weapon. It was found to be a very effective anti-personnel weapon during the North African campaigns of 1941–42: here it was fired at rocks over or near a concealed enemy, the resultant rock splinters acting as anti-personnel fragments. The Boys also found its way into US Marine Corps hands during the Philippines

A French officer about to receive the hefty recoil of the Boys anti-tank rifle. The French army used a number of these rifles in 1940 provided by the British in exchange for a number of 25-mm (0.98-in) Hotchkiss anti-tank cannons. This example is the original Mk 1 with the monopod supporting leg.

SPECIFICATION	
Northover Projector	**Boys Anti-Tank Rifle Mk 1**
Calibre: 63.5-mm (2.5-in)	**Calibre:** 13.97-mm (0.55-in)
Weights: projector 27.2 kg (60 lb); mounting 33.6 kg (74 lb)	**Length overall:** 1625 mm (64 in)
Range: effective 90 m (100 yards); maximum 275 m (300 yards)	**Length of barrel:** 914 mm (36 in)
	Weight: 16.33 kg (36 lb)
	Muzzle velocity: 991 m (3,250 ft) per second
	Armour penetration: 21 mm (0.827 in) at 300 m (330 yards)

The Northover Projector was a weapon developed in 1940 to equip the Home Guard. It was supposed to be used as an anti-tank weapon to fire the No. 76 bottle grenade filled with phosphorus. There was no recoil mechanism as the frame carriage was supposed to absorb the recoil, and the propelling charge was black powder.

campaign of early 1942, when some were used very sparingly against dug-in Japanese infantry positions. Captured Boys rifles also saw limited service with the Germans for a short while after Dunkirk as the **13.9-mm Panzerabwehrbüchse 782(e)**.

In 1940 there were plans to produce a Boys Mk 2 as a shortened and lightened version for airborne forces, but it did not get very far before the project was terminated.

Northover Projector

In the aftermath of Dunkirk the British army was left with virtually no anti-tank weapons. With invasion imminent there was a need for an easily produced weapon that could be used to equip the army and also the newly formed Local Defence Volunteers, later to become the Home Guard. One of the weapons that was rushed into production was the Northover mortar, also known as the bottle

mortar but later designated the **Northover Projector**. This was was little more than a steel pipe with a rudimentary breech at one end. The ammunition consisted of orthodox hand and rifle grenades that were propelled from the muzzle by a small black-powder charge. Later the No. 76 phosphorus grenade was fired, and it was this that gave rise to the name bottle mortar. There was no appreciable recoil, the sights were basic but accurate enough up to about 90 m (100 yards), and the maximum range was about 275 m (300 yards).

For some time after 1940 the Northover Projector was a standard Home Guard weapon, and it was also issued to many army units for a while. In practice the Northover was only as good

as the projectiles it fired, and as these were orthodox hand or rifle grenades their efficiency against most tanks was doubtful. The use of the white phosphorus grenade would no doubt have been more successful, but this was not a popular weapon with the projector crews for the simple reason that the glass bottle often broke inside the barrel on firing. The usual crew was two men, with possibly another in charge of the weapon. Many Home Guard units introduced their own local modifications to enable the Northover to be moved around more easily. To make the normal four-legged carriage easier to handle, a lightened **Northover Projector Mk 2** was introduced during 1941

Anti-tank grenades

The British army used three types of anti-armour hand grenade. The first was the **Grenade, Hand, Anti-tank, No. 73**, known as the 'Thermos' bomb from its shape and size. It was a pure blast weapon which often had little effect on armour, so it was mainly used for demolition work. More common during the early war years was the infamous **Grenade, Hand, Anti-tank, No. 74 (ST)**, the 'sticky bomb' which was coated in a gooey adhesive to make it stick to the side of a tank after landing: the sticky surface was normally contained within two shell halves which were removed just before throwing. The No. 74 was a most unpopular weapon as the sticky substance tended to make it stick to anything, even before throwing, and the type was used as little as possible.

The best of the British anti-tank grenades was the **Grenade, Hand, Anti-tank, No. 75,**

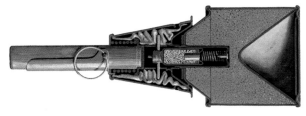

Left: The RPG 1943 was the Soviet equivalent of the German Panzerwurfmine, but in flight was reliant on a fabric strip stabiliser tail to keep the hollow charge warhead pointing toward the target tank. The tail was ejected from the throwing handle after the grenade had been thrown and after the arming pin had been removed.

Left: The Soviet RPG-6 was a late-war version of the RPG 1943. It used a revised warhead shape and four fabric tails to stabilise the warhead in flight. The revised warhead also had a very useful fragmentation effect, so it could also be used as an anti-personnel weapon. It was used for many years after 1945.

otherwise known as the **Hawkins Grenade**. It was intended to be either thrown or laid as a mine to blow off a tank's tracks. It used a crush igniter fuse and about half of its weight of 1.02 kg (2.25 lb) was made up of the bursting charge. The type was often used in clusters for better effect, and the Germans captured so many of them before Dunkirk that they were later used as part of the minefields defending the Atlantic Wall with the designation **Panzerabwehrmine 429/1 (e)**.

The **Grenade, Rifle, Anti-tank, No. 68** was a rifle grenade fired from a muzzle cup fitted to the No. 1 Mk III rifle. It was

withdrawn after 1941 as it was not much use against anything other than very light armour. It weighed 0.79 kg (1.75 lb) and could also be fired from the Northover Projector.

American grenades

The American equivalent of the No. 68 was the **Antitank Rifle Grenade M9A1**, a much more successful grenade that could be fired from an M7 launcher fitted to the M1 Garand rifle or an M8 launcher fitted to an M1 carbine. The M9A1 weighed 0.59 kg (1.31 lb) and had an 0.113-kg (0.25-lb) warhead behind a thin steel metal nose fitted with an impact fuse. Its capability

against tanks was somewhat limited, but it was retained in service for some time as it was a very useful weapon against targets such as pillboxes. A ring tail was used for inflight stabilisation.

Soviet grenades

As with the anti-tank rifle, the Soviets tended to neglect the anti-tank grenade and had to rush something into service in rather a hurry in 1940. Their first attempt was the **RPG 1940**, which resembled a short stick grenade and relied mainly on blast for its effect; it was not a great success and was gradually replaced. The contemporary

VPGS 1940 was a rifle grenade which featured a long rod that fitted into the rifle barrel before firing. It too was no great success. The best of the wartime Soviet anti-tank grenades was the **RPG 1943** of 1943. This was a hand-thrown grenade which in some ways imitated the German Panzerwurfmine, but had a tail unit that trailed on two canvas strips to keep the warhead with its hollow charge pointed towards the target. The RPG 1943 weighed 1.247 kg (2.75 lb), and was thus quite a weight to throw, but it had a heavy explosive content and could be very effective. It was retained is use after 1945.

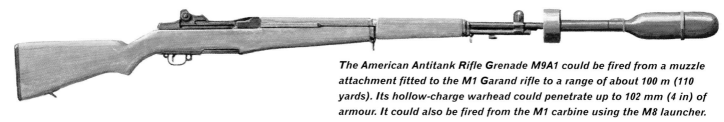

The American Antitank Rifle Grenade M9A1 could be fired from a muzzle attachment fitted to the M1 Garand rifle to a range of about 100 m (110 yards). Its hollow-charge warhead could penetrate up to 102 mm (4 in) of armour. It could also be fired from the M1 carbine using the M8 launcher.

PIAT

While others went for rocket-propelled hollow-charge anti-tank bombs, the British used the Projector Infantry Anti-Tank – the PIAT. This was a form of spigot mortar using a powerful central spring to fire its projectile from a front-mounted 'trough'. It was not a popular weapon, but it could kill tanks.

The **Projector, Infantry, Anti-Tank Mk 1 (PIAT)** was a British anti-tank weapon that somehow bypassed the usual stringent weapon selection procedures used by the War Office as it was a product of the unusual department known colloquially as 'Winston Churchill's Toy

Shop'. It was designed to exploit the armour-piercing effect of the hollow-charge warhead, and fired a useful grenade that could penetrate almost any contemporary tank's protection. Thus it came into the same general category as the bazooka and Panzerfaust.

However, the PIAT relied upon coiled-spring rather than chemical energy to deliver its grenade, for the weapon worked on the spigot mortar principle. In this launching method, the PIAT grenade was projected from an open trough and supported for the initial part of its travel by a

central spigot. Pulling the trigger released a powerful main spring and this spring enabled the spigot to strike the grenade's propelling charge to fire it from the trough. The propelling charge also recocked the main spring ready for another grenade to be loaded.

Multi-role weapon

The PIAT was intended primarily as an anti-tank weapon, but it could also fire HE and smoke grenades, which made it much more versatile than many of its contemporaries. It was a very useful weapon in house-to-house and urban combat, for the forward monopod could be extended to provide a fair degree of elevation for use in confined spaces.

The PIAT replaced the Boys anti-tank rifle as the infantry's standard anti-tank weapon, and it was issued widely throughout the British and some Commonwealth armies. However, it cannot be said to have been very popular for it was bulky and needed a two-man team to handle it. The main point of unpopularity was the powerful mainspring. This generally required the efforts of two men to cock it. If a grenade failed to fire the weapon was all but useless, for recocking the PIAT when the enemy was nearby was a very risky

business. The use of the PIAT spread outside the ranks of the infantry, for it was often the main armament of light armoured vehicles such as light armoured cars. There was also some limited use of the weapon on carriers, which mounted up to 14 PIATs on a multiple mounting as a mobile mortar battery.

The PIAT was the British army's standard squad anti-tank weapon after 1941, and was carried and used by most combat arms and services. It was a rather hefty load to carry, but it could knock out most enemy tanks at close ranges and could also fire HE and smoke bombs.

The PIAT remained in service with the British army for some years after World War II. Although it was an effective tank-killer, it used a principle that was not adopted by any other

designers. However, it did have the advantage that it could be produced in quantity and at a relatively low cost at a time when anti-tank weapons of any type were in great demand.

Here the crew members of a knocked out British tank are covering their position armed with a PIAT until a recovery vehicle can arrive to retrieve the damaged vehicle. The men are from the 13/18th Hussars, and the location is near Mount Pincon, northern France, July 1944. Note the No. 4 rifle near the PIAT.

SPECIFICATION	
PIAT	**Muzzle velocity:** 76–137 m (250–450 ft) per second
Length: overall 990 mm (3 ft 0 in)	
Weights: launcher 14.51 kg (32 lb); grenade 1.36 kg (3 lb)	**Ranges:** combat 100 m (110 yards); maximum 340 m (370 yards)

Bazooka

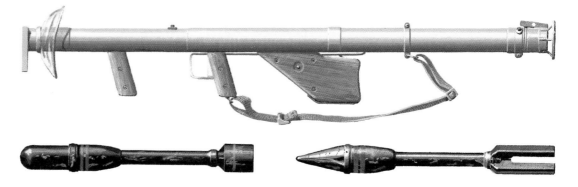

The American **Bazooka** was one of the more original weapons of World War II and was founded on basic rocket research that had been conducted at the Aberdeen Proving Ground, Maryland, since 1933. The active service development of the weapon began in earnest early in 1942, and led to the creation of a weapon whose first examples were introduced straight into combat in North Africa during November 1942 within the context of the Allies' Operation 'Torch' landings in north-west Africa. However, it was the following year before any found their way into action against Axis armour.

The full designation of the first model was **2.36-in Rocket Launcher, M1**. The 60-mm (2.36-in) rocket fired from the tube launcher was the **M6A3**, and the practice rocket was known as the **M7A3**.

The bazooka was a very simple weapon, being nothing more than a steel tube that was open at each end and along which the rocket-propelled weapon was launched. A shoulder rest or wooden stock was provided, together with two grips, to facilitate the aiming of the tube; the rear grip included the trigger group. Once loaded, the rocket was fired electrically. In low temperatures, however, not all the propellant was consumed before the rocket left

SPECIFICATION	
M1A1	
Calibre: 60-mm (2.36-in)	**Range:** maximum 595 m (650 yds)
Length: 1384 mm (4 ft 6.5 in)	**Muzzle velocity:** 82.3 m (270 ft) per second
Weights: launcher 6.01 kg (13.25 lb); rocket 1.54 kg (3.4 lb)	**Armour penetration:** 119.4 mm (4.7 in) at 0°

the launcher, allowing unburnt powder to be blasted into the firer's face. To prevent this it was possible to fit a small circular wire mesh screen just behind the muzzle. In practice the bazooka could be used at point targets up to 274 m (300 yards) distant, but for most purposes the range was confined to about 90 m (100 yards) as the rocket was not notably accurate in its flight.

Improved models

Soon after the M1 bazooka entered service it was replaced by the essentially similar **M1A1**. It was a popular weapon that could knock out any enemy tank and was normally served by a two-man team, one aiming and the other loading the rockets and connecting their electrical firing circuits. The versatility of the weapons soon meant that the

bazooka found a great number of battlefield tasks other than its designed anti-tank role: this was the result of the use of a hollow-charge warhead in the rocket, and this was very good at knocking out pillboxes of all kinds, and could even blast holes through barbed-wire obstacles; the bazooka could be used against area targets such as vehicle parks at ranges up to 595 m (650 yards), and at times the weapon was also used to clear combat lanes through minefields. There are even records of the bazooka being used against artillery pieces at close ranges.

Tank killer

But it was in the war against the tank that the bazooka made its main mark, and so successful was the bazooka in this task that

The American 2.36-in (60mm) Rocket Launcher M1 was the first of the bazookas and was used by the Germans as the original for their RP series. The M1 used a one-piece barrel that could not fold and early versions (shown here) used a wire mesh shield around the muzzle to protect against rocket blast.

the Germans seized upon the concept as the design basis of their own Raketenpanzerbüchse series after examples of the M1 had been captured in Tunisia early in 1943. Although the German counterparts were much larger in calibre, the Americans stuck to their 60-mm (2.36-in) calibre until after 1945.

By then they had introduced a new model, the **M9**, that differed from the M1 in being breakable into two halves for ease of carrying. Smoke and incendiary rockets were developed and used before 1945. As the war ended the all-aluminium **M18** launcher was being introduced to service.

Below: The original M1 bazooka is shown on the left and the M9 on the right. The M9 could be broken down into two halves, which greatly assisted carriage and stowage inside vehicles. By the time the war ended, a version of the M9 was being produced in aluminium for lightness; this was the M18.

Above: The rocket fired from the American bazookas was fin-stabilised and weighed 1.53 kg (3.4 lb). It had a maximum range of 640 m (700 yds), but was accurate only to ranges much shorter than that.

German flamethrowers

The first time the German army used flamethrowers was in 1914, when early weapons of this type were used against the French during the fighting in the Argonne region, but their first large-scale use was once again against the French, this time during the 1916 Verdun campaign. These early flamethrowers were large items of equipment requiring up to three men to handle them, but development led to a much lighter version that weighed 'only' 35.8 kg (79 lb).

Nazi expansion

Based on the flamethrower introduced to German service in 1918, this was the **Flammenwerfer 35**, which was issued to units of the new and much expanded German army during the 1930s. In design terms the Flammenwerfer 35

The Flammenwerfer 41, seen here resting on its side, used a hydrogen ignition system that proved to be too unreliable under the extreme winter conditions of the Eastern Front and was later replaced by a cartridge ignition system. The larger of the two tanks contained the fuel, and the other compressed nitrogen propellant.

owed much to the World War I equipment, and remained in production into 1941.

Steady evolution

From this year the Flammenwerfer 35 was gradually supplemented by later models.

The first of these was the **Flammenwerfer klein verbessert 40,** a much lighter 'lifebuoy' model that carried less inflammable fuel. Relatively few of these equipments were produced as the type was soon replaced in manufacture and

service by the improved **Flammenwerfer 41**. This reverted to the arrangement of the Flammenwerfer 35, with side-by-side fuel and compressed-gas propellant tanks, and was the standard German flamethrower of the

Right: A Flammenwerfer 35 is seen in action against a concrete emplacement in Poland after the 1939 campaign. The Flammenwerfer 35 had a range of 25.6 to 30 m (28 to 33 yards) and carried enough fuel for 10 seconds of use, but it weighed 35.8 kg (79 lb) and so was often carried into action by two men.

Left: The fearsome blast of a man-pack flamethrower is seen during a night attack at Stalingrad. Flamethrower operators had to be well protected by friendly infantry as they were both vulnerable and conspicuous.

rest of World War II. One important modification was introduced after the grim winter of 1941–42, when the intense cold prevented the normal flame ignition system from working. This system was replaced by a cartridge ignition device that was much more reliable at other temperatures as well. When full this version, the **Flammenwerfer mit Strahlrohrpatrone 41,** which was otherwise identical to the standard 1941 model, weighed 18.14 kg (40 lb) and the range at

best was 32 m (35 yards).

Single-shot weapon

These multiple-burst weapons were complemented by an odd model for airborne and assault unit troops. This was a single-shot model known as the **Einstoss Flammenwerfer tragbar** which delivered a 0.5-second burst of fire to a range of about 27 m (30 yards). Not many were produced.

It should not be thought that the above were the only German

flamethrower equipments for the Germans proved themselves extremely prolific, as indeed they did with virtually all their weapon types, in the creation of derived and separate models of greater or lesser practicality. In addition to the Flammenwerfer 35 back-pack equipment mentioned above, for instance, there was also a two-man version known as the **mittlerer Flammenwerfer,** whose main fuel tank was carried on a small trolley: the fuel capacity of this equipment was thus increased to 30 litres (6.6 Imp gal) from the Flammenwerfer 41's figure of 7 litres (1.54 Imp

gal). As if this was not enough, there was also a much larger model carried on a trailer towed behind a light vehicle: this carried enough fuel to produce flame for 24 seconds. Finally, for use in static situations there was a device known as the **Abwehrflammenwerfer 42**, a single-shot device to be buried into the ground with only the flame projector nozzle above ground and pointing towards a target area. This was set off by remote control as an enemy approached. Needless to say, the Germans made much use of captured equipments.

SPECIFICATION	
Flammenwerfer 35	**Range:** 25.6 to 30 m (28 to
Weight: 35.8 kg (79 lb)	33 yards)
Fuel capacity: 11.8 litres	**Duration of fire:** 10 seconds
(2.6 Imp gal)	

A German assault pioneer team is seen with one member of the team carrying the weight and bulk of a Flammenwerfer 35. This equipment was an awkward load for a single man, especially in an assault situation, but the equipment remained in production until 1941.

Lanciafiamme
Modello 35 & 40

The Italian L3 Lanciafiamme carried its fuel in a trailer connected to the flame gun by a flexible hose. The propellant gas was contained in a cylinder on the rear of the chassis, but later versions carried both fuel and gas actually on the hull exterior. The L3 Lanciafiamme was the most widely used of the Italian mobile flamethrowers.

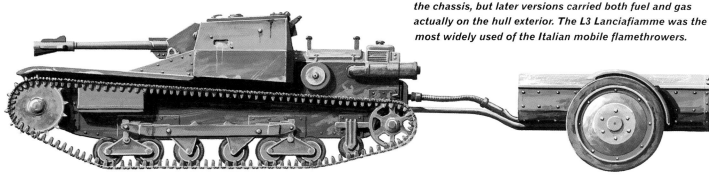

As its designation implies, the Italian **Lanciafiamme modello 35** entered service in 1935, just in time to make its operational debut during the Italian invasion of Abyssinia, in which it proved a major success. In design terms, there was nothing really remarkable about the modello 35. It was a relatively portable twin-cylinder backpack equipment that used a rather cumbersome flame projector. This projector was fitted at the end with a large collar housing

the flame ignition system. For various reasons this ignition system was not considered sufficiently reliable, so it was modified to produce the **Lanciafiamme modello 40**. In general appearance and use the modello 40 was otherwise identical to the modello 35.

These flamethrowers were used by special troops known as Guastori, or assault pioneers, who had to wear thick protective clothing with their faces covered by normal service gas

respirators. When so clothed their operational mobility and vision was restricted, so they were usually guarded by teams of supporting infantry. On the move their flamethrower equipments were usually carried on special brackets fitted to trucks or, if the formation was

not mechanised, mules with special harnesses. The fuel for the flamethrowers was carried in specially marked containers.

Africa and Russia

Both flamethrower types were used in some numbers by Italian troops operating in North Africa

SPECIFICATION	
Lanciafiamme modello 35	**Range:** about 25 m (27 yards)
Weight: 27 kg (59.5 lb)	**Duration of fire:** 20 seconds
Fuel capacity: 11.8 litres	
(2.6 Imp gal)	

The flame projector of the L3 Lanciafiamme was mounted in place of the machine gun carried on the L3 tankettes. These Italian flamethrower tanks were of very limited tactical value as they were very lightly armoured and had a crew of only two.

and on the Eastern Front. In both theatres the modello 35 and 40 worked well enough, but it was increasingly noticed that the equipments lacked range by comparison with contemporary equivalents, and especially the later German designs.

The success of the flamethrower in Abyssinia moved the Italian army authorities to fit a special version of a lanciafiamme, much larger than the man-pack version, to the L3 tankette. As space within the low hull of this **L3-35Lf** vehicle was very limited, the fuel was carried externally in a lightly armoured trailer, with a corrugated pipe passing the fuel from the trailer to the projector. There was also a version that dispensed with the trailer and carried a much smaller flat fuel tank over the top of the vehicle's rear. Although much was made of these two flamethrowing tankettes, they appear to have been little used.

Portable flamethrower
Types 93 & 100

The Japanese Model 93 and Model 100 portable flamethrowers were almost identical – this is the Model 93 – and differed only in the shape of the flame gun and other minor changes. Two tanks held the fuel and the other was the nitrogen pressure tank, providing a flame jet duration of 10 to 12 seconds.

The first Japanese flamethrower of World War II was the **Portable Flamethrower Type 93**. This was first issued during 1933 and was an orthodox design that made much use of German experience in World War I. It used three cylinders on a rather awkward back-pack arrangement, two of the cylinders containing the fuel and the central (and smaller) cylinder containing the compressed gas propellant.

From 1939 a small petrol-driven air compressor was issued with each equipment.

It was never satisfactory, and in 1940 was replaced by the outwardly similar **Portable Flamethrower Type 100**. The new flame gun was 0.9 m (35.5 in) rather than 1.2 m (47.125 in) long, and had a nozzle that could easily be changed, whereas that

of the Type 93 was fixed.

Although the Japanese infantry made some use of flamethrowers, the Japanese tank formations made only limited use of the weapon. Apparently only one attempt was made to produce a flamethrower tank, which was used by a small unit encountered on the Philippines island of Luzon in 1944. These turretless tanks were fitted with obstacle clearing equipment on the front hull, and mounted a single flamethrower forward. Both internal and external fuel tanks were carried. The tank used as the basis appears to have been the Medium Tank Type 98, and the only other armament was a single MG.

SPECIFICATION	
Portable Flamethrower Type 100	**Range:** about 23 to 27 m (25 to 30 yards)
Weight: 25 kg (55 lb)	
Fuel capacity: 14.77 litres (3.25 Imp gal)	**Duration of fire:** 10 to 12 seconds

If war-time propaganda photographs are to be believed, the Japanese army and marines made extensive use of flamethrowers during World War II. This impression came from a series of 'official' photographs, which were taken during Japan's long war against China, where weapons such as flamethrowers had a psychological effect that far outweighed their real utility as combat weapons.

Lifebuoy Flamethrower

Development of what was to become officially known as the **Flame-Thrower, Portable, No. 2 Mk I** began during 1941. This British flamethrower appears to have been influenced by the German Flammenwerfer 40, but the basic design of any portable flamethrower is fixed by physical constraints. This results from the fact that for a vessel that has to contain gas at high pressure, a sphere is the best possible shape. On a flamethrower the fuel tank has to contain as much fuel as possible within as small a volume as can be managed. These design criteria virtually dictate the shape of the equipment, i.e. a central sphere containing pressurised gas in the centre of a doughnut-shaped fuel tank. This produces the classic shape which gave the British equipment its **Lifebuoy** nickname, a name that stuck.

Over-hasty production

The first pilot model was ready by mid-1942 and production orders followed before troop and other trials had been completed. This was unfortunate, for after only a short time in service the Lifebuoy began to demonstrate a number of serious defects, many of them caused by hurried manufacture of the tanks' complex shapes. Ignition proved to be somewhat unreliable, and the position of the fuel valve under the tanks proved to be awkward. As a result the production run of the Mk I

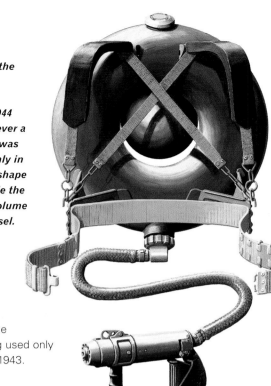

The Mk II version of the Lifebuoy became the standard British flamethrower from 1944 onward, but it was never a popular weapon and was used operationally only in limited numbers. Its shape was chosen to provide the maximum possible volume inside a pressure vessel.

weapon was short, the equipment then being used only for training from mid-1943.

Improved model

It was not until the following year that there appeared the improved **Flame-Thrower, Portable, No. 2 Mk II**. It was this version that the British army used until the end of World War II and for many years after it. In appearance there was little to differentiate the Mk I from the Mk II. This was ready for service by June 1944, and was used during and after the Normandy landings, and in the Far East. The British army was never really enthusiastic about the portable flamethrower, however, and decided that not many would be required: manufacture of the Mk

II ended as early as July 1944, after 7,500 had been made. Even the Mk II proved to be generally unreliable as it depended on a small battery to ignite the flame, and in the wet or after even a short period of use the battery often failed. In an effort to reduce weight, there was developed the smaller **Ack-Pack** device, which weighed 21.8 kg (48 lb). In the event the Ack-Pack was developed so slowly that it was not produced until after the war's end.

SPECIFICATION

Lifebuoy	**Range:** 27.4 to 36.5 m (30 to
Weight: 29 kg (64 lb)	40 yards)
Fuel capacity: 18.2 litres (4 Imp gal)	**Duration of fire:** 10 seconds

The Mk I version of the Flame Thrower, Portable, No. 2 was usually known as the Lifebuoy from its shape. It was not a great success and saw only limited operational use before being replaced in late 1944 by the Mk II.

Below: The operator of a Lifebuoy flamethrower brings up the rear of a file of British infantrymen moving up toward the front line somewhere in northwestern Europe.

Flame-Thrower M1 & M2

When the US Army requested a man-portable flamethrower in July 1940, the Chemical Warfare Service had no knowledge base upon which to work. From the **Portable Flame-Thrower E1** development model the service evolved the **E1R1** for troop trials, some of which were carried out under combat conditions in Papua. The E1R1 was easily broken and its controls were difficult to reach, but a more rugged version was accepted for service as the **M1**. This was much like the E1R1 in that it had two tanks, one for fuel and the other for compressed hydrogen.

The M1 went into production in March 1942, and the weapon was in action during the Guadalcanal operations of June 1942. It proved to be something of a disappointment: the ignition circuit used electrical power supplied by batteries that often failed under service conditions, and the tanks were liable to pin-hole corrosion spots that allowed pressure to escape.

Improved but flawed

By June 1943 the new **M1A1**, of which 14,000 were made, was in service. This was the M1 modified for use of fuels thickened by the additives and

giving better flame effects and a range of up to 46 m (50 yards) compared with the 27.5-m (30-yard) maximum of the M1. Unfortunately the troublesome ignition system was not improved in any way.

By mid-1943 the Chemical Warfare Service had a much better idea of what kind of portable flamethrower the troops required. Based on the **E3** experimental design, the **M2-2** featured several improvements. The M2-2 used the new thickened fuel but was a much more rugged weapon carried on a back-pack frame (very similar to that used to carry ammunition) and with a cartridge ignition system using a revolver-type mechanism that allowed up to six flame jet shots before new cartridges had to be inserted.

The M2-2 was first used in action on Guam in July 1944 and by the time the war ended almost 25,000 had been produced.

Continued progress

Although the M2-2 was an improvement over the M1 and

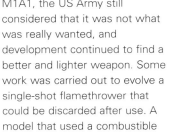

The Portable Flame-Thrower M2-2 was produced by the Americans in greater numbers than any other type, and was first used on Guam in July 1944. It was destined to remain the standard US flame weapon for many years after 1945 and saw action in Korea. Its maximum range under good conditions was 36.5 m (40 yards).

M1A1, the US Army still considered that it was not what was really wanted, and development continued to find a better and lighter weapon. Some work was carried out to evolve a single-shot flamethrower that could be discarded after use. A model that used a combustible

powder to produce pressure to eject 9 litres (2 Imp gal) of thickened petrol-based fuel from a cylinder was under development as the war ended, but the project was then terminated. It would have had a maximum range of 27.5 m (30 yards).

SPECIFICATION	
M1A1	**M2-2**
Weight: 31.8 kg (70 lb)	**Weight:** 28.1 to 32.7 kg (62 to 72 lb)
Fuel capacity: 18.2 litres (4 Imp gal)	**Fuel capacity:** 18.2 litres (4 Imp gal)
Range: 41 to 45.5 m (45 to 50 yards)	**Range:** 22.9 to 36. 5 m (25 to 40 yards)
Duration of fire: 8 to 10 seconds	**Duration of fire:** 8 to 9 seconds

Below: In addition to their noise, flamethrowers had a powerful visual effect on morale, and the mere sight of their flame jets was often enough to make even the strongest men quail. This is an American M2-2 in action on Ie Shima in June 1945.

Above: The American M1 Flame-Thrower was a development of the earlier E1R1 which, although technically an experimental model, was used in action in 1943. The M1 was used for the first time during the Guadalcanal campaign, and used the original 'thin' fuel.

World War II Artillery

Much of the general purpose artillery used by combatants in the early stages of World War II dated back to World War I. Most had been fitted with more efficient mounts, however, and motor vehicles took the place of the teams of horses formerly used to move them.

It would not be long before guns were being mounted on armoured, tracked chassis of their own, giving the new self-propelled artillery pieces the same mobility as the armoured forces which now dominated the field of battle. But warfare was changing and there were new threats to be faced by all armies.

Anti-aircraft artillery and anti-tank guns both light and heavy became an essential component in any army's inventory. Among the most effective was the outstanding German 8.8-cm (3.46-in) Flak gun, which proved lethal as an anti-aircraft gun, as an anti-tank weapon, and as the main armament of the Wehrmacht's massive Panzer VI Tiger tank.

Left: A 5.5-inch medium gun of the British Army opens fire on Axis positions in the desert near El Alamein in the Autumn of 1942. Artillery was one of the few areas in which Allied equipment was generally superior to that of the Wehrmacht during World War II.

Canon de 75 mle 1897 75-mm field gun

During World War I the French '75' or, more formally, the **Canon de 75 modèle 1897**, passed into French national legend as the gun that enabled the French to win the war. It was famous even before 1914 as what may now be regarded as the first of all modern field artillery designs: it coupled a highly efficient recoil mechanism with a rapid-action breech design and a carriage that enabled hitherto unheard-of rates of fire to be maintained. Before 1914 the 75 was a virtual state secret but once in action it more than proved its worth, to the extent that the French army depended on its high rate of fire to make up for deficiencies in the availability of heavier artillery weapons.

The Canon de 75 mle 1897 was still in widespread service in 1939; this example has been fitted with large pneumatic tyres for mechanised traction. Not all World War II examples were so fitted, but in any form the old 75 was still a viable field gun in 1939 and went on to serve with the Germans after 1940.

Overseas service

By 1939 the 75 was rather past its best, and was outranged by more modern field gun designs, but the French still had well over 4,500 of them in front-line use. Other nations also used the 75. The list of these nations was long for it included the US (which was producing its own **75-mm M1897A2** and **75-mm M1897A4** versions), Poland (**armata polowa wz 97/17**), Portugal, many of the French colonies, some Baltic states, Greece, Romania, Ireland and many other nations. The 75 of 1918 was also very different from the 75 of 1939 in many cases. The Americans and Poles had introduced split trail carriages to the 75 in place of the original pole trail, and many nations (including the French) had introduced rubber-tyred wheels for motor traction in place of the original spoked wheels.

The 75 also underwent some other changes in role. Before 1918 many 75 barrels had been placed on rudimentary anti-aircraft carriages, both static and mobile, and despite their limited value many were still around in 1939. The 75 also underwent some adaptation as a form of tank weapon, but it was to be left to the Americans to make the full development of this possibility when they later adapted the type as the main gun for their M3 and M4 tank series. In France the 75 was updated to **Canon de 75 modèle 1897/33** standard with a new split trail carriage, but by 1939 there were few of these weapons still in front-line service.

In the shambles of May and June 1940 huge numbers of 75s fell into the hands of the Germans, who were only too happy to use many of them for their own purposes as the **7.5-cm FK 231(f)** or, more commonly, as the **7.5-cm FK 97(f)**. At first many were issued to occupation garrisons and second-line formations, while others were later incorporated into the beach defences of the Atlantic Wall. Many more were stockpiled ready to be on hand when some use could be found for them. That came during 1941 when it was discovered the hard way that the armour of the T-34/76 Soviet tank was invulnerable to nearly all the German anti-tank weapons. As a hasty stopgap improvisation the stockpiled 75s were taken from the storerooms, fitted with strengthening bands around the barrel and placed on 5-cm Pak 38 anti-tank gun carriages. A muzzle brake was fitted and special armour-piercing (AP) ammunition was hastily produced. The results were rushed to the Eastern Front and there they proved just capable of tackling the Soviet tank armour. This rushed improvisation was

Not all the mle 1897 field guns were fitted with tyres for pneumatic traction, as demonstrated by this example on tow behind a Citroen-Kegresse halftrack.

known to the Germans as the **7.5-cm Pak 97/38** and was really too powerful for the light anti-tank gun carriage, but it worked for the period until proper anti-tank guns arrived on the scene.

Anti-ship weapon

The 7.5 cm Pak 97/38 was not the 75's only wartime development, for later the Americans developed the 75 to the stage where it could be carried in B-25 Mitchell bombers as an anti-ship weapon. After 1945 the 75 lingered on with many armies, and remained in service for many years. In its day it was an excellent artillery piece that deserved its famous reputation.

SPECIFICATION	
Canon de 75 modèle 1897	
Calibre: 75 mm (2.95 in)	**Traverse:** 6°
Length of piece: 2.72 m (8ft 11.1 in)	**Muzzle velocity:** 575 m (1,886 ft) per second
Weight: travelling 1970 kg (4,343 lb) and in action 1140 kg (2,514 lb)	**Range:** 11110 m (12,140 yards)
Elevation: -11° to +18°	**Shell weight:** 6.195 kg (13.66 lb)

Canon de 105 mle 1913 Schneider 105-mm field gun

The Canon de 105 mle 1913 had its origins in a Russian design, but it was a thoroughly modern weapon that was still good for service in 1939-45. Despite its age (the gun was first accepted for service in 1913) it was a good-looking gun with a good performance, and after 1940 it was pressed into service by the occupying German army.

In the first decade of the 20th century the French Schneider concern took over the Russian Putilov armaments factory as part of a deliberate plan of commercial expansion. Putilov had for long been the main Russian armament concern, but during the early 1900s had been restricted in its expansionist ideas by the backwardness of the Russian commercial scene, so the infusion of French capital was a decided advantage.

Among the designs found on the Putilov drawing boards was an advanced design of 107-mm (4.21-in) field gun that appeared to offer considerable increase in range and efficiency over comparable models. Schneider eagerly developed the model and offered it to the French army, which was at first not interested as the 75 was all it required and there was no need for heavier weapons. But eventually the Schneider sales approach triumphed and in 1913 the Russian design was adopted by the French army as the **Canon de 105 modèle 1913 Schneider**, more usually known as the **L 13 S**. The events of 1914 rammed home to the French the fact that the 75 was not capable of supplying all the artillery fire support required, and that heavier guns would be necessary. Thus the L 13 S was given a higher priority and large numbers began to roll off the Schneider production lines.

Good performance

Between 1914 and 1918 the L 13 S provided sterling service. It was a handsome gun with a long barrel and a conventional box trail that provided enough elevation for the 15.74-kg (34.7-lb) shell to reach a range of 12000 m (13,130 yards). After 1918 the L 13 S became a French export as it was either sold or handed on to numerous armies under French influence. These nations included Belgium, Poland and Yugoslavia but it was in Italy that the L 13 S achieved its main market penetration. There the L 13 S became the **Cannone da 105/28**, and it remained one of the main field guns of the Italian forces until 1943. The Poles modified their L 13 S guns to take a new split trail design, and this **armata wz 29** was in service when the Germans attacked in 1939.

After 1940 the Germans found that the L 13 S was a viable weapon and out of the 854 still in French service in May 1940 they captured many that were still intact. Large numbers were handed over to various occupation units but it was not until 1941 that a real use was found for the bulk of the booty. When the Atlantic Wall was ready to be armed the L 13 S was decided upon as one of the primary weapons to be used. There were enough on hand to become a standard weapon, and there were stockpiles of ammunition ready for use. Thus the L 13 S became the German **10.5-cm K 331(f)** and was ready to play its most important part in World War II. Ex-Belgian guns were designated **10.5-cm K 333(b)**.

Turntable mounting

The Germans took the guns off their carriages and mounted them on special turntables protected by curved or angled armour shields. These were placed in bunkers all along the French and other coasts, and many of the bunkers can still be seen among the Atlantic sand dunes to this day. As a beach defence gun the L 13 S was more than suitable, and the bunkers were hard targets for any attacking force to destroy. Fortunately the Normandy landings of June 1944 bypassed most of these bunkers. Not all the guns in these bunkers were directly ex-French; some found their way into the defences from as far away as Yugoslavia and Poland. Captured guns used by the Germans were the **10.5-cm K 338(i)** and **10.5-cm K 338(j)** Italian and Yugoslavian weapons, while unmodified and modified Polish weapons were the **10.5-cm K 13(p)** and **10.5-cm K 29(p)** respectively.

SPECIFICATION	
L 13 S	
Calibre: 105 mm (4.13 in)	**Muzzle velocity:** 550 m (1,805 ft) per second
Length of piece: 2.98 m (9 ft 9.3 in)	**Range:** 12000 m (13,130 yards)
Weight: travelling 2650 kg (5,843 lb) and in action 2300 kg (5,070 lb)	**Shell weight:** 15.74 kg (34.7 lb) for French guns and 16.24 kg (35.8 lb) for Italian guns
Elevation: 0° to +37°	
Traverse: 6°	

Canon de 105 court mle 1935 B 105-mm howitzer

By the mid-1930s the French artillery park was beginning to appear very dated. The vast bulk of the weapons in service were items retained from World War I, and if not already obsolete were at best obsolescent. Most of the weapons involved were 75s, which despite their one-time excellence had their limitations by the 1930s and were also unable to produce the plunging fire that was so often required when attacking fixed defences. Thus the need was forecast for a new field piece capable of easy transport for the support of mechanised forces, and two weapons were produced as the result of this forecast.

Orthodox design

The first was a weapon known as the **Canon de 105 court modèle 1934 S**. It was a Schneider design which was entirely orthodox in design and appearance yet possessing a relatively short barrel. Although the mle 1934 was designated a gun, it had more in common with a howitzer. The mle 1934 was ordered into production, but only at a low priority as more was expected of a slightly better design.

The better design was a product of the state-run Atelier Bourges and appeared during 1935, hence the designation **Canon de 105 court Modèle 1935 B** (*court*, for short, and B for Bourges). The mle 1935 was a very advanced design for its day, and it too had a relatively short barrel, shorter in fact even than that of its Schneider equivalent. The carriage had a split trail which, when opened, also splayed the wheels outwards to improve crew protection. Once spread the trails were held in place with large spades that were pushed down into the ground through the trail extremities. The wheels

could be either large steel items with solid rims or more modern designs with pneumatic tyres for towing by Laffly tractors. The rate of fire was about 15 rounds per minute, which was quite high for a weapon of its calibre.

Into production

The mle 1935 was ordered into production, but this was slow to the extent that although 610 were initially ordered this total was never reached. Instead production was terminated in 1940 in order to permit the production of more anti-tank guns, which were by

then realised as having a higher operational priority. Thus there were only 232 mle 1935s in service when the Germans attacked in May 1940 (and only 144 of the Schneider mle 1934s). In action they proved to be excellent small field pieces, so much so that the Germans took over as many as they could. The Germans recognised the mle 1935 for what it was and gave it a howitzer designation as the **10.5-cm leFH 325(f)**. The

This photograph of a Canon de 105 mle 1935 B howitzer provides a good indication of how the steel carriage wheels were 'toed in' to provide extra protection for the carriage and the gun crew.

weapons were used for training purposes and by various second-line occupation units. Some were incorporated into coastal and beach defences.

SPECIFICATION	
Canon de 105 court mle 1935 B	
Calibre: 105 mm (4.13 in)	**Traverse:** 58°
Length of piece: 1.76 m (5 ft 9.3 in)	**Muzzle velocity:** 442 m (1450 ft) per second
Weight: travelling 1700 kg (3,748 lb) and in action 1627 kg (3,587 lb)	**Range:** 10300 m (11,270 yards)
Elevation: -6° to +50°	**Shell weight:** 15.7 kg (34.62 lb)

Skoda 76.5-mm kanon vz 30/100-mm howitzer vz 30
Field gun and howitzer

When the Austro-Hungarian Empire vanished in the aftermath of World War I, the new state of Czechoslovakia was left with the huge Skoda arms manufacturing complex at Pilsen. The newly independent state was thus poised to become a major supplier of all manner of arms to Central European nations. But in the years after 1919 the arms market was sated with the residue of World War I, and the only way to break into the market was to offer something that was not already on the market. By 1928 the Skoda felt it had found the breakthrough.

Weapon proposal

What the Skoda designers discovered was that there was a definite market for a gun that could be 'all things to all men'.

Their suggestion was for a field gun with a high angle of barrel elevation, which would enable the weapon to be used as an anti-aircraft gun or alternatively as a useful mountain gun. At that time the limitations imposed by the requirements of the antiaircraft weapon were still not fully appreciated, so the Skoda proposal met with significant interest. The new weapon was produced in two forms, namely a 75-mm (2.95-in) anti-aircraft and field gun, and a 100-mm (3.9-in) howitzer that could be used in a mountain role.

The first two weapons of this type were known as the **75-mm kanon vz 28** and

The Skoda 76.5-mm kanon vz 30 was an attempt to produce a field gun with enough barrel elevation for it to be used as an anti-aircraft gun. While it was a sound enough field gun, it proved to be of little use as an anti-aircraft weapon, but the type was used by the Czechoslovak and other armies.

SPECIFICATION	
76.5-mm kanon vz 30	**Elevation:** -8° to +80°
Calibre: 76.5 mm (3.01 in)	**Traverse:** 0°
Length of piece: 3.61 m (11 ft 10.1 in)	**Muzzle velocity:** 600 m (1,968 ft) per second
Weights: travelling 2977 kg (6,564 lb) and in action 1816 kg (4,004 lb)	**Range:** 13505 m (14,770 yards)
	Shell weight: 8 kg (17.64 lb)

100-mm houfnice vz 28 as they were produced during 1928. Both types found ready markets in Yugoslavia and in Romania, and were each based on a carriage that was conventional in appearance. What was not immediately obvious was that the barrel could be elevated to +80°. A firing table could be placed under the spoked-wheel carriage, enabling the barrel to be traversed rapidly enough to track aerial targets. Needless to say, the performance of the

guns against aircraft was less than satisfactory, and by the late 1920s it was finally being recognised that there was more to an anti-aircraft capability than merely pointing a muzzle skyward. But as a field and mountain gun the vz 28 weapons were more than adequate, and the anti-aircraft role was dropped. Instead the weapons' multi-role capability was enhanced by making the carriage easy to dismantle into three loads that could be carried

on three horse-drawn carts for the mountain warfare role.

Modification

In 1930 the Czechoslovak army decided to adopt the two Skoda equipments as their vz 30 weapons. The main change from the export models was the alteration of the gun's calibre to 76.5 mm (3.01 in) to suit Czechoslovak standard calibre requirements, resulting in the **76.5-mm kanon vz 30**. The **100-mm houfnice vz 30** was fitted with a new pattern of rubber-tyred wheels. The result was a more than adequate pairing of field gun and howitzer to arm the field batteries of the Czechoslovak army.

These weapons never got a chance to prove their worth in

Czechoslovak hands. Their two-part seizure of Czechoslovakia in 1938 and 1939 meant that the Germans were able to take over the large Czechoslovak army gun parks and the assets of the Skoda complex at Pilsen without a shot being fired. All the Czechoslovak guns and the bulk of the various export models eventually found their way into German army service, and Skoda was forced to supply ammunition, spares and even more guns for the German army. In German service the **7.65-cm FK 30(t)** gun and **10-cm leFH 30(t)** howitzer were used by various units from front-line batteries to beach defence positions along the Atlantic Wall.

Skoda 100-mm howitzer vz 14 and howitzer vz 14/19
Field howitzers

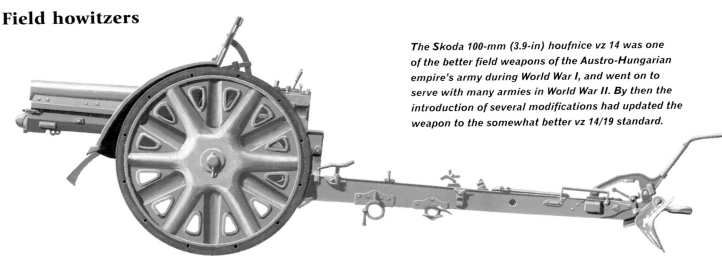

The Skoda 100-mm (3.9-in) houfnice vz 14 was one of the better field weapons of the Austro-Hungarian empire's army during World War I, and went on to serve with many armies in World War II. By then the introduction of several modifications had updated the weapon to the somewhat better vz 14/19 standard.

In the days of the Austro-Hungarian empire the name Skoda ranked second only to that of Krupp in European armaments manufacture, and the armies of many European nations armed themselves almost entirely with weapons produced at the massive Skoda works at Pilsen. By 1914 Skoda's designs were as good as any produced anywhere, and the range of weapon products was greater than that of most as Skoda also specialised in mountain guns. One of its products was a 100-mm (3.9-in) mountain howitzer mounted on

a special carriage that could be broken down into loads for carrying over difficult terrain, and this weapon attracted the attention of many armies. Unfortunately they did not like the idea of the special carriage which was heavier than many would want for field artillery use, so the adoption of a new field carriage produced the **100-mm houfnice vz 14**.

Major Italian service

The vz 14 was destined to be used mainly by the Italian army, which received large numbers in the upheavals of the break-up

of the empire in 1918–19. The type became a standard Italian weapon as the **Obice da 100/17 modello 14**, which was still in large-scale service in 1940. The numbers involved were so large that the Italians produced their own spare parts and ammunition, and the type saw action in North Africa and served with Italian units on the Eastern Front alongside the Germans. But in 1943 the Italians withdrew from the conflict and their modello 14 howitzers were taken over by the German forces and remained in use until 1945

under the designation **10-cm leFH 315(i)**, supplementing similar weapons taken over from the Austrians as the **10-cm leFH 14(ö)**. The type was also in service with the Polish and Romanian armies.

When Skoda resumed production in newly independent Czechoslovakia, the vz 14 was one of the first weapons placed back into production. However, the opportunity was taken to modernise the design, the main change being to the barrel length which was increased from L/19 to L/24, i.e. the length of the barrel was increased to 24 times the calibre (100 mm x 24 for 2.4 m/7 ft 10.5 in). This improved the range, and new ammunition was also introduced to provide the new design, soon known as the **100-mm houfnice vz 14/19**, with improved all-round capability.

The vz 14/19 was soon in demand and numbers were exported to Greece, Hungary, Poland (**Haubica wz 1914/1919**) and Yugoslavia (**M.1914/19**). Italy also acquired the parts to modernise a proportion of its modello 14s and the Czechoslovak army also adopted the vz 14/19 as one of its standard field pieces. All in all, the vz 14/19 became one of the most important Central European field pieces, and by 1939 the howitzer was in service in numbers that ran into the thousands. It was a stout weapon with few design frills, and it was capable of prolonged hard use. Many Italian examples were fitted with rubber-tyred wheels for motor traction (**Obice da 100/24**), but even after 1939 many examples retained their original spoked wheels and were pulled into action by horse teams.

In German hands

After 1940 many vz 14/19 weapons passed into service with the German army. By this date the stocks of Czechoslovak army weapons had already passed into German hands and indeed full service as a result of Germany's two-part takeover of Czechoslovakia in 1938 and 1939. Thus the vz 14/19 howitzer was widely used during the French campaign of May and June 1940 as the **10-cm leFH 14/19(t)**. Many more of these useful howitzers were used during the initial stages of the German invasion of the USSR during 1941, but thereafter the vz 14/19 weapons were gradually relegated to second-line use. Many were incorporated into the Atlantic Wall defences of France. Examples taken over from Greece received the designation **10-cm leFH 318(g)**, those from Poland **10-cm leFH 14/19(p)** and those from Yugoslavia **10-cm leFH 316(j)**.

SPECIFICATION	
100-mm houfnice vz 14/19	
Calibre: 100 mm (3.9 in)	**Traverse:** 5.5°
Length of piece: 2.4 m (7 ft 10.5 in)	**Muzzle velocity:** 415 m (1,362 ft) per second
Weight: travelling 2025 kg (4,465 lb) and in action 1505 kg (3,318 lb)	**Range:** 9970 m (10, 905 yards)
Elevation: -7.5° to +48°	**Shell weight:** 14 kg (30.86 lb)

7.5-cm Feldkanone 16 nA and leichte Feldkanone 18
Field guns

Almost as soon as the German army began to introduce new field guns in the late 19th century it adopted 77 mm (3.03 in) as its standard field gun calibre. In 1896 the Germans produced the **C/96** in this calibre, and in 1916 updated and revised the weapon to produce the **7.7-cm FK 16** (Feldkanone, or field gun, with 16 standing for 1916).

After 1918 there was a drastic rethink of German weapon practices, and among the changes that emerged from this study was the adoption of 75 mm (2.95 in) as the field gun calibre. This was (and to a limited extent has been until recently) a standard field gun calibre, so the Germans were following a well trodden path. The Treaty of Versailles had left the rump of the German army with a stockpile of the old

FK 16 guns, and in a modernisation effort these were rebarrelled with new 75-mm barrels to create the **7.5-cm FK 16 nA** (neuer Art, or new pattern).

New issue

The rebarrelled guns were issued during 1934, initially to horse-drawn batteries supporting cavalry units. The Germans continued to use horse cavalry units until 1945, but by then the FK 16 nA had fallen out of use, for it was really a relic of a past era and was as such too heavy and lacking in mobility for the cavalry role. Instead many were

The 7.5-cm leFK 18 offered many advantages over the FK16 nA, but was expensive to produce and also provided a notably shorter range with the same shell.

This 7.5-cm (2.95-in) FK 16 nA field gun is being used to train members of the Indian Legion, one of the units raised by the Germans from disaffected prisoners of war to fight against their former comrades.

relegated to the training role or were issued to second-line units. Large numbers were still in service when the war ended, though, and one fired its way into history when it held up an Allied armoured formation for some time during the fighting near the Normandy beach-heads in June 1944: the gun was not destroyed until it had knocked out at least 10 Allied tanks.

Modern field gun

Even while the rebarrelling of the old FK 16 carriages was under way, a call for a new design of cavalry gun was put out. During 1930 and 1931 both Krupp and Rheinmetall produced designs, and although the Krupp design was finally chosen it was not until 1938 that the first examples were issued for service. The new design became the **7.5-cm leFK 18** (leichte Feldkanone, or light field gun), and this had modern features such as a split-trail carriage to increase the on-carriage traverse (so useful in the anti-armour role) and a range of ammunition that included a hollow-charge warhead for use against tanks. The leFK 18 was judged to be a great success, though its range was less than that of the weapon it was intended to replace, and the complex carriage made it an expensive and difficult item to produce. Consequently not many were produced and the emphasis for field artillery calibres changed to 105 mm (4.13 in). However, the leFK 18 was kept in production for export to gain influence. Some sales were made to South American countries.

SPECIFICATION	
FK 16 nA	**Traverse:** 4°
Calibre: 75 mm (2.95 in)	**Muzzle velocity:** 662 m (2,172 ft) per second
Length of piece: 2.7 m (8 ft 10.3 in)	**Range:** 12875 m (14,080 yards)
Weight: travelling 2415 kg (5,324 lb) and in action 1524 kg (3,360 lb)	**Shell weight:** 5.83 kg (12.85 lb)
Elevation: -9° to +44°	

15-cm schwere Infantriegeschütz 33 Infantry howitzer

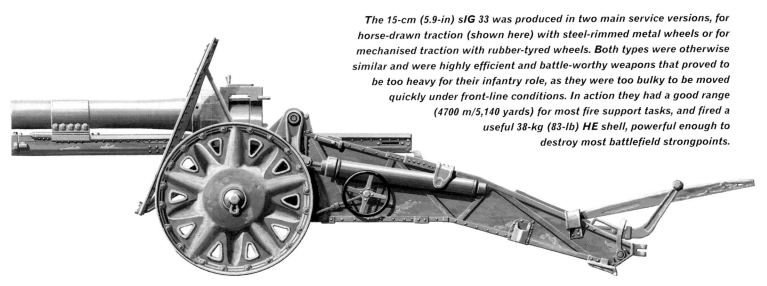

The 15-cm (5.9-in) sIG 33 was produced in two main service versions, for horse-drawn traction (shown here) with steel-rimmed metal wheels or for mechanised traction with rubber-tyred wheels. Both types were otherwise similar and were highly efficient and battle-worthy weapons that proved to be too heavy for their infantry role, as they were too bulky to be moved quickly under front-line conditions. In action they had a good range (4700 m/5,140 yards) for most fire support tasks, and fired a useful 38-kg (83-lb) HE shell, powerful enough to destroy most battlefield strongpoints.

When the German army issued its infantry gun requirements during the early 1920s, two types of weapon were requested. One was to be a 75-mm (2.95-in) gun and the other a 15-cm (5.9-in) howitzer to act as a heavier counterpart to the light gun. Development of this heavy weapon commenced in 1927 at a leisurely pace, so that it was not finally approved for service until 1933. Even then it was 1936 before the first examples came off the production lines and they were then issued at the rate of two to each infantry battalion.

To confuse matters somewhat this 15-cm howitzer was actually designated as a gun, i.e. **15-cm schwere Infantriegeschütz 33** or **15-cm sIG 33** (15-cm heavy infantry gun model 1933). It was definitely a howitzer, however, with a short barrel set on a heavy box-trailed carriage. Early examples had pressed steel wheels with metal rims for horse traction, but later examples intended for use with the motorised formations had wheels with rubber rims.

Heavyweight weapon

Once again Rheinmetall-Börsig was responsible for the basic design (although production was carried out by several other manufacturers), and for once no

Red Army soldiers examine a pair of 15-cm sIG 33 infantry howitzers, with the soldier in the background wielding a rammer for some destructive purpose. Note the heavy carriage and large breech of the weapon in the foreground. Many of these weapons were lost to the enemy, as they were too difficult to move.

SPECIFICATION	
sIG 33	**Muzzle velocity:** 240 m (787 ft) per second
Calibre: 150 mm (5.9 in)	
Length: barrel 1.65 m (5 ft 5 in)	**Maximum range:** 4700 m (5,140 yards)
Weight: in action 1750 kg (3,858 lb)	**Projectile weight:** HE 38 kg (83.8 lb)
Elevation: 0° +73°	
Traverse: 11.5°	

unnecessarily complex features were introduced, the design of the sIG 33 being straightforward and orthodox. If anything it was too orthodox for the infantry gunners, for the adherence to standard design meant that the sIG 33 was really too heavy for the infantry role. It required a large horse team to drag the weapon, and once the sIG 33 was emplaced it was a slow and hard task to move it out. Some attempts were made before 1939 to lighten the heavy carriage by the use of light alloys, but these were in overall

short supply and earmarked for the Luftwaffe so the heavy design had to be tolerated.

Throughout the war most sIG 33s were towed by horse teams, although trucks or halftracks were used whenever possible. Even with a tractor it was still a job to handle the weapon in action, and it was not until the sIG 33 was placed upon a tracked self-propelled chassis that the weapon could give its full potential. It was then much more appreciated as a powerful support weapon firing a wide array of projectiles. Most of the

tracked chassis used for the self-propelled role were old tank chassis that were no longer large or powerful enough for armoured warfare; in fact the very first attempt to mount a sIG 33 on a PzKpfw I hull resulted in the very first German self-propelled artillery weapon, and this was used during the 1940 campaign in France.

As with all other weapons of its era, the sIG 33 was supposed to have an anti-tank capability and was accordingly issued with hollow-charge projectiles. In use these proved to be less than fully effective, for even a normal 150-mm HE shell striking a tank could be effective and a lot less trouble to manufacture and issue. But for really strong

15-cm sIG 33s of a motorised infantry unit are seen in action on the Eastern Front. The wheels of these weapons have rubber tyres, denoting that they were towed by some form of mechanised tractor.

targets the sIG 33 could fire a muzzle-loaded stick bomb known as a Stielgranate 42. This had only a short range and was guided by fins (which stabilized the stick bomb) towards its target, which was usually a blockhouse, bunker or some other strongpoint.

The crew of a 15-cm sIG 33 undergoes training in 1938. The layer is adjusting the dial sight, while two members of the crew prepare to traverse the heavy carriage using a lever over the trail spade.

10.5-cm howitzers German field artillery family

The 10.5-cm (4.13-in) leFH 18 in its original form with no muzzle brake, pressed steel wheels of typical German form and the original heavy carriage. This was a Rheinmetall design that proved sound but too heavy for the mobile role intended, especially in the muddy conditions encountered on the Russian front.

The German army had chosen the calibre of 105 mm (4.13 in) for its standard field howitzers

well before World War I, and then stuck with it. During World War I the standard field

howitzer had been the 10.5-cm leFH 16 (leichte FeldHaubitze, or light field howitzer) which used the same carriage as the then-standard 7.7-cm FK 16. After 1918 numbers of these howitzers remained with the rump of the German army and were used to train the generation of gunners who were to be the battery

commanders and NCOs of World War II.

The operational analysis carried out by German war planners during the 1920s indicated that in future conflicts a 105-mm projectile would be far more effective than the 75-mm (2.95-in) equivalent for no great cost in delivery system weight, that is the artillery piece

SPECIFICATION	
10.5-cm leFH 18/40	**Traverse:** 60°
Calibre: 105 mm (4.13 in)	**Muzzle velocity:** 540 m (1,770 ft) per
Length of piece: 3.31 m (10 ft	second
10.3 in)	**Range:** 12325 m (13,478 yards)
Weight: travelling and in action	**Shell weight:** 14.81 kg (32.65 lb)
1955 kg (4,310 lb)	
Elevation: -5° to +42°	

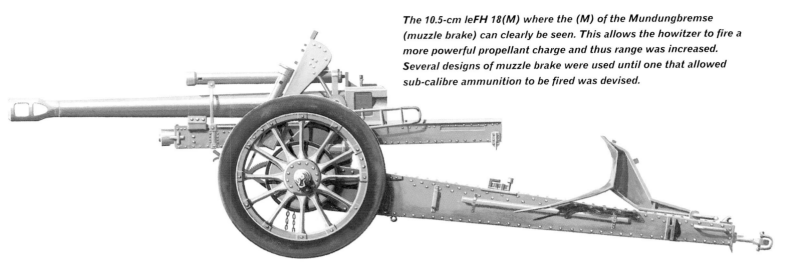

The 10.5-cm leFH 18(M) where the (M) of the Mundungbremse (muzzle brake) can clearly be seen. This allows the howitzer to fire a more powerful propellant charge and thus range was increased. Several designs of muzzle brake were used until one that allowed sub-calibre ammunition to be fired was devised.

Abandoned 10.5-cm leFH 18(M) howitzers in Normandy in June 1944. Note the obvious bulk and weight of the trail legs and spades that combined to make this howitzer much too heavy for the mobile field role.

involved. Thus they plumped for a new 105-mm howitzer, and design work started as early as 1928–29. Rheinmetall was the project leader, and the result of its efforts was ready for service in 1935.

The new weapon was the **10.5-cm leFH 18**, a conventional and sound howitzer with a useful projectile weight and adequate range. If there was a fault with the leFH 18 it was that it was so soundly constructed that it was rather heavy, but as motor traction was expected to provide the bulk of the pulling power that was no great disadvantage, at

least in theory. The leFH 18 became a valuable export item, and numbers were sold to Spain, Hungary, Portugal and some South American nations; large numbers also came off the production lines to equip the expanding German forces.

Muzzle brake

As ever the gunners were soon asking for more range, and as a result an increased propellant charge was introduced for the leFH 18. This dictated the introduction of a muzzle brake which meant a change of designation to **10.5-cm leFH 18(M)**, the suffix for

10.5-cm leFH 18s in action in France during May 1940 when these howitzers, towed into action by halftracks, consistently outfought the more numerous French artillery units as they swept across France.

Mundungbremse, or muzzle brake. The introduction of this muzzle attachment meant that a special sabot sub-calibre 88-mm (3.46-in) projectile could not be fired until a new revised design was introduced slightly later.

Thus the leFH 18 series went to war and proved itself efficient enough until the winter campaign in the Soviet Union took its toll in 1941–42. During the thaws involved in that

campaign large numbers of 105-mm howitzers were lost because the weights involved were too great for the available towing vehicles to drag weapons clear of the all-prevailing mud. Thus the overweight howitzers showed their disadvantage, and a hurried search for some form of alternative carriage then began.

The result was an unsatisfactory improvisation. The carriage of the 7.5-cm Pak 40 anti-tank gun was simply taken as the new mount for the leFH 18(M) gun, its associated cradle and the large shield. The result was slightly lighter than the original (but not by very much), and the improvised arrangement gave constant problems that were never properly eradicated. It was intended that the new howitzer/carriage combination, designated **10.5-cm leFH 18/40**, would become the standard field howitzer for all the German army, but this never happened.

Cannone da 75/27 75-mm modello 06 and modello 11 field guns

One of the most elderly of all field artillery pieces still in service during World War II was the Italian army's **Cannone da 75/27 modello 06** (model 1906 75-mm L/27 gun) in the Italian standard system of artillery nomenclature. This was originally a German Krupp export model adopted by the Italian army in 1906 for licensed manufacture, and then retained until Italy's 1943 armistice with the Allies.

The original Krupp designation was **M.06**, and the weapon was an entirely orthodox design with little of note other than a sound and sturdy construction. The carriage used a form of one-piece pole trail which restricted elevation and thus range, but for all that the 75/27 still had a useful reach for a field gun. Not surprisingly, the original models had wooden-spoked wheels for horse traction, but by 1940 some had been modified to take rubber-tyred steel wheels for powered traction. It was this latter pattern that was most usually encountered outside the Italian mainland.

Gun deployment

The steel-wheeled gun was widely used throughout the North African and other Italian colonial campaigns, and was at one point issued to German field batteries in North Africa when their own equipment was not available. The Germans even supplied the 75/27 with their own designation, **7.5-cm FK 237(i)**. So widespread was the use of the 75/27 modello 06 in Italian service that special versions were even produced for use in fixed fortifications.

Model variations

The modello 06 was not the only 75/27 in Italian service. To confuse matters somewhat there was also a **Cannone da 75/27 modello 11**. This was another licence-built gun, this time from a French source, namely the Deport design centre. The 75/27 modello 11 had one unique feature, namely the original design of recoil and recuperator mechanism. On nearly all artillery pieces the recoil/recuperator mechanism is situated alongside the barrel, either above or below it and in some cases both. On the modello 11 the mechanism stayed in the horizontal position and the barrel elevated independently. The operation of

An American soldier examines a captured Cannone da 75/27 modello 11. This had a barrel that elevated independently of its recoil mechanism.

SPECIFICATION	
Cannone da 75/27 modello 06	
Calibre: 75 mm (2.95 in)	**Traverse:** 7°
Length of piece: 2.25 m (7 ft 10.6 in)	**Muzzle velocity:** 502 m (1,647 ft) per second
Weight: travelling 1080 kg (2,381 lb) and in action 1015 kg (2,238 lb)	**Range:** 10240 m (11,200 yards)
Elevation: -10° to +16°	**Shell weight:** 6.35 kg (14 lb)

the system was in no way impaired, but the feature did not catch on with other designers and soon fell into abeyance.

Nevertheless the modello 11 was still in widespread Italian service in 1940 and was used mainly in support of cavalry units, although some were issued to field batteries. As with the modello 06, some were modified to take rubber-tyred steel wheels for powered traction, and some were also used by the Germans with the designation **7.5-cm FK 244(i)**.

Obice da 75/18 modello 35 75-mm light field howitzer

Ever since the establishment of Italy as a nation, a certain sector of its armed forces has associated itself with the specialised art of mountain warfare. This has required the provision of special types of artillery adapted for the mountain role. Many of these mountain artillery pieces came from the Austrian firm of Skoda, and during World War I the Italians were happily firing Austrian mountain guns at their former suppliers.

In contrast with many other Italian artillery pieces of World War II, the Obice da 75/18 modello 35 was a very modern and useful light field piece. Designed by Ansaldo, it was the field howitzer version of a mountain howitzer design and thus lost the facility to be broken down into several pack loads.

Italian gunners undergo training on an Obice da 75/18 modello 35. The box by the wheel contained the sights, not ammunition. That no firing was intended can be deduced by the fact that a dust cover is still in place over the muzzle. The small size of this howitzer can be clearly seen.

Weapon redesign

By the 1930s much of this mountain artillery was obsolescent and thoroughly overdue for replacement. The Italian firm Ansaldo thus undertook to produce a new mountain howitzer design. By 1934 this had emerged as the **Obice da 75/18 modello 34**, a sound and thoroughly useful little mountain-warfare howitzer that could be broken down into eight loads for pack transport. In the interests of standardisation and logistics, it was decided that the 75/18 was just what was required as the light howitzer component of the normal field batteries, moreover, and thus the weapon was ordered for these as well, but this time with a more orthodox carriage without any provision for being broken down into loads. This field version was designated as the **Obice da 75/18 modello 35**.

Production difficulties

The modello 35 was ordered into full-scale production but, like its virtual contemporary, the modello 37 gun, could not be produced in the numbers required. This was the case despite the fact that the carriage used by the modello 35 howitzer had many features in common with that of the later modello 37 gun, as well as exactly the same barrel and recoil mechanism as used in the mountain howitzer.

The supply situation was not eased by the need for the Italians to make part of the modello 35's production available for the export market in an effort to raise much-needed foreign currency. In 1940 a sizeable batch of the weapons was sold to Portugal, and more went to a number of South American states to pay for Italian imports of raw materials. More production capacity was diverted to the production of versions for use on various forms of Italian *semovente* (self-propelled) carriages, but very few of these self-propelled equipments ever reached the hands of the front-line forces. Those that did proved to be as efficient as any of the comparable German *Sturmgeschütze* (assault guns).

After Italy's 1943 armistice, the Germans took modello 35 equipments under their control as swiftly as they took over the rest of the available Italian gun parks, and the diminutive howitzers took on a new guise as **7.5-cm leFH 255(i)** weapons.

SPECIFICATION	
Obice da 75/18 modello 35	
Calibre: 75 mm (2.95 in)	**Traverse:** 50°
Length of piece: 1.557 m (5 ft 1.3 in)	**Muzzle velocity:** 425 m (1,395 ft) per second
Weight: travelling 1850 kg (4,080 lb) and in action 1050 kg (2,315 lb)	**Range:** 9565 m (10,460 yards)
Elevation: -10° to +45°	**Shell weight:** 6.4 kg (14.1 lb)

Cannone da 75/32 modello 37 75-mm field gun

The Cannone da 75/32 modello 37 was another Ansaldo design, and was a good modern weapon that could stand comparison with any of its contemporaries. Its main fault for the Italian army was that there were never enough to go round. After 1943 the Germans took over, for their own use, as many as they could find.

When Italy emerged from World War I its economy, never particularly sound, was in no state to support any form of rearmament programme, and thus the weapons of World War I were bulked out by reparations from the defeated Austro-Hungarian empire, and the army was otherwise left to cope with what it already had. By the 1930s it had been realised that even the large numbers of weapons at hand constituted no real answer to more modern designs of the types fielded by a number of possible opponents, so a programme of new weapon design and manufacture was undertaken. The first weapons to be considered were those of the field artillery, and thus the first wholly new artillery design to be introduced since the end of World War I in 1918 was a light field gun known as the **Cannone da 75/32 modello 37**.

This new gun was an Ansaldo design. It was of good, sound and modern concept and was intended from the outset for powered traction. It had a long barrel fitted with a muzzle brake, and had a muzzle velocity high enough that the weapon could be usefully employed on occasion in the anti-tank role.

When the split trail was deployed it provided a traverse of 50°, which was no doubt useful in armoured warfare, but this was rather negated by the use of large trail spades that were hammered down into the ground through the trail legs, and thus a rapid change of traverse through a large angle wasn't easy. Even with this disadvantage, the modello 37 was a very useful field gun, and the Italian gunners clamoured for as many as they could get.

Pressure on resources

Unfortunately they clamoured in vain, for Italian industry was in no position to provide the numbers of such weapons that were required. There was quite simply no industrial potential to spare to produce the guns, and the raw materials, or at least the bulk of them, had to be imported. Thus gun production got under way at a time when all other arms of the Italian forces were rearming: the air force was given far higher priority than the artillery, and the Italian navy was also absorbing a large proportion of the few available manufacturing and raw material resources. So demand for the modello 37 constantly exceeded supply, and by 1943 most of the Italian artillery park was still made up of weapons that dated from World War I or even earlier.

In 1943 Italy signed an armistice with the Allies. The Germans had already noted the finer points of the modello 37, and as Italy withdrew from the Axis the Germans moved swiftly to take over the Italian armoury – or at least as much of it as they could lay their hands on. In this grab for possession, large numbers of modello 37s on the Italian mainland changed their designation to **7.5-cm FK 248(i)**. The Germans used their booty until the war ended, not only in Italy but also in the confused Balkan campaigns against the Greek and Yugoslavian partisans.

SPECIFICATION	
Cannone da 75/32 modello 37	**Traverse:** 50°
Calibre: 75 mm (2.95 in)	**Muzzle velocity:** 624 m (2,050 ft) per
Length of piece: 2.574 m (8 ft 5.3 in)	second
Weight: travelling 1250 kg (2,756 lb)	**Range:** 12500 m (13,675 yards)
and in action 1200 kg (2,646 lb)	**Shell weight:** 6.3 kg (13.9 lb)
Elevation: -10° to +45°	

70-mm Battalion Gun Type 92 Field howitzer

The little **70-mm Battalion Gun Type 92** was one of the most successful infantry support weapons of World War II, despite its rather odd appearance. It was issued to every Japanese infantry battalion and could be used in several ways, as a battery weapon or, more frequently, as an individual weapon to produce harassing fire.

Modern design

Despite its unusual look, the Type 92 was a thoroughly modern design. Much of the unusual appearance came from the use of a short barrel on a carriage travelling on large steel disc wheels. Normally the gun was towed by horses or mules, but in typical Japanese fashion there were various holes and brackets on the carriage through which long poles could be inserted to act as man-carrying handles for short moves. The shield could be removed to save weight when required, and the wheels were supported on cranked axles that could be turned through 180° to lower the silhouette of the gun when occasion demanded. Although it was a small weapon, the Type 92 required a crew of 10 men, most of these being used for manhandling or carrying the gun and acting as ammunition suppliers. In action the maximum number required was only five.

The Type 92 fired the usual HE projectiles along with smoke and shrapnel for close-range use against personnel in the open. There was also a rather ineffective armour-piercing projectile. The maximum range was rather short, being only some 2745 m (3,000 yards), and the effective range was only about half that, but as the Type 92 had only very simple sights and was rarely used against targets other than those clearly visible. This mattered little in action, and the Type 92 was certainly used well forward. Its direct or plunging fire could be very effective, in both defence and attack, and

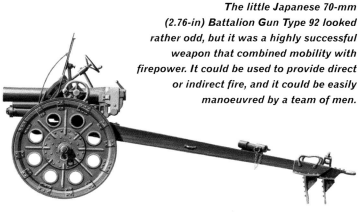

The little Japanese 70-mm (2.76-in) Battalion Gun Type 92 looked rather odd, but it was a highly successful weapon that combined mobility with firepower. It could be used to provide direct or indirect fire, and it could be easily manoeuvred by a team of men.

some Allied reports speak of the Type 92 being used in the same manner as a mortar. One operational method that was developed to a fine art by the Japanese for the Type 92 was harassing fire in jungle warfare. A small team would drag or carry the Type 92 forward, fire off a few rounds at a known target and then move hastily to a new fire position or out of the area altogether. A single gun could keep large bodies of Allied soldiers awake and alert by the employment of tactics as simple as this.

Short range

Although labelled as a gun, the Type 92 used a variable propellant charge system and could be fired in the upper register (i.e. above an elevation angle of 45°) to drop projectiles onto targets as close as 100 m (110 yards) away. On target the HE projectiles were very destructive, and the shrapnel shell often proved to be very effective in breaking up massed infantry attacks such as those sometimes used by the Chinese army. There was even a version of the Type 92 developed for use in some experimental tanks, but only a few of these (known as the Type 94) were actually produced.

The Type 92 was a small artillery piece but it often had an effect on its enemies that was quite out of proportion to its size, range and projectile weight. Many of them are still highly prized as evocative museum pieces.

SPECIFICATION	
Battalion Gun Type 92	**Traverse:** 90°
Calibre: 70 mm (2.76 in)	**Muzzle velocity:** 198 m (650 ft) per
Length of barrel: 0.622 m (2 ft 0.5 in)	second
Weight: in action 212.47 kg	**Maximum range:** about 2745 m
(468.4 lb)	(3,000 yards)
Elevation: -10° to +50°	**Projectile weight:** HE 3.795 kg (8.37 lb)

75-mm Field Gun Type 38 (Improved) Field artillery

75-mm Field Gun Type 38 (Improved) was a title given by Western intelligence agencies to a field gun that was in widespread use with the Japanese field batteries between 1935 and 1945. The gun had its origins in a Krupp design that was obtained for licence production as far back as 1905. This was the original Type 38, and during World War I the Japanese had observed enough of artillery developments elsewhere to be able to make improvements to the original design.

Box trail

Perhaps the most obvious of these Japanese innovations was the introduction of a form of box trail in place of the original Krupp pole trail. This innovation made possible extra elevation, and the range was increased accordingly. Other alterations were made to alter the balance

of the barrel on its cradle, and yet more minor changes were made to the recoil mechanism. Although the updated gun was given the full title Field Gun Type 38 (Improved) by the Allies, by 1941 few, if any, of the Type 38 guns had been left unmodified, so the extra terminology was superfluous.

Mule teams

Despite the changes introduced to the Type 38 by the Japanese, the overall design was unremarkable, and the overall performance was also unimpressive. Through-out its service life the gun was never adapted for vehicle traction, so horse or mule teams were used right up to 1945. In appearance

The Japanese Field Gun Type 38 dated back to the Krupp design of 1905, but by World War II it had been modernised to obtain the (Improved) designation. Although an unremarkable gun, the Japanese were so short of artillery production facilities that the type was produced until the end of the war.

the gun was archaic, and it was indeed a design relic of a former era, maintained in service as the Japanese were never able to develop the industrial potential to produce artillery in the amounts required. Although much more modern and powerful field guns (with calibres of 75 mm/2.95 in and upwards) were produced right up to the beginning of World War II, they were never produced in numbers sufficient to permit the replacement of the Type 38. Thus, in the absence of anything else, Japanese gunners were saddled with obsolete equipment.

During the initial stages of the Japanese war against the Chinese during the 1930s the Type 38 proved more than adequate for all the operational tasks demanded of it, but once

the Allies joined in the conflict after 1941 things were very different. Following initial easy successes, the Japanese gunners constantly found themselves outgunned by even small forces of Allied artillery, and in these circumstances the Type 38 did not shine. In fact the Type 38 became something of a liability for, being horse-drawn, it was easily rendered immobile by enemy action or terrain conditions, and many precious Japanese guns were lost or knocked out simply because they could not be moved rapidly enough. After 1945 quantities of Type 38 guns passed into the hands of various forces in South-East Asia, some official and others unofficial, and the weapon used against French forces in Indo-China.

SPECIFICATION	
Field Gun Type 38 (Improved)	**Elevation:** -8° to +43°
Calibre: 75 mm (2.95 in)	**Traverse:** 7°
Length of piece: 2.286 m (7 ft 6 in)	**Muzzle velocity:** 603 m (1,978 ft) per
Weights: travelling 1910 kg	second
(4,211 lb) and in action 1136 kg	**Range:** 11970 m (13,080 yards)
(2,504 lb)	**Shell weight:** 6.025 kg (13.3 lb)

Bofors 75-mm Model 1934 Mountain howitzer

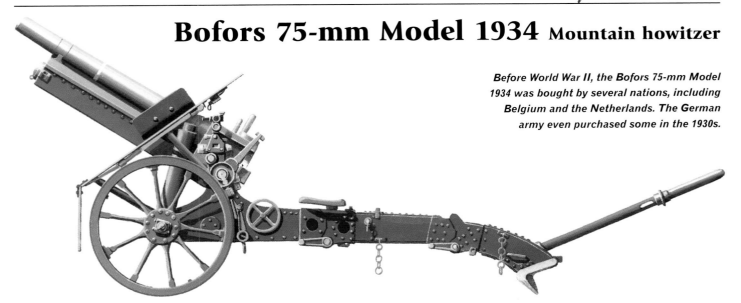

Before World War II, the Bofors 75-mm Model 1934 was bought by several nations, including Belgium and the Netherlands. The German army even purchased some in the 1930s.

The **Bofors 75-mm Model 1934** was originally designed as a mountain howitzer and was

placed on the market in the 1920s. At that time the artillery markets around the world were

awash with the surplus of World War I, but there was a small demand for specialised weapons

and the Bofors 75-mm howitzer fell into this category. As with all products from the Bofors plant at Karlskroga, the 75-mm howitzer was well made from the finest materials, and was based on a sound and well considered design. And it was just what was required by the Dutch armed forces.

One would have thought that the last thing wanted by a nation as well endowed with flat terrain as the Netherlands was a mountain howitzer, but the Dutch needed the gun not for service at home but away on the other side of the world in the Dutch East Indies. At that time the Netherlands maintained a sizeable force of troops in the islands that now make up much of Indonesia, and as the terrain is either very overgrown or mountainous, some form of pack artillery was required.

Four-horse team

The Bofors gun was apparently just what was needed and a batch of the howitzers was duly acquired. The Bofors weapon could be broken down into eight loads, carried in special harnesses by mules, but for normal towing a four-horse team was used, with a further six mules carrying ammunition and other bits and pieces; the gunners themselves had to walk. These guns were still in use when World War II reached the Pacific, and with the Japanese invasion the guns had a brief period of action before falling into Japanese hands. Their new masters used the guns for their own purposes until the ammunition stocks ran out, and by 1945 few were left.

Some of these Bofors 75-mm howitzers were sold to Turkey in the years leading up to World War II, but the main customer was yet another unlikely client for a mountain gun. This time the recipient was Belgium, for which a special version was produced as the **Canon de 75 modèle 1934**.

This time the gun was for use by the Belgian troops based along the borders in the Ardennes region, but as this area was reasonably well provided with roads and tracks, there was no need for the full pack transport facility. Instead the modèle 1934s were produced as 'one-piece' weapons, the only feature designed to save towing length being a section of the box trail that could be folded upward. The Belgian models were intended for towing by light tracked tractors and were delivered with rubber-tyred steel disc wheels.

A Dutch army Bofors 75-mm (2.95-in) Model 1934 howitzer is readied for action against the Japanese in the Dutch East Indies early in 1942.

SPECIFICATION	
Model 34 Mountain Howitzer	**Traverse:** 8°
Calibre: 75 mm (2.95 in)	**Muzzle velocity:** 455 m (1,493 ft) per second
Lengths: piece overall 1.8 m (5 ft 10.9 in); barrel 1.583 m (5 ft 2.3 in)	**Maximum range:** 9300 m (10,170 yards)
Weight: in action 928 kg (2,046 lb)	**Projectile weight:** 6.59 kg (14.53 lb)
Elevation: -10° to +50°	

The Netherlands army used its Bofors 75-mm Model 1934 howitzers in the Dutch East Indies, where they were carried into action by pack mules.

76.2-mm Field Gun Model 1936 Light artillery piece

By the early 1930s the Red Army artillery staff was becoming aware that its field gun park was falling behind those of the rest of Europe in terms of power and efficiency. So the USSR began a programme to create new weapons. One early effort, made in 1933, was the placing of a new 76.2-mm (3-in) barrel on the carriage of a 122-mm (4.8-in) field gun, but this was only a stopgap pending the introduction of what was intended to be one of the best all-round field guns in the world.

Impressive gun

The new gun was introduced in 1936, and was thus known as the **76.2-mm Field Gun Model 1936**, usually known as the **76-36**. It was an excellent design that made quite an impression on artillery designers elsewhere when the details became known. The 76-36 had a very long and slender barrel mounted on a deceptively simple split-trail carriage that provided a large traverse angle. This had been deliberately designed into the weapon as the Red Army's anti-tank philosophy had reached the point at which every Soviet gun and howitzer had to have an anti-tank capability. Even the standard HE shell of the 76-36 had a very powerful anti-armour effect.

The 76-36 first saw active service against Finland in the 'Winter War' of 1939–40. It performed effectively in this campaign, but did not fare so well in its second campaign, the German invasion of the USSR. It was not so much that the 76-36 did not perform well, but rather that it had little chance to do anything. The advancing Germans moved so fast that whole Soviet armies were cut off and destroyed. Huge numbers of 76-36s fell into German hands and, more disastrously for the Soviets, the Germans also captured a great deal of the plant that produced the guns. Thus almost their whole stock of 76-36 artillery was lost to the Soviets within a very short time.

Firing trials

German artillery experts swarmed over the captured guns, taking measurements and carrying out their own firing trials before they came up with two suggestions. One was that the 76-36 should become a standard German field gun, the **7.62-cm Feldkanone 296(r)**, as there was enough ammunition to hand to make these weapons useful for some time as longer-term plans were laid to produce the ammunition in Germany.

The second suggestion, also implemented, was that the

76-36 should be converted into a specialised anti-tank gun for use against even the most powerfully armoured Soviet tanks. Large numbers of 76-36 guns were therefore taken to Germany, where they were modified to take new ammunition and thus emerge with the revised designation **7.62-cm Panzerabwehrkanone 36(r)**, which proved itself one of the best all-round anti-tank guns of World War II. The changes for the antitank role also involved some on-carriage changes (such as all the fire-control wheels being used by the layer instead of the original two men) and a few other modifications.

A long way from home, this 76.2-mm Field Gun Model 1936 was captured on the Eastern Front by the Germans in 1941 and then converted for use as a very effective anti-tank gun before arrival in North Africa.

Thus a Soviet field gun was used as much by the Germans as by the Soviets. With the disruption of the German advances, the 76-36 was never put back into full production, although spare parts were made for use on the few 76-36s in Soviet hands. By 1944 the 76-36 was no longer a Red Army weapon, for by then the Soviets had a new gun in service.

SPECIFICATION	
76.2-mm Field Gun Model 1936	
Calibre: 76.2 mm (3 in)	**Elevation:** -5° to + 75°
Length of piece: 3.895 m (12 ft 9.3 in)	**Traverse:** total 60°
Weight: travelling 2400 kg (5,292 lb); in action 1350 kg (2,977 lb)	**Muzzle velocity:** 706 m (2,316 ft) per second
	Range: 13850 m (15,145 yards)
	Shell weight: 6.4 kg (14.1 lb)

76.2-mm Field Gun Model 1942 Light artillery piece

With much of their production facilities lost to the advancing German forces during the second half of 1941, Soviet staff planners had some difficult decisions to make. Vast stockpiles of weapons of all kinds had been lost to the Germans, and the manufacture of new weapons demanded that production capacity had to be improvised hurriedly in outlying areas where factories currently did not even exist. In the Soviets' favour was the fact that their gun design bureaux were inherently

conservative, preferring not large-scale innovation but a process of gradual evolution and the combination of a new gun or carriage with an existing carriage or gun.

Smaller design

This served the Soviets well after 1941, for in 1939 they had introduced a new gun known as the **76.2-mm Field Gun Model 1939**, or **76-39**. This reflected the realisation that, good as it was, the 76-36 was too bulky in

76-42 guns with boxed ammunition and rounds ready for loading. Each artillery division had a light brigade of three (later two) 24-gun regiments.

The 76.2-mm (3-in) Field Gun Model 1942 was produced in greater numbers than any other artillery weapon of World War II. Also known as the 76-42 or ZIS-3, the Model 1942 was a very sound design with no frills and a good performance, firing a 6.21-kg (13.7-lb) shell to a maximum range of 13215 m (14,450 yards).

Above: Soviet troops are instructed on the use of the 76-42. This excellent weapon was allocated to the field artillery batteries of rifle (infantry) and tank units as well as to artillery formations.

Left: A 76.2-mm Field Gun Model 1942 in action in the ruins of the Tractor Works in Stalingrad during the ferocious fighting in the winter of 1942-43. Both sides exploited this weapon's anti-tank capability.

tactical terms, and thus a smaller design was desirable. The 76-39 used a shorter barrel on the carriage derived from that of the 76-36.

When the Germans struck in 1941 they did not capture the main plant for 76-39 barrels, though they did take the carriage plant for the 76-36. Thus it was possible to use the barrel and recoil mechanism of the 76-39 on a new carriage to allow production to get under way once more. The result was the **76.2-mm Field Gun Model 1942**, later known as the **76-42** or **ZIS-3**.

The 76-42 was to achieve fame through production in numbers greater than that of any other gun of World War II. It was produced in its thousands, and if this had not been enough it turned out to be an excellent all-round weapon capable of being used not only as a field gun but an anti-tank gun, a form of tank gun and a self-propelled gun. The new carriage was a very simple but sturdy affair using split pole trails and a simple flat shield. The gun

assembly was modified to take a muzzle brake to reduce firing stresses and so allow the carriage to be lightened, and throughout the design process emphasis was given to ease of mass production. In action the 76-42 proved light and easy to handle, and also had excellent range. To simplify the Red Army's logistic load the ammunition was ruthlessly standardised to the point at which the 76-42 fired the same ammunition types as the 76.2-mm gun of the T-34 medium tank and many other similar guns. Only two types of projectile were generally used in World War II, namely HE and AP, though

smoke was fired on some occasions.

Still in service

The Germans used captured examples of the 76-42 as the **7.62-cm FK 288(r)**. The 76-42 was produced in numbers so great that it remains in service with some nations to the present. Examples were encountered in Korea and Indo-China, and the gun is still fielded in Africa and the Far East. The 76-42 was widely delivered to guerrilla groups such as the PLO in the Middle East and SWAPO in South-West Africa, and there seems to be no time limit on its active life.

Numerous attempts were made to mount the 76-42 on self-propelled carriages but only one was ever produced in any quantity. the SU-76.

October 1944, and men of the US Army fire a Soviet Model 1942 gun against the Germans. Thus the gun, a product of one Allied nation, was used by another against the Axis power which had first captured it.

SPECIFICATION	
76.2-mm Field Gun Model 1942	**Traverse:** total 54°
Calibre: 76.2 mm (3 in)	**Muzzle velocity:** 680 m (2,230 ft) per second
Length of piece: 3.246 m (10 ft 7.8 in)	**Range:** 13215 m (14,450 yards)
Weight: travelling and in action 1120 kg (2,470 lb)	**Shell weight:** 6.21 kg (13.7 lb)
Elevation: -5° to +37°	

Ordnance, Q.F., 25-pdr

Gun/howitzer

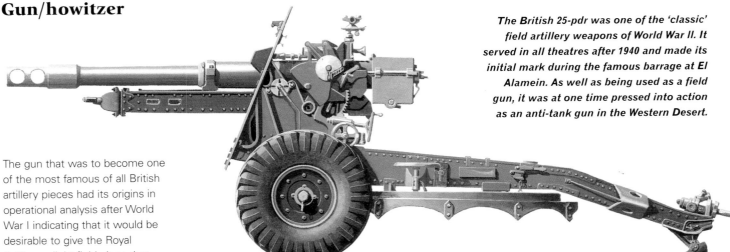

The British 25-pdr was one of the 'classic' field artillery weapons of World War II. It served in all theatres after 1940 and made its initial mark during the famous barrage at El Alamein. As well as being used as a field gun, it was at one time pressed into action as an anti-tank gun in the Western Desert.

The gun that was to become one of the most famous of all British artillery pieces had its origins in operational analysis after World War I indicating that it would be desirable to give the Royal Artillery a light field piece that could combine the attributes of a gun and a howitzer. In the mid-1930s the go-ahead was given to develop the new weapon to replace the British Army's ageing stock of 18-pdr field guns and 114-mm (4.5-in) howitzers.

Dunkirk

There were large stocks of the old 18-pdr guns still around in the 1930s and the Treasury insisted that a way be found to use them. From this came the **Ordnance, Q.F., 25-pdr Mk 1**, which was a new barrel placed on an 18-pdr carriage. It was with this gun that the BEF went to war in 1939. The old carriages had been updated with new pneumatic wheels and other changes, but the 25-pdr Mk 1 had little chance to shine before most of them were lost at Dunkirk.

By then the **25-pdr Mk 2 on Carriage 25-pdr Mk 1** was on the scene. This was a purpose-built weapon which would replace the old pieces and can be described as a gun-howitzer. It used an ammunition system with variable charges as in a howitzer but could also be used for lower register firing with no loss in

efficiency. The barrel itself was orthodox and used a heavy vertical sliding breech mechanism, but the carriage had some unusual features. It was a humped box trail carried on a circular firing table that enabled one man to make large changes of traverse easily and quickly. The gun was intended from the start for powered traction, the usual tractor being one of the large 'Quad' family.

Muzzle brake

Almost as soon as the first 25-pdr guns saw action in North Africa they were pressed into use as anti-tank guns. It was then that the circular firing table came into its own, for the guns could be rapidly moved from target to target, but the 25-pdr had to rely on shell power alone for its effects as there was no armour-piercing ammunition. Such a round was developed,

but it entailed the use of an extra charge which in turn dictated the use of a muzzle brake, and in this form the 25-pdr was used throughout the rest of World War II.

Some changes were made to the carriage design to suit local requirements. A narrower version was developed for jungle and airborne warfare (**25-pdr Mk 2 on Carriage 25-pdr Mk 2**) and a version with a hinged trail (**25-pdr Mk 2 on Carriage 25-pdr Mk 3**) was produced to increase elevation for hill warfare. The Australians produced a drastic revision for pack transport, and there was even a naval version mooted at one time. The 25-pdr

went self-propelled in the Canadian Sexton carriage and there were numerous trial and experimental versions, one classic expedient being the stopgap mounting of 17-pdr anti-tank barrels on 25-pdr carriages. Captured examples were designated **8.76-cm FK 280(e)** by the Germans,

The 25-pdr provided sterling service. It had a useful range and the gun and carriage proved capable of absorbing all manner of punishment. It remained in service with a number of armies for many years after 1945. The 25-pdr was a 'classic' gun, and many former gunners remember the weapon with much affection.

SPECIFICATION	
Q.F., 25-pdr Mk 2	**Traverse:** on carriage 8°; on firing table 360°
Calibre: 87.6 mm (3.45 in)	**Muzzle velocity:** 532 m (1,745 ft) per second
Length of piece: 2.4 m (7 ft 10.5 in)	
Weight: travelling and in action 1800 kg (3,968 lb)	**Range:** 12253 m (13,400 yards)
Elevation: -5°to +40°	**Shell weight:** 11.34 kg (25 lb)

25-pdrs on a training range are manned by Canadian gunners, the 25-pdr being the standard field gun for many Commonwealth armies. This photograph probably dates from mid-1943.

Ordnance, Q.F., 25-pdr Mk 2

The finest all-round piece of British field artillery in World War II, the 25-pdr Field Gun was a gun/howitzer providing first-class capabilities in the direct-fire gun and indirect-fire howitzer roles. The first such weapon was the 25-pdr Mk 1, which was the 18-pdr gun bored out to take the 25-pdr separate-loading ammunition and mounted on a box or split-trail carriage. The definitive 1940 model was the classic 25-pdr Mk 2 with a new and higher-elevating ordnance mounted on a box-trail carriage whose wheels could be located on a turntable for rapid changes in bearing.

Left: It is thought that the last occasion in which the 25-pdr Field Gun saw extensive action was during the 1971 war between India and Pakistan, in which both sides used the weapon. This weapon however, is seen in the hands of the South African Defence Force as late as the 1980s.

Above: The 25-pdr Field Gun Mk 2 in action. The weapon's one major limitation was its weight, which precluded the development of a version for the use of airborne forces, but in overall terms the weapon served the British and their allies well in World War II and for a long period after the end of that conflict.

Above: The muzzle flash of a 25-pdr Field Gun firing at night reveals the gap between the two sides of the box trail, which allowed the ordnance to be elevated to +40°.

Right: A 25-pdr Field Gun Mk 2, in a camouflaged position and identifiable by its lack of a muzzle brake, is seen in the recoiled position with propellant gases still streaming from the muzzle.

Above: The rate of fire of a 25-pdr Field Gun served by a willing and well-trained crew could be very high, and this imposed a great strain on the logistical organisation charged with keeping the guns fed.

Below: Artillery batteries were a favoured target for bombers and fighter-bombers, so it was only sensible for the crews of weapons such as this 25-pdr gun to conceal their charges under outline-breaking camouflage netting.

SPECIFICATION	
Ordnance, QF, 25-pdr Mk 3 (otherwise 25-pdr Field Gun Mk 3 on Carriage 25-pdr Mk 1)	
Gun	
Calibre: 87.6 mm (3.45 in)	
Barrel length: 2.35 m (7 ft 8.5 in)	
Muzzle brake: double-baffle type	
Weight	
Travelling and in action (complete with turntable): 1801 kg (3,970 lb)	
Dimensions	
Length travelling: 7.924 m (26 ft)	
Width travelling: 2.12 m (6 ft 11.5 in)	
Height travelling: 1.65 m (5 ft 3 in)	
Height of bore axis (firing with barrel horizontal): 1.168 m (3 ft 10 in)	
Ground clearance: 0.342 m (1 ft 1.5 in)	
Wheel track: 1.778 m (5 ft 10 in)	
Tyres	
9.00x16	
Elevation/traverse	
Elevation: -5° to +40°	
Traverse: 8° on carriage and 360° on turntable	
Ammunition types	
HE, AP (solid shot), Canister, Smoke, Coloured Smoke, and Illuminating	
Range	
12250 m (13,400 yards)	
Rate of fire	
Nominal: 5 rounds per minute	
Detachment	
6 men	

Above: The crew of a 25-pdr Field Gun ready their weapon for action. It was important that the turntable on which the gun sat was firmly bedded into the ground to absorb the recoil forces without moving and to allow rapid training.

Left: The 25-pdr gun was not best suited to jungle operations as a result of its weight and width. The Australians therefore developed a 'baby' version for pack transport.

95-mm Infantry Howitzer Mk II Light howitzer

At some point during 1942 a decision was made to produce a light howitzer for use by British infantry battalions but at that time the infantry themselves had not been consulted: perhaps the planners were influenced by the use of infantry artillery in nations such as Germany and the US. In order to conserve production facilities it was decided that the new weapon would incorporate features from a number of existing weapons. The barrel was to be machined from a 94-mm (3.7-in) anti-aircraft gun liner, the breech mechanism would come from the 25-pdr field gun and the recoil system and cradle came from 6-pdr anti-tank gun components. To simplify matters the new weapon would fire the same ammunition as the old 32-inch Pack Howitzer and the close-support howitzers fitted in some tanks. The term **95-mm Infantry Howitzer Mk II** was applied to the project, the 95-mm being chosen to differentiate between this and other 94-mm weapons.

Not a success

The Mk II Howitzer was not one of the success stories of World War II. The amalgamation of components from a variety of weapons allied to a new welded steel box carriage looked rather odd, and performed poorly. The 6-pdr recoil system was simply not up to the task of absorbing the recoil loads and frequently broke. The wheel track was too narrow, leading to tow instability. The poor overall construction, designed for pack transport in 10 loads, was such that components could be shaken loose in prolonged firing. More development could have eliminated many of these defects, but by the time they

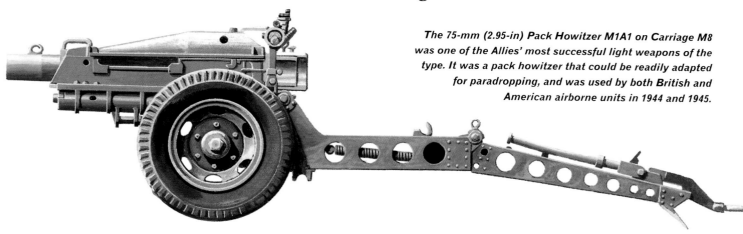

The experimental 95-mm (actually 3.7-in/ 94-mm) Infantry Howitzer was created using various parts of existing weapons. This howitzer was not a great success, especially since the infantry did not particularly want it, so the weapon was never accepted for full-scale military service.

emerged the weapon was already in production.

Not wanted

It was at this point that the infantry were drawn into the programme. They quickly announced that they did not want the new weapon. They had not been consulted in its development, and they already had quite enough weapon types within their battalions.

This finally killed off the 95-mm Infantry Howitzer project altogether, and the majority of the equipments produced were never issued. They were scrapped after 1945.

Only two projectiles were produced for use with this weapon, High Explosive and

smoke. There were plans for an antitank HEAT projectile, but that was an offshoot of the 95-mm tank howitzer programme. Mention also can be found of a proposed flare shell. These projectiles were to be fired using a three-charge system. The entire 95-mm Infantry Howitzer project now seems like a textbook example of how not to go about the design, development and production of a new military weapon system.

SPECIFICATION	
95-mm Infantry Howitzer	**Traverse:** 8°
Calibre: 94 mm (3.7 in)	**Muzzle velocity:** 330 m (1,083 ft) per second
Lengths: barrel 1.88 m (6 ft 2 in); bore 1.75 m (5 ft 8.9 in)	
Weight: in action 954.8 kg (2,105 lb)	**Maximum range:** 5486 m (6,000 yards)
Elevation: -5° to +30°	**Projectile weight:** 11.34 kg (25 lb)

75-mm Pack Howitzer M1A1 Light howitzer

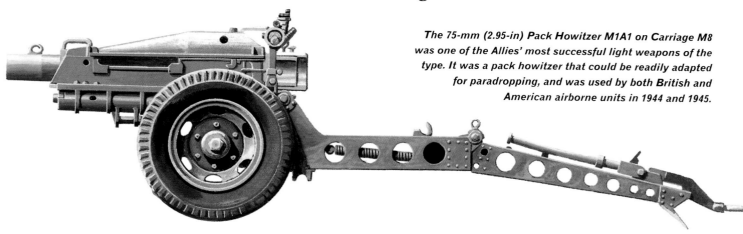

The 75-mm (2.95-in) Pack Howitzer M1A1 on Carriage M8 was one of the Allies' most successful light weapons of the type. It was a pack howitzer that could be readily adapted for paradropping, and was used by both British and American airborne units in 1944 and 1945.

In the aftermath of World War I the 1920 Westervelt Board recommended the design of a new 75-mm (2.95-in) light howitzer for mountain warfare and as a general-issue pack howitzer. This was one of the few proposals that was actually pursued at the time, and by 1927 the **75-mm Pack Howitzer Mk 1** had been standardised; some later production changes altered the designation to **M1A1**.

Carriage

The howitzer was mounted on a carriage of ingenious design that could be easily broken down into six loads. The howitzer itself could be broken down in constituent parts for transport, and was so arranged that the barrel was held in a trough and kept in place by a cover along the top: this gave the weapon a distinctive appearance. A screw mechanism aided the traverse

and the cradle carried the elevation mechanism.

The first M1A1s were mounted on the Carriage M1, which was intended for animal traction and so had wooden

spoked wheels. The introduction of mechanised traction led to the adoption of the Carriage M8, which used rubber-tyred metal wheels. This little howitzer became one of the

SPECIFICATION	
M1A1	**Traverse:** 6°
Calibre: 75-mm (2.95-in)	**Muzzle velocity:** maximum 381 m (1,250 ft) per second
Lengths: piece 1.321 m (4 ft 4 in); barrel 1.194 m (47 in)	
Weight: complete 587.9 kg (1,296 lb)	**Maximum range:** 8925 m (9,760 yards)
Elevation: -5° to +45°	**Projectile weight:** 6.241 kg (13.76 lb)

first Allied airborne artillery weapons, for it was issued to nearly every Allied airborne formation, including the British airborne divisions. But it should not be thought that the M1 carriage went out of fashion: many were produced during World War II for issue to Allied armies such as the Chinese, who also used the howitzer.

On either carriage the M1A1 was a very useful weapon. It was easy to serve in action, and

it could be used to provide fire support at ranges up to 8925 m (9,760 yards).

Despite its light weight, conversions to the self-propelled role were made with some being mounted on half-tracks, and it was just as successful in that guise.

Partisan use

One role for which the M1A1 was not much used, ironically, was in mountain warfare. There

were few campaigns where mountain weapons were needed by the Allies. One exception was Yugoslavia. There, partisan troops were trained on the M1A1 by British officers, and the partisans made good use of the guns during the later stages of their war of self-liberation.

It was as one of the first Allied airborne artillery pieces that the M1A1 will probably be best remembered. It was used

at Arnhem when some were landed from General Aircraft Hamilcar gliders, but the howitzer could also be broken down into nine loads for paradropping.

Not all M1A1s had such an adventurous life. Many were used simply as infantry support weapons or as pack artillery in the dense jungles of the Far East. However, the M1A1 was light enough to take part in amphibious assaults.

105-mm Howitzer M2A1 Field howitzer

When the US entered World War I in 1917 the US Army was poorly equipped. The Americans decided to equip themselves with the French 75 and began production in the USA for their own use. Production was just getting under way when the war ended, leaving the US Army with a huge stockpile of 75s that was to last until 1942.

Early origins

The Westervelt Board of 1919 recommended a 105-mm (4.13-in) howitzer. At the time little was done to put the suggestions into practice, so it was not until 1939 that the design was completed. The weapon was placed into production the following year and thereafter the **105-mm Howitzer M2A1** poured off the American production lines by the thousand.

The M2A1 was destined to become one of the most widely used of all American

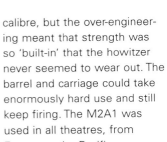

Although proposed as far back as 1919, the first examples of the M2A1 were not ready until 1939. Thereafter it was produced by the thousand, and it became the standard USA army field artillery howitzer. Rugged and basically simple, it was able to withstand all manner of hard use.

weapons in World War II.

The M2A1 was an orthodox piece of artillery, with little of note in its overall design. The associated **Carriage M2A2** was a split-trail design with the gun assembly mounted in such a way that the centre of balance was just forward of the breech. The weapon was never intended for animal traction and so was fitted with rubber-tyred wheels from the outset. The M2A1 was heavy for its

calibre, but the over-engineering meant that strength was so 'built-in' that the howitzer never seemed to wear out. The barrel and carriage could take enormously hard use and still keep firing. The M2A1 was used in all theatres, from Europe to the Pacific.

Wartime development

Through the war years the basic design was the subject of numerous trials and improvements, and the

ammunition underwent the same development process. By the time the war ended the ammunition fired by the M2A1 ranged from the usual HE through various smoke marker shells to non-lethal tear gas shells. Not all of the 105-mm howitzers were towed. Some of them were fitted to self-propelled carriages, one of the most widely used being the M7, known to the British gunners who used it as the 'Priest'.

SPECIFICATION	
Howitzer M2A1	**Traverse:** 45°
Calibre: 105-mm (4.13-in)	**Muzzle velocity:** 472 m (1,550 ft) per
Length of piece: 2.574 m (8 ft 5.3 in)	second
Weight: travelling and in action	**Range:** 11430 m (12,500 yards)
1934 kg (4,260 lb)	**Shell weight:** 14.97 kg (33 lb)
Elevation: -5° to +65°	

A 105-mm (4.13-in) M2A1 in action during the Korean War. Taken in 1950, this photo is typical of many of the actions in which it was used. Eventually re-designated M101, at the beginning of the 21st century the gun is still in service with the US Marine Corps and with more than 50 other countries worldwide.

Skoda 149-mm vz 37 howitzer (K4) Heavy field howitzer

By the early 1930s the Skoda company at Pilsen in Czechoslovakia was in a position to design, develop and produce entirely new artillery pieces that owed nothing to the obsolescent World War I weapons that had hitherto been the company's main output. By 1933 Skoda had produced, among other things, an entirely new 149-mm (5.87-in) range of howitzers known as the K series. The first of these, the **K1**, was produced in 1933 and the entire output of these **vz 33** (*vzor*, or model) weapons went for export to Turkey, Romania and Yugoslavia. The K1 was a thoroughly modern piece with a heavy split trail, and was designed for either horse or motorised traction. For the latter the piece could be towed as one load, but for the former the barrel could be removed to be towed as a separate load.

Further development

Despite the success of the K1, the Czechoslovak army decided that the weapon did not meet its exact requirements and therefore funded further development. This led to the **K4** model, which fully met the

specification. The K4 had much in common with the K1, but had a shorter barrel and, as the Czechoslovak army was making considerable strides towards full mechanisation, no provision for separate movement of the barrel. The K4 also had pneumatically tyred wheels in place of the K1's steel wheels with solid rubber tyres, and a number of other modifications were introduced to suit the equipment for towing by an artillery tractor.

Replacement

The Czechoslovak army decided to adopt the K4, with these changes, as its standard heavy field howitzer to replace the large range of elderly weapons remaining from World War I. The K4 was given the army designation **15-cm hrubá houfnice vz 37**, vz 37 denoting the equipment's acceptance for service in 1937. Skoda drew up production plans, but this lengthy process was overtaken by the Germans' 1938 occupation of the Sudetenland border region of Czechoslovakia. Production planning then became even more frantic but,

with the Sudetenland line of defences occupied, Czechoslovakia was wide open to further aggression and in 1939 the Germans marched in to take over the rest of the country.

The Germans also secured the Skoda works, finding on the production lines the first full-production vz 37 weapons. Only a few examples had been produced by this time, and these the German army tested on its ranges back in Germany, discovering that the vz 37 was a sound and serviceable howitzer with a good range of 15100 m (16,515 yards) and the ability to fire a very useful 42-kg (92.6-lb) projectile. Thus the Germans decided to keep the vz 37 in production at Pilsen for their own requirements, the vz 37 thereupon becoming the German army's **15-cm schwere Feldhaubitze 37(t)**, or 15-cm heavy field howitzer model 1937 (Czechoslovak), the (t) denoting *tschechisch*. In the German army

The high water mark of German success on the Eastern Front came in the late summer of 1942 as elements of Army Group 'A' penetrated more than 300 km (185 miles) to the south-east of Stalingrad. Here an sFH 37(t) 15-cm howitzer pounds Soviet positions in the foothills of the Caucasus mountain range.

the **sFH 37(t)** became a standard weapon of many formations, forming part of the divisional artillery equipment and being used even by some corps batteries. The howitzer was used during the French campaign of May and June 1940, and later in the invasion of the USSR during 1941. Some equipments were still in service on the Eastern Front as late as 1944, but by then many had been passed to the various Balkan forces under German control and operating within what was later Yugoslavia; the Slovak army was another one of the recipients.

SPECIFICATION	
sFH 37(t)	
Calibre: 149.1 mm (5.87 in)	**Traverse:** 45°
Length of piece: 3.6 m (11 ft 9.7 in)	**Muzzle velocity:** 580 m (1,903 ft) per second
Weight: travelling 5730 kg (12,632 lb) and in action 5200 kg (11,464 lb)	**Maximum range:** 15100 m (16,515 yards)
Elevation: -5° to +70°	**Shell weight:** 42 kg (92.6 lb)

Skoda 220-mm howitzer Heavy howitzer

Whereas the Skoda vz 37 howitzer was a completely new design, the slightly earlier **Skoda 220-mm howitzer** was a product that could trace its origins back to

somewhat earlier days and an older pattern of warfare. In the period up to 1918, when Skoda had been the largest armament producer for the army of the

Austro-Hungarian empire in World War I, the Pilsen works had been only slightly behind the German Krupp concern in the manufacture of really heavy artillery, and the heavy Skoda howitzers were second to none in overall capability. Thus, when the Skoda works started production again in what was then an independent Czechoslovakia, the 'classic' howitzer became one of the

company's primary product ranges.

However, the accent in heavy artillery was no longer just on a very large calibre. Despite their dreadful efficiency in demolishing fortifications, as proved in World War I on both the Western and Eastern Fronts, such equipments were ponderous beasts to move and their rate of fire was also extremely slow. Moreover, they were fearfully expensive to buy

SPECIFICATION	
Skoda 220-mm howitzer	
Calibre: 220 mm (8.66 in)	**Traverse:** 350°
Length of piece: 4.34 m (14 ft 2.9 in)	**Muzzle velocity:** 500 m (1,640 ft) per second
Weight: travelling 22700 kg (50,045 lb) and in action 14700 kg (32,408 lb)	**Maximum range:** 14200 m (15,530 yards)
Elevation: +40° to +70°	**Shell weight:** 128 kg (282.2 lb)

and to use. So when some of the new nations formed after World War I's end started to arm themselves against a difficult future they still wanted heavy artillery, but not too heavy. An interim calibre of about 220 mm (8.66 in) was still adequate for the task of destroying fixed fortifications and other heavy structures, but it was necessary that the howitzer itself should not be too ponderous. Skoda sensed the needs of this new market and produced the required 220-mm design incorporating much of its considerable experience in such matters, and it was not long before customers arrived.

The first was Yugoslavia, formed from several of the pre-World War I Balkan states. The new nation decided it had much to fear from its neighbours, and thus became involved in numerous purchases of weapons of all kinds throughout Europe. Yugoslavia was a good customer of Skoda, and in 1928 took delivery of a batch of 12 220-mm Skoda howitzers under the designation **M.28**. Another customer was Poland, which ordered no fewer than 27. These latter featured prominently in many pre-war propaganda photographs

Skoda produced some of the best heavy artillery pieces of World War I, and continued the tradition with the 220-mm howitzer, which was exported to both Poland and Yugoslavia. After the Germans had invaded and seized much of eastern and southern Europe, they used the captured weapons against the Soviet fortress city of Sevastopol in the Crimea.

of the Polish army. All of these photographs had one feature in common: the breech mechanism was always obscured in some way, usually by a soldier, as part of the normal Polish security procedure in any artillery illustration intended for publication.

Useful weapon

It did the Poles no good, for in 1939 the Germans invaded Poland, and in a one-month campaign destroyed or captured the entire Polish gun park. The unfortunate Yugoslavs suffered the same fate just over 18 months later. Thus the Germans found themselves with a useful quantity of 220-mm howitzers, which promptly became part of their army's inventory. There was

not much of a role for such a relatively heavy piece in the German *Blitzkrieg* concept, so the captured howitzers were distributed mainly to garrison and static units in the occupied territories. Some of these were as distant as Norway, but late in 1941 a number of the howitzers

were gathered for the siege train that was sent to invest the Soviet fortress of Sevastopol in the Crimea. This was the last classic investment of a fortress by the age-old method of assembling and using a siege train, and the fortress fell after the howitzers had played a useful part.

10.5-cm Kanone 18 and 18/40 Field guns

Among the requirements for a new German artillery park to replace the weapons lost in World War I was that for a new long-range gun to be used by

corps rather than field artillery batteries. This project was one of the very first put out to the underground German armaments industry, for by

A 10.5-cm K 18 stands in splendid isolation in the middle of an abandoned German field position in the Western Desert. In the background is one of the famous '88' Flak guns, giving an indication that the position was intended to be some form of strongpoint.

1926 both Krupp and Rheinmetall had produced specimen designs, and by 1930 were ready with prototype hardware.

Standard weapon

As it turned out, the German army could not decide which design to approve, resulting in the compromise adoption of the Rheinmetall barrel on the Krupp carriage. This latter was destined to become one of the most widely used of all the German artillery carriages, for it was the same as that used on the larger 15-cm sFH 18 howitzer series. It was 1934 before the first guns actually reached the troops and for a while the new gun, known as the **10.5-cm K 18** (*Kanone*, or gun), was the standard weapon of the medium artillery batteries.

This state of affairs did not last long, for the choice of 105-mm (4.13-in) calibre for a medium gun proved to an unhappy one. In a nutshell the gun was too heavy for the weight of projectile fired. The larger 150-mm (actually 149-mm/5.87-in)

howitzers fired a much more efficient projectile over almost the same range and at no great increase in weapon weight. There was also another snag: when the K 18 entered service it was at a time when the German army had yet to become even partially mechanised, so the guns had to be pulled by horse teams: the gun was too heavy for one horse team to tackle, so the barrel and carriage had to be towed as separate loads, which was a bit much for a 105-mm gun. Later, the introduction of half-tracked tractors enabled the piece to be towed in one load, but by then the K 18 was on a very low production priority.

Upgraded version

In order to make the K 18 a more powerful weapon, the German staff planners called for

British infantry examine a 10.5-cm K 18, which is notable for its sheer size. In the foreground is a handspike, used to move the trail legs either for a rapid change of traverse or to join them together in preparation for a move to a new position.

an increase in range. There was no way to produce this increase without increasing the length of the barrel from the original L/52 to L/60. The first of these improved models was ready in 1941 and was known as the **10.5-cm K 18/40**, but it was not put into production until much later when the designation had been changed yet again to **10.5-cm sK 42** (*schwere Kanone*, or heavy gun). Very few were produced.

By 1941 the disadvantages of the 105-mm gun in its K 18 and later versions had been recognised, but there remained a role for them for any task in which their considerable weight and bulk would be only a

relatively minor disadvantage. This task was coast defence. Weapons for Germany's Atlantic Wall defences in France, at that time still under construction, were in both great demand and short supply, so the K 18 was assigned to that relatively static role. As a coast defence weapon, the piece had a considerable advantage in its long range, even though the projectile weight was still rather low for the anti-ship role. To enable it to be used to greater advantage when firing at long ranges against maritime targets, a new range of ammunition was introduced, including a special sea marker shell for ranging purposes.

SPECIFICATION	
10.5-cm K 18	
Calibre: 105 mm (4.13 in)	**Elevation:** 0° to +48°
Length of piece: 5.46 m	**Traverse:** 64°
(17 ft 11 in)	**Muzzle velocity:** 835 m (2,740 ft) per
Weight: travelling 6434 kg	second
(14,187 lb) and in action 5624 kg	**Range:** 19075 m (20,860 yards)
(12,400 lb)	**Shell weight:** 15.14 kg (33.38 lb)

15-cm schwere Feldhaubitze 18 Heavy field howitzer

Within Germany the two major artillery manufacturing concerns had been Krupp and Rheinmetall since the turn of the century. Both firms survived World War I intact, but with their usual markets shattered both decided to start again with new products. Thus for both the 1920s was a period of retrenchment and research so that by the time the Nazi party came to power in 1933 both were ready to supply their new customer. The new customer was shrewd enough to invite both parties to submit designs for every new artillery requirement made by the

Shown here in an Eastern Front camouflage scheme, the 15-cm sFH 18 was a compromise between Krupp and Rheinmetall design and became the standard German heavy field ordnance of World War II.

expanding German forces, and thus when a call was made for a new heavy field howitzer each company had a ready design.

The trouble for the army selectors was that the submissions were as good as each other. Therefore, the eventual equipment was a compromise, the Rheinmetall ordnance being placed on the Krupp carriage. This selection was made in 1933

and given the designation of **15-cm schwere Feldhaubitze 18** (**15-cm sFH 18**), although the actual calibre was 149 mm (5.87 in). The howitzer quickly became the standard German heavy field howitzer and it was churned out from numerous production lines all over Germany.

sFH 18 variants

The first version of the sFH 18 was intended for horse traction and was towed in two loads, namely barrel and carriage. However, before long a version intended to be towed by a half-track tractor was produced, and this soon became the more common version. It proved to be a sound and sturdy howitzer and served well throughout all of Germany's World War II campaigns. Once the invasion of the Soviet Union was under way in 1941, however, it soon became apparent to the Germans that the piece was outranged by its Soviet 152-mm (6-in) equivalents. Various attempts were made to increase range, including two more powerful propellant charges to be added to the six already in use. These extra charges worked

to a limited extent but caused excessive barrel wear in the process and also overstrained the carriage recoil mechanism. To overcome the latter problem some howitzers were fitted with a muzzle brake to reduce recoil forces, but this modification was no great success and the idea was dropped; weapons so modified received the designation **15-cm sFH 18(M)**.

As the war went on the sFH 18 was placed on a self-

propelled carriage known as the Hummel (bumblebee), and thus formed part of the artillery component of a few Panzer divisions. Not all sFH 18 weapons were used in the field role. Divisions that found themselves installed along the Atlantic Wall defences used their sFH 18s to bolster coastal defences, usually under German navy control. Some sFH 18s were handed out to some of Germany's allies, notably Italy (where the type recived the local designation **obice da 149/28**) and, for a while, Finland (as the **m/40**).

The sFH 18 was still in use in very large numbers when the war ended in 1945 and for a period the howitzers were

This sFH 18 is being towed into an Me 323 transport by an SdKfz 7 halftrack. The majority of German artillery was horse-drawn, but the 15-cm howitzer was modified early in the war to be towed by vehicles.

used by many armies. Remarkably, Czechoslovakia used an updated version of the sFH 18 until relatively recently, and the type was also used by the Portuguese army for a considerable period. Some examples survived in parts of Central and South America into the 1980s, and the sFH 18 has proved to one of the soundest and sturdiest of all German artillery pieces.

SPECIFICATION	
15-cm sFH 18	**Traverse:** 60°
Calibre: 149 mm (5.87 in)	**Muzzle velocity:** 520 m (1,706 ft) per
Length of piece: 4.44 m (14 ft 6.8 in)	second
Weight: travelling 6304 kg	**Maximum range:** 13325 m (14,570
(13,898 lb) and in action 5512 kg	yards)
(12,152 lb)	**Shell weight:** 43.5 kg (95.9 lb)
Elevation: -3° to +45°	

15-cm Kanone 18 Heavy field gun/coastal defence gun

When a German army requirement for a heavy gun to arm the new divisional artillery batteries was made in 1933, Rheinmetall was able to land the contract. Using the same carriage as that submitted for the 15-cm sFH 18 competition, Rheinmetall designed a long and well proportioned gun with a range of no less than 24500 m (26,800 yards), which was well in excess of anything else available at the time. Production did not begin immediately for at the time priority was given to the sFH 18. It was not until 1938 that the army received its first **15-cm Kanone 18 (15-cm K 18)**.

When the German army began to receive the 15-cm K 18

weapon it was very impressed with the range and the projectiles, but was less than enchanted with some of the features of the carriage. One of these was the fact that as the

A 15-cm K 18 forms the centrepiece of a German artillery park captured by the British in Libya. This Rheinmetall design had an impressive range, but was dangerously time-consuming to deploy or withdraw.

gun was so long the gun and carriage could not be towed together except over very short distances. For any long move the barrel had to be withdrawn from the carriage and towed on its own special transporter carriage. The carriage itself was towed on its own wheels and a small limber axle carrying another two wheels. All this preparation for travel took a good deal of time, an undesirable feature when the troops needed to get the gun into and out of action rapidly, and this time was increased by another carriage feature, the use

of a two-part turntable onto which the gun was lifted to provide 360° traverse. This too had to be got into and out of action, and the carriage was equipped with ramps and winches so that even when sectionalised for towing it made up into two heavy loads.

Poor rate of fire

As if the time-consuming installation and removal drawbacks were not enough, the rate of fire of the K 18 was at best two rounds per minute. Not surprisingly, the gunners requested something better but

in the interim the gun was in production and the gunners had to put up with things as they were. As things turned out, many of the K 18s were allocated to static coastal defence batteries or garrison divisions where their relative lack of mobility was of small account. Not surprisingly, the coastal batteries soon found that the K 18 made an excellent coastal gun: its long range and the easily traversed carriage made it ideal for the role, and it was not long before special marker projectiles using red dyes were produced specially for the marking and ranging of the guns.

Production of the 15-cm K 18 ended well before the end of the war in favour of heavier weapons. However, for the guns already in the field a range of ammunition in addition to the marker shells was made

available. There was a special concrete-piercing shell with a much reduced explosive payload, and another was tailored to produce just the opposite effect, being a thin-walled shell with an increased explosive content for enhanced blast effect.

Assessment

On paper the K 18 should have been one of Rheinmetall's better designs, as it had an excellent range and fired a heavy (43-kg/94.8-lb) projectile. However, for the gunners who served this weapon it must have provided a great deal of hard work. Gunners are trained to get in and out of action as rapidly as possible, whatever weapon they are using, but the K 18 seems to have provided them with something that only hard work could turn into an acceptable battlefield weapon.

SPECIFICATION	
15-cm K 18	
Calibre: 149.1 mm (5.87 in)	**Traverse:** on platform 360° and on carriage 11°
Length of piece: 8.2 m (26 ft 10.8 in)	**Muzzle velocity:** 865 m (2,838 ft) per second
Weight: travelling 18700 kg (41,226 lb) and in action 12460 kg (27,470 lb)	**Maximum range:** 24500 m (26,800 yards)
Elevation: -2° to +43°	**Shell weight:** 43 kg (94.8 lb)

15-cm Kanone 39 Coastal defence gun/heavy field gun

The gun that became known to the Germans as the **15-cm Kanone 39** (**15-cm K 39**) came to them via a circuitous route. The gun was originally designed and produced by Krupp of Essen for one of its traditional

customers, Turkey, during the late 1930s. The gun was intended to be a dual field/ coastal defence gun and so used a combination of split-trail carriage allied with what was then an innovation, namely a portable turntable onto

which the gun and carriage would be hoisted to provide 360° traverse, a feature very useful in a coastal defence weapon. Two of the ordered batch had been delivered in 1939 when World War II broke out, and there was then no easy way of delivering any more to Turkey. With a war on its hands the German army decided it needed as many new field guns as possible and the design was taken into German service without modification as the 15-cm Kanone 39, and the type remained on the production lines at Essen for the German army alone.

Thus the German army found itself with a large and useful gun that had to be transported in three loads: barrel, carriage and turntable. For most purposes the turntable was not really necessary and was only used when the gun was emplaced for

coastal defence; the unit consisted of a central turntable onto which the carriage was placed, a series of outrigger struts and an outer traversing circle. The whole turntable was made of steel, and in use was anchored in place. The spread trails were secured to the outer traverse circle, and the whole gun and carriage could then be moved by using a hand crank arrangement. This platform attracted a great deal of attention from many other design teams, including the Americans who used it as the basis for the 'Kelly Mount' used with 155-mm (6.1-in) M1 guns.

The K 39 could fire conventional German ammunition, but when first introduced into service it came with sizable stocks of ammunition produced for Turkish use and to Turkish specifications. This involved

SPECIFICATION	
15-cm K 39	
Calibre: 149.1 mm (5.87 in)	**Traverse:** on turntable 360° and on carriage 60°
Length of piece: 8.25 m (27 ft 0.8 in)	**Muzzle velocity:** 865 m (2,838 ft) per second
Weight: travelling 18282 kg (40,305 lb); in action 12200 kg (26,896 lb)	**Maximum range:** 24700 m (27,010 yards)
Elevation: -4° to +45°	**Shell weight:** 43 kg (94.8 lb)

The 15-cm Kanone 39 was a Krupp design commissioned by Turkey. Only two examples had been supplied when war broke out and the German army adopted it instead, along with large stocks of ammunition built to Turkish specifications.

a three-charge system and included a high explosive shell and a semi- armour-piercing projectile originally intended by the Turks to be used against warships. All this non-standard ammunition was gradually used up before the Germans switched to their normal ammunition types.

By that time the K 39 was no longer in use as one of the standard weapons of the German army. The full production run for the army amounted to only about 40 units, and this was understandably thought to be too awkward a number for logistical comfort. Thus the K 39s were diverted to the training role and then to the Atlantic Wall

defences, where they reverted to their intended purpose. On the static Atlantic Wall sites the turntables could be carefully emplaced to best effect.

A 15-cm K 39 lies abandoned on the frozen steppes, providing a subject of interest for the columns of Soviet troops marching westwards. The K 39 was eventually withdrawn to a training role for logistic reasons. Some were emplaced in the Atlantic Wall as a coastal defence gun – the weapon's original role.

17-cm Kanone 18 and 21-cm Mörser 18 Heavy howitzers

When it came to artillery design in the years during both world wars, Krupp of Essen can be regarded as the virtual leaders. The company's sound approach, coupled with the thorough development of innovations, led to some of the most remarkable artillery pieces in use anywhere in their day, and one of these innovations featured on what were two of the most remarkable artillery pieces in service during World War II. This innovation was the 'double recoil' carriage on which the normal recoil forces were first taken up by the orthodox recoil mechanism close to the barrel and then by the carriage sliding inside rails set on the bulk of the travelling carriage. In this way all the recoil forces were absorbed with virtually no movement relative to the ground, and firing accuracy was thus enhanced. Further improvements also ensured that the entire barrel and carriage could rest on a light

firing platform that formed a pivot for easy and rapid traverse.

Krupp weapons
This double-action carriage was used mainly with two Krupp weapons. The smaller was the **17-cm Kanone 18** (the actual calibre of which was 172.5 mm/ 6.79 in) and the larger the **21-cm Mörser 18** (the Germans often followed the continental practice of calling heavy howitzers a mortar). These two weapons were first introduced in 17-cm (6.8-in) form in 1941 and in 21-cm (8.3-in) form in 1939. Both proved to be excellent weapons and demand was such that Krupp had to delegate extra production to Hanomag at Hannover. Of the two weapons priority was at first given to the **21-cm Mrs 18**, and a wide range of special projectiles was developed for this weapon, including concrete-piercing shells. But with the advent of the **17-cm K 18** it soon became apparent

that the 17-cm shells were only marginally less effective than their 21-cm equivalents, and that the 17-cm gun had a much greater range (29600 m/ 32,370 yards as opposed to 16700 m/18,270 yards). Thus in 1942 priority was given to the 17-cm K 18, production of the 21-cm Mrs 18 ceasing.

However, the 21-cm Mrs 18 remained in use until the end of the war, as did the 17-cm K 18 which continued to impress all who encountered it, either as recipients of the 68-kg (149.9-lb) shell or as gunners. In fact the Allies sometimes acted as gunners, for in 1944 some Allied batteries used captured 17-cm K 18s when ammunition supplies for their normal charges were disrupted by the long logistical train from Normandy to the German border. For all their weight and bulk, both the 17-cm (6.8-in) and 21-cm pieces were fairly easy to handle. A full 360°

As the 8th Army advanced deeper into Tunisia, this 17-cm K 18 was captured intact and used against its Afrika Korps former owners. Longer ranged than the 21-cm Mrs 18, production facilities were devoted exclusively to the K 18 after 1942.

traverse could be made by only one man, and although both pieces had to be carried in two loads the carriage was well equipped with winches and ramps to make the process of removing the barrel from the carriage a fairly rapid task. For short distances both weapons could be towed in one loader.

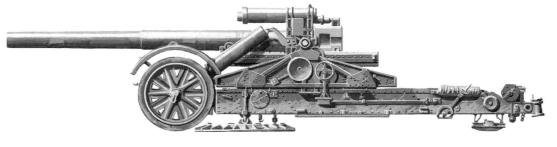

A 21-cm Mörser, so called because the Germans referred to their heavy howitzers as mortars, used the same carriage as the 17-cm K 18.

24-cm Kanone 3 and 35.5-cm Haubitze M.1

German ultra-heavy guns

During 1935 Rheinmetall began design work on a new heavy gun to meet a German army requirement for a long-range counterbattery gun firing a heavy projectile. The first example was produced during 1938, and a small batch was ordered soon after as the **24-cm Kanone 3** (**24-cm K 3**). The K 3 was a fairly massive piece of artillery that used the 'double recoil' carriage coupled to a firing table that could be easily traversed through 360°. The barrel could be elevated to 56° and thus fired in the upper register to ensure that plunging fire against fortifications and field works would make the shells as effective as possible.

The K 3 carriage was well endowed with all manner of technical novelties. In order to make the gun as mobile as possible the whole gun and carriage were broken down into six loads, and assembly on site was made as easy and rapid as possible by a number of built-in devices such as ramps and winches. Various safety measures were incorporated in case assembly was in some way incorrect; for instance, incorrect breech assembly left the gun unable to fire. Other safety measures ensured that if a winch cable broke the component involved could not move far enough to cause any damage. For all these measures it took some 25 men 90 minutes to get the gun into action. Once the gun was in action a generator, an integral part of the carriage, was kept running to provide power for the gun's services. Not many K 3s were produced; most references mention eight or 10. They were all used operationally by one unit, schwere Artillerie Abteilung (mot) 83. This motorised artillery battalion had three batteries (each with two guns), and it was in action all over Europe from the USSR to Normandy.

Sabot projectiles

The K 3 was the subject of much experimentation by German designers. Special barrels were produced in order to fire experimental projectiles with body splines that aligned with the barrel rifling as the projectile was rammed into the chamber. Other barrels fired projectiles fitted with sabots to increase range, and there was even a device fitted over the muzzle that 'squeezed' back skirts around special sub-calibre projectiles, again in an attempt to increase range. Some smooth-bore barrels were produced to fire the long-range *Peenemünder Pfeilgeschosse* (arrow shells).

By a quirk of production schedules the Rheinmetall-designed K 3 weapons were actually manufactured by Krupp of Essen. The Krupp engineers were not highly impressed by the engineering of the K 3 and decided they could do better, so producing their own version, the **24-cm K 4**. This was a very advanced design with the mounting carried on the move between two turretless Tiger tanks. There was even supposed to be a self-propelled version, but in 1943 the prototype was destroyed during an air raid on Essen and the whole project was terminated. The K 3 was still in action when the war ended and at least one example fell into

The career of the monstrous 35.5-cm H M.1, seen here in action on the Eastern Front, is still shrouded in mystery. Several of them were used to pulverise the Soviet fortifications at Sevastapol.

US Army hands. This was taken to the United States and underwent a great deal of investigation. Once the trials were over it went to Aberdeen Proving Grounds in Maryland, where it can still be seen.

In 1935 the German army asked Rheinmetall to produce an enlarged version of its 24-cm K 3, and although the design of that gun was still at an early stage, the Rheinmetall company went ahead and produced a new design with an actual calibre of 355.6 mm (14 in). The first example was produced ready to enter service in 1939, and emerged as a scaled-up version of the 24-cm (9.37-in) design. The new weapon was designated the **35.5-cm Haubitze M.1** (**35.5-cm H M.1**) and incorporated many of the features of the 24-cm design including the double-recoil carriage. The weapon was even carried in six loads, but an extra load had to be involved for the special gantry needed to assemble and disassemble the massive weapon. This gantry used electrical power from a generator carried on the same 18-tonne halftrack tractor that towed the disassembled gantry. Other 18-tonne halftracked

tractors were used to tow the other components; these were the cradle, top carriage, barrel, lower carriage, turntable and rear platform.

There appears to be no record of how long it took to get the H M.1 into action, but the time involved must have been considerable. It is known that the weapon was used by only one unit, namely 1 Batterie der Artillerie Abteilung (mot) 641. This motorised artillery battery was certainly involved in the siege of and assault on Sevastopol, but its exact whereabouts at other times are not certain.

Manufacture

There are still a number of unknown facts regarding the service career of the H M.1. Even the exact number produced is uncertain. It is known that the weapon was manufactured by Rheinmetall at Dusseldorf, but the number completed varies from three to seven depending on the reference consulted. The projectiles fired included a 575-kg (1,267.6-lb) HE shell, and there was also a 926-kg (2,041.5-lb) concrete-piercing shell. It was possible to effect 360° traverse on the carriage platform by using power jacks.

SPECIFICATION	
24-cm K 3	**35.5-cm H M.1**
Calibre: 238 mm (9.37 in)	**Calibre:** 356.6 mm (14 in)
Length of piece: 13.104 m (42 ft 11.5 in)	**Length of piece:** 10.265 m (33 ft 8 in)
Weight: travelling (six loads) 84636 kg (186,590 lb) and in action 54000 kg (119,050 lb)	**Weight:** travelling 123500 kg (272,271 lb) and in action 78000 kg (171,960 lb)
Elevation: -1° to +56°	**Elevation:** +45° to +75°
Traverse: on turntable 360° and on carriage 6°	**Traverse:** on platform 360° and on carriage 6°
Muzzle velocity: 870 m (2,854 ft) per second	**Muzzle velocity:** 570 m (1,870 ft) per second
Maximum range: 37500 m (41,010 yards)	**Maximum range:** 20850 m (22,800 yards)
Shell weight: 152.3 kg (335.78 lb)	**Shell weight:** HE 575 kg (1,267.6 lb) and anti-concrete 926 kg (2,041.5lb)

For all its weight and bulk, the range of the H M.1 was limited, so the efficiency of the weapon must have been questionable. It now seems doubtful that the considerable investment of money, manpower and equipment in a howitzer with such a range was worth the efforts involved. But the H M.1 fired a shell that must have been devastating in effect when it landed on target. Even the strongest fortification would be hard put to remain operational after a few hits from such a shell, and this no doubt made the howitzer a viable weapon. But there were few such targets for the H M.1 to pulverise, and the only time that the howitzers were put to any great use was at Sevastopol. There are records of these howitzers firing 280 rounds, which must have taken some time, for the rate of fire of the H M.1 was at best one round every four minutes.

Obice da 210/22 modello 35
Italian heavy howitzer

Most of Italy's 210-mm howitzers found their way into Hungarian hands for service on the Eastern Front. Those still in Italy at the time of the surrender were promptly manned by Germans, and made their contribution to the tenacious defence of the peninsula until 1945.

During the late 1930s the Italian army decided to attempt to replace the bulk of its heavy artillery park, which by that time resembled an oversize artillery museum. It selected two good and thoroughly modern designs, one a gun with a calibre of 149 mm (5.87 in) and the other a howitzer with a calibre of 210 mm (8.26 in). The howitzer was designed by an army organisation known as the Servizio Tecnici Armi e Munizioni (STAM), but production was carried out by Ansaldo at Pozzuoli.

The howitzer was known as the **Obice da 210/22 modello 35**. Although shown in prototype form in 1935, it was not accepted for service until 1938 when a production order for no less than

346 was placed. The modello 35 was a very sound and modern design. It used a split-trail carriage with two road wheels on each side. When the howitzer went into action these wheels were raised off the ground and the weight was assumed by a firing platform under the main axle. The entire weapon could then be traversed easily through 360° once the stakes that anchored the trail spades to the ground had been raised.

The main problem for the Italians was that having designed a first-rate howitzer they could not produce it quickly enough. Despite the good intentions of the Italian army, it had to enter the war with its antique gun park still largely undisturbed by modern equipments, and by the autumn of 1942 the grand total of modello 35s was still only 20, five of them in Italy and the rest in

SPECIFICATION	
Obice da 210/22	**Traverse:** 75°
Calibre: 210 mm (8.26 in)	**Muzzle velocity:** 560 m (1,837 ft) per second
Length of piece: 5 m (16 ft 4.8 in)	
Weight: travelling (two loads) 24030 kg (52,977 lb) and in action 15885 kg (35,020 lb)	**Maximum range:** 15407 m (16,850 yards)
Elevation: 0° to +70°	**Shell weight:** 101 or 133 kg (222.7 or 293.2 lb)

action in the Soviet Union. Part of this state of affairs was due to the fact that despite the requirements of the Italian army, modello 35s were sold to Hungary as they came off the production line, no doubt in exchange for raw materials and food products. The Hungarians found it necessary to make their own carriage modifications to suit this **21-cm 39.M** to the rigours of their service and eventually set up their own **21-cm 40.M** and finally **21-cm 40a.M** production line in 1943.

Service history
In service the modello 35 was successful enough. It could be transported in two loads, but for prolonged moves it could be further broken down into four loads with an extra load for assembly equipment and accessories. The modello 35 attracted the attentions of the Germans, and when the Italians surrendered in September 1943, the Ansaldo concern was forced to continue production for German units based in Italy. Thus the modello 35 became the **21-cm Haubitze 520(i)** and was still in action with the Germans when the war ended.

After 1945 attempts were made by Ansaldo to sell the modello 35 on the home and export markets. There were no takers as the home market was sated with American equipment and war surplus equipment was widely available elsewhere.

Italy made extensive use of heavy artillery in World War I, but by the 1930s these big guns were obsolete and new weapons were ordered. The 210-mm howitzer was an excellent design, but Italian industry could not produce the guns with sufficient speed.

Soviet 152-mm guns Models 1910/30, 1937 and 1910/34

The 152-mm gun-howitzer M 1937 had a box-section split trail carriage, and its double tyres were filled with sponge rubber. On the move, a two-wheeled limber was secured under the trails.

When considering Soviet artillery development it is as well to remember that the Soviet artillery design teams rarely produced anything innovative. Instead they placed great emphasis upon a steady programme of development in which a new piece of ordnance was placed on an existing carriage, or in which a new carriage was allied to an existing gun or howitzer. Their continual aim was to produce an artillery piece that was as light as possible but firing as heavy a projectile as possible to as great a range as possible.

Principal types

This was particularly true of the Soviet 152-mm (6-in) heavy guns. There were three main types of these, although others existed and the earliest of them could trace its origins back to 1910. Despite its age this weapon, designated the **152-mm Pushka obr. 1910g**, was updated in 1930 to become the **152-mm Field Gun Model 1910/30**. In this form it was still in service when the Germans invaded in 1941. The Model 1910/30 was an unremarkable piece of artillery, so heavy that it had to be carried in two loads. This was considered to be too much of a disadvantage for modern use, and by 1941 the Model 1910/30 was being phased out of use. The Germans designated captured equipments **15.2-cm K 438(r)**.

In 1937 the Soviet design teams came up with a replacement. This was the **152-mm Gaubitsa-Pushka obr. 1937g** (**182-mm Gun-Howitzer Model 1937**) which emerged as a new and rather long gun barrel mounted on the carriage of an existing piece, the 122-mm (4.8-in) Field Gun Model 1931/37. This combination was a gun-howitzer rather than a gun, and turned out to be a very versatile and powerful weapon, known to the Germans as the **15.2-cm K 433/1(r)** in captured service.

Carriage combination

The Soviets wanted vast numbers, but the Artillery Plant Number 172 at Perm could not produce enough so another source of these gun-howitzers was sought. This turned out to be the same barrel as the Model 1937 but mounted on the carriage of an earlier 122-mm field gun, the Model 1931. This combination was known for some reason as the **152-mm Gun-Howitzer Model 1910/34** to the Soviets and as the **15.2-cm K 433/2(r)** to the Germans.

There was also one other Soviet 152-mm field gun about which little is now known. This was apparently a long 152-mm naval barrel placed on the carriage of the 203-mm (8-in) howitzers produced as a form of emergency design in 1941–42. Few details of this weapon now exist.

These two major field gun designs, the Model 1937 and the Model 1910/34, formed the mainstay of the heavy field gun batteries of the Red Army throughout the war. Later development tended to concentrate on howitzers, but the field guns proved to be very useful weapons. They were often able to outrange their German

Seen here in German hands as a coastal defence piece, the Soviet 152-mm gun was a tough and reliable weapon and was produced in vast numbers. Massed batteries of heavy artillery played a vital role in driving the Germans back from Moscow to Berlin.

counterparts and so impressed the German gunners that they used as many captured Soviet 152-mm guns as they could lay their hands on. Many of these captured weapons were used against their former owners and as many again were diverted to the Atlantic Wall defences.

Perhaps the best indication of how good the Model 1937 gun-howitzer was at the time it was introduced can be seen by the fact that it was still in widespread use throughout the Cold War. Known as the **ML-20**, it remained in service with many Soviet-influenced armies throughout the world until relatively recently.

SPECIFICATION	
Model 1937	
Calibre: 152.4 mm (6 in)	**Elevation:** -2° to +65°
Length of piece: 4.925 m (16 ft 1.9 in)	**Traverse:** 58°
Weight: travelling 7930 kg (17,483 lb) and in action 7128 kg (15,715 lb)	**Muzzle velocity:** 655 m (2,149 ft) per second
	Maximum range: 17265 m (18,880 yards)
	Shell weight: 43.5 kg (95.9 lb)

Soviet 152-mm howitzers Models 1909/30, 1910/30 1938 and 1943

The Soviet Union not only produced some of the best artillery designs of World War II but also manufactured big guns in prodigious quantities. The 152-mm howitzer series was even used in the anti-tank role.

In 1941 the Red Army still had substantial numbers of short 152-mm (6-in) howitzers such as the **Field Howitzer Model 1909/30** and **Field Howitzer Model 1910/30**, but these were long in the tooth and despite an interim updating programme carried out after 1930 they lacked range. It was realised that these howitzers would have to be replaced and in 1938 the replacement appeared. For once this weapon was an all-new design combining a long 152-mm barrel with a sturdy and steady split-trail carriage. It went into production at two artillery factories, Artillery Plant Number 172 at Perm and Artillery Plant Number 235 at Volkinsk. The **Field Howitzer Model 1938**, later known as the **M-10**, turned out to be a great success and was widely used, later becoming one of the main types in Red Army service throughout the war. The Red Army came to value the flexibility of the

howitzer over the long-range capabilities of the gun to a great extent, and found during the early days of the war with the invading German army that the heavy 51.1-kg (112.6-lb) high explosive shell was also a powerful anti-tank weapon.

Anti-tank service

The use of the 152-mm howitzer in the anti-tank role derived from the Red Army practice of using every available field piece as an anti-tank weapon, and was so successful that a special solid-shot projectile was introduced for use by the Model 1938. This weighed 40 kg (88.2 lb) and could knock out any known tank. The Germans also prized the Model 1938 highly, using as

many as they could capture under the designation **15.2-cm sFH 443(r)**, either in the Soviet Union or as part of the Atlantic Wall defences. More turned up in Italy and France.

In their constant striving to make their progeny as light and efficient as possible, the Soviet artillery designers later converted the Model 1938 to be mounted on the carriage of the 122-mm (4.8-in) Model 1938 howitzer. A larger muzzle brake was fitted to reduce, at least in part, the recoil forces of the heavier barrel, and the new combination became the **152-mm Field Howitzer Model 1943**. As its designation implies this new howitzer/carriage combination was first produced in 1943 and soon replaced the earlier Model 1938 in production. It continued to fire the same range of ammunition as the Model 1938 and the range capabilities remained the same. By 1945 it was in service with the Red Army in huge numbers

and was later designated the **D-1**.

Post-war service

Post-war the Model 1938 and Model 1943 went on to serve in many more conflicts. Gradually the Model 1938 faded from use and it was last used in a front-line capacity by Romania, but the Model 1943 remained very much in evidence. It was still in Red Army service into the early 1980s, although only with reserve units. The weapon was bestowed the accord of being thought fit to be copied by the Chinese army, which produced its own version, known as the **Type 64**. The Model 43 was used by nearly every nation that came under Soviet influence, ranging from Czechoslovakia to Iraq and from Cuba to Vietnam. It even appeared in Ethiopia and Mozambique.

SPECIFICATION	
Model 1943	**Traverse:** 35°
Calibre: 152.5 mm (6 in)	**Muzzle velocity:** 508 m (1,667 ft) per second
Length of piece: 4.207 m (13 ft 9.6 in)	**Maximum range:** 12400 m (13,560 yards)
Weight: travelling 3640 kg (8,025 lb) and in action 3600 kg (7,937 lb)	**Shell weight:** HE 51.1 kg (112.6 lb)
Elevation: -3° to +63.5°	

203-mm Howitzer Model 1931 Heavy howitzer

The heaviest of the field-type weapons used by the Soviets between 1941 and 1945 was the **203-mm Howitzer Model 1931**, also known as the **B-4**. This was a powerful but heavy weapon that is now generally remembered as being one of the few artillery weapons to use a carriage that ran on caterpillar tracks. This was an outcome of the huge Soviet investment in tractor factories during the 1920s

and 1930s, and the use of these tractor tracks was thus an obvious and economic measure for the Soviet carriage designers to take. The use of these tracks meant that the Model 1931 could traverse very bad or soft terrain where other weapons of similar weight could not venture.

This was an important point for the Model 1931, which was a heavy piece. It was so heavy that although most versions could be

towed for short distances in two loads, long moves involved the breaking down of the weapon into as many as six separate loads. Some versions could move

in five loads but there were about six different variants of the Model 1931. All of them used the tracked carriage but varied in the way they were towed.

SPECIFICATION	
Model 1931	**Traverse:** 8°
Calibre: 203 mm (8 in)	**Muzzle velocity:** 607 m (1,991 ft) per second
Length of piece: 5.087 m (16 ft 8.3 in)	**Maximum range:** 18025 m (19,712 yards)
Weight: in action 17700 kg (39,022 lb)	**Shell weight:** 100 kg (220.46 lb)
Elevation: 0° to +60°	

The mighty 203-mm howitzer M1931 was still in service with some heavy artillery units of the Soviet army up until the early 1980s, although it no longer used its tracked chassis. The Germans were pleased to use any they captured, and fielded them not only in the Soviet Union but against the Allies in Italy and northwestern Europe.

Movement of the Model 1931 involved the use of a limber onto which the split trails were lifted to be towed, usually by some form of heavy tracked tractor with (again) agricultural origins. Some of these limbers used tracks again and some had large single road wheels. Others had twin road wheels of smaller diameter.

In action

To the soldier at the front all these variations made little difference as the howitzer itself remained much the same throughout its service life. It was rather a ponderous weapon to use in action, and the rate of fire was usually limited to one round every four minutes, although higher rates could be attained. It made a powerful barrage weapon but was also used for the demolition of heavy strongpoints, a heavy 100-kg (220-lb) high explosive shell being provided for the role. But

essentially it was a weapon for static use, being limited on the move to a maximum speed of no more than 15 km/h (9.3 mph). Not surprisingly, whenever mobile warfare was possible, the Model 1931 was at a disadvantage and consequently many fell into German hands as they could not be moved quickly enough. The Germans were so short of heavy artillery that they used as many as they could, mainly in the Soviet Union but also in Italy and in north west Europe after 1944, under the designation **20.3-cm H 503(r)**.

Later service

After 1945 the Model 1931 appeared to fade from service but in later years it once again emerged. It remained part of the equipment of the Red Army heavy artillery brigades into the early 1980s, and would have been used for the destruction of

strongpoints that it might have encountered. By this stage it had lost the tracked travelling arrangements and in their place had a new wheeled road-wheel suspension with two wheels in tandem on each side. This form of carriage allowed the Model 1931 to be towed in one load. The arrival of the 203-mm 2S7 (M-1975) self-propelled gun from the mid-1970s finally made the Model 1931 redundant.

The heaviest Soviet gun in field use during the war, the 203-mm Howitzer Model 1931 was mounted on converted agricultural tractor tracks widely available in the Soviet Union as a result of Stalin's lopsided industrialisation programme. It fired a 100-kg (220-lb) shell to a maximum range of 18 km (11 miles).

4.5-in Medium Gun Mk 2 Medium artillery

By the late 1930s, British gunnery staff officers were aware that something better would soon be required for their medium gun regiments. It was proposed that a new 4.5-in (114-mm) gun sharing the same carriage as a proposed 5.5-in (139-mm) howitzer would be suitable, and this proposal was adopted, the required range being 20,000 yards (18290 m).

Service entry

The design phase of the gun itself was straightforward and

gun production commenced during late 1940. Thanks mainly to a period of difficulty with carriage production, it was mid-1941 before the first examples were given to gunners. This was just in time for the latter phases of the North African campaigns. It was not long before the old 4.5-in Mk 1 guns were relegated to the training role back in the United Kingdom.

Apart from the ordnance, the **4.5-in Mk 2** gun (the Mark 2 differentiating it from the

A British 4.5-in gun fires on the Anzio beachhead, 17 March 1944. The shell from this mission reportedly scored a direct hit on a house that was being used by the Germans as a command post.

Mark 1, a converted 60-pdr gun with limited range performance) and 5.5-in howitzer were visually almost identical, the gun barrel of the 4.5-in gun being only marginally longer than that of the howitzer. The 4.5-in ordnance fired a 24.97-kg (55.04-lb) high-explosive projectile to 18758 m (20,513 yards), compared to the 14823 m (16,210 yards) achieved by the 5.5-in howitzer.

Limited firepower

However, there was one significant drawback to the 4.5-in projectile as far as the gunners were concerned. For various reasons its high-explosive payload was small in comparison with the projectile weight so the destructive effects on the target proved to be less than might have been wished. For this reason the 5.5-in howitzer became the preferred weapon, especially as it fired a useful 36.32-kg (80.07-lb) projectile with an excellent on-target performance. Production priorities therefore switched to the howitzer, although in-service guns continued to be employed in the important counter-battery role. The 4.5-in Mk 2 gun was not used by any other army other than the British, and no other projectile apart from high explosive was developed for it.

The carriage of the 4.5-in Mk 2 gun had a few minor modifications from that of the howitzer to accommodate the different weight and length of the gun barrel, but it remained of the split-trail type with the barrel's muzzle preponderance balanced by two prominent equilibrator pillars. Barrel traverse was 30° right and left.

Normandy 1944, and the Allies advance on Tilly-sur-Seulles. Here a 4.5-in gun is seen firing in support of British infantry. A crew of up to eight was required to manhandle the 4.5-in gun carriage in action.

Gun handling

The equipment proved to be sturdy and largely trouble-free once a few early carriage problems had been eliminated. Handling the relatively heavy carriage by the crew of up to eight or so was greatly assisted by the balance of the equipment over its two prominent pneumatic-tyred wheels, although opening and closing the split-trail legs could be a heavy task. The gun was fired 'off its wheels', all recoil forces being absorbed by the hydro-pneumatic recoil system and two large recoil spades at the extreme ends of the trail legs.

Although the 4.5-in Mk 2 gun was withdrawn from service soon after the war ended in 1945, small numbers were retained as training weapons until at least the late 1950s, largely to consume the stockpiles of 4.5-in ammunition.

The 4.5-in Medium Gun Mk 2 first saw combat during the closing stages of the campaign in North Africa.

SPECIFICATION	
4.5-in Gun Mk 2	**Traverse:** 30°
Calibre: 114 mm (4.5 in)	**Muzzle velocity:** up to 686 m (2,250
Length of piece: 4.764 m (15 ft 7 in)	ft) per second
Weight: in action 5842 kg (12,879.4 lb)	**Maximum range:** 18758 m (20,513.9 yards)
Elevation: -5° to +45°	**Shell weight:** 24.97 kg (55 lb)

7.2-in Howitzers Mks I-V and 6 Heavy artillery

Between the wars the British Army tended to neglect artillery, so when heavy artillery was required in 1940 all that there was to hand was a quantity of World War I 8-in (203-mm) howitzers with ranges too short for the conditions. As a stopgap it was decided to reline existing 8-in barrels to a calibre of 7.2 in (183 mm) and to develop a new range of ammunition. The original 8-in carriages were retained, with new pneumatic balloon-tyred wheels added to what became known as the **7.2-in Howitzer**.

Fearsome recoil

The new ammunition provided a useful increase in range, but when the weapon fired the full charge the recoil forces were too much for the carriage to absorb. Firing the 7.2-in howitzer on full charge was risky, for the whole equipment tended to rear up and jump backwards. Some of this unwanted motion could be partly overcome by placing behind each wheel wedge-shaped ramps, but sometimes even these were insufficient and the howitzer would jump over them. But the conversion proved to be an excellent projectile-delivery system capable of good range

The story of British heavy artillery after 1918 is the familiar one of inaction and neglect. When war broke out again, heavy guns had to be improvised by re-lining old 8-in howitzers to a calibre of 7.2-in to give them a respectable range.

and accuracy, to the extent that the gunners in the field called for more.

In order to provide more, the number of 8-in howitzer conversions eventually ran to six marks depending on the original barrel and type of conversion; some of the 8-in barrels came from the US. The first 7.2-in howitzers were used in action during the latter period of the war in North Africa and were later used following the Normandy landings.

But by 1944 numbers of 7.2-in barrels were being placed on imported American M1 carriages. These excellent carriages proved to be just as suitable for the 7.2-in howitzer as they were for the American 155-mm (6.1-in) gun and 203-mm howitzers, and the first

combination of a 7.2-in barrel with the M1 carriage was the **7.2-in Howitzer Mk V**. Few, if any such combinations were made as it was obvious that the M1 carriage was capable of carrying more than the original conversion. Thus a much longer 7.2-in barrel was placed on the M1 carriage and this was the **7.2-in Howitzer Mk 6**. The longer barrel produced a considerable range increase to

17985 m (19,667 yards) and the carriage was much more stable than the old 8-in carriage. As more M1 carriages became available they were used to mount the new Mk 6 barrels, and by the end of 1944 there were few of the original 8-in carriages left. With the increased stability came increased accuracy, and the Mk 6 howitzer gained an enviable reputation for good shooting.

The 7.2-in howitzer could be as terrifying to its crew as to the target. Seen here in action at Routot, France, in September 1944, the 10-ton gun leaps into the air after firing at full charge. Surprisingly for such a makeshift design, the 7.2-in proved fairly efficient.

SPECIFICATION	
7.2-in Howitzer Mks I-V	**Traverse:** 0
Calibre: 183 mm (7.2 in)	**Muzzle velocity:** 518 m (1,700 ft) per second
Length of piece: 4.343 m (14 ft 3 in)	**Maximum range:** 15453 m (16,900 yards)
Weight: in action 10387 kg (22,900 lb)	**Shell weight:** 91.6 kg (202 lb)
Elevation: 0° to +45°	

240-mm Howitzer M1 Heavy artillery

In 1939 the US Army resurrected a joint project for a 203-mm gun/240-mm howitzer on a common carriage that had been first suggested in 1919. The first 203-mm (8-in) guns were not issued until 1944, but the 240-mm (9.4-in) howitzer was less problematic and was ready by May 1943. This **240-mm Howitzer M1** was a fairly

massive piece of artillery using what was virtually an enlarged M1 carriage as used on the 155-mm (6.1-in) Gun M1. But the 240-mm howitzer carriage did not travel with barrel fitted, instead it travelled on a six-

Weighing over 30 tons, the US 240-mm howitzer originated from a project begun after World War I, but little progress had been made before 1940, and America had been at war 18 months before the 240-mm weapon was ready. However, once in action it proved very useful against German emplacements in Italy and northwestern Europe.

wheeled carriage and once on site its wheels were removed. The barrel was towed on a form of semi-trailer. At the chosen site the carriage was emplaced and a pit was dug to permit barrel recoil at full elevation. The barrel was then lifted into position, usually by a mobile crane that was also used to place the carriage into position and spread the trails.

Once in place the howitzer proved to be a powerful weapon and was used whenever the fighting settled down behind static lines for any time. There was little call for the type to be employed whenever fighting was fluid as it took too long to emplace the weapons or get them out of action, but when they were used the heavy 163.3-kg (360-lb) high-explosive shells were devastating weapons. The howitzers were used by both the US and British armies into the 1950s.

A 240-mm howitzer prepared for action: it travelled on a six-wheel carriage, which was emplaced over a pit dug to absorb the recoil.

SPECIFICATION	
240-mm Howitzer M1	**Traverse:** 45°
Calibre: 240 mm (9.4 in)	**Muzzle velocity:** 701 m (2,300 ft) per second
Length of piece: 8.407 m (27 ft 7 in)	
Weight: complete 29268 kg (64,525 lb)	**Maximum range:** 23093 m (25,255 yards)
Elevation: +15° to +65°	**Shell weight:** 163.3 kg (360 lb)

155-mm Gun M1 Heavy gun

The 155-mm (6.1-in) M1 gun in travelling mode, trails together and connected to the limber. Still used by more than a dozen countries into the 1980s, it was served by a 14-man crew and could maintain a rate of fire of two rounds per minute.

When the US entered World War I in April 1917 its army was ill-equipped with heavy artillery, and as a result received various types of Allied artillery, including the French 155-mm (6.1-in) GPF (Grand Puissance Filloux). This was one of the best guns of its type at that time, but in the years after 1918 American artillery designers

A 155-mm (6.1-in) 'Long Tom' gun fires in the Nettune area of the Allied 5th Army's Anzio beach head in Italy during the first part of 1944. Longer-range weapons such as the M1 gun were vital in such campaigns to keep the Germans from swamping the beach head.

sought to improve the overall efficiency of the gun and carriage by introducing a series of prototypes throughout the 1920s. Sometimes this programme stood in abeyance for years, but by the late 1930s the new design (very basically the original GPF barrel equipped to accommodate an Asbury breech mechanism) was accepted for standardisation as **the 155-mm Gun M1 on Carriage M1**, and production of

this 6.1-in weapon started at a steady pace at several American arsenals.

The M1 gun and carriage combination was very much an overall improvement on the French GPF design, but

introduced some new features. The barrel was an L/45 unit, and the carriage was of a heavy split-trail type carried on four double-tyred road wheels forward. This carriage arrangement meant that in action the wheels were lifted to allow the carriage to rest on a forward-firing platform: in use this proved to be an excellent arrangement offering great stability. This made the gun very accurate, and eventually the carriage was adopted by the British for use with their 7.2-in (183-mm) howitzer. For towing, the trail legs were hitched up onto a limber device. There were two of these, the M2 and the M5, the latter having a rapid up-and-over lift arrangement that permitted quick use in action but which could also be dangerous to an untrained crew. For this reason the M2 limber was often preferred.

Improved models

The M1 was gradually developed into an **M1A1** form and then, late in 1944, into the **M2**. The changes were limited mainly to production expedients

The gunner covers his ears as his 155-mm (6.1-in) 'Long Tom' gun blasts off a round against Japanese artillery positions in the hills beyond Dulag on the Filipino island of Leyte during 1944. Its long range made the M1 an excellent counter-battery weapon.

and did not affect the gun's performance, which proved to be excellent: a 43.1-kg (95-lb) shell could be fired to a range of 23220 m (25,395 yards).

The M1 soon became one of the standard heavy guns of the US Army, and its combination of accuracy and range meant that it was often used for counter-battery work. Numbers of the guns were issued to Allied nations, and the M1 was soon part of the British Army gun park, seeing active service in Europe from the time of the June 1944 Normandy landings onward.

The M1 also went self-propelled. This was carried out using a much-modified M4A3E8 Sherman tank chassis with the gun mounted in an open super-structure, and in this form the

vehicle/gun combination was known as the **M40**. It was 1945 before the M40 entered production, so its main career was post-war but it was widely used by many nations, again including the UK.

Revised designation

After 1945 the US Army underwent a period of internal reorganisation and in the process the M1 and M2 guns became the **M59**. The post-war period also saw the end of the

limber devices after it was discovered that, with most of the heavy tractors then in service, all that was needed was to join the trails and connect them direct to the tractor towing eye, usually with chains. In this form the 155-mm (6.1-in) M59 served on into the 1990s with many armies around the world, and is still in limited service as it is considered to be a good gun, albeit a piece of ordnance rather lacking in range and range flexibility.

SPECIFICATION	
155-mm Gun M1A1	
Calibre: 155 mm (6.1 in)	**Muzzle velocity:** 853 m (2,800 ft) per second
Length of piece: 7.366 m (24 ft 2 in)	**Maximum range:** 23221 m (25.395 yards)
Weight: travelling 13880 kg (30,600 lb) and in action 12600 kg (27,778 lb)	**Shell weight:** 42 kg (92.6 lb)
Elevation: -2° to +65°	
Traverse: 60°	

8-in Howitzer M1 Heavy howitzer

After the US entry into World War I, among the various types of heavy artillery its army received in France were the British 8-in Howitzer Mks VII and VIII, which were incidentally being produced in the US to a British order. The US Army took to this howitzer with a will, for it soon discovered that it was a

very accurate weapon. In the years after 1918 the army set about producing its own version. This was under the aegis of an advisory body known as the Westervelt Board, which also recommended the introduction of the 155-mm Gun M1. The board also recommended that the 155-mm

A view of the interrupted-screw breech mechanism of an 8-in (203-mm) howitzer in action. Four crew members prepare to lift the 90.7-kg (200-lb) shell, whose size gives some clue as to why the maximum rate of fire was just one round per minute.

SPECIFICATION	
8-in Howitzer M 1	**Elevation:** -2° to +65°
Calibre: 203 mm (8 in)	**Traverse:** 60°
Length of piece: 5.324 m (17 ft 5.6 in)	**Muzzle velocity:** 594 m (1,950 ft) per second
Weights: travelling 14515 kg (32,000 lb) and in action 13471 kg (29,698 lb)	**Maximum range:** 16595 m (18,150 yards)
	Shell weight: 90.7 kg (200 lb)

In addition to receiving the French 155-mm (6.1-in) gun, the US Army in France received during 1918 the British 8-in (203-in) howitzer, which was subsequently used as the basis for post-war US heavy howitzer design. The M1 howitzer resulted from years of intermittent, underfunded research and was not standardised until 1940. Once in action, however, it was an impressive piece. Accurate and hard-hitting, it is still in extensive service, and was developed into the M110 self-propelled equipment.

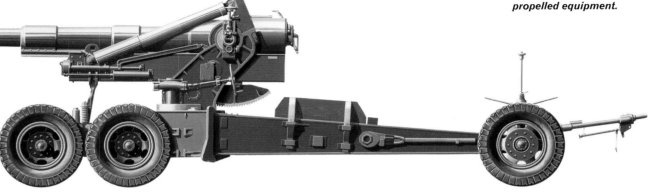

(6.1-in) gun and the 203-mm (8-in) howitzer should share the same carriage, and thus the new howitzer used the same M1 carriage as the 155-mm Gun M1.

Slow development

Despite the recommendations of the Westervelt Board, however, the development of the new howitzer was slow and erratic, and at times ceased altogether for years on end. So it was 1940 before the howitzer was standardised as the **8-in Howitzer M1**. This owed much to its British origins, but was longer, and as it used the M1 carriage it was still more accurate than its predecessor. It should not be thought, however, that because the 8-in Howitzer M1 and the 155-mm Gun M1 shared the same carriage that the two barrels were readily interchangeable: an exchange of the two barrels involved a great deal of

workshop time and a great deal of trouble.

Once the powerful Howitzer M1 had been introduced to service, it quickly became a very popular weapon. Its accuracy allowed it to be used to bring down heavy fire on spot targets quite close to friendly troops, and it was frequently used thus to destroy strongpoints and bunkers. The shell fired by the M1 was initially a 90.7-kg (200-lb) high explosive shell also used by 203-mm (8-in) coast guns, but this was later replaced by a special HE shell known as the M106, which had the same weight as the earlier shell but

Driving through the bitter December 1944 weather of western Europe, these 8-in (203-mm) howitzers are travelling through Belgium to join the US 1st Army. Artillery was particularly effective in areas like the Ardennes, where roads were few and chokepoints obvious.

could be fired to a range of 16596 m (18,150 yards). The M106 is still in service with the Howitzer M1 which, in a post-war designation reshuffle, became the **M115**.

Like the 155-mm Gun M1, the Howitzer M1 also went self-propelled, although the first version did not appear until 1946. This was the **M43** which used a much-modified M4A3E8 tank chassis as the carrier. Subsequent development along

these lines led to the M110 series which originally used the 8-in howitzer in a form virtually unchanged from its towed version but which was then developed to the M110A2 using a much lengthened howitzer.

The M115 towed howitzer is still in widespread service with eight armies. Thus the 8-in howitzer can lay claim to being one of the longest-lived of all the world's modern heavy artillery pieces.

The blast effect of an 8-in (203-mm) howitzer firing hits not just the ears but the whole body as the shock wave passes outward. This is the first 8-in howitzer in action in Normandy during 1944, firing during the barrage the Americans organised for Independence Day on 4 July.

Semovente da 149/40 Self-propelled gun

The Italian army was not far behind the Germans in realising the need for assault guns, and developed a string of vehicles that outwardly resembled the German StuG III. These Italian assault guns were produced in appreciable numbers, for they were better armoured and in relative terms quicker to produce than contemporary Italian tanks. But by the time significant numbers had been issued Italy was effectively out of the war, and most of these Italian assault guns fell into German hands.

High demand

The majority of Italian self-propelled weapons, known as *semovente*, mounted 75-mm (2.95-in) or 105-mm (4.13-in) guns and howitzers of varying lengths, but since these were direct-fire mounts, the Italian artillery arm still required self-propelled artillery weapons to support the armoured formations. Accordingly Ansaldo diverted some of its precious development facilities to design

a powerful artillery weapon that could be carried on a trucked chassis. In the end Ansaldo plumped for an existing weapon, the long Canone da 149/40 modello 35, and decided to place it on a much modified Carro Armato M.15/42 tank chassis. The selection of these two items of equipment was made in order to produce as good a carriage/ weapon combination as possible, but the snag was that the Italian army was already crying out for large numbers of both the gun and tank. Italian industry quite simply could not keep up with the existing demands and so the new self-propelled weapon, known as the **Semovente da 149/40** got off to a shaky start.

Unprotected weapon

The Semovente da 149/40 was a completely unprotected weapon as the long gun barrel was placed on an open mounting carried on the turretless tank chassis. The gun crew stood in the open to serve the gun,

which had its trunnions mounted right to the rear to absorb some of the recoil forces produced on firing. It was late 1942 before the first prototype was ready for prolonged firing trials, but even before these were over, unsuccessful attempts were being made to start production. Before the lines could start rolling the Italians surrendered to the Allies, and the Germans took over what was left of the Italian economy. Thus the Semovente da 149/40 prototype remained the sole example of what seemed to be a promising design. The gun of the Semovente da 149/40 was certainly a useful weapon: it could fire a 46-kg (101.4-lb) projectile to a range of 23700 m

The long, lean lines of the Italian Semovente da 149/40 can be seen at the Aberdeen Proving Grounds in Maryland. It still looks very serviceable as a modern artillery weapon despite the lack of crew protection and stowage on the vehicle for ammunition and other items.

(25,919 yards), at which distance the lack of protection for the gun crew would have been of relatively little importance.

The prototype survived the war, and can now be seen at the Aberdeen Proving Grounds in the US. It still looks a thoroughly modern piece of equipment that would not be too out of place in many modern gun parks.

SPECIFICATION	
Semovente da 149/40	**Dimensions:** length 6.6 m (21 ft 7.8 in); width 3 m (9 ft 10 in); height 2 m (6 ft 6.7 in)
Crew: (on gun) 2	
Weight: 24000 kg (52,911 lb)	
Powerplant: one SPA petrol engine developing 186.4 kW (250 hp)	**Performance:** maximum road speed 35 km/h (21.75 mph)
	Armament: one 149-mm (5.87-in) gun

Type 4 HO-RO Self-propelled howitzer

The Type 97 mounted a short Type 38 howitzer with limited range, but the Japanese were never able to produce the numbers required and they were mainly used in ones and twos as local fire-support weapons.

The Type 97 had its 150-mm (5.9-in) howitzer mounted in place of the turret normally carried. The howitzer was meant to be used as a form of mobile field artillery but was normally used as close support artillery.

The Japanese were behind in armoured warfare development throughout all their World War II campaigns. Their early military excursions into China and Manchuria misled them into disregarding the need for heavy armoured vehicles, and instead they concentrated on what were regarded elsewhere as light tanks and tankettes. This approach was supported by the state of Japanese industry, which was still in a relatively early state of industrial development and lacked large-scale production capability. Thus it was that the Japanese army fell way behind in the development of self-propelled artillery, and ultimately only a small number of equipments were produced.

Howitzer conversion

One of these was the **Type 4 HO-RO**, a self-propelled howitzer that allied the Type 38 150-mm (5.9-in) howitzer with the Type 97 medium tank. The conversion to the self-propelled role was a straightforward design task in which the howitzer was mounted in a shield which provided forward and side armour protection while leaving the top and rear open; the side armour, it is worth noting, did not extend even to the rear of the fighting compartment. The howitzer dated from 1905 and was derived from a Krupp design. It fired a 35.9-kg (79.15-lb) projectile to a range of 5900 m (6,452 yards), but most of these weapons were so old and worn that they had been withdrawn from general use after about 1942. They had a slow rate of fire as a result of the type of breech mechanism employed, but they were apparently thought good enough for the self-propelled role.

The chassis used for the Type 4 was the Type 97 CHI-HA, a medium tank by Japanese standards and dating from 1937. It was a mobile enough vehicle, but showed a relative lack of development in its thin armour, which was only about 25 mm (1 in) thick on the gun shield frontal armour, and in its overall riveted construction. The use of rivets in tank construction had elsewhere long disappeared, but the Japanese had no option but to retain the method as they lacked any other form of construction capability.

Limited production

They also lacked the ability to produce the Type 4 HO-RO in anything but small numbers. Even those were virtually hand-built, with few pretensions to mass production. Even then the Japanese did not concentrate on the Type 4 HO-RO alone, for they also produced a version known as the Type 2 mounting a 75-mm (2.95-in) gun and designed to double as a self-propelled artillery platform and a tank-killer. The Type 4 HO-RO vehicles appear not to have been organised into anything larger than four-howitzer batteries. No records survive of larger formations and most accounts refer to these vehicles being captured or knocked out in ones or twos. Very often they were assigned for island defence in the amphibious campaign leading to the Japanese mainland, and only a few were captured intact.

SPECIFICATION	
Type 4 HO-RO	2 in); width 2.286 m (7 ft 6 in);
Crew: 4 or 5	height to top of shield 1.549 m (5 ft
Weight: not recorded, but about	1 in)
13600 kg (29,982 lb)	**Performance:** maximum road speed
Powerplant: one V-12 diesel	38 km/h (23.6 mph)
developing 126.8 kW (170 hp)	**Armament:** one 150-mm (5.9-in)
Dimensions: length 5. 537 m (18 ft	howitzer

sIG 33 auf Geschützwagen Self-propelled infantry support howitzer

The German infantry battalions each had a small artillery complement of four 7.5-cm (2.95-in) light howitzers and two 15-cm (5.9-in) infantry howitzers for their own local fire support. The 15-cm howitzer was known as the schwere Infantrie Geschütz 33 (sIG 33, or heavy infantry gun) and was a very useful and versatile weapon, but it was heavy and the only 'equipment' allocated to most infantry formations for the movement of the weapons were horse teams. Thus when an increasing degree of mechanisation began to filter through the German army the sIG 33 was high on the list for consideration.

Mobile weapon

The first form of mobile sIG 33 was used during the French campaign of May 1940. It was one of the simplest and most basic of all the German self-propelled equipments, for it consisted of nothing more than a sIG 33 mounted complete with carriage and wheels on to a turretless PzKpfw I light tank as the **15-cm sIG 33 auf Geschützwagen I Ausf B**. Armoured shields were provided for the crew of four, and that was that. It was not a very satisfactory conversion as the centre of gravity was rather high and the chassis was overloaded. Moreover, the armour protection was not good, and so in 1942 the PzKpfw II was the subject for conversion. This **15-cm sIG 33 auf Geschützwagen II ausf**

SPECIFICATION	
SdKfz 138/1	height 2.4 m (7 ft 10.5 in)
Crew: 4	**Performance:** maximum road speed
Weight: 11500 kg (25,353 lb)	35 km/h (21.75 mph); maximum
Powerplant: one Praga 6-cylinder	road range 185 km (115 miles)
petrol engine developing 111.9 kW	**Fording:** 0.914 m (3 ft)
(150 hp)	**Armament:** one 15-cm (5.9-in)
Dimensions: length 4.835 m (15 ft	howitzer
10.4 in); width 2.15 m (7 ft 0.6 in);	

C SdKfz 121 conversion had the howitzer mounted low in the chassis, and was so successful that during 1943 a version with a lengthened hull was produced as the **15-cm sIG 33 auf Fgst PzKpfw II (Sf) Verlänget**.

The ex-Czech PzKpfw 38(t) was also converted to act as a sIG 33 carrier. In 1942 the first of a series of vehicles known collectively as the **15-cm sIG 33 (Sf) auf PzKpfw 38(t) Bison SdKfz 138** were produced. The first series had the sIG 33 mounted forward on the hull top behind an open armoured superstructure, and this weapon/vehicle arrangement proved to be so successful that it was formalised in 1943 by the production of a new version. This was a factory-produced model rather than a conversion of existing tanks and had the vehicle engine mounted forward (instead of at the rear as

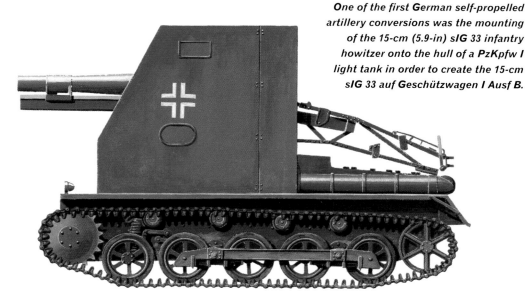

One of the first German self-propelled artillery conversions was the mounting of the 15-cm (5.9-in) sIG 33 infantry howitzer onto the hull of a PzKpfw I light tank in order to create the 15-cm sIG 33 auf Geschützwagen I Ausf B.

originally located), this entailing the movement of the fighting compartment to the hull rear. This was the **SdKfz 138/1** (SdKfz for *Sonder Kraftfahrzeug*, or special vehicle) and it was this vehicle that was retained as the German army's standard sIG 33 carrier until the end of the war. The SdKfz 138/1 had a crew of four men

including the driver, and 15 shells were carried on the vehicle. There was no room for more because the fighting compartment was rather restricted for space.

Different version

There was one other sIG 33 self-propelled version, this time on a PzKpfw III chassis. This **15-cm sIG 33 auf PzKpfw III** appeared in 1941 and used a large box

Taken from a German newsreel, this shot clearly shows how high and awkward the mounting of the 15-cm howitzer really was on the PzKpfw I chassis. The crew had only limited protection and stowage was minimal, but it provided the Germans with an indication of what would be required in future.

superstructure on a PzKpfw III to house the sIG 33. This proved to be rather too much of a good thing, for the chassis was really too large for the weapon which could be easily carried by lighter vehicles. Thus production never got properly under way, being terminated after only 12 conversions had been made. These vehicles were used in action on the Eastern Front.

All the sIG 33 self-propelled equipments were used for their original role, i.e. the direct fire-support of infantry units. Perhaps the most successful of these self-propelled carriages were the Bison and the later SdKfz 138/1. Over 370 of the vehicles were produced.

Wespe Self-propelled field howitzer

Even as early as 1939 it was obvious that the days of the little PzKpfw II tank were numbered, for it lacked both armament and armour. However, it was in production and quite reliable, so when the need arose for self-propelled artillery the PzKpfw II was selected to be the carrier for the 10.5-cm (4.13-in) leFH 18 field howitzer. The conversion of the tank hull to carry the howitzer was quite straightforward, as the howitzer was mounted behind an open topped armoured shield towards the rear of the hull and the area where the turret had

been was armoured over and the space used for ammunition stowage. The maximum armour thickness was 18 mm (0.7 in).

Cumbersome

The result was the self propelled howitzer known as the **Wespe** (wasp), although its full official designation was the rather more cumbersome **leFH18/2 auf Fgst PzKpfw II (Sf) SdKfz 124 Wespe**, but to everyone it was just the Wespe. It was a very popular self-propelled weapon that soon gained a reputation for reliability and mobility. The first

This shot of a Wespe on the move shows that the top of the fighting compartment was open, but protection was provided at the rear. Note how small the vehicle actually was by comparing it to the stature of the gun crew in the compartment.

of them were based on the PzKpfw II Ausf F chassis and went into action on the Eastern Front during 1943. On this front they were used by the divisional artillery batteries of the Panzer and Panzergrenadier divisions. They were usually organised into batteries of six howitzers with up to five batteries to each separate Abteilung (battalion). The rationale behind their deployment was to provide all mobile formations with proper and effective indirect fire support.

Wasp's nest

The Wespe was so successful in its artillery support role that Hitler himself made an order that all available PzKpfw II chassis

production should be allocated to the Wespe alone, and the many other improvised weapons on the PzKpfw II chassis were dropped or their armament diverted to other chassis. The main Wespe construction centre was the Fame plant in Poland, and there production was so rapid that by mid-1944 682 examples had been built. Some time around that date manufacture of the Wespe ceased, but not before 158 had been completed without howitzers; these vehicles had the gap in the armour plate for the howitzer sealed off, the space behind the armour being used for resupply ammunition.

A typical Wespe went into action carrying its crew of five,

The SdKfz 124 Wespe was a purpose-built carrier for a light 105-mm (4.13-in) howitzer, based on the chassis of the PzKpfw II light tank. It was first used during 1942 and had a crew of five.

including the driver, and 32 rounds of ammunition. A Wespe battery was completely mobile, although some of the vehicles were soft-skinned trucks for carrying ammunition and other supplies. The forward observers were usually carried in light armoured vehicles although some batteries used ex-Czech or captured French tanks for this purpose. Fire orders were relayed

back to the battery by radio, and from the battery fire command post the orders were relayed to the gun positions by land lines. The standard 10.5-cm leFH 18 as used by towed batteries was carried by the Wespe, although most were fitted with muzzle brakes, and they used the same ammunition. They also had the same range of 10675 m (11,675 yards).

Hummel Self-propelled field howitzer

The Hummel (bumble bee) was a purpose-built self-propelled artillery piece that used chassis components from both the PzKpfw III and IV. Used on all fronts, it was a successful weapon that remained in production until the war ended. It had a crew of five.

The self-propelled artillery vehicle that became known as the **Hummel** (bumble bee) was a hybrid combining components of the PzKpfw III and PzKpfw IV tanks into a new vehicle known as the **Geschützwagen III/IV**. The first of these hybrids was produced during 1941 and used a lengthened PzKpfw IV suspension and running gear combined with the final drive

assemblies, track and transmission of the PzKpfw III. Onto this new hull was built an open superstructure formed with light armour plates, and two types of weapon were mounted.

Vehicles intended for use as tank destroyers mounted a version of the 88-mm (3.46-in) anti-tank gun, but vehicles intended for use as self-

propelled artillery mounted a special version of the 15-cm (5.9-in) FH 18 field howitzer.

The FH 18 vehicle was the **15-cm Panzerfeldhaubitze 18M auf GW III/IV SdKfz 165 Hummel**, and it formed the heavy field artillery element of the Panzer and Panzergrenadier divisions from 1942 onwards. The ordnance was known as the Panzerfeldhaubitz 18/1,

and could fire a 43.5-kg (95.9-lb) projectile to a range of 13325 m (14,572 yards). The first howitzers produced for the self-propelled role were fitted with large muzzle brakes, but experience demonstrated that these were not really necessary and were accordingly left off later production versions. The armour was 50 mm (1.97 in) thick.

A battery of four Hummels stand ready for action on the Russian steppe in 1942. The closeness of the guns and the overall lack of concealment demonstrates that the Luftwaffe had air superiority at this time, otherwise the guns would have been much more widely dispersed and better camouflaged.

Driver luxury

The Hummel had a crew of five, including the driver who sat in an armoured position forward. The provision of an armoured compartment for the driver alone was considered a luxury in war-production terms, but instead of eliminating this feature the designers made the whole thing cheaper by enlarging the armoured position and employing more flat steel plates. Thus more internal space was provided for one of the crew members.

The Hummel could carry only 18 rounds of ammunition so more had to be kept nearby and brought up when necessary. Trucks were often of little value for this task, so by late 1944 no less than 150 Hummels were produced without the howitzer and the divided front armour plates replaced by a single plate. These vehicles were used as ammunition carriers for the Hummel batteries.

Ostkette

By late 1944 no less than 666 Hummels had been produced and the type remained in production until the end of the war. They proved to be useful and popular weapons, and were used on all fronts. Special versions with wider tracks known as Ostkette were produced for use during the winter months on the Eastern Front, and the open superstructures were often covered with canvas tarpaulins to keep out the worst of the weather. The gun crew generally lived with the vehicle, so many Hummels were festooned not only with camouflage of all kinds but also with bed rolls, cooking pots and items of personal kit.

The Hummel was one of the Germans' best examples of purpose-built self-propelled artillery. It had plenty of room for the crews to serve the gun, and the carriage gave the howitzer the desired mobility to keep up with the Panzer divisions.

SPECIFICATION	
Hummel	**Performance:** maximum road speed 42 km/h (26.1 mph); road range 215 km (134 miles)
Crew: 5	
Weight: 24000 kg (52,911 lb)	**Fording:** 0.99 m (3 ft 3 in)
Powerplant: one Maybach V-12 petrol engine developing 197.6 kW (265 hp)	**Armament:** one 15-cm (5.9-in) howitzer with 18 rounds of ready use ammunition and one 7.92-mm (0.31-in) machine gun
Dimensions: length 7.17 m (23 ft 6.3 in); width 2.87 m (9 ft 5 in); height 2.81 m (9 ft 2.6 in)	

Waffentrager Self-propelled howitzer carrier

The **Waffentrager** (literally 'weapons carrier') was a novel concept for the Germans when it was first mooted during 1942. The idea was that the Waffentrager was to be not so much a form of self-propelled artillery but a means of carrying an artillery piece in a turret into action, where it would be removed from the tank, emplaced, used in action, and picked up again when no longer required. The exact tactical requirement for this arrangement is still uncertain, for in 1942 the Panzer divisions were still dictating mobile warfare to all opponents and the need for a static artillery piece seems remote.

Conversions

Be that as it may, a series of eight vehicles known generally as **Heuschrecke IVB** (locust) were produced during 1942. These vehicles were converted PzKpfw IV tanks with a gantry at the rear to lift off the turret mounting a 10.5-cm (4.13-in) light field howitzer. The turret could be emplaced on the ground for action or it could be towed behind the vehicle on wheels carried on the rear specifically for this purpose; this arrangement allowed the vehicle to be used as an ammunition carrier for the turret.

The eight vehicles produced were no doubt used in action, for one of them was captured and is now in the Imperial War Museum in London, but at the time no more were requested.

German defensive

By 1944 things had changed somewhat. The German army was everywhere on the defensive and anything that could hold up the advancing Allies was investigated. The Waffentrager concept came within this category, and more designs were initiated. One was an interim design in which a normal field howitzer, a 10.5-cm leFH 18/40, was carried in an armoured super-structure on top of a modified Geschützwagen III/IV (normally used for the Hummel). The howitzer could be fired from the vehicle, but it was also designed to be removed from

This Heuschrecke prototype was one in which a 105-mm (4.13-in) field howitzer was carried on a chassis produced from PzKpfw III and IV components. The design called for the howitzer to be lowered to the ground when in a selected firing position.

the carrier using a block and tackle and mounted on the ground as a normal field piece once the wheels and carriage trails had been fitted. This design did not get far for it was overtaken by a series of design projects that were in turn overtaken by the end of the war.

These late-1944 and early-1945 Waffentrager all adopted the removable turret concept used in the 1942 Heuschrecke IVB. They had a variety of chassis, including both the modified PzKpfw IV and Geschützwagen III/IV. The artillery pieces involved ranged from 10.5-cm to 15-cm (5.9-in) howitzers. One that got as far

SPECIFICATION	
Heuschrecke NB	(9 ft 5 in); height 2.25 m (7 ft 4.6 in)
Crew: 5	
Weight: 17000 kg (37,479 lb)	**Performance:** maximum road speed 45 km/h (28 mph); road range 250 km (155 miles)
Powerplant: one Maybach petrol engine developing 140.2 kW (188 hp)	
Dimensions: length 5.9 m (19 ft 4.3 in); width 2.87 m	**Armament:** one 10.5-cm (4.13-in) howitzer

as model form was to have carried either the 10.5-cm or 15-cm howitzer on a cruciform carriage that would have been used with the '43' series of weapons had they ever advanced further than the prototype stage. These howitzers were mounted in an open-backed turret, and could be fired from the carrier or from a ground mounting. They could also be towed behind the carrier on their field carriages. It was all rather complicated and over-engineered as it involved the use of ramps and winches, and the concept was typical of many that never got to the hardware stage. But a few such equipments were built only to be overtaken by the end of the war, being scrapped in the immediate post-war years.

The Heuschrecke was one of a number of experimental German vehicles that were meant to carry an artillery piece to a firing site and then lower the piece to the ground for firing. The Heuschrecke was the only one of many similar designs to be produced.

Karl series Self-propelled siege howitzers

The weapons known as **Karl** were originally devised as anti-concrete weapons for the demolition of the Maginot Line forts and other such fortified locations. They were produced during the 1930s following a great deal of mathematical and other theoretical studies carried out during the 1920s. Work on the actual hardware began during 1937, and the first equipment was ready by 1939.

The Karl series must be regarded as being the largest self-propelled artillery weapons ever produced. There were two versions. One was the **60-cm Mörser Gerät 040** which mounted a 60-cm (23.62-in) barrel and the other the **54-cm Mörser Gerät 041** which mounted a 54-cm (21.26-in) barrel. Both weapons were also known as the **Thor** in service with the German army.

'Bunker-busters'

Both weapons fired special concrete-piercing projectiles. The range of the Gerät 040 was 4500 m (4,921 yards) and that of the Gerät 041 6240 m (6,824

yards). Both could penetrate between 2.5 and 3.5 m (8 ft 2.4 in and 11 ft 6 in) of concrete before detonating to produce maximum effect. These projectiles were massive items. The 60-cm shell weighed no less than 2170 kg (4,784 lb), although a lighter version was also used. The smaller-calibre 54-cm shell weighed 1250 kg (2,756 lb).

Both Karl weapons were huge, ponderous equipments. Although technically self-propelled, their mobility was limited by their sheer weight and bulk and the tracked carriages were meant for only the most local of moves. It is reported that the Karl was capable of creeping along at only 4.8 km/h (3 mph) on the 432.5 kW (580 hp) provided by their tracked carrier's diesel engines. For long-distance travel they were carried slung between special railway trucks. Shorter moves were made by removing the barrel from the carriage and placing both the barrel and the carriage on separate special trailers towed by heavy tractors.

Assembly and break-down was carried out using special mobile gantries. The whole process was difficult to an extreme, but the Karl weapons were not intended for mobile

The massive 60-cm and 54-cm Karl howitzers were really fortification-smashing equipments, and had only limited tactical mobility.

SPECIFICATION	
Gerät 041	m (36 ft 7 in); track 2.65 m (8 ft 8.3 in)
Crew: around 30	
Weight: 124000 kg (273,373 lb)	**Performance:** maximum speed around 4.8 km/h (3 mph)
Powerplant: one V-12 petrol engine developing 894.8 kW (1,200 hp)	
Dimensions: length of barrel 6.24 m (20 ft 6 in); length of carriage 11.15	**Armament:** one 54-cm (21.26-in) howitzer/mortar

The Karl howitzers had to be carried to the firing positions by special trailers and assembled on site. For this purpose, they were aided by the ammunition carrier version of the PzKpfw IV.

warfare. They were produced to reduce fortresses and that meant a long, planned approach to the firing site, a slow rate of fire (the best was one round every 10 minutes) and a steady withdrawal once the fortress had been reduced. A ground crew of

109 was needed to support the Karl howitzer in action, of which about 30 were needed for the support of the carriage.

Siege of Sevastopol
The Karls were too late for the Maginot Line, which fell along

with the rest of France in 1940. Their first real engagement was the siege of Sevastopol in exactly their designed role. Following the successful end of that siege more Karls were used during the Warsaw uprising when they were used to demolish the centre of Warsaw and crush the Polish underground fighters.

By then it was 1944. Most of the early 60-cm barrels had then

been replaced by 54-cm barrels, but Warsaw was their last period in action. The increasing mobile warfare of the last year of the war gave the Karls no chance to demonstrate their destructive powers, and most were destroyed by their crews in the last stages of the war. Only a few of the special PzKpfw IV ammunition carriers produced to carry projectiles for the Karls survived for Allied intelligence staffs to examine. It is possible that one example of the Karl may survive as a museum piece in Russia.

Brummbär Self-propelled heavy assault howitzer

Despite their overall success, the StuG III assault guns were considered by 1943 as being too lightly armoured for the assault role, and a new heavy assault vehicle was required. The existing 15-cm (5.9-in) sIG 33 self-propelled equipments lacked the armour protection required for the close-support role and so, with the PzKpfw IV tank gradually being replaced by the Panther and Tiger tanks, there was the chance to produce a purpose-built vehicle using the later versions of the PzKpfw IV as a basis.

The first examples of this new vehicle appeared during 1943 under the designation **Sturmpanzer IV Brummbär** (grizzly bear). The Brummbär used a box structure formed from sloping armour plates set over the front of a turretless PzKpfw IV, and mounted a

Most German self-propelled equipments carried only light armour, so when a call was made for a special close-support assault gun the result was the heavily armoured Brummbär.

specially developed howitzer in a ball mounting on the front plate. This howitzer was known as the Sturmhaubitze 43 and

was a shortened version, only 12 calibres long, of the 15-cm sIG 33. Armour was provided all round (the frontal armour being 100 mm/2.54 in thick), so the crew of five men were well protected. Later stand-off side armour was added, and most vehicles acquired a coating

of Zimmerit plaster paste to prevent magnetic charges being stuck on to the hull by close-in tank killer squads. A machine gun was mounted on the hull front plate on late production models, earlier versions having lacked this self-defence weapon.

SPECIFICATION	
Brummbär	2.52 m (8 ft 3 in)
Crew: 5	**Performance:** maximum road speed
Weight: 28200 kg (62,170 lb)	40 km/h (24.85 mph); maximum
Powerplant: one Maybach V-12	road range 210 km (130 miles)
petrol engine developing 197.6 kW	**Fording:** 0.99 m (3 ft 3 in)
(265 hp)	**Armament:** one 15-cm (5.9-in)
Dimensions: length 5.93 m (19 ft 5.5	howitzer and one or two 7.92-mm
in); width 2.88 m (9 ft 5 in); height	(0.3-in) machine guns

The Brummbär was normally used when close-in infantry tank-killer squads were likely to be encountered, and often in street fighting. It was therefore liberally covered with a plaster-like substance known as Zimmerit that prevented magnetic charges from sticking to the hull.

The roomy fighting compartment of the Brummbär could accommodate up to 38 rounds of 15-cm ammunition. The commander sat to the rear of the howitzer using a roof-mounted periscope to select targets. Two men served the gun and handled the ammunition, while another acted as the gun layer. The driver normally remained in his seat at the left front. Most targets were engaged with direct fire, but provision was made for indirect fire.

Production

About 313 Brummbär vehicles were produced before the war ended, and most appear to have been used in direct support of Panzergrenadier and infantry units. The vehicles moved forward with the first waves of attacking troops and provided fire to reduce strongpoints and smash bunkers. Infantry had to remain close to prevent enemy tank-killer squads from coming too close to the Brummbär vehicles, which were always vulnerable to close-range anti-tank weapons, especially as some of their side armour was as thin as 30 mm (1.18 in). Brummbär vehicles were generally used in ones and twos split up along an area of attack. As defensive weapons they were of less use, for the short howitzer had only a limited performance against armour as its prime mission was the delivery of blast effect HE projectiles. One factor that restricted the Brummbär's overall mobility was its weight, which gave the vehicle a rather poor ground-pressure 'footprint': it was fast enough on roads, but across country it could get bogged down in soft or muddy ground.

The Brummbär was a well-liked vehicle that often provided exactly the degree of fire support required by infantry. On the debit side it was heavy, rather ponderous and the early examples lacked close-in protection. But they were well protected against most weapons.

Sturmtiger Assault gun

Stalingrad taught the German army many lessons, not least of which was that the Germans were ill-equipped for the art of close-quarter street fighting. In typical fashion they decided to meet any future urban warfare requirements by a form of overkill by using a super-heavy weapon that would do away with the need for house-to-house fighting by simply blowing away any defended houses or structures. This they decided to do with a land version of a naval weapon, the depth charge.

In 1943 the Germans produced a version of the Tiger tank known by several names including **38-cm Sturmmörser**, **Sturmpanzer VI** and **Sturmtiger**. Whatever the designation, the weapon was a Tiger tank with the turret replaced by a large box-shaped superstructure with a short barrel poking through the front sloped plate. This barrel was not

Largest of all the German close-support weapons was the Sturmtiger, carrying a 38-cm (15-in) rocket projector that fired a form of naval depth charge to demolish buildings. They were designed for urban warfare. This example has been captured by American troops.

a gun but a 38-cm (15-in) Raketenwerfer 61 rocket projector of an unusual type, for it fired a rocket-propelled depth charge that weighed no less than 345 kg (761 lb). As this projectile was based upon the design of a naval depth charge nearly all the weight was high explosive; the effect of this upon even the stoutest structure can well be imagined. The rockets had a maximum range of 5650 m (6,180 yards), and the projector barrel was so arranged that the rocket efflux gases were diverted forward to vent from venturi around the muzzle ring. The Sturmtiger was very well armoured, with 150 mm (5.9 in) at its front and between 80 and 85 mm (3.15 and 3.35 in) at the side.

Crew

The Sturmtiger had a crew of seven including the commander, a fire observer and the driver carried within the large armoured superstructure. The other four men served the rocket projector. Because of their massive size, only 12 projectiles could be carried inside the superstructure, with the possibility of one more inside the projector. Loading the rockets into the vehicle was helped by a small crane jib mounted on the superstructure rear, and a small hatch nearby allowed access to the interior. Once inside overhead rails assisted in the movement of the rockets to and from their racks along each side, and loading into the projector was carried out using a loading tray.

Although the Sturmtiger prototype was ready by late 1943, it was not until August 1944 that production of this massive vehicle got under way. Only about 10 were ever produced, and these were used in ones and twos on most fronts but in situations where

their powerful armament was of little advantage. Consequently most were soon either knocked out in action or simply abandoned by their crews once their fuel allocation had been used.

In action

Used as they were in isolation and in such areas as the North Italian campaign, the hulks fascinated the Allies who encountered them and many detailed intelligence reports were written on them. Most

realised that the Sturmtiger was a highly specialised weapon that was simply pushed into the field during the latter stages of the war in the German effort to get any weapon into action. If the

Sturmtigers had been used as intended for street fighting, they would have been formidable weapons. Instead, by the time they were ready the time of concentrated urban warfare had passed.

SPECIFICATION	
Sturmtiger	height 2.85 m (9 ft 4 in)
Crew: 7	**Performance:** maximum road speed
Weight: 65000 kg (143,300 lb)	40 km/h (24.86 mph); road range
Powerplant: one Maybach V-12	120 km (75 miles)
petrol engine developing 484.7 kW	**Fording:** 1.22 m (4 ft)
(650 hp)	**Armament:** one 38-cm (15-in) rocket
Dimensions: length 6.28 m (20 ft	projector and one 7.92-mm (0.3-in)
7 in); width 3.57 m (11 ft 8 in);	machine gun

Sturmgeschütz III Assault gun

Following from its experiences in World War I, the German army saw the need for an armoured mobile gun that could follow infantry attacks and provide fire support and the firepower to knock out strongpoints and bunkers. During the late 1930s such a gun was developed using the chassis, suspension and running gear of the PzKpfw III tank. This armoured gun was known as the **Sturmgeschütz III** though its formal designation was **Gepanzerte Selbstfahrlafette für Sturmgeschütz 7.5-cm Kanone SdKfz 142**, and it had the usual upper hull and turret of the tank replaced by a thick carapace of armour with a short 75-mm (2.95-in) gun mounted in the front. This weapon was first issued for service in 1940 (**StuG III Ausf A**) and was soon followed by a whole series of vehicles that gradually incorporated overall and detail improvements, to the extent that when the war ended in 1945 many were still in service on all fronts. The 1941 models

were the **StuG III Ausf B**, **C** and **D**, while the slightly improved **StuG III Ausf E** appeared in 1942.

Upgunned models

The main change to the StuG III series was a gradual programme of upgunning. The original short 75-mm gun was an L/24 weapon (i.e. the length

of the barrel was 24 times the calibre) and had limitations against many targets except at short ranges. Thus it was replaced by longer guns with improved performance, first an L/43 (**StuG III Ausf F**) and then an L/48 gun (**StuG III Ausf G**). The latter gun also provided the StuG III series with an anti-tank capability, and this was in a way to the detriment of the original assault support concept, for it was far easier to produce a StuG than it was a tank, so many StuG IIIs with L/48 guns were diverted to the Panzer divisions in place of battle tanks. Used as a tank-killer the StuG III had its moments, but it lacked traverse and adequate

Two StuG IIIs move forward in the Soviet Union in 1944. They are armed with 75-mm (2.95-in) anti-tank guns and are carrying extra lengths of track links for added protection. More protection comes from the stand-off side plates known as 'Schützen' carried to defeat close-range hollow-charge anti-tank warheads.

protection for the task. It had to be retained as such, however, for German industry simply could not supply enough tanks for the Panzer divisions.

As an assault gun the StuG III series was far more successful. Eventually the type was upgunned to the stage late in

A StuG is seen on the Eastern Front against a distant target. In order to better observe the fire, one of the gun crew is using the hull roof for observation. The vehicle is equipped with 'Ostkette' tracks for use on snow and soft ground.

75-mm gun
Initially fitted with a short 75-mm gun, the F model shown here was introduced in 1942 and carried a long 75-mm weapon, significantly improving anti-tank capability.

Tank destroyer
The G model with its 75-mm L/48, heavier armour and smoke dischargers, was designed more as a tank destroyer than a self-propelled gun. By contrast, as early as 1941 variants were in production mounting a 105-mm (4.1-in) howitzer.

The Sturmgeschütz Sdkfz 142 was based on the chassis of the PzKpfw III with the gun mounted in the hull. The driver's station was unaltered from the tank, but behind was now a large but cramped fighting compartment. Absent from this vehicle, armoured skirts were fitted as standard from 1943.

the war when many StuG IIIs were armed with the powerful 10.5-cm (4.13-in) Sturmhaubitze, a special assault howitzer produced for the **StuG III für 10.5-cm StuH 42**. The first of these was completed in 1943, but manufacture of this variant was initially slow. Instead the version with the 75-mm L/48 gun was rushed off the production lines for the Panzer divisions.

The StuG III had a crew of four and extra machine guns were often carried behind a shield on the roof. The protective mantlet for the main gun underwent many changes before it ended up as a *Saukopf* ('pig's head') mantlet which proved very good protection. More protection against short-range hollow-charge warheads was provided with the addition of Schützen ('skirts') along both sides. These were simply sheets of stand-off armour

to detonate the warheads before they hit the vehicle armour, and were used on many

German tanks after 1943.

As a close-range assault support weapon the StuG III series was an excellent vehicle/weapon combination. It was relatively cheap and easy to produce, and in wartime Germany that mattered a lot. Therefore the series was built in some numbers and numerically it was one of the most important German armoured vehicles.

A StuG III Ausf F, with a PzKfw I mounting a 4.7-cm (1.85-in) gun approaching (centre background). The divisional emblem identifies the StuG as belonging to the elite SS Adolf Hitler Division.

SPECIFICATION	
StuG III Ausf E	height 2.16 m (7 ft 1 in)
Crew: 4	**Performance:** maximum speed
Weight: 23900 kg (52,690 lb)	40 km/h (24.9 mph); road range
Powerplant: one Maybach V-12	165 km (102 miles)
petrol engine developing 197.6 kW	**Fording:** 0.8 m (2 ft 7.5 in)
(265 hp)	**Armament:** one 75-mm (2.95-in) gun
Dimensions: length 6.77 m (22 ft	and two 7.92-mm (0.3-in) MG34 or
2.5 in); width 2.95 m (9 ft 8 in);	MG42 machine guns

StuG III in combat

Moving into action in a StuG III cannot have been a very pleasant experience. Like those of most armoured vehicles, the interior of the StuG III was cramped and uncomfortable. Much of the interior of the main fighting compartment was taken up by the breech of the 7.5-cm gun. Ammunition racks lined the lower portion of the white-

Designed to meet a 1936 Wehrmacht requirement for an armoured close support vehicle, the StuG III was introduced in 1940 and fought in all theatres until 1945, both in an artillery and tank destroyer role.

painted walls, while radios and other black boxes occupied what was left of the bulkhead space. The driver sat in his own position to the left front, most of the time peering through his armoured vision slits and trying to make out where he was going. Generally the driver was guided by orders from the commander, who sat under his cupola behind the driver. When possible the commander kept his hatch open and raised his head for better vision, but in action and closed down he could often see little more than the driver. The loader sometimes aimed and fired the 7.92-mm (0.31-in) machine gun by controls from within the vehicle. When occasion allowed this was usually used from behind a shield on the roof. To the right of the commander sat the loader, who had his own overhead hatch that was seldom used in action; he also had a small hatch in the rear wall through which spent cases were despatched. Just in front of the commander and almost in his lap sat the gun layer with his gun controls. His outlook was limited to what he could see through his sighting devices: a small panoramic telescope was set in the roof for laying indirect fire and a telescope was placed in front for direct aiming. Given the noise of the engine, the constant jolting from the suspension, and the fumes and smells of the gun and fuel, life for the StuG crews must have been very unpleasant. But they could take heart that they at least had more armour around them than most of their tankborne colleagues, and that many tank interiors were even more cramped than that of the StuG III.

StuG crews were considered the elite of the artillery units and were issued special field grey uniforms. StuG IIIs had accounted for an impressive 20,000 enemy tanks by spring 1944.

SU-76 76.2-mm self-propelled gun

The Soviet SU-76 was a wartime and rather rushed conversion of the T-70 light tank to carry a 76.2-mm (3-in) field gun, and although it was produced in large numbers it was little liked by its crews, who called it the 'Bitch'.

During the desperate days of 1941 the Red Army lost so much materiel that Soviet planners were forced to list mass production as their top priority, and in order to cut down the numbers of different equipments being produced only a few types were selected for future use. One of these types was the superlative ZIS-3 76.2-mm (3-in) gun, which was not only an excellent field piece but for that period also a good anti-tank gun. Thus when it was decided to adopt the ZIS-3 in quantity the Red Army had a very good weapon for the future, especially when the chance arose to make the weapon a self-propelled one.

The events of 1941 had shown the Red Army that its light tanks were virtually useless and the type was scheduled for withdrawal from production and service. A production line was available for the T-70 light tank, however, and it was decided to convert the T-70 to take the ZIS-76 gun as a highly mobile anti-tank weapon. Thus was born the **SU-76** (SU for *Samokhodnaya Ustanovka*, or self-propelled mounting). The conversion to take the 76.2-mm gun and 62 rounds of ammunition was a simple one, but the T-70 chassis had to be widened somewhat and an extra road wheel was added to take the additional weight. The first

examples had the gun mounted centrally, but later models had the gun offset to the left. Maximum armour thickness was 25 mm (0.98 in).

Fire-support role

It was late 1942 before the first SU-76s were produced, and it was mid-1943 before they had entered Red Army service in any appreciable numbers. By that time the ZIS-3 gun had lost much of its edge against the ever-thickening German tank armour, and thus the SU-76 was gradually phased over to the direct fire-support of Red Army infantry formations. Some anti-tank capability was retained when new anti-armour ammunition was introduced, but by the end of the war the SU-76 was being phased out in favour of vehicles with larger-calibre guns. By June 1945, over 14,000 SU-76s had been constructed, at Factory 30 in Kirov; Factory 40 in Mytischchi and the GAZ Factory in Gorkii. Once the guns had entered service in the summer of 1943, they were initially sent to mixed self-propelled artillery regiments, with each unit having 21 vehicles, which included four batteries of five vehicles and a

commander's vehicle, although after a while it was realised that the gun was better suited to the close support of the infantry. To this end, by 1944 many guns were allotted to light self-propelled artillery batteries of 16 vehicles each which would operate with the regular infantry divisions.

Many SU-76s were pressed into other roles by 1945. The usual process was to remove the gun and use the vehicle as a supply and ammunition carrier, as an artillery tractor and as a light armoured recovery vehicle. Some were fitted with anti-aircraft cannon.

The 'Bitch'

After 1945 there were still many SU-76s to hand, and the Soviets handed them on to many friendly nations including China and North Korea with whom the type saw another bout of action during the Korean War that started in 1950. More went to some of the Warsaw Pact armed forces. It is doubtful that the new recipients welcomed

Red Army soldiers attack under the close supporting fire of SU-76 76.2-mm guns, providing a graphic example of what close-range artillery support really means. By 1945 the SU-76 was used almost exclusively in this role after being used at one point as a mobile field artillery piece.

the SU-76 for it was very much a wartime expedient vehicle with no crew comforts whatsoever. Apart from a few examples that had an armoured roof, the crew compartment of the SU-76 was open to the elements and the driver had to sit next to the twin engines with no intervening bulkhead. The Red Army referred to the SU-76 as the *Sukarni* (Bitch).

Thus the SU-76 started life as a mobile anti-tank weapon and ended up as an artillery support weapon. It was no doubt a very useful weapon in the latter role, but essentially it was a hasty expedient rushed into production at a time of desperate need.

SPECIFICATION	
SU-76	in); height 2.17 m (7 ft 1.4 in)
Crew: 4	**Performance:** maximum road speed
Weight: 10800 kg (23,810 kg)	45 km/h (28 mph); road range 450
Powerplant: two GAZ 6-cylinder	km (280 miles)
petrol engines each developing	**Fording:** 0.89 m (2 ft 11 in)
52.2 kW (70 hp)	**Armament:** one 76.2-mm (3-in) gun
Dimensions: length 4.88 m	and one 7.62-mm (0.3-in) machine
(16 ft 0.1 in); width 2.8m (8 ft 11.5	gun

ISU-122 and ISU-152 122-mm and 152-mm self-propelled guns

The first of the heavy Soviet self-propelled artillery carriages was the SU-152, which first appeared in 1943, just in time to take part in the tank battles at Kursk. It was built onto a KV-2 heavy tank chassis and was typical of later World War II designs in that the tank chassis was taken virtually unchanged and a large armoured box was built on to the front of the hull. The weapon was a 152-mm (6-in) M-1937 howitzer mounted in a large and heavy mantlet on the front superstructure plate and there were roof hatches, one of which had provision for mounting an anti-aircraft machine gun.

This first vehicle was intended for use as much as an anti-armour weapon as a heavy assault weapon, for the Red Army made no differentiation between anti-tank and other weapons when it came to tactics. The SU-152 relied upon sheer projectile weight and kinetic power to defeat enemy armour.

When the KV tank series was replaced in production by the IS series, these too were used for

the SU self-propelled role. The conversion closely followed that of the original SU-152, and the IS-based conversion was known as the **ISU-152**. To the average observer the SU-152 and ISU-152 were visually identical but the ISU-152 mounted a more modern howitzer, known as the ML-20S (with 20 rounds), technically a gun/howitzer and a very powerful weapon, especially at the assault ranges favoured by Red Army tactics. The weapon was protected by an armoured box made up from sloping plates of thick armour, with hand rails around the edge of the roof for use by 'tank descent' infantry who used the vehicles to carry them into action. Maximum armour thickness was 75 mm (2.95 in).

The ISU-152 was joined by the **ISU-122**, a virtually identical vehicle carrying a powerful 122-mm (4.8-in) gun known as the M-1931/4 or A-19S (with 30 rounds), the ordnance being a modification of the then-standard 122-mm M-1931/37, though there was also another gun known as the D-25S which was ballistically identical to

The ISU-152 was a straight-forward conversion of an IS series heavy tank to carry a 152-mm (6-in) howitzer as a powerful close-support artillery weapon; it was also a powerful tank killer. The howitzer was housed in a thick superstructure with dense frontal armour.

the A-19S but differed in the way it was constructed. Numerically the ISU-122 was less important than the ISU-152, but the 122-mm version was potentially the more powerful weapon as it fired a higher-velocity projectile than the heavier 152-mm weapon, which relied more upon shell weight for its destructive effects.

Battle for Berlin
During 1944 and 1945 the ISU-152 and ISU-122 were in the vanguard of the Red Army advances through Germany towards Berlin. Some of the first Red Army units entering Berlin were ISU-152 units, which used their howitzers to blast away strongpoints at close ranges and clear the way to the remains of the city centre.

If the ISU weapons had a fault it was that they lacked internal

ammunition stowage space. Thus they had to have a virtual constant supply of ammunition brought forward by armoured carriers, which was often a hazardous undertaking. But the massive weapons carried by the ISU vehicles were considered to be of great value in the direct support of Red Army tank and motorised infantry divisions.

Mass production of the ISU-152 continued until 1955 by which time 2,450 vehicles had been built, in addition to the 4,075 vehicles produced during the war. Production of the ISU-122 had been terminated at the end of the war, although it was restarted in 1947.

The IS chassis was later utilised for carriage of the R-11 (SS-1b 'Scud-A') ballistic missile, although these launchers were later replaced by the more familiar MAZ wheeled launchers.

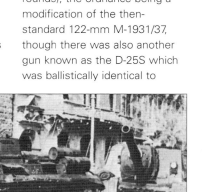

Above: ISU-152s were still in front-line service in 1956 when the Red Army ruthlessly crushed the Hungarian uprising. In the streets of Budapest the lack of traverse proved a serious disadvantage. The gun mechanism was never modernised; elevation and loading was done by hand.

SPECIFICATION	
ISU-122	height 2.52 m (8 ft 3.2 in)
Crew: 5	**Performance:** maximum road speed
Weight: 46430 kg (102,361 lb)	37 km/h (23 mph); road range 180
Powerplant: one V-12 diesel	km (112 miles)
developing 387.8 kW (520 hp)	**Fording:** 1.3 m (4 ft 3.2 in)
Dimensions: length overall 9.8 m	**Armament:** one 122-mm (4.8-in) gun
(32 ft 1.8 in) and hull 6.805 m (22 ft	and one 12.7-mm (0.5-in)
3.9 in); width 3.56 m (11 ft 8.2 in);	anti-aircraft machine gun

The ISU-122 was a conversion of the IS tank to accommodate a front-mounted 122-mm (4.8-in) howitzer in a well-armoured and well-sloped superstructure. It was produced in large numbers for the close-support role, but could also be used for stand-off artillery fire.

Sexton Self-propelled gun-howitzer

The Sexton mounted the British 25-pdr gun and was a well-liked and reliable vehicle that served on for many years after World War II with many armies. It was still used by India into the 1980s.

During early 1941 the British Purchasing Commission in Washington asked the Americans if the M7 Priest could be altered to allow it to carry the British 25-pdr gun-howitzer. While the British appreciated the amenities of the M7 Priest, it had the major disadvantage of mounting a 105-mm (4.13-in) howitzer that was not a standard British weapon calibre at that time. The Americans accordingly produced the M7 with the 25-pdr and named it the T51, but at the same time announced that there was no way that they could produce it in quantity as they had their production hands full already. The British accordingly looked around and noted that the Canadians had set up a production line for the Ram tank, a type that was soon to be replaced by the American M3 and M4. The Ram was accordingly altered to accommodate the 25-pdr, and thus was born the **Sexton**.

The Sexton used the overall layout of the M7 Priest, but many changes were introduced to suit British requirements. These included the movement of the driver's position to the right-hand side. The Sexton lacked the pronounced 'pulpit' of the M7, but the fighting compartment was left open with only a canvas cover to provide weather protection for the crew. The Sexton had a crew of six and much of the interior was taken up with lockers for ammunition and some of the crew's personal kit; more stowage was provided in boxes at the rear. Maximum armour thickness was 32 mm (1.25 in).

Anti-tank capability

The 25-pdr gun-howitzer was carried in a special cradle produced by the Canadians specifically for the Sexton. This allowed a traverse of 25° left and 40° right, which was very useful for the anti-tank role (18 AP rounds) but in the event the Sexton had little need of this facility. Instead it was used almost exclusively as a field artillery weapon (87 HE and smoke rounds) supporting the armoured divisions in north-west Europe from 1944 onwards. There were several variations, all of them incorporating the production changes progressively introduced on the lines of the Montreal Locomotive Works at Sorel. Production continued there until late 1945, by which time 2,150 Sextons had been manufactured.

The Sexton was a well-liked and reliable gun and weapon combination that proved so successful that many remained in use in odd corners of the world for many years after the war. One example is preserved as a museum piece at the Royal School of Artillery at Larkhill, Wiltshire.

There were a few in-service variants of the Sexton, some being converted to 'swim' for possible use on D-Day, but none appear to have been used in this role on the day. A more common conversion was the replacement of the gun-howitzer by extra map tables and radios in the **Sexton Gun Position Officer** command vehicle; there was usually one of these to a battery. In post-war years some Sextons were handed over to nations such as Italy.

Above: The British Army used the Sexton until the late 1950s, an example seen here taking part in early combined operations with a Hoverfly Mk II helicopter.

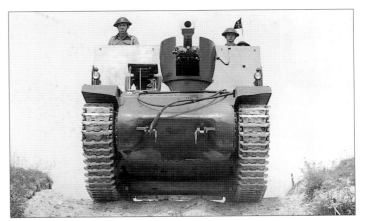

Operated by a crew of six (commander, driver, gunner, gun layer, loader and radio operator), the Sexton self-propelled gun-howitzer was used almost exclusively for artillery support of armoured divisions.

SPECIFICATION	
Sexton	**Performance:** maximum road speed
Crew: 6	40.2 km/h (25 mph); road range
Weight: 25855 kg (57,000 lb)	290 km (180 miles)
Powerplant: one Continental	**Fording:** 1.01 m (3 ft 4 in)
9-cylinder radial piston engine	**Armament:** one 25-pdr gun-howitzer,
developing 298.3 kW (400 hp)	two unmounted 0.303-in (7.7-mm)
Dimensions: length 6.12 m (20 ft 1	Bren Guns and (on some vehicles)
in); width 2.72 m (8 ft 11 in); height	one pintle-mounted 0.5-in
2.44 m (8 ft)	(12.7-mm) Browning machine gun

Bishop Self-propelled gun-howitzer

The vehicle that became known as the **Bishop** was conceived at a time when 25-pdr batteries in the North African desert were perforce used as anti-tank weapons and were taking a terrible pounding as a result. It was decided to place the 25-pdr on a mobile carriage to increase protection for the gun crews, and it was soon clear that the Valentine infantry tank would make a good basis for such a conversion. Unfortunately the exact role of this gun/tank combination was uncertain from the start. The tank exponents saw it as a variant of the heavy-gun tank theme, while the gunners wanted a self-propelled carriage. These arguments were never really solved, and the result was something of a compromise even though the gunners won in the end.

Valentine conversion

The Valentine 25-pdr emerged as a straightforward conversion (officially the **Mounting, Valentine, 25-pdr Gun Mk I on Carrier, Valentine, 25-pdr Gun, Mk I**), the usual turret being replaced by a much larger turret mounting the 25-pdr. This new turret was fixed, and was a large slab-sided design too large for battlefield concealment and too small to allow much room inside for the gun crew. The turret design also had one major disadvantage for the gunners in that it restricted the elevation of the barrel and thus curtailed range to only 5852 m (6,400 yards) which was a considerable reduction from the normal 12253 m (13,400 yards). The only way to increase this performance was the tedious and tactically-hampering construction of earth

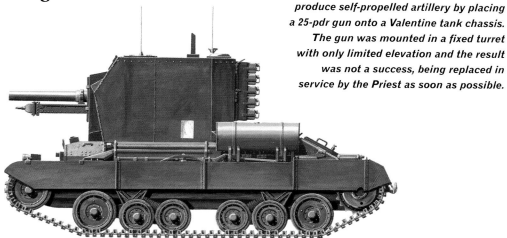

The Bishop was an early British attempt to produce self-propelled artillery by placing a 25-pdr gun onto a Valentine tank chassis. The gun was mounted in a fixed turret with only limited elevation and the result was not a success, being replaced in service by the Priest as soon as possible.

ramps up which the vehicle could be driven to increase the elevation angle. Traverse was also severely restricted, to a maximum of 4° to each side. Internal ammunition stowage was 32 rounds but more could be carried in a limber towed behind the vehicle. Armour varied in thickness from 8 mm (0.315 in) to 60 mm (2.36 in).

The 25-pdr Valentine went into action in North Africa during the latter stages of the campaign in that theatre, by which time the 25-pdr was no longer in use as an anti-tank gun, so the vehicles were used as self-propelled artillery with no distraction and the Royal Artillery learned a lot from their use. The type was eventually named Bishop, and it went on to be used in Sicily and the Italian mainland during the opening stages of these campaigns.

Throughout these campaigns the Bishop demonstrated all its several drawbacks, but also provided an indication of the potential of self-propelled artillery for it was the first British self-propelled weapon to see active service. The need for supporting logistics was more than emphasised, as was the

A Bishop in action near Naples during the later stages of its operational career. The gun number is passing ammunition to the gun turret after taking it from the ammunition limbers, one of which can be seen in the foreground and was normally towed behind the vehicle.

need for improved radio links with forward observers.

The Bishop also demonstrated things to avoid in future designs. The most obvious one was for the gun to have its full range of movement if it was to be of any use; additionally, more room was needed to serve the gun, for the turret of the Bishop was

cramped and ill-ventilated. More internal ammunition stowage was needed and the carrier had to be fast enough to keep up with tanks. Being an infantry tank, the Valentine chassis was too slow to keep up with armoured formations.

All these things were put right when the gunners were issued numbers of M7 Priests. The gunners took to the Priest with a will, and before long the Bishops had been discarded. They may have been less than perfect, but the Bishop has the distinction of being the British Army's first self-propelled artillery piece.

A Bishop on the ranges with the gun detachment commander outside the fixed turret, as there was room for only two gunners inside. The fixed turret restricted the barrel elevation and thus range.

SPECIFICATION	
Bishop	3.05 m (10 ft)
Crew: 4	**Performance:** maximum road speed
Weight: 7911 kg (17,440 lb)	24 km/h (15 mph); road range 177
Powerplant: one AEC 6-cylinder	km (110 miles)
diesel developing 97.7 kW (131 hp)	**Fording:** 0.91 m (3 ft)
Dimensions: length 5.64 m (18 ft 6	**Armament:** one 25-pdr
in); width 2.77 m (9 ft 1 in); height	(87.6-mm/3.45-in) gun-howitzer

M7 Priest 105-mm self-propelled howitzer

Experience gained with 105-mm (4.13-in) howitzers mounted on halftracks enabled the US Army to decide that it would be better if the howitzer was mounted in a fully tracked carriage, and accordingly an M3 medium tank chassis was modified to take such a weapon. The M3 chassis was considerably reworked to provide an open-topped superstructure with the howitzer mounted in its front. The development vehicle was known as the **T32**, and following trials which added a machine gun mounting to the right-hand side, the vehicle was adopted for service as the **Carriage, Motor, 105-mm Howitzer, M7**. The maximum armour thickness was 25.4 mm (1 in).

The British gunners nicknamed the American M7 the 'Priest' after seeing the pulpit that housed the 0.5-in (12.7-mm) machine gun for anti-aircraft and local defence.

Priest in action

The first production examples were for the US Army, but many were soon diverted to the Lend-Lease programme for the Allies, among them the British Army. The British soon named the M7 the **Priest**, a popular myth being that the prominent machine gun mounting gave the impression of a pulpit. The British gunners adopted the M7 with enthusiasm, and the type first went into action with them at the Second Battle of El Alamein in October 1942. The British asked for 5,500 M7s to be produced for their use alone by the end of 1943, but this order was never completed in full. The figure nonetheless provides an indication of the success of the M7 with the British gunners. They appreciated the space and mobility of the carriage and also the extra space for personal stowage. The one snag was that the howitzer was not a standard British Army type: thus ammunition (stowage was provided for 69 rounds on each vehicle) had to be supplied separately for the M7 batteries, which made for a considerable logistic complication. This was not resolved until the first

Left: The M7's weight of 22967 kg (50,634 lb) caused some difficulties for the mobility of the vehicle, and hampered wartime operations in mountainous areas.

Above: An M7 tank destroyer is seen here with US Army markings, although many of the vehicles were supplied to the UK under the Lend-Lease agreement.

Left: An M7 in action in the Ardennes in 1945, with the open fighting compartment covered by a tarpaulin to keep out the worst of the bitter weather. The tank obstacles behind the M7 were taken with ease.

SPECIFICATION	
M7	developing 279.6 kW (375 hp)
Crew: 5	**Performance:** maximum road speed
Weight: 22967 kg (50,634 lb)	41.8 km/h (26 mph); maximum
Dimensions: length 6.02 m (19 ft 9	range 201 km (125 miles)
in); width 2.88 m (9 ft 5.4 in);	**Fording:** 1.22 m (4 ft)
height 2.54 m (8 ft 4 in)	**Armament:** one 105-mm (4.13-in)
Powerplant: one Continental R-975	M2 howitzer and one 0.5-in
air-cooled 9-cylinder radial engine	(12.7-mm) M2 machine gun

Sextons with 25-pdr weapons were issued in 1944. The British M7s were used all through the Italian campaign, and some were landed in Normandy in June 1944, though they were soon replaced by the Sexton equipments.

The M7 then began a new service career in a revised form: the howitzer was removed and the hull was used as an armoured personnel carrier nicknamed the **Kangaroo**. This soon became a normal fate for unwanted M7s, and the idea soon spread to Italy.

American service

The US Army also made wide use of the M7, although production for the US Army was not a constant process. After 1942 M7 production proceeded in fits and starts. At one stage the original M3 chassis was replaced by the later M4A3 Sherman chassis, and such M7s were known by the designation **M7B1**. After 1945 large numbers of M7s were handed over to other countries such as Brazil and Turkey. The M7 was also used during the Korean War. The 105-mm howitzer is still a standard weapon worldwide. Throughout their service life the M7s gave outstanding reliability, and demonstrated their ability to cross rough terrain, although performance in mountainous areas was disappointing.

Carriage, Motor, 155-mm Gun, M40 Self-propelled gun

Although the M40 arrived on the scene late in World War II, it was one of the best of all wartime self-propelled guns and went on to enjoy a long post-war career. It used the chassis of the M4 tank as its basis.

The first 155-mm (6.1-in) self-propelled gun produced in quantity by the Americans during World War II was the **M12**, a design originally known as the **T6** and built on a converted M3 medium tank chassis. Starting in December 1943 a new weapon/carriage combination was initiated. The gun was the 155-mm M1A1 known as the 'Long Tom' (with 20 rounds) and the carriage was based on the chassis of the M4A3 medium tank, though much widened and fitted with new suspension springing. The engine was moved from the rear to a new forward position, and a spade which could be lifted for travel was added to absorb some of the recoil. A working platform under the breech was also provided. The gun had a range of 23514 m (25,715 yards) and fired a projectile weighing 43.1 kg (95 lb), which made it a useful counter-battery and

The M40's driver sat at the front of the vehicle with the engine behind him. Two roof hatches were fitted for access to the front of the vehicle.

The M40 was unusual by today's standards in having an open fighting compartment. This was rendered useless by the advent of nuclear weapons.

long-range bombardment weapon. Armour thickness was 12.7 mm (0.5 in).

The development of this **Carriage, Motor, 155-mm Gun, M40** took rather longer than expected, so it was not until January 1945 that the first production examples rolled off the lines. They were rushed across the Atlantic in time to see the end of the war in Germany.

M40s took part in the bombardment of Cologne and the short campaigning after this. Between January and May 1945 no less than 311 M40s were built, and production continued after the war. The M40 then saw service during the Korean conflict.

On the M40 there was no protection for the crew as the equipment was intended for use so far behind the front

When the M40's 155-mm gun was being fired, the members of the gun's crew stood on a hinged platform over the spades at the rear of the vehicle.

line that none would be necessary. The M40 had a crew of eight and there was provision on the carriage for their weapons and kit. The same carriage was also used to mount an 8-in (203-mm) howitzer, but this version (the **Carriage, Motor, 8-in Howitzer,**

M43) was not used in great numbers; only 48 were built. After 1945 M40s were distributed to other armies. The British Army used the type for some years. More were used by nations such as France, where the type saw extensive service in Indo-China. There

was one variant, the **Cargo Carrier T30**, which could be used as a supply carrier though its normal deployment was for the delivery of ammunition to M40 batteries.

The M40 was significant in that it paved the way for the generation of self-propelled weapons that saw service into the 1990s. The M40 proved that the only proper protection comes from an armoured turret, and modern self-propelled weapons now use this design feature.

SPECIFICATION	
M40	air-cooled radial engine developing
Crew: 8	294.6 kW (395 hp)
Weight: 37195 kg (82,000 lb)	**Performance:** maximum road speed
Dimensions: length overall 9.04 m (29	38.6 km/h (24 mph); maximum
ft 8 in); width 3.15 m (10 ft 4 in);	range 161 km (100 miles)
height 2.84 m (9 ft 4 in)	**Fording:** 1.07 m (3 ft 6 in)
Powerplant: one Continental R-975	**Armament:** one 155-mm (6.1-in) gun

Ordnance, Q.F., 2 pdr

40-mm static anti-tank gun

The **2-pdr** anti-tank gun (or more formally the **Ordnance, Q.F., 2 pdr**) is one of those unfortunate weapons that has been given a bad reputation for no real reason other than it had to be used at a time when it was no longer a viable weapon. In its day it was as good as any contemporary design, but the increases in tank armour thicknesses during the late 1930s rendered it obsolete just at a time when it was being placed into widespread service.

The 2-pdr had its origins in a British staff requirement dated

2-pdr gun crews undergo training during a chemical warfare exercise. The gun in the foreground shows the ammunition box carried on each weapon.

1934. Much of the original development was carried out by Vickers-Armstrongs, and the first guns and carriages were produced for commercial sales. Some went to Spain, but the main recipient was the British Army which received its first examples during 1938. Further development was required until the full Army specification could be met and it was not until 1939 that the most commonly encountered carriage (the **Carriage, 2 pdr, Mk III**) was issued.

Compared with many other designs then in existence, the 2-pdr was a complex piece of ordnance and it was almost twice as heavy as any other gun in its class. The main reason for this weight was the carriage which, in action, rested on a low tripod carriage that provided the gun with 360° traverse. A high shield was provided for the gun crew and there was provision for an ammunition chest to be carried on the back of the gun shield. The philosophy behind the design differed from contemporary thought as well.

A drill-book photograph of a 2-pdr gun and crew in action with the gun about to be loaded. Note that the ammunition is being passed from a box to the rear as the box on the gun shield was for emergencies only.

Many European armies intended the anti-tank gun to be used in a mobile attacking role, but the 2-pdr was intended for use in static defensive positions. The type was also manned by specialist anti-tank personnel from the Royal Artillery.

Shortcomings

The events of 1940 showed the 2-pdr to be at best obsolescent, and the BEF had to leave the bulk of its 2-pdr guns behind at Dunkirk. The gun lacked the power to punch through the thick armour of most of the German tanks, and the effective range was too short for tactical comfort; the projectiles were too light to cause damage at ranges outside the machine gun range of the target tanks, and many gun crews were thus decimated before they could fire a useful shot. In the United Kingdom, however, the production facilities to produce any modern form of anti-tank gun for the Army that was almost devoid of any form of defence against tanks was quite simply not available. Industry had therefore to carry on producing the 2-pdr at a time when it was

realised that it was no longer an effective weapon. The results of this had to be borne during the North African campaigns of 1941–42, when the 2-pdr proved to be almost useless against the Afrika Korps, to the extent that the 25-pdr field piece had to be used for anti-tank work in its place.

All manner of remedies to make the 2-pdr more successful were tried, one measure being the placement of the gun on the back of an open truck to provide a mobile platform, and another the development of the Littlejohn Adaptor, a squeeze-bore device attached to the muzzle and firing special skirted projectiles to improve projectile performance.

Neither of these measures saw much use, however, and after 1942 the 2-pdr was withdrawn from use and passed to infantry units for their anti-tank defences. The type did not remain in use for long in that role, but in the Far East the 2-pdr remained in service until 1945, for there the target tanks were generally lighter and the gun could still cope with them.

SPECIFICATION	
Ordnance, Q.F., 2 pdr	**Elevation:** -13° to +15°
Calibre: 40 mm (1.575 in)	**Muzzle velocity:** AP 792 m (2,626 ft) per second
Length of piece: 2.082 m (6 ft 10 in)	
Length of rifling: 1.672 m (5 ft 5.84 in)	**Maximum effective range:** 548 m (600 yards)
Weight: complete 831.6 kg (1,848 lb)	**Projectile weight:** 1.08 kg (2.375 lb)
Traverse: 360°	**Armour penetration:** 53 mm (2.08 in) at 455 m (500 yards)

A 2-pdr ready to be towed, usually by a small truck or Jeep. The 2-pdr was a rather complex weapon with a tripod carriage and was too heavy for its tactical role when compared with other designs of the time. By 1941 it was rendered almost useless by increases in enemy tank armour, but was passed to infantry units for their anti-tank defences, and was used in the Far East. Later marks were able to remove the road wheels to aid concealment.

Ordnance, Q.F., 6 pdr 57-mm anti-tank gun

British weapon planners had foreseen the need for an anti-tank gun more powerful than the 2-pdr as early as April 1938, but it took time to develop and then to produce the new gun. During late 1940 production was delayed as 2-pdr guns occupied the production lines, so that it was not until late 1941 that the new gun reached the troops. This new weapon had a calibre of 57 mm (2.244 in) and fired a projectile weighing about 6 lb (2.72 kg) so the new gun was known as the **6-pdr**.

By the time the 6-pdr reached the troops it was sorely needed, and once in action it proved to be effective against the enemy tanks then in use. Compared with the 2-pdr, the 6-pdr was much more conventional and used a split-trail carriage that gave a useful 90° traverse. There were two main variants, the **Ordnance, Q.F., 6 pdr Mk II** and **Ordnance, Q.F., 6 pdr Mk IV**; the **Ordnance, Q.F., 6 pdr Mk I** was used for training only, and the Mks III and V were tank guns. The main difference

between the Mks II and IV was barrel length, that of the Mk IV being slightly longer. Some slight carriage variations were produced but the most drastic was the **Carriage, Q.F., 6 pdr, Mk III**, which was developed for use by airborne units. This was narrower than the norm and the trail legs could be shortened for stowage in gliders; a number of these special conversions were used at Arnhem.

The 6-pdr provided some sterling service in North Africa, but once the Tiger tank appeared on the scene it was realised that the day of the 6-pdr was almost over, for the 2.85-kg (6.28-lb) projectile was unable to penetrate the thick frontal armour of the Tiger and only a lucky shot to the side could be effective. As a result, the 6-pdr was gradually withdrawn from Royal Artillery use from 1943 onwards. They were issued instead to infantry anti-tank companies and with the infantry the 6-pdr saw out the war. Many were supplied to units in the Red Army.

31 May 1942, and a truck-mounted 6-pdr goes into action near Tobruk. Within a month Rommel would have taken the town, and at the same time forced the 8th Army back towards Mersa Matruh and El Alamein.

SPECIFICATION	
Ordnance, Q.F., 6 pdr, Mk IV	**Traverse:** 90°
Calibre: 57 mm (2.244 in)	**Elevation:** -5° to +15°
Length of piece: 2.565 m (6 ft 8.95 in)	**Muzzle velocity:** 900 m (2,700 ft) per second
Length of rifling: 2.392 m (7 ft 10.18 in)	**Projectile weight:** 2.85 kg (6.28 lb)
Weight: complete 1112 kg (2,471 lb)	**Armour penetration:** 68.6 mm (2.7 in) at 915 m (1,000 yards)

The Soviets were not the only recipients of the 6-pdr, for the type was adopted by the Americans also. When the Americans realised that they too would need a heavier anti-tank gun than their 37-mm (1.46-in) M1 they saw that the easiest way to produce something was to copy the 6-pdr, and in early 1941 they obtained a set of drawings from the British and adapted them to suit their own production methods. The result was the **57-mm Antitank Gun M1**. At first the American carriage had a handwheel traverse in place of the shoulder pad of the British original, but in

time the Americans adopted the shoulder pad also and in this form the **M1A2** was used until the war ended in 1945. However, it was as a weapon mounted on a self-propelled carriage that the American gun was most important. Large numbers of M1 guns were produced for mounting on half-tracks and in this form the American guns were widely used by the British Army and many other Allied forces as well as by the US Army. The 6-pdr may have been outclassed by heavy tanks such as the Tiger, but against nearly all other German tanks it proved to be effective enough. It was also quite a light and handy weapon.

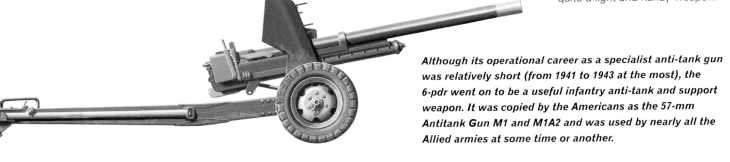

Although its operational career as a specialist anti-tank gun was relatively short (from 1941 to 1943 at the most), the 6-pdr went on to be a useful infantry anti-tank and support weapon. It was copied by the Americans as the 57-mm Antitank Gun M1 and M1A2 and was used by nearly all the Allied armies at some time or another.

Ordnance, Q.F., 17 pdr 3-in anti-tank gun

By 1941, the rapid increase in the armour protection of tanks was being forecast to the extent where it was realised that not even the 6-pdr would be able to cope. To deal with the expected armour increases it was decided to produce the next generation of anti-tank guns with a calibre of 3-in (76.2-mm) to fire a projectile weighing no less than 17 lb (7.65 kg). It was realised that the resultant gun would be a fair-sized piece of artillery but at the time there seemed to be no other option open, and the development of the gun proceeded with haste.

The first guns, soon known as the **Ordnance, Q.F., 17 pdr** or **17-pdr**, were made as early as August 1942 but these guns were prototypes only and getting the gun into full production took more time. This was to have dramatic results for from North Africa came news that the first consignment of Tiger tanks was expected in the theatre in the

very near future. At that time some guns were ready but they had no carriages. To get some form of heavy anti-tank weapon into the hands of the troops it was decided to fly 100 guns to North Africa, where they were hastily fitted onto 25-pdr field gun carriages to produce a hybrid known as the **17/25-pdr**. The conversions were made just in time, for a few weeks later the first Tigers appeared and the 17/25-pdr was on hand to tackle them. These 17/25-pdr guns served until 'proper' 17-pdr guns were to hand during the early stages of the Italian campaign in 1943.

When the 17-pdr guns arrived the overall design was low and not too cumbersome. The carriage had long and angled split trails and a large double-thickness armoured shield was fitted. The gun was proportionately long, and was fitted with a muzzle brake and a large and heavy vertical block breech mechanism.

To handle the gun a detachment of at least seven men was required, and more were needed if any man-handling was necessary. In mitigation of this factor the gun proved capable of firing a projectile that could penetrate any enemy tank at long ranges and the rate of fire was such that 10 rounds per minute were not uncommon.

By 1945 the 17-pdr was the standard anti-tank gun of the Royal Artillery anti-tank batteries and many had been handed on to Allied armed forces. The 17-pdr proved to be the last of the British Army's conventional anti-tank guns (a 32-pdr with a calibre of 94-mm/3.7-in was proposed but a 120-mm/4.72-in recoilless gun was selected instead), and many served on until the 1950s with the British Army. Various types of 17-pdr tank guns were produced as well.

First introduced into service in small numbers in late 1942, the 17-pdr went on to be one of the most powerful Allied anti-tank guns. Although rather heavy and awkward to move, the 17-pdr had a calibre of 3 in (76.2 mm) and could penetrate up to 130 mm (5.12 in) of armour at about 1000 m (1094 yards). It was used on occasion as a field gun firing HE shells.

SPECIFICATION	
Ordnance, Q.F., 17 pdr	**Traverse:** 60°
Calibre: 3 in (76.2 mm)	**Elevation:** -6° to +16.5°
Length of piece: 4.443 m (14 ft 6.96 in)	**Muzzle velocity:** 950 m (2,900 ft) per second
Length of rifling: 3.562 m (11 ft 8.25 in)	**Projectile weight:** 7.65 kg (17 lb)
Weight: in action 2923 kg (6,444 lb)	**Armour penetration:** 130 mm (5.12 in) at 915 m (1,000 yards)

By September 1944 the 17-pdr had proved an extremely effective weapon, and in the 8th Army's assault on the Gothic line was well to the fore to deal with German heavy armour.

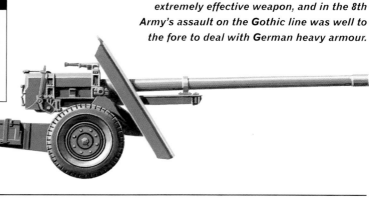

3.7-cm Pak 35/36 Anti-tank gun

The origins of the gun that was to become the **3.7-cm Pak 35/36** (Pak standing for *Panzerabwehrkanone*, or anti-tank gun) can be found in

1925. In this year Rheinmetall began the creation of a new anti-tank gun. Manufacture began in 1928, and as the German army was at that time

still largely horse-oriented the gun was fitted with spoked wheels for horse traction. In its design the gun was a very modern weapon for the period, and used a well-sloped shield, tubular split-trail legs and a long slender barrel.

Expanded production

At first production was relatively limited, but once the Nazi party came to power in 1933 production was greatly

accelerated. In 1934 there appeared the first version with steel wheels and pneumatic tyres suitable for vehicle traction, and the designation 3.7-cm Pak 35/36 was formally assigned to the gun in 1936.

It was in 1936 that the Pak 35/36 first saw action, during the Spanish Civil War. Here the small gun proved eminently capable against the relatively light armoured vehicles used during the conflict. It also

SPECIFICATION	
3.7-cm Pak 35/36	**Muzzle velocity:** 760 m (2,495 ft) per second with AP ammunition
Calibre: 37 mm (1.46 in)	**Maximum range:** 7000 m (7,655 yards)
Length of gun: 1.665 m (5 ft 5.6 in)	
Length of rifling: 1.308 m (4 ft 3.5 in)	**Projectile weight:** AP 0.354 kg (0.78 lb) or HE 0.625 kg (1.38 lb)
Weights: travelling 440 kg (970 lb) and in action 328 kg (723 lb)	**Armour penetration:** 38 mm (1.48 in) at 30° at 365 m (400 yards)
Traverse: 59°	
Elevation: -8° to +25°	

proved successful in 1939 against the lightly armed Polish forces, but in 1940 the Pak gun crews encountered the more heavily armoured French and British tanks and had the unfortunate experience of seeing their carefully aimed armour-piercing projectiles bouncing off the hulls of attacking tanks. The truth was that by 1940 the Pak 35/36 had had its day. It was no longer powerful enough to penetrate the armour of the more modern tanks, and larger-calibre weapons had to take its place. However, these latter could not be produced quickly enough, so the 37-mm (1.46-in) guns had to be rushed to action during the German invasion of the USSR – Operation Barbarossa – in June 1941: here the Pak 35/36 provided to by wholly incapable against the T-34/76 tank. Some attempts were made to prolong the service life of the gun by firing large stick bombs

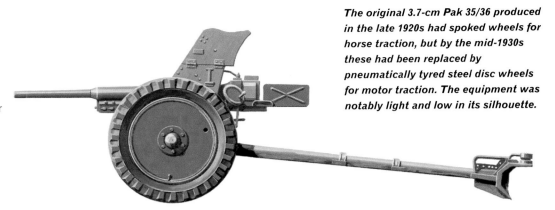

The original 3.7-cm Pak 35/36 produced in the late 1920s had spoked wheels for horse traction, but by the mid-1930s these had been replaced by pneumatically tyred steel disc wheels for motor traction. The equipment was notably light and low in its silhouette.

that fitted over the muzzle: these projectiles, although effective, were essentially close-range missiles of dubious combat worth. Consequently the Pak 35/36 was passed to second-line and garrison units, and to some training schools, so the type was still in limited service in 1945. Many carriages were later converted to take 75-mm (2.95-in) barrels for service in the infantry support task.

Export success

The Pak 35/36 was widely exported before 1939, and the design was copied in Japan as the **Type 97**.

Other recipient nations were Italy (**Cannone contracarro da 37/45**), the Netherlands (**37-mm Rheinmetall**) and also the USSR. In this last the Pak 35/36 was known as the **M30**, it was widely copied and formed the basis for a whole

family of 37-mm and 45-mm (1.77-in) anti-tank guns that served on for many years even after 1945. The design was also copied in the US to create the 37-mm Antitank Gun M3, although only the concept was copied as the M3 had many detail differences from the German original. At one point the Germans produced a special version of the Pak 35/36 for paradropping.

5-cm Pak 38 Anti-tank gun

The 5-cm Pak 38 was light and possessed a low silhouette, facilitating movement and concealment. A removable dolly wheel under the trail spades eased manhandling. The extensive use of light alloys in the manufacture of its carriage also meant that the gun was easily handled.

By 1940 the 3.7-cm Pak 35/36 was of very limited value against the armour of the most modern tanks. Fortunately for the German army this had been foreseen as early as 1937, and by 1938 Rheinmetall-Borsig had developed a new gun in 50-mm (1.97-in) calibre. By 1939 the gun was ready for production, but it was not until the mid summer of 1940 that the first examples reached the troops. By then the new gun, designated the **5-cm Pak 38**, was too late to take part in any western European campaign,

and it was not until 1941 that the new gun saw its first use in a major campaign.

Soviet tank killer

That was the invasion of the USSR, and by that time the new gun had been supplied with a new type of tungsten-cored ammunition known as AP40. This ammunition had been developed from captured Czechoslovakian and Polish ammunition, and was adopted because the dense tungsten core of the new projectiles

offered a considerable increase in armour penetration. This was just as well, for when the Soviet T-34/76 appeared on the battlefield the Pak 38 firing AP40 ammunition proved to be the only gun/projectile combination capable of penetrating the Soviet tank's thick hide. However, the numbers of Pak 38s in the field were limited, the gun could not be everywhere and it was some time before extemporised conversions of old French 75-mm (2.95-in) guns could be hurried up to fill the many gaps

in the anti-tank defence lines. After that the 50-mm gun proved good enough to remain in use for the rest of the war, although later it was replaced by heavier-calibre weapons.

The Pak 38 had a curved shield, steel wheels and a tubular split-trail carriage that locked out the torsion-bar suspension when the trail legs were spread. Light alloys were used throughout the construction of the carriage, which made it easy to handle, and a small dolly wheel was mounted under the trail legs for manhandling. The barrel had a muzzle brake.

The Pak 38 was one of the German army's standard anti-tank guns and was further developed with an automatic feed device for the ammunition. The provision of this system allowed the gun to be used as a heavy aircraft weapon, and at one point a variant was fitted to a variant of the Me 262 jet fighter. This same weapon was further adapted for service as a ground-based anti-aircraft gun, but that was only late in the war and it seems that no production was undertaken. There was also a tank gun equivalent of the Pak 38 that was produced in a number of models, many of these weapons finding their way into service as beach-defence guns in Germany's 'Atlantic Wall'.

The Pak 38 was mounted on a number of tracked Panzerjäger carriages. At one point the British captured so many of these weapons that they were stockpiled as contingency weapons in the event of a crisis in the manufacture of British anti-tank guns.

SPECIFICATION	
5-cm Pak 38	per second, and HE 550 m (1,805 ft) per second
Calibre: 50 mm (1.97 in)	**Maximum range:** HE 2650 m (2,900 yards)
Length of piece: 3.187 m (10 ft 5.5 in)	
Length of rifling: 2.381 m (7 ft 9.7 in)	**Projectile weight:** AP 2.06 kg (4.54 lb), AP40 0.925 kg (2.04 lb) and HE 1.82 kg (4 lb)
Weights: travelling 1062 kg (2,341 lb) and in action 1000 kg (2,205 lb)	
Traverse: 65°	**Armour penetration:** AP40 101 mm (3.98 m) at 740 m (820 yards)
Elevation: -8° to +27°	
Muzzle velocity: AP 835 m (2,903 ft) per second, AP40 1180 m (3,870 ft)	

7.5-cm Pak 40 Anti-tank gun

The Pak 40 was considered an excellent weapon and became the German army's 'standard' anti-tank gun. The weapon was first used in action late in 1941.

By 1939 intimations regarding the next generation of Soviet tanks were filtering back to the German war planner staffs in Berlin. Although the new 50-mm (1.97-in) Pak 38 gun had yet to reach the troops, it was felt that something heavier would be needed to counter the armour of the new Soviet tanks, and consequently Rheinmetall-Borsig was asked to produce a new design. In basic terms what Rheinmetall did was to scale up the Pak 38 to 75-mm (2.95-in) calibre with an L/46 length. The resulting weapon was adopted in 1940 as the **7.5-cm Pak 40**, but it was not until late in the following year that the first examples off the production line reached the hard-pressed troops on the Eastern Front.

Pak 38 origins

In appearance the Pak 40 resembled its predecessor, but there were many differences apart from the scale. The basic layout of the 50-mm gun was retained, but as the expected shortages of many raw materials (especially light alloys that had been earmarked for the Luftwaffe production requirements) were becoming apparent, the Pak 40 was constructed mainly of steel and was thus proportionately much heavier than the smaller gun. To simplify and speed production the shield was formed from flat instead of curved plates, and there were several other such alterations including the omission of the dolly wheel that had made it easy to manoeuvre the trail spades of the Pak 38. However, the result was an excellent gun, able to tackle virtually any Allied tank encountered on all fronts.

The Pak 40 was destined to remain in production until the end of World War II in 1945. It had a tank gun equivalent that was progressively developed, but the Pak 40 itself remained in service virtually unchanged. A version intended for use as an aircraft weapon was developed as the **Bordkanone 7.5**, and the carriage was even adapted to allow short 75-mm (2.95-in) barrels to be fitted and so create a hybrid infantry support and anti-tank gun to be used by infantry formations. The gun itself was even placed on a 105-mm (4.13-in) howitzer carriage to form a light field artillery piece, though another approach was to use the Pak 40 itself as a field gun: by 1945 there were several artillery formations using this gun as the **7.5-cm FK 40** (FK standing for *Feldkanone*, or field gun).

But it was as an anti-tank gun that the Pak 40 was most important. Many German gunners rated it their best all-round weapon, and many Allied tank crews had occasion to agree with them. The Pak 40 fired a wide range of ammunition, varying from the straightforward solid armour-piercing (AP) shot to the tungsten-cored AP40 projectile. Also available were high explosive (HE) shells that carried enough payload to make the type a useful field artillery piece, and various hollow-charge projectiles. A measure of the gun's efficiency can be seen in its range/armour penetration figures: at a range of 2000 m (2,185 yards) the AP40 projectile could penetrate no less than 98 mm (3.86 in) of armour plate, and a combat range in the order of 500 m (545 yards) this figure increased to 154 mm (6.06 in).

In the German army the Pak 40 replaced the earlier 3.7-cm (1.46-in) and 5-cm weapons with specialist battalion and brigade anti-tank units, and was widely used until the end of the war. German anti-tank gun tactics saw Pak 40s distributed to fill the gaps between the heavier 88-mm guns.

SPECIFICATION	
7.5-cm Pak 40	per second and HE 550 m (1,805 ft) per second
Calibre: 75 mm (2.95 in)	**Maximum range:** HE 7680 m (8,400 yards)
Length of piece: 3.7 m (12 ft 1.7 in)	
Length of rifling: 2.461 m (8 ft)	**Projectile weight:** AP 6.8 kg (15 lb), AP40 4.1 kg (9.04 lb) and HE 5.74 kg (12.65 lb)
Weight: travelling 1500 kg (3,307 lb) and in action 1425 kg (3,141.5 lb)	
Traverse: 45°	**Armour penetration:** 98 mm (3.86 in) at 2000 m (2,185 yards)
Elevation: -5° to +22°	
Muzzle velocity: AP 750 m (2,460 ft) per second, AP40 930 m (3,050 ft)	

8.8-cm Pak 43 and 8.8-cm Pak 43/41 Anti-tank guns

The success of the 8.8-cm Flak 18 (Flak for *Fliegerabwehrkanone*, or anti-aircraft gun) as an anti-tank weapon led to the development of a similar weapon for use as a tank gun to arm the large Tiger tank. Further design thought ran along the lines of developing a comparable family of guns for tank, anti-tank and anti-aircraft use. From this came a series of design studies known as the *Gerät* 42 (*Gerät* was the designation for equipments still in the design stage), but in the event the anti-aircraft gun specification was pitched at a level where the 88-mm (3.46-in) calibre could not cope and thus the designers concentrated on the tank and anti-tank guns.

Krupp was given the eventual production contract for the new anti-tank gun, and in 1943 produced the **8.8-cm Pak 43**. This was a truly superb gun, but it was also a fairly large one. To move it required a powerful tractor and a large gun team, and once emplaced the gun was removed from its twin-axle carriage to rest upon a large cruciform carriage. It thus lacked the mobility of the smaller anti-tank guns, which had a greater range of movement around the battlefield, but could knock out virtually any tank likely to enter its sights, even at ranges of over 2500 m (2,735 yards). The Pak 43 bristled with advanced features such as a semi-automatic breech mechanism, an electrical firing circuit with safety cut-outs to prevent firing over unsafe arcs, and a low turntable carriage. It was also difficult to produce in

quantity, a factor not helped by the continuous attention given to the various Krupp factories by the Allied bomber fleets, so output was constantly disrupted.

Service entry

When the Pak 43 appeared in service, commanders on all fronts called for more and more of the type and demand consistently outstripped supply. In typical German fashion an extemporised way was found out of this situation by asking Rheinmetall-Borsig to produce its own version from existing resources. The result was the **8.8-cm Pak 43/41**, a combination of various weapons cobbled together to provide the required gun. The basic ordnance of the Pak 43 was retained, but in this instance placed on a new single-axle carriage with a conventional split trail. The carriage came from one gun, the wheels from another and various other components were derived from other sources. A new

shield was produced and the result was a most cumbersome and ungainly design that had one saving grace, the fact that it worked. For despite being very difficult to handle and emplace, the gun retained the power of the original Pak 43. Thus it was tolerated but never gained the respect and praise bestowed upon the superb Pak 43.

A small number of halftrack conversions mounting the '88' on a 12-ton chassis were made, and served in France in 1940.

Tank gun

By 1945 both guns were still in production. The Pak 43 was modified for use on various self-propelled carriages and as the 8.8-cm **KwK 43** tank gun was the main armament of the powerful Tiger II tank. The ammunition fired by these

The German 8.8-cm Pak 43 on its carriage. At the 1000-m (1094-yard) plus range favoured, it was capable of knocking out virtually any Allied tank. However, demand constantly outstripped supply – much to the relief of Allied tank crews.

weapons was different from the 88-mm (3.46-in) ammunition fired by the earlier anti-aircraft guns that were the origins of the '43' family, and used a more powerful propellant system.

This ammunition was considered suitable for use in the field artillery role and despite the desperate need for anti-tank guns on all fronts by 1945 many of these guns were used by field artillery batteries.

SPECIFICATION	
8.8-cm Pak 43	**Muzzle velocity:** AP 1130 m (3,707 ft) per second, and HE 950 m (3,118 ft) per second
Calibre: 88 mm (3.46 in)	
Length of piece: 6.61 m (21 ft 8 in)	
Length of rifling: 5.13 m (16 ft 10 in)	**Maximum range:** HE 15150 m (16,570 yards)
Weight: travelling 4750 kg (10,472 lb) and in action 3650 kg (8,047 lb)	**Projectile weight:** AP 10.16 or 7.3 kg (22.4 or 16.1 lb), and HE 9.4 kg (20.7 lb)
Traverse: 360°	**Armour penetration:** 184 mm (7.244 in) at 2000 m (2,190 yards)
Elevation: -8° to +40°	

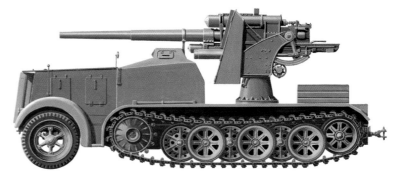

This self-propelled anti-tank carriage was an early attempt to place the famous '88', the 8.8-cm Flak 18, onto a mobile platform, in this case a 12-ton artillery tractor halftrack.

'88' in action From Flak to tank-killer

One of the oddest facts relating to anti-tank guns in service during World War II is that the most famous such weapon was not an anti-tank gun at all but an anti-aircraft (AA) gun. This was the famous (or infamous) '88', the gun that could knock out any tank it could see at ranges well outside those of normal anti-tank guns. The weapon gained for itself a reputation that in some ways overshadowed the disadvantages of the gun, but the fact was that the '88' was used as an anti-tank gun on the very day World War II started and it was still knocking out tanks when the war ended.

Above and below: The key to the success of the '88' was the very high velocity of its shells. It could damage most Allied tanks even when firing high-explosive rounds, and with armour-piercing shot it was lethal. Anti-tank guns and AA guns have a number of key features in common – both are designed to fire projectiles at high velocities with flat trajectories. Give an AA gun the right kind of ammunition, and it becomes a highly effective tank killer. However, at the outbreak of the war, the only AA gun equipped to fight tanks was the Flak 18.

8.8-cm Flak 18

Designed by a Krupp team in Sweden (in order to circumvent the conditions of the Treaty of Versailles) the 8.8-cm Flak 18 (right) entered production in 1933, and with the National Socialist state was to become legendary. Originally made with a one-piece barrel, later models were equipped with multi-sectioned barrels to allow replacement of worn sections. Seen here on the Sonderhanger 201 carriage (the later model 202 travelled with the barrel to the rear), the Flak 18 was usually towed by the eight-tonne SdKfz 7 halftrack.

Improving the '88'

One of the earliest measures taken to improve the '88' was the introduction of a new model, the 8.8-cm Flak 41. This was an entirely new gun designed and developed by Rheinmetall-Borsig, but despite the facts that it had excellent all-round performance and fired an entirely new range of ammunition, it had too many technical faults (which proved to be inherent) and the bulk of those produced were assigned to anti-aircraft defences only. Shortly after the 8.8-cm Flak 41 entered service, Krupp was asked to develop a new design of gun that could be used as an anti-aircraft, anti-tank and tank gun. Krupp assigned the new design the cover name Gerät 42. This emerged as the 8.8-cm Pak 43 anti-tank gun.

8.8-cm Flak 41

The 8.8-cm Flak 41 (right) was never really free from problems in its service career, as a result of its complicated construction. Seen here dismounted from its Sonderhanger carriage, the Flak 41 was usually retained for service within the Reich. In spite of operational difficulties, it was widely regarded as the finest of the German heavy AA weapons. Although capable of firing 25 rounds per minute, and with a muzzle velocity of 1000 m (3,280 ft) per second giving a maximum effective ceiling of 14700 m (48,320 ft), the complexity of manufacture allowed only 318 pieces to see operational deployment.

Eisenbahn '88'

The '88' was also adopted as a railway gun. Although in this role the '88' was used only for anti-aircraft work, large numbers were used on special trains that were pulled around the Reich to defend areas affected by Allied air attacks.

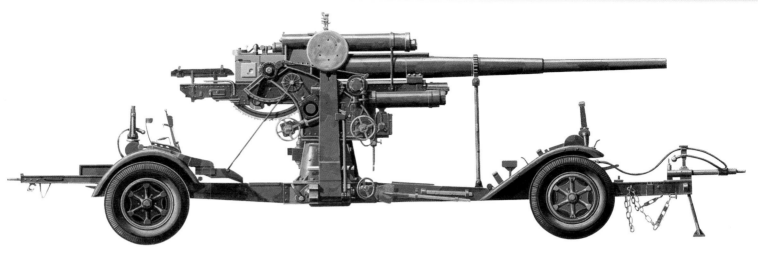

An '88' is put on tow after its capture by the 7th Army in January 1945. For a brief period, these guns were used by the US Army. A rear-pointing barrel was the identifying feature of the Sonderhanger 202 wheeled carriage.

An 8.8-cm Flak 36 anti-aircraft gun is seen in action during the Soviet campaign. After the tribulations of the bitter winter of 1941, the German army had by now become more familiar with sub-zero fighting.

Mobile '88's

Early on in the life of the 8.8-cm Flak 18 attempts were made to convert the guns for the self-propelled role. One of the earliest of these involved the use of a wheeled bus chassis, but by 1940 the '88' was carried into action in France mounted on halftrack chassis (heavy halftracks were also used to tow '88s'). After the introduction of the 8.8-cm Pak 43, numerous tracked chassis were converted to carry the gun in a self-propelled role. One of the earliest of these was the Elefant, which proved to be a spectacular failure during the Battle of Kursk in 1943. Later vehicles were more successful, while others never passed the project stage. One of the best of the self-propelled '88's was the Jagdpanther, which mounted a special version of the 8.8-cm Pak 43 in a well-sloped superstructure built onto the chassis of a Panther tank. This combination was by far the best all-round tank destroyer design of World War II.

Early development

The '88' was designed and developed as an anti-aircraft gun, the actual design and development of the gun being carried out not in Germany but in Sweden during the 1920s when gun designing was forbidden to Krupp by the terms of the Treaty of Versailles. Krupp got around this by setting up a design team based in Sweden but funded by the German army. By 1932 they had produced an excellent anti-aircraft gun carried between two bogie axle units and pivot-mounted on a cruciform carriage when emplaced. The barrel was long and slender and it had a high muzzle velocity between 820 and 840 m (2,690 and 2,755 ft) per second. The projectile weighed 9.6 kg (21.16 lb) and the maximum ceiling to which this projectile could be fired was 10600 m (34,775 ft). For the period, this performance was little short of excellent and when the new German army started to re-arm during 1933, numbers of '88's were already coming from the Krupp production lines at Essen.

Taper-bore anti-tank guns

The German taper-bore guns were an odd off-shoot from the main avenue of anti-tank development that, although successful, foundered for the simple fact that the German war economy could not afford the raw materials required to produce them. Three guns were produced and issued for service, and all relied on what is commonly known as the Gerlich principle. In simple terms this involved the use of a small projectile core made from tungsten, a hard and very dense metal ideal for punching a way through armour plating. In order to provide this tungsten core with the maximum punch the Gerlich system involved the use of guns with calibres that tapered downwards in size from the breech to the muzzle. The special projectiles involved used flanged or 'skirted' forms that allowed the flanges to fold back as the bore narrowed. This had the advantage of increasing the emergent velocity of the projectile, enabling it to travel farther and to hit the target harder. The principle was attractive to the German

ordnance designers who adapted it for the anti-tank gun, but the principle had some disadvantages: to ensure the maximum power of the gun expensive and relatively rare tungsten had to be used for the projectile core, and the guns themselves were costly to produce.

The first of the taper-bore guns to enter service was the **2.8-cm schwere Panzerbüchse 41 (2.8-cm sPzB 41)**, which was really little more than a heavy anti-tank rifle, with a bore that tapered from 28 mm (1.1 in) at the breech to 20 mm (0.787 in) at the muzzle. It used a light carriage, but an even lighter version of the carriage was produced for the German airborne formations. Both types were still in use at the end of the war.

Light anti-tank gun

Second in this series of taper-bore guns was the **4.2-cm leichte Panzerabwehrkanone 41 (4.2-cm lePak 41**, or light anti-tank gun 41). This used the carriage of the 3.7-cm Pak 35/36

powerful and advanced gun in which the bore decreased from 75 mm (2.95 in) to 55 mm (2.16 in). At one time this gun showed so much promise that it almost took over from the 7.5-cm Pak 40 as the standard German anti-tank gun, but despite having a better armour-piercing performance it was passed over because of the German tungsten shortage. Tungsten was normally used for the machine tools to produce

The 2.8-cm schwere Panzerbüsche 41 was the smallest of the German taper-bore guns, and was produced in two forms: one had large road wheels while a special airborne version, shown here, had small wheels and a light tubular alloy carriage.

SPECIFICATION	
7.5-cm Pak 41	**Elevation:** -10° to +18°
Starting calibre: 75 mm (2.95 in)	**Muzzle velocity:** AP 1230 m (4,035
Emergent calibre: 55 mm (2.16 in)	ft) per second
Length of barrel: 4.32 m (14 ft 2 in)	**Projectile weight:** AP 2.5 kg
Weight: in action 1390 kg	(5.51 lb)
(3,064 lb)	**Armour penetration:** 171 mm (6.73
Traverse: 60°	in) at 455 m (500 yards)

more weapons, but the raw materials had to be brought into Germany by blockade runners and when these were repeatedly intercepted on the high seas the supplies dwindled. It was a choice between anti-tank guns and machine tools, and the result had to be the machine tools. Thus production of the taper-bore guns ceased. Only 150 Pak 41s were produced,

A 2.8-cm sPzB 41 is carried on a Kfz 15 light signals vehicle in order to provide a useful boost in firepower to a normally lightly-armed unit. The gun is carried complete with its light wheeled carriage.

and once their ammunition stocks had been expended they passed from use.

SPECIFICATION	
2.8-cm sPzB 41	**Muzzle velocity:** AP 1400 m (4,593
Starting calibre: 28 mm (1.1 in)	ft) per second
Emergent calibre: 20 mm (0.787 in)	**Projectile weight:** AP 0.124 kg (0.27
Length of barrel: 1.7 m (5 ft 7 in)	lb)
Weight: in action 223 kg (492 lb)	**Armour penetration:** 56 mm (2.205
Traverse: 90°	in) at 365 m (400 yards)
Elevation: -5° to +45°	

The 7.5-cm Pak 41 was the largest of the German taper-bore guns, but was prevented by the general tungsten shortage then prevalent in Germany from becoming the standard German army heavy anti-tank gun.

but the ordnance was tapered from 40.3 mm (1.586 in) at the start to 29.4 mm (1.157 in) at the muzzle. These guns were issued to airborne units, namely the Luftwaffe's Fallschirmjäger.

Largest of the trio was the **7.5-cm Pak 41**. This was a very

SPECIFICATION	
4.2-cm lePak 41	**Traverse:** 60°
Starting calibre: 40.3 mm	**Elevation:** -8° to +25°
(1.586 in)	**Muzzle velocity:** 1265 m (4,150 ft)
Emergent calibre: 29.4 mm	per second
(1.157 in)	**Projectile weight:** AP 0.336 kg (0.74
Length of barrel: 2.25 m (7 ft 4.6 in)	lb)
Weight: in action 560 kg	**Armour penetration:** 72 mm (2.835
(1,234.5 lb)	in) at 455 m (500 yards)

Böher 4.7-cm Austrian anti-tank gun

The diminutive **Böhler 4.7-cm** (1.85-in) anti-tank gun was first produced in 1935, and is thus sometimes known as the **Model 35**. It was first produced in Austria but its use soon spread outside that nation and licences to produce the gun were taken up by Italy. In fact the Italian production run reached the point where the Böhler gun became regarded almost as an indigenous Italian weapon, designated as the **Cannone da 47/32 M35**.

The Böhler gun was a useful weapon that was soon diverted into other roles. It was widely issued as an infantry gun and as it could be rapidly broken down into a number of pack

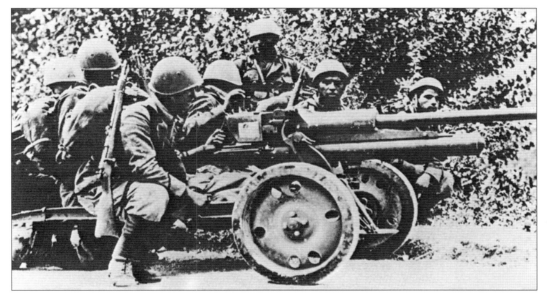

loads it was also employed as a mountain gun. But though, as it turned out, the Böhler was something of a multi-purpose weapon, it was not entirely successful in any of these extra roles. It did prove to be a fairly effective anti-tank gun, however, and was widely used during the early war years by a number of nations. Italy was the main user, but others were employed by the Netherlands (**Kanon van 4.7**), and Romania, and the type also turned up in the Soviet Union (in relatively small quantities) as the **M35B**. Some also found their way into

German army service when Austria came under German domination after 1938, receiving the designation **4.7-cm Pak**.

There were several developments on the basic Böhler theme that issued from the company's Kapfenberg works. Although the basic gun remained unchanged, there were numerous variations on such things as types of carriage wheel, the width of the carriage axle and so on. Some models had muzzle brakes while others did not. All models had a feature whereby

the wheels could be removed and the gun then rested on the trail legs and a small platform under the axle for firing. This gave the gun a lower silhouette for firing and concealment. The gun could fire both armour piercing and high explosive

Above and left: In action the 4.7-cm (1.85-in) Böhler anti-tank gun was often used with the wheels removed and with the forward part of the carriage resting on a firing platform. A periscope sight was used, even for anti-tank use, and no shield was usually fitted. The gun could be broken down into loads for pack transport on mules.

projectiles, the latter having a range of 7000 m (7,655 yards) to provide the gun with a useful infantry support role. As the armour thicknesses of tanks increased, the Böhler increasingly assumed this infantry support role.

There was one odd sideline to the story of the Böhler that is still little known. In 1942 the Allied armies in North Africa were still relatively short of many weapons and the large

SPECIFICATION	
Cannone da 47/32 M35	**Muzzle velocity:** AP 630 m (2,067 ft) per second and HE 250 m (820 ft) per second
Calibre: 47 mm (1.85 in)	
Length of barrel: 1.68 m (5 ft 6 in)	
Length of bore: 1.525 m (5 ft)	**Maximum range:** HE 7000 m (7,655 yards)
Length of rifling: 1.33 m (4 ft 4.4 in)	
Weight: travelling 315 kg (694.5 lb) and in action 277 kg (610.6 lb)	**Projectile weight:** AP 1.44 kg (3.175 lb) and HE 2.37 kg (5.225 lb)
Traverse: 62°	**Armour penetration:** 43 mm (1.7 in) at 500 m (550 yards)
Elevation: -15° to + 56°	

numbers of captured Italian Böhler guns were a useful windfall. About 100 were refurbished at a Captured Weapons Depot in Alexandria and issued to various units for second-line service. But perhaps the oddest item in this story was that 96 were actually converted by the British for use by airborne forces: the fire-control system of the original gun was altered so that one man could lay the gun, and the carriage was modified to allow dropping by parachute; a rifle telescope for aiming and a shoulder pad from a 6-pdr

gun were also added. These proved, according to the records, 'very popular'.

Unfortunately it has not yet been possible to trace the units involved, but these Böhler guns

must have been among the first guns adopted for the airborne role.

Skoda 47-mm kanon P.U.V. vz 36 Czech anti-tank gun

The Czech 47-mm Model 1936 looked archaic, mainly because of the small spoked wheels and long trails, but the gun was one of the most powerful of its day. Many were taken over by the German army who used the type in large numbers, often mounted on special tank destroyer self-propelled carriages. A version of the gun was also produced for use in fortifications.

The Czech firm of Skoda, based at Pilsen, was one of the first European armaments manufacturers to turn its attention to the production of specialised anti-tank guns. All through the 1920s Skoda's technicians and designers carried out a long chain of experiments and design studies to formulate a viable anti-tank gun, and in 1934 the company produced a gun with a calibre of 37 mm (1.46 in). For various reasons this weapon was not widely adopted (it was generally felt that something heavier would be needed) and in 1936 there appeared the **Skoda**

An illustration from a Skoda brochure that advertised their 47-mm Model 1936 anti-tank gun for export sale. The gun is here being towed using drag ropes.

German soldiers manhandle their 4.7-cm Pak 36(t) during training prior to the 1940 invasion of France. The soldiers are wearing drag-rope slings for towing the gun, and a full gun crew would comprise at least four men.

47-mm kanon P.U.V. vz 36 (vz for *vzor*, or model). The vz 36 had a calibre of 47 mm (1.85 in) and was immediately ordered into production by the Czech army.

In its day the vz 36 was one of the most powerful and hardest-hitting of all the contemporary European anti-tank guns. It fired a relatively heavy projectile, weighing 1.65 kg (3.6 lb), and this projectile could penetrate any tank then in service at ranges of up to 640 m (700 yards) at a time when most similar guns were confined to targets no more than 186 to 275 m (200 to 300 yards) distant.

But despite this power the vz 36 appeared a rather clumsy design. It had anachronistic spoked wheels and a very long trail which split to form two legs when in the firing position. The crew was protected by a shield that had over the wheel flaps that were folded out in action, but an oddity was that the upper rim of the shield was finished off as an asymmetric curved line to aid concealment, the wavy line breaking up the outline. The gun had a prominent recoil cylinder over the barrel and another recognition feature was the single-baffle muzzle brake.

vz 36 in service

Production for the Czech army proceeded at a high priority rate, and a few guns were exported to Yugoslavia at one point. In service the vz 36 was issued to the specialist anti-tank companies of the Czech army, but was found to be a bit of a handful for the infantry anti-tank units, for whom a developed version of the earlier 37-mm gun was placed in production. This became the **kanon P.U.V. vz 37** and although this gun followed the same general lines as the larger 47-mm model it was recognisable by the use of more modern steel wheels with rubber tyres.

The vz 36 was destined never to fire a shot for its Czech masters, for the Munich Agreement of 1938 allowed the Germans to take over the Czech Sudetenland defences without a shot being fired. This allowed the Germans to impress large numbers of a very special version of the vz 36 that had been developed for use in static fortifications, but large numbers of the wheeled vz 36 fell into German hands during the following year when Germany took over control of the rest of Czechoslovakia. The vz 36 then became the **43-cm Pak 36(t)** and was eagerly added to the German gun parks. The Czech gun became a virtual standard weapon with the German army and remained in use with some of their second-line units until the end of the war in 1945. It was mounted on several types of tracked chassis to become the armament of several German Panzerjäger and proved itself to be a very viable anti-armour weapon.

However, the vz 37s did not remain in German service for very long after 1941.

SPECIFICATION	
Kanon P.U.V. vz 36	
Calibre: 47 mm (1.85 in)	**Muzzle velocity:** AP 775 m (2,543 ft) per second
Length of barrel: 2.04 m (6 ft 8 in)	**Maximum range:** 4000 m (4,375 yards)
Weight: travelling 605 kg (1,334 lb) and in action 590 kg (1,300 lb)	**Projectile weight:** AP 1.64 kg (3.6 lb) and HE 1.5 kg (3.3 lb)
Traverse: 50°	**Armour penetration:** 51 mm (2 in) at 640 m (700 yards)
Elevation: -8° to +26°	

47-mm Anti-tank Gun Type 1 Japanese anti-tank gun

As with so many other weapons, Japan was short of anti-tank guns and had only a limited capacity to produce the numbers required. In 1934 it had introduced the 37-mm Gun Type 94 for use by infantry units, but realised even then that this gun would have only a limited performance, and it was therefore supplemented by the licence production of the 37-mm Anti-tank Gun Type 97, the origin of which was the German 3.7-cm Pak 35/36.

It was not until 1941 that a heavier gun was introduced in the form of the **47-mm Anti-tank Gun Type 1**. In overall design terms the Type 1 was entirely orthodox and used a split-trail carriage and a well-sloped shield. Compared with designs then being produced in Europe the Type 1 was not very powerful, but the Japanese considered it adequate as it had the advantage of a semi-automatic sliding breech carried over from the 47-mm (1.85-in) German gun, giving it a relatively high rate of fire; this was a possible 15 rounds a minute.

As with many other Japanese weapons ease of handling was given high priority, and the Type 1 proved to be easy to handle in action and it was relatively light. In combat this advantage was often squandered for as the Allies advanced these guns were often statically emplaced and

were manned by crews who favoured death rather than capture.

Extreme measures

Production of the Type 1 was never sufficient to meet the needs of hard-pressed Japanese army units as the Allies advanced on all fronts, and as the Allies deployed increasing amounts of armour in its amphibious landings. Consequently the Japanese were forced to use all manner of improvised anti-tank methods, ranging from pressing into use naval and anti-aircraft guns to the extreme of suicide attackers armed with pole charges and

explosive blocks. By 1945 the use of such measures was becoming commonplace, and they cost the operators dearly.

Despite the fact that the Japanese learned early on in the conflict that their small tanks were likely to be of very limited use against their Allied equivalents, they still diverted a proportion of the Type 1 gun

production towards producing a tank gun for their Type 97 tank. The Type 1 was regarded as the standard Japanese anti-tank gun, and most of them were issued to regimental and divisional anti-tank battalions. The 47-mm Anti-tank Gun Type 1 remained in production from 1941 until the war ended in 1945.

SPECIFICATION	
47-mm Anti-Tank Gun Type 1	**Muzzle velocity:** AP 824 m (2,700 ft) per second
Calibre: 47 mm (1.46 in)	
Length of barrel: 2.527 m (8 ft 3.5 in)	**Projectile weight:** APHE 1.528 kg (3.37 lb) and APHE 1.4 kg (3.08 lb)
Weight: in action 747 kg (1,660 lb)	
Traverse: 60°	**Armour penetration:** 51 mm (2 in) at 915 m (1,000 yards)
Elevation: -11° to +19°	

The Japanese Anti-tank Gun Type 1 was the only indigenous Japanese weapon produced exclusively for the anti-tank role, and although it was effective against most light Allied armour it was never produced in significant enough numbers to make any overall impression.

Soviet 45-mm anti-tank guns Models 1932, 1937, 1938 & 1942

The Soviet Union purchased a batch of 37-mm (1.46-in) Rheinmetall anti-tank guns as early as 1930, and standardised the type as the M30 well before the German army adopted the identical model as the 3.7-cm Pak 35/36. The Soviets decided to licence-produce the 37-mm gun, but in 1932 produced their own variant with a calibre of 45 mm (1.77 in). This was the **M1932**, and this could be identified by the wire-spoked wheels that were fitted to the otherwise unchanged Rheinmetall-based carriage. By 1940 there were large numbers of these guns in service with the Red Army and some had even

been used in action on the Republican side during the Spanish Civil War.

In 1937 the slightly revised

A Model 1942 in action in early 1945 on the final approaches to Danzig as the Red Army advanced westwards during the last winter of the war. The Model 1942 was still in large scale Red Army use at this time and remained so post-war.

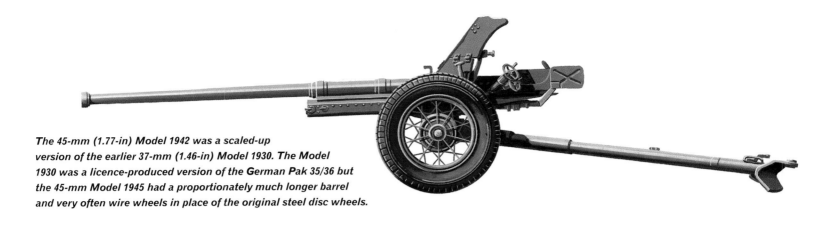

The 45-mm (1.77-in) Model 1942 was a scaled-up version of the earlier 37-mm (1.46-in) Model 1930. The Model 1930 was a licence-produced version of the German Pak 35/36 but the 45-mm Model 1945 had a proportionately much longer barrel and very often wire wheels in place of the original steel disc wheels.

Model 1937 appeared, and in the following year a tank gun variant, the **M1938**, was produced. These two guns first saw major action during the short but intense war with Finland during 1939 and 1940, but in many ways this war gave the Red Army the wrong impression of the effectiveness of their guns. The Finns had only small numbers of light armoured vehicles and the M1932 and M1937 proved quite effective against these. But when the Germans invaded the Soviet Union in 1941, the Red Army found out the hard way that its guns could not penetrate the armour of most German tanks. The only way the Red Army could stop the German attacks was to use massed artillery fire against the German formations, and

although there was an obvious need for heavier anti-tank guns the Soviet war industry was in no position to produce any such new weapons. The huge German advances had overrun many of the Soviet military industrial centres, and it took time to set up new facilities deep in the hinterland of the Soviet Union.

Lengthened model

When a new gun did appear it was nothing more than a lengthened version of the existing gun. The original M32 had a barrel that was about 46 calibres long (L/46) while the new gun had a barrel that was 66 calibres long. This extension of barrel length increased the muzzle velocity and provided the projectile with more penetrating

power. The new and longer gun was produced some time during 1942 and was thus named the **M1942**, but it took time for appreciable numbers to reach the front line. In the meantime the M1938 tank gun was called upon partially to fill the gaps. Numbers of these tank guns were placed on simple improvised carriages and rushed into action. These conversions were of limited value as they had only a small traverse arc, but they did work and as such were better than nothing.

SPECIFICATION	
45-mm M1942	**Muzzle velocity:** 820 m (2,690 ft) per second
Calibre: 45 mm (1.77 in)	
Length of barrel: 2.967 m (9 ft 8.8 in)	**Projectile weight:** 1.43 kg (3.151 lb)
Weight: in action 570 kg (1,257 lb)	**Armour penetration:** 95 mm (3.74 in) at 300 m (330 yards)
Traverse: 60°	
Elevation: -8° to +25°	

M1942 in service

When the M1942 did get into the front line it proved to be more effective than the earlier guns, but only marginally so, yet the Soviets continued to produce large numbers throughout the war. These M1942 guns had pressed steel wheels in place of the earlier wire-spoked units, and the trail legs were longer, but the Rheinmetall origins could still be seen. Although it would appear that the M1942 had only a limited performance against the later tanks the type long remained in service with some of the smaller Soviet-influenced armies following the war.

In 1941, the Soviet weapons designers followed the increase in anti-tank calibres prevalent elsewhere. The first gun to be introduced had a calibre of 57 mm (2.24 in) and is known as the M1941 and in 1944 a massive gun with a calibre of 100 mm (3.94 in) was introduced as the M1944.

A Soviet 45-mm anti-tank gun in action. Copied and enlarged from a German design, the weapon was really too small for use against heavier German armour, but was retained in use.

Soviet 76.2-mm guns Models 1936, 1939, & 1942

One of the most widely used of the German heavy anti-tank guns was not originally a German weapon at all but a Soviet design. This hybrid weapon was originally designed as a field gun and was known as the 76.2-mm (3-in) **M1936**. It was the latest in a line of gun designs that stretched back many years, and the first of them were issued to the Red Army during 1939. The M1936 was a rather heavy gun for the field role and it possessed a long slender barrel mounted on a heavy but strong carriage that was ideally suited to the harsh conditions of the Soviet terrain.

In 1941 the lack of a suitable anti-tank gun other than the 45-mm (1.77-in) M1932 led to the simple expedient of using field guns for defence against tanks. In this role the M1936 proved itself to be an excellent anti-armour gun and, even firing high-explosive shells, was powerful enough to inflict damage on German tanks of all kinds. This fact was duly noted by the Germans when they came to contemplate a use for the huge stockpiles of M1936 guns that they captured during 1941 and 1942. Many were simply turned around against their former owners, but large numbers were returned to Germany where they were

Right: A Model 1936 field gun in service with the Germans in North Africa converted for anti-tank use as the 7.62-cm Pak 36(r), a role in which the gun excelled.

reconditioned and altered to accommodate German ammunition. A muzzle brake was added and the fire controls altered for the anti-tank role, the result being the **7.62-cm Pak 36(r)**, an excellent heavy anti-tank gun that was used on all fronts from North Africa to the Soviet Union.

Back in the Soviet Union, as early as 1939, a new field gun lighter than the M1936 was produced as the **M1939**. This was smaller overall than the M1936 with a shorter barrel. Again, many fell into German hands in 1941, and these were converted for German use, some as anti-tank guns. The Soviet designers produced other 76.2-mm field guns in 1941 and at one desperate point were even placing 76.2-mm tank guns on lash-up carriages in order

The Soviet 76.2-mm gun made a superb specialist anti-tank gun and was considered by many to be one of the best all-round anti-tank guns of the war.

to produce something to keep the advancing German army forces at bay, but in 1942 came the first of what can be regarded as dual-purpose guns.

Dual-role gun

This was the 76.2-mm **M1942**, or **ZiZ-2**, a versatile light field gun that could be readily used as an anti-tank gun if and when necessary. The M1942 had a light carriage that used split tubular trails, and the gun barrel was fitted with a muzzle brake. By the time it first appeared at the front, the Red Army was well versed in the art of using field artillery against attacking

armoured vehicles and during many battles the Red Army relied on field guns alone for defence. They simply turned their guns, of all calibres, against the target and started firing. The well-balanced M1942 was ideal for this type of employment. It was also very sturdy, and as it fired a shell weighing 6.21 kg (13.69 lb), it could pack a useful punch when fired against tanks. The M1942 turned out to be one of the best artillery pieces ever produced in the Soviet Union, where the type was churned out in thousands, and the type continued to remain a front-line equipment with many armies around the world during the Cold War. Between 1943 and 1945, the German also found any captured examples very useful indeed.

SPECIFICATION	
7.62-cm Pak 36(r)	**Muzzle velocity:** AP40 990 m (3,250 ft) per second
Calibre: 76.2 mm (3 in)	**Maximum range:** HE 13580 m (14,585 yards)
Length of piece: 4.179 m (13 ft 8.5 in)	**Projectile weight:** AP 7.54 kg (16.79 lb) and AP40 4.05 kg (8.9 lb)
Length of rifling: 2.93 m (9 ft 7.4 in)	
Weight: in action 1730 kg (3,770 lb)	**Armour penetration:** AP40 98 mm (3.86 in) at 500 m (545 yards)
Traverse: 60°	
Elevation: -6° to +25°	

The Soviet 76.2-mm Model 1942 ZiZ-2 field gun was not intended primarily to be an anti-tank gun, but on many occasions it was used as such and proved to be very effective. Firing mainly HE shells it was able to knock out nearly all contemporary tanks or at least inflict severe damage.

37-mm Antitank Gun M3 Anti-tank gun

When the US Army Ordnance Department decided to develop an anti-tank gun before 1939 it obtained an example of the German 3.7-cm Pak 35/36, and using this as a starting point proceeded to design a similar weapon, also in 37-mm (1.46-in) calibre. The result was outwardly different from the German original but was in fact closely influenced by it. The American gun was designated the **37-mm Antitank Gun M3**, but only a few had been made before it was decided to fit the gun with a muzzle brake, the change making the M3 the **M3A1**.

The muzzle brake was fitted in an attempt to reduce the recoil forces on the carriage, which was even lighter than the German original, but as it was soon discovered that the muzzle brake was unnecessary it was removed, though the guns were still produced with the fixtures on the muzzle for ease of production. The rest of the gun and carriage was quite unremarkable. The carriage used the usual split trails but the main carriage axle was rather wider than on other similar designs. A small flat shield was provided for the gun crew and the breech mechanism was copied directly from the German gun and remained a vertical drop block.

Pacific service

By the time the diminutive M3A1 had been taken into service it was obsolete. By 1941 events elsewhere had demonstrated that something larger than 37 mm would be required to penetrate the

Although it appeared to be a very different weapon, the 37-mm M3A1 was closely influenced by the German Rheinmetall 3.7-cm Pak 35/36. Soon overtaken by armour increases in Europe, many were used as infantry support weapons in the Pacific.

armoured hides of in-service enemy tanks and although the M3A1 was used in North Africa by the US Army the type was withdrawn there and replaced by heavier guns. However, it was a different scenario in the Pacific theatre where the expected enemy tanks were light (and in any event few and far between), so a place could be found for the M3A1 as an infantry support weapon. HE and canister rounds were developed for use during the various island-hopping campaigns and the armour-piercing (AP) projectiles were often called upon during 'bunker-busting' operations. The light weight of the gun proved to be highly effective during these amphibious operations, so production continued specifically for the Pacific operations. By

1945 no fewer than 18,702 M3s had been produced. A tank gun version was also produced for use in American light tanks and armoured cars.

After 1945 many M3A1s were handed out to nations friendly to the Americans, and many long remained in use in some Central and South American states. Numbers were also converted to become saluting guns with blank cartridges.

During World War II many attempts were made to turn the M3A1 into a self-propelled anti-tank weapon, but very few were ever used operationally for the simple reason that the gun lacked the power to tackle the tanks it was likely to encounter in the field. However, as an infantry support gun it proved to be excellent.

Although the European war had shown it to be obsolete, the M3 was still in US Army service at the Kasserine Pass in 1943, where it proved disastrously inadequate against the veteran Afrika Korps armour.

SPECIFICATION	
37-mm Antitank Gun M3A1	per second
Calibre: 37 mm (1.45 in)	**Maximum effective range:** 457 m
Length of piece: 1.98 m (6 ft 6 in)	(500 yards)
Weight: travelling 410.4 kg (912 lb)	**Projectile weight:** 0.86 kg (1.92 lb)
Traverse: 60°	**Armour penetration:** 25.4 mm (1 in)
Elevation: -10° to +15°	at 915 m (1,000 yards)
Muzzle velocity: AP 885 m (2,900 ft)	

3-in Antitank Gun M5 Anti-tank gun

When the US Army Ordnance Department decided in 1942 to produce a new heavy anti-tank gun it took a course of action that had already been taken elsewhere: it decided to combine existing weapon components to produce a new gun. The gun itself was taken

from the 3-in (76.2-mm) Antiaircraft Gun M3 but the chamber had to be altered slightly to take different ammunition. The new gun was modified to take the breech mechanism of the 105-mm (4.13-in) Howitzer M2A1, then in full-scale production, and the

same howitzer was used to supply the carriage and the recoil system. The new carriage became the **Gun Carriage M1** and in this form the original straight shield of the 105-mm howitzer was retained but in time the shield was modified to have sloping shield plates and

this became the **Gun Carriage M6**.

Penetration power

The new gun itself became the **3-in Antitank Gun M5**, and it turned out to be a remarkably workmanlike-looking weapon. It was rather large and heavy for

SPECIFICATION

3-in Antitank Gun M5
Calibre: 76.2 mm (3 in)
Length of piece: 4.02 m (13 ft 2.3 in)
Weight: travelling 2653.5 kg (5,850 lb)
Traverse: 46°
Elevation: -5.5° to +30°
Muzzle velocity: AP 793 m (2,600 ft)

per second; APC 853 m (2,800 ft) per second
Maximum effective range: 1830 m (2,000 yards)
Projectile weight: AP and APC 6.94 kg (15.43 lb)
Armour penetration: 84 mm (3.31 in) at 1830 m (2,000 yards)

its role, but in this respect was no worse than many of its contemporaries and in action soon proved capable of being able to penetrate up to 84 mm (3.3 in) of sloping armour at ranges of almost 2000 m (2,190 yards). Not surprisingly the M5 proved to be a popular weapon with

the anti-tank batteries of the US Army, and the type was used in all theatres of the war. Numerous types of armour-piercing ammunition were developed for the M5, but one of the more widely used was the capped armour-piercing (APC) projectile known as the

M62. However, the M5 did have a disadvantage and that was its weight. Rapid movement of the M5 proved to be a major task, and a heavy 6x6 truck had to be used to tow the weapon although lighter tractors could be used on occasions where the terrain permitted.

The first M5s were issued for service in December 1941 but it took time for the weapon to be issued widely. The M5 was also in demand as the armament for a series of self-propelled tank destroyer projects, the most important of which turned out to be the M10A1, an

open-topped M4 Sherman variant that mounted the M5 in a special turret. The importance of this demand can be seen as 2,500 M5s were completed for the anti-tank gun role compared to 6,824 guns produced for the M10A1.

Withdrawal

Once the war ended the M5 was gradually withdrawn from US Army service and passed to reserve units. It was overtaken by more technologically advanced forms of anti-tank weapon and few examples remained in use after 1950.

The 3-in Antitank Gun M5 was an improvised weapon using the barrel of an anti-aircraft gun and the breech and carriage of a 105-mm howitzer together with some new components. The resultant weapon worked surprisingly well and proved to be a very effective tank destroyer although it was rather cumbersome to move in a hurry.

French 25-mm anti-tank guns SA-L mle 1934/1937

The first of two French 25-mm (0.98-in) anti-tank guns (in many references the correct term should be cannon instead of guns as the calibre of 25 mm is generally considered too light to apply to a gun) was the **Canon léger de 25 antichar SA-L mle 1934**. Produced by Hotchkiss et Cie, this weapon was based on the design of a gun originally intended for use in World War I tanks but too late for that conflict as its development was not

completed until 1920. In 1932 Hotchkiss conceived the idea of placing the design on a light wheeled carriage in response to a French army requirement. The design was adopted in 1934 (hence the mle 1934 in the designation), and by 1939 there were well over 3,000 such equipments in service with the French army.

The other French 25-mm. gun was the **Canon léger de 25 antichar SA-L mle 1937**. This

was a later arrival, designed and developed by the Atelier de Puteaux (APX), and first offered for service in 1937. It was not adopted for service until 1938 and the numbers produced for service never approached those of the mle 1934. In appearance the mle 1937 looked very similar

to the mle 1934, but it was much lighter and had a slightly longer barrel. In fact the two guns were intended for different service roles: the mle 1934 was issued to nearly all French army armoured units and specialised anti-tank units, while the mle 1937 was intended for use by the

Left: Seen in a retouched image, the Canon léger de 25 antichar SA-L mle 1934 proved to be virtually useless against even light tank armour in 1940.

Above: Too flimsy for towing, the 25-mm Hotchkiss anti-tank gun, once issued to the BEF, was light enough to be carried on a 15-cwt truck.

support companies of infantry battalions. The latter equipments were towed by horses, one horse pulling the gun towed behind a small limber vehicle, this carrying the ammunition and all the gun crew's kit and equipment. When the mle 1937 was towed in this fashion the cone-shaped muzzle brake was removed and stowed over the breech.

British Army use

The mle 1934 was a serviceable enough weapon, but its calibre was too small for the gun to be of much use against the German armour that swept across France in 1940. By that time the mle 1934 was also in use with the British Army. In a show of Allied co-operation it had been decided that the BEF would use the mle 1934 as its anti-tank gun but this did not turn out well in practice. The BEF was the only all-mechanised formation in Europe at that time and when it tried to tow the mle 1934s behind its vehicles the guns very quickly proved to be too flimsy to withstand the hard knocks involved. Thus the BEF carried the guns on its vehicles and the mle 1934 became the first British portée gun.

The mle 1937 fared even less well in service. It was even less stoutly built than the mle 1934 and ran into weakness problems even when confined to the horse-drawn role. The main problem with both guns was that the round they fired was too small to make any sort of impact on attacking armour and their combat ranges were limited to something like 300 m (330 yards). Even in 1940 this was far too low for tactical comfort, but the French army had invested heavily in the 25-mm guns, so all too often they were the only such weapons available.

In the 1940 campaign large numbers of these 25-mm guns fell into the hands of the Germans, who retained some as **2.5-cm Pak 112(f)** and **2.5-cm Pak 113(f)** to provide their occupation divisions with some form of anti-tank weapon. They do not appear to have been used long after 1942.

SPECIFICATION	
Canon léger de 25 antichar SA-L mle 1937	**Muzzle velocity:** 900 m (2,953 ft) per second
Calibre: 25 mm (0.98 in)	**Maximum range:** 1800 m (1,968 yards)
Length of barrel: 1.925 m (6 ft 4 in)	**Projectile weight:** AP 0.32 kg (0.7 lb)
Weight: in action 310 kg (683.5 lb)	**Armour penetration:** at 25° 40 mm (1.57 in) at 400 m (440 yards)
Traverse: 37°	
Elevation: -10° to +26°	

Canon de 47 antichar SA mle 1937 French anti-tank gun

The best of the French anti-tank guns was the **Canon de 46 antichar SA mle 1937**, designed by the Atelier de Puteaux. It was developed rapidly and introduced into service once the French army had become aware of the armour thickness of the PZKpfw IV tank. Considering the rush with which the mle 1937 was developed it was one of the best anti-tank weapons in service anywhere in 1939. The main trouble for the French army was that there were not enough of them to hand in May 1940.

The mle 1937 was introduced into limited service in 1938, but the main production run was in 1939. The type was issued to artillery batteries operating in support of army divisions and brigades, and was operated in batteries of six guns each. The guns were usually towed into action behind Somua halftracks, and in action their low profile made them easy to conceal. They were capable of penetrating the armour of any tank likely to be put into action against them. In appearance the mle 1937 looked powerful and low. The gun carriage used pressed steel wheels with solid rubber rims. On top of the shield was a corrugated outline to break up the shape.

Along with production of the towed model went production of a similar gun for use in the permanent fortifications of the Maginot Line. This version lacked the carriage of the towed version and instead was swung into its firing position (through specially constructed firing slits) suspended from overhead rails. In 1939 there appeared a slightly revised version known as the

The Puteaux mle 1939 was a more involved development of the 47-mm mle 1937 using a complex all-round traverse carriage, although some were produced with normal wheeled carriages.

Canon de 47 antichar SA mle 1937/39, with detail differences. In 1940 there appeared the **Canon de 47 antichar SA mle 1939**. This used the original gun mounted on a new tripod carriage so arranged that once it was emplaced the gun could be swung through 360°. To emplace the gun a forward leg of the tripod was swung down, the trail legs were spread and the wheels were then raised to positions on each side of the shield. This concept never saw service, for the events of May 1940 intervened before production could start.

May and June 1940 saw the bulk of the mle 1937s pass into German hands. The Germans regarded the mle 1937 highly, and after 1940 they used the mle 1937 widely as the **4.7-cm Pak 141(f)**; the gun was still in service when the Allies landed in Normandy in June 1944. The Germans also used the mle 1937 to arm many early Panzerjäger conversions produced from captured French tanks.

SPECIFICATION	
Canon de 47 antichar SA mle 1937	**Muzzle velocity:** 855 m (2,805 ft) per second
Calibre: 47 mm (1.85 in)	**Maximum range:** 6500 m (7,110 yards)
Length of barrel: 2.49 m (8 ft 2 in)	**Projectile weight:** 1.725 kg (3.8 lb)
Weight: travelling 1090 kg (2,403 lb) and in action 1050 kg (2,315 lb)	**Armour penetration:** 80 mm (3.15 in) at 200 m (220 yards)
Traverse: 68°	
Elevation: -13° to +16.5°	

15-cm Wurfgranate 41 HE/smoke artillery rocket

The 15-cm (5.9-in) German artillery rockets were the mainstay of the large number of German army Nebelwerfer (literally smoke-throwing) units, initially formed to produce smoke screens for various tactical uses but later diverted to use artillery rockets as well. The 15-cm rockets were extensively tested by the Germans at Kummersdorf West during the late 1930s and by 1941 the first were ready for issue to the troops.

The 15-cm rockets were of two main types: the **15-cm Wurfgranate 41 Spreng** (high explosive) and **15-cm Wurfgranate 41 w Kh Nebel** (smoke). In appearance both were similar and had an unusual layout, in that the rocket venturi that produced the spin stabilisation were located some two-thirds of the way along the rocket body with the main payload behind them. This ensured that when the main explosive payload detonated the remains of the rocket motor added to the overall destructive effects. In flight the rocket had a distinctive droning sound that gave rise to the Allied nickname 'Moaning Minnie'. Special versions were issued for arctic and tropical use.

Launcher types

The first launcher issued for use with these rockets was a single-rail device known as the **'Do-Gerät'** (after the leader of the German rocket teams, General Dornberger). It was apparently intended for use by airborne units, but in the event was little used. Instead the main launcher for the 15-cm rockets was the **15-cm Nebelwerfer 41**.

Above: The 15-cm Panzerwerfer 42 was not only more mobile, but more survivable; rockets betrayed their position the moment they fired, so to avoid enemy artillery fire they needed to change position rapidly.

This fired six rockets from tubular launchers carried on a converted 3.7-cm Pak 35/36 anti-tank gun carriage. The tubes were arranged in a rough circle and were fired electrically one at a time in a fixed sequence that lasted around 10 seconds. It was recommended that the launcher crew withdrew to a distance of at least 15 m (16 yards) prior to firing.

The maximum range of these rockets was variable, but usually about 6900 m (7,545 yards), and they were normally fired en masse by batteries of 12 or more launchers. When so used the effects of such a bombardment could be devastating as the rockets could cover a considerable area of target

The 15-cm (5.9-in) rockets were among the earliest in widespread use by the German army, following an extensive pre-war test programme. Originally fired from a 6-barrel mount converted from the Pak 35/36 anti-tank gun carriage, by 1942 the 10-tube launcher had been developed.

terrain and the blast of their payloads was powerful.

Halftrack carriers

On the move the Nebelwerfer 41s were usually towed by light halftracks that also carried extra ammunition and other equipment, but in 1942 a half-tracked launcher was issued. This was the **15-cm Panzerwerfer 42** which continued to use the 15-cm rocket with the launcher tubes arranged in two horizontal rows of five on the top of an Opel SdKfz 4/1 Maultier armoured halftrack. These effective vehicles were used to supply

supporting fire for armoured operations, and their mobility ensured them greater survivability than static projectors. The Panzerwerfer 42 could carry up to 10 rockets in the launcher and a further 10 weapons inside. Later in the war similar launchers were used on armoured schwere Wehrmachtschlepper (SWS) halftracks that were also used to tow more Nebelwerfer 41s. The SWS could carry up to 26 rockets inside its hull. The 15-cm rockets were also used with the launchers intended for the 30-cm (11.8-in) rockets using special adapter rails.

SPECIFICATION	
15-cm Wurfgranate 41 Spreng	**15-cm Wurfgranate 41 w Kh Nebel**
Dimensions: length 979 mm (38.55 in); diameter 158 mm (6.22 in)	**Dimensions:** length 1.02 m (40.16 in); diameter 158 mm (6.22 in)
Weights: overall 31.8 kg (70 lb); propellant 6.35 kg (14 lb); filling 2.5 kg (5.5 lb)	**Weights:** overall 35.9 kg (79 lb); propellant 6.35 kg (14 lb); filling 3.86 kg (8.5 lb)
Performance: initial velocity 342 m (1,120 ft) per second; range 7055 m (7,715 yards)	**Performance:** initial velocity 342 m (1,120 ft) per second; range 6905 m (7,550 yards)

21-cm Wurfgranate 42 HE artillery rocket

The 21-cm rocket superficially resembled a conventional artillery round, but its streamlined nose was hollow and its base had 22 angled venturi to produce spin stabilisation.

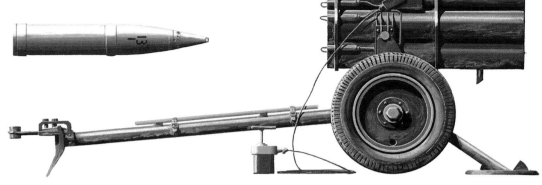

Following on from the success of their 15-cm (5.9-in) rockets, German designers decided to produce a larger rocket which by 1941 emerged as a 210-mm (8.27-in) design. At first sight this rocket, known as the **21-cm Wurfgranate 42 Spreng**, looked exactly like a conventional artillery projectile, but closer examination showed that the base had 22 angled venturi to impart the important spin stabilisation. The long streamlined nose was also deceptive, for it was hollow and the warhead proper was located some distance from the tip. This rocket contained no less than 10.17 kg (22.4 lb) of high explosive which on detonation produced a powerful blast effect. The weapon was so successful in this destructive role that only high explosive versions were produced.

Rocket projector

The 21-cm rocket was used with only one type of projector, the **21-cm Nebelwerfer 42**. The first such equipment appeared in action in the Soviet Union during 1943 as it took some time to finalise the launcher design.

Originally this was to have been a simple enlargement of the existing 15-cm Nebelwerfer 41 complete with six launcher tubes, but the larger calibre gave rise to some imbalance problems when the launcher was being towed and fired, so the number of tubes was eventually reduced to five and that solved the problems. In all other respects the carriage was the same as the earlier design and was a modification of the 3.7-cm Pak 35/36 anti-tank gun carriage. As with the 15-cm rockets the firing of the 21-cm weapon was by electrical means. Once the rockets had been loaded in their tubes the launcher crew withdrew to a safe distance (or even took cover), and on receipt of the firing order one of the crew operated a special switch-gear box and the full load of rockets were fired one at a time in a fixed sequence.

The salvo firing of the rockets produced a considerable amount of smoke and dust that revealed the launcher and battery position to the enemy, and during their trajectory the rockets produced their characteristic moaning noise that made them so distinctive as a weapon. This combination of smoke, dust and

Right: Entering service in 1943, the 21-cm Wurfgranate 42 was to have used the same carriage as the 15-cm (5.9-in) rocket, but the number of tubes had to be reduced to five to compensate for the increased charge. The Americans were so impressed by the 21-cm weapon that they copied it.

noise meant that the Nebelwerfer troops had to be experts at getting in and out of action quickly, for any firing of the large salvoes necessary to cover a target quickly produced counterbattery artillery or rocket fire that could have the effect of neutralising the launcher units.

US copy

The 21-cm rockets made a considerable impression on all who had to endure their effects, and the Americans in particular considered the rocket and launcher design to be so far in advance of anything they could produce that they took some examples back to the US and copied them. The US version was the 210-mm (8.27-in) **T36**, which was used for a series of trials that did nothing to produce an operational weapon but which added considerably to the Americans' knowledge of artillery rockets.

SPECIFICATION	
21-cm Wurfgranate 42 Spreng **Dimensions:** length 1.25 m (49.21 in); body diameter 210 mm (8.27 in) **Weights:** overall 109.55 kg (241.5 lb); propellant 18.27 kg (40.25 lb);	explosive 10.17 kg (22.4 lb) **Performance:** initial velocity 320 m (1,050 ft) per second; range about 7850 m (8,585 yards)

28-cm and 32-cm Wurfkörper HE/incendiary artillery rockets

The 28-cm (11-in) and 32-cm (12.6-in) rockets preceded the 15-cm (5.9-in) rockets in service with the German army, the first of them being issued for use during 1940. The two rockets shared the same rocket motor, but differed in their payload.

Both were awkward and bulky rockets with a poor ballistic shape, but both had powerful payloads.

The smaller weapon was the **28-cm Wurfkörper Spreng**, which used a heavy high explosive warhead, while the larger weapon was the **32-cm Wurfkörper M F1 50** with an incendiary warhead in heavy liquid form. Both had a range limitation of just over 2000 m (2,185 yards) and were highly inaccurate despite their spin stabilisation, and were

consequently used en masse whenever possible. Counterbalancing these disadvantages was the fact that both were devastating in their effects if they hit a target, and the high explosive rocket was highly regarded for use in urban

The short-ranged but powerful 28-cm (11-in) and 32-cm (12.6-in) rockets were among the first to be fitted to vehicles, in this case the ubiquitous SdKfz 251 halftrack. This conversion was known as the 'Foot Stuka' or 'Howling Cow'.

fighting where houses or other structures had to be demolished.

Launching methods

Both rockets were issued to the troops in wooden carrying crates, or **Packkiste**. These crates doubled as launching frames and were fitted with simple forward supporting legs for rudimentary aiming purposes. In this form both rockets could be used by assault pioneers to demolish bunkers or strongpoints, but more often the rockets were used in batches of four resting on simple launcher frames known as the **schweres Wurfgerät 40** or **schweres Wurfgerät 41**, which differed from each other only in that the latter was tubular steel-framed rather than wooden-framed. Both could be used for pre-arranged barrages, as during the siege of Sevastopol in 1942. However, this launching method was static, and to provide some form of mobility the **28/32-cm Nebelwerfer 41** was developed.

This was a simple trailer with frames for six rockets in two superimposed rows of three, and after the 15-cm Nebelwerfer 41, this launcher was the most important early equipment of the Nebelwerfer units.

Halftrack launcher

Another and still more mobile launcher for these rockets was the **schwerer Wurfrahmen 40**, in which six launcher frames were mounted on the sides of an SdKfz 251/1 halftrack. The rockets were mounted on the side frames still in their carrying crates. Aiming was achieved by simply pointing the vehicle towards the target, and the rockets were then fired one at a

time in a set sequence. This rocket/vehicle combination had several names but was often known as the **'Stuka-zu-Fuss'** or **'heulende Kuh'** ('Foot Stuka' or 'Howling Cow') and was often used to support Panzer operations, especially in the early days of Operation Barbarossa, the invasion of the Soviet Union. Later in the war

other vehicles, usually captured French or other impressed vehicles, were used to bulk out the numbers of mobile launchers available. All manner of light armoured vehicles were used in this role, some carrying a reduced load of four launchers. Many of these improvised launcher vehicles were used during the fighting in Normandy.

SPECIFICATION	
28-cm Wurfkörper Spreng	**32-cm Wurfkörper M F1 50**
Dimensions: length 1.19 m (46.85 in); body diameter 280 mm (11 in)	**Dimensions:** length 1.289 m (50.75 in); body diameter 320 mm (12.6 in)
Weights: overall 82.2 kg (181 lb); propellant 6.6 kg (14.56 lb); filling 49.9 kg (110 lb)	**Weights:** overall 79 kg (174 lb); propellant 6.6 kg (14.56 lb); filling 39.8 kg (87.7 lb)
Performance: range about 2138 m (2,337 yards)	**Performance:** range about 2028 m (2,217 yards)

30-cm Wurfkörper 42 Artillery rocket

Compared with 28-cm (11-in) and 32-cm (12.6-in) rockets which preceded it, the **30-cm Wurfkörper 42 Spreng** (also known as the **Wurfkörper Spreng 4491**) was a considerable improvement on the earlier designs when it appeared on the artillery scene during late 1942. Not only was it in aerodynamic terms a much smoother and cleaner design, but it had a much higher propellant/payload ratio than any other German artillery rocket. However, to the troops in the fields these technicalities were far less important than the fact that the more advanced type of propellant used with the new

rocket produced far less smoke and exhaust trails than the other rockets, and was thus far less likely to give away the firing position. But for all this improvement the 30-cm (11.8-in) rocket did not have any marked range advantages over the existing rockets. It had a theoretical range of some 6000 m (6,560 yards), but practical ranges were of the order of 4550 m (4,975 yards).

Rail launcher

The first launcher used with the new 30-cm rockets was the **30-cm Nebelwerfer 42**. This was a simple conversion of the 28/32-cm Nebelwerfer 41 with

A gunner places some rather optimistic camouflage over a 30-cm (11.8-in) rocket launcher. Initially fired from modified 28/32-cm launchers, the 30-cm rocket was soon provided with its own carriage, based on that of the 5-cm (1.97-in) Pak 38 anti-tank gun.

the simple rail launching frames altered to accommodate the new rocket shape and size. But this simple conversion did not last long, for almost as it was issued a new programme of rationalisation was drawn up and the special trailer of the Nebelwerfer 41 and 42 was eliminated. Instead, a new trailer based on the carriage of the 5-cm (1.97-in) Pak 38 anti-tank gun was placed into production and the 30-cm

launcher frames were placed on this to produce the **30-cm Raketenwerfer 56**; to ensure that the new launcher could be used to the maximum each was provided with a set of launcher rail inserts to allow 15-cm (5.9-in) rockets to be fired if required. When not in use, these 15-cm rails were stacked on top of the 30-cm frames.

Yet another rationalisation was that the 30-cm rockets could also

be fired from the schwerer Wurfrahmen launcher frames of the SdKfz 251/1 halftrack, originally intended for use by the 28-cm and 32-cm rockets. When launched from these frames, the 30-cm rockets were fired from their carrying crates or Packkiste, and no doubt the 30-cm rockets were used by assault pioneers for direct firing from their crates in the same manner as the earlier 28-cm and 32-cm weapons.

Limited action

Despite its relative improvements over the earlier artillery rockets, the 30-cm rocket was not used in very great

numbers. The earlier rockets remained in service right until the end of the war despite a late attempt to replace all existing weapons, including the 30-cm type, by an entirely new 12-cm (4.72-in) spin-stabilised design. This decision was made too late in the war for anything actually to reach the troops.

One unusual installation for the 30-cm 42 Wurfkörper Spreng was on the submarine *U-511*, which received an experimental rack for six such weapons in summer 1942. Launches were conducted from a depth of 12 m (39 ft) with the aim of creating a powerful shore-bombardment weapon.

SPECIFICATION	
30-cm Wurfkörper 42 **Dimensions:** length 1230 mm (48.44 in); body diameter 300 mm (11.8 in) **Weights:** overall 125.7 kg (277 lb);	propellant 15 kg (33.07 lb); explosive 44.66 kg (98.46 lb) **Performance:** initial velocity 230 m (754 ft) per second; range about 4550 m (4,975 yards)

Japanese rockets 20-cm and 44.7-cm rockets

The Japanese recognised the value of the artillery rocket to their under-armed forces and carried out considerable design and development work in order to provide a weapon that could make up for their lack of industrial capacity. Unfortunately for them their results were patchy and well behind the work carried out by the Allies. To add to the lack of Japanese success there were often development programmes carried out in opposition to each other, and typical of these were the projects to develop a 20-cm (7.87-in) rocket by both the army and the navy.

The **Army 20-cm Rocket** may be regarded as the better of the two projects. It was a spin-stabilised rocket using six base vents to impart propulsion and spin, and had an overall resemblance to an artillery projectile. To fire this rocket the army provided what appeared to be an oversize mortar known as the **Type 4 Rocket Launcher**.

The rocket was inserted into the 'barrel' by raising part of the upper section of the barrel and part of the tube base was open. This launcher was supposed to deliver the rocket relatively accurately, but few equipments appear to have been issued and most of these were used for coastal defences.

The **Navy 20-cm Rocket** resembled the army weapon in many respects, but was intended for launching from troughs made from simple wooden planks, or in some cases more sophisticated metal troughs. At times the rockets were simply emplaced to be launched directly from holes dug in the ground. A more conventional launcher used in small numbers only was a simple barrel on a light artillery-type carriage.

Rocket motor

These 20-cm rockets formed the bulk of the Japanese rocket

Japan undertook considerable development work on rockets, but lagged behind the other belligerent nations and produced few usable weapons. This 20-cm army rocket was one of the small number to see action.

programmes but there were others. One was the **Type 10 Rocket Motor** which was a simple propulsion unit designed to push aircraft bombs along ramps or troughs to launch them. At least two versions of the Type 10 existed but they were very inaccurate and had a maximum range of only 1830 m (2,000 yards). The launchers used for these rocket motors were often improvised, and improvisation was also used in at least one case where the conventional fins of an aircraft 250-kg (551-lb) bomb were replaced by a large rocket motor for launching from a simple wooden trough. Some intelligence reports from the period (1945) speak of these

launchers mounted on trucks, but no confirmation of this has been found.

The largest of all the Japanese rockets had a diameter of 44.7 mm (17.6 in), and this **44.7-cm Rocket** was a somewhat crude spin-stabilised design that was used in action on Iwo Jima and Luzon. It had a range of 1958 m (2,140 yards) at best, and was launched from short wooden racks or frames. It was wildly inaccurate, but it did have a warhead weighing 180.7 kg (398 lb). By the time these rockets were used, Japanese industry was in such a state that the conventional HE warheads often had to be replaced by simple picric acid.

SPECIFICATION	
Army 20-cm Rocket **Dimensions:** length 984 mm (38.75 in); diameter 202 mm (7.95 in) **Weights:** overall 92.6 kg (44.95 lb); filling 16.2 kg (35.7 lb)	**Navy 20-cm Rocket** **Dimensions:** length 1041 mm (41 in); diameter 210 mm (8.27 in) **Weights:** overall 90.12 kg (198.5 lb); propellant 8.3 kg (18.3 lb); filling 17.52 kg (38.6 lb) **Performance:** range 1800 m (1,970 yards)

M-8 Soviet 82-mm rocket

During the 1920s and 1930s the Soviet Union used a great deal of its research potential to determine exactly how propellants suitable for rockets could be mass produced. Even before 1918 the Russians had been great advocates of the war rocket, and after this the Soviets were determined to remain in the forefront of rocket technology despite the fact that they were hampered by a lack of industrial potential, which in turn led to their selection of the simpler and more easily produced fin-stabilised over the more accurate spin-stabilised rockets. One of their very first designs, produced during the late 1930s, was one of their most famous rockets, namely the 82-mm (3.23-in) **M-8** weapon.

The M-8 rocket was an off-shoot of an aircraft rocket programme. The aircraft rocket was the RS-82, and such was the state of the Soviet rocket development programme that it actually entered service after the 132-mm (5.2-in) rocket. The M-8

was a small rocket with a maximum range of 5900 m (6,455 yards) that carried a fragmentation warhead. It was carried on and fired from a series of rails carried on 6x6 trucks, and these rail launchers were just one type of the series of weapons known as **Katyusha**. One of the first of these multiple launchers was carried on a ZiS-6 6x6 truck. As this arrangement could carry and launch up to 36 M-8 rockets it was known as the **BM-83-6**, the BM denoting 'combat vehicle' as a cover name.

The BM-83-6 was not the only vehicle that fired the M-8 rocket, for when sufficient US-supplied Lend-Lease trucks became available these too were used as M-8 launcher vehicles: typical of these was the Studebaker 6x6, which was large enough to take rails for 48 rockets and thus became the **BM-8-48**. Being wheeled, these launchers could not always traverse the rough terrain of the Soviet Union or keep up with the tank units they were meant to support. At one

Seen here mounted atop a T-70 light tank, the M-8 82-mm rocket had its origins in an aircraft rocket programme; it proved an enormous success and served throughout the war. The Waffen-SS were so impressed that they copied it.

point experiments were made to fit single-rail launchers to the sides of tank turrets, but they came to nothing. Instead numbers of the T-60 light tank, which had proved to be of little combat value in its designed role, were converted to take rails for 24 M-8 rockets and the type thus became known as the **BM-8-24**.

Mountain rocketry

There were other launchers for the M-8 rocket, including a special eight-rocket frame intended for use by mountain troops. On all of the M-8

launchers the rockets were fired not in a massed salvo but in ripples under the control of an electrical rotary switch box.

The M-8 rockets had quite an effect on the recipient German troops who had to endure the high fragmentation warheads. The Waffen-SS was so impressed that it decided to copy the design direct (along with the launcher rails) as its own 'Himmlerorgel'. The M-8 rocket remained in service throughout the war, but following 1945 they were gradually phased out from use in favour of the heavier Soviet war rockets.

SPECIFICATION	
M-8	
Dimensions: length 660 mm (26 in); body diameter 82 mm (3.23 in)	explosive 0.5 kg (1.1 lb)
Weights: overall 8 kg (17.6 lb); propellant 1.2 kg (2.645 lb);	**Performance:** initial velocity 315 m (1,033 ft) per second; maximum range 5900 m (6,450 yards)

M-30 and M-31 Soviet 300-mm rockets

The **M-30** 300-mm (11.8-in) rocket was introduced during 1942 when it was appreciated that good as the M-8 and M-13 rockets were, a heavier explosive warhead would be an advantage. The M-30 used a modified M-13 rocket motor allied to a bulbous warhead that contained 28.9 kg (63.7 lb) of explosive, which more than met the requirement, although the range was limited to no more than 2800 m (3,060 yards).

The first M-30s were fired from their carrying crates with the aid of a frame known as **Rama**, which was a close copy of

the German method of using the Packkiste for launching from the schwere Wurfgerät. These Ramas were cumbersome devices that were laborious to set up close to the front line, and were little liked by the Red Army troops. But they did like the M-30 rocket for its powerful effects, even going to the extent of using the M-30 for ambushes against tanks or for house-to-house fighting. When used in this role the M-30 was simply aimed at the target while still in its carrying crate and fired at very close range.

By the end of 1942 a newer type of 300-mm rocket was ready

and this was known as the **M-31** to differentiate it from the earlier model. The M-31 had an improved rocket motor that gave a range of 4300 m (4,705 yards). This rocket could be fired from the Rama frames in the same manner as the M-30, but later Ramas could take six M-31s or

M-30s in place of the original four. By March 1944 the first mobile launchers for the M-31 appeared. These could carry up to 12 M-31s (the short range of the M-30 ruled out their use with the mobile launchers), and the type was thus known as the **BM-31-12**.

SPECIFICATION	
M-30	**M-31**
Dimensions: length 1200 m (47.24 in); body diameter 300 mm (11.8 in)	**Dimensions:** length 1760 mm (69.3 in); body diameter 300 mm (11.8 in)
Weights: overall 72 kg (158.7 lb); propellant 7.2 kg (15.87 lb); explosive 28.9 kg (63.7 lb)	**Weights:** overall 91.5 kg (201.7 lb); propellant 11.2 kg (24.7 kg); explosive 28.9 kg (63.7 lb)
	Performance: initial velocity 255 m (836 ft) per second

Truck launchers

Early versions of this launcher were carried by the ZiS-6 6x6 truck, but most wartime production examples were carried on Lend-Lease Studebaker US-6 6x6 trucks. These American trucks were fitted with steel shutters over the cab windows for protection against blast when the rockets were fired.

After 1945 the M-31 rockets did not survive for many years as they were essentially short-range weapons, and as such often suffered from counter-battery fire. But the basic M-31 did undergo some development before it was dropped.

There was an **M-31-UK** which used some of the efflux gases to impart a measure of spin for increased stabilisation and hence accuracy. Range was slightly

Entering service in 1942, the M-30 300-mm rocket carried almost six times as much explosive as the M-13, but its heavy payload reduced its range to under 3 km (1.8 miles). The first mobile launchers were introduced in 1944.

reduced, but the M-13-UK could greatly decrease the area of ground covered by a battery and thus increase the amount of explosive falling upon a point target. The M-30 and M-31 rockets were fitted only with HE

warheads. They were undoubtedly powerful projectiles with a considerable explosive effect, but they lacked range and for much of the war their mobility was virtually nonexistent as they had to be fired from the static

Rama frames. It was not until the later stages of the war that they were provided with mobility in the form of the BM-31-12, a tardiness for which the German troops on the Eastern Front were no doubt grateful.

M-13 132-mm rocket

The most widely used of all the Soviet war rockets during World War II was the **M-13** 132-mm (5.2-in) weapon. It was designed during the late 1930s, and when the Germans invaded the Soviet Union in 1941 there were only a few production launchers and a small stock of rockets to hand. These were pressed into service as an emergency measure and first went into action on the Smolensk front in July 1941, when they caused near-panic among the hapless German troops. This is hardly surprising, for in a period of under 10 seconds a single M-13 battery could swamp a large area in high explosive to an extent hitherto unseen in warfare.

Katyusha in action

These first M-13 batteries were very much special units. The launchers for the M-13 fin-stabilised rockets were carried by ZiS-6 6x6 trucks with rails for 16 rockets. The rails were known as 'Flute' launchers to the Soviet troops as a result of their perforated appearance, but they soon gained the name **Katyusha**

('Little Katy'), and at one time were known as 'Kostikov guns' after their supposed designer. For security purposes the launchers were usually shrouded in tarpaulins when not in use, and the crews were culled from Communist Party members in order to maintain tight security. But it was not long before the M-13 launchers were in widespread use and their secrets became common knowledge.

In for the kill, steel shutters down, Katyushas bombard the last pocket of German resistance near the Reichstag itself in March 1945. Such was the power of the Soviet industry that by 1945 some 10,000 launchers had been produced along with over 12 million rockets.

SPECIFICATION	
M-13	explosive 4.9 kg (10.8 lb)
Dimensions: length 1.41 m (55.9 in); body diameter 132 mm (5.2 in)	**Performance:** initial velocity 355 m (1,165 ft) per second; range 8500 m (9,295 yards)
Weights: overall 42.5 kg (93.7 lb); propellant 7.2 kg (15.87 lb);	

Rocket design

The basic M-13 rocket had a range of about 8000 to 8500 m (8,750 to 9,295 yards). The usual warhead was of the HE fragmentation type, and as always with fin-stabilised rockets accuracy was not of a high order. But as the M-13s were usually used in massed barrages this last mattered only little. Later versions of the M-13 used a form of efflux diversion to introduce more spin for increased accuracy, but this measure reduced the range slightly. As mentioned above, the first launcher type used 16 rails and was known as the

BM-13-16, but when supplies of Lend-Lease trucks became available they too were used as Katyusha carriers. Several types of truck, including Studebakers, Fords, Chevrolets and Internationals, were so used, along with STZ-5 artillery tractors and other vehicles. These BM-13-16 launchers had no traverse and only limited elevation, and were laid by pointing the carrier vehicle towards the target. Some carrier vehicles used steel shutters to protect the cab and crew in the launching sequence.

Warhead types

As the war progressed more types of M-13 warhead were introduced, including armour-piercing to break up tank formations, flare for night illumination, incendiary and signal. One variation was the

M-13-DD, which used two rocket motors burning together at launch to produce a possible range of 11800 m (12,905 yards), and this rocket was launched from the upper rails of the launcher only. The M-13-DD had the greatest range of all

Below: Shunted off the road and abandoned, this is the most famous of the war rockets: the truck-mounted Katyusha. Because of the distinctive moaning sound the missiles made in flight, the Germans dubbed the weapon 'Stalin's organ'.

Above: Original World War II Katyushas and their modern launchers remained favourites of the Palestine Liberation Organisation into the 1980s. Also, after the Israelis crushed the PLO in Beirut in 1982, they captured many Katyushas that they subsequently used themselves.

Left: M-13 132-mm rocket launchers in action on the outskirts of Berlin. The dreadful noise and clouds of smoke produced by these rockets, combined with the shock effect of mass detonations, frequently induced panic amongst the defenders.

For the awesome barrages that heralded a Red Army offensive, rockets would be massed on static launchers close to the front. Here the first salvoes blast off against the doomed men of the German 6th Army trapped in Stalingrad, January 1943.

solid-propellant artillery rockets in World War II.

After 1945 the M-13 rocket batteries remained in Red Army use right up to 1980, when the last examples were finally replaced by later models. However, the M-13 remained in service with many countries after this date, although more modern trucks were used as carriers in place of the old wartime models. In fact the service life of the basic M-13 continued into the 21st century, for the Chinese continue to use the design as a form of minelet-laying device known as the **Type 74**. This system is mounted on the rear of a CA-30A 6x6 truck.

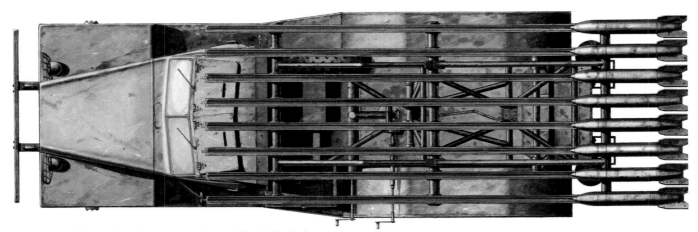

Introduced in conditions of great secrecy and crewed by dedicated party members, the first Soviet rocket launchers were tested in combat on 7 July 1941. Called Kostikov guns to conceal their real nature, they were soon nicknamed Katyusha ('Little Katy') after a popular song of the time. Rockets were mounted on a wide variety of vehicles from obsolescent light tanks to ZiS-6 lorries, but one of the most common combinations was the M-13 132-mm rocket on American Studebaker 6x6 trucks. Note the steel shutters over the windscreen to protect the cab from the ferocious backblast.

2-in rocket Anti-aircraft rocket

During the late 1930s the need for improved defence of the United Kingdom against air attack was finally appreciated, but at the time it was thought that to produce enough anti-aircraft guns to meet immediate needs would take too long. Thus the rocket was investigated to see if it could provide a cheap and easily-manufactured alternative to the gun, and among the first designs investigated was a type known as the **2-in Rocket**. As things turned out the later 3-in rocket was to prove more promising, but at the time the smaller rocket seemed quite encouraging and work went ahead on the design with some momentum.

The 2-in (51-mm) rocket was a simple device that used a propellant known as solventless cordite or SCRK. The overall simplicity of the weapon could be seen in the fact that the earliest designs used a

direct-action wind vane on the nose to arm the fuse after firing, with a self-destruct timer to destroy the weapon after it had been in flight for 4.5 seconds, by which time it would have reached a maximum height of about 1370 m (4,500 ft).

Naval applications

In the event the 2-in rocket was used mainly to arm light naval vessels and some merchant shipping. There were many and various simple naval mountings such as the basic vertical launchers that were mounted on each side of the bridge on many light vessels. These were supposed to launch their rockets as a low-flying aircraft attacked the ship. As the rockets rose they were designed to carry aloft a length of light wire that would enmesh itself in the aircraft's propellers and bring it down. The system never worked and neither did many other similar and somewhat optimistic

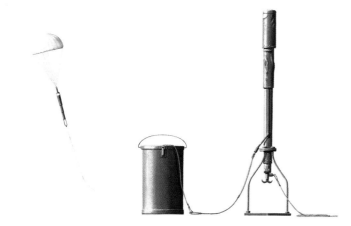

The 2-in Rocket was an ingenious AA rocket, being designed to destroy low-flying aircraft by fouling their propellers with the long wire it left in its wake.

devices. There was a high explosive version that could carry a 0.25-kg (0.56-lb) warhead, but by the time this was ready it was appreciated that the larger 3-in (76-mm) rocket was much better for this role and relatively few 2-in rockets were produced.

Pillar Box

One naval mounting that was used on land was the one known as the **2-in Rocket Mounting Mk II, Pillar Box**. This was used during the desperate days of 1940-41 to provide at least a measure of coastal AA defence, and could launch up to 20 rockets. The rockets were

arranged in two vertical rows of five on each side of a central drum housing in which the aimer operated the simple controls. This drum housing gave the Pillar Box mounting its name. The aimer could fire all 20 of the rockets in one salvo or two salvoes of 10 rockets using electrical ignition. Other forms of land-mounted 2-in rocket launchers existed and were used as temporary defensive measures. The 2-in rocket was really too small and light to have any great destructive effect, but the lessons learned in the design of war rockets had a good effect on later designs.

SPECIFICATION	
2-in Rocket	**Weights:** overall 4.88 kg (11 lb); warhead 0.25 kg (0.56 lb)
Dimensions: length 914 mm (36 in); body diameter 57 mm (2 in)	**Performance:** initial velocity 457 m (1,500 ft) per second

3-in rocket Anti-aircraft rocket

Design work on British artillery rockets started as early as 1934, though only on a low-priority basis, and by 1937 had reached the position where a **3-in Rocket** was proposed as an alternative to the anti-aircraft gun; indeed, the rocket used the same warhead weight as the 3.7-in (94-mm) AA shell. Under strict security conditions, development of the new rocket went ahead with the **UP (Unrotated Projectile)** cover name. Early firings were made at Aberporth in Wales, and by

1939 the final test firings were being made in Jamaica. Interestingly it was the trial battery at Aberporth that claimed the first 'kill' of a Luftwaffe bomber. These trials led to the establishment of the first operational battery near Cardiff in South Wales, where it was known as a Z battery.

This first Z battery used a single-rail launcher known as the **Projector, 3-in, Mk 1**. It was a very simple, even crude device and it was produced for both the Army and the Royal Navy,

The 36-round Projector, Rocket, 3-in, No 4 Mks 1 and 2 was mobile as it was carried on converted 3-in (76-mm) anti-aircraft artillery platform trailers.

although in the event most of the Royal Navy's allocation went to the merchant navy. The rocket was a simple fin-stabilised tube containing a motor and the same SCRK cordite used on the 2-in (51-mm) rocket. These early designs were somewhat erratic in performance, and accuracy was such that huge salvoes had to be fired from all the projectors in a Z battery in order to have some chance of hitting an aircraft target. They did have their successes, but they were few and did not improve until the **Projector, Rocket, 3-in, No. 2 Mk 1** came along. This used a two-rail launching system and was produced in some numbers, still firing the 3-in (76-mm) rocket but fitted with more sophisticated fusing systems including early attempts at

proximity fusing and other electro-magnetic devices. Some of these No. 2 projectors saw action in North Africa, including port defence at Tobruk.

Ripple fire

The next improvement in launching methods was the **Projector, Rocket, 3-in, No. 4 Mk 1** and **Mk 2**. This had no fewer than 36 launcher rails to fire nine rockets in a ripple sequence. Again some of these projectors were used in North Africa. The largest of all the British 3-in rocket projectors was the **Projector, Rocket, 3-in, No. 6 Mk 1**, which could fire 20 rockets in four salvoes. This entered service in 1944 and was intended for use in static locations for home defence. One unexpected offshoot from the

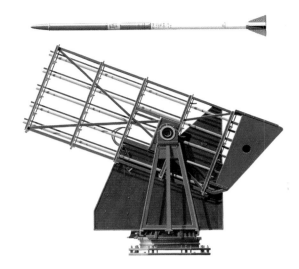

Designed originally as an anti-aircraft system, the 3-in rocket achieved modest success as a ground weapon. However, it is better known as an air-to-ground weapon, fired from Hawker Typhoons over Normandy during D-day.

AA rocket programme was that the ground-launched 3-in rocket was taken up as an aircraft weapon. Fired from short launcher rails it proved to be a devastating ground-attack missile, especially against tanks, and during 1944 proved to be one of the most powerful of all anti-tank weapons when

used by 'cab-rank' Hawker Typhoons over the Normandy battlefields. By the time the war ended the airborne 3-in rocket was even being used to sink U-boats. In a different installation towards the close of the war, the Coldstream Guards even fitted two 3-in aircraft rockets to their tank turrets.

SPECIFICATION	
3-in Rocket	
Dimensions: length 1.93 m (76 in); body diameter 82.6 mm (3.25 in)	**Performance:** maximum velocity 457 m (1,500 ft) per second; service ceiling 6770 m (22,200 ft); horizontal range 3720 m 4,070 yards)
Weights: overall 24.5 kg (54 lb); propellant 5.76 kg (12.7 lb); warhead 1.94 kg (4.28 lb)	

LILO Short-range rocket

By 1944 the Allies were becoming accustomed to the Japanese tactic of using heavily-protected bunkers to delay Allied advances, not only on the Pacific Islands but also in the land warfare raging in South East Asia. The only effective way to demolish these formidable defensive works was by the use of heavy artillery at close ranges, but the Japanese did not always build their bunkers where such heavy weapons could get at them. The rocket was obviously a relatively portable method of dealing with such obstacles, and thus there emerged a programme known by the cover name **LILO**.

Bunker-buster

LILO was a very simple single-barrel launcher designed to fire a rocket at short range against

bunker-type targets. It fired a projectile powered by the Motor, Rocket, 3-in, No. 7 Mk 1 to which two types of warhead could be fitted. Both were HE types, one weighing 17.8 kg (39.25 lb) complete and the other 35.5 kg (78.25 lb) complete. The idea was that the LILO projector could be carried to its firing location by one man, with another carrying a rocket on a suitable backpack. The projector was then set up as close to its intended target as possible and

As the Allies drove the Japanese back towards their homeland, numerous expedients were tried to knock out the toughly-constructed bunkers that were the hallmark of Japanese positions. One such was LILO – a short-range single-shot 60-lb (27.2-kg) rocket.

the rocket loaded into the launcher tube from the front. Open sights were used to aim the weapon, the back legs of the launcher being moved for changes in elevation. When all was ready the rocket was fired electrically, using a light 3.4-volt battery.

The LILO rockets were capable of penetrating 3.05 m (10 ft) of earth plus a layer of logs, so they could normally penetrate any Japanese bunker. But the main problem was hitting the target: despite the fact that a degree of spin was imparted to the rocket as it was launched, the inherent inaccuracy of the rocket was such that to ensure a 95 per cent chance of hitting a point target distant only some 45 to 50 m (49 to 55 yards), five rockets had to be fired. This may sound uneconomic but the alternative was to bring up heavy artillery with all its attendant risks and labour.

US equivalent

The Americans also used a short-range rocket for the same purpose as LILO. Their device was known as the **M12 Rocket**

Launcher which fired a 4.5-in (114-mm) rocket, and this resembled LILO in many ways apart from the fact that the first launcher tubes used were plastic and were discarded after firing. Such a system proved to be too wasteful, even for the US war economy, so a later version was developed as the **M12E1** which used a magnesium alloy tube that could be reloaded and reused. These projectors were used on Okinawa to blast the Japanese soldiers from heavily-defended caves.

SPECIFICATION	
LILO rocket (9.53-kg/21-lb warhead) **Dimensions:** length 1.24 m (49 in); body diameter 83 mm (3 in) **Weights:** overall 17.8 kg (39.25 lb); propellant 1.93 kg (4 lb); explosive 1.8 kg (4 lb)	**LILO rocket (27.2-kg/60-lb warhead)** **Dimensions:** length 1.32 m (52 in); body diameter 152 mm (6 in) **Weights:** overall 35.5 kg (78.25 lb); propellant 1.93 kg (4 lb); explosive 6.24 kg (14 lb)

Land Mattress Artillery rocket

Although early development of the war rocket in the United Kingdom was initially to produce an anti-aircraft weapon, some consideration was also given to producing an artillery rocket. One early attempt at this was a design for a 5-in (127-mm) rocket which was rejected by the Army but adopted by the Royal Navy for use in modified landing craft for the saturation of landing beaches and approaches by massed rocket fire. This eventually evolved as the **Mattress**, but range was limited. However, further trials revealed that the range could be improved by introducing, at launch, a degree of spin which would also improve accuracy, and this was simply achieved by using an aircraft 3-in (76-mm) rocket motor attached to a

naval 13-kg (29-lb) warhead. This increased range to a possible 7315 m (8,000 yards), making the artillery rocket a viable proposition once more. Thus Mattress became **Land Mattress**. The first Army launchers for these new Land Mattress rockets had 32 barrels, but a later version had 30 barrels. Demonstrations of this launcher greatly impressed Canadian army staff officers, who requested a 12-launcher battery which in the event was ready for action on 1 November 1944.

First action

This battery went into action during the crossing of the River Scheldt and was a great success, to the extent that more were requested and

Loading 30.5-kg (67-lb) rockets into the 32-round launchers was an exhausting job, but to be effective rockets had to be fired in big volleys. The first Land Mattress battery fired over 1,000 rounds in six hours during the crossing of the River Scheldt.

produced. The Land Mattress launcher was limited in its elevation capabilities to between 23° and 45°, and this not only limited the maximum range to 7225 m (7,900 yards) but also limited the minimum range to 6125 m (6,700 yards). To reduce the minimum range possible, a system of rotary spoilers over the rocket exhausts was formulated and put into use. The rotary spoiler disturbed the exhaust gases by closing off their efflux by varying amounts, and thus

reduced the minimum range to 3565 m (3,900 yards).

For all the success of the Land Mattress, not many equipments were used in action before the war ended in Europe in May 1944. By that time many were only just emerging from the factories ready to be sent off to South East Asia, but their use there was very limited, as a result mainly of the weight and bulk of the projectors. A special 16-barrel version was developed for towing by a Jeep, but never saw service.

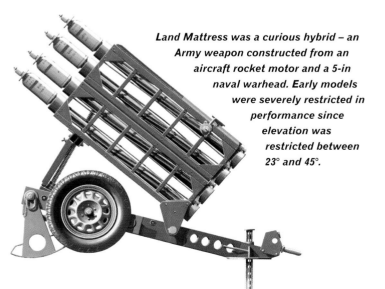

Land Mattress was a curious hybrid – an Army weapon constructed from an aircraft rocket motor and a 5-in naval warhead. Early models were severely restricted in performance since elevation was restricted between 23° and 45°.

SPECIFICATION	
Land Mattress (rocket) **Dimensions:** length 1.77 m (70 in) **Weights:** overall 30.5 kg (67 lb); propellant 5 kg (11 lb); payload 3.18 kg (7 lb)	**Performance:** maximum velocity 335 m (1,100 ft) per second; maximum range 7.2 km (4.4 miles)

Rocket, HE, 4.5-in, M8 & M16 Fin- and spin-stabilised rockets

When the US entered World War II in December 1941, its armed forces had no rockets at all in service or even in prospect. But with typical energy, the Americans used their considerable technical knowledge and industrial potential to remedy this deficit with great speed. In what seemed like no time at all they had erected huge facilities for the production of rocket propellants of all kinds (the first deliveries being accomplished even before the factories had been completed) and were busy designing and producing rockets for a host of purposes.

Mass production

One of these rockets was a relatively straightforward fin-stabilised weapon known during its development and trials periods as the **T12** but then standardised for service as the **Rocket, HE, 4.5-in, M8**.

Looking toward German positions in front of the Canadian 1st Army's XII Corps in January 1945, a fire controller prepares to unleash part of a barrage.

This 114.3-mm rocket carried a nose-fused warhead and tail-mounted folding fins for stabilisation, and was destined to be manufactured in numbers larger than those for any other World War II artillery rocket with the probable exception of the Soviet 82- and 132-mm (3.23- and 5.2-in) weapons: no fewer than 2.537 million had been produced by the end of World War II in 1945. Used in exactly the same fashion as the M8, the **M8A1**, **M8A2** and **M8A3** were slight variations of the baseline M8, the first having a strengthened motor body for service

When the US entered World War II it had no rocket weapons. A high-speed programme then saw the creation of the M8 and M16 (seen) and their launchers.

in a wider range of climates, the second having a smaller warhead with thicker walls providing a superior fragmentation effect, and the third being the M8A2 with slightly modified fins.

Technical details

The M8 was powered by 30 sticks of ballistite propellant exhausting through a single venturi nozzle in the tail, and

was firing by an electrical circuit, or a percussion cap, or a black powder igniter depending on the type of launcher being employed.

Being fin- rather than spin-stabilised, the M8 was inherently inaccurate as any slight trajectory deviation as the rocket left the launcher was amplified by range, and was accordingly used not for the engagement of point targets

Armed with an M1 carbine personal weapon, a US Army soldier loads a 4.5-in (114.3-mm) M8 rocket into its tube on a frame launcher unit.

but for the saturation of large areas. Thus it was used extensively for the mass bombardment of target areas before amphibious landings or as a supplement to massed artillery bombardments. Even at short ranges its accuracy was erratic, so nearly all the launchers used with the M8 were of the multiple type to ensure that the target area was saturated with fire.

Special launcher

Typical of these types was the **T27 Multiple Rocket Launcher**, which fired eight M8 rockets and was carried on the back of a GMC or Studebaker 2.5-ton truck on a mounting that provided an elevation arc of 50 degrees (-5 to +45 degrees) to vary the range. The launcher was moved onto the right bearing by alignment of the truck, and sighting was entrusted to the M6 telescopic sight. There were two variations of this launcher,

namely the **T27E1** that could be disassembled for transport and the **T27E2** with capacity for up to 24 rockets in three layers of eight tubes each.

The **T34** or **Calliope** was a large launcher carried over the turret of an M4 Sherman

medium tank. The Calliope had no fewer than 60 launching tubes (two upper layers each of 18 tubes and two divided bottom layers each comprising upper and lower six-tube units) and was constructed from ply-wood as it was a one-shot

weapon for use against strongpoints. Measuring some 3.05 m (10 ft) in length, the Calliope was traversed by movement of the turret, and elevated by a link to the gun barrel, and after firing or in an emergency the whole device could be jettisoned to leave the Sherman unencumbered for its gun tank role. Variants of the T34 were the **T34E1** and the **T34E2**. The former had two 16-tube upper rows and two divided lower rows each comprising seven-tube upper and lower layers. The T34E1 provided lower dispersion than the T34. The latter had square- rather than round-section tubes.

The **T44** was even larger than the Calliope as it had 120 launcher tubes, and was designed for installation in the cargo area of a DUKW

A gunner checks the sight of a simple T27 eight-tube launcher, generally mounted in the cargo area of GMC or Studebaker 21/2-ton trucks. The M8 was also fired from DUKWs for beach assault.

SPECIFICATION	
Rocket, HE, 4.5-in, M8 **Dimensions:** length 838 mm (33 in); diameter 114.3 mm (4.5 in) **Weights:** overall 17.5 kg (38.5 lb); propellant 2.16 kg (4.75 lb);	explosive 1.95 kg (4.3 lb) **Performance:** maximum velocity 259 m (850 ft) per second; maximum range 4205 m (4,600 yards)

This T34 (Calliope) 60-tube launcher for M8 artillery rockets is fitted not on the standard M4 medium tank, but on a captured German halftrack.

Improved accuracy

Despite the fact that it was made in very large numbers and saw extensive service in the European and Pacific theatres, the M8 was so inaccurate that the rocket was considered inadequate for use as a genuine artillery rocket. Using knowledge gained from trials of captured German rockets, the Americans developed a spin- rather than fin-stabilised weapon known as the **Rocket, HE, 4.5-in, M16**. This had an overall length of 787 mm (31 in) and a weight of 19.3 kg (42.5 lb) including 2.16 kg (4.75 lb) of propellant and 2.36 kg (5.2 lb) of HE, and its other data included a maximum velocity of 253 m (830 ft) per second and a maximum range of 4805 m (5,250 yards).

Dedicated launcher

The M16 was fired from the **Launcher, Rocket, Multiple 4.5-in, T66**. This was an arrangement of three layers of tubes, each with a circular-section interior and hexagonal-section exterior, carried on a two-wheel carriage towed by a light truck. The launcher was trained in azimuth by movement of its trail, and could be elevated between 0 degrees and +45 degrees. The launcher weighed 544 kg (1,200 lb) empty and 1007 kg (2,220 lb) with its 24 rockets, which were loaded from the front rather than the rear, which was the case with the M8 rocket's launchers. It took some 90 seconds to load the T66 launcher, and the 24 rockets could then by discharged in a rippled salvo of two seconds.

This combination arrived at the front late in the war and was used during only one engagement in Germany, by the 282nd Field Artillery Battalion of the US 1st Army's VIII Corps, before the end of hostilities in Europe. The M16 weapon was not used at all in the Pacific theatre.

amphibious truck or LVT amphibious vehicle. The T44 was a simple area-saturation launcher, so there was no method of varying elevation or traverse. A similar device known as the **Scorpion** but mounting 144 launcher tubes was used on DUKW amphibious trucks in the Pacific theatre. The **T45** was a twin 14-tube launcher system that could be fitted to the sides of various vehicles, including light trucks, the M24 light tank and the LVT amphibious vehicle: there were no traverse controls, but the paired launders could be elevated between 0 degrees and +35 degrees. Yet another launcher that fired the M8 rocket was the **M12** (developed and trialled as the **T35**) which was a single-shot 'bunker-buster' (also possessing capability against Japanese cave positions) along the lines of the British LILO, with a plastic launcher tube supported on one rear and two front legs. Complete with one M8 rocket, the equipment weighed 23.6 kg (54 lb). The **M12A1** was an improved M12, while the **M12E1** had a tube made of magnesium alloy rather than plastic and so could be reused.

Above: The firing of any artillery rocket weapon is always an impressive sight and sound, all the more so when multiple launchers are used to fire area-saturation salvoes from wheeled or tracked vehicles.

Left: These M4 Sherman medium tanks each carry the 60-tube T34 launcher generally known as the Calliope. Intended for only a few firings at most (the whole launcher was often jettisoned after only one salvo to allow the tank to function in its primary role), the launcher was based on the use of plywood tubes.

Post-War Small Arms

After World War II, the bolt-action rifle was replaced by automatic assault rifles, optimised for combat at real battlefield ranges of up to 300 metres (328 yards). Manufacture also changed: instead of being machined from high-quality steel, most weapons were made from pressed steel or high impact plastics, greatly reducing the cost of production.

The post-war years also saw the introduction of a wide range of infantry support weapons, including mortars, grenade launchers, and man-portable anti-tank and anti-aircraft weapons. By the end of the 20th century a new generation of personal weapons had entered service, but the biggest change has been in infantry equipment.

The combat riflemen of the future will look more like a Starship Trooper than the soldiers of the past, having helmets with built in night vision sensors, equipped with computerised communications and navigation systems, wearing lightweight personal body armour and using weapons with night sights and individual laser range finders.

Left: In service for more than 40 years, the M16 is the US Army's standard assault rifle. One of the first of the modern small-calibre weapons to enter sevice, the M16 is much lighter and is easier to handle than the heavy M14 rifle which preceded it.

Glock Self-loading pistol

When it first appeared in the early 1980s, the Glock pistol seemed to break all the rules. Largely made of plastic, its design made no concessions to the popular view of what a pistol should look like. When it first appeared, there were wide-spread press reports about this sinister plastic pistol. Why plastic? Was it deliberately designed to be smuggled through security checkpoints at airports – was the Glock intended as the latest weapon in the terrorist arsenal?

In fact the Glock is firmly on the side of law and order. The slide, barrel and trigger group are all metal, so it is not X-ray proof. And the Glock is now in widespread service with armies and police forces worldwide, with over two million having been manufactured. Around 40 per cent of American law enforcement agencies that use automatic pistols have adopted the Glock.

Non-traditional

Part of the reason for the Glock's unusual features comes from the fact that it was not designed by a traditional firearms maker. Glock was founded in Austria by Gaston Glock, an engineer who specialised in the manufacture of plastic and steel components. When the Austrian Army held a competition to find a new service pistol in the 1980s, Glock entered his revolutionary pistol design.

The Glock's receiver is made of tough plastic, resistant to both heat and cold. The old military adage of 'Keep It Simple' has been rigorously applied in the design of the Glock. It has only 33 parts, and can be stripped in a matter of seconds. Best of all, it has no

The Glock is an extremely simple design, with only 33 component parts. It is easy to strip and clean, which is a major plus for military use.

Operation
The Glock is recoil operated; the reaction to firing forces the slide back and allows another round to be chambered.

Ammunition
The Glock 17 fires NATO standard 9x19-mm Parabellum ammunition. Other popular calibres include 10-mm, 0.40 S&W and 0.45 ACP.

Magazine
The Glock uses a double-row magazine holding 17 rounds.

Slide
Manufactured from high-strength polymer plastic, the Glock's slide will withstand temperatures ranging from -50° to +200°C.

Safety
The Glock has no manual safety catch; an automatic firing pin lock prevents the pistol from firing unless the trigger is pulled. The firing pin lock is disengaged by the simple catch mounted on the front of the trigger.

Weight
The use of plastic and light alloy means that the Glock is lighter than most pistols of similar size and ammunition capacity.

SPECIFICATION	
Glock 17	**Weights:** empty 0.63 kg (1 lb 5 oz);
Calibre: 9x19 mm Parabellum	loaded 0.88 kg (1 lb 15 oz)
Length: overall 186 mm (7.32 in);	**Muzzle velocity:** 350 m (1,148 ft) per
Barrel length: 114 mm (4.48 in)	second
	Magazine: 17 rounds

external safety catch to release and so nothing to remember in the stress of action. Unlike almost all pistols in military service, the Glock is ready to fire from the moment it leaves your holster; draw and fire is all you need to do. A group of internal safety mechanisms keeps the weapon in a safe condition until the trigger is pulled.

Military use
The 9-mm **Glock 17** is the most widely used version. Adopted by the Austrian army and by armies and special operations units all over the world, it is an

outstanding handgun. The Glock 18 is a fully automatic version, used as a compact machine pistol. To prevent unauthorised conversions, the operating parts are not interchangeable with the Glock 17.

Its greatest commercial success has been in the United States, with police and civil users. To meet the needs of this

rapidly expanding market, the basic design has been adapted to other calibres. Glock were one of the first manufacturers to launch a 10-mm (0.39-in) pistol, the **Glock 20**. One more step in search of the ultimate pistol cartridge, the 10-mm is a far more lethal round than the standard 9-mm (0.35-in) Parabellum used by most

armies. The Glock 21 is chambered for the .45 ACP round, while the **Glock 22** and **23** fire the popular .40 Smith and Wesson round. Smaller examples of the Glock have been manufactured in all calibres, primarily for plain-clothed police officers to carry concealed. World-wide success speaks for its quality.

Light in weight, very tough, and accurate enough for all combat uses, the Glock is a firm favourite with military, special forces and law enforcement shooters.

Browning High Power Self-loading pistol

The **Browning High Power** was the last firearms design to come from the fertile brain of J.M. Browning, who died in 1926. His design was produced by Fabrique Nationale (FN) of Herstal, in Belgium. Serving through World War II on both sides, the High Power has been produced by the million, and is still in production.

The main producer is still FN, although spares are made in Canada following extensive World War II production in that country.

During the 1990s, assembly was at a plant in Portugal from Belgian parts, but the factory was closed and full production has moved back to Herstal.

Variants

FN has made several variants of the basic High Power. All are virtually identical internally, using the same basic Browning short recoil method of operation and the double-row magazine which made the High Power the first modern high-capacity pistol. However, the exterior fittings and finish vary considerably.

The military variants, the **High Power Mk 2** and **Mk 3**, are updated versions of the original with more modern finish and grip shape. The **High**

Power Standard is the commercial model, while the **High Power Practical** is optimised for competition shooters.

Compact carry

In recent years other versions of the High Power have appeared, some with specially lightened slides and components made from light alloys,

Below: Hard-hitting and with a large magazine capacity, civilian High Powers have found a ready market with bodyguards all over the world.

Above: Millions of High Powers have been made, and countless accessories have been produced. This example has non-slip grips and a 'Red Dot' sight on the slide.

SPECIFICATION	
FN High Power	**Weights:** empty 0.88 kg (1 lb 15 oz);
Calibre: 9x19 mm	loaded 1.04 kg (2 lb 4 oz)
Length: overall 200 mm (7.85-in)	**Muzzle velocity:** 350 m (1,148 ft) per
Barrel length: 118 mm (4.65-in)	second
	Magazine capacity: 14 rounds

The reliability of the High Power made it the weapon of choice for Britain's SAS when the regiment set up one of the world's first hostage rescue teams.

to reduce weight. All these versions fire the 9-mm (0.35-in) Parabellum cartridge and all have found ready buyers, even in a world market sated with more modern pistol designs.

A double-action development, the BDA, was introduced in various calibres in the early 1980s, but did not sell as well as the original single-action pistol did.

One factor that has consistently sold the classic Browning design has been the series' extreme robustness. The pistols can accept very hard use and

will fire under the most adverse conditions, always providing that they are properly maintained and are loaded with decent ammunition.

The High Power can be a bit awkward to handle, especially for those with small hands, as the butt is rather wide to accommodate the double-stack box magazine. However, this does not detract from the pistol's many other virtues, and the Browning High Power has become the standard military issue sidearm in more than 50 countries.

Below: The axis of the High Power's bore sits low on the shooter's hand, reducing muzzle flip on firing. The well-positioned safety catch automatically drops the thumb into firing position when disengaged.

9-mm FN High Power Belgian-made Browning

The **Browning High Power** pistol was created in 1925 by John Moses Browning, the famous American weapons designer, but the type is still in production and service to this day. The main producer of this fine weapon is still the Fabrique Nationale (FN) organisation of Herstal in Belgium, where manufacture began in 1935, although spares are also made in Canada following World War II production in that country by the Inglis company.

FN now makes several variants of the High Power in addition to the basic military version. All of these variants use the same basic Browning short recoil method of operation, and can easily be

recognised as coming from the same stable. One notable modern variant is the **High Power Mk 2**, which can be regarded as an updated version of the original, characterised by a more modern finish and grip shape but retaining the original, reliable and well-proved operation without any significant modification. The **High Power Mk 3** is basically the High Power Mk 2 with an automatic firing pin safety

This cutaway of the Browning High Power shows all the working parts of this automatic pistol. The name High Power was applied by the Belgians because it out-performed anything they had used previously.

device. The FN-made High Power carries the legend 'FABRIQUE NATIONALE HERSTAL BELGIUM

BROWNING'S PATENT DEPOSE FN (year)' on the slide.

There are three versions of the standard military model. The

SPECIFICATION	
9-mm FN High Power	**Weight:** empty 0.882 kg (1.94 lb);
Cartridge: 9 mm (0.35 in)	loaded 1.04 kg (2.29 lb)
Length overall: 200 mm (7.87 in)	**Muzzle velocity:** 350 m/s
Length of barrel: 118 mm (4.65 in)	**Magazine:** 13-round box

basic military model is now known to FN as the **BDA-9S**. The smaller **BDA-9M** uses the same frame as the BDA-9S but in combination with a shorter slide and barrel. The shorter slide and barrel are also used in the compact version of the family, the **BDA-9C**. This is a very small pistol for its calibre and has a much shortened butt holding only seven rounds instead of the 14 that are standard for the other models. The BDA-9C is intended as a 'pocket pistol' for use by plain clothes police units and by those involved in specialist tasks such as VIP protection.

In recent years other versions of the High Power have appeared, some with specially lightened slides to reduce weight and others with components made from light alloys, again to reduce weight. All these versions fire the standard 9-mm (0.35-in) Parabellum cartridge and all have found ready buyers, even in a world market that would appear to have been saturated with more modern pistol designs. One factor that has consistently boosted sales of the High Power pistol has been its reputation for robustness and reliability. Both of these factors are inherent in Browning designs, and also in weapons of FN manufacture. The pistols are capable of accepting very hard use and will fire under the most adverse conditions, with the proviso – as with all weapons – that they are properly cleaned and maintained, and are also loaded with decent ammunition.

The High Power pistol can be a bit awkward to handle, for on all but the BDA-9C model the butt is wide, which results directly from the use of a double-stack box magazine to provide accommodation for the very useful total of 13 rounds. However, this has not prevented the High Power being used as a target pistol by some enthusiasts.

Czech pistols CZ 75 and family

The design and manufacture of land warfare weapons, especially small arms and artillery, has long been a Czech speciality. The city of Brno in the central Czech republic is recognised as a centre of excellence for the manufacturer of small arms. Brno gave its name to the 'Br' part of the Bren gun. The Brno-based armaments firm, Ceská zbrojovka organisation, generally known as CZ, has been responsible for most of the country's pistol designs.

The first Czechoslovakian semi-automatic pistol was the VZ.22 recoil-operated weapon chambered for the 9.65-mm (0.38-in) short cartridge, but this was made only in small numbers before being replaced by the VZ.24 with a slightly modified locking and firing mechanisms. Next came the VZ.27, which was made in larger numbers that any other Czechoslovakian pistol of the period before World War II. Chambered for the 7.65-mm (0.32-in) ACP (Automatic Colt Pistol) cartridge, of which eight rounds were carried in the detachable inline box magazine, which fits inside the butt, the VZ.27 fitted was a blowback operating system which had used the momentum of the round leaving the chamber to

Above: Demonstrating the blowback mechanism, a second round can be seen underneath the main bullet which is ready to fire. The weapon is notably jam-resistant.

extract another cartridge from the magazine. Made only in small numbers, the VZ.38 was chambered for the 9-mm (0.35-in) short cartridge, and was also a blowback weapon.

The next Czechoslovakian pistol to enter production was the 7.65-mm (0.30-in) VZ.50 with blowback operation and an eight-round magazine, and then came the VZ.52 firing the

Left: The CZ 75 features a large grip that fills the hand and greatly improves both the handling and accuracy of the pistol. Note the adjacent double-row magazine.

SPECIFICATION	
CZ.75B	**Weight:** 1 kg (2.2 lb) with empty
Cartridge: 9-mm (0.35 in)	magazine
Length overall: 206 mm (8.1 in)	**Muzzle velocity:** around 370 m/s
Length of barrel: 120 mm (4.7 in)	**Magazine:** 11- or 16-round box

This CZ 75 is ready to fire with a 9-mm (0.35-in) cartridge in the chamber. This pistol borrows much of its design from Browning. The ammunition of the basic model is carried in a 16-cartridge magazine.

Czechoslovakian VZ.48 cartridge offering greater power than the Soviet Type P cartridge of the same calibre; the VZ.52 was a recoil-operated weapon with an eight-round magazine. One of the best pistols to be created in Europe after World War II, the **VZ.75**, increasingly known as the **CZ 75**, has been made in large numbers and has also been widely copied. This excellent 9-mm (0.35-in) Parabellum pistol is clearly derived from Browning design thinking with features from several other weapons. It is available in semi-automatic and automatic variants, and has a 16-round magazine. The **CZ 85** is basically similar to the **CZ 75** except for its ambidextrous safety catch and slide stop. The **CZ 85B** version adds a firing pin safety to enhance the drop safety of the pistol. The **CZ 85 Combat** is a CZ 85 development with additional features including an adjustable rear sight.

Blowback

The **CZ 83** is a double-action pistol chambered for the 7.65-mm (0.30-in) ACP, 9-mm (0.35-in) short or 9-mm (0.35-in) Makarov rounds, of which 15, 13 or 13 respectively are carried. The **CZ 83** is a 'pocket' weapon with blowback operation; the trigger guard is large enough to admit a gloved finger.

The **CZ 92** is designed for personal defence, and is a double-action pistol working on the blowback system. The pistol is not equipped with a manual safety; after each shot the hammer returns to its released position, which enhances its safety against accidental discharge. The pistol is also fitted with a magazine safety catch so that removal of the magazine automatically blocks the trigger mechanism.

Belonging to a new range of pistols firing from a locked breech, the **CZ 100** is notable for its modern concept and the use of a high-impact plastic and steel slide for reduced weight. The trigger mechanism is of the double-action type and incorporates a firing pin safety, the pistol also being equipped with a single side slide stop and a magazine catch – the slide is locked open when the last round has been fired. The shaping of the weapon facilitates shooting with gloved hands, while the ergonomic shaping allows shooting with either hand.

Finally, the **CZ 110** is based on the **CZ 100** but has semi-automatic and double-action firing modes. One major advantage of the weapon is that the pistol can be carried safely even with a cartridge in the chamber.

French automatic pistols Model 1950 and PA15

The French **MAS Model 1950** 9-mm (0.35-in) pistol was designed by Nationale d'Armes, St-Étienne, eastern France, and manufactured at the Nationale d'Armes factory, Châtellerault, western France. From 1950 onwards it became the standard service pistol for the French army and the armies of several former French colonies.

The pistol is loaded by inserting nine 9-mm Parabellum cartridges into the magazine. A cartridge is positioned into the chamber by pulling back the slide and then releasing it. The gun's safety catch is located on the left rear side of the slide. If the safety catch lever is horizontal it indicates that the pistol is safe.

The locking ribs on top of the barrel are fitted into the grooves on the inside of the slide, causing the barrel to move backwards with the slide. The lower rear end of the barrel is attached to the receiver by means of a swinging link. The barrel and slide move back together for a short distance and then, since the lower portion of the link is attached to the non-recoiling frame, the link pulls the rear end of the barrel down. This separates the locking ribs of the barrel from the recesses inside the slide and, when the locking system is disconnected, the barrel is at rest and the slide continues to the rear under its own momentum. The empty cartridge case comes out on the breach face and stays there until it strikes the fixed ejector.

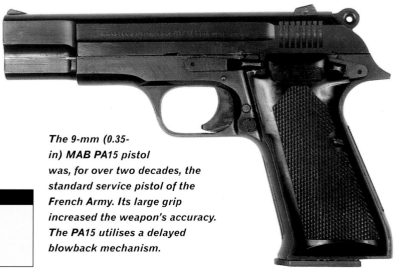

The 9-mm (0.35-in) MAB PA15 pistol was, for over two decades, the standard service pistol of the French Army. Its large grip increased the weapon's accuracy. The PA15 utilises a delayed blowback mechanism.

SPECIFICATION	
MAB PA15	
Cartridge: 9 mm (0.35 in)	**Weight:** 1.09 kg (2.43 lb)
Length overall: 203 mm (7.99 in)	**Muzzle velocity:** 350 m/s
Length of barrel: 114 mm (4.49 in)	**Magazine:** 15-round box

The weapon is reloaded when the return spring forces the slide forward and the face of the breech block carries the top cartridge in the magazine forward into the chamber. The breech block contacts the barrel and pushes it forward where the link raises the breech and the ribs on the top of the barrel enter the grooves on the slide, locking the two together. Forward movement ceases when the lug on the bottom of the barrel contacts the slide stop pin.

MAB PA15

The MAB PA15 pistol was designed and introduced into the French Army in 1970 as the standard service pistol. It has a characteristic bulky grip giving better handling and increased accuracy, and the grip is also long enough to accommodate a magazine containing 15 9-mm (0.35-in) Parabellum cartridges. The weapon features a prominent spur towards the rear of the receiver; it also features a ring-type hammer.

Production of the MAB PA15 was terminated in the late 1980s, but it was announced in late 1991 that a deal had been

Until the appearance of the MAB PA15 in 1970, the MAS Model 1950 was the standard service pistol of the French Army and of several former French colonial nations. The safety catch is located on the left rear side of the slide.

SPECIFICATION	
MAS Model 1950	
Cartridge: 9-mm (0.35 in)	**Weight:** 0.86 kg (1.89 lb)
Length: 195 mm (7.68 in)	**Muzzle velocity:** 354 m/s
Length of barrel: 112 mm (4.41 in)	**Magazine:** 9-round box

concluded between the French and Yugoslav governments permitting the licensed manufacture of the MAB PA15 by Zastava Arms of Serbia. The gun is believed to be in service with some of the armies within the former Yugoslavia.

The MAB PA15 has a frame-mounted safety catch on the left frame, and also features an internal magazine safety catch. This prevents the gun being fired if the magazine is removed. The reload of the chamber is by delayed blowback action.

Heckler & Koch pistols

Heckler & Koch GmbH was established in the 1950s and produced a pistol based on the Mauser HSc but with thumb-rests on the grip and a modernised profile. Manufactured in four calibres, the **HK4** was marketed in the US in the late 1960s but was not a great commercial success and manufacture ceased in the 1980s. The company, however, went from strength to strength after it won the contract to develop the G3 rifle for the newly established West German army. In 1990 the revolutionary G11 rifle was finally rejected as a replacement for the G3, however, and the company got into financial difficulty. It was bought by Royal Ordnance plc, a subsidiary of British Aerospace which already manufactured a number of Heckler & Koch weapons under licence.

The **P9** pistol has a delayed blowback action derived from that of the G3 rifle, involving a roller-locked breech block. Available in 7.65-mm (0.301-in) and 9-mm Parabellum (0.354-in) calibres, it has an internal hammer with a de-cocking lever on the left side of the receiver. The **P9S** is a double-action version. Both have been sold to a number of armies and paramilitary units, and a version chambered for the 0.45-in ACP (11.43-mm) cartridge was introduced in 1977 for the US market. The US Marine Corps acquired a number of P9s fitted with threaded barrels to accept a silencer. The P9 was taken out of production in 1990.

VP70

From 1970 until the mid-1980s, Heckler & Koch manufactured a double-action automatic with a three-round burst facility. The **VP70** came with a detachable shoulder stock and it was intended for the military market. Sales were limited to a few third-world armies, and neither this nor a 'civilian' version without the burst facility is widely encountered today.

Above: The P9 employs a version of the roller and block delayed-locking system as used in the family of Heckler & Koch rifles.

Below: A demonstration of the P7 variant.

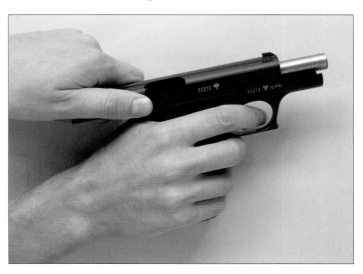

P7 variant

The **P7** was designed to a specification issued by the then West German police for an automatic that could be drawn and fired without releasing an external safety catch. Full production began in 1979, and the weapon is used by the German police and also by the Border Guard. Immediately recognisable by its grip, the P7 has a cocking lever built into the front of the handgrip: this must be squeezed in order for the pistol to operate. Releasing the grip disconnects the firing pin from the trigger rendering the weapon safe. The **P7K3**, chambered for the 9-mm Short (0.38-in) cartridge, is a simple blowback pistol adopted by the German army and some paramilitary forces. The **P7M8** and **P7M13** are models with 8- and 13-round magazines respectively, as well as a gas piston and cylinder for the delayed blowback action demanded by its more powerful 9-mm Parabellum cartridge. In 1987 the **P7M45** was introduced for the US market; chambered for the 0.45-in ACP cartridge, it uses an oil-filled cylinder rather than gas cylinder to delay the recoil of the slide, an interesting adaptation of an artillery mechanism to a hand gun. This made the P7M45 an expensive weapon and, at a time when competition was extremely fierce, its commercial failure could not have been a total surprise.

Developed in the 1980s was the **Mk 23**, which won a US Special Operations Command competition for a handgun for special forces missions, and entered service is 1996. Chambered for 0.45-in ACP, this large automatic has a double-action only trigger with safety and de-cocking levers. The frame is polymer with steel inserts and the pistol is built to mount laser aiming devices and/or tactical flashlights. The barrel is threaded to accept a silencer.

Heckler & Koch's other military pistol of recent years is a derivative of the **Universal Selbstlade Pistole** (universal self-loading pistol) that has been made in many variants in the last decade. A general purpose law enforcement and self-defence weapon, the USP includes sporting versions and the **USP Tactical**, a 0.45-in automatic used by some US Special Forces units instead of the huge Mk 23. The German army has acquired the USP which it designates **P8**, and the German police employs the **USP Compact** as the **P10** (both guns are 9mm).

SPECIFICATION	
P7M8	**P9**
Calibre: 9-mm Parabellum	**Calibre:** 9-mm Parabellum
Weights: 0.8 kg (1.76 lb) empty; 0.95 kg (2.09 lb) loaded	**Weights:** 0.88 kg (1.94 lb) empty; 1.07 kg (2.35 lb) loaded
Lengths: overall 171 mm (6.73 in); barrel 105 mm (4.13 in)	**Lengths:** overall 192 mm (7.56 in); barrel 102 mm (4 in)
Muzzle velocity: 350 m (1,150 ft) per second	**Muzzle Velocity:** 350 m (1,150 ft) per second
Magazine capacity: 8 rounds	**Magazine capacity:** 9 rounds
VP70	**USP**
Calibre: 9-mm Parabellum	**Calibre:** 9-mm Parabellum, 0.40-in S&W, 0.45-in ACP, 0.357-in SIG
Weights: 820 g (1.81 lb) empty; 1.14 kg (2.51 lb) loaded	**Weight:** 720 g (1.59 lb)
Lengths: overall 204 mm (8.03 in); barrel 116 mm (4.57 in); with stock fitted 545 mm (21.45 in)	**Magazine capacity:** 15 rounds (9-mm version)
Muzzle velocity: 360 m (1,180 ft) per second	**Mk 23**
Magazine capacity: 18 rounds	**Calibre:** 0.45-in ACP
	Weight: 1100 g (2.425 lb) empty
	Length: 245 mm (9.65 in) overall
	Magazine capacity: 12 rounds

Walther PP and PPK

Walther introduced its **PP** (**Polizei Pistole**) pistol in 1929, and the weapon is still in production. It was widely used by the German armed forces and their allies during World War II. The **PPK** (**Polizei Pistole Kurz**, or short police pistol) was a more compact version for the use of the police, and especially the plain clothes police, of which Germany had something of a surplus during the 1940s. Introduced in 1931, it has also been waved about in many a spy movie from James Bond down.

(Bond has just upgraded to the more recent Walther P99). These were the first successful double-action automatics. Production ceased after the war but resumed in the mid-1960s, and the PP and PPK have remained in widespread service ever since. The original PP was offered in the 7.65-mm (0.301-in) and 9-mm Short (0.38-in) calibres; since the 1960s a version in 0.22-in Long Rifle (5.59-mm) calibre has been widely sold for plinking. A handful of PPs were made in 6.35-mm (0.25-in) calibre before the war.

Small, light and possessing no significant features to snag in clothes, the PP and its smaller half-brother, the PPK, were designed for police and paramilitary use rather than the more arduous demands of front-line military forces.

SPECIFICATION	
PPK	**Length:** 154 mm (6 in) overall; barrel 84 mm (3.31 in)
Calibre: 7.65-mm	
Weight: 0.58 kg (1.28 lb) empty	**Magazine capacity:** 7 rounds

One oddity is the **PPK/S**, a PP frame with the barrel and slide of the PPK: this was built to get around the 1968 US gun control laws which introduced a minimum size for imported handguns. The **PP Super** has a trigger guard designed for two-handed use, and fires the 9-mm Police cartridge. The diminutive **TP** and **TPH** versions were discontinued in the 1970s, although they were manufactured under licence for a period in the United States.

All the models operate on a straightforward blowback principle, and good safety arrangements are incorporated as standard. One of these safeties has been widely copied: a block is placed in the way of the firing pin when it moves forward, and is removed only when the trigger is given a definite pull. Another innovation in the weapon is the incorporation of a signal pin above the hammer, which protrudes when a round is actually in the chamber to provide a positive 'loaded' indication. This feature was omitted from production in the course of World War II.

Modern Walther pistols P5, P88, and P99

Walther's P38 automatic pistol of World War II fame was revived as a production item in the course of 1979, the modernised version being designated as the **P5**. The main improvements are to the weapon's safety. Used by police arms including German and Dutch forces, and ordered by several African armies, the P5 is also manufactured in a compact format with a length of 169 mm (6.65 in) and an 8-round magazine.

In 1988 Walther departed from its standard operating design feature, the wedge lock, and produced a pistol with Colt/Browning toggle locking. This **P88** was tested by a number of armies looking for a new service sidearm, including the British Army. However, it did not attract sufficient interest to warrant a large-scale production programme.

The **P99** began life in the mid-1990s in an effort to overcome the problems of the P88: it is much cheaper than the P88

and yet incorporates the simple features modern armies prefer. It has no manual safeties, instead using three automatic safety features: trigger safety, out-of-battery

The latest Walther semi-automatic pistols, such as the P99, are notable for their excellent design and high manufacturing qualities. These make Walther pistols reliable and safe. The P99 entered production in 1999 and is also available as the double action only P990 model.

safety, and striker safety. There is a de-cocking button in the upper part of the slide. The 'military' version's polymer slide is coloured olive green rather than the standard black.

The redoutable Smith & Wesson manufactures the weapon under licence in the US as the **S&W99**: the frame and action are German-made, while the United States manufacturer supplies the slide and undertakes final assembly of the weapon for the local market. The version chambered for the 0.40-in S&W cartridge has the reduced magazine capacity of 12 rounds.

SPECIFICATION	
P5	barrel 102 mm (4 in)
Calibre: 9-mm Parabellum	**Weight:** 0.9 kg (1.98 lb)
Lengths: overall 180 mm (7.09 in); barrel 90 mm (3.54 in)	**Magazine capacity:** 15 rounds
Weight: 0.795 kg (1.75 lb)	**P99**
Magazine capacity: 8	**Calibre:** 9-mm Parabellum
	Weight: 0.72 kg (1.59 lb) unloaded
P88	**Lengths:** overall 180 mm (7.09 in); barrel 102 mm (4 in)
Calibre: 9-mm Parabellum	**Magazine capacity:** 16 rounds
Lengths: overall 187 mm (7.36 in);	

The P38 and its linear descendant, the P5, represent a continuous line of design thinking between the middle of the 1930s and the late 1970s, when the P5 was introduced as a modernised P38. The legend on the left-hand side of the slide, to the rear of the Walther banner emblem, reads 'P5/Carl Walther Waffenfabrik Ulm/Do'. The weapon's serial number is marked on the right-hand side of the frame. The Walther P5's basic specification was provided by the German police.

IMI Desert Eagle Pistol

The automatic pistol produced by Israel Military Industries and known as the **IMI Desert Eagle** was originally an American design proposed by M.R.I. Limited of Minneapolis, Minnesota. The basic concept has been developed in Israel to the point where the Desert Eagle is an extremely advanced and powerful weapon. Predictably, it has captured the imagination of film makers and has been wielded on screen in many an action movie.

The Desert Eagle can be converted to fire either the 0.357-in Magnum (9-mm) cartridge or the even more powerful 0.44-in Magnum

IMI entered the pistol field with the Desert Eagle, an automatic chambered for the ever-popular 0.357-in Magnum cartridge. The Desert Eagle is fitted with an ambidextrous safety catch on the rear of the slide which locks the firing pin and disconnects the trigger from the hammer mechanism. Military interest remains speculative.

(10.92-mm) round; the latter cartridge is one of the most powerful pistol rounds available. All that is required to convert the pistol from one calibre to the other is the replacement of a few parts. To ensure complete safety when using these large rounds the Desert Eagle uses a rotating bolt for a maximum locking action, The safety catch can be engaged by either the right or left hand, and when in position on 'Safe' the hammer is disconnected from the trigger and the firing pin is immobilized.

Extended barrels

The pistol uses a 152-mm (6-in) barrel as standard, but this basic barrel is interchangeable with

SPECIFICATION	
Desert Eagle	**Muzzle velocity:** 0.357 Magnum 436 m (1,430 ft) per second; 0.44 Magnum 448 m (1,470 ft) per second
Calibre: 0.357 in (9-mm) or 0.44 in (10.92-mm) Magnum	
Weight: empty 1.701 kg (3.75 lb)	**Magazine capacity:** 0.357 Magnum 9 rounds; 0.44 Magnum 7 rounds
Lengths: overall with 6-in barrel 260 mm (10.25 in); barrel 152.4 m (6 in)	

barrels 203 mm (8 in), 254 mm (10 in), and 356 mm (14 in) long. The extended barrels are intended for long-range target shooting and may be used with a telescopic sight fitted to a

mounting on top of the receiver. No special tools are required to change the barrels. Several other options are available for the Desert Eagle. The trigger can be made adjustable and several

different types of fixed sight can be fitted. The trigger guard is shaped to be used with a two-handed grip, although special grips can be fitted if required. The normal construction is of high-quality steels, but an aluminium frame can be supplied.

To date the Desert Eagle has been marketed with the civilian target shooter or enthusiast in mind, but it could also make a powerful military or police weapon. However, most military

The 0.357 Magnum is the cartridge favoured by most US police units and significantly outperforms the 9-mm Parabellum and 0.38 special. Recoil is sharp but controllable, despite gas operation.

authorities usually frown upon the use of Magnum cartridges as they are too powerful for general military use because they require a great deal of training for their best capabilities to be realised. It is one of the ironies of the modern military that pistols, issued as sidearms to personnel who are not normally expected to get into a firefight, actually require more training than any other firearm for a shooter to become proficient. Regular practice is essential. Even among well trained military forces, accidents with pistols are depressingly common. Thus weapons such as the Desert Eagle seem destined to remain with special police units and enthusiasts who simply want the best and most powerful hand-guns available.

Beretta Model 1951/Beretta 9-mm Model 92 series
Pistol

The **Model 1951** retained the Beretta open-topped slide, but early hopes that this slide could be made from aluminium did not materialize and most production models use an all-steel unit.

The first examples of the Model 1951 did not appear until 1957 as a result mainly of attempts to develop a satisfactory light slide. In more recent years the aluminium slide has become available as an option.

Standard pistol

The 9-mm (0.354-in) Model 1951 became the standard service pistol of Israel and Egypt as well as Italy. A production line was established in Egypt to manufacture the type and it is known in Egypt as the **Helwan**. The Model 1951 uses the basic Beretta layout, despite the adoption of the locked breech system. The recoil rod and spring are located under the largely open barrel, and the well-sloped butt holds the box magazine containing eight rounds. There is an

The Beretta Model 1951 was the standard pistol of the Italian armed forces, although numbers are now declining, and has been exported to a number of countries, including Israel and Egypt. This is an example manufactured in Egypt, where the locally produced model is called the Helwan.

external hammer and the safety catch engages the sear when in use. Both rear and fore sights are adjustable on most versions.

New types

In 1976 Beretta placed in production two new families of automatic pistols, the **Model 81** which used a blowback system and was chambered for

calibres such as 7.65 mm (0.301 in), and the much larger **Beretta Model 92** which fires the usual 9-mm (0.354-in) Parabellum cartridge. One of its variants, the **Model 92F** or **M9**, is the US Army's standard pistol and replaced the M1911A1.

Slide safety catch

Starting from the basic Model 92, the **Model 92S** has a

revised safety catch on the slide rather than below it as on the basic Model 92. This allows the hammer to be lowered onto a loaded chamber with complete safety as the firing pin is taken out of line with the hammer.

The **Model 92SB** is essentially similar to the Model 92S, but the slidemounted safety catch can be applied from each side of the slide. The **Model 92 SB-C** is a more compact and handier version of the Model 92SB.

US Army variant

The Model 92F was a development of the Model 92SB for the US Army and has been produced in both Italy and the US. The main changes from the Model 92SB are a revised trigger guard outline to suit a two-handed grip, an extended magazine base, revised grips and a lanyard ring. The bore is chrome-plated for durability and the exterior is coated in a Teflon-type material.

Introduced in 1976, the Model 92 has proved a logical successor to the Modello 1951. This has a frame-mounted safety catch (later models have the catch on the slide). The Model 92 is operated by the Italian army.

Following on from the Model 92F there is a **Model 92F**

Compact, designed along the same lines as the Model 92 SB-C but using the features of the US Army's Model 92F.

Also produced along the same lines is the **Model 92 SB-C Type M** which has an eight-round magazine instead of the 15-round magazine. There are also two more models based on the

Model 92 series but in a smaller calibre: the **Model 98 and Model 99** (no longer in production), both in 7.65-mm calibre and based on the Model 92 SB-C and Model 92 SB-C Type M respectively.

SPECIFICATION	
Model 1951	**Model 92F**
Calibre: 9 mm (0.354 in)	**Calibre:** 9 mm (0.354 in)
Weight: empty 0.87 kg (1.918 lb)	**Weight:** loaded 1.145 kg (2.524 lb)
Lengths: overall 203.2 mm (8 in); barrel 114.2 mm (4.45 in)	**Lengths:** overall 217 mm (8.54 in); barrel 125 mm (4.92 in)
Muzzle velocity: 350 m (1,148 ft) per second	**Muzzle velocity:** about 390 m (1,280 ft) per second
Magazine capacity: 8 rounds	**Magazine capacity:** 15 rounds

Beretta 9-mm Model 93R Pistol

With the **Beretta Model 93R** one is back in that no-man's land between true machine pistols and selective-fire pistols, for the Model 93R is another modern pistol design intended to fire three-round bursts. Derived from the Beretta Model 92, the Model 93R can be handled and fired as a normal automatic pistol, but when the three-round burst mode is selected, the firer has to use both hands to hold the pistol steady.

Grip arrangement

To do this Beretta has designed a compact grip system on which the right hand carries out its normal function of operating the trigger and grasping the butt. For the left hand a small forehand grip is folded down from in front

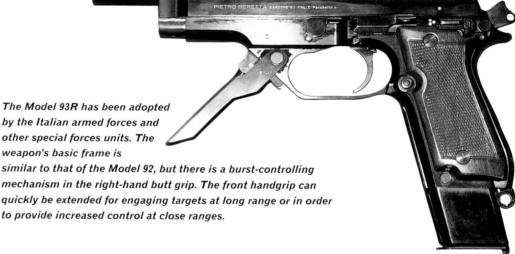

The Model 93R has been adopted by the Italian armed forces and other special forces units. The weapon's basic frame is similar to that of the Model 92, but there is a burst-controlling mechanism in the right-hand butt grip. The front handgrip can quickly be extended for engaging targets at long range or in order to provide increased control at close ranges.

of the elongated trigger guard. The left thumb is inserted into the front of the trigger guard and the rest of the fingers grasp the forehand grip. For additional

assistance in holding the pistol steady during firing, the end of the protruding barrel is equipped with a muzzle brake that also acts as a flash hider.

Folding stock

To provide even more firing stability it is possible to fix a metal folding stock to the butt. When not in use this can be carried in a special holster, and when mounted on the pistol can

be extended to two lengths to suit the firer.

Two types of box magazine can be used with the Model 93R, one holding 15 rounds and the other holding 20. The usual 9-mm (0.354-in) Parabellum cartridge is used.

The design detail incorporated into the Model 93R is considerable and one item that will no doubt be seen on future

SPECIFICATION	
Model 93R	
Calibre: 9 mm (0.354 in)	**Lengths:** pistol 240 mm (9.45 in); barrel 156 mm (6.14 in)
Weights: loaded with 15-round magazine 1.12 kg (2.47 lb); loaded with 20-round magazine 1.17 kg (2.58 lb)	**Muzzle velocity:** 375 m (1,230 ft) per second
	Magazine capacity: 15 or 29 rounds

A self-loading weapon capable of firing three-round bursts, the Model 93R is more accurately a 'machine pistol', although it is carried and handled in the manner of a conventional pistol.

designs is the use of the foregrip in front of the trigger guard. This is so arranged that the two-handed grip derived from its use is much steadier than the usual two-handed grip with both hands wrapped around what is often a bulky pistol butt.

Using this foregrip it is quite possible to provide reasonably accurate burst fire as both hands are 'spaced' to produce a longer holding base and yet are close enough to prevent either hand wavering. It is possible to fire bursts without using the metal extending stock, but for really accurate fire (even with single shots) its use is recommended.

The Model 93R has now progressed from the development stage and is available on the open market. However, one problem encountered with the pistol seems to be that the three-round burst mechanism is rather compli-cated and at present requires the services of a trained technician, rather than the operator, to carry out maintenance and repairs.

Once this difficulty has been ironed out, the Model 93R will certainly make a formidable close-quarter self-defence weapon.

Makarov 9-mm pistol

The **Makarov** automatic pistol was developed in the USSR in the early 1950s and entered production during 1952, although it was first noticed by various Western intelligence agencies only during the early 1960s. In design terms it is believed to be an enlarged version of the German Walther PP, a semi-automatic pistol introduced in 1929 and since that time acknowledged to be one of the best weapons of its type. It is worth noting, however, that there are other suggestions for the design origins of the Makarov pistol. The Makarov uses a 9-mm (0.354-in) x 18 cartridge which, though of nominally the same dimensions as the Western 9-mm Police

cartridge, is in fact different from any other in use. Developed for use from 1951 in the Stechkin machine pistol (basically a scaled-up Walther PP with full-automatic fire capability and a 20-round magazine), this cartridge is intermediate in power between the 9-mm Parabellum and the 9-mm Short. The Soviet cartridge appears to have been based on a German design of World War II, known as the Ultra: this was not accepted for German wartime service, but attracted some attention in the West for a while. The Ultra has not been produced in the West in any form, but the Soviets took to it

The Makarov is a simple semi-automatic pistol working on the blowback principle and apparently based in general terms on the Walther PP and PPK designs, closely related German pistols of the period before World War II.

into their thinking, for use in unlocked-breech weapons.

Simple action

The availability of this cartridge made it possible for the Makarov

to be designed on the basis of a straightforward blowback operating mechanism without the complications that would be needed with a more powerful cartridge. Another difference

SPECIFICATION	
Makarov	**Length of barrel:** 91 mm (3.58 in)
Calibre: 9-mm (0.354-in) Makarov	**Muzzle velocity:** 315 m (1,033 ft) per second
Weight: empty 0.663 kg (1.46 lb)	
Length overall: 160 mm (6.3 in)	**Magazine:** 8-round detachable box

between the PP and the Makarov is the latter's trigger mechanism: this is simpler than that of the Walther pistol, but this simplicity was purchased only at the price of a very poor double-action pull.

The Soviets introduced the Makarov as the **PM** (**Pistole Makarova**). As well as being issued to all the branches of the Soviet armed forces, the Makarov was also used by the forces of virtually all the other countries of the Warsaw Pact organisation, and by a great many of the Eastern bloc police forces as well.

The Makarov is a sound, rugged and simple weapon that can be relied upon to operate even under severe conditions. Most accounts state that the pistol is rather awkward to handle as the butt is rather thick, but this is presumably no problem for Eastern bloc soldiers, many of whom have to wear heavy gloves during much of the year.

The Makarov has also been manufactured outside the USSR. One of the largest producers has been China, where the weapon is known as the **Type 59**. China has made some efforts to secure export orders for its Type 59 in direct competition to the USSR, which frequently included the Makarov within the context

of its military aid packages. East Germany was another non-Soviet manufacturer of the Makarov pistol, producing a weapon that was virtually identical to the Makarov but known as the **Pistole M**, while Poland turned out yet another Makarov lookalike known as the **P-64**. The special Makarov ammunition has also been produced in all three of these countries.

Unadopted successor

The primary limitations of the Makarov pistol are a relatively small magazine capacity and an underpowered cartridge. The Soviets appreciated this fact and from the early 1980s attempted unsuccessfully to overcome these shortcoming in the **PMM** (PM Modified) pistol with a 12-round double-stack magazine, and a cartridge based on a lighter bullet fired by a heavier propellant load for a muzzle velocity increased by 100 m (328 ft) per second.

An officer of the Soviet Naval Infantry prepares to fire his 9-mm Makarov pistol. The Naval Infantry was small by comparison with most Soviet arms, but for its size was regarded as one of the most effective fighting forces possessed by the USSR.

PSM 5.45-mm pistol

In the 1970s the Soviet authorities decided that a new, notably compact and light-weight semi-automatic pistol was needed as the personal defence weapon to be carried by senior military and security officers. The requirement demanded that the weapon be as slim as possible and lacking in external excrescences that

might catch in clothing, the object clearly being the creation of a weapon that could be carried under clothing as unobtrusively as possible yet still possessing the capability for being drawn quickly and smoothly.

The new weapon was created round a newly developed cartridge, the

5.45-mm (0.215-in) x 18 round with a bottle-necked case and a spitzer-pointed jacketed bullet to provide capability superior to those offered by the 0.22-in (5.59-mm) LR and Browning 0.25-in (6.35-mm) ACP cartridges. Although this round offers only a modest muzzle velocity, the bullet is claimed by some sources to possess remarkable penetrative capabilities against some types of body armour.

Small and light

The weapon designed to fire this useful cartridge is the

Pistolet Samozaryadnii Malogabaritnii (PSM, or small self-loading pistol), which entered production in 1980 and reached service shortly after this time. The PSM is a perfectly conventional blowback-operated weapon with a double-action trigger and a manually operated safety catch (pulled back to make the weapon safe) mounted on the left-hand side of the slide's rear portion. There is no slide stop. The weapon is made primarily of steel, but the grip sideplates are fabricated from thin aluminium alloy in an effort to

SPECIFICATION	
PSM	**Length overall:** 155 mm (6.1 in)
Calibre: 5.45-mm (0.215-in) x 18 MPT	**Length of barrel:** 85 mm (3.35 in)
Weight: empty 0.46 kg (1.014 lb); loaded 0.51 kg (1.124 lb)	**Muzzle velocity:** approximately 315 m (1,033 ft) per second
	Magazine: 8-round detachable box

The PSM was designed from the outset for concealed carriage, and is a notably slim semi-automatic pistol without the excrescences typical of larger pistols which can catch in clothing when the weapon is being drawn. As well as being operated by the Russian miliatry, the PSM is in service with Bulgarian armed forces.

reduce weight and width, the latter being a mere 18 mm (0.71 in) and facilitating the weapon's easy concealment under the wearer's outer clothes.

The trigger guard is accommodated neatly on the underside of the weapon with curves optimised to ease the drawing of the weapon, the barrel has six rifling grooves with a right-hand twist, and the magazine is carried in the weapon's butt, as is standard for modern semi-automatic pistols.

Small magazine

The magazine carries only eight rounds, a figure deemed acceptable for a snugly carried self-defence weapon, and is unloaded after its catch, in the heel of the butt, has been operated. Once the magazine has been removed, the weapon can be made safe and also checked as safe by pulling back the slide to eject (via the ejector port in the weapon's right-hand side) any round that may be in the chamber, looking through the ejector port to ensure that there is no round in the chamber, and finally releasing the slide before pulling the trigger. The PSM is still in modest production.

SIG-Sauer P220 series Convertible-calibre pistols

For very many years the Schweizerische Industrie-Gesellschaft (SIG) has been producing excellent weapons in its production facility located at Neuhausen Rhinefalls. The company has always been restricted by the strict Swiss laws governing military exports from making any significant overseas sales, however, so by joining up with a German company, J. P. Sauer und Sohn, SIG was finally able to transfer production to West Germany and thus gain access to more markets. This was the original of the SIG-Sauer concern.

One of the first military pistols developed by the new organization was the **SIG-Sauer P220**, a mechanically locked single- or double-action semi-automatic pistol. When dealing with the P220 it is difficult to avoid superlatives, for in many ways this is a truly magnificent pistol. Its standards of manufacture and finish are superb, despite the extensive

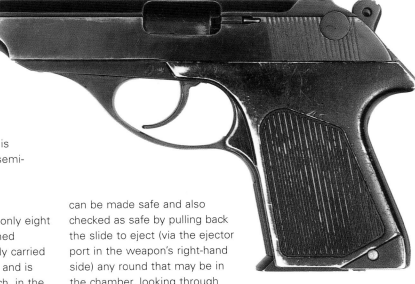

The superb SIG-Sauer P220 resulted from a collaborative effort between the Swiss SIG company and J. P. Sauer und Sohn to produce a pistol for export, unfettered by Swiss government restrictions. The P220 is available in up to five calibres: 0.45 ACP, 0.38-in Super, 9-mm Parabellum, 7.65-mm Parabellum and even 0.22-in LR.

use of metal stampings and an aluminium frame to keep down weight and cost. The pistol handles very well, being one of those weapons that immediately feels 'right' in the hand as soon as it is picked up. It is accurate, and the overall design is such that it is difficult for dirt or dust to find its way into the interior and thereby cause stoppages. Despite this factor, the pistol is still easy to strip and maintain, and has all the usual pistol safeties.

Four calibre options

One notable feature of the P220 in overall terms is the fact that it can be supplied in any one of four calibres, a fact that significantly increases the pistol's marketability across an international customer base.

These calibres are the usual 9-mm (0.354-in) Parabellum, 7.65-mm (0.301-in) Parabellum, 0.45-in (11.27-mm) ACP and 0.38-in Super (9-mm, but not to be confused with 9-mm Parabellum). It is possible to convert the P220 from one calibre to another, and there are also kits to convert the pistol to fire 0.22-in Long Rifle (5.59-mm) for training purposes. In its form to fire the 9-mm Parabellum cartridge, the pistol has a magazine holding nine rounds,

SPECIFICATION	
9-mm Pistole 75	**Weight:** empty 0.83 kg (1.83 lb)
Calibre: 9-mm (0.354-in)	**Muzzle velocity:** 345 m (1,132 ft) per second
Length overall: 198 mm (7.8 in)	
Length of barrel: 112 mm (4.4 in)	**Magazine:** 9-round detachable box

Well over 150,000 examples of the SIG-Sauer P220 series have been produced, including 35,000 9-mm Pistole 75s for Swiss military use. The design has also apparently influenced the Iranian ZOAF pistol. This P226 is a limited edition, marking the Swiss concern's 125th anniversary in 1985.

but when firing 0.45-in ACP the magazine holds only seven.

The excellence of the P220 has rewarded SIG-Sauer with a

stream of orders. The P220 is in service with the Swiss army as the **9-mm Pistole 75**, a designation which sometimes provides the P220 with the name **Model 75**.

There is a later version of the P220 known as the **P225** which is a slightly more compact weapon chambered only for the 9-mm Parabellum cartridge. This has been selected for Swiss and West German police as the **P6**.

The 9-mm Parabellum **P226** was developed with a 15-round magazine for the US competition to find an M1911A1 successor but proved too expensive. The **P228** was introduced in 1989 as a compact version of the P226 with a smaller magazine and was adopted as the US Air Force's **M11**, and the **P229** is the P228 chambered for 0.40-in SW.

American Self-loading pistols

Although there are several American manufacturers who produce semi-automatic pistols of the type likely to be used by military, security and law enforcement bodies, the two with the largest grip on the market are Ruger and Smith & Wesson.

The most advanced of the Ruger pistols entered production in 1987 as the **Ruger P-85** in 9-mm (0.354-in) Parabellum, and the series has remained in manufacture since that time in a number of developed forms. All of the weapons are of the recoil-operated type, fire from a locked breech and, with the exception of the polymer-framed 9-mm **P-95** and 0.45-in (11.43-mm) **P-97**, are based on an aluminium frame.

The weapons differ from each other mainly in the details of their triggers, barrel lengths and magazine capacities. Taken out of production in 1991, the P-85 has a double-action trigger, 114-mm (4.5-in) barrel and 15-round magazine; the 9-mm **P-89** entered production in 1991 and differs in its options of double-action, double-action with decocker and double-action only

The AMT On Duty pistol is typical of modern semi-automatic designs. Chambered for 9-mm or .40 S&W, it has a machined aluminium frame and other parts are made from steel castings. It can hold 15 rounds in its 9-mm version, with a capacity of 11 in the more powerful S&W .40 calibre.

trigger; the **P-90** is a 0.45-in weapon with double-action and double-action with decocker trigger options, and a seven-round magazine; the **P-91** in 0.4-in (10.16-mm) calibre was made between 1992 and 1994 with a 110-mm (4.33-in) barrel, double-action with decocker and double-action only options, and an 11-round magazine; the 9-mm **P-93** of 1994 has a 99-mm

(3.9-in) barrel, double-action with decocker and double-action only options, and a 10-round magazine; the 9-mm **P-94** and 0.4-in **P-944** of the same year have 108-mm (4.25-in) barrels, all three trigger options and a 10-round magazine; the 9-mm P-95 of 1996 has a 99-mm barrel, all three trigger options and a 10-round magazine; and finally the 0.45-in **P-97** of 1998

also has a 99-mm barrel, all three trigger options and an eight-round magazine.

S&W pistols

Smith & Wesson has also produced large numbers of semi-automatic pistols, starting with the 9-mm **Smith & Wesson Model 39** of 1949, based on a recoil-operated mechanism and steel, stainless

SPECIFICATION	
Ruger P-97	**Weight:** 0.86 kg (1.9 lb)
Calibre: 0.45-in (11.43-mm)	**Muzzle velocity:** not available
Length overall: 185 mm (7.28 in)	**Feed:** 8-round straight box
Length of barrel:: 99 mm (3.9 in)	magazine

steel and aluminium alloy construction. The Model 39 and companion **Model 59** with a 14- rather than eight-round magazine were the first-generation of S&W semi-automatic pistols, and were taken out of production in 1980. The second generation of S&W pistols was introduced in 1980 on the basis of the Models 39 and 59, had three-digit model numbers and different frame materials, and with double-stack magazines and traditional double-action triggers with safety/decockers. The key to understanding second-generation model numbers is a first digit of 4, 5 or 6 indicating an aluminium alloy, carbon steel or stainless steel frame; second and third digits indicating magazine capacity and frame size (59 for 9-mm and double-stack, 39 for 9-mm and single-stack magazines, 69 for 9-mm compact size and double-stack magazine).

The third-generation pistols were made from 1990 and have four-digit model numbers, an ambidextrous safety/decocker lever, double-action only and decocker only models, and calibres such as 0.4-in, 0.45-in and 10-mm (0.39-in). The key to third-generation pistols is the first two digits for the calibre and frame type (39 for 9-mm with single stack magazine, 59 for 9-mm with double-stack magazine, 69 for 9-mm compact with a double-stack magazine etc), third digit for the trigger type and frame size (5 for double-action only and compact etc), and a fourth digit for frame material (3 and 6 for aluminium alloy and stainless steel).

Above: Pistols have always had marginal military use, being primarily issued as personal protection weapons. However, they are much more important as police and paramilitary weapons, and constant training is essential to maintain proficiency.

Right: Colt's venerable Model 1911 has been updated by a number of arms makers as well as by Colt. The Delta Elite is a modernised version of the M1911, rechambered to fire the powerful 10-mm round now popular with law-enforcement officers.

Smith & Wesson, Colt, and Ruger Revolvers

Smith & Wesson no longer manufactures a revolver specifically for military use, but many armed forces use Smith & Wesson revolvers, generally for the military and security police roles.

Top of the current list come the weapons chambered for Magnum cartridges offering prodigious stopping power. Primary among these is the **No. 29** firing the 0.44-in (10.92-mm) Magnum round and introduced in 1955. The No. 29 is too much of a handful for most users since its recoil is very considerable, so the **No. 57** was introduced in 1964 to use the less potent 0.41-in (10.41-mm) Magnum round. This revolver has the same overall dimensions as the No. 29, and retains much of its stopping power, but is rather more manageable.

Smith & Wesson also offers several 0.38-in (9-mm) revolvers. A typical weapon is the **No. 38 Bodyguard**, a snub-nosed revolver with a shrouded hammer and a five-round cylinder. The generally similar **No. 49** differs only its its steel rather than aluminium alloy body.

Colt revolvers

Modern Colt military revolvers are double-action designs. The best known of these weapons is the **Python**. Introduced in 1955, this has a shrouded barrel with a distinctive appearance and is chambered for one cartridge

SPECIFICATION	
No. 38 Bodyguard	**Weight:** 1.022 kg (2.253 lb)
Calibre: 0.38-in (9-mm)	**Muzzle velocity:** about 436 m (1,430 ft) per second
Length overall: 165 mm (6.5 in)	**Chamber capacity:** 6 rounds
Length of barrel: 51 mm (2 in)	
Weight: 0.411 kg (0.9 lb)	
Muzzle velocity: 260 m (853 ft) per second	**0.38-in Service-Six**
Chamber capacity: 5 rounds	**Calibre:** 0.38-in (9-mm)
	Length overall: 235 mm (9.25 in)
Lawman Mk III	**Length of barrel:** 102 mm (4 in)
Calibre: 0.357-in (9-mm)	**Weight:** 0.935 kg (2.06 lb)
Length overall: 235 mm (9.25 in)	**Muzzle velocity:** 260 m (853 ft) per second
Length of barrel: 51 mm (2in)	**Chamber capacity:** 6 rounds

only, the 0.357-in Magnum. The Python is a very powerful weapon, but to absorb some of the effects of the heavy cartridge load it has to be constructed in an equally heavy fashion – it is thus very heavy (1.16 kg/2.56 lb). The Python is available in two barrel lengths, 102 and 152 mm (4 and 6 in).

Appearing in 1953, the **Trooper** was available in a variety of barrel lengths and in various calibres. The Trooper was replaced by the **Lawman Mk III**, which is produced only in 0.357-in Magnum and with barrels as short as 51 mm (2 in).

Ruger revolvers

When planning its revolver range, Sturm, Ruger and Co. decided to examine the fundamental design aspects of the revolver and came up with what was a very modern version of a weapon that had been around for nearly a century. New types of steel and other materials (especially springs) were introduced and the manufacture was developed into a modular system in which components could be added or subtracted to form any particular model.

Ruger revolvers are offered with various barrel lengths and in varying finishes, including stainless steel. The revolvers are also available in a wide range of calibres from 0.38-in Special up to the Magnums. Typical of the service revolvers is the **Service-Six** chambered for either the 0.38 Special or 0.357 Magnum cartridges. The Service-Six can be fitted with either a 70- or 102-mm (2.75- or 4-in) barrel, while the generally similar **Security-Six**, intended for police use, can have even longer barrels.

The trigger actions of both are single- and double-action. Some Ruger revolvers fire rimless 9-mm Parabellum ammunition, so for loading these rounds special 'half moon' clips, each holding three rounds, have to be used to put the rounds in place.

A Ruger revolver that caused quite a stir on its introduction in 1955 is the **Blackhawk** firing the 0.44-in Magnum round. This was too much for most users – the recoil bordered on the painful – so the Blackhawk range was extended to include other less potent cartridges. The quality of the weapons means it is still in great demand by many pistol enthusiasts.

Above: The Ruger Speed-Six is known to the US Army as the GS-32N. It is made in two versions: one for 0.357-in Magnum/0.38-in Special and one for 9-mm Parabellum. The 9-mm is a rimless cartridge, so three-round 'half-moon' clips are used to ensure ejection.

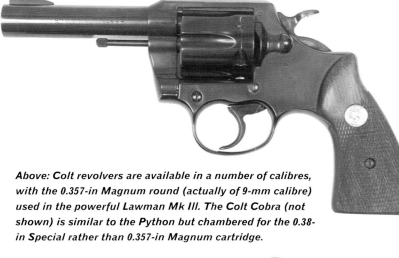

Above: Colt revolvers are available in a number of calibres, with the 0.357-in Magnum round (actually of 9-mm calibre) used in the powerful Lawman Mk III. The Colt Cobra (not shown) is similar to the Python but chambered for the 0.38-in Special rather than 0.357-in Magnum cartridge.

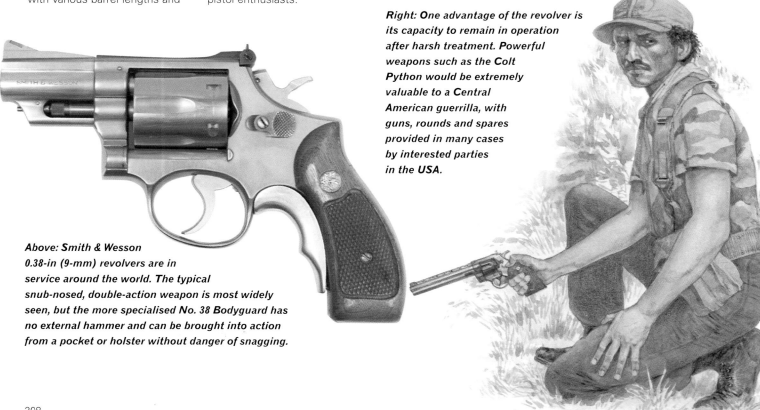

Above: Smith & Wesson 0.38-in (9-mm) revolvers are in service around the world. The typical snub-nosed, double-action weapon is most widely seen, but the more specialised No. 38 Bodyguard has no external hammer and can be brought into action from a pocket or holster without danger of snagging.

Right: One advantage of the revolver is its capacity to remain in operation after harsh treatment. Powerful weapons such as the Colt Python would be extremely valuable to a Central American guerrilla, with guns, rounds and spares provided in many cases by interested parties in the USA.

Stechkin in operation Fully automatic machine-pistol

The Stechkin is a fully automatic pistol that was issued to Soviet forces beginning in the 1950s. As such it is one of the few successful 'machine-pistol' designs: not too large to be used as a pistol, yet still effective as a fully automatic weapon.

The Stechkin is a curious combination of the old and new: some features of the weapon are old-fashioned, yet the final product remains a very useful weapon for special forces. Issued with a wooden holster that doubles as a shoulder stock, the Stechkin can be fired like a sub-machine gun and the sights go up to 200 m (656 ft). It is similar to the Beretta 93R, but the Italian pistol's metal skeleton stock looks more modern than the huge lump of wood tacked onto the back of the Stechkin.

Unusually among Soviet infantry weapons, the Stechkin was never exported to Warsaw Pact armies. Nor was it supplied to the armies of client states in the Third World – although a few examples in presentation boxes were given to particularly favoured leaders.

When Stechkins left the USSR they did so only in the hands of Soviet soldiers. For the Stechkin is a fine weapon, superbly engineered with a blued finish. The light recoil of the 9-mm (0.354-in) Makarov cartridge is absorbed well and during full-auto short bursts it can be kept on a man-sized target at up to 25 m (82 ft). The Stechkin was issued to specialist units including KGB and MVD detachments: a Bulgarian arrested for spying on NATO facilities in the Netherlands during 1989 had a loaded Stechkin in the cab of his lorry.

The Stechkin operates by direct blowback using an unlocked breech. Its 9-mm cartridge is relatively low-powered so a locked breech is not necessary. When the Stechkin is fired, the breech remains closed, held by its weight and the recoil spring.

Top: The Stechkin is often considered somewhat of a failure. But if this were altogether true it would not have been issued to front-line units and to special operations forces, who were the main users of the weapon within the Soviet military.

Above: Although the Stechkin is fairly large for a hand-held weapon, especially compared to the Makarov service pistol (bottom right) or the PSM police pistol (top), it is not excessively so, and can be easily handled by any competent operator.

Gas pressure eventually overcomes the resistance, propelling the slide to the rear, cocking the hammer and ejecting the empty cartridge case. The recoil spring then drives the slide forward again, chambering another round and shutting the breech. When the selector is positioned for fully automatic fire, the hammer is tripped as the breech closes. On semi-automatic, the trigger stays disengaged until pressed again.

Stechkin: Soviet special forces machine-pistol

The 9-mm Stechkin pistol is an extremely well-made example of a pistol capable of full-automatic fire. Although large, it is not too big to be handled as an ordinary pistol, when it displays notable accuracy. By switching to fully automatic fire and with the attachment of the solid wooden holster/stock, it can function as a reasonably effective short-range machine-pistol or as a sub-machine gun.

Barrel

The Stechkin has a 127-mm (5-in) barrel, which is the same length as that of the Model 1911 Government Colt. In fact, the pistol is about the same size as the Government Colt. It has four-groove rifling with a right-hand twist. Like the Walther PP, which seems to have been an influence, the Stechkin's recoil spring is wrapped around the barrel.

Sights

The Stechkin has a conventional blade front sight and a flip-over 'L' rear sight. With the shoulder-stock attached it is quite capable of hitting man-sized targets at 100 m (328 ft) or more, although 25 m (82 ft) is a more reasonable range when firing full-auto.

Action

The Stechkin is a conventional blowback weapon. Gas pressure forces the slide to the rear, ejecting the spent case and cocking the weapon. In semi-automatic mode the hammer is then held back until the trigger is pulled. When the selector lever at the left-rear of the slide is switched to full-auto the hammer is released automatically as the breech closes as long as the trigger is held down.

Ammunition

The Soviets followed the policy of using different ammunition to the rest of the world. The 9-mm x 18 round used in the Stechkin was developed for the contemporary Makarov pistol. Intermediate in power between 9-mm Short (.380 ACP) and 9-mm Parabellum, it is about as powerful as a blowback mechanism can handle.

Left: The holster supplied with the Stechkin is hardly a quick-draw device, being a bulky wooden item. It doubles as a detachable stock, however.

Left: The Stechkin fires the 9-mm x 18 Makarov round. This is a little less powerful than the NATO 9-mm Parabellum, and makes controlling the weapon on full-auto a little easier.

The Stechkin is also available in a silenced version. The KGB unit that stormed the Afghan Presidential Palace in 1979 made plentiful use of silenced Stechkins during the initial assault. The Stechkin silencer fits on without obstructing the sights. Instead of the wooden holster/shoulder-stock unit, the silenced Stechkins have a collapsible wire stock, providing a special forces assault team with a very compact automatic weapon.

Accuracy

The Stechkin has a rear drum sight which can be set for 25, 50, 100 or 200 m (82, 164, 328 or 656 ft), although even with a shoulder stock attached, 200 m is wildly optimistic. It takes little practice to shoot the Stechkin accurately at 100 m. The hammer drop safety/fire-selector can be set for single shots or fully automatic fire. A weight forced against the hammer spring serves to reduce the rate of fire to a controllable level by delaying the hammer release. It also works as a buffer, slowing the movement of the slide. However, although the Stechkin is one of the most controllable full-auto weapons, it has a severe disadvantage as an automatic weapon. Rapid reloading – an essential feature – is rendered impossible by the location of the magazine release latch in the heel of the grip.

Reloading

At its cyclic rate of about 750 rounds per minute, a Stechkin empties its 20-round magazine in less than two seconds. The decision to favour magazine security over rapid reloading left special forces with a clumsy reload procedure.

The Stechkin was replaced as a machine-pistol in Soviet service by the AKSU cut-down Kalashnikov rifle. For airborne forces, tank crew or other specialists, the AKSU provides considerably greater firepower and longer-range accuracy and it is no larger than a conventional

Above: The Stechkin comes with a 20-round magazine. The release is located at the heel of the butt, which is secure but a little too awkward to permit rapid magazine changes.

Right: Stechkin pistols are very well made, and although somewhat large they can be handled like a normal pistol. In trained hands, the Stechkin can hit targets at ranges of up to 100 m (328 ft).

SMG. However, the Stechkin – especially when silenced – remains a useful weapon for special forces and will be encountered for some time.

F1 Sub-machine gun

Lieutenant Evelyn Owen created the sub-machine gun that bears his name, and this was used by Australian soldiers during World War II and for many years after. One of the most recognisable features of the Owen sub-machine gun was the vertical magazine, a feature with no particular merit or demerit but one that the Australians found very much to their liking. When the Australian army began searching for a new sub-machine gun, it was therefore not averse to choosing a design with an overhead vertical magazine.

Before selecting the design now known as the **F1**, the Australians looked at a number of experimental weapons that rejoiced in names such as 'Kokoda' and 'MCEM'. Some of these experimental designs had a number of advanced features, but they were generally regarded as not being 'soldier-proof' enough to suit Australian conditions. But in 1962 a design known as the **X3** was selected for production, and this became the F1. The predilections of the Australian military were very evident, for the F1 has a vertical magazine but in order to allow a certain amount of interchange-ability with other weapons the

Replacement for the extremely popular Owen sub-machine gun in Australian service, the F1 retains the uniquely Australian feature of a vertical top-loading magazine. The F1 is otherwise similar to the Sterling.

magazine is now curved and identical to that of the British Sterling and the Canadian C1.

This interchangeability factor is also evident in several other features of the F1. The pistol grip is the same as that used on the L1A1 7.62-mm (0.3-in) NATO rifle, and the bayonet is another Sterling component. In fact it is tempting to regard the F1 as an Australian Sterling, but there are too many differences to support such a claim. The F1 uses a simple 'straight-through' design with the butt fixed in line with the tubular receiver, and the pistol grip group is arranged differently from that of the Sterling. The overhead magazine does produce one difficulty, namely sighting. In action deliberate aiming is not common but has to be taken into account, so a form of offset sighting

system had to be introduced. On the F1 this comprises an offset leaf sight (folding down onto the tubular receiver) and an offset fixed foresight.

Protective feature

The F1 has one unusual, yet simple and effective safety feature: on a short-barrel weapon it is often too easy to place the forward grip over the

muzzle or too close to it for safety, but on the F1 a simple sling swivel bracket prevents the hand from getting too close to the muzzle.

The F1 has some other interesting design features. One is the cocking handle, which exactly duplicates the position and action of its counterpart on the L1A1 rifle: this handle has a cover which prevents dirt and debris getting into the action, though if enough dirt does get into the action to prevent the bolt closing, the cocking handle can be latched to the bolt for the firer to force it closed in an emergency.

For all its many attributes the F1 has not been bought outside Australia and some of its associated territories. At one time there was talk of replacement by the American M16A1 rifle, but the F1 is still used.

Simple and effective, the F1 in its prototype X3 form performed extremely well in the Mekong Delta during the Vietnam War. Modern construction made it almost 1 kg (2.2 lb) lighter than its World War II ancestor.

SPECIFICATION	
F1	
Calibre: 9-mm (0.354-in)	**Muzzle velocity:** 366 m (1,200 ft) per second
Length overall: 714 mm (28.1 in)	**Rate of fire, cyclic:** 600–640 rounds per minute
Length of barrel: 213 mm (8.386 in)	**Feed:** 34-round curved magazine
Weight: loaded 4.3 kg (9.48 lb) with bayonet	

FMK-3 Sub-machine gun

The FMK-3 has a straight-through design with a telescoped wrap-around bolt, retractable wire buttstock, plastic fore grip and metal rear grip carrying the magazine.

From 1943 the Halcon small arms company of Buenos Aires in Argentina produced a series of blowback-operated sub-machine guns chambered for the 9-mm (0.354-in) Parabellum and 11.43-mm (0.45-in) ACP cartridges. None of them was ever adopted as a first-line weapon by the Argentine forces, but the weapons did see a measure of second-line and police use. The first of the weapons was the Model 1943 with a very distinctive appearance as a result of the fact that its buffer cap overhung a buttstock with a pistol grip built into its forward end. The Model 1946 differed mainly in having a metal rather than wood buttstock. The Light Model 57

marked a shift in design thinking, for the barrel lacked cooling fins, the receiver was cylindrical rather than rectangular, and the magazine was curved rather than straight. The final Light Model 60 was based on the Model 57 but with the fire selector removed from the receiver and a two-trigger arrangement introduced.

Manufactured by the Fabrica Militar de Armas Portatiles of Rosario, the PAM was a shorter and lighter variant of the American M3A1, and was produced in two models as

SPECIFICATION	
FMK-3	**Weight:** empty 3.4 kg (7.5 lb)
Calibre: 9-mm (0.354-in)	**Muzzle velocity:** 400 m (1,312 ft) per
Length overall: 693 mm (27.3 in)	second
with the buttstock extended and	**Rate of fire, cyclic:** 650 rounds per
523 mm (20.6 in) with the	minute
buttstock retracted	**Feed:** 25-, 32- and 40-round straight
Length of barrel: 290 mm (11.42 in)	box magazine

the PAM-1 capable only of automatic fire, and the PAM-2 with full selective-fire capability.

Advanced design

FMAP then moved forward to the creation of a more modern sub-machine as the PA3-DM. Like the PAM, it is a blowback-operated weapon firing the 9-mm Parabellum cartridge. This selective-fire weapon has a 25-round detachable and straight box magazine that slides into the pistol grip, and a plastic fore grip under the receiver. The weapon was produced in two variants: one has a fixed wooden buttstock, and the other a sliding wire buttstock modelled on that of the M3. Other features of the PA3-DM include the use of a metal pressing at the body, a screw-threaded cap at the front for easy removal of the barrel, a wrap-around bolt and a cocking handle on the left-hand side of the receiver with a slide that covers the cocking handle's slot to keep out dirt and thus reduce

the chances of the weapon jamming under adverse conditions.

The PA3-DM was accepted for first-line service with the Argentine forces, and was followed in the mid-1970s by the **FMK-3**. Produced by what is now the Fabricaciones Militares organisation, this sub-machine gun can be regarded as a modernised development of the PA3-DM, and is a selective-fire weapon that has also been produced in semi-automatic form as the **FMK-5** for sale to civilians.

Used by the Argentine army and also by the country's police, the FMK-3 is based on the use of a telescoped bolt that sleeves round the rear part of the barrel when closed, a double-row magazine, a receiver and pistol grip fabricated from steel stampings, and a safety and fire-selector switch on the left-hand side of the weapon above the pistol grip, which incorporates a grip safety in its rear. The FMK-3's sights are of the flip-up type, with a rear sight blade of the L type and calibrated for 50- and 100-m (55- and 110-yard) ranges. The buttstock is of the retractable sliding steel wire type derived ultimately from that of the American M3.

The FMK-3 is a wholly conventional and utilitarian sub-machine gun that was designed and manufactured in Argentina for the country's armed forces.

MPi 69 Sub-machine gun

Designed by a team under the supervision of Hugo Stowasser, the **MPi 69** (Maschinen-Pistole 1969) is a product of Steyr-Daimler-Puch AG (now known as Steyr-Mannlicher AG). This Austrian sub-machine gun bears a strong visual affinity to the Uzi weapon of Israeli design, but differs in a number of important respects and is in fact a simpler weapon than the Israeli gun. The MPi 69 is no longer in production, having been superseded by two other Steyr weapons, the TMP and AUG/Para.

The MPi 69 works on the blowback principle, and is a selective-fire weapon offering a choice between single shot and full automatic. The forward end of the sling is attached to the simple pressed steel cocking piece, which is therefore operated by a tug on the sling.

The weapon's receiver is a pressing of light-gauge steel sheet which is welded into a hollow box with two openings (one in the middle to serve as the ejection port and one near the front to accept the barrel seating, barrel release catch and barrel locking nut) on its right-hand side. The ejector is a simple steel strip bent to the right shape and rivetted into position on the base of the receiver to run in a groove let into the bottom of the breech block. Attached by spot welds under the rear of the receiver are the guides for the telescoping steel-wire buttstock and its release plungers, and also at the rear is the strip-down catch. Screws attach the optional Singlepoint sight to the top of the receiver, while under the receiver is a moulded nylon receiver cover that carries the trigger mechanism and the pistol grip complete with the magazine housing.

The Austrian-designed MPi 69 was clearly influenced by the Uzi sub-machine gun of Israel, and fires the virtually universal 9-mm Parabellum cartridge.

Cold-forged barrel

The barrel is cold-forged on a mandrel in a process that is notably cheap and clean in its results. The breech block has a fixed firing pin on the bolt face, itself located at about the mid-point of this wrap-around unit, which is cut away on its right-hand side for ejection purposes. The fresh round is kept out of alignment with the firing pin until it is fully chambered, and this considerably enhances safety in conjunction with the applied safety device. A light pull on the trigger produces single-shot fire, while a strong pull generates automatic fire.

A later variant is the **MPi 81**, which differs in having a conventional cocking handle on the left of the receiver, and the rate of fire boosted to 700 rounds per minute.

Above: The MPi 69 is a sub-machine gun of straight-through concept, and the 25- or 32-round box magazine is loaded into the weapon's pistol grip.

The MPi 69 has a sliding wire buttstock, the spent cases are ejected from a port on the weapon's right side, and the swivels for the sling are located on the left.

SPECIFICATION	
MPi 69	
Calibre: 9-mm (0.354-in)	**Muzzle velocity:** 381 m (1,250 ft) per second
Length overall: 673 mm (26.5 in) with the buttstock extended and 470 mm (18.5 in) with the buttstock retracted	**Rate of fire, cyclic:** 550 rounds per minute
Length of barrel: 260 mm (10.24 in)	**Feed:** 25- or 32-round straight box magazine
Weight: loaded 3.52 kg (7.76 lb)	

Steyr TMP 9-mm Tactical Machine Pistol

The Austrian 9-mm (0.354-in) calibre **Steyr Tactical Machine Pistol** (**TMP**) could equally be considered as a pistol, but the weapon's full-automatic capability and general configuration places it into the 'personal defence weapon' category and gives it equal credence as a sub-machine gun. In effect, the TMP has pistol dimensions but offers the firepower of a sub-machine gun.

TMP components

The Tactical Machine Pistol is a locked-breech weapon in 9 x 19-mm (0.354-in x 0.7-in)

The TMP has replaced the MPi 69 and the MPi 81 as Steyr's standard production sub-machine gun. A folding forward hand-grip is provided and a sound suppressor can be added.

Parabellum calibre, although other calibres are planned, one possible cartridge being the 10-mm (0.39-in) Auto developed in the US. There are only 41 component parts and the frame and top cover are made from a strong polymer-based material. The receiver is almost entirely fabricated from synthetic materials. An integrated mounting rail is provided over the receiver for the installation of various optical and electro-optic sighting devices according to user choice, although conventional 'iron' sights are also provided. The overall outlines are smooth while the fore-grip allows the weapon to be kept under control and on target even when firing bursts. This can be accomplished without a butt-stock installed, although one available combat accessory is a detachable shoulder-stock made from robust plastic-based materials, the use of which provides for even steadier sustained firing.

The locking system uses a rotating barrel, controlled by a single lug which engages in a groove in the frame to turn the barrel and thus unlock it from the bolt. The cocking handle is at the rear of the weapon, beneath the rear-sight, and is pulled back

The TMP is seen with the detachable shoulder-stock fitted. This attachment provides for more steady burst firing, resulting in increased accuracy. The TMP entered production in 1993.

SPECIFICATION	
TMP	
Calibre: 9 mm (0.354 in) Parabellum	**Weight:** empty, 1.3 kg (2.87 lb)
Length overall: 282 mm (11.1 in)	**Rate of fire, cyclic:** around 900 rpm
Length of barrel: 130 mm (5.12 in)	**Feed:** 15- or 30-round box magazine

to cock. Selection of single shot or semi-automatic fire is performed by a three-position safety bar. Box magazines hold 15 or 30 rounds and are inserted into the weapon through the pistol grip.

Compact dimensions

An indication of the compact nature of the Steyr TMP is that its size (minus the optional shoulder-stock) allows it to fit within the dimensions of a sheet of standard A4 paper. The TMP has facilities for attaching a sound suppressor or other muzzle

attachments such as laser target indication devices. It is understood to be in production but no known users have yet emerged. A licence to manufacture the TMP has been obtained by SME Ordnance BHD of Malaysia. The TMP is also produced in semi-automatic only form, whereupon it becomes the **Steyr Special Purpose Pistol** (**SPP**). The single-shot SPP lacks the folding fore-grip of the TMP and has a prominent muzzle attachment for the barrel, but is externally identical and uses the same 15- or 30-round magazines.

FN Herstal P90 5.7-mm sub-machine gun

The **FN Herstal P90** sub-machine gun and its 5.7 x 28-mm (0.2 x 1.1-in) SS190 cartridge were developed by FN Herstal to equip military personnel who would not normally operate small arms. The P90 is also suitable for special forces who require compact firepower, and has police and paramilitary applications.

The P90 is a blow-back weapon firing from a closed bolt. The overall design places great reliance on ergonomics to the extent that the pistol grip, with a thumb-hole stock, is well forward on the receiver so that,

when gripped, the bulk of the receiver lies along the firer's forearm. The controls are fully ambidextrous; a cocking handle is provided on each side and the selector/safety switch is a rotary component located under the trigger. Even the forward sling swivel can be located on either side of the weapon as required.

Intended for use as a military self-defence weapon, the P90 sub-machine gun has an effective combat range of 200 m (219 yards) and a maximum range of 1790 m (1,958 yards).

Magazine

The magazine lies along the top of the receiver, above the barrel, and the cartridges are aligned at 90° to the weapon axis. The 50 rounds lie in double-row configuration and, as they reach the mouth of the magazine, they are ordered into a single row by a fixed ramp. A spiral ramp then turns the round through 90° as it is being guided down into the feedway so that it arrives in front of the bolt correctly oriented for chambering. The magazine itself is made from translucent plastic so its contents can be visually checked at any time.

The integral reflex sight unit has a circle and dot; in low light a tritium-illuminated cross-hair appears. The sight can be used with both eyes open and allows very rapid acquisition of the target and accurate aiming. Two sets of 'iron' sights are machined into the sight base, one being located on each side.

The weapon strips easily into three basic groups for field maintenance. Much of the body and internal mechanism is of high-impact plastic material, only the bolt and barrel being of steel. Empty cartridge cases are ejected downwards through the pistol grip.

Externally mounted tactical lights and laser aiming devices can be located either side of the sight assembly on an accessory rail. Also available is a combat sling, a blank firing attachment, a cleaning kit and a magazine pouch and filler. A special-to-type sound suppressor that screw-clamps over the muzzle attachment is available.

Two special forces variants of the P90 are offered, each with a laser target designator. It is also possible to mount various forms of night sight and image intensifier on the P90.

SPECIFICATION	
P90	
Calibre: 5.7 mm (0.224 in)	with empty magazine, 2.68 kg
Length overall: 500 mm (19.69 in)	(5.91 lb); with full magazine, 3 kg
Length of barrel: 256.5 mm (10.1 in)	(6.61 lb)
Weight: empty, 2.54 kg (5.6 lb);	**Rate of fire, cyclic:** 900 rpm
	Feed: 50-round magazine

Croatian sub-machine guns Zagi and ERO

The 1990s break-up of Yugoslavia into its current independent states resulted in a long period of inter-ethnic strife during which the procurement of weapons for everything from local defence to arming irregular formations came to be very difficult for those concerned. Croatia was better able than most to produce weapons using only its own skills and resources, for the country has long been technically skillful in the production of small arms. Among the several types of weapon devised were

The Mini-ERO is based on the Israeli Mini-Uzi and, although dimensionally smaller than the standard weapon, it fires the same 9-mm Parabellum cartridge as the full-size ERO.

sub-machine guns.

First generation

At first, the sub-machine guns were manufactured in whatever premises were available, from machine-tool plants to back-street garages. Not surprisingly the number of types was legion. Many of the results were crudely made and not particularly reliable. On the other hand, some displayed modern ergonomic plastic furniture and relatively fine finishes. Many of them never received formal designations. Those that did include the **Zagi**, **Sokacz** and

The Zagi is typical of the first types of SMG developed in Croatia after 1991. The Zagi M91 is a well-made weapon with a long 32-round magazine housing that also serves as a fore-grip. A push-through safety catch is fitted, but the weapon can only fire on full-auto.

Agram, but there were many others. This 'first generation' of Croatian sub-machine guns had two features in common. They fired 9 x 19-mm (0.354 x 0.7-in) Parabellum ammunition and were made in only small numbers.

With time, most of these first generation sub-machine guns were withdrawn, many ending up in criminal hands all over Europe. They were largely replaced by a more sophisticated design known as the **ERO**.

Right: The ERO is a direct copy of Israel's ubiquitous Uzi SMG. As a result, the ERO weapon is almost indistinguishable from its forebear. Production of the weapon began in 1995.

The design of the ERO 9-mm calibre sub-machine gun was obviously based on that of the Israeli IMI Uzi 9-mm sub-machine gun, so the principle of operation and general mechanical details are similar to those of the Uzi. The location of the cocking handle over the receiver makes operation simple for both left- and right-handed users, while the ERO has a double safety system. An automatic safety located in the rear of the pistol grip prevents both cocking the action and firing until the firer tightens their hand pressure on the grip and thus releases the safety. The ordinary safety acts directly on the trigger and is operated by the change-over lever on the left-hand side above the pistol grip.

The ERO became so well established that it was offered for export, some local states obtaining the type. There is a more compact version, the **Mini-ERO,** with a short barrel, a vestigial telescopic wire butt-stock and an extremely high cyclic rate of fire, but still carrying over the design of the Uzi. In addition to export use, the ERO has been issued to Croatian military police units.

SPECIFICATION	
Zagi M91	**ERO**
Calibre: 9 mm Parabellum	**Calibre:** 9 mm Parabellum
Length overall: stock extended, 850 mm (33.46 in); stock retracted, 565 mm (22.24 in)	**Length overall:** 650 mm (25.59 in)
Length of barrel: 220 mm (8.66 in)	**Length of barrel:** 260 mm (10.24 in)
Weight: empty, 3.41 kg (7.52 lb)	**Weight:** 3.73 kg (8.22 lb)
Rate of fire, cyclic: 600 rpm	**Rate of fire, cyclic:** 650 rpm
Feed: 32-round box	**Feed:** 32-round box

Steyr AUG Para Sub-machine gun

The family kinship of the AUG Para sub-machine gun to the AUG assault rifle is evident, although the sub-machine gun has a shorter barrel and fires a larger-calibre round at lower velocity.

Entering production in 1988, the **Steyr AUG Para** from the Steyr-Daimler-Puch AG is an Austrian sub-machine gun derived very simply from the same company's AUG (Armee Universal Gewehr) assault rifle. The process of converting the assault rifle, chambered for the NATO or SS109 5.56-mm (0.219-in) cartridge, into a sub-machine gun chambered for the 9-mm (0.354-in) Parabellum cartridge was essentially simple: a shorter barrel in the new calibre was introduced, the bolt assembly was changed, an adapter was added to allow the weapon to accept the 25- or 32-round magazine of the MPi 69 sub-machine gun, and the gas-operated mechanism of the assault rifle was disabled so that the weapon would operate on the blowback principle that is a standard physical feature of all modern sub-machine guns.

Closed-bolt firing

Notable features of the AUG Para include firing from the closed bolt position for greater accuracy and safety, and a barrel that is longer than those of most sub-machine gun barrels and therefore provides a higher muzzle velocity (and therefore greater range and increased accuracy) than is usual among weapons chambered for the 9-mm Parabellum cartridge. The interior of the chamber is chromed for longer life and the useful advantage of reduced cleaning requirements.

The AUG Para, which is otherwise known as the **AUG 9**, also has a muzzle threaded to accept any of several types of silencer, and provision for the installation of a device to launch CS or CN grenades, or alternatively for the mounting of a bayonet, an item not frequently found on a sub-machine gun.

Pioneering move

The Steyr company was one of the first small arms manufacturers to make the commercially and militarily sensible adaptation of an assault rifle to sub-machine-gun standard. A major attraction of the concept is that there is need for only a small number of different parts, which greater eases the operating service's spares holding and logistics requirements. To improve the versatility of the AUG assault rifle and AUG Para sub-machine gun family, the manufacturer also offers a kit of three major parts to allow the conversion of the weapon between the two primary standards in as little as 10 minutes.

The AUG Para retains the AUG's fixed optical sight over the rear part of the barrel and forward part of the receiver (with mechanical sights retained for emergency use) and its straight-through 'bullpup' design with the magazine located behind the trigger group and aiming accuracy enhanced by the provision of a forward pistol grip.

Safety and firing

The safety arrangements are based on a cross-bolt safety catch above the trigger: this is pushed firmly from right to left to make the weapon safe, and from left to right to allow the weapon to be fired. There is a firing pin safety integrated with this mechanism. The AUG 9 Para can be fired in two modes: the first pressure on the trigger fires the weapon in semi-automatic mode, while the second pressure yields fully automatic fire.

SPECIFICATION	
AUG Para	**Muzzle velocity:** not available
Calibre: 9-mm (0.354-in) Parabellum	**Rate of fire, cyclic:** 700 rounds per minute
Length overall: 665 mm (26.18 in)	
Length of barrel: 420 mm (16.54 in)	**Feed:** 25- or 32-round straight box magazine
Weight: empty 3.3 kg (7.28 lb)	

CZ vz 61 Skorpion Sub-machine gun/Machine-pistol

Stock fully extended, the Type 61 can shoot with reasonable accuracy at up to 200 m (220 yards). It uses a simple blowback operation, but the empty case is ejected directly upwards.

A weapon that was manufactured in the period from about 1960 to 1975, the **Ceska Zbrojovka vz 61 Skorpion** is of Czechoslovak design and manufacturing origins, and lies in that no-man's land of small arms capability in

The Model 61 Skorpion is a favourite weapon of the Palestine Liberation Organization, its small size making for easy concealment.

which a weapon that is neither a pistol nor a true sub-machine gun is described as a 'machine pistol'. Such a weapon is small enough to be carried and fired as a pistol, but is also capable of fully automatic fire when this is required. Thus the vz 61 has the advantages and disadvantages of both types of weapon, and is perhaps below par in both capacities, but is nevertheless one of the most feared of all 'underground' arms, despite the fact that it was intended to be a standard service weapon for the conventional Czechoslovak armed forces and also for special forces requiring a close-combat weapon that could be concealed with ease.

Personal weapon

The Skorpion was designed for use by tank crews, signallers and other personnel who have no normal need for anything larger than a pistol. But since a pistol is essentially a short-range weapon, the introduction of a fully automatic feature provided this small weapon with a considerable short-range firepower. The Skorpion resembles a pistol, though the magazine is not in the butt, but forward of the trigger assembly, and a folding wire butt is provided for aimed fire. The overall appearance is short and chunky, and the weapon is small enough to be carried in a somewhat oversized belt holster.

When fired in fully automatic mode the weapon has a cyclic rate of about 840 rounds per minute, which makes it formidable at short ranges, but this advantage is offset by two

factors. One is that the firing of any machine pistol on full automatic makes the weapon almost impossible to aim accurately: the forces above the position of the hands and shoulder of the firer cause the muzzle to climb and judder, making it all but impossible to hold the weapon on the target for anything other than an instant. The other is that the Skorpion uses magazines with only 10- or 20-round capacities, and on automatic either is soon exhausted. But while the Skorpion fires, it creates an alarming swathe of fire.

The Skorpion operates on the blowback principle. Single shots can be selected, and the folding wire butt helps in aiming. The basic vz 61 Skorpion fires the American 0.32-in (7.65-mm) cartridge – the only Warsaw Pact weapon to use this round – but the **vz 63** uses the 9-mm Short (0.38-in) round and the **vz 68** the 9-mm (0.354-in) Parabellum cartridge. There is also a silenced version.

Terrorist weapon

Apart from its use by Czechoslovakia, the Skorpion was also sold to some African nations, but its main impact has been in the hands of guerrillas, terrorists and 'freedom fighters'. The Skorpion is easily concealed and its impact at short range is considerable, which suits the requirements of assassination and terror squads, so the type is much favoured by such groups. With them it has turned up in parts of the world from Central America to the Middle East.

SPECIFICATION	
vz 61 Skorpion	**Weight:** loaded 2 kg (4.4 lb)
Calibre: 0.32-in (actual 7.65-mm)	**Muzzle velocity:** 317 m (1,040 ft) per second
Length overall: 513 mm (20.2 in) with butt extended and 269 mm (10.6 in) with butt folded	**Rate of fire, cyclic:** 840 rpm
Length of barrel: 112 mm (4.4 in)	**Feed:** 10- or 20-round straight box magazine

Skorpion in operation The terrorist's choice

The Skorpion is the size of a large pistol, yet it is fully automatic and can take a 20-round magazine. Its folding wire stock allows accurate fire to about 100 m (110 yards) in the hands of a practised user.

Although it gained a notorious reputation for its terrorist use, the Skorpion actually started out as a military firearm. The weapon was designed in Czechoslovakia during the late 1950s after the communist seizure of power. Although the new regime abandoned many weapons then in development, it did initiate several projects with remarkable speed. Among them was a scheme for a self-defence weapon for issue to tank crews and the drivers of armoured personnel carriers.

Tank crews forced to bale out near enemy infantry have always been vulnerable. Foot soldiers are only too happy to have their revenge on men who,

The Skorpion machine-pistol is small and easy to conceal, which made it a favourite weapon of Arab terrorists during the 1970s and 1980s. It is seen here without its wire stock or the silencer that is often fitted.

Left and below: The Skorpion is a straightforward weapon to learn how to shoot. With a little practice (and the wire stock extended) it can hit a man-sized target some 75-100 m (80-110 yards) distant.

Left and below: Firing the Skorpion (in this case the weapon is actually the Yugoslav-made Model 61) can be a difficult experience as it spits its empty cases vertically upward. It should never be fired from the hip.

a few moments earlier, may have been firing on them from the safety of a armoured vehicle. During World War II, the Soviet army jealously guarded its trained tank crews, because it did not want to waste the precious time and effort that had been spent teaching them their job. The Soviets even provided special hospitals with burns specialists to get wounded tank drivers back into action as fast as possible. After the war they looked at possible weapons to give to tank crews as a means of defending themselves if their vehicles was disabled close to the enemy. The Soviets developed the Stechkin and, inspired by similar thoughts, Czechoslovak engineers were put to work on a machine-pistol for the vehicle crews.

Personal defence

The interiors of all armoured vehicles are notoriously cramped, and those of Soviet AFVs were especially so. With available space at a premium, no vehicle crew could afford to pack any defensive weapon much larger than a pistol. It takes a lot of time and effort to learn to shoot a pistol with any accuracy, however, and the pistol is of limited value to men who have little time to train with it. The Skorpion is a small sub-machine gun of the type usually referred to as a machine-pistol. An inexperienced shooter, firing it from the shoulder using the wire stock, is probably more likely to hit something than if he was using an ordinary handgun. The compact dimensions of the Skorpion allowed it to be carried by tank crew without much difficulty.

Unfortunately for the reputation of the Skorpion, one man's self-defence weapon is another man's concealable murder weapon. Being manufactured in Eastern Europe at the height of the Cold War meant that batches of Skorpions were soon travelling the world in diplomatic bags. The ease with which the weapon can be silenced further endeared it to the terrorist community and it became a favourite with the members of the Palestine Liberation Organisation.

The Skorpion is a simple weapon and is straightforward to shoot, disassemble and maintain. There is a fire selector marked '0' for safe, '1' for single shot and '20' for fully automatic. Curiously for a Soviet-bloc weapon, it is chambered for the .32 ACP (Automatic Colt Pistol) cartridge – known to the communists as 7.65-mm x 17. This has the advantage of being readily available, and suggests that the designers were either very alert to the export potential or that special forces usage was anticipated.

Pistol operation

The low recoil of the .32 ACP round allows direct blowback operation to be employed. The pressure of the expanding gases produced on firing drives back the case in the chamber against the bolt. This overcomes the inertia of the bolt and twin drive springs, and so pushes the bolt backward. The extractor ejects the case vertically upward, which makes the Skorpion an uncomfortable weapon to fire from the hip.

Rate of fire

The bolt is very light, partly to keep down weight and partly to reduce the disturbance to the aim caused by its movement. But unless some other feature was included, the rate of fire

Identifiable by its black pistol grip, the Model 61(i) is the Yugoslav-made version of the Czechoslovak Skorpion machine-pistol, which is more formally known as the CZ vz 61. This diminutive weapon was manufactured in Czechoslovakia between 1960 and 1975.

backplate. At the same time the bolt drives down a spring-loaded weight into the pistol grip. This goes down, rebounds and rises again to release the hook holding the bolt. Of course, the delay is only measurable in hundredths of a second, but it reduces the cyclic rate of fire to about 840 rounds per minute.

Although the Czechoslovakians did experiment with versions in .380 ACP and 9-mm Makarov calibres, the .32 ACP type is by far the most common. It has the advantage of producing no more recoil than a .22 pistol, so it is extremely easy to shoot and no problem to silence. In fact, it produces less muzzle energy than a high-velocity .22 rifle round. The .32 ACP cartridge

makes the Skorpion one of the least powerful pistols in the world. Defeated by almost any body armour and deflected by light cover or even car doors, the .32 is no 'man-stopper'. However, at pointblank range the Skorpion is as effective as many larger weapons.

The Skorpion went out of production in Czechoslovakia several years before the end of communist rule in that country. Zastava, the then Yugoslav arms industry in Belgrade, purchased some tooling equipment, however, and began to manufacture the weapon as the Model 61(i) machine pistol. This is identical to the Czech weapon except for the black plastic grips that replace the plywood ones.

would be over 1,000 rounds per minute and the weapon would be uncontrollable. Therefore, the Skorpion has a 'rate reducer'

fitted in the butt. When the bolt reaches the backward limit of its travel, it is caught by a spring-loaded hook mounted on the

SKORPION: CZECHOSLOVAK MACHINE-PISTOL

Subsequently manufactured in Yugoslavia, where it served with all sides during the civil war fighting of the 1990s, the Skorpion was designed and made in Czechoslovakia during the 1960s and 1970s. Without the silencer and with the wire stock folded over the top of the weapon the Skorpion is only 269 mm (10.6 in) long. The ease with which the weapon can be con-cealed made it a favourite with several terrorist organisations. With the stock

fully extended the Skorpion can fire with reasonable accuracy out to 100 m (110 yards). This is fairly good for a weapon not much bigger than a handgun. However, on full automatic its light weight and high rate of fire of 840 rounds per minute make it inaccurate at any but the shortest ranges.

Vertical ejection
The Skorpion is one of the relatively few weapons that eject their empty cases directly upwards. Firing it from the hip is not recommended.

Wire stock
When swung into position, the wire stock increases the overall length of the Skorpion to 513 mm (20.2 in). It allows the weapon to be comfortably fired from the shoulder — the only way to hit anything more than 30 m (33 yards) away — although it is not suited to people with long arms.

Pistol grip
The Skorpion can be fired one- or two-handed like a pistol, but this exposes its relatively poor accuracy. Like most machine-pistols it is a poor pistol in terms of accuracy, and as an automatic weapon it is not as effective in overall terms as a true sub-machine gun.

Madsen Sub-machine guns

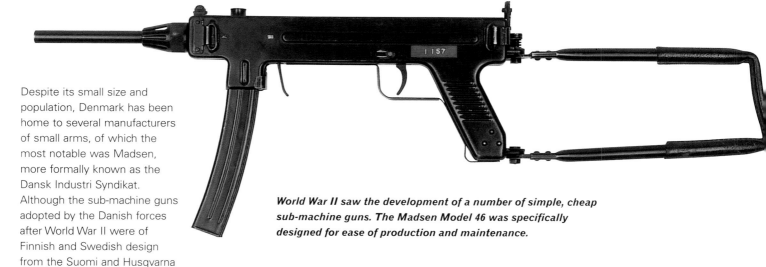

World War II saw the development of a number of simple, cheap sub-machine guns. The Madsen Model 46 was specifically designed for ease of production and maintenance.

Despite its small size and population, Denmark has been home to several manufacturers of small arms, of which the most notable was Madsen, more formally known as the Dansk Industri Syndikat. Although the sub-machine guns adopted by the Danish forces after World War II were of Finnish and Swedish design from the Suomi and Husqvarna organisations, Madsen had some export success with its own weapons.

The first Madsen sub-machine gun to appear after World War II was the **Model 45**, which had a number of interesting features but was not a success, but the following **Model 1946, Model 1950** and **Model 1953** were altogether more profitable for the company.

The Model 1945 (or **P13**) was chambered for the 9-mm (0.354-in) Parabellum cartridge, of which 50 were carried in a box magazine below the receiver. Despite the fact that the weapon had wooden furniture, the designers achieved the low empty weight of 3.2 kg (7.1 lb). Unusual features included a cocking slide rather than handle, a recoil spring wound round the barrel below this cocking slide, and a light breech block whose inertia was boosted by the mass of the moving spring and slide.

Rapid obsolescence

The Model 1945 was rendered obsolete only a year later by the Model 1946 (or **P16**). This was schemed for ease of production, and the weapon's body comprised two pressed steel frames hinged together at the rear and held together at the front by the barrel locking nut. The butt comprised a length of metal tube bent into a rectangle open at the forward end, where its ends were hinged to the rear of the body and the heel of the pistol grip allowing the butt to be folded to the right so that it rested alongside the weapon's body. Like the Model 1945, the Model 1946 was chambered for the 9-mm Parabellum cartridge, of which 32 rounds were carried. The Model 1946's cyclic rate of fire was 480 rounds per minute rather than the Model 1945's figure of 850 rounds per minute. The Model 1946 also had a lower muzzle velocity than the Model 1945, the respective figures being 380 and 400 m (1,247 and 1,312 ft) per minute. The Model 1946 weighed only 3.175 kg (7 lb) without its magazine.

The Model 1946 had basically the same cocking arrangement as the Model 1945, namely a slide on the upper part of the body's rear with a pair of milled flanges extending outward and downward for the firer to grip. On the Model 1950 the flanges were replaced by a knob on top of the slide, which was integral with the bolt. The weapon had the same type of folding butt as the Model 1946, and was supplied with 32 rounds of ammunition from a straight, flat-sided box magazine under the weapon. Other details included a weight of 3.175 kg (7 lb), muzzle velocity of 380 m (1,247 ft) per second, and cyclic rate of around 550 rounds per minute.

British interest

The Model 1950 was demonstrated in many countries and secured some orders. The British at one time wanted to adopt this weapon for use by second-line troops as the EM-2 was adopted for first-line forces, but plans for both these weapons were abandoned, and the British instead adopted the Sterling sub-machine gun.

The one major change that the British had demanded for the Model 1950 was the replacement of the Madsen type of single-row magazine by a double-row magazine that was curved and fullered to make it easier for the magazine spring to lift the rounds and for dirt and debris to fall to the bottom of the magazine without interfering with the gun's operation.

This type of magazine was adopted for the definitive Model 1953 sub-machine gun, which was otherwise still very clearly a linear descendant of the Model 1946 via the Model 1950. A closer examination revealed a reversal of the previous system to lock the two halves of the body to the rear of the barrel. Now the barrel locking nut screwed onto the barrel rather than onto the the front of the receiver as had been the case with the Models 1946 and 1950. Also the rotation of the locking nut drew the barrel forward until a flange on the rear of the barrel met the inside of the body, in the process holding the whole assembly in a stronger and more rigid arrangement.

Another internal change was the improved shaping of the bolt for better functioning. An optional extra was a removable barrel jacket to which a special short bayonet could be attached. Like the other Madsen sub-machine guns, the Model 1953 was generally produced as an automatic weapon with provision for an alternative selective-fire mechanism, and had comprehensive safety features preventing, amongst other things, the accidental discharge of the weapon should it be jarred or dropped.

SPECIFICATION	
Model 1953	**Weight:** loaded 4 kg (8.82 lb)
Calibre: 9-mm (0.354-in)	**Muzzle velocity:** 385 m (1,263 m)
Length overall: 808 mm (31.8 in) with butt extended	per second
Length of barrel: 213 mm (8.4 in)	**Rate of fire, cyclic:** 600 rpm
	Feed: 32-round curved magazine

Jati-Matic
Sub-machine gun

During the 1970s Jaati Tumari was working in Finland to design a highly accurate 0.22-in (5.59-mm) semi-automatic (self-loading) pistol for target shooting. While being test fired, the new pistol suddenly unleashed a burst of fully automatic fire, and on investigating the resulting impacts through the target Tumari found that the holes were very tightly grouped. Such are the semi-accidental design origins of the **Jati-Matic** sub-machine gun, which is chambered for the universally accepted 9-mm (0.354-in) Parabellum cartridge, and is certainly one of the most unusual-looking weapons of its type currently to be found in service anywhere in the world.

Odd appearance

The striking and somewhat disconcerting appearance of the Jati-Matic is derived from the apparent misalignment of the barrel and the body of the weapon. This is the result of Tumari's patented inclined bolt system. Rather than operating in the same plane as the barrel, the Tumari type of bolt recoils up an inclined ramp, which helps to retard the bolt's movement to the rear, and at the same time forces the weapon down. This angling of elements in the receiver also permits the grip to be located in a position higher than would otherwise have been possible, and therefore in line

with the barrel and the weapon's recoil. The result is a virtual elimination of the muzzle-climb tendency evident in most of the other sub-machine guns to be found anywhere in the world, which makes it virtually impossible for the firer to hold the target in his sights during a protracted burst of fire. On the Jati-Matic the higher grip ensures that the recoil force does not compel the weapon to rotate muzzle-upward in the firer's hands, but rather to push straight back and therefore leave the sights on the target. The one major limitation of the arrangement is that it reduces the natural 'pointability' of the sub-machine gun.

Other features of the Jati-Matic include a foregrip that is hinged at its upper end to fold to the rear, when it serves as a safety, provision for 20- and 40-round magazines inserted into the weapon just forward of the trigger group, and a trigger on which the first pressure yields single-shot fire and the second pressure produces fully automatic fire.

Blowback operation

The Jati-Matic is a blowback-operated weapon, the receiver is

The Jati-Matic certainly offers a very unusual appearance from the side as it appears to be bent, with the barrel not aligned with the receiver.

SPECIFICATION	
Jati-Matic	**Muzzle velocity:** not available
Calibre: 9-mm (0.354-in) Parabellum	**Rate of fire, cyclic:** 650 rounds per
Length overall: 400 mm (15.75 in)	minute
Length of barrel: not available	**Feed:** 20- or 40-round straight box
Weight: empty 1.65 kg (3.64 lb)	magazine

made of pressed steel with a hinged cover, the foregrip serves as the cocking handle when lowered into the open position, and there is no stock, fixed or folding, control of the weapon being exercised by means of the foregrip and the pistol grip.

The Jati-Matic was manufactured in modest numbers between 1980 and

1987 by the Tampeeren Asepaja Oy, and then re-entered production in 1995 by Finnish concern, the Oy Golden Gun Ltd. The model manufactured from 1995 is the **GG-95 PDW** (Personal Defence Weapon). This is a development of the Jati-Matic revised to eliminating much of the weapon's unpopular angularity.

Above: The complete 'kit' for the Jati-Matic sub-machine gun includes a night sight, holsters, 20- and 40-round magazines, a carrying sling, and cleaning and maintenance equipment.

Left: The foregrip of the Jati-Matic serves as a cocking handle when opened, and as a safety when closed. The blade on the lower part of its rear edge engages in the weapon's mechanism to prevent any movement of the bolt.

MAT 49
Sub-machine gun

In the immediate aftermath of World War II the French armed forces were equipped with a variety of weapons from a remarkable miscellany of origins and sources. As far as sub-machine guns were concerned, some of these were of French design and manufacture dating from before the start of World War II in 1939, and others were American and British weapons delivered to the revised French forces from the United States and the United Kingdom. While the weapons themselves were serviceable enough, the range of ammunition calibres and types was considered too large for logistical convenience and cost-effective stores holding. A selection and standardisation programme was therefore launched, resulting in the authorities' decision to standardise on the 9-mm (0.354-in) Parabellum cartridge for future sub-machine gun developments.

Entering French service in 1949, the 9-mm (0.354-in) MAT 49 is an extremely rugged design, made from heavy-gauge steel stampings. The pistol grip/magazine housing hinges forward for stowage and transport.

New weapon

A new sub-machine gun of wholly French origin was also demanded, and three arsenals responded with new designs. That created by the Manufacture d'Armes de Tulle (hence MAT) was selected for service, and the new weapon went into production during 1949 within the context of re-equipping and strengthening the French armed forces with more capable weapons that were, wherever possible, of French design and manufacture.

This **MAT 49** sub-machine gun is still in fairly extensive service, for it is an efficient weapon that is also, unlike many other sub-machine guns of the period, very well manufactured. Although it uses the now commonplace constructional practice of parts and assemblies fabricated from steel from stampings, those of the MAT 49 were made from heavy-duty steels and are thus very strong and capable of absorbing a great deal of hard use. This was a factor of primary importance to the French, whose forces were committed to a large number of operations over the following 15 years or so, many of them in parts of the world (such as Indo-China and North Africa) notably inhospitable to the continued smooth functioning of weapons.

Proven mechanism

The design uses the blowback principle but, in place of what is now described as a 'wraparound' breech block, to reduce the length of the receiver the MAT 49 has an arrangement in which a sizeable portion of the breech block enters the barrel chamber to have much the same effect. No other design uses this feature. There is another aspect of the MAT 49 which is typically French. This is the magazine housing, which can be folded forward with the magazine inserted to reduce the bulk of the weapon for stowage and transport. This feature is a carry-over from the pre-war MAS 38, and was considered so effective by the French army that it was retained in the MAT 49: a catch is depressed and the magazine housing (with a loaded magazine in place) is folded forward to lie under the barrel, while to use the weapon again the magazine is simply pulled back into place so that the housing acts as a foregrip. This foregrip is made all the more important by the fact that the MAT 49 can be fired only in full automatic mode, so

Designed with colonial service in mind, the MAT 49 was used extensively in Indo-China, as well as by the paratroops so notably involved in the bloody conflict in Algeria. It withstood such stern tests successfully.

a firm grip is needed to keep the weapon under control when it is fired.

Considerable pains were taken in the design of the MAT 49 to ensure that dust and dirt were kept out of the weapon's mechanism: this too was another historical carry-over from previous times as the MAT 49 was intended for use in the deserts of North Africa. Even when the magazine is in the forward

position a flap moves into position to keep out foreign matter. If repairs or cleaning are required, the weapon can be easily stripped without tools. In action a grip safety locks both the trigger mechanism and any possible forward movement of the bolt.

Overall the MAT 49 is a sturdy weapon. It is still used in limited numbers by the French armed forces and also by various of the

French police and para-military units. It was also exported to many of the ex-French colonies. The numbers in French service declined after the introduction of

the 5.56-mm (0.219-in) FA MAS assault rifle, but there are enough operators left to ensure that the MAT 49 will remain around for some time.

SPECIFICATION	
MAT 49	**Muzzle velocity:** 390 m (1,280 ft) per second
Calibre: 9-mm (0.354-in) Parabellum	
Length: 720 mm (28.34 in) with butt extended and 460 mm (18.1 in) with butt closed	**Rate of fire, cyclic:** 600 rounds per minute
Length of barrel: 228 mm (8.97 in)	**Feed:** 20- or 32-round straight box magazine
Weight: loaded 4.17 kg (9.19 lb)	

Walther MP-K and MP-L 9-mm sub-machine guns

By 1963 the Carl Walther Waffenfabrik of Ulm in Germany were anxious to make a greater impact on the small arms market rather than just relying on sales of their various police and military pistols.

New version

Following years of development and testing dating back to the late 1950s, they therefore introduced a sub-machine gun design to their product range to be available in two basic forms. These were the **MP-K**, with the K denoting *Kurz* or short, and the **MP-L** with the L denoting *Lange* or long. Both weapons were identical, the main difference being the length of barrel and the associated hand guard shroud wrapped around almost the entire length of the barrel.

The MP-K and MP-L both fired the 9 x 19-mm Parabellum pistol cartridge and were selective fire (single shot or automatic) blowback weapons firing from the open bolt position. One marketing option was the availability of models firing either fully automatic (no single shot) or semi-automatic (single shot) only. The bolt was located over the barrel, overlapping it at the chamber end when the breech was closed. A guide rod carried both the bolt and the main operating spring. Grooves were machined into the bolt body into which intrusive dirt or debris could be directed to proven jamming. One unusual design

The Walther MP was a competent weapon, but was overshadowed by competition from the more complex but more accurate Heckler & Koch MP5, as well as cheaper designs dating from the World War II period. The MP-L model is illustrated: its overall length is 737 mm (29 in) with the butt extended and 455 mm (17.9 in) with the butt retracted. The barrel length is 257 mm (10.1 in).

feature was that the cocking handle on the left-hand side of the receiver did not reciprocate with the bolt yet it could be pushed down to manually actuate the bolt to clear ammunition jams. The fire control switch was ambidextrous. Field stripping for cleaning and maintenance was simple and rapid.

Construction was of robust, hard-wearing steel stampings with the 32-round box magazines inserted upwards into the receiver through a magazine well located just forward of the pistol grip. A steel skeleton outline butt stock could be folded forward to locate along either the right- or left-hand side of the receiver for carrying convenience. Sling swivels were provided for a webbing sling.

One sighting novelty was a two-part leaf sight at the rear. It had a simple notch that aligned with the top of the foresight housing for rapid sighting at ranges up to about 75 m (82 yards). For more accurate fire at the longer ranges, optimistically stated to be up to 150 m (164 yards), the notch was folded down to reveal an aperture sight to be aligned with a barleycorn foresight. A sound suppressor or blank firing attachment could be secured over the muzzle while provision was made for mounting a

tactical light under the front hand guard.

The MP-K and MP-L were extensively tested by numerous police and armed forces but significant orders did not materialise. Both were sound weapons with many attractive features but they appeared at a time when the potential market was still sated with the legacy of already available weapons from World War II. It has been reported that small numbers were procured by a few West German police forces.

SPECIFICATION	
MP-K	**Weight:** empty 2.8 kg (6.17 lb)
Calibre: 9 mm (0.354 in) x 19 Parabellum	**Muzzle velocity:** 356 m (1,168 ft) per second
Lengths: butt extended 653 mm (25.7 in); butt retracted 368 mm 14.5 in); length of barrel 171 mm (6.7 in)	**Cyclic rate of fire:** 550 rpm
	Magazine: 32-round box

Heckler & Koch MP7 4.6-mm Personal Defence Weapon

Left: The MP7 is designed for use as a close-range self-defence weapon by military personnel who by the nature of their duties are not able to carry a full-sized weapon such as an assault rifle, or even a conventional sub-machine gun.

Right: The Heckler & Koch MP7 with both the telescopic butt-stock and the foregrip in the folded position. The main combat cartridge for the MP7 is a BAE Systems-developed Ball round with a steel bullet and with an overall weight of 6.3 g (0.22oz).

The **Heckler & Koch MP7** falls into the category of the Personal Defence Weapon (PDW). The 4.6-mm (0.18-in) PDW is a controversial innovation intended to be carried by those who have to carry a defensive weapon but, due to their military activities, cannot carry an assault rifle or sub-machine gun, yet they still have to have something better than a short-range pistol. Numerous military personnel are potential PDW users, from radio operators to drivers and clerks, who may have to carry their PDW at all times for months on end yet when they need it their PDW has to be lethal and easy to fire accurately at ranges up to 200 m (219 yards).

Ease of use

To this end the Heckler & Koch MP7 is a compact and light weapon with rounded lines that enable it to be carried either slung over a shoulder, or in some form of holster, while imposing the minimum of encumbrance to the user. To

In addition to iron sights, the MP7 is provided with red dot optical sights, while a universal rail allows the addition of alternative sighting systems. The cocking lever/bolt closure is ambidextrous.

ensure a good ballistic capability at the combat ranges envisaged, Heckler & Koch developed a new 4.6 x 30-mm round specially for the MP7 and have already developed several forms of what seems to be a very small cartridge weighing just 6.3 g (0.22oz). The main combat cartridge uses a special copper-coated steel Ball bullet weighing 1.6 g (0.05oz) capable of penetrating 1.5 mm (0.06 in) of titanium plus 20 layers of Kevlar at 100 m (109 yards). This means it can penetrate most types of military body armour. Other cartridges include a Tracer and a special Ball Spoon Nose cartridge with a copper bullet that will deform on impact. Also available are low cost Ball Training, Ball Frangible, Blank and Drill cartridges. Other types are under development.

The MP7 itself is a gas-operated weapon with a rotary locking bolt. Considerable use is made of synthetic polymer materials to keep the weight down. The body is only 380 mm (15 in) long with the telescopic shoulder stock

The MP7 can be fired using only one hand, although it is preferable to use a two-handed grip with the use of the folding foregrip in front of the trigger. A telescopic shoulder stock is provided for long-range fire up to a range of 200 m (219 yards).

retracted. It can be fired in pistol fashion from one hand but for more controlled fire the butt is extended (to make the overall length 590 mm/23.2 in) and a forward handgrip is folded down. Weight empty is just 1.6 kg (3.5 lb), plus box magazines inserted upwards through the pistol grip, each holding 20 or 40 rounds. Cyclic rate of fire is about 950 rpm and there is a single shot facility.

A length of Picatinny sight mounting rail is provided over the receiver to allow a wide range of optical sights to be employed – iron sights are also provided. Most users seem to have opted for some form of red dot reflex sight. All safety and fire controls, magazine

release and cocking devices are ambidextrous. MP7 combat accessories include a sound suppressor over the muzzle and a tactical light secured to one side of the receiver.

It is known that German special forces make use of the

MP7 and it has undergone prolonged testing in several other countries, especially in the United Kingdom where the armed forces have stated an initial requirement for about 14,000 weapons of the PDW type.

SPECIFICATION	
MP7	**Weight:** empty 1.6 kg (3.5 lb)
Calibre: 4.6 mm (0.18 in) x 30	**Muzzle velocity:** 750 m (2,461 ft) per second
Lengths: butt extended 590 mm (23.2 in); butt retracted 380 mm (15 in); length of barrel 180 mm (7 in)	**Cyclic rate of fire:** 950 rpm
	Magazine: 20- or 40-round box

Heckler & Koch MP5 Sub-machine gun

Since World War II, the German concern of Heckler und Koch has become one of Europe's largest and most important small-arms manufacturers. Its success has been based soundly on the production of its G3 rifle, which was a standard NATO weapon and is still in use all over the world. In the 1960s the company used the G3 as a basis on which to produce the **Heckler und Koch MP5** sub-machine gun

Rifle-based

The MP5 was designed to fire the standard 9-mm (0.354-in) X 19 Parabellum cartridge. Although this is a relatively low-powered pistol round, the MP5 uses the same roller and inclined ramp locking mechanism as the G3, which fires a full-power rifle round. The complexity of this

Heckler & Koch MP5A3

This MP5A3 is fitted with a sliding metal strut stock which can allow a considerable reduction in length. Early MP5s used a straight magazine.

Heckler & Koch MP5A2

This MP5A2 has a fixed plastic stock. After 1978 all MP5s were fitted with a curved magazine to improve cartridge feed.

system is more than offset by its increased safety. Unlike other machine pistols, the MP5 fires from a closed bolt – the breech block is in the forward position when the trigger is pulled so there is no forward-moving mass to disturb the aim. This makes the MP5 much more accurate than other SMGs. The resemblance to the G3 is maintained by the use of many G3 components on the MP5.

Used by military and law enforcement units in more than 50 nations, the MP5 is firmly established as the world's pre-eminent sub-machine gun. Over 120 variants of the MP5 are available to address the widest range of tactical requirements. The weapon's unique modular design and a variety of optional buttstocks, forearms, sight mounts, and other accessories gives the MP5 extraordinary flexibility to meet almost any mission.

The main versions of the MP5 include the **MP5A2** with a fixed butt stock and the **MP5A3** with a sliding metal strut stock. The **MP5A4** and the **MP5A5** are the same weapons with the addition of a three-round burst fire capability.

The **MP5SD** is a silenced weapon for use in special or anti-terrorist warfare. The removable sound suppressor is integrated into the design and conforms to the normal length and profile of an unsuppressed weapon. The MP5SD uses an integral aluminum or optional wet technology stainless steel sound suppressor. Unlike most silenced weapons, it does not

Heckler & Koch MP5K

require use of subsonic ammunition for effective sound reduction.

Hideaway guns

The **MP5K** was introduced for use by special units, where weapon concealment is often essential. It is a very short version of the basic MP5, only 325 mm (12.8 in) long and recognizable by a small foregrip, under the almost non-existent muzzle. The **MP5KA1** is a special version of this variant with no protrusions so that it can be carried under clothing or in a special holster.

The **MP5N** or 'Navy' model is made for US Navy SEALs. Fully 'marinised' for operations in seawater, it comes standard with an ambidextrous trigger group and threaded barrel.

In spite of its complexity, the MP5 has proved to be an excellent and reliable sub-machine gun. Its first users were West German police

agencies and border guards, and soon numbers were purchased by Swiss police and the Netherlands armed forces. Single fire variants are widely used by law-enforcement officers in crowded public areas such as airports.

However, it is since the MP5 was adopted by the British SAS

that it has become the weapon of choice for special forces worldwide. The MP5 is inherently accurate because it fires from a closed bolt, and pinpoint accuracy is an essential requirement of any weapon used in a hostage rescue, where innocent lives are at risk from inaccurate fire.

SPECIFICATION	
MP5A2	**Muzzle velocity:** 375 m (1,230 ft) per second
Calibre: 9 mm (0.354-in) Parabellum	**Magazine:** 15- or 30-round box
Weight: loaded 2.97 kg (6 lb 8 oz)	
Length: 680 mm (26.77 in); length of barrel 225 mm (8.85 in)	**MP5SF**
Muzzle velocity: 400 m (1,312 ft) per second	**Calibre:** 0.40-in S&W
Rate of fire: 800 rpm cyclic	**Weight:** loaded 2.54 kg (5 lb 7 oz)
Magazine: 15- or 30-round box	**Length:** 712 mm (28 in); length of barrel 225 mm (8.85 in)
	Muzzle velocity: 330 m (1,083 ft) per second
MP5K	**Rate of fire:** semi-auto only
Weight: empty 2.1 kg (4 lb 7 oz)	
Length: 325 mm (12.8 in); length of barrel 115 mm (4.53 in)	

Sir John Stevens, the Commissioner of the London Metropolitan Police, holds a Heckler & Koch MP5 sub-machine gun, during a visit to the force's new firearms and public order training centre.

Heckler & Koch MP5A3

Lugs for barrel attachments

Front sling attachment

Handguard locking pin

Cocking lever

Handguard locking pin

Barrel extension

9-mm Parabellum round

30-round magazine

Firing pin

Recoil spring

Magazine release lever

Rotary rear aperture sight

Sear

Trigger

Receiver

Trigger spring

Trigger housing

Pistol grip

Buttstock release lever

Folding butt

Sliding buttstock

Law-enforcement special

To satisfy US law-enforcement demand, in 1991 H&K introduced an MP5 chambered to fire 10-mm (0.39-in) Auto, followed by versions firing .40 calibre S&W and .45 Colt. The MP5SF (single fire) carbine is semi-automatic only. It is popular as a squad car weapon, to supplement or replace police shotguns. It has less recoil, greater range, and more ammunition capacity than a shotgun and is especially suitable for small stature officers.

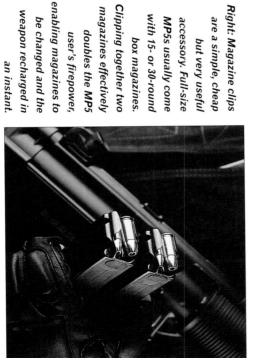

Left: Heckler & Koch have developed a whole range of accessories for the MP5. A variety of laser sights and torches have been developed for police use.

Above: A selection of optional trigger groups allow for single fire only, full automatic, 2-round, and 3-round burst options. The selector switch is easy to use, even in gloves.

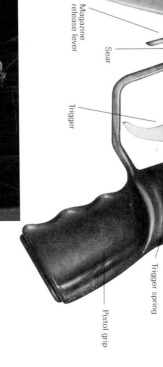

Right: Magazine clips are a simple, cheap but very useful accessory. Full-size MP5s usually come with 15- or 30-round box magazines. Clipping together two magazines effectively doubles the MP5 user's firepower, enabling magazines to be changed and the weapon recharged in an instant.

Modular weapon system

The modular design of the Heckler & Koch MP5 consists of six main assembly groups, not including the carry sling. The variety of optional buttstocks, forearms, sight mounts, and other accessories provides an unmatched degree of flexibility, as these groups can be exchanged with other groups to cover almost any operational requirements. This design also allows assemblies to be repaired separately from the weapon, which can be fitted with a new group and immediately returned to service.

Daewoo K7 9-mm silenced sub-machine gun

Announced as recently as 2003, the 9-mm (0.354-in) calibre **Daewoo K7** silenced sub-machine gun is a South Korean weapon. It was created specifically for the use of that nation's special forces, and was conceived in a fashion that reduces its firing report to a level at which little sound is transmitted, and then only in a form that bears no real resemblance to the conventional report of a firearm being discharged.

Despite this novel aspect and its particular capabilities, the K7 is not a wholly new design, but is based on an existing weapon, the Daewoo K1A short assault rifle designed to fire the 5.56 x 45-mm (0.219-in) NATO cartridge, which is now a world standard for assault rifles.

Weapon potential

While the sub-machine gun uses the same receiver and telescopic butt-stock as the short assault rifle, its operating system has been much altered. For a start, the type of cartridge fired has been changed from the K1A short rifle's 5.56-mm (0.219-in) round to a special low-powered cartridge. This 9 x 19-mm cartridge fires a fully metal jacketed bullet at subsonic speed, which reduces

the bullet's lethality at all but short ranges. However, the bullet's low velocity and the low pressure of the gases that propel it combine to reduce the weapon's potential firing signature to a very marked degree. Moreover, the little sound that is produced is almost entirely removed by the large sound suppressor. This is a cylindrical unit secured around the short barrel. The suppressor not only eliminates most of the weapon's audible firing signature but also, and just as important, contains all of the muzzle flash within the body of the suppressor, thus ensuring that the firer's position cannot be detected visually even at night.

Ammunition

The low-velocity ammunition also removes the need for the weapon to use the gas-operated system of the K1A rifle. In place of the assault rifle's Kalashnikov-derived gas operation with a rotary locking bolt, therefore, the K7 works on the pure blow-back principle, the mass of the forward-moving breech block overcoming the rearward momentum on firing until the chamber pressure has fallen to a safe level following the

The K7 sub-machine gun, fabricated in South Korea by the Daewoo company, is notably quiet in operation but pays the penalty in short range and reduced lethality. However, this is of little consequence in a weapon intended primarily for special forces use.

bullet's departure from the muzzle.

Ammunition is fed into the weapon from a 30-round vertical box magazine. As the original K1A rifle magazine well was retained, a special internal modification has been introduced to accommodate the smaller magazine. Three fire modes are provided. The mode likely to be used most often is single-shot, but there are also three-round burst and fully automatic modes. Prolonged use of the fully automatic mode soon damages the suppressor baffles, however, especially as the cyclic rate of fire is stated to be 1,150 rounds per minute, a remarkably high rate and the result of the use of a light bolt assembly and breech block.

Revised sights

Compared with those of the K1A rifle, the K7's sights have been much revised to cater for the low velocity of the ammunition. Using these sights the maximum effective range is 135 m (150 yards), though most

engagements would be at shorter ranges. A night sight can be fitted, the only other available combat accessory being a carrying sling.

One of the units most likely to make use of the K7 is the 707th Special Missions Battalion, which is an element of the South Korean army's Special Warfare Command. The battalion is South Korea's primary counter-terrorist and quick-reaction force. The unit's personnel wear a distinguishing black beret and are entrusted with the fulfilment of urban counter-terrorist missions and, in time of war, clandestine special warfare assignments.

This elite force was established after the disaster of the Arab terrorist attack on the Olympic Games in Munich in 1972, after which the South Korean government realised that it needed to raise a special unit to handle emergent threats. These ranged from North Korean special operations forces to the operations of foreign terrorists on South Korean soil.

New operations

In 1982 the South Korean government tasked the battalion with providing a counter-terrorist response to any terrorist attack during the 1988 Olympic Games in Seoul. The unit immediately began a programme to boost its strength and overall capabilities, and virtually tripled in size. The battalion provided security for important persons and sites in the Asian and Olympic Games of 1986 and 1988. The battalion has also seen considerable service against North Korean infiltrators, it is believed, and unconfirmed reports suggest the launching of several operations on the North Korean mainland.

Based at Songham City, the battalion numbers some 300 operational personnel divided into six companies, of which only two are specifically dedicated to the counter-terrorist role. Each counter terrorist team comprises four 14-man teams aided by support and demolitions teams. The battalion reportedly maintains a group of female operators for use in situations in which a woman might not be suspected by a terrorist group of posing a threat. Candidates for the battalion are drawn only from qualified special forces personnel. Special forces training and selection last one year, and include six months of basic infantry combat training followed by six months of special warfare and parachute training. During the special warfare portion of their training the men receive instruction in basic parachute techniques, rappelling and mountain warfare, martial arts, fire arms instruction, and demolitions.

The troops of the South Korean special forces are well known for their physical toughness, and the personnel of the 707th SMB are still tougher. The training regime emphasises physical fitness, standard elements including calisthenics in the snow or temperatures well below freezing point, and swimming in freezing lakes without protection.

Specialised training

Members of the special forces who volunteer for service with the battalion must first pass an extensive background check and complete a 10-day selection process that eliminates all but 10 per cent of the applicants. The battalion's counter-terrorist training is intensive, and a person accepted into the battalion receives additional instruction in a comprehensive range of combat skills.

Reportedly one of the finest in the world, the battalion's training facility has an extensive network of range facilities allowing for the development of the unit personnel's skill.

As well as working with other South Korean special operations forces, the battalion maintains close ties with similar units in other nations, including the Singaporean STAR team and the Australian SAS Regiment's Tactical Assault Group, though the unit's closest links are with the US Army's 1st Special Forces Group and 'Delta Force'.

Funding for training and operations is generous, and as a result the battalion has access to a large variety of foreign and domestically produced weapons. Pistols include modified versions of the 0.45-in Colt M1911A1 and 9-mm Daewoo DP51. The Heckler & Koch MP5 is the primary sub-machine gun for assault purposes, with the Daewoo K7 used for lower-profile roles. The Daewoo K1 and K2 assault rifles are used in forms modified by the addition of forward pistol grips and low-light vision devices. Rearguard elements are trained in the use of the Benelli Super 90 shotgun with pistol grips. For shorter-range sniping the 7.62-mm Heckler & Koch PSG1 and M24 rifles are standard, and for longer-range work there is the 0.5-in RAI rifle. For heavier firepower the battalion has 40-mm M203 grenade launchers, and 7.62-mm M60E3 and K3 belt-fed machine-guns. The battalion has also deployed the Javelin man-portable SAM against air attackers.

SPECIFICATION	
Daewoo K7	**Muzzle velocity:** about 295 m (968 ft) per second
Calibre: 9 mm (0.354 in)	**Rate of fire, cyclic:** 1,150 rounds per minute
Length overall: 606 mm (23.9 in) with butt retracted; 788 mm (31 in) with butt extended	**Effective range:** 135 m (150 yards)
Length of barrel: 134 mm (5.3 in)	**Magazine:** 30-round box
Weight: empty 3.4 kg (7.5 lb)	

PM-63 (Wz 63) 9-mm machine pistol

Designed by a team under the leadership of Professor Piotr Wilniewzyc, one of the designers of the the ViS 35 pistol, the **PM-63 (Wz 63)** is primarily a weapon used by the Polish special, airborne and armoured forces. It is popularly known as the **RAK (Reczny Automat Komandosa)**, and fires the Soviet 9 x 18-mm (0.354-in) Makarov cartridge. The weapon was manufactured by Z. M. Lucznik of Radom, and went out of production in 1980.

More of a machine pistol than a true sub-machine gun, the PM-63 combines the principal features usually considered characteristic of the self-loading pistol and the fully automatic sub-machine gun.

Thus the PM-63 has the advantage that single shots can be fired using only one hand, but if fully automatic fire is needed the shoulder stock can be pulled out and the fore-end dropped to provide a steady right-hand hold.

Two magazines

The magazine catch is at the heel of the pistol grip, as is typical of communist bloc weapons of the period, and the weapon can accept double-column magazines of the 15- and 25-round types. Since it operates on the simple blow-back principle, the gun fires from the open breech position, so the slide must be pulled back to cock the action or, alternatively, the compensator can be placed against a vertical surface and the gun pushed forward to achieve the same result.

When the trigger is pulled (a short pull for semi-automatic fire, and a long pull for fully automatic fire in the absence of any selector), the slide is released and driven forward by the spring, stripping a round from the magazine and feeding it into the chamber. As soon as the cartridge is lined up with the chamber the extractor grips the cartridge rim and the gun fires while the slide is still

SPECIFICATION	
PM-63	**Muzzle velocity:** 323 m (1,060 ft) per second
Calibre: 9 mm (0.354 in)	**Rate of fire, cyclic:** 600 rounds per minute
Length overall: 333 mm (13 in) with butt retracted; 583 mm (23 in) with butt extended	**Effective range:** about 175 m (190 yards)
Length of barrel: 152 mm (6 in)	**Magazine:** 15- or 25-round box
Weight: empty 1.8 kg (3.97 lb)	

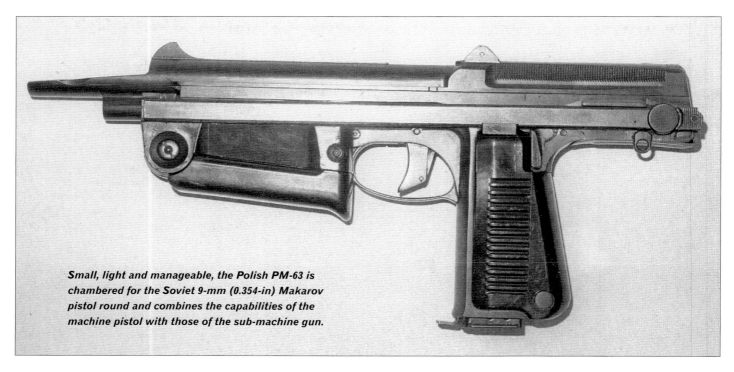

Small, light and manageable, the Polish PM-63 is chambered for the Soviet 9-mm (0.354-in) Makarov pistol round and combines the capabilities of the machine pistol with those of the sub-machine gun.

moving forward. The firing impulse then checks and halts the slide before driving it back against the pressure of the return spring. During this process the extractor holds the empty case until the ejector pushes it through the ejection port in the right-hand side of the slide. The slide continues to the rear and the return spring, which is located under the barrel, is fully compressed during the process.

Retarding action

The slide then rides over a retarder lever which snaps up and holds the slide to the rear. The retarder, an inertia pellet in the rear of the slide, continues rearward under its own momentum and compresses its own spring. When the spring is fully compressed it throws the retarder forward and this pushes the retarder lever down out of engagement with the slide and, provided the trigger

The upper example shows the PM-63 in its most compact form with the stock folded, while the lower example shows the weapon's extended form for shoulder firing and therefore somewhat greater accuracy.

is still depressed and ammunition remains in the magazine, the slide goes forward to repeat the cycle. The retarder keeps the weapon's cyclic rate of fire down to 600 rounds per minute from an un-retarded rate that would be about 840 rounds per minute. This helps to make the PM-63 a very controllable weapon despite its small size.

The above should not be allowed to convey the impression that the PM-63 is a perfect weapon of its type,

however, for this interesting weapon does have a few drawbacks and limitations. In the first place, it was difficult to make and therefore expensive to manufacture, this being especially true of the complex one-piece slide. In the second place, the sights move during firing, a fact that makes it almost impossible to adjust the fall of shot during burst firing.

Continued service

What cannot be denied, however, is the fact that the

PM-63 has withstood the test of time: the weapon was introduced to service during 1963, and is still in limited but useful service with the Polish armed forces in the first decade of the 21st century.

It is worth noting that for some reason the Chinese Norinco state-owned manufacturing concern has chosen to manufacture and market this Polish design without change and, probably, without any licence agreement in place.

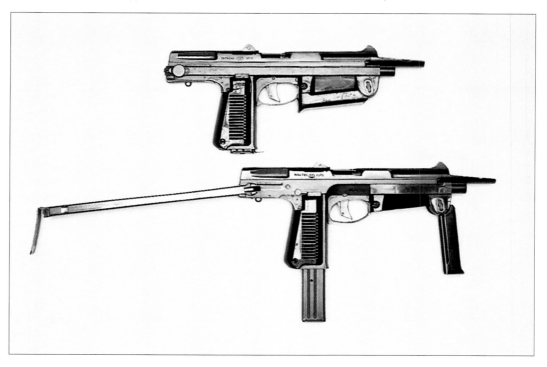

Israel Military Industries Uzi
Sub-machine gun

Above: The original Uzi sub machine gun came with a conventional wooden stock, but most weapons are now seen with a folding metal device for compactness.

Below: Mechanically identical to the full size gun, the Mini Uzi has a shorter barrel and a lighter bolt, giving a high rate of fire.

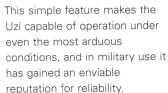

Even though its design dates back more than half a century, the **Uzi** remains one of the most effective sub-machine guns ever built. Named after designer Uziel Gal, the compact weapon was developed at a time when Israel was beset by enemies, yet had little in the way of manufacturing facilities. As a result the gun is largely made from cheap pressed-steel parts, easy to make and easy to maintain.

Gal was influenced by the pre-war Czech CZ 23. This featured a bolt that wrapped around the barrel, placing the mass well forward, while the breech remained at the rear. Although of short overall dimensions, the Uzi's barrel is actually longer than that of more conventional weapons.

Cheaply made

The Uzi is made largely from welded steel pressings. The main body is made from a single sheet of heavy gauge sheet steel, with grooves pressed into the sides to take any dust, dirt or sand that might get into the works.

This simple feature makes the Uzi capable of operation under even the most arduous conditions, and in military use it has gained an enviable reputation for reliability.

The barrel is secured to the body by a large nut just behind the muzzle. The trigger group is situated centrally, and the box magazine is inserted through the pistol grip. This makes reloading very easy in the dark, for 'hand will naturally find hand'. The normal combat magazine holds 32 rounds, but a common practice is to join two magazines together using a cross-over clip or tape to allow rapid changing. A grip safety is incorporated into the pistol grip, and a change lever just above the grip can be used to select semi-automatic (single-shot) fire. Originally built with a sturdy wooden butt stock, production was quickly switched to a version with a metal butt, which can be folded under the receiver to reduce overall length.

Even with the folding stock, there were many users who wanted an even more compact weapon. The **Mini-Uzi** was developed by Israel Military Industries from the full scale

Uzis fire from an open bolt, so they will never be blindingly accurate. However, at combat ranges they shoot straight enough to do the job.

Uzi and differs from the original only in dimensions and weights. A few modifications have been introduced to the basic design, but these are only superficial while the operating system of the original has been retained unchanged. As the weapon is lighter than the full-size version, its breech block is lighter too and this provides a cyclic rate of fire of 950 rounds per minute, which is much higher than on the original. The most obvious difference is that the normal folding metal butt has been replaced by a single-strut butt stock that folds along the right hand side of the body. When folded the butt plate acts as a rudimentary foregrip.

Reduced scale

The **Micro-Uzi** is even smaller, having been developed primarily for clandestine or security use. Barely larger than a heavy pistol, the small size and weight of the bolt would create an unacceptably high rate of fire, so a tungsten insert has been added to increase the mass. Even so, the Micro Uzi has a cyclic rate of more than 1,200 rounds per minute.

Other Uzi variants include the semi-automatic **Carbine UZI**, which has been produced to conform with the legal requirements of some American states that ban the private ownership of fully-automatic weapons. An Uzi pistol has also been developed.

The Uzi became one of the symbols of Israeli military prowess, but Israel is not the only nation to use the type – it has been sold to police and military forces in at least 30 countries. The West German police and military forces bought large numbers of the gun, which was given the designation **MP2**. This model was produced under licence by FN in Belgium.

Had he not been close enough to be tackled, would-be assassin John Hinckley would undoubtedly have been killed by the Uzis carried by President Ronald Reagan's Secret Service bodyguards.

SPECIFICATION	
Uzi	**Mini Uzi**
Calibre: 9 mm (0.354 in) Parabellum	**Calibre:** 9 mm (0.354 in) Parabellum
Weight: loaded with 32-round magazine 4.1 kg (9 lb)	**Weight:** loaded with 20-round magazine 3.11 kg (6.85 lb)
Length: 650 mm (25.59 in) with wooden stock; 470 mm (18.5 in) with folding stock, retracted	**Length:** with stock extended 600 mm (24 in) and with stock folded 360 mm (14 in)
Length of barrel: 260 mm (10 in)	**Length of barrel:** 197 mm (7.75 in)
Muzzle velocity: 400 m (1,312 ft) per second	**Muzzle velocity:** 352 m (1,115 ft) per second
Effective range: 200 m (656 ft)	**Cyclic rate of fire:** 950 rpm
Cyclic rate of fire: 600 rpm	**Magazine:** 20-, 25- or 32-round box
Magazine: 25- or 32-round box	

Beretta Model 12 Sub-machine gun

During World War II, Beretta sub-machine guns were among the most highly-prized of all war trophies. They remained in service with both military and paramilitary formations for many years. After the war, Beretta introduced a new naming system, and post war weapons were known as the Models 4 and 5. The last of the variants on pre-war design came in 1949. It was extremely well-made – too well-made, in fact, since it was slow and expensive to produce.

Modern design

During the 1950s, the company set about producing an entirely new submachine gun. The **Beretta Model 12** was introduced in 1958. This owed nothing to previous designs, and for the first time Beretta adopted the tubular receiver and stamped component construction that had long been employed by many other manufacturers.

Although it looked simple, the Model 12 was still a Beretta product, and was made to the customary high standard of finish and quality.

The Model 12 was of fairly orthodox construction, although it was one of the earlier sub-machine guns to employ the 'wrap-around' or telescoping bolt that has now become commonplace. This allowed it to be short and handy, qualities enhanced by the fact that it could be fitted with a folding metal stock as well as a fixed stock. It was chambered for the 9-mm Parabellum cartridge fed from a 20, 30 or 40 round magazine.

Overseas sales

The Model 12 was a commercial success, sold extensively to

SPECIFICATION	
Beretta Model 12S	
Calibre: 9 mm (0.354 in) Parabellum	**Length of barrel:** 200 mm (7.87 in)
Weight: loaded with 32-round magazine 3.81 kg (8.4 lb)	**Muzzle velocity:** 381 m/1,250 ft per second
Length: with stock extended 660 mm (26 in) and with stock folded 418 mm (16.45 in)	**Cyclic rate of fire:** 500–550 rpm
	Magazine: 20-, 32- or 40-round box

The BM12S can be distinguished from the earlier Model 12 by the single-lever fire-selector and safety. The white 'S' is for safe, 'I' is for semi-automatic and 'R' is for full-auto fire.

nations in South America, Africa, the Middle East and Southeast Asia. Beretta was able to negotiate licence production of the Model 12 in Indonesia and Brazil for local sales and export. However, the Italian armed forces, who bought the weapon in 1961, acquired relatively small numbers, primarily for use by special units.

Production of the Model 12 continued until 1978, when it was eventually replaced by the improved Model 12S. Externally the **Model 12S** looks very like the Model 12 but there are some detail differences. The most obvious is the epoxy-resin finish, making the metal resistant to corrosion and environmental wear.

The fire selector mechanism on the Model 12 was of the 'push through' type, operated by pushing a button from either side of the receiver just over the pistol grip. The Model 12S has a conventional single-lever mechanism with a safety catch that locks both the trigger and the grip safety.

Modifications

The folding butt now has a more positive lock for both the open and the closed positions, giving greater rigidity, and some changes have been made to the sights. One laudable feature that has been carried over from the original Model 12 is the retention of the raised grooves that run along each side of the tubular receiver. These grooves act as catchers for any dirt or debris that find their way into the interior, and enable the Model 12S to operate under adverse conditions.

The Model 12S has been purchased by the Italian armed forces and by several other armies. A production licence was taken out by FN of Herstal, Belgium, and the type is also manufactured by Forjas Taurus of Brazil.

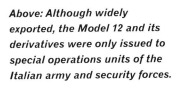

Above: Although widely exported, the Model 12 and its derivatives were only issued to special operations units of the Italian army and security forces.

Left: Very different from pre-war Beretta designs, the Model 12 uses heavy sheet metal stampings to form the magazine housing and receiver.

Spectre Sub-machine gun

Created by the SITES company of Italy from the late 1970s and first offered for sale in 1983, the **Spectre** sub-machine gun is a capable weapon that is somewhat underrated and has therefore failed to gain the commercial success that its technical capabilities should have commanded. The weapon was designed for the close-range role, as are all sub-machine guns, but optimised for the police and anti-terrorist tasks rather than the battlefield role. This optimisation led to the evolution of a weapon notable for its compact overall dimensions, capability for being brought into action at a moment's notice, and high degree of safety in carriage and operation.

The Spectre has been offered in four different forms; as the **Spectre HC** semi-automatic pistol, **Spectre H4** fully automatic sub-machine gun, **Spectre PCC** with a 230 mm (9.06 in) barrel fitted with a silencer, and **Spectre Carbine** that has reached only prototype form with a 407-mm (16.02-in) barrel.

Easy concealment

The Spectre is designed for maximum capability rather than

The Spectre sub-machine gun is shown here as a silenced weapon, but in typical sales format with the high-capacity magazine removed from its housing in the fore grip.

lowest cost, even though its price is still lower than that of 'blue-ribband' weapons such as the Heckler & Koch MP5. It has a stamped steel receiver, polymer grips and a butt that folds flat over the top of the receiver and barrel jacked without protrusions that could catch in clothing, and then unfolds upward and rearward to lock into position as a brace against the shoulder.

The Spectre is a recoil-operated weapon that fires from a closed bolt, and is hammer-fired. Both of these are factors that enhance the weapon's safety. The weapon's action is controlled by two springs, and the fact that it fires from a closed bolt also enhances the

weapon's stability when firing, in which there is a significantly lower level of vibration and muzzle climb than in most other sub-machine guns. The trigger group is more characteristic of the typical semi- automatic pistol than the standard type of sub-machine gun, and the trigger is of the double-action variety, the only known instance of this in a sub-machine gun. There is no manual safety on the weapon, but rather a de-cocking lever, whose use makes the accidental discharge of the weapon impossible. The Spectre can therefore be carried safely with a round in the chamber and the hammer down, but then be fired without delay by pressure on the trigger.

Men of an African country's army receive instruction in the firing of the Spectre, which is a safe and highly cost-effective weapon of the sub-machine class but optimised for para-military service.

The provision of two grips and a shoulder stock combines with the weapon's action to make the Spectre easy to hold on the target even when firing in full automatic mode.

Cooling arrangement

A particular feature of the bolt is that its action doubles as an air pump to drive air through the the barrel's shroud and thus improve the cooling of the barrel and action when long bursts are fired. Another notable feature embodied in the overall design of the Spectre is the compact magazine. This carries four rows of cartridges in an arrangement that makes the magazine comparatively wide but also fairly short: the 50-round magazine of the Spectre is about the same length as the 30-round magazine of the MP5. This is a notable advantage when concealed carriage of the weapon is desirable.

In an effort to maximise the Spectre's sales potential, the manufacturer also offers the weapon in calibres other than the standard 9-mm (0.354-in), including 0.4-in (10.16-mm) S&W and 0.45-in (11.43-in) ACP.

SPECIFICATION	
Spectre H4	**Weight:** 2.9 kg (6.39 lb)
Calibre: 9-mm (0.354-in)	**Muzzle velocity:** not available
Length overall: 580 mm (22.835 in) with stock extended and 350 mm (13.78 in) with stock closed	**Rate of fire, cyclic:** 850 rounds per minute
Length of barrel: 130 mm (5.12 in)	**Feed:** 30- or 50-round straight box magazine

m/45 Sub-machine gun

The 9-mm (0.354-in) **m/45** sub-machine gun was originally produced by the Karl Gustav Stads Gevärsfaktori (now part of the FFV consortium), and is thus widely known as the **Carl Gustav**. The m/45 is an entirely orthodox design with no frills, and uses a simple tubular receiver and barrel cover with a simple folding butt hinged onto the pistol grip assembly. The usual blowback operating principle is employed, and in overall terms there is nothing remarkable about the m/45.

But the weapon does have one interesting point, namely its magazine. On many sub-machine guns the magazine is usually one of the most trouble-prone components, for the magazine relies upon simple spring pressure to push the rounds towards the receiver, whence they are fed into the firing system. It is all too easy for rounds to become misaligned or

forced together, and the result is then a misfeed or jam, which can happen at inopportune moments in combat. On the original m/45 the magazine was that once used on the Suomi Model 37-39 of the period before World War II, a 50-round magazine considered at

Used by many countries, including Egypt (in the 1967 war with Israel) and the USA (in a silenced version by special forces in Vietnam), the Carl Gustav remains in large-scale service with the Swedish forces.

the time to be one of the best in use. But in 1948 a new magazine was introduced: this held 36

rounds in twin rows that were carefully tapered into a single row by a wedge cross-section.

Problem-free feed

This new magazine proved to be remarkably reliable and trouble-free in use, and was soon being widely copied elsewhere. Production examples of the m/45 were soon being offered with a revised magazine housing to accommodate either the Suomi magazine or the new wedge-shaped magazine, and this version was known as the **m/45B**. Later production models made provision for the wedge-shaped magazine only.

The m/45 and m/45B became one of Sweden's few major export weapons. Numbers were sold to Denmark and some other nations such as Eire. Egypt produced a licensed version of the m/45B as the **Port Said**, and copies were also produced in Indonesia. Perhaps the oddest service use of the m/45B was in Vietnam. Numbers of these weapons were obtained by the Central Intelligence Agency and converted in the USA with a special silenced barrel. These weapons were used in action in Vietnam by the US Special Forces on undercover missions. According to most reports the silencers were not particularly effective, and the weapons did not survive long in service.

Numerous accessories have been produced for the m/45, one of the oddest being a muzzle attachment that doubles as a blank firing device or a short-range target training device. The attachment is used with special plastic bullets which for safety are shredded as they leave the muzzle. These bullets generate enough gas pressure to operate the mechanism and if required enough pressure is available to project a steel ball from the attachment itself. This reusable steel ball can thus be used for short-range target practice.

The m/45 is often known as the Carl Gustav. The weapon has been in service since 1945, and has been exported widely. The 9-mm (0.354-in) Parabellum round is known as the m/39B in Sweden.

SPECIFICATION	
m/45B	**Weight:** loaded 4.2 kg (9.25 lb)
Calibre: 9-mm (0.354-in)	**Muzzle velocity:** 365 m (1,198 ft) per second
Length: 808 mm (31.8 in) with butt extended and 551 mm (21.7 in) with butt folded	**Rate of fire, cyclic:** 550–600 rounds per minute
Length of barrel: 213 mm (8.385 in)	**Feed:** 36-round straight box magazine

Z-84 Sub-machine gun

The **Z-84** sub-machine gun was developed in the mid-1980s by the Star Bonifacio Echeverria SA company of Spain as successor to the Z-62 and Z-70B but, unlike these weapons, probably chambered only for the 9-mm (0.354-in) Parabellum round.

Compact, light and comfortable to handle and fire, the Z-84 is of modern concept

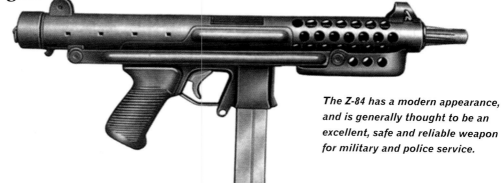

The Z-84 has a modern appearance, and is generally thought to be an excellent, safe and reliable weapon for military and police service.

and construction with a two-piece stamped steel receiver and the magazine housing built into the forward grip. The weapon works on the blowback principle, and has a wrap-around bolt that sleeves round the barrel for most of the bolt's length. The bolt travels on two guide rails, and the good clearance between the bolt and the inside of the receiver ensures that the

SPECIFICATION	
Z-84	**Weight:** empty 3 kg (6.61 lb)
Calibre: 9-mm (0.354-in)	**Muzzle velocity:** not available
Length overall: 615 mm (24.21 in) with stock extended and 410 mm (16.14 in) with stock folded	**Rate of fire, cyclic:** 600 rounds per minute
Length of barrel: 215 mm (8.465 in)	**Feed:** 25- or 30-round straight box magazine

weapon continues to work even when highly fouled.

Safety features

The weapon fires from an open bolt, the safety is located inside the trigger guard to the rear of the trigger to lock the trigger when engaged and other safety features include interceptor notches on the bolt to catch the bolt if the cocking handle slips while the weapon is being cocked, and an inertia lock to hold the bolt in its forward position. On the left-hand side of the receiver is a fire selector offering single-shot or automatic fire.

The Z-84 is easy to handle, and is sighted to 200 m (220 yards). The weapon is seen here with its butt in the open position.

BXP 9-mm sub-machine gun

When the South African armed forces decided to update its armoury during the 1960s in the face of a major increase in the level of insurgency in the country (conducted with the support of governments of countries on its borders), an early realisation was that a modern sub-machine gun was a primary requirement. The first step in this direction was the obtaining of a licence from IMI to manufacture the Uzi, firing the ubiquitous 9 x 19-mm Parabellum round. The resulting weapon entered South African manufacture and service with the local designation S-1.

Wear and tear

In the following 20 years the combination of very extensive operational use and only limited production meant that many of the country's S-1 weapons were becoming worn out. Faced with the prospect of having to resume S-1 manufacture, or of acquiring the design of a more modern weapon for licensed or unlicensed manufacture in the face of a United Nations embargo on military sales to the country, South Africa decided to adopt a third course, namely the manufacture of a weapon that would be designed within the country and therefore be fully optimised for South Africa's precise needs.

The task was entrusted to Mechem, and the result is a weapon that bears a significant similarity to the Uzi and also to an American-made sub-machine gun, the Ingram Model MAC10, in its basic configuration and

also more specifically in the design of the bolt and receiver, but with a number of individually small but cumulatively significant improvements.

Design influences

Intended for police use as well as service with the South African forces, the weapon that emerged from this process is the **BXP** firing the standard 9-mm Parabellum cartridge. The new gun was based on a design finalised in the 1980s (for manufacture from 1988), along the same general lines as the Uzi. The BXP is thus a conventional weapon working on the blow-back principle and therefore firing from an open bolt, with the bolt enveloping the rear end of the barrel as a means of keeping the weapon's overall length short but at the

*The South African **BXP** sub-machine gun is a weapon of notably high quality, and can be supplied with a number of accessories including a carrying case, a flash suppressor and several muzzle attachments.*

same time allowing the incorporation of the longest possible barrel in what is still a notably compact weapon. The enveloping bolt arrangement also has the significant advantage of maintaining the weapon's centre of gravity above the pistol grip, so it is entirely possible to deliver accurate fire using the pistol grip alone and without resort to the folding butt-stock for additional stability. This means that the plate of the butt-stock, which folds under and then up, can be used as a fore-grip when the butt is retracted, keeping the firer's hand away from the barrel and the heat that is generated as the weapon is fired.

As with the Uzi, the straight box magazine (of two types with 22- and 32-round capacities) is inserted through the pistol grip, again helping to maintain the centre of gravity.

Construction

The BXP is constructed largely from stainless-steel stampings and precision castings, employment of which minimises the amount of machining required and therefore helps to keep manufacturing costs down to the lowest possible figure: the receiver, for example, comprises just upper and lower halves. Metal parts are coated with a rust-resistant finish that also serves as a life-long dry lubricant,

The BXP was configured in its design to meet the particular needs of South Africa's defence forces, and is a very reliable and easily maintained weapon.

reducing routine cleaning and maintenance tasks to a minimum. Moreover, when the BXP is carried with its bolt in the forward position, all the receiver's apertures are sealed, which helps to ensure that dirt and debris are kept out of the weapon's mechanism, in the process boosting longevity and reducing the chances of a jammed action. The weapon can be stripped in a few seconds, and is therefore well suited to demanding field operations.

Operating the BXP sub-machine gun is extremely simple. Although a 22-round magazine is available, the 32-round unit is far more frequently used, and once the magazine has been inserted through the pistol grip the action is cocked using a handle located over the receiver so that it can be operated by either hand. The ambidextrous operating facility is enhanced by the provision of a fire/safety lever on both sides of the receiver behind the trigger: this is an important improve-ment over the MAC10, which can be operated effectively only by a right-handed shooter. When the safety mode is selected it locks the trigger, sear and bolt, the latter in either the forward or rear position. One further safety feature is that the weapon will not fire if dropped or if the firer's hand slips during the cocking operation.

There is no fire mode selector once the safety has been set to the 'fire' position: a slight pressure on the trigger produces a single shot, while a more pronounced trigger pressure results in fully automatic fire at a cyclic rate of some 800 rounds per minute, although a cyclic figure of 1,000 rounds per minute has also been quoted.

Muzzle attachments

At the front of the barrel, which has a length of 208 mm (8.19 in), the muzzle is threaded to allow the addition of several types of muzzle attachment. The most common of these is a perforated jacket to serve as a heat shield and so protect the firer's forward hand from barrel heat. A similar attachment can be used to reduce muzzle jump during firing. Another attachment, most unusual for a sub-machine gun, is a rifle grenade launcher tube which can fire numerous types of grenade by the use of blank cartridges, including some carrying riot-control agents. The muzzle can also accept a firing signature suppressor that largely eliminates firing sounds and muzzle flash: for optimum performance from this device, however, special subsonic ammunition should be fired.

Other accessories include a holster, a carrying bag and a sling. 'Iron' sights are integral with the weapon but one locally produced option is the Armson Occluded Eye Sight (OES) which projects a red dot to infinity to act as the aiming mark.

Also available is a semi-auto-matic version of the BXP, which is intended for civilian sales. The main change is that this single-shot model fires from a closed breech as a means of enhancing accuracy.

SPECIFICATION	
BXP	
Calibre: 9 mm (0.354 in)	**Muzzle velocity:** about 380 m (1,247 ft) per second
Length overall: 387 mm (15.24 in) with butt retracted; 607 mm (23.9 in) with butt extended	**Rate of fire, cyclic:** 800–1,000 rounds per minute
Length of barrel: 208 mm (8.19 in)	
Weight: empty 2.6 kg (5.73 lb)	**Magazine:** 22- or 32-round straight box

Colt 9-mm sub-machine gun series

The Colt 9-mm sub-machine gun is clearly a close relative of the M16 series of assault rifles, but it is shorter overall, is fitted with a telescopic butt-stock, and is also capable of accepting a number of different types of sighting device.

The **Colt** sub-machine gun in 9-mm (0.354-in) calibre is a light and compact blow-back-operated weapon based on exactly the same 'straight-line' construction and design as embodied in the company's M16 series of assault rifles in 5.56-mm (0.219-in) calibre. The lower recoil impulse of the SMG's 9 x 19-mm Parabellum cartridge, coupled with the straight-line configuration, provides highly accurate fire with reduced muzzle climb.

Rigorous testing
The US Drug Enforcement Agency (DEA) adopted the weapon after conducting extensive tests that included other 9-mm sub-machine guns.

Other US law enforcement agencies and military forces (including special forces) also use the weapon, which has been evaluated by various governmental agencies throughout the world. This has happened despite the growing acceptance of short assault rifles that combine the

The weapons of the Colt 9-mm sub-machine gun family are in more widespread service with law enforcement agencies than with armed forces. A Colt 9-mm weapon is seen here in the hands of the officer on the right. The weapon entered production in 1990.

firepower of a 5.56- or 5.45-mm (0.214-in) rifle cartridge with the dimensions and performance of a sub-machine gun. However, for many missions the sometimes excessive power of a rifle cartridge makes the use of a lower-powered 9 x 19-mm cartridge preferable.

As with the M16 rifle, the Colt 9-mm sub-machine gun is fired from a closed bolt, with the bolt remaining open after the last round has been fired. This feature, which is also standard on assault rifles of the M16 series, allows the user to replace magazines and re-open fire more rapidly. The weapon is equipped with a three-position telescopic butt-stock, which facilitates the effective use of the weapon by persons of different statures, and is readily field-stripped without the need for any special tools. Operation and training are

similar to those of the rifles and carbines of the M16 series, which eliminates the need for extensive cross-training of operators.

The Colt sub-machine gun fires standard 9-mm Parabellum ammunition fed from 20- or 32-round box magazines. The magazine is inserted through the original 5.56-mm M16 series magazine well. This is adapted by the installation of an internal assembly suitable for accepting and handling the Parabellum cartridge, which was designed for use in pistols and then became virtually standard for sub-machine guns of Western origin. A hydraulic buffer is available from the manufacturer to reduce the recoil felt by the firer and also to trim the weapon's cyclic rate of fire by some 100 rounds to 200 rounds per minute. These factors combine to improve

accuracy, provide additional control and reduce the time needed for the firer of the Colt SMG to recover their aim on the target.

For aiming, the weapon's rear sight is adjustable for windage and incorporates two flip-up apertures, one for shorter ranges (from zero to 50 m/55 yards) and the other for longer ranges (50 to 100 m/109 yards). The fore-sight is adjustable for elevation. There is also provision for the installation of optional sights on the optical, reflex and night-vision types.

Numerous versions

There are several models of Colt 9-mm sub-machine gun. The **Model RO635** has safe, semi-automatic and fully automatic fire modes. The **Model 639** is basically similar to the Model RO635 except for its safe, semi-automatic and three-round burst fire modes. There is also a **Model AR6451** intended for police and para-military forces and this is capable only of single-shot fire. This model has replaced the earlier **Model 634**.

There are two further variants of the Colt 9-mm sub-machine gun family, but these

are no longer available from the manufacturer. The **Model RO633HB** has a barrel only 178 mm (7 in) long by comparison with the figure of 267 mm (10.5 in) for that of the Model RO635, and also incorporates a hydraulic buffer to reduce stresses produced by the action during firing. The base-line **Model RO633**, in contrast, has a simple mechanical buffer.

As a result of the open availability, in very substantial numbers, of the basic M16 design in the US, many gun-making concerns have manufactured the type more or less as a clone of the original. This extends to variants of the Colt 9-mm sub-machine gun, and several manufacturers have either proposed or produced weapons in this calibre, usually with enhancements or alterations compared to the original weapon. These additional manufacturers have included Bushmaster and La France Specialities. The latter concern offers the **M16K**, which fires the Parabellum cartridge and has a sleeve round the barrel, the latter being only 184 mm (7.25 in) long. The barrel also features a flash suppressor.

SPECIFICATION	
Colt Model RO635	magazine 3.19 kg (7.03 lb)
Calibre: 9 mm (0.354 in)	**Muzzle velocity:** about 396 m (1,300
Length overall: 650 mm (25.6 in)	ft) per minute
with stock retracted; 730 mm	**Rate of fire, cyclic:** 800–1,000
(28.75 in) with stock extended	rounds per minute
Length of barrel: 267 mm (10.5 in)	**Effective range:** 100 m (110 yards)
Weight: without magazine 2.61 kg	**Magazine:** 20- or 32-round box
(5.75 lb); with loaded 32-round	

9-mm L2A3 Sterling Sub-machine gun

Replacing the ubiquitous Sten in British Army service, the Sterling 9-mm (0.354-in) sub-machine gun, seen here with the stock extended, has proved effective and reliable under the most extreme conditions.

The sub-machine gun that is now almost universally known as the **Sterling** entered British Army use in 1955, although an earlier form, known as the **Patchett**, underwent troop trials during the latter stages of World War II. It was intended that the Patchett would replace

the Sten gun, but in the event the Sten lasted in service until well into the 1960s.

The British Army model was designated the **L2A3** and equated to the **Sterling Mk 4** produced commercially by the Sterling Armament Company of Dagenham, Essex. This weapon

is one of the major export successes of the post-war years, for it was sold to over 90 countries and in 2002 it remained in production in India. The basic service model is of simple design with the usual tubular receiver and a folding metal butt stock, but where the

Sterling differs from many other designs is that it uses a curved box magazine that protrudes to the left. This arrangement has proved to be efficient in use and it has certainly created no problems for the army in India, or in Canada where the design was produced as the **C1** with some slight modifications.

Blowback operation

The Sterling is a simple blow-back weapon with a heavy bolt, but this bolt incorporates one of the best features of the design in that it has raised and inclined

Left: The Sterling saw considerable service in Malaya and Borneo, where the inherent inaccuracy of the sub-machine gun proved no handicap.

splines that help to remove any internal dust or dirt and push it out of the way. This enables the Sterling to be used under the worst possible conditions. The usual magazine holds 34 rounds, but a 10-round magazine is available along with a string of accessories including a bayonet.

The weapon can be fitted with any number of night vision devices or sighting systems, although these are not widely used. Several variants of the Sterling exist. One model of the gun is the silenced version that was known to the British Army as the **L34A1**.

This uses a fixed silencer system allied to a special barrel that allows the firing gases to leak through the sides of the barrel into a rotary baffle silencer that is remarkably efficient and almost silent in use. There is also a whole range of what are known as paratrooper's pistols that use only the pistol group and the receiver allied to a short magazine and a very short barrel. These are available in single-shot or machine pistol types.

The Sterling in all its forms has proven to be a very

SPECIFICATION	
L2A3	**L34A1**
Calibre: 9 mm (0.354 in)	**Calibre:** 9 mm (0.354 in)
Weight: 3.47 kg (7.65 lb)	**Weight:** loaded 3.6 kg (7.93 lb)
Length: with stock extended 690 mm (27.16 in) and with stock folded 483 mm (19 in)	**Length:** with stock extended 864 mm (34 in) and with stock folded 660 mm (26 in)
Length of barrel: 198 mm (7.88 in)	**Length of barrel:** 198 mm (7.88 in)
Muzzle velocity: 390 m (1,280 ft) per second	**Muzzle velocity:** 293–310 m (961–1,017 ft) per second
Cyclic rate of fire: 550 rpm	**Cyclic rate of fire:** 515–565 rpm
Magazine: 10- or 34-round box	**Magazine:** 34-round box

reliable and sturdy weapon. With many armies the weapon has been used to arm second-line personnel who do not have to carry normal service rifles, and on vehicles it can easily be folded away to take up very little stowage space. With the

British Army the L2A3 was slowly replaced by the 5.56-mm (0.219-in) Individual Weapon, but the large numbers of Sterlings still going strong around the world mean that it will remain a widely used type for some years to come.

The Sterling as seen on exercise in the UK, at Bassingbourn. The Sterling was replaced by the improved 5.56-mm (0.219-in) L85 Individual Weapon.

Ingram Model 10 9-mm and 0.45-in sub-machine gun

There have been few weapons that have 'enjoyed' the attentions of the Press and Hollywood to such an extent as that lavished on the Ingram sub-machine guns. Gordon B. Ingram had designed a whole string of sub-machine guns before he

produced his **Ingram Model 10**, which was originally intended to be used with the Sionics Company suppressor. First produced during the mid-1960s, the diminutive Ingram Model 10 soon attracted a great deal of public attention because of its

rate of fire, coupled with the highly efficient sound suppressor.

Hollywood and television films added their dramatic commentaries and the Ingram Model 10 soon became almost as widely known as the old Thompson sub-machine guns of the 1920s.

Exceptional weapon

The Ingram Model 10 is indeed a remarkable weapon. It is constructed from sheet metal but manufactured to a very high standard and is extremely

robust. This has to be, for it fires at a cyclic rate of over 1,000 rounds per minute, yet control of the weapon is still relatively easy thanks to the good balance imparted by the centrally-placed pistol group through which the box magazine is inserted. Most versions have a folding metal butt but this may be removed, and many weapons not fitted with the long tubular suppressor use a forward webbing hand-strap as a rudimentary foregrip. The muzzle on most models is threaded to

SPECIFICATION	
Model 10 (0.45-in model)	
Calibre: 0.45 in (11.43 mm)	**Length of barrel:** 146 mm (5.75 in)
Weight: loaded with 30-round magazine 3.818 kg (8.4 lb)	**Length of suppressor:** 291 mm (11.46 in)
Length: with stock extended 548 mm (21.575 in) and with stock folded 269 mm (10.59 in)	**Muzzle velocity:** 280 m (918 ft) per second
	Cyclic rate of fire: 1,145 rpm
	Magazine: 30-round box

accommodate the suppressor, and when fitted this is covered with a heat-resistant canvas or plastic webbing to allow it to be used as a forward grip. The cocking handle is on top of the slab-sided receiver and when turned through 90° acts as a safety lock. As this handle is slotted for sighting purposes the firer can soon notice if this safety is applied, and there is a normal trigger safety as well.

Model 10

The Model 10 may be encountered chambered for either the well-known 0.45-in (11.43-mm) cartridge or the more usual 9-mm (0.354-in) Parabellum. The latter round may also be used on the smaller **Model 11** which is normally chambered for the less powerful 9-mm Short (0.380 ACP). In all these calibres the Ingram is a dreadfully efficient weapon and unsurprisingly it has been sold widely to customers ranging from paramilitary forces to bodyguard and security agencies.

Covert operators

Military sales on any large scale have been few but several nations have acquired numbers for 'testing and evaluation'. The British SAS is known to have obtained a small quantity for testing. Sales have not been encouraged by the fact that the ownership and manufacturing rights have changed hands several times, but both the Model 10 and Model 11 are now effectively back in production as the **Cobray M11**. This, again, is available in either 9-mm Short or 9-mm Parabellum versions.

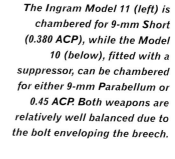

In order to keep sales rolling several variants of the basic Ingram design were made. Versions firing single-shot only and without the folding butt are available, and at one point a long-barrelled version was produced, though only in limited numbers as the type did not find a ready market.

In the meantime Ingrams can be found in countries as diverse as Greece, Israel and

Ingram fire selection is determined by the pressure put on the trigger: the initial pressure produces single shots, whilst more pressure gives automatic fire.

Portugal, while the weapon is also retained in small numbers by the US Navy. Many of these fearsome weapons been sold to Central and South American nations.

Above: Its efficient suppressor makes the Ingram a useful weapon for the Special Forces. By reducing the escaping gas to subsonic speed and eliminating flash, the position of the firer can remain a mystery to the target, until hopefully it is too late.

The Ingram Model 11 (left) is chambered for 9-mm Short (0.380 ACP), while the Model 10 (below), fitted with a suppressor, can be chambered for either 9-mm Parabellum or 0.45 ACP. Both weapons are relatively well balanced due to the bolt enveloping the breech.

AKSU Sub-machine gun

The AKSU, otherwise known as the AKS-74U, is the sub-machine gun development of the AKS-74, and was created as a weapon to arm the personnel of armoured vehicles as well as other specialised and second-line troops.

Just as the major armies of the West switched from the full-calibre 7.62-mm (0.3-in) cartridge to the smaller 5.56-mm (0.219-in) cartridge better suited to the shorter-range engagements that had been recognised as typical of modern infantry combat, the USSR switched from its 7.62-mm (0.3-in) x 39 M1943 cartridge to the 5.45-mm (0.215-in) x 39 M1974 cartridge; this was both lighter and lower-powered than its predecessor. This required the development and introduction of a new series of weapons chambered for the smaller cartridge. As they were content with the basic performance and capabilities of their current Kalashnikov assault rifle in its AK-47 standard and product-improved AKM forms, they opted for the simplest course, namely the scaling down of the basic Kalashnikov concept to chamber the new round.

The result was the **AK-74** and folding-stock **AKS-74** that were adopted in 1974. The weapons have the same gas-operated action and rotary bolt as the AKM, and though sighted to 1000 m (1,095 yards), they are typically used only at ranges considerably shorter than this. The AK-74 and AKS-74 have been produced in very large numbers for the Soviet forces and the armies of the USSR's allies and adherents, both within and outside of the Warsaw Pact organisation, and in combat have revealed themselves to be formidable rivals to the American M16 series of assault rifles. The Soviet arms are slightly less accurate than the M16, but provide somewhat better reliability and robustness and well as the capacity for easier battlefield cleaning and maintenance.

Weapon development

Though happy with the AK-74 and AKS-74 for their infantry, the Soviets appreciated that specialised troops, such as tank crews, signallers and artillery crews, as well as second-line troops, needed a more compact weapon. This led to the development of the **AKSU**, otherwise known as the **AKS-74U**. This is generally regarded more as a sub-machine gun than as a short assault rifle, and is known to those armed with it as the 'spitter'. Like its longer half-brother, the AKSU is reliable and easy to maintain, but is not notably accurate and therefore suited more to the requirements of troops than to those of security and police organisations.

There have also been a large number of other developments based on the Kalashnikov gas-operated action with a rotary two-lug bolt. The **AK-101**, for example, was designed in an effort to boost international sales and is basically a development of the AK-47 to chamber the 5.56-mm x 45 NATO cartridge. This results in a weapon 943 mm (37.125 in) long with its butt extended and 700 mm (27.56 in) long with the butt folded. The weapon has a 415-mm (16.34-in) barrel and a weight of 3.4 kg (7.5 lb), and fires from a 30-round magazine at a cyclic rate of 600 rounds per minute.

The same basic desire to expand the market for Russian small arms has led to other developments, such as the **AK-103** that is in effect the AK-47 chambered for the 7.62-mm x 39 NATO cartridge but also incorporating a number of improvements suggested by operational experience as well as the availability of better materials and manufacturing techniques. The **AK-102**,

Like other members of the Kalashnikov family of small arms, the AKSU is strong and reliable. The latter stems from a well-designed and well-made mechanism that is capable of operating efficiently under the most adverse of conditions.

AK-104 and **AK-105** are variants of the same basic compact design chambered for the 5.56-mm x 45, 7.62-mm x 39 and 5.45-mm x 39 cartridges respectively, all fired from a 30-round magazine, and their data includes an empty weight of 3 kg (6.61 lb) and length of 824 mm (32.44 in) with the stock extended and 586 mm (23.07 in) with the stock folded. The barrel is 314 mm (12.36 in) long and the rate of fire is 600rpm. The 5.45-mm **AK-107** and 5.56-mm **AK-108** are more advanced in basic concept as they work on the basis of a balanced operating system with two pistons operating in opposite directions (one driving the bolt carrier and the other a compensating mass) so that the weapons' centres of gravity are not altered as they fire.

SPECIFICATION	
AKS-74U **Calibre:** 5.45-mm (0.215-in) **Length overall:** 735 mm (28.94 in) with the stock extended and 490 mm (12.29 in) with the stock folded **Length of barrel:** 210 mm (8.27 in) **Weight:** empty 2.71 kg (5.97lb) **Muzzle velocity:** not available **Rate of fire, cyclic:** not available **Feed:** 20- or 30-round curved box magazine	**AK-107 and AK-108** **Calibre:** 5.56-mm (0.219-in) **Length overall:** 943 mm (37.13 in) with the stock extended and 700 mm (27.56 in) with the stock folded **Length of barrel:** 415 mm (16.34 in) **Weight:** 3.4 kg (7.5 lb) **Muzzle velocity:** not available **Rate of fire, cyclic:** 850 rounds per minute for the AK-107 and 900 rounds per minute for the AK-108 **Feed:** 30-round curved box magazine

Modern Russian sub-machine guns

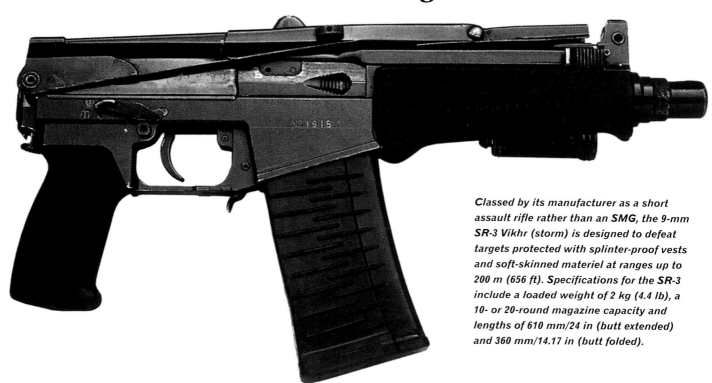

Classed by its manufacturer as a short assault rifle rather than an SMG, the 9-mm SR-3 Vikhr (storm) is designed to defeat targets protected with splinter-proof vests and soft-skinned materiel at ranges up to 200 m (656 ft). Specifications for the SR-3 include a loaded weight of 2 kg (4.4 lb), a 10- or 20-round magazine capacity and lengths of 610 mm/24 in (butt extended) and 360 mm/14.17 in (butt folded).

Throughout the world the general opinion is that sub-machine guns are on their way out in favour of short assault rifles. However, the Russians have other opinions. They continue to develop and market a whole array of sub-machine gun designs, some of them with unusual characteristics.

Top of the unusual list must come the 9-mm (0.354-in) **PP-90M**. As with most Russian sub-machine guns it fires the 9 x 18 mm Makarov pistol cartridge although more and more Russian sub-machine gun designs can now be supplied chambered for 9 x 19 mm Parabellum (9-mm Luger) ammunition to suit Western tastes (in this case the **PP-90M1**) and support export sales. When carried the PP-90M resembles something like a rifle magazine and has the same dimensions. When needed it hinges open to become a close-range personal defence weapon, although it has been seen with accessories such as a sound suppressor and red dot sight. Production of the PP-90 series may now have ended, reportedly as a result of it being found unsatisfactory for Russian Federation armed forces service.

To confuse matters there is another PP-90M1, this time chambered only for 9 x 19 mm Parabellum. This model is unusual in that it can have either a conventional 32-round straight box magazine or a helical magazine containing 64 rounds. The magazine arrangements can be altered by the user to suit the particular mission in progress.

A helical magazine also features on the **Bizon** (bison) which has a permanent 64-round magazine under the barrel (53 rounds when using the 9 x 19

SPECIFICATION	
PP-90M **Calibre:** 9-mm (0.354-in) Makarov **Length overall:** 490 mm (19.29 in) with stock extended and 270 mm (10.63 in) with stock folded **Weight:** empty 1.83 kg (4.03 lb) **Muzzle velocity:** 320 m (1,050 ft) per minute **Rate of fire, cyclic:** 600–700 rounds per minute **Feed:** 30-round folding box magazine	**OTs-22** **Calibre:** 9-mm (0.354-in) Makarov **Length overall:** 460 mm (18.11 in) with stock extended and 250 mm (9.84 in) with stock folded **Weight:** empty 1.2 kg (2.65 lb) **Effective range:** 100 m (328 ft) maximum **Rate of fire, cyclic:** 800–900 rounds per minute **Feed:** 20- or 30-round detachable box magazine

Magazine options for the 9-mm PP-90M1 sub-machine gun comprise a 64-round helical magazine (shown in position) and an alternative 32-round box magazine (detached).

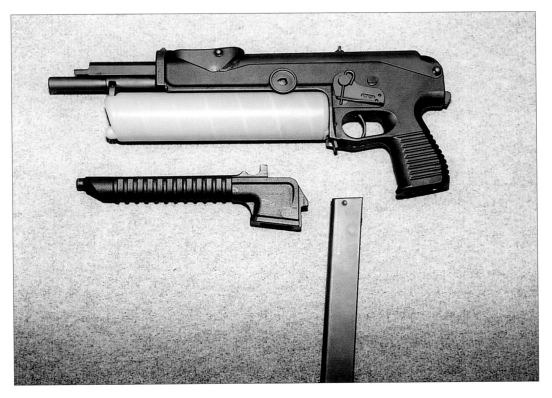

mm Parabellum cartridge). For commercial sales the Bizon can be chambered for a wide range of ammunition, including the old 7.62 x 25 mm Tokarev round.

Special forces SMGs

Other Russian products are more conventional, apart from the potent 9-mm **SR-2**. This weapon is intended for special forces use and fires a special 9 x 21 mm cartridge family which includes rounds intended to pierce body armour.

As with most Russian sub-machine guns the SR-2 has a folding metal butt stock to save carrying space. Another special forces weapon is the 9 x 19 mm Parabellum only **OTs-22** that resembles the Israeli Uzi in outline by having its 20- or 30-round box magazine inserted through the pistol grip. The same magazine feed layout is also used by the larger **Kovrov AyeK-919 Kashtan** (chesnut) which has been used operationally by

Russian Federation forces in Chechnya. Apart from being larger than the OTs-22, the Kashtan has a telescopic wire butt stock.

The Uzi layout crops up again with the 9-mm **PP-93**, a compact design seemingly designed for mass production as it is constructed mainly from steel pressings. It fires only the 9 x 18 mm Makarov round, including

the latest enhanced performance cartridge, the 57-N-181SM.

Then there is also the **OTs-02 Kiparis** (cypress). This resembles an oversize machine pistol and was designed for special forces use as long ago as 1972.

For some reason it was not placed in production until 1991. The Kiparis is deployed with Russian Federation Interior Ministry forces and can feature a sound suppressor and/or a laser aiming device.

The folding 9-mm PP-90 complete with sound suppressor and red dot sight. Both the PP-90 and PP-90M are primarily close-quarter weapons intended to be fired from the hip in emergency situations.

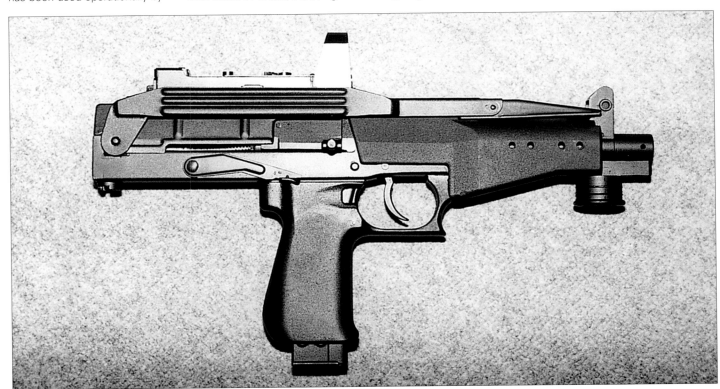

CETME Modelo 58 Assault rifle

The core of the Mauser team which designed the German Sturmgewehr 45 decamped to Spain after the war and developed a new assault rifle based on the StG 45's layout. The Modelo 58 is made of low-grade steel and built with the emphasis on cheapness and reliability rather than looks.

The **CETME Modelo 58** has a long history stretching back to the German Sturmgewehr 45 (StG 45) of World War II. This was an attempt by Mauser designers to produce a low-cost assault rifle incorporating a novel system using rollers and cams to lock the bolt at the instant of firing. After World War II's end the nucleus of the StG 45 design team moved to Spain and established a design team under the aegis of the Centro de Estudios Tecnicos do Materiales Especiales (CETME), outside Madrid.

With CETME the roller locking system was gradually perfected. The resulting assault rifle looked nothing like the StG 45 starting point, but the original low-cost manufacturing target was met. The assault rifle produced by CETME was made from low-grade steels and much of it was stamped and shaped using sheet steel. An automatic-fire capability was featured, and in overall terms the weapon was simple and basic.

Initial German sale

It was 1956 before the first sales were made to West Germany. This involved a batch of only 400 rifles, but the Germans decided that some modifications to the rifle were needed to enable the weapon to meet their requirements. By a series of licence agreements (between a CETME licensed production offshoot in the Netherlands and Heckler & Koch) the CETME rifle became the Heckler & Koch G3, although the Spanish appear to have gained little from the deal.

In 1958 the Spanish army decided to adopt the CETME rifle in a form known as the **Modelo B**, and this became the Modelo 58. The Modelo 58 fired a special cartridge outwardly identical to the standard NATO 7.62-mm (0.3-in) cartridge but using a lighter bullet and propellant charge. This made the rifle much easier to fire (as a result of the reduced recoil) but also made the cartridge non-standard as far as other NATO cartridge users were concerned. In 1964 the Spanish adopted the NATO cartridge in place of their own less powerful product, and rifles adapted or produced to fire the NATO round became the **Modelo C**.

The Modelo 58 has since been produced in several versions, some fitted with bipods, some with semi-automatic mechanisms and others with folding butts, and there has even been a sniper version fitted with a telescopic sight. The latest version is the **Modelo L** chambered in the NATO standard 5.56 mm (0.219 in), but the basic 7.62 mm Model 58 is still available from CETME.

The Spanish army adopted the CETME as its standard rifle in 1958, initially buying the Modelo B, chambered for a unique, light, 7.62-mm (0.3-in) round. In 1964 Spain decided to adopt the more powerful 7.62-mm NATO cartridge, and CETME modified their design accordingly to make the Modelo C.

SPECIFICATION	
Modelo C	**Muzzle velocity:** 780 m (2,559 ft) per second
Calibre: 7.62-mm (0.3-in)	
Length overall: 1016 m (40 in)	**Rate of fire, cyclic:** 600 rounds per minute
Length of barrel: 450 mm (17.7 in)	
Weight: 4.49 kg (9.9 lb)	**Feed:** 20-round straight box

SIG Assault rifles

The Swiss were rather slow to work their way round to designing an assault rifle, but when they did produce one it turned out to be a decidedly superior weapon. This had its origins in a weapon known as the **Sturmgewehr Modell 57** (or **StuG57**) that took advantage of the delayed-blowback roller breech locking system pioneered by the Spanish CETME rifles. This rifle was produced by SIG for the Swiss army calibred for the national 7.5-mm (0.295-in) rifle cartridge, and even carried over the fluted chamber of the CETME rifle.

First-class handling

At first sight the StuG57 looked odd and awkward. In use it was quite the opposite. As always, the high standard of SIG manufacture made it a good weapon to handle, and Swiss soldiers liked the integral bipod and grenade launcher. The use of the Swiss cartridge limited sales, so SIG went one stage further and developed the **SG510** series of rifles to fire more internationally accepted cartridges. In many ways the SG510 was identical to the StuG57 and carried over the extremely high standards of workmanship which, in their turn, meant that although the weapon was a soldier's dream, it was very expensive. As a result sales were few. The Swiss army purchased the larger batches, but some went to African and South American nations.

Numerous variants

This was not for want of trying on the part of the SIG designers. They produced

SIG produced one of the most unusual post-war rifles, the AK 53, which used a stationary bolt and a moving barrel, reducing the overall length of the gun. The disadvantages of this operation include potential cook-off and a tendency to jam.

several versions. The first was the **SG510-1** chambered for the 7.62-mm (0.3-in) NATO cartridge. The **SG510-2** was a lighter version of the SG510-1. The **SG510-3** was produced to fire the Soviet 7.62-mm short cartridge used on the AK-47. The **SG510-4** was another 7.62-mm NATO round model, and there was also a single-

shot only sporting version known as the **SG-AMT** which was sold in large numbers to Swiss target-shooters.

The SG510-3 and SG510-4 had some extra features. One was an indicator on the magazine to show how many rounds were left and another was a folding winter trigger. The bipod (folding up over the

barrel) was retained, and both had provision for optical sights for night vision or sniping. The StuG57 and SG510 can still be

found hanging on the walls of many Swiss army reservists, and numbers of the SG510 are still in use in Bolivia and Chile.

SPECIFICATION	
SG510-4	**Muzzle velocity:** 790 m (2,592 ft) per second
Calibre: 7.62-mm (0.3-in)	
Length overall: 1016 m (40 in)	**Rate of fire, cyclic:** 600 rounds per minute
Length of barrel: 505 mm (19.8 in)	
Weight: 4.45 kg (9.81 lb)	**Feed:** 20-round straight box

Beretta BM59
Rifle

The BM59 is based on the US M1 Garand self-loading rifle, which Beretta was producing under licence when NATO adopted the 7.62-mm x 51 cartridge. Beretta modified the M1 design to accept the new round.

In 1945 Beretta started the licensed manufacture of the American M1 Garand semi-automatic rifle for the Italian armed forces, and by 1961 had made about 100,000, some for export to Denmark and Indonesia. The introduction of the NATO 7.62-mm (0.3-in) cartridge meant that these rifles would have to be replaced (they fired the American World War II 0.3-in round), for a rechamber-ing of the existing Garands would have meant that the Italian army would have been saddled with a rifle of outdated design for years to come.

'Breathed on' Garand
The Beretta designers had for some time before 1961 been contemplating a revision of the basic Garand design to produce a selective-fire weapon using as much as possible of the existing mechanism. The result was the **Beretta BM59**, which was the Garand at heart but modified to provide the required automatic-fire feature. It fired the NATO standard 7.62-mm cartridge, of which 20 were carried in a detachable box magazine replacing the old eight-round magazine. Some other slight alterations were introduced, but

basically the BM59 was a 'breathed-on' Garand.

Special-role variants
Almost as as soon as the BM59 was placed in production for the Italian armed forces a number of variants began to appear. The basic model was the **BM59 Mk 1**, issued to most of the Italian army. Then came the **BM59 Mk 2** with a pistol grip and a light bipod. The next two variants were virtually identical: the **BM59 Mk 3 Paracudisti** for use by airborne units had a removable grenade launcher at the muzzle, while the **BM59 Mk 3 Alpini** model for mountain troops had a fixed grenade launcher. These two versions both had folding skeleton butts and light bipods. On the **BM59 Mark 4** the bipod was much more robust, for this version

was intended as a squad fire-support weapon. The Mk 4 also had a heavier barrel and a butt strap to allow it to be used for its fire-support role.

The BM59 proved to be an excellent modification of an existing design and it is still in use by the Italian armed forces. It was built at one time under licence in Morocco and Indonesia, and Nigeria planned to produce the BM59 as well, though the Biafran War put paid to that project.

The two drawbacks to the BM59 when compared with many contemporary designs are its heavy weight and the need for extensive machining during the manufacturing process. For all that the BM59 is a very robust, powerful and reliable weapon that still has some service life left to run.

SPECIFICATION	
BM59 Mk 1	**Muzzle velocity:** 823 m (2,700 ft) per second
Calibre: 7.62-mm (0.3-in)	
Length overall: 1095 m (43.1 in)	**Rate of fire, cyclic:** 750 rounds per minute
Length of barrel: 490 mm (19.3 in)	
Weight: unloaded 4.6 kg (10.14 lb)	**Feed:** 20-round curved box

Fusil Automatique Modèle 49 Rifle

The FN mle 49 is the ancestor of the FN FAL, designed before the war by Dieudonné Saive, who escaped to the UK when the Germans overran Belgium. While in England, Saive continued to develop his designs, and after the war the mle 49 was sold to Egypt and Latin America.

Left: Weapons produced to a high standard often lose potential sales to cheaper weapons, but FN managed to sell its mle 49 to several different armies, offering it in many calibres. This Egyptian carries the 7.92-mm (0.312-in) model.

Made by the Fabrique Nationale d'Armes de Guerre organisation based at Herstal in Belgium, the **Fusil Automatique Modèle 49** was known by several other names: to some it was the **Saive**, to others the **SAFN (Saive Automatique, FN)** and to more as the **ABL (Arme Belgique Legère)**. The weapon was actually designed before World War II, but the arrival of the war led to the temporary shelving of the project, ready for it to be revived as soon as peace had arrived once more. The weapon was designed by one D. J. Saive, who moved to the UK when the Germans arrived in Belgium during May 1940 and spent the rest of World War II working on small arms designs for the British. In 1945 he offered his pre-war design to the British army, which tested it but then turned down the offer.

Return to Belgium

Once the new rifle's design had been returned to Belgium, the weapon entered production by FN, and much of the company's growing prosperity from the late 1940s started with the good sales record of the new rifle.

Sound design

By whatever name it was called, the Modèle 49 was a basic and functional design of gas-operated self-loading rifle. The locking of the bolt was achieved by the operation of cams in the sides of the receiver, which caused the bolt to tilt into the locked position at just the correct instant. This action was notably strong and dependable, and could therefore absorb a great deal of hard use, but it also meant that the rifle's entire mechanism had to be very carefully machined out of high-quality materials.

The combination of high-grade materials and the use of extensive machining rendered the weapon rather expensive to manufacture, but when the Modèle 49 was placed on the open market in 1949 it sold surprisingly well. This was the result partially of the fact that the Modèle 49 was offered in a variety of calibres, ranging from 7-mm (0.275-in) and 7.65-mm (0.301-in), which were both well established calibres on the continent of Europe, to 7.92-mm (0.312-in) which was then widely used as a legacy of the German control of most of Europe in World War II, and the American 0.3-in (7.62-mm). In all these well-established calibres, the Modèle 49 was firing full-power rifle cartridges, making it a potent long-range weapon.

The Modèle 49 was sold not only in Europe but also to Venezuela and Colombia in South America and to Indonesia in South-East Asia. One of the largest sales was made to Egypt, where the Modèle 49 remained in use for some time.

But perhaps the most important impact made by the ABL was that it was used as the design starting point for the FN FAL (Fusil Automatique Legère), destined to be one of the most important rifles within NATO and elsewhere for the following decades.

SPECIFICATION	
Fusil Automatique Modèle 49	
Calibres: 7-mm (0.275-in), 7.65-mm (0.301-in), 7.92-mm (0.312-in) and 0.3-in (7.62-mm)	**Length of barrel:** 590 mm (23.2 in) **Weight:** 4.31 kg (9.5 lb) **Muzzle velocity:** dependent on cartridge fired
Length overall: 1116 m (43.94 in)	**Feed:** 10-round box

Samonabiject Puska vz 52

For a few years after the end of World War II Czechoslovakia was a completely independent nation and for a while returned to the importance of the pre-war days when its armament industry was one of the leaders in Europe.

World War II

The Czech armaments industry had been heavily used by the Germans during World War II. Experienced small arms designers were available, together with extensive facilities.

One of the first major small-arms developed during the early post-war period was a 7.62-mm (0.30-in) self-loading rifle known as the **Samonabiject Puska vz 52** (vz for *vzor* or model) that followed many of the design trends initiated by late war German automatic rifles. The Czechs also developed a new short assault rifle cartridge (also known as the vz 52) based on German *kurz* cartridge experience for use in the new rifle. The lower-powered cartridges evolved after German

Although it looked very like the standard wartime rifles that had preceded it, the vz 52 was in fact an early example of what would come to be known as the assault rifle, firing a low-powered 7.62-mm rifle round.

combat analysis showed that standard rifle rounds, accurate to a thousand metres or more, were far too powerful for most infantry combat, which rarely took place at ranges of more than 300 m (984 ft), and which often were fought at less than 100 m (328 ft).

Czech individuality

As always the Czechs followed their own design paths and the vz 52 rifle had some unusual features, not the least of which was a method of tipping the bolt to lock the mechanism.

There was also a permanently-fixed bayonet, and the 10-round box magazine was filled using chargers. The gas-operated mechanism used a gas piston system wrapped around the barrel. Hardly

innovative was the trigger mechanism, which was a direct lift of that used on the American MI (Garand) rifle.

Overall the vz 52 was rather heavy but this made it easy to fire as recoil was limited. Even so the vz 52 took up quite a lot of manufacturing potential, and was really too complex a weapon for the period.

Only the Czech army took the vz 52 into service for a while, and when other better weapons came along (such as the vz 58 assault rifle) the vz 52s were withdrawn and sold on the international arms markets.

Warpac conversion

By the time the vz 52s were deleted the Czechs had been drawn into the Soviet sphere of influence. The Czech 7.62-mm

SPECIFICATION	
vz 52	**Length overall:** bayonet folded
Calibre: 7.62-mm (0.30-in)	1.003 m (39.49 in); bayonet
Weights: empty 4.281 kg (9.44 lb),	extended 1.204 m (47.4 in);
loaded 4.5 kg (9.92 lb)	**Length of barrel:** 523 mm (20.6 in)
	Muzzle velocity: about 744 m (2,441
	ft) per second
	Feed: 10-round box

vz 52 cartridge had nothing in common with the Soviet equivalent, although both had been designed from the same starting point. The Soviet military authorities were very strict regarding standardisation throughout the armies under their control, and the Czechs were thus forced to abandon their cartridge and convert to the Soviet equivalent.

Since the Czech and Soviet short cartridges were far from interchangeable, this meant the

vz 52 rifles had to be modified accordingly, and late vz 52s with alterations to use the Soviet ammunition were known as the vz 52/57.

Export vz 52s

Many of the VZ-52s were placed into storage by the Czechs. Large numbers were exported to Soviet and Third World client states, notably to Cuba and Egypt, and many of those were passed on to guerrillas.

Fusil Mitrailleur Modèle 49 (MAS 49) Rifle

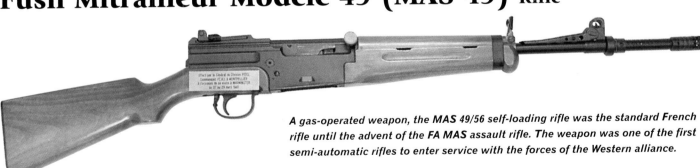

*A gas-operated weapon, the **MAS 49/56** self-loading rifle was the standard French rifle until the advent of the **FA MAS** assault rifle. The weapon was one of the first semi-automatic rifles to enter service with the forces of the Western alliance.*

Designed by the Manufacture d'Armes de St Etienne, the **Fusil Mitrailleur Modèle 49 (MAS 49)** was one of the first semi-automatic rifles to enter service after World War II. Although it resembles the MAS 36 bolt-action rifle, it was not created as an automatic version of the earlier weapon but as a completely new design. At over 4.5 kg (10 lb) it is no lightweight, but its strength proved itself invaluable in the French

campaigns in Indo-China and Algeria during the 1950s and 1960s. In French service the MAS 49 was replaced by the FA MAS assault rifle from 1979.

Gas operation

The MAS 49 was based on work in the earlier part of the 20th century on direct-impingement operating systems. Prototypes were produced in the 1920s and 1930s, and a few examples of

the MAS 44 type were made after the Germans had been driven from France in 1944, primarily for service trials. The MAS 49 is thus a gas-operated weapon, but uses no cylinder or piston. In this system propellant

gas is tapped off from the barrel and ducted into a tube that directs it to the face of the bolt carrier where it expands and forces back the carrier. The system has often been eschewed because it can

SPECIFICATION	
MAS 49/56	**Weights:** 3.9 kg (8.6 lb) empty and
Calibre: 7.5-mm (0.295-in)	4.34 kg (9.52 lb) loaded
Length overall: 1010 mm (39.8 in)	**Muzzle velocity:** 817 m (2,680 ft) per
Length of barrel: 521 mm (20.5 in	second
	Feed: 10-round box magazine

produce excessive fouling, but the MAS 49 did not suffer unduly from the problem. The breech is locked in the same simple manner as on the Fabrique Nationale mle 49, simply by tilting the breech block.

New magazine

Though the MAS 49 was derived from the MAS 44, it differed from its predecessor in having a detachable rather than integral box magazine. This magazine holds 10 rounds and can be replaced when empty, but there are stripper clip guides machined into the front of the bolt carrier, and this provision allows two five-round clips to be loaded straight into the magazine. Somewhat unusually, the MAS 49 also has an integral grenade launcher, with a dedicated sight fitted on the left-hand side.

Above: Legionnaires of the 2nd REP are seen with a MAT 49 sub-machine gun (left) and a MAS 49/56 rifle (right). The rifle fired the standard 7.5-mm (0.295-in) x 54 ball cartridge, and there were also armour-piercing and tracer rounds.

Left: French soldiers cautiously approach a possible 'freedom fighter' in one of their African colonies. The man in the foreground has a MAS 49/56 rifle.

The MAS 49 was modified in 1956 to produce the **MAS 49/56**, which is the variant that was generally supplanted by the FA MAS. The MAS 49/56 is easily distinguished from the earlier weapon: the wooden forestock is much shorter and the barrel has a combined muzzle-brake/grenade-launcher with raised foresight. The length of the whole weapon was reduced by 90 mm (3.54 in) and that of the barrel by 60 mm (2.36 in), and provision was made for the mounting of a spike bayonet. Like the MAS 49, the MAS 49/56 has a mounting rail machined into the left-hand side of the receiver for an APX L mle 1953 telescopic sight with x3.85 magnification. The standard sights, calibrated to a range of 1200 m (1,315 yards), comprise a hooded front sight on the front stock band and an aperture rear sight above the receiver.

Obsolete cartridge

The French obstinately stuck with the obsolete 7.5-mm x 54 mle 1929 cartridge, but a few MAS 49/56 assault rifles were experimentally modified to fire the NATO standard 7.62-mm (0.3-in) cartridge. Armour-piercing ammunition was also produced, but this proved very unkind to the barrels.

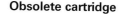

A French infantry patrol on the move, the weapons evident including the MAS 49, complete with a rifle grenade, carried by the point man.

Rifle M14

The rifle that was eventually to be the standard American service rifle for most of the late 1950s and 1960s had a simple origin but a most convoluted development period. When the American military planners virtually imposed their 7.62-mm (0.3-in) cartridge upon their NATO partners, they had to find their own rifle to fire it, and quickly.

For various reasons it was decided simply to update the existing M1 Garand rifle design to fire the new ammunition, and also to add a selective-fire mechanism. Unfortunately these innovations proved difficult to achieve, for the evolution from the M1 had to progress through a number of intermediate 'T' trials models.

Two models planned

Eventually, in 1957, it was announced that a model known as the **T44** had been approved for production as the **Rifle M14**. A planned heavy-barrel version, the M15, did not materialise. The assembly lines began to hum, at one time involving four different manufacturing centres.

Updated Garand

The M14 was basically the M1 Garand semi-automatic rifle updated to take a new 20-round box magazine and selective-fire mechanism. The M14 was long and rather heavy, but well made, involving a great deal of machining and handling during manufacture at a time when other weapon designers were moving away from such methods. But the Americans could afford it and the soldiers liked the weapon. In service

there were few problems, but the selective-fire system that had needed so much development time was usually altered so that automatic fire could not be produced: the US Army had soon discovered that prolonged bursts overheated the barrel and that ammunition was in any event wasted firing non-productive bursts.

Major production

Production of the basic M14 ceased in 1964, by which time 1,380,346 had been made. In 1968 a new version, the **M14A1**, was introduced. This had a pistol grip, a bipod and some other changes. It was intended as a squad fire-support weapon producing automatic bursts but the bursts had to be short as the barrel could not be changed when hot. Also produced were experimental folding butt versions and the **M21** sniper model.

The M14 is no longer used by first-line US forces, surviving last with the National Guard and other reserve formations. As the M14 was replaced by the M16, many were passed to nations such as Israel, where they stayed in service until replaced by the Galil assault rifle.

Rebel Filipino soldiers fire on loyalist forces during the last days of the Marcos regime. Note the spent case being ejected from the M14 (higher weapon).

Once NATO had adopted the American-developed 7.62-mm (0.3-in) cartridge, most NATO countries opted for a variant of the Belgian FAL rifle. The USA, however, was still in thrall to the 'not invented here' syndrome and wanted an American rifle, developed from the M1 as the recalibred M14 with a larger magazine.

SPECIFICATION	
Rifle M14	second
Calibre: 7.62-mm (0.3-in)	**Rate of fire, cyclic:** (M14A1)
Length overall: 1120 mm (44.0 in)	700–750 rounds per minute
Length of barrel: 559 mm (22.0 in)	**Feed:** 20-round straight box
Weight: 3.88 kg (8.55 lb)	
Muzzle velocity: 853 m (2,798 ft) per	

The M14A1 was created as the squad fire-support variant of the M14 rifle with an automatic action, bipod and a combination of pistol and fore grips.

Stoner 63 System

Eugene Stoner was one of the most influential and innovative weapon designers of the 1950s and 1960s, and his hand can still be discerned in many small arms types in use today. His innovatory thinking was such that at one point Stoner was involved in developing a modular weapon system that not surprisingly became known as the **Stoner 63 System**.

Produced not long after Stoner had left Armalite Inc in the late 1950s, the Stoner 63 System was based on 17 modular units that could be arranged and assembled in ways that allowed the creation of a whole series of small arms. The basis for the system was the rotary lock mechanism first used on the AR-10 rifle and later on the AR-15/M16 rifle. However, the Stoner 63 used a different method of gas operation based on a long-travel piston.

Above: Seen mounted on a tripod for evaluation by the US Marine Corps, this is the medium machine gun variant of the Stoner 63 System.

The light machine gun variant of the Stoner 63 System, normally fitted with a bipod, is seen here in its belt-fed form with an open box of disintegrating metal-linked ammunition.

Kits of components

The only components common to all weapons in the system were the receiver, bolt and piston, return spring and trigger mechanism. To these core elements could be added, such as buttstocks, feed devices, various barrels and items including bipod or even tripod mountings to produce the weapon types required in any of the many possible tactical situations in which an operator might find himself involved.

Originally the Stoner 63 System was developed to use the 7.62-mm (0.3-in) NATO cartridge, but when it became clear that the 5.56-mm (0.219-mm) calibre was destined to overtake this, Stoner revised the system to accommodate the lighter round. This change had the benefit of making many of the components considerably lighter, and as a result the weapons themselves were also lighter, with obvious tactical advantages.

The basic weapon was a carbine with a folding butt. and then came an assault rifle; magazine- and belt-fed light machine guns using bipods were next, while the addition of a heavy barrel, belt feed and tripod finally produced a medium machine gun. It was even possible to produce a solenoid-fired machine gun for co-axial use in AFVs.

Stoner pedigree

Given its provenance and also its manifest overall advantages, the Stoner 63 System attracted a great deal of attention. The system was put into small-scale production by Cadillac Gage, the company under whose aegis Stoner had

US Navy SEAL (SEa-Air-Land) special forces teams used the Stoner 63 System weapons in the Vietnam War. This is a belt-fed light machine gun with 100-round plastic ammunition boxes.

SPECIFICATION	
Stoner 63 System assault rifle	**Muzzle velocity:** about 1000 m (3,280 ft) per second
Calibre: 5.56-mm (0.219-in)	**Rate of fire, cyclic:** 660 rounds per minute
Length overall: 1022 mm (40.23 in)	
Length of barrel: 508 mm (20.0 in)	**Feed:** 30-round curved box
Weight loaded: 4.39 kg (9.68 lb)	

developed the project. Plans were made with a Dutch firm for licensed production, but military interest was not so forthcoming. The US Marines carried out a series of trials, and more trials were carried out in Israel. The system performed well throughout all these trials, but no large-scale procurement resulted. Exactly why this happened is not easy to determine, but the main

reason was perhaps the fact that for a set of components to be produced to perform so

many roles, a number of the parts had to be something of a compromise and thus less

successful than a purpose-built design. The Stoner System gradually faded from the scene.

This is the fixed-stock assault rifle member of the Stoner 63 Weapon family. The magazine is a 30-round unit, and at the muzzle is a combined flash suppressor and grenade launcher.

Armalite AR-10 Assault rifle

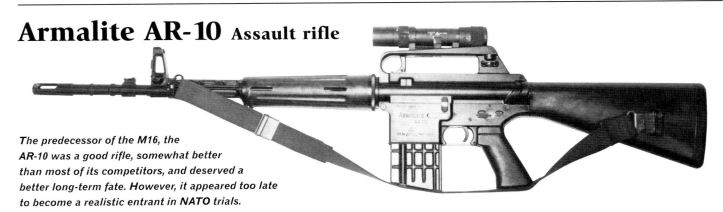

The predecessor of the M16, the AR-10 was a good rifle, somewhat better than most of its competitors, and deserved a better long-term fate. However, it appeared too late to become a realistic entrant in NATO trials.

In 1954 the newly formed Armalite Division of the Fairchild Engine & Airplane Company started development of an assault rifle firing the World War II 7.62-mm (0.3-in) rifle cartridge. By 1955 Eugene Stoner had joined the company and development had switched towards using the new 7.62-mm NATO cartridge, though the Armalite team, greatly influenced by Stoner, was not restricted to using established small arms design conventions. The team thus evolved an innovative 'all-in-line' configuration with the sights above the weapon, but perhaps the concept's most important contribution to small arms design was the reintroduction of the rotary-bolt locking system that has now become virtually standard on

assault rifle designs throughout the world.

Lightweight rifle

The new rifle emerged during 1955 as the **Armalite AR-10**. This made great use of aluminium in its construction, and steel was used only for the barrel, bolt and bolt carrier. This made the weapon light, or perhaps too light as its tendency to 'rear' when fired automatically meant that a muzzle compensator had to be fitted to overcome this failing. The cocking lever was on top of the receiver, protected by a carrying handle that also carried the rear sight. Originally it was planned that there would be sub-machine gun and light machine-gun variants of the AR-10, but only prototypes were produced.

The Armalite team found that marketing its product was rather more difficult than designing it. Tooling up for production was slow, and sales were not helped by the fact that the NATO nations had already made their various new rifle decisions by the time the AR-10 appeared. The Dutch seemed to offer hope of sales, and arrangements were made with a Dutch company, NWM, for licensed production of the AR-10, but that project finally came to nothing despite a great deal of preparatory work.

This was a pity, for the AR-10 was really far better than any weapon then in NATO use and far more advanced than most. It was simple, easy to handle and had much potential. Some sales were made, by far the largest to Sudan, Portugal bought 1,500 examples and other batches went to Burma and Nicaragua.

Perhaps the greatest importance of the AR-10, whose production ended in 1961, was that it paved the way for the AR-15 (M-16), one of history's seminal firearms.

SPECIFICATION	
AR-10	**Muzzle velocity:** 845 m (2,772 ft) per second
Calibre: 7.62-mm (0.3-in)	
Length overall: 1029 mm (40.5 in)	**Rate of fire, cyclic:** 700 rounds per minute
Length of barrel: 508 mm (20.0 in)	
Weight loaded: 4.82 kg (10.63 lb)	**Feed:** 20-round straight box

The innovative AR-10 made extensive use of aluminium alloy for most of its metal parts, exceptions being the steel barrel, bolt and bolt carrier. Light weight also meant a muzzle-climb tendency, however.

Valmet/Sako Rk.60 and Rk.62 Assault rifles

Although it was not a member of the Warsaw Pact, its proximity to the USSR meant that despite its neutrality Finland inevitably had to go along with the Soviet way of doing things in some matters through most of the 20th century's second half. Thus, when it decided to adopt a new service rifle in the late 1950s, the Finnish army not surprisingly opted for the Soviet AK-47 assault rifle and its ammunition, and Finland therefore negotiated a manufacturing licence for both. Once the AK-47 design was in their hands, Finnish small arms designers at the Valmet company made changes to create the **Valmet m/60** rifle, later redesignated as the **Rk.60**.

AK-47 origins

Its AK-47 origins can readily be discerned in the Rk.60, but the reworking of the basic design resulted in a much better all-round weapon. The Rk.60 has no wood in its construction, the wooden furniture of the AK-47 being replaced by plastics or metal tubing. The tubular butt of the Rk.60 is thus easier to produce and is also more robust as well as carrying the cleaning tools and equipment. The pistol grip and forestock are cast from hard plastic, while the trigger is left virtually unguarded to allow the wearing of gloves.

Other changes from the AK-47 include slightly altered sights, a three-pronged flash hider at the muzzle, and a revised bayonet mounting bracket to accommodate the Finnish bayonet. Internally the mechanism of the AK-47 is left virtually unchanged apart from the introduction of a few manufacturing expedients, and the curved magazine and its housing are also unaltered to allow use of AK-47 magazines.

The Rk.62 is an improved Finnish development of the Soviet AK-47 optimised for manufacturing capabilities and operating conditions in Finland

The later **m/62** or **Rk.62** is virtually the same as the Rk.60 apart from a few extra cooling holes in the forestock and the introduction of a vestigial trigger guard. Export variants were also created in 5.56-mm (0.219-in) calibre.

Improved variants

After Valmet's merger with Sako, the small arms team created modernised variants of the Rk.62 as the **Rk.76** and **Rk.95TP**. The former has a stamped rather than machined receiver, much reducing weight, and the option of four buttstocks (fixed wooden, fixed plastic, fixed tubular and folding tubular in the **Rk.76W**, **Rk.76P**, **Rk.76T** and **Rk.76TP** respectively). Also known as the **Sako Rk.75**, the latter has a machined receiver but a folding skeleton buttstock, and new handguards.

The m/60 was in effect the production prototype of the m/62 that became better known as the Rk.62. This appears to be a non-standard example with a trigger guard.

The large trigger guard of the Rk.62 was designed to allow the weapon's use in winter conditions by a soldier wearing gloves.

SPECIFICATION	
Rk.62	**Muzzle velocity:** 719 m (2,359 ft) per second
Calibre: 7.62-mm (0.3-in)	**Rate of fire, cyclic:** 650 rpm
Lengths: overall 914 mm (36.0 in) and barrel 420 mm (16.54 in)	**Feed:** 30-round curved box
Weight loaded: 4.7 kg (10.36 lb)	

Samozaryadnyi Karabin Simonova (SKS) Rifle

The SKS almost has the appearance of a bolt-action rifle, but is in fact a gas-operated self-loading weapon with a 20-round integral magazine.

The semi-automatic rifle known as the **SKS (Samozaryadnyi Karabin Simonova obrazets 1945g**, or Simonov self-loading carbine type 1945) was designed in World War II, but was not placed in production until some time after this war's end. The designer was Sergei Gavrilovich Simonov, who was responsible for many important Soviet small arms, but in the SKS Simonov decided to play things safe and thus created what was in fact a relatively uninspired design.

Conservative design

The SKS was the first weapon designed to use the new Soviet 7.62-mm (0.3-in) cartridge derived from the German 7.92-mm (0.312-in) *kurz* (short) round of World War II.

The SKS was based on the use of a gas-operated mechanism with a simple tipping bolt locking system. So conservative was the overall design that the SKS even outwardly resembled a conventional bolt-action rifle, complete with extensive wooden furniture. A fixed folding bayonet was fitted under the muzzle and the box magazine could hardly be seen: it held only 10 rounds and was fixed to the receiver. Loading was by chargers or insertion of single rounds; to unload, the magazine was hinged downward, allowing the rounds to fall free. In typical Soviet fashion the SKS was very strongly built, so much so that many Western observers derided it as being far too heavy for the relatively light cartridge it fired.

Knockbacks

Despite this, the SKS was well able to withstand the many knocks and rough treatment likely to be encountered during service use, and the SKS was the standard rifle of the Warsaw Pact nations for years until the arrival in adequate numbers of the AK-47 assault rifle and the later AKM firing a smaller-calibre round.

Phased out of service

By the mid-1980s the SKS was no longer in Warsaw Pact service other than as a ceremonial weapon for parades or 'honour guards'. However, it may somewhat improbably still be encountered elsewhere as enormous numbers were produced, not only in the USSR but in East Germany and Yugoslavia where it was known as the **Karabiner-S** and **m/59** respectively; a variant of the m/59 was produced as the **m/59/66** with a spigot-type grenade launcher attached permanently to the muzzle.

The communist Chinese have produced a slightly revised version of the SKS known as the **Type 56** which features a spike rather than blade bayonet.

With so many SKS rifles produced, it is not surprising that many remained in use throughout the Middle and Far East until recent times. Large numbers of the weapon were encountered by US and South Vietnamese forces during the Vietnam conflict, and from there many passed into the hands of irregular forces. Being simple and robust weapons, they are easy to use after a minimum of training, and the SKS will be around for several years to come.

SPECIFICATION	
SKS	**Muzzle velocity:** 735 m (2,411 ft) per second
Calibre: 7.62-mm (0.3-in)	**Feed:** 20-round integral box
Length overall: 1021 mm (40.2 in)	
Length of barrel: 521 mm (20.5 in)	
Weight empty: 3.85 kg (8.49 lb)	

The Type 65 is the Chinese-made SMS, and while many of the weapons are virtually indistinguishable from the Soviet version, this has a spike bayonet.

Steyr AUG
Assault rifle

The 'Star Wars' look of the **AUG (Armee Universal Gewehr**, or army universal rifle) is one of the most striking of all modern assault rifles. But it has been around for a surprisingly long time: it first entered service with the Austrian army in 1977.

Bull-pup design

Manufactured by the old-established Steyr concern, the AUG is a 'bull-pup' design, with the trigger group forward of the magazine. This makes for a compact, handy weapon. The modern appearance is enhanced by the liberal use of nylonite and other non-metallic materials in the rifle's construction.

The only metal parts are the barrel and the receiver with the internal mechanism; even the receiver is an aluminium casting. All the materials are very high quality. The magazine is made from tough clear plastic,

Steyr AUG-A1

The original AUG assault rifle has proven extremely tough in operational service: in tests, one example remained fireable even after being repeatedly run over by a 10-tonne truck! The only damage it received was a crack in the plastic receiver cover.

Steyr AUG-P

The police version of the AUG has a shorter barrel than the assault rifle, and is usually supplied in black plastic. Most law enforcement examples are semi-automatic, capable of single-shot fire only.

this has the advantage that a soldier can see at a glance how many rounds the magazine contains.

Weapon system

The Steyr AUG is the heart of a modular weapon system. By changing the barrel, working parts or magazine, it can be converted to a sub-machine gun, a carbine, a specialist sniper rifle, or a light machine gun. By changing the fittings on the

*Left: The **AUG** has been exported to a number of nations around the world, including the Malaysian armed forces.*

*Above: In spite of its space-age appearance, the **AUG** has been in service with the Austrian army since 1977.*

receiver the AUG can be fitted with a wide range of night sights or sighting telescopes, but the usual sight is a simple optical telescope with a graticule calibrated for normal combat ranges.

Stripping the AUG for cleaning is rapid and simple, and cleaning is facilitated by the use of a chromed barrel interior. Repairs can be easily effected by changing an entire module.

Full production of the AUG began in 1978, and since that date Steyr has been kept busy supplying the Austrian army, various Middle Eastern, African and South American armed forces, as well as the armed forces of Australia, New Zealand and Ireland. The AUG is also in the armouries of special forces all over the world, and has been used by the British SAS and the German GSG-9 hostage rescue units.

The AUG weapon is popular with law enforcement agencies in a number of countries, and has been a commercial success in the US.

SPECIFICATION	
Steyr AUG (assault rifle)	
Calibre: 5.56 mm (0.22 in)	**Weight loaded:** 4.09 kg (9 lb)
Length: 790 mm (31 in)	**Magazine:** 30-round box
Length of barrel: 508 mm (20 in)	**Rate of fire, cyclic:** 650 rpm

FN FAL, L1 and FNC Assault rifles

Produced by Fabrique Nationale in Belgium, the **FN FAL** (Fusil Automatique Légère, or light automatic rifle) was originally produced in 1948. The prototypes fired the German 7.92-mm (0.312-in) *kurz* (short) cartridge, but later attempts at NATO standardisation meant that the FAL was revised for the standard 7.62-mm (0.3-in) cartridge. The rifle was then widely adopted not only throughout NATO but by many other nations, and has been licence-produced by nations as diverse as South Africa and Mexico. Many of these overseas production models differ in detail from the original FAL but the overall appearance is the same.

The FAL is a sturdy weapon based on the use of high-grade materials and extensive

machining. The action is gas-operated via a gas regulator that taps propellant gases from above the barrel to operate a piston that pushes back the bolt action for unlocking the breech.

The unlocking system has a delay action built in for increased safety. Automatic fire is possible on most models by use of a selector mechanism located

Dutch Marines on exercise in Norway aim their FALs. The rifle's popularity is a reflection of its ability to be used in any climate and terrain.

Although most FALs are capable of automatic fire, only those fitted with heavy barrels and bipods are really controllable. This heavy barrelled version (top), together with the folding-stocked para rifle, were captured by the British in the Falklands.

SPECIFICATION	
FN FAL	
Calibre: 7.62 mm (0.3 in)	**Magazine:** 20-round box
Length: 1143 mm (45 in)	**Rate of fire:** 30–40 rpm (single shot) or 650–700 rpm (FAL, cyclic)
Length of barrel: 554 mm (21.8 in)	**Muzzle velocity:** 838 m (2,750 ft) per second
Weight loaded: 5 kg (11 lb)	

near the trigger group.

The FAL models are many and varied. Most have solid wooden or nylonite butts and other furniture, but some models (usually issued to airborne forces) have folding butts. An overall sturdiness is a feature of the FAL.

British model

One version of the FAL that deserves further mention is the British **L1A1**. This was adopted by the British forces only after a lengthy series of trials and modifications that resulted in the elimination of the automatic fire feature and the introduction of some other differences. The L1A1 has been adopted by many other nations, including India, for licensed production. Australia also adopted the type and even produced a shorter version, the **L1A1-F1**, to suit the stature of the New Guinea troops.

Both the FAL and the L1A1 are equipped to fire rifle grenades. A bayonet can also be fitted, and some versions of the FAL have heavy barrels and bipods to enable them to be

Australian infantry with their version of the L1A1 manufactured locally at Lithgow in New South Wales. The Australians also produced a short version called the L1A1-F1 for use by local troops in New Guinea. They also use the M16A1.

Above: The L1A1, once the standard British infantry weapon and lacking automatic fire capability.

Above: Short-barrel FAL.

Below: Argentine FAL with folding butt and, like the FAL, capable of automatic fire.

used as light machine guns. Night sights are another optional fitting. The trend in assault rifle design is now toward the 5.56-mm (0.219-in) calibre, and a new model in this calibre is now in production as the **FN Carbine**.

The **FNC** first appeared in 1978, and has since been adopted by Belgium, Indonesia and Sweden, the latter two making the weapon under licence as the **Bofors AK-5** and **Pindad SS1**. The FNC is based on a rotary bolt, and is a light weapon through the use of features such as a stamped steel upper receiver, aluminium alloy lower receiver, plastic pistol grip and fore end, and plastic-coated steel folding buttstock; a fixed buttstock is optional. The FNC fires in single-shot, three-round burst and full-automatic modes.

SPECIFICATION	
FNC	
Calibre: 5.56-mm (0.219-in)	**Muzzle velocity:** not available
Length overall: 997 mm (39.25 in)	**Rate of fire, cyclic:** about 650
Length of barrel: 449 mm (17.68 in)	rounds per minute
Weight empty: 4.06 kg (8.95 lb)	**Magazine:** 30-round curved box

Above: The FNC drew its inspiration from weapons such as the AK-47, M16 and Galil, and is a gas-operated weapon with a rotary bolt. This is the standard weapon with the folding buttstock, and there is also a shortened Para model for the use of airborne troops.

FA MAS Assault rifle

For some years after World War II the French armaments industry lagged in the design of small arms, but with the **FA MAS**, or in full the **Fusil d'Assaut de la Manufacture d'Armes St Etienne**, it has made up that leeway with a vengeance. The FA MAS is a thoroughly modern and effective assault rifle, and yet another example of the overall compactness that can be achieved by using the 'bullpup' layout that was initially unorthodox but has now became virtually standard. This 'bullpup' layout located the trigger group in front of the magazine, allowing the weapon to be made very short in overall terms. Even by the standards of this abbreviated concept, the FA MAS is very short and handy, and must be one of the smallest in-service assault rifle designs of all.

Small but capable

Developed from 1972, the **FA MAS F1** baseline model was accepted in 1978 as the standard service rifle for the French armed forces and therefore ensuring a lengthy production run at St Etienne for many years.

The first FA MAS F1 rifles were issued to some paratroop and specialist units, and the

The French 5.56-mm (0.219-in) FA MAS F1 is one of the smallest and most compact of modern assault rifles. The magazine has been removed, but note that the carrying handle contains the sights and that the cocking lever is just underneath; note also the folded bipod legs.

type was initially used in combat by French troops in Chad and the Lebanon in 1983.

The FA MAS F1 is easy to spot, for in appearance it is quite unlike any other assault rifle. It fires the American 5.56-mm (0.219-in) M193 cartridge and over the top of the receiver there is a long handle that doubles as the base for both the rear and fore sight units. The buttstock is prominent and chunky, and from the front of the weapon's main bulk there protrudes a short length of barrel with a grenade-launching attachment.

Three fire options

There is provision for a small bayonet, and folding bipod legs are provided as standard. The fire selector has three positions: single-shot, three-round burst, and automatic. The mechanism to control this last feature is housed in the buttstock along with the rest of the rather complex trigger mechanism. The FA MAS F1's operating system is of the delayed blowback type. Use is made of plastics where possible and no

particular attention is paid to detail finish: for instance, the steel barrel is not chromed.

Despite its unusual appearance, the FA MAS F1 is comfortable to handle and fire, and presents no particular problems in use. Great attention was given to features such as grenade sights and generally easy sighting. The weapon has proved easy to handle and training costs have been reduced by the use of a version employing a small sparklet gas

cylinder to propel inert pellets for target training: this version is otherwise identical to the full service version.

Developed via the **FAS MAS F2** interim model, the latest variant is the **FA MAS G2** with the bipod replaced by a sling swivel (though a bipod can still be attached), the grenade launcher removed, the trigger guard extended to cover the whole grip and the magazine housing modified to accept NATO-standard magazines.

Although the rifle grenade has fallen from favour as a battlefield weapon, it still retains a limited utility for tasks such as persuading the skippers of small vessels to halt and undergo a search by naval or coast guard forces.

*This **FA MAS F1** is fitted with a TN21 night sighting infra-red spotlight under the muzzle. This equipment has a useful range of 150 m (165 yards), and the soldier picks up the IR reflections in the night vision binoculars held over his eyes. This equipment is in service with the French army.*

SPECIFICATION	
FA MAS F1	**Muzzle velocity:** 960 m (3,150 ft) per second
Calibre: 5.56-mm (0.219-in)	**Rate of fire, cyclic:** 1,000 rounds per minute
Length overall: 757 mm (29.8 in)	**Magazine:** 25-round straight box
Length of barrel: 488 mm (19.21 in)	
Weight loaded: 4.59 kg (10.12 lb) with sling	

Chinese assault rifles Type 56, Type 56 carbine, and Type 95 series

Despite the introduction of several alternatives over the years, in numerical terms the Chinese assault rifle most likely to be encountered continues to be the 7.62-mm (0.3-in) calibre **Type 56** weapon.

There are several models in the Type 56 family, all of them based closely on the Soviet 7.62-mm Kalashnikov AK-47 and AKM weapons. Early Type 56 production models were based on the AK-47, the improved manufacturing details of the AKM then being gradually phased into production. All models in the Type 56 series have slight differences from the Kalashnikov original, but the weapon operates along the same lines, and all models fire the Soviet 7.62 x 39-mm M1943 cartridge.

The basic Type 56 rifle can be recognised by the combination of a fixed wooden butt-stock and a permanently fixed bayonet, which folds back under the barrel. The Type 56 is the most prolific weapon of the series, production of the weapon extending into the millions. The **Type 56-1** has a folding metal butt and no fixed bayonet. The **Type 56-2** also lacks

Norinco produces the Type 56 weapon for PLA infantry and special forces units. The design is simply a Chinese copy of the Soviet AK-47/AKM assault rifle; the weapon has an effective range of up to 400 m (437 yards). Note the folded bayonet.

the bayonet but the stock folds along the right side of the receiver. The latest production model is the **Type 56C**, a more compact version of the Type 56 making use of plastic furniture and other detail modifications, and again without a fixed bayonet. The Type 56C does not appear to have been manufactured in quantity as yet.

Type 56 carbine

One earlier Chinese rifle that may still be encountered is the **Type 56** carbine. This is not related to the assault rifle of the same name and is a Chinese derivative of the Soviet SKS. Although termed as a carbine, this earlier Type 56 is in fact some 151 mm (5.9 in) longer than the Type 56 assault rifle. Entering production

in 1956, the Type 56 carbine has a 10-round magazine for 7.62 x 39-mm M1943 cartridges.

Since the introduction of the Type 56 assault rifle during the 1950s the manufacturer, Norinco, has introduced several other assault rifles, none of which has been adopted for indigenous service since the models were all intended for export sale. These include the **Type 81** and **WQ 314**, both in 7.62-mm calibre, and the **CQ** that is virtually a direct copy of the US 5.56-mm (0.219-in) calibre M16. Norinco also produces the 5.8-mm (0.228-in) calibre **Type 95**, a light and compact 'bullpup' rifle owing little to other designs produced elsewhere. The Type 95 fires a 5.8 x 38-mm cartridge optimised to meet Chinese

The 7.62-mm Type 56-1 assault rifle. Note the folding metal butt-stock which passes over the receiver and the magazine placed forward of the trigger assembly. The Type 56-1 and 56-2 both lack a folding bayonet.

armed forces specifications, and is built in several forms. Apart from the basic assault rifle, there is also a light support weapon with a bipod and heavy barrel, a carbine, and a marksman rifle with bipod and telescopic sights.

The Type 95 has been issued only to elite units, and it will be years before it is deployed throughout the Chinese armed forces. It has all the features expected of a modern assault rifle, such as plastics-based furniture, ergonomic outlines, a rifle grenade launcher at the muzzle, and the facility for the installation of an under-barrel grenade launcher. An export version of the weapon has been planned. Dubbed the **Type 97**, this will be chambered for the 5.56 x 45-mm cartridge.

SPECIFICATION	
Type 56 assault rifle	**Weight:** 3.8 kg (8.4 lb) empty; 4.19 kg (9.2 lb) loaded
Calibre: 7.62 mm (0.3 in)	**Rate of fire:** 40 rpm single-shot, or 90–100 rpm burst-fire
Length overall: 874 mm (34.4 in) with bayonet folded and 1100 mm (43.3 in) with bayonet extended	**Muzzle velocity:** 710 m (2,329 ft) per second
Length of barrel: 414 mm (16.3 in)	**Magazine:** 30-round curved box

Shanghai girls receive combat drill instruction using Type 56 carbines fitted with bayonets, in May 1973. Later Type 56 models were fitted with a folding spike rather than a folding sword-type bayonet.

INSAS 5.56-mm assault rifle/light support weapon

The INSAS light support weapon is fitted with a 30-round plastic box magazine, although this can also be mounted on the baseline assault rifle. The light support weapon has no three-round burst fire mode.

The **INSAS (Indian Small Arms System)** assault rifle in 5.56-mm (0.219-in) calibre is one member of a family of weapons derived from the same basic design. The other family members are a light support weapon/light machine gun and a short assault rifle/ carbine.

Developed since the mid-1980s, the INSAS rifle is intended to replace all existing rifles in service with the Indian armed forces. The intended service debut was initially delayed by the lack of an indigenous facility for the manufacture of the 5.56 x 45-mm ammunition round for which the INSAS was designed. This Indian cartridge was in turn based on the NATO SS109. By 1995 it was estimated that the INSAS programme was running almost four years behind schedule and, by 2000, further slippages had occurred.

However, by February 1999, more than 30,000 INSAS rifles had entered service with the Indian army and, out of a planned requirement for

528,000 weapons, more than half had been delivered by mid-2001, most of them subsequently being issued to units based in Kashmir. However, a 2001 report relating to the INSAS revealed that various technical problems were still prevalent and remained to be eliminated.

The short assault rifle/ carbine variant is still under continued development as technical problems have also plagued the finalisation of this variant.

Despite these drawbacks, early in 1999 an export version of the INSAS rifle was announced.

INSAS operation

The INSAS assault rifle is a gas-operated, selective-fire weapon that displays an interesting combination of features derived from a variety of sources, and which reflect the diverse range of military suppliers that have provided small arms equipment to the Indian armed forces. The receiver and pistol grip show

AK-47 influence; the butt, gas regulator and flash hider show FN FAL influence; the fore-end appears to rely upon that of the AR-15/M16; and the forward cocking handle is based on Heckler & Koch practice. The gas system operates the usual front-locking rotating bolt. Sheet metal pressings are used for the receiver, and the barrel bore and firing pin are chrome plated. All of the furniture is made from a plastics-based material. The dimensions of the magazine housing are designed to accommodate standard US M16 magazines, though the intended INSAS magazine is made of semi-transparent plastic and holds 20 rounds. The 30-round magazine used with the INSAS light machine gun/light support weapon may also be used.

The gas piston drives the bolt carrier and rotating bolt, in the normal manner found on modern weapons of this class. Drawing upon Indian army experience in Sri Lanka, the fire selector mechanism allows single-shot fire or bursts of three rounds; full-automatic fire is not available on the assault rifle. A large thumb-operated safety catch is located on the left side of the receiver, above the pistol grip. The fire selector lever is located alongside the safety.

One most surprising feature of the INSAS assault rifle is the retention of the butt-plate from the Lee-Enfield No. 1 Mk III rifle, which was licence-produced in Indian factories. This butt-plate provides a trap for the oil bottle

and associated cleaning materials, including a barrel pull-through.

Provision is made for mounting various types of passive night sight or optical sights. The muzzle attachment doubles as a flash eliminator and rifle grenade launcher. Both fixed-butt and tubular steel folding-butt (Para) versions of the INSAS assault rifle have been produced. Accessories include a blank firing attachment, a multi-purpose bayonet and a carrying sling.

Squad support

In addition to the INSAS assault rifle, the same weapon forms the basis for a light machine gun/light support weapon, again in 5.56-mm calibre. The INSAS light support weapon is the basic assault rifle with the addition of a heavier barrel in order to permit sustained fire; both fixed- and folding-butt versions are again available. The weapon retains the same gas operation and rotating bolt, and can deliver either single shots or automatic fire at a cyclic rate of 650 rounds per minute, the same rate as the INSAS assault rifle. The light support weapon differs only in its provision for a bipod and in its barrel design. The latter is internally chromed and uses a different rifling contour (four grooves, right-hand turn as opposed to six grooves, right-hand turn for the assault rifle). The different con-tour is tailored to develop improved ballistic performance when firing at the longer ranges usually encountered in the light-machine gun role. The barrel cannot be rapidly changed and a 30-round magazine is carried as

SPECIFICATION	
INSAS assault rifle	**INSAS light machine gun**
Calibre: 5.56 mm (0.219 in)	**Calibre:** 5.56 mm (0.219 in)
Length overall: 945 mm (37.2 in) fixed-butt, or 750 mm (29.53 in) in folding-butt form folded and 960 mm (37.8 in) extended	**Length overall:** 1050 mm (41.3 in) fixed-butt, or 890 mm (35 in) in folding-butt form folded and 1025 mm (40.4 in) extended
Length of barrel: 464 mm (18.3 in)	**Length of barrel:** 535 mm (21 in)
Weight: 3.2 kg (7 lb) without magazine; 4.1 kg (9 lb) loaded	**Weight:** 6.23 kg (13.7 lb) fixed-butt empty; 5.87 kg (12.9 lb) folding-butt empty; both 6.73 kg (14.8 lb) loaded
Rate of fire, cyclic: 650 rpm	**Rate of fire, cyclic:** 650 rpm
Muzzle velocity: 915 m (3,002 ft) per second	**Muzzle velocity:** 925 m (3,035 ft) per second
Magazine: 20-round curved box or 30-round curved box	**Magazine:** 30-round curved box

standard. The INSAS light support weapon also makes use of an unexpected influence: in this case it is the bipod, which is of the same type as that manufactured in India for use with the Bren and Vickers-Berthier weapons of World War II.

The INSAS light support weapon has 'iron' sights calibrated for ranges of up to 1000 m (1,904 yards) and the muzzle is designed to allow NATO grenades to be launched, using the standard diameter of 22 mm (0.87 in).

In common with the INSAS assault rifle, the light support weapon has been approved for service with the Indian armed forces, but its delivery has been delayed by a shortage of appropriate ammunition.

The INSAS assault rifle is the replacement for the Indian army's licence-manufactured 7.62-mm FN FAL. The assault rifle entered service with NATO-standard ammunition before the local round became available.

Heckler & Koch G3 Assault rifle

The Heckler & Koch HK 21 is the 7.62-mm (0.3-in) light machine gun version of the basic G3. This version uses a belt feed which can be altered to take a 20-round box magazine if required. This weapon has been produced in Portugal and has been widely sold in Africa.

The **Heckler & Koch G3** assault rifle is a development of the CETME design created in Spain by a team largely of German small arms designers, and was adopted by the West German Bundeswehr during 1959. In many ways the G3 has proved to be one of the most successful of all the post-war German weapon designs, and it has been manufactured in Germany not only for that nation's forces but in several other countries desirous of manufacturing their own weapons under licence. Within a total of 13 countries that have made the G3, these nations include Greece, Mexico, Norway, Pakistan, Portugal, Saudi Arabia and Turkey. The G3 has served with the armed forces of some 60 countries in all.

Low-cost manufacture

Although the maker would not like it to be said, the G3 can be regarded as virtually the nearest that small arms designers have come to the concept of the 'use-and-throw-away' rifle. Despite the cost the G3 is a weapon designed from the outset for mass production using as much simple machinery as possible and thus reducing the need for expensive machining tools and operations. On the basis of the CETME design Heckler & Koch developed the design so that cheap and easily produced materials such as plastics and pressed steel were used wherever possible. The locking roller system developed by CETME was retained to provide a form of delayed blow-back operation after the weapon has been fired.

The G3 possesses a general resemblance to the FN FAL in its overall configuration, but there are many differences between the two weapons. The G3 is a whole generation ahead of the FAL, and this significant fact is reflected not only in the G3's general construction and materials but also in the development of the whole family of variants based on the basic G3

assault rifle. There are carbine versions, some with barrels so short they could qualify as sub-machine guns, sniper variants, light machine gun versions with bipods and heavy barrels, and so on. There is also a version for use with airborne or other such troops: this is the **G3A4**, which has a butt that telescopes onto either side of the receiver.

Special features

For all its overall simplicity, the G3 nonetheless possesses some unusual features. One is the bolt, which was designed so that it locks with the bulk of its mass forward and over the chamber to act as an extra mass to move when unlocking. Stripping is very simple and there are only a very few moving parts. With very few changes the basic G3 can be produced

Using the same basic layout as the G3, this 5.56-mm (0.219-in) version is known as the HK 33. It can take a 20- or 40-round magazine, and exists in several versions, including a special sniper's rifle and a version with a telescopic folding butt. Most versions can fire rifle grenades.

with a calibre of 5.56 mm (0.219 in), and this version is manufactured as the **HK 33**.

The success of the G3 can be seen in the number of nations that have adopted the type. The G3 was prominent in the overthrow of the Shah of Iran's regime by the Moslem fundamentalist revolution of 1979, and was also one of the weapons obtained despite sanctions by Rhodesia when defying the world by a unilateral

SPECIFICATION	
Heckler & Koch G3A3	
Calibre: 7.62-mm (0.3-in)	**Muzzle velocity:** 780–800 m (2,560–2,625 ft) per second
Length overall: 1025 mm (40.35 in)	**Rate of fire, cyclic:** 500–600 rounds per minute
Length of barrel: 450 mm (17.7 in)	
Weight: loaded 5.025 kg (11.08 lb)	**Feed:** 20-round box magazine

Carrying the launcher for a rocket-propelled anti-tank weapon with the pack on his back, this German soldier has a variant of the G3 with a telescoping butt as his personal weapon.

declaration of independence before the war that led to the creation of Zimbabwe. Some nations find it profitable to produce the G3 under licence for export rather than the use of their own forces, and in this category were France and the United Kingdom.

Popular weapon

In many ways the G3 can be regarded as one of the most important of all modern assault rifles, but it uses the over-powerful NATO 7.62-mm (0.3-in) x 51 cartridge, in common with other designs such as the FAL. Despite this it remains a popular assault rifle and one that will remain in service for some time.

Heckler & Koch HK 53 Assault rifle

The **Heckler & Koch HK 53** is a highly capable weapon that falls in classification terms into the borderland between the sub-machine gun and the assault rifle, most commentators placing it on the assault rifle side of the border because of the cartridge it fires.

The HK 53 is one of a series of weapons derived from the operating system that was first adopted by the manufacturer for the 7.62-mm (0.3-in) G3 assault rifle. This delayed-blowback action is based on a two-part bolt comprising a bolt head and a heavier bolt body behind it. The bolt head carries two vertically aligned rollers: when the weapon is ready to fire, these rollers are driven out into recesses in the barrel extension by a wedge-shaped extension of the bolt body, which pushes forward during the chambering of the cartridge to drive the rollers outward. When the cartridge is fired, the gas pressure in the barrel tries to force the bolt head backward,

but the movement is limited until the rollers are driven inward by the shaping of the recess walls. The inward movement of the rollers is further checked by the wedge-shaped extension of the bolt body, backed by the return spring. As the rollers are forced inward, the bolt body is accelerated to the rear as the rollers push the wedge-shaped extension rearward: so the bolt body moves swiftly as the bolt head is still checked and so withstands the gas pressure. By

The HK 53 is a cross between an SMG and a rifle, being fractionally larger than the MP5 but firing the powerful 5.56-mm NATO round. This can lead to control difficulties, requiring experienced hands to allow the weapon to be used to good effect.

the time the rollers have been driven fully inward, the buller has

SPECIFICATION	
Heckler & Koch HK 53 **Calibre:** 5.56-mm (0.219-in) **Length overall:** 780 mm (30.71 in) with the butt extended and 565 mm (23.23 in) with the butt retracted **Length of barrel:** 211 mm (8.31 in)	**Weight:** empty 3 kg (6.61 lb) **Muzzle velocity:** not available **Rate of fire, cyclic:** 750 rounds per minute **Feed:** 25-, 30- or 40-round curved box magazine

departed from the muzzle and the two parts of the bolt move backward together under the force of the residual gas pressure. There follow the extraction and ejection as the return spring is compressed, and then the bolt is driven forward to chamber a fresh round and become locked as the rollers are driven outward once more.

Selective fire

If the fire selector lever is set for 'auto', pressure on the trigger releases the hammer to fire the weapon, but if the selector lever is set for 'single shot', the presence of a disconnector makes it necessary to release the pressure on the trigger

The very rare firing port variant of the HK53 is designed to be used from within an armoured vehicle. The foresight is removed, and a bag is fitted to prevent spent cartridges from bouncing dangerously around the inside of the APC.

between shots. This means that the weapon fires from a close breech, which leads to a greater consistency of operation on the one hand, but also to the possibility of a round 'cooking off' if the chamber is hot from previous burst firing.

Related models

The HK 53 is closely related to the **HK 33** developed from the mid-1960s for production from 1968 as a scaled-down version of the G3 rifle. The HK 33 was developed for the then-new 5.56-mm x 45 (actual 0.223-in) Remington cartridge, and was exported to countries such as Chile, Malaysia and Thailand. Since 1999 the HK 33 has also been made under licence in Turkey. The HK 33 is still in German production, and has served as the basis for developments such as the G41

assault rifle and HK 53 compact assault rifle, which is known to its manufacturer as a sub-machine gun.

The HK 53 is an ultra-compact version of the HK 33, which can be categorised as a compact (short) assault rifle by the fact that its fires the intermediate rifle round. The HK 53 was developed in the mid-1970s.

The HK 33 is a selective-fire rifle. The receiver is of stamped steel, and the HK 33 is available with either a fixed plastic butt (HK 33A2) or retractable metal butt (HK 33A3). A carbine version of the HK33 is also available as the HK 33k with a shorter barrel and similar fixed or retractable butts as the HK 33kA2 and HK 33kA3 respectively. The HK 33 variants are available with different trigger units, with or without a three-round burst mode.

The HK 53 is internally similar to the HK 33 but cannot fire rifle grenades, or carry an under-barrel 40-mm grenade launcher, or be equipped with a bayonet. The weapon features a long, four-pronged flash hider. Both the HK 33 and HK 53 use 25-, 30- and 40-round magazine, but the last has been out of production for some time.

The emphasis in the creation of modern battlefield weapons such as the HK 33 and HK 53 series is on the reduction of weapon weight and size. Also important is maximising firepower flexibility by the introduction of larger magazines and more comprehensive firing options.

Heckler & Koch G36 Assault rifle

In the late 1960s Heckler & Koch launched development of the G11 rifle after the West German army had decided to replace its G3 rifle with a lighter weapon offering a considerably greater hit probability. The company's initial studies led to the concept of a small-calibre rifle firing caseless ammunition (created by Dynamit Nobel) for a high rate of fire and, to provide sufficient stopping power despite the use of a small-calibre bullet, a three-round burst capability and a large-capacity magazine.

The G11 was of notably advanced concept and, in its official evaluation from the late 1980s, proved an excellent weapon. But then the whole programme was cancelled for economic and NATO standardisation reasons.

Second-line rifle

While the G11 was envisaged as the personal weapon of first-line German forces, a G41 rifle was planned as the equivalent for second-line units. This G41 was developed in the early 1980s from the HK-33E assault rifle, and the cancellation of the G11 sealed the fate of the G41 for German service. The G41 was in effect a further development of the G3 rifle based on the same roller-delayed blowback action but chambered for 5.56-mm (0.219-in) ammunition.

Current weapon

The **G36** assault rifle was created at the **HK-50** project in the early 1990s, and in 1999 the weapon was adopted by the German army as successor to the G3. The G36 differs from earlier Heckler & Koch assault rifles in having a gas-operated operating system with a rotating bolt locking into the barrel extension. The receiver is made from steel-reinforced plastic, the trigger unit is contained inside the plastic pistol grip and there are variants with or without a three-burst fire capability. The charging handle is attached to the top of the bolt carrier and can be hinged to the left or right.

The G36 is fed from a polymer magazine with translucent walls, and this magazine has inbuilt clips to connect magazines one to another for faster reloading. The plastic buttstock folds to the side. Above the receiver is a large carrying handle with built-in sights. The standard G36 has dual sights: an x3.5 compact scope is coupled to an x1 'red-dot' sight for faster short-range target acquisition. The **G36E**

The G36 reflects the state-of-the-art production for assault rifles, and is a thoroughly workmanlike and reliable weapon offering light weight, adequate magazine capacity, a good rate of fire, accuracy and imponderables such as 'user friendliness'.

export and **G36K** carbine versions have only one sight, an x1.5 scope. The G36 has NATO-standard muzzle brake for launching rifle grenades, and can be equipped with a bayonet or 40-mm (1.57-in) grenade launcher.

There is also a somewhat smaller **G36C** close assault model created for the use of special forces and the like.

SPECIFICATION	
Heckler & Koch G36	**Weight empty:** 3.6 kg (7.94 lb)
Calibre: 5.56-mm (0.219-in)	**Muzzle velocity:** not available
Length overall: 998 mm (39.3 in) with the buttstock extended	**Rate of fire:** 750 rounds per minute
Length of barrel: 480 mm (18.9 in)	**Magazine:** 30-round curved box

Galil & R4 Assault rifles

The exact provenance of the Israeli **Galil** assault rifle is more than a trifle clouded, for although it is claimed that the design was created as an indigenous Israeli effort, there are some obvious likenesses to the Finnish Valmet assault rifles that were produced in a variety of models and calibres. Things are made more confused by the fact that the Valmet rifles were themselves modelled on the Soviet AK-47 in its original form with a machined rather than stamped steel receiver unit. Though it would be an oversimplification to state that the Galil is a direct derivative of the AK-47, there are certainly some resemblances in operation (the usual rotating bolt) and general layout, but these are now common to many designs. The situation is further complicated by the fact that the Galil was initially manufactured on tooling supplied by Valmet and with Valmet's type of manufacturing documentation.

The Galil assault rifle has been produced in both 5.56-and 7.62-mm (0.219- and 0.3-in) calibres, and is now one of the most widely used weapons issued to the various Israeli armed forces. It is produced in three forms: one is known as the **Galil ARM**, which has a bipod and a carrying handle and is the all-purpose weapon; another is the **Galil AR**, which lacks the bipod and handle; and the third is the **Galil SAR**, which has a shorter barrel and no bipod or carrying handle. All three have folding stocks. The bipod on the ARM can be used as a barbed wire cutter, and all three versions have a bottle cap opener fitted as standard to prevent soldiers using other parts of the weapon as bottle openers (e.g. the magazine lips).

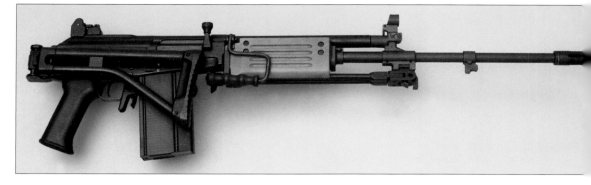

*The Israeli **Galil ARM** assault rifle with the metal stock folded forward to reduce the length. This version cannot be used to fire rifle grenades and does not have the bipod fitted to the longer models. It can be found in variants calibred for 5.56-mm (0.219-in) and 7.62-mm (0.3-in) ammunition.*

A fixture over the muzzle acts as a rifle grenade launcher.

Three magazine sizes

In its full ARM version the Galil can be used as a form of light machine gun, and 35- and 50-round magazines are produced; there is also a special 10-round magazine used to contain the special cartridges for launching rifle grenades. As usual a bayonet can be fitted.

The Galil has proved to be very effective in action and has attracted a great deal of overseas attention. Some have been exported and the design has also been copied – the Swedish 5.56-mm **FFV 890C** is obviously based on the Galil.

One nation that negotiated a licence for local production was South Africa, which then manufactured a version known as the **R4**, which is the standard rifle for the front-line units of the South African defence forces. The R4 is produced in 5.56-mm calibre and differs in some details from the original, the changes resulting mainly from operational experience in the South African and Namibian bush.

SPECIFICATION	
Galil ARM (5.56-mm)	with 35-round magazine
Calibre: 5.56-mm (0.22-in)	**Muzzle velocity:** 980 m (3,215 ft) per
Length overall: 979 mm (38.54 in)	second
Length of barrel: 460 mm (18.1 in)	**Rate of fire, cyclic:** 650 rpm
Weight loaded: 4.62 kg (10.19 lb)	**Magazine:** 35- or 50-round boxes

*Key features of the **Galil ARM** include a straight-through design, the gas system above the barrel, an inbuilt bipod folding into the underside of the fore grip and the location of the magazine forward of the trigger group.*

SPECIFICATION	
Galil ARM (7.62-mm)	**Weight loaded:** 4.67 kg (10.30 lb)
Calibre: 7.62-mm (0.3-in)	**Muzzle velocity:** 850 m (2,790 ft) per
Length: 1050 mm (41.34 in)	second
Length of barrel: 533 mm	**Rate of fire, cyclic:** 650 rpm
(20.98 in)	**Magazine:** 20-round curved box

Beretta AR70 & AR90 Assault rifles

The **AR70** was developed by Beretta of Italy following a series of manufacturer's in-house trials involving several types of assault rifle designs, and from these evolved a gas-operated design using the rotary-bolt locking principle but in a very simple form. To provide increased safety, Beretta decided to strengthen the locking system with extra metal around the chamber area. The result is a functional and well-made weapon that can be stripped down into its few operating parts with ease.

Normal options

There are three production versions of the AR70: one is the AR70 proper, which has a nylonite stock and furniture; the **SC70** with a folding buttstock constructed from shaped steel tubing; and the **SC70 Short** that is a version of the SC70 with a shorter barrel for the soldiers of special forces units. While the AR70 and SC70 can fire 40-mm (1.57-in) rifle grenades, the SC70 Short lacks this capability.

The AR70 is as good as any assault rifle on the market, and is notable for the high standard of care that is taken in its manufacture, which is a hallmark of Beretta small arms design and manufacture.

For some reason the AR 70 series has yet to make any large impact on the market for small arms. Modest numbers have been adopted by the Italian

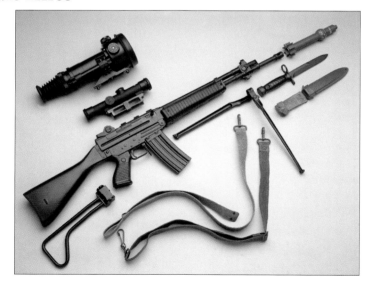

*The **AR70** has several equipment options, including the fitting of night sights, a bayonet or a **MECAR** rifle grenade launcher. The butt can easily be removed and replaced with a skeleton butt to convert the rifle to **SC70** standard.*

SPECIFICATION	
AR70	**Muzzle velocity:** 950 m (3,115 ft) per
Calibre: 5.56-mm (0.22-in)	second
Length overall: 955 mm (37.6 in)	**Rate of fire, cyclic:** 650 rpm
Length of barrel: 450 mm (17.72 in)	**Magazine:** 30-round curved box
Weight loaded: 4.15 kg (9.15 lb)	

This Beretta AR70 assault rifle, fitted with a 20-round magazine reveals the weapon's clean overall lines and good finish. It is used by some Italian anti-guerrilla special units and has been sold in Jordan and Malaysia, but large-scale sales have not been made.

special forces, and some weapons have also been exported to Jordan and Malaysia, but in none of these cases have the numbers involved been large. This is rendered even more odd when it is realised that the care in design and construction is such that the weapons of the AR70 series are notably accurate – accurate enough for a telescopic sight to be fitted to standard production versions if required.

In the early 1980s the Italian army's requirement for a new 5.56-mm rifle was met by the

AR90 derivative of the AR70. Entering service in the 1990s, this has a carrying handle and fixed sight above the receiver. The standard model has a longer barrel and fixed buttstock, but there are also long-/short-barrel models with folding stocks.

The Beretta AR70 in service in the Malaysian jungles; note the applied camouflage paint scheme. The AR70 weighs only 4.15 kg loaded with 30 rounds and is thus a fairly handy weapon for the small-statured men of Asian armies to handle.

ST Kinetics assault rifles Singapore 5.56-mm rifle series

The first assault rifle produced by Chartered Industries of Singapore (now Singapore Technologies Kinetics, or ST Kinetics) was the 5.56-mm (0.219-in) **SAR80** designed in the UK under contract for the Singaporean company by Sterling. The first prototypes appeared in 1978.

Above: Designed in the UK by Sterling, the SAR80 was the first attempt by Chartered Industries of Singapore (later ST Kinetics) to break into the potentially lucrative but difficult small arms market.

The design emphasis was on ease of production with a gas-operated system, with a rotary bolt, based around that of the American M16. The M16 had been manufactured under licence in Singapore for the local armed forces. Although ordered in quantity, the SAR80 did not completely supplant the M16 in

The SAR21 is a modern assault rifle of the 'bullpup' type. The weapon strips down into barrel, bolt, upper receiver and lower receiver groups as well as the magazine.

local use. Despite intensive marketing no sales of the SAR80, other than those for local use, resulted.

Steady evolution

The Singaporean company's next foray into the small arms market involved the 5.56-mm **SR88** and the subsequent **SR88A**. This could be regarded in design terms as an enhanced export model based around the SAR80 with numerous detail design changes. There was also a shortened carbine model. Once again there were no export sales

269

so the SR88A, the final offering, was withdrawn.

Its successor seems certain to attract far more sales interest. It is the 5.56-mm **SAR21**, designed from about 1995 onwards in the light of the company's intention of producing a rifle which could replace all the rifles then in service with the Singapore armed forces. It was first demonstrated publicly during 1999 and is now in series production. The SAR21 has a bullpup layout, with the magazine behind the trigger group, to ensure a compact and handy weapon. Great use is made throughout the design of composite materials and plastics for enhanced handling ergonomics.

Construction is modular to assist maintenance, the rifle stripping down into only five sub-assemblies, one of which is the 30-round box magazine. Gas operation and the rotary bolt locking system are carried over from earlier designs. Aiming is carried out using a x1.5 telescopic sight permanently mounted over the receiver.

Derived models

The SAR21 assault rifle is only one of a series of variants. One is the **SAR21 P-Rail**, an assault rifle model with the usual sight replaced by a length of Picatinny Rail onto which various optical or night sights can be fitted.

The **SAR21/40 mm** has provision for mounting a 40-mm grenade launcher under the barrel, while the **SAR21 Sharp Shooter** has a x3 optical sight for use by dedicated marksmen. There is also a SAR21 light machine gun with a heavy barrel, bipod and automatic fire only – all other models can be fired as single shot when required. The weapon's cyclic rate of fire is 450-650 rounds per minute.

SPECIFICATION	
SAR80 **Calibre:** 5.56 mm (0.219 in) **Length:** 970 mm (38.19 in) **Length of barrel:** 459 mm (18.07 in) **Weight:** empty 3.7 kg (8.16 lb) **Magazine capacity:** 30 rounds **Rate of fire:** 600–800 rpm **SR88A** **Calibre:** 5.56 mm (0.219 in) **Length:** 960 mm (37.8 in) **Length of barrel:** 460 mm (18.11 in)	**Weight:** empty 3.68 kg (8.11 lb) **Magazine capacity:** 30 rounds **Rate of fire:** 700–900 rpm **SAR21** **Calibre:** 5.56 mm (0.219 in) **Length:** 805 mm (2 ft 7.7 in) **Length of barrel:** 508 mm (31.69 in) **Weight:** empty 3.82 kg (8.42 lb) **Magazine capacity:** 30 rounds **Rate of fire:** 450–650 rpm

CETME Model L/LC
Spanish 5.56-mm assault rifles

Production of the 5.56-mm (0.219-in) assault rifles generally known as the **CETME** family ended under another manufacturer's designation, that of Santa Barbara (now owned by General Dynamics) at the Oviedo arsenal. The rifle had design origins dating back to 1945 as it employed a German delayed-blowback locking system based on gas operation and rollers moving outward into slots in the receiver walls at the instant of firing. This system was used in Spain for a series of 7.62-mm and 7.92-mm (0.3-in and 0.312-in) CETME rifles (and in Germany by Heckler & Koch) before Spanish attentions turned to producing a 5.56-mm rifle.

Above: Two versions of the CETME 5.56-mm selective fire assault rifle were built: a standard model with a fixed butt stock (the Model L) and a short-barrelled version with a telescopic stock (Model LC). A 20-round magazine was originally fitted.

CETME stood for Compañia de Estudios Técnicos de Materiales Especiales, the name of a design bureau that modified the 7.62-mm rifle designs into a lighter, handier and more compact 5.56-mm assault rifle. Two models resulted – the **Model L** with a fixed butt stock and the **Model LC** with a telescopic butt stock. The Model LC was also slightly shorter overall with the butt stock extended and the barrel was shorter, resulting in a higher cyclic rate of fire.

Spanish production

Production of these weapons for service with the Spanish armed forces took place between 1986 and 1991, and a key feature of the basic design was the extensive use in much of the weapons' exteriors on the basis of various composite

Left: The Model LC is readily distinguishable from its Model L half-brother by its telescopic butt. Though mainly successful, the Model L series has revealed a tendency toward damage.

SPECIFICATION

Model L
Calibre: 5.56 mm (0.219 in)
Length: 925 mm (36.42 in)
Barrel length: 400 mm (15.75 in)
Weight: empty 3.4 kg (7.5 lb)
Magazine capacity: 30 rounds
Rate of fire: 600–750 rpm

Model LC
Calibre: 5.56-mm (0.219 in)
Length: 860 or 665 mm (33.86 or 26.18 in)
Barrel length: 320 mm (12.6 in)
Weight: empty 3.4 kg (7.5 lb)
Magazine capacity: 30 rounds
Rate of fire: 650–800 rpm

material mouldings. Early production models were supplied with a 20-round box magazine, but this was later altered to allow M16 pattern 30-round magazines to be employed. The 30-round magazine then became standard, although a 10-round box was occasionally seen.

Another production change was to the sights. These were altered from the original four-position sight graduated up to 400 m (440 yards), to a far simpler flip-over sight assembly graduated only for 200 m (220 yards) and 400 m. Another change was to the fire-control lever: the rifle was originally produced with a three-round burst limiter device in addition to the usual safe, single shot and fully automatic selections, but this was omitted from late-production weapons (the limiter was deemed unnecessary).

The CETME 5.56-mm rifles were sold only to the Spanish armed forces. In service the rifles proved to be somewhat prone to damage, requiring care and maintenance. The only complete answer was a replacement rifle, so in mid-1998 it was revealed that the replacement would be the Heckler & Koch G36. The forecast requirement was then for about 115,000 rifles, and so a factory is being constructed in Spain in order to carry out licensed manufacture.

SIG SG550 Assault rifle

The **SG550** series of 5.56-mm (0.219-in) assault rifles was developed to meet a Swiss army requirement for an assault rifle to replace the service's 7.5-mm (0.295-in) Sturmgewehr 57 (Stgw 57, otherwise the SG510-4). The two basic SIG models originally involved were the **SG550** and **SG551**. The Swiss army designation for the SG550 is **Sturmgewehr 90 (Stgw 90)**, while the SG551, also in Swiss army service, is shorter and lacks the fittings for a bipod. Both models were accepted for service during 1984, and remain in production.

A number of related models have since appeared. The **SG550 SP** and **SG551 SP** are semi-automatic sporting rifles for the large Swiss target rifle market. A **SG551 SWAT**, virtually identical to the SG551, is intended mainly for special forces or special law enforcement agencies, and

has provision for the installation of optical sights and, under the barrel, a 40-mm grenade launcher. The **SG550 Sniper** rifle is a specialised semi-automatic rifle with a longer barrel, a telescopic sight and numerous other associated refinements. This variant is also used by the Jordanian police. The **SG552 Commando**, launched during mid-1998, is a much lighter and more compact model, also with a folding butt stock, intended for special forces. It has provision for a number of optical sights.

High specification

The SG550 series is one where superlatives can be liberally lavished. The overall standard of construction and ease of handling are excellent. As is usual these days, extensive use is made of plastics-based materials to save weight wherever possible. The method of operation is the usual gas-operated rotary-locking bolt.

Noticeable on all models is the attention to design detail in features such as the translucent plastic magazines that allow the magazine contents remaining to be instantly assessed. The 20- or 30-round magazines also have studs and lugs on the

This SG550 (Stgw 90) assault rifle reveals the facility for the carriage on the weapon of three plastic magazines to provide a large quantity of ready-use ammunition.

sides to allow a number of magazines to be clipped together in such a way that as one magazine is emptied the firer can pull the assembly out, shifting its sideways and then pushing in one of the still-loaded magazines. The provision of 60 or possibly even 90 ready-use rounds has obvious tactical advantages. A five-round magazine containing rifle grenade-launching cartridges is

The SG550 Sniper retains the 20- or 30-round magazine of the basic model but has a number of different features, including an adjustable stock and telescopic sight, to optimise the weapon for improved accuracy at longer ranges.

SPECIFICATION	
SG550	**SG551**
Calibre: 5.56 mm (0.219 in)	**Calibre:** 5.56 mm (0.219 in)
Length: 998 mm (39.29 in)	**Length:** 827 mm (32.56 in)
Length of barrel: 528 mm (20.47 in)	**Length of barrel:** 372 mm (14.65 in)
Weight: empty 4.1 kg (9.04 lb)	**Weight:** empty 3.4 kg (7.5 lb)
Magazine capacity: 20 or 30 rounds	**Magazine capacity:** 20 or 30 rounds
Rate of fire: 700 rpm	**Rate of fire:** 700 rpm

also available. The butt stock can be folded to the right hand side of the receiver to reduce carrying or stowage length.

It is claimed that the balance of the rifle with the stock folded is such that firing with reasonable accuracy at combat ranges is possible. The sights are particularly easy to utilise and have luminous spot facilities for night firing. A telescopic sight mounting is provided, as is a three-round burst limiter for controlled automatic fire.

T86 5.56-mm assault rifle

The Taiwanese 5.56-mm (0.219-in) **T86** assault rifle, also known as the **Type 86**, is a weapon that generally resembles the US M16 but carries over several features of the earlier T65 assault rifle. In fact the T86 is a 'repackaged' T65, although the overall dimensions are much reduced. The T65, also a 5.56-mm weapon, became the standard Taiwanese service rifle. It was manufactured in Taiwan by the Hsin Ho Machinery Corporation using machine tools

Betraying its M16 lineage in its side profile, the Taiwanese T86 assault rifle's underslung T85 40-mm grenade launcher and trigger assembly can be seen under the barrel of the gun.

originally obtained to manufacture M16 series rifles, although the upper receiver was more typical of the commercial Stoner AR-18 rifle. The T65 rifle

remains in service, having been only partially supplemented by the T86, which is also manufactured by Hsin Ho.

The design of the T86 is described as modular to assist maintenance and logistic support, so component and

*The T86 can be equipped with a wide variety of accessories, the weapon here being seen with the bipod fitted on to the barrel behind the flash hider. In addition, a scope and **C-MAG** 100-round drum magazine have been added.*

Taiwanese troops exercise with their T86 rifles. The design owes much of its development to the expertise Taiwan received from the US during local M16 production.

assembly interchange between rifles is greatly facilitated. The 30-round curved box magazine is of the widely adopted M16 attern. The barrel is rifled for one turn in 178 mm (7 in) for the latest NATO-standard SS109 type 5.56 x 45-mm ammunition.

Accessories

Compared to the earlier T65, the T86 has a much shorter barrel with a muzzle-located flash hider and features a retractable elescopic butt-stock. The rotary locking bolt and gas operating system remain much as they were on the T65 and US M16

series. Other design features include an optical sight, mounted above what would normally be the carrying handle over the receiver. The top of the carrying handle can be used to mount various types of sight other than optical – numerous types of reflex, red dot and night sights are options. A laser target indicator can be mounted on a bracket close to the muzzle and the same location can be used to mount a high-intensity tactical flashlight for night operations. A quick-release bipod can be attached, as can a sling. The T86 can be fitted with a sound

suppressor and can also accept commercially procured 100-round C-MAG magazines from the US, although bursts should be limited when using the latter as otherwise the barrel will overheat. One further combat accessory is the locally produced 40-mm (1.57-in) T85 grenade

launcher, the Taiwanese counter-part to the US 40-mm M203.

A carbine version of the T86 has been developed with an even shorter barrel, although few details are available. Doubtless developed for use by Taiwan's special forces, it does not appear to have been produced in quantity.

SPECIFICATION	
T86	
Calibre: 5.56 mm (0.219 in)	**Rate of fire, cyclic:** 600–900 rpm
Length overall: stock extended, 880 mm (34.6 in); stock retracted, 800 mm (31.5 in)	**Muzzle velocity:** 840 m (2,756 ft) per second
Length of barrel: 375 mm (14.8 in)	**Maximum effective range:** 800 m (875 yards)
Weight: without magazine, 3.17 kg (7 lb)	**Magazine:** 30-round detachable box or 100-round C-MAG

Diemaco C8 5.56-mm assault carbine

The **Diemaco C8** 5.56-mm (0.219-in) assault carbine is a compact version of the Canadian forces' basic C7 assault rifle, itself a Diemaco product manufactured under licence from Colt of the US and based on the M16A2 rifle. The C8 features a three-position telescopic butt-stock and a shortened barrel, while retaining all normal field-replaced parts common with the C7 and M16 series rifles. The C8 carbine is issued to CAF armoured vehicle crews and to special forces and other users requiring a more compact

Above: The C8A2 carbine is a version of the C8 with a heavy barrel. A tactical mount can also be fitted, adapting the weapon to carry accessories including flashlights, lasers and forward grips.

personal weapon than the full-length C7. The C8 is also in service with the Dutch special forces and with Denmark and Norway. The **C8A1** is a lighter version with standard carbine barrel, while the **C8A2** has a heavy barrel for sustained firing and can mount the M203A1 grenade launcher and various other accessories.

In spite of the shortened barrel, in service the C8 has demonstrated accuracy nearly equivalent to the C7 and it shares most of the firing and handling characteristics of the rifle. The carbine uses the same

Left: Norwegian special forces troops armed with the Special Forces Weapon, which is derived from the basic C7 assault rifle. This variant is fitted with a multi-position butt-stock and a high-performance buffer.

A Canadian soldier in winter camouflage and armed with a C8A2 assault carbine. The C8A2 firing mechanism offers single-shot, fully automatic or three-round burst fire modes.

hammer-forged barrel as the rifle, for superior longevity and accuracy, and also accepts all C7 accessories. C8 carbines employed by UK special forces may carry a Heckler & Koch AG36 pattern 40-mm (1.57-in) grenade launcher.

CQB weapon

Canadian special forces have adopted the C8 but configured in a manner originally developed by and for US Special Forces personnel.

The latter devised what is loosely termed as a Close Quarters Battle (CQB) weapon configuration and kit that allows the user to install or remove combat accessories as a particular mission dictates. The kit associated with the shortened, lightweight **C8CQB** is carried in a protective case and includes items such as reflex, optical and night sights, a 40-mm grenade launcher, a forward hand grip, infra-red and laser target pointers, tactical lights, a sound suppressor, a sling and several other combat accessories. It should be emphasised that not all the accessories have to be used at once: they are selected to suit a particular mission and once removed are returned to the kit case.

The modified C7 with a 400 mm (15.7 in) long barrel, known as the **Special Forces Weapon**, is very similar to the US M4A1 CQB weapon, a variant of the standard M4A1 carbine. The Special Forces Weapon features 'flat top' rails over the receiver and along the forward hand guard that allow combat accessories to be rapidly installed or removed. The rails are so arranged that various forms of sight can be installed without affecting the weapon's aiming zero.

SPECIFICATION	
C8	**Weight:** 2.7 kg (6 lb) empty; 3.2 kg (7 lb) loaded
Calibre: 5.56 mm (0.219 in)	**Rate of fire, cyclic:** 900 rpm
Length overall: butt retracted, 760 mm (29.9 in); butt extended, 840 mm (33.1 in)	**Muzzle velocity:** around 920 m (3,018 ft) per second
Length of barrel: 370 mm (14.6 in)	**Magazine:** 30-round box

Kalashnikov AK-47 Assault rifle

The **Avtomat Kalashnikova AK-47** is one of the most successful and widely used small arms ever produced. It is used all over the world, and even after more than half a century variants of the type are still in production in one form or another in many countries.

The first AK-47 was designed around a short 7.62-mm (0.3-in) calibre cartridge that owed much to the German 7.92-mm (0.31-in) *kurz* round. The Red Army was often on the receiving end of the German assault rifle family (the MP 43, MP 44 and StuG 44) and asked for their own counter. The result was the 7.62-mm x 39 cartridge and the AK-47. The designer was Mikhail Kalashnikov and the rifle is universally known by his name.

The first experimental examples were issued for service during 1947, though the weapon did not enter wide scale service until the 1950s. The AK-47 gradually became the standard weapon of the Warsaw Pact. The production lines were huge, but such was the demand that most Warsaw Pact nations set up their own production facilities. From this sprang the large numbers of AK-47 sub-variants that continue to delight the gun research buff to this day.

Reliable quality

The basic AK-47 is a sound and well-made weapon that carried over few of the mass production expedients employed by its German wartime

Original AK-47
One of the most popular variants of the Kalashnikov, fitted with a folding metal buttstock.

Modernized AKM
Identifiable by different muzzle brake attachment and hand-grip on forestock

Chinese Type 56
The Chinese version of the AK-47 with its own integral bayonet seen folded under the forestock.

Built in larger numbers than any other firearm in history, the Kalashnikov assault rifle has been used in virtually every conflict fought in the second half of the twentieth century.

SPECIFICATION	
AK-47	**AKM**
Calibre: 7.62 mm (0.3 in)	**Calibre:** 7.62 mm (0.3 in)
Length: 869 mm (34.21 in)	**Length:** 876 mm (34.49 in)
Length of barrel: 414 mm (16.30 in)	**Length of barrel:** 414 mm (16.30 in)
Weight loaded: 5.13 kg (11.31 lb)	**Weight loaded:** 3.98 kg (8.77 lb)
Magazine: 30-round box	**Magazine:** 30-round box
Rate of fire: cyclic, 600 rpm	**Rate of fire:** cyclic, 600 rpm
Muzzle velocity: 710 m (2,330 ft) per second	**Muzzle velocity:** 710 m (2,330ft) per second

equivalents. The AK-47 receiver is machined, and good-quality steel is used throughout with wooden furniture as standard. The result is a weapon that can absorb any amount of hard use and mishandling.

As there are few moving parts and stripping is very simple, maintenance is also simple and can be accomplished with even a minimum of training.

Numerous variants of the basic AK-47 emerged over the years, one of the most common was a version with a folding butt. All these different versions used the same mechanism, a simple rotary bolt that was

Egyptian troops are pictured here during the 1973 Yom Kippur War. Their weapons are AKMs with the characteristic angled muzzle attachment and the handgrip grooved into the stock. The AKM was the standard Egyptian rifle for over 20 years.

cammed into corresponding grooves in the receiver by bolt cams. Operation is by gas tapped from the barrel via a gas port.

World manufacture

AK-47s were produced in China, Poland and East Germany and the operating system was copied by several countries, emerging as the Finnish Valmet and the Israeli Galil.

For all its success, it was finally admitted during the late 1950s that production of the AK-47 involved too much use of manufacturing facilities. A redesign produced the **Avtomat Kalashnikova Moderniziro-van-nyi** or **AKM**, which outwardly resembles the earlier design but is generally revised to facilitate production.

The most obvious external change is to the receiver, which is formed from a steel stamping in place of the former machined equivalent, but internally the locking system has been revised

AK-47s, AKMs and local variants of the design were made in almost every country of the Warsaw Pact. This East German infantryman would have been armed with the MPiKM version, made in the GDR. Eastern Europe was one of the major markets for export of Russian AKs, and the rugged nature of the weapons was ideally suited to the often poor standards of weapons training.

to make it simpler. There are numerous other differences but the overall changes are in manufacturing methods.

The AKM did not immediately take the place of the AK-47, being used more as a supplement to numbers. The other Warsaw Pact production lines gradually switched to the AKM,

some nations (such as Hungary) even going so far as to modify the basic design to produce their own version, which often differs in many ways from the original (the Hungarian **AKM-63** even looks different but retains the basic mechanism of the AKM). A version with a folding steel butt is known as the **AKMS**.

Huge numbers

More than 50 million AK-47s and variants have been produced, and the AK-47 and AKM will remain in service until well into the 21st century, if not beyond. This longevity must be partially attributed to widespread availability and the numbers produced, but the basic fact is that the AK-47 and AKM are both sound and tough weapons that are easy to use and simple to maintain.

The durability of the AK weapons has consequently caused a headache for security organisations around the world. It is impossible to know how many people have died from AK fire, but it must number millions.

A Shi'ite Moslem militiaman fires his AK-47 during skirmishes with Druse irregulars in West Beirut in 1987. This was during a week-long battle to gain control of Beirut's Moslem sector.

A signature weapon of the Afghan conflict, the AK-47 was the most widely used rifle of the war. Soviet Kalashnikovs were deployed along with Chinese copies and home-made Pakistani versions. This picture shows three Mujahideen guerillas; the nearest to the camera aims his AK-47 to his right, his comrade aims his Lee Enfield 303 rifle.

AK-47

Manufactured in the USSR, Eastern Europe and China, the AK-47 series is the most widely manufactured rifle in history, with well over 50 million examples having been made. Although it is not the most accurate rifle available, the AK is incredibly strong and very reliable.

Gas operation

When the bullet passes the gas block in the barrel, some of the propellant gases driving it forward are diverted into the tube above. This contains a spring-loaded piston which cycles back and forth under pressure form the gas, keeping the weapon firing while the trigger is held back.

Piston extension

The bolt carrier is built into the piston extension. A peg on the bolt engages a curved slot in the carrier.

Rear sight and fire selector bar

The rear sight is shown here in its most common position – folded flat. This is for ranges of 200 m (656 ft) or less; the slide and ramp arrangement allows it to be sighted up to 800 m (2,625 ft), but with most firefights conducted at under 30 m (98 ft), it is often irrelevant.

The fire selector bar above the trigger sets the AK to fire single shots when pushed fully down. In the middle position, the AK will fire fully automatically. On its top setting, it locks the trigger and prevents the bolt from coming all the way back. The firer can still pull back the cocking handle to see if there is a round in the chamber.

Folding bayonet

Pulling the base of the bayonet towards the muzzle and rotating it through180° will snap it into position. Various models of Chinese AKs are fitted with fixed triangular bayonets.

Above: Ammunition for the AK is officially designated Model 1943, although the Soviets had no weapon capable of firing it at that time. The cartridge gives good performance for its size, whilst the magazines are solidly built.

Wooden butt

AK-47s have been manufactured in numerous different versions. Many are fitted with collapsible metal stocks instead. This saves room – important in a vehicle or for airborne troops; but folding stocks have a tendency to wobble after a while, making accurate shooting more difficult. Some Eastern European versions of the AK have plastic stocks and foregrips. Even the wooden ones vary in appearance, from dark colours to garish plywood finishes seen especially on some Chinese versions. In 1990 the Russian army began to receive the modernised AK-74M sub-machine gun, fitted with a folding plastic butt. East German MPiKM models were fitted with a studded plastic stock.

Viet Cong guerrillas attack up a blasted slope after a mine has been triggered. Surprise attacks and ambushes were the Viet Cong's stock-in-trade and the Kalashnikov allowed operations to be conducted with minimum logistical support.

A militiaman of the mainstream Shi'ite Moslem Amal movement opens fire on Palestinian guerrillas entrenched in houses at the edge of a Beirut refugee camp. The AK-47 was widely used during the vicious 15-year civil war in Lebanon between rival Christian and PLO-backed Islamic factions.

AKs around the world

It is not only its ubiquity that has made the AK-47 weapon of choice for guerrillas around the world. Almost foolproof, it can be dropped in the mud and still fire thousands of rounds without cleaning. It can be easily maintained, spare parts are relatively easy to acquire and almost anyone – even someone without formal weapon training – can be taught to use it.

Right: This haul of AKMs was discovered in a warehouse by US troops during Operation Urgent Fury in 1983. The US was convinced of the threat posed by the Cuban and Soviet presence in Grenada, but the invasion uncovered only around 50 Cuban 'military advisers'.

Above: Syrian commandos charge across the desert during a training exercise in Saudi Arabia in September 1990. These soldiers were some of 1,500 Syrian troops deployed as part of the Arab forces protecting the country against Iraqi attack.

Left: This North Vietnamese sentry is armed with an original AK-47, as evidenced by the longer groove just forward of the magazine and the absence of any groove in the foregrip. Initially operated by the NVA, and later by guerrillas in the South, the AK-47 was the single most important weapon provided by the USSR.

Above: During the long holy war mounted against the Soviet occupation in Afghanistan, Afghan guerrillas and Islamic volunteers used almost every version of the AK-47. The Mujahideen pictured carries an AKMS captured from the enemy. This is a version of the AKM fitted with a folding butt-stock.

Right: The traditional guerrilla weapon for over 40 years, the AK-47 was the standard weapon for SWAPO, ZANLA, ZIPRA, FRELIMO, UNITA, FAPLA and other insurgent forces operating in southern Africa. Its reliability in the field, combined with its ease of use and low maintenance, resulted in a variety of modifications – such as this model with a folding stock – to make the weapon suitable for different combat situations. Despite its popularity, many guerrilla fighters have tended to rely too much on the weapon's spectacular but inaccurate firepower.

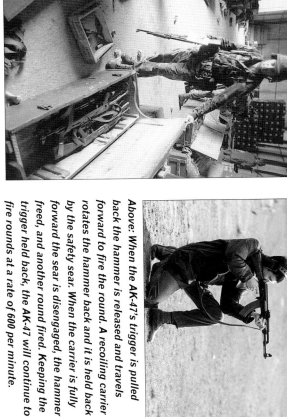

Above: When the AK-47's trigger is pulled back the hammer is released and travels forward to fire the round. A recoiling carrier rotates the hammer back and it is held back by the safety sear. When the carrier is fully forward the sear is disengaged, the hammer freed, and another round fired. Keeping the trigger held back, the AK-47 will continue to fire rounds at a rate of 600 per minute.

SPECIFICATION

AK-47
Calibre: 762 mm (0.3 in)
Length: 880 mm (34.6 in)
Length of barrel: 415 mm (16.3 in)
Weight: 4.3 kg (9.5 lb) loaded
Muzzle velocity: 715 m/s
Rate of fire, cyclic: 600 rds/min
Feed: 30-round detachable box magazine

AKM
Calibre: 762 mm (0.3 in)
Length: 880 mm (34.6 in)
Length of barrel: 415 mm (16.3 in)
Weight: 3.86 kg (8.5 lb) loaded
Muzzle velocity: 715 m/s
Rate of fire, cyclic: 600 rds/min
Feed: 30-round detachable box magazine

AK-74M
Calibre: 5.45 mm (0.215 in)
Length: 943 mm (37.1 in) butt extended
Length of barrel: 415 mm (16.3 in)

Weight: 3.7 kg (8.2 lb) loaded
Muzzle velocity: 900 m/s
Rate of fire, cyclic: 650 rds/min
Feed: 30-round plastic box magazine

AKS-74U
Calibre: 5.45 mm (0.215 in)
Length: 730 mm (28.7 in) butt extended
Length of barrel: 206.5 mm (8.1 in)
Weight: 3.2 kg (7 lb) loaded
Muzzle velocity: 735 m/s
Rate of fire, cyclic: 650–735 rds/min
Feed: 30-round curved box magazine

AK101
Calibre: 5.56 mm (0.219 in)
Length: 943 mm (37.1 lb) butt extended
Length of barrel: 415 mm (16.3 in)
Weight: 3.63 kg (8 lb) loaded
Muzzle velocity: 910 m/s
Rate of fire, cyclic: 600 rds/min
Feed: 30-round plastic box magazine

Kalashnikov AK-74 Assault rifle

Left: A Soviet rifleman circa 1988, dressed in leaf pattern camouflage, with a gas mask and NBC oversmock. He is armed with a standard AK-74 rifle, which by this time had replaced the AK-47 in front line Soviet military units.

Right: An AK-74 (top), with an AK-47 for comparison beneath. The AK-74 has a skeleton butt, but note the prominent muzzle brake and the brown plastic magazine. Note also the size difference between the two cartridges.

The Soviet Union was surprisingly slow in following the Western adoption of small-calibre cartridges for its future weapon designs. Perhaps the huge numbers of AK-47s and AKMs already in service made such a change a low priority, so it was not until the early 1970s that any intimation of a new Warsaw Pact cartridge was given. In time it emerged that the new cartridge had a calibre of 5.45 x 39 mm and the first examples of a new weapon to fire it were noted.

In time the weapon emerged as the **AK-74**, which entered full-scale production to meet the requirements of the Red Army; as with earlier designs, variants were manufactured in other Warsaw Pact countries.

The AK-74 is basically an AKM revised to suit the new cartridge. It is almost identical to the AKM in appearance, weight and overall dimensions. Some changes, such as a plastic magazine, have been introduced and there is a prominent muzzle brake. There are versions with the usual wooden stock and with a folding metal stock.

One matter relating to the AK-74 that deserves special mention is the bullet used. To gain maximum effect from the high-velocity 5.45-mm (0.215-in) calibre bullet, the designers have adopted a design that is very effective but outlawed by international convention, for the steel-cored projectile has a hollow tip and the centre of gravity far to the rear. This has the effect that when the nose strikes a target it deforms, allowing the weight towards the rear to maintain the forward impetus and so tumble the bullet. In this way the small-calibre bullet can have an effect on a target far in excess of its cross sectional area. Some high-velocity projectiles can display this nasty effect, but on some, such as the M193 5.56-mm (0.219-in) cartridge, it is an unintended by-product. On the Soviet 5.45-mm the effect has been deliberately designed into the projectile.

New Kalashnikovs

The end of the Soviet era has seen cosmetic modification of the Kalashnikov design, and it is being sold for export under 'Series 100' designations. The **AK101** fires the 5.56 x 45 NATO rounds, while the **AK 102** is a short-barrelled variant. The **AK103** fires the original 7.62 x 39 cartridge used by the AK-47, while the **AK105** is a short barrelled update of the AK-74 firing the high-velocity 5.45 x 39 round.

The AK-74's combat debut came during the conflict in Afghanistan in the 1980s, where captured examples soon fell into the hands of the Mujahideen.

SPECIFICATION	
AK-74	**Magazine:** 30-round box
Calibre: 5.45 mm (0.215 in)	**Rate of fire:** 650 rpm
Length: 930 mm (36.61 in)	**Muzzle velocity:** 900 m (2,955 ft) per
Length of barrel: 400 mm (15.75 in)	second
Weight unloaded: 3.6 kg (7.94 lb)	

Armalite AR-15/M16
Assault rifle

The **M16** assault rifle was created by the noted designer Eugene Stoner. Derived from the Armalite AR-10, a revolutionary full-power battle rifle developed in the mid-1950s, the new design emerged as a 5.56-mm (0.22-in) calibre weapon known as the **Armalite AR 15**.

The AR-15 was submitted for a competition to decide the new standard rifle for the US armed forces. Before the competition was decided, the British army took a batch of 10,000, making it one of the first customers to purchase significant quantities of the new design. The US Air Force bought soon afterwards in 1961.

Standard rifle

The AR-15 was selected by the US Army to become its new standard rifle, the M16. Production was then switched to the Colt Firearms Company, which took out a production and sales contract with Armalite.

The M16 became the **M16A1** in 1966 with the addition of a bolt closure device, fitted as the result of experience in Vietnam. There had been a number of problems encountered during initial fielding, especially in combat situations, but better training, preventive maintenance, and several design changes resulted in the weapon that has become the standard issue rifle of the US Army.

Since then more than three million M16s have been manufactured, and the rifle has been widely issued and sold to nations all around the world. Numerous developments have been produced and tried,

The original M16 became famous as an icon of the Vietnam War. The standard rifle was used by tens of thousands of infantrymen, but the short-barrelled, sliding-stocked Colt Commando was used primarily by special operations forces.

including a light machine gun variant with a heavy barrel and a bipod, and short-barrel versions for special forces.

Operation

The M16 is a gas-operated weapon that uses a rotary bolt locking system. A carrying handle over the receiver also acts as the rear-sight base, and nylonite is used for all the furniture. The plastic gave it something of the feeling of a toy to soldiers accustomed to the heavy wood of previous generation weapons like the M14, but the M16 was far from a toy. The use of 5.56-mm ammunition meant that the soldier could carry more rounds than before, and the reduced power of the rounds meant that for the first time ordinary soldiers could be issued with a fully automatic weapon.

M16A2

In the 1980s a product-improved version of the rifle was introduced. The most obvious change is the redesigned handguard with a tougher round contour which provides a better grip. Less obvious is the heavier barrel with a 1 in 7 twist to fire NATO-standard SS109-type (M855) ammunition which is also fired from the M249 Squad Automatic Weapon (SAW). This increases the range and penetration.

The **M16A2** will also shoot the older M193 ammunition

Above: The rifle used to develop the US Army's 'Land Warrior' infantry system for the twenty-first century is the M4 carbine version of the M16 assault rifle.

M16-armed troopers in combat near Dak To during Operation Hawthorne, during the Vietnam War in 1966.

designed for a 1 in 12 twist. It also incorporates a burst control device that limits automatic fire to three-round bursts, which increases accuracy while greatly reducing wasteful ammunition expenditure.

M4/M4A1

The **M4/M4A1** 5.56-mm Carbine is a carbine variant of the

M16A2. It is designed to provide heavyweight firepower to individual soldiers working in close quarters. The M4 Carbine shares most (over 80 per cent) of its parts with the M16A2. The M4 Carbine has replaced 45-cal sub-machine guns and some pistols with troops such as armour crews and special operations forces.

SPECIFICATION	
M16A2 Assault rifle	less than 200 m (656 ft)
Calibre: 5.56 mm (0.22 in)	**Muzzle velocity:** 853 m (2,800 ft) per second
Length: 1006 mm (39.63 in)	
Barrel length: 508 mm (20 in)	**Rate of fire:** 800 rounds per minute cyclic; 45 rounds per minute semi-auto; 90 rounds per minute burst fire
Weight: loaded: 3.99 kg (8.79 lb)	
Range: maximum 3600 m (11,811 ft); effective 550 m (1,804 ft); normal combat range	
	Magazine capacity: 30 rounds

Armalite AR-15/M16

Nylonite buttstock

Rear sling swivel

Action spring

Take-down pin

Cocking handle

Selector lever

Cocking lever

Pistol grip

Rear sight

Trigger

Sear

Hammer spring

Hammer

Magazine

Carrying handle

Magazine platform

Bolt

7.62-mm 0(.30-in) round

Magazine spring

Bolt head

Pivot pin

5.56-mm (0.22-in) calibre barrel

Gas pipe

Nylonite hand guard

Forward sling swivel

Fixed post foresight

Flash suppressor

Gas port

M16 in action

The prototype M16 used exceptionally clean ammunition, and it quickly became known as the 'no-clean' rifle. However, service ammunition created much more fouling, which meant that inexperienced troops who did not clean their weapons regularly experienced endless stoppages. Professional troops had few such troubles.

Ammunition

The main advantage of adopting a smaller-calibre rifle like the M16 (ammunition and magazine at right) is that any soldier so armed can carry twice as much ammunition as one equipped with a full-power 7.62-mm (0.30-in) rifle.

Right: The AR-15 (far right) was developed from the AR-10 rifle of the 1950s (near right). The AR-10, chambered for the 7.62-mm NATO round, was one of the first rifles to make extensive use of plastic and aluminium parts.

Below: By releasing the take-down pin and swivelling the fore-end on the pivot pin, the working parts of the M16 rifle become easy to extract at any time for cleaning, maintenance or repair.

5.56 x 45-mm M193 cartridges

Ten-round ammo clips

Magazine platform

40-round magazine

Five-round ammo clips

7.62 x 51-mm NATO cartridges

Magazine platform

20-round magazine

SA80 British Army rifle

The British Army's standard rifle is the **SA80**, more formally known as the **L85A1** in its initial form. This is accurate and in theory is easy to maintain, and is a pleasure to shoot. Its light recoil allows the soldier to keep the weapon on target with the minimum of problems, and a special optical sight gives the soldier a clear view even in poor light. The most striking feature of the SA80 is its compactness. The 'bullpup' layout means that the magazine is located behind the trigger group, which opens the way to the inclusion of a relatively long barrel into a weapon of small overall dimensions. The barrel of the SA80 is only a little shorter than that of the SLR (Self-Loading Rifle) it has replaced, but the complete weapon is 30 per cent shorter. As a result, the SA80 is easy to handle, especially in confined spaces such as an APC.

The compact size of the SA80 is important for the British soldier: thus the SA80 is ideal

for troops entering action in the Warrior infantry fighting vehicle, which was used for the movement of British infantry in the course of Operation Desert Storm.The SA80 also works well in house-to-house fighting, and

its sling arrangement has proved popular; the SA80 can be slung across the chest, the back or to one side to leave the soldier's hands free, but still ensure that the weapon can still be brought into action without undue delay, simply by unclipping the sling at the top.

Because of its 'bullpup' design, the SA80 ejects its empty cases from a port opposite the firer's face, so it can only be fired right-handed mode.

SUSAT sight

The SA80 is one of the first combat rifles to be issued with a telescopic sight as a standard fitting. This SUSAT (Sight Unit, Small Arms, Trilux) gives x4 magnification and comes with

The ergonomic nature of the SA80 suits the weapon well to the demands of modern warfare by aiding fast movement and prone firing.

a comfortable rubber eyepiece through which the soldier sees a pointer (dark in daylight, illuminated by the radioactive Trilux lamp in poor light) that he places over the target.

A selector lever set at R (Repetition) provides the soldier with a single-shot capability, while the A (Automatic) setting provides for continuous fire as long as the trigger is pulled and there are rounds in the magazine.

The SA80 fires a 5.56-mm (0.22-in) round that is light enough for each man to carry

Shown here, infantrymen carrying the SA80 on patrol. This rifle has become a signature weapon of the Northern Ireland conflict.

SPECIFICATION	
L85A1 (SA80)	**Magazine:** 30-round detachable box
Calibre: 5.56 mm (0.22 in) x 45 mm NATO	**Rate of fire, cyclic:** 610–775 rounds per minute
Length: 85 mm (30.91 in)	**Muzzle velocity:** 940 m (287 ft) per second
Length of barrel: 518 mm (20.39 in)	**Range:** 300 m (984 ft) typical and 500 m (545 yards) effective
Weight: 3.80 kg (8.38 lb) without magazine and optical sight	
Weight loaded: 4.98 kg (10.98 lb)	

eight 30-round magazines plus an ammunition bandolier. Light as it is, the bullet is effective at up to 500 m (1,640 ft), although in practice small arms fire is rarely used at ranges over 300 m (984 ft). A strong wind can affect the flight of the bullet, however, and at long ranges the soldier needs to adjust his aim to compensate for this factor.

The SA80 replaces three weapons in the infantry armoury: the SLR, the 9-mm Sterling sub-machine gun and the 7.62-mm (0.31-in) General Purpose Machine-Gun. To take the GPMG's place there is another version of the SA80 which has a heavy barrel and a bipod. Known as the **Light Support Weapon**, this **L86A1** is otherwise virtually identical to the SA80, so the soldier only needs to be familiar with one weapon instead of three.

The SA80 assault rifle has proved far from popular in service, and first-line use has uncovered a number of problems. Much of the SA80's mechanism was therefore redesigned by Heckler & Koch to create the **L85A2** version. This is more reliable than the L85A1, but there have been complaints that reliability is still poor under dusty conditions.

Left: The small size of the SA80 is an advantage for troops who typically ride into battle in the confined troop compartment of armoured personnel carriers.

Above: A problem faced by the designers of small arms is the need to make weapons usable under all conditions, including those typical of high-technology battlefields where NBC protection may be worn.

Armalite AR-18
Paramilitary rifle

Once the Armalite concern had cleared its design desks of the AR-15, with production under way by Colt Firearms of the M16 series, it decided to look to the future for new products. With the 5.56-mm (0.22-in) round well established, Armalite decided that what was needed was a notably simple and therefore reliable and easily produced weapon that could fire this cartridge. While the AR-15 was a sound weapon, it was not easy to produce without sophisticated machine tools, and throughout much of the world these machine tools were not available. Thus the need for a weapon which could be simply produced by Third World nations was recognised, and a drastic revision of the AR-15 design was undertaken.

The result was the **Armalite AR-18**, which is very basically an AR-15 adapted for manufacture by the now-familiar production expedients

This AR-18 was originally manufactured in Japan but was captured from the IRA in Belfast. It is the standard production model with a folding butt.

of pressed steel, plastics and castings. For all these expedients the AR-18 is a sound design that is easy to produce, maintain and use. In general

appearance and layout the AR-18 is similar to the AR-15, but the stamped steel receiver gives it a bulkier outline. The plastic butt is designed to fold

alongside the receiver for stowage or firing from the hip.

Completed design

Once the AR-18 design was complete, Armalite attempted to find purchasers, but with the AK-47 and the M16A1 flooding the world's markets, there were few takers. An arrangement to produce the AR-18 in Japan fell through and for some years the design

was in abeyance. Then the Sterling Armaments Company of the UK took out a licence, undertaking some production and at one time moving production to Singapore. Some sales were then made locally, but more importantly the local defence industry took the design as the basis for its own weapon designs, the AR-18 now living on disguised in many forms and under various labels.

SPECIFICATION	
AR-18	**Magazine:** 20-, 30- and 40-round detachable box
Calibre: 5.56 mm (0.22 in)	**Rate of fire:** 800 rpm cyclic
Length: 940 mm (37 in) extended or 737 mm (29 in) folded	**Muzzle velocity:** 1000 m (3,280 ft) per second
Weight loaded: 3.48 kg (7.67 lb) with 20-round magazine	

Ruger Mini-14 Paramilitary and special forces rifle

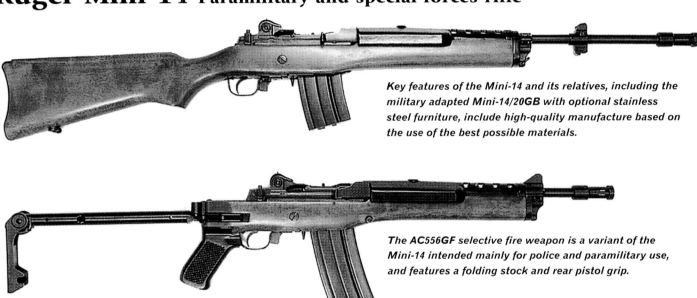

Key features of the Mini-14 and its relatives, including the military adapted Mini-14/20GB with optional stainless steel furniture, include high-quality manufacture based on the use of the best possible materials.

The AC556GF selective fire weapon is a variant of the Mini-14 intended mainly for police and paramilitary use, and features a folding stock and rear pistol grip.

When it was first produced in 1973, the **Ruger Mini-14** marked a significant turn away from the mass production methods introduced during World War II, towards the fine finish and attention to detail that was formerly the hallmark of the gunsmith's art. The Mini-14 is an unashamed example of how guns used to be made before the concepts of steel stampings and die-cast alloys came upon the scene.

Variant

From a design viewpoint, the Mini-14 is a 5.56-mm (0.22-in) version of the 0.3-in (7.62-mm) Garand M1 service rifle of World War II. By adopting the Garand action, Ruger managed to combine a sound and well-engineered design with the

ammunition of a new technology. Allied to craftsmanship and a deliberate appeal to those who look for that something extra in a weapon, the result is a remarkable little rifle.

In appearance the Mini-14 has the characteristics of a previous age. The materials used are all high quality and in an age where plastics have now taken over, the furniture is all manufactured from high-grade walnut. But visual appeal has not been allowed to take precedence over functional safety, for the Mini-14 has been carefully engineered to prevent dust and debris entering the action. Some degree of visual appeal has been allowed to affect the finish, for the weapon has

been carefully blued all over, and there is even a stainless steel version that sells very well in the Middle East.

Export

The Mini-14 has not yet been adopted by any major armed forces but it has been sold to such establishments as police forces, personal bodyguard units and to many special forces who prefer a well-engineered and balanced weapon to the usual 'tinny' modern products. To suit the

requirements of some armed forces Ruger later developed a special version that should appeal to many soldiers. This is the **Mini-14/20GB** with a bayonet lug. Police forces have been catered for by the introduction of the **AC-566** with glass fibre furniture, and another innovation is the **AC556GF** with a folding stock and a shorter barrel. The two versatile AC-556 designs can be used to either fire on single shot or full automatic for bursts.

SPECIFICATION	
Mini-14	**Magazine:** 55-, 20- or 30-round detachable box
Calibre: 5.56 mm (0.22 in)	**Rate of fire:** 40 rpm
Length: 946mm (37.24 in) overall	**Muzzle Velocity:** 1005m (3,300 ft) per second
Weight loaded: 3.1 kg (6.8 lb) with 20-round magazine	

SSG 69 Sniper rifle

SSG 69 is the Austrian army's designation for the Steyr-Mannlicher sniper rifle the service adopted in 1969, the SSG prefix standing for *Scharfschützengewehr* (sharp-shooters' rifle). It has been widely adopted as both a military and police marksman's rifle and is available in numerous versions, from the 'Police' type with extra-heavy barrel and oversize match-type bolt handle to the latest sniper/sports rifle version, the **SSG P11**.

However, the fundamental design of the rifle dates back to the beginning of the 20th century: the bolt and magazine are little changed from a weapon made by Steyr for the Greek army, the Mannlicher-Schoenauer Model 1903. The bolt is manually operated, locked by six symmetrically positioned rear locking lugs.

Rear locking lugs

Rear lock-up, pioneered so successfully on the famous Lee-Enfield, is theoretically dangerous as the whole length of the bolt – rather than just the bolt head – is placed under compressive stress during firing. Yet in practice neither the Mannlicher nor the Lee-Enfield has suffered notable problems and the benefit is appreciated by many shooters: the cartridges feed directly into the chamber without having to traverse space for forward-locking lugs.

Loading is thus smoother and faster, aided by the spool magazine that feeds more consistently than a stacked, spring-loaded magazine. On the other hand, some shooters believe the multiple lug system to be less accurate, and it can make it harder to use re-loaded brass.

The barrel is 650 mm (26 in) long with a heavy contour and a target crown. The rifling consists of four lands and grooves, and the twist rate is one turn in 305 mm (12 in). The barrel is cold-forged, that is, the tube of metal that will form the barrel is placed over a mandrel (a steel bar with the rifling in raised relief) and a rotary hammer is used to forge the barrel both internally and externally. The hammering hardens the barrel internally and externally as it forms the rifling.

Spiral-shaped barrel

This process was developed by Steyr and has since been employed by many other manufacturers. It gives the barrel a characteristic spiral appearance and there is a faintly discernible taper from breech to bore. The barrel is screwed into the receiver for 57 mm (2.24 in), which is farther than on most other rifles. Once the barrel is in place, a concentric press is used to apply considerable pressure round the join between barrel and receiver, which makes for a fantastic, rigid action, albeit making it next to impossible to change the barrel other than by returning it to the factory.

The bolt action of the SSG 69 is pleasantly smooth and even more so now it is teflon-coated. A cocking indicator is provided. The two-position safety is a sliding type safety catch on the right-hand side of the receiver. With the safety 'on', the bolt

cannot be operated, which is a mixed blessing. However, the safety is at least silent, so there is no tell-tale 'click' when the firer is ready to take a shot. The safety can be operated whether or not the weapon is cocked.

The P11 is optionally available with a double trigger, which is really suitable only if the firer has small hands. The modular assembly of the rifle permits a change in trigger assembly very easily, although second assemblies are not cheap.

The standard magazine holds five rounds and is made of plastic with a transparent plate so that the firer can see how many rounds are inside it. Unlike most magazines with detachable floorplates, the rounds are directly on top of each other and are held securely so bullet tips cannot get damaged during

firing. Also available is a 10-round magazine, but this protrudes from the weapon for some way. The accuracy of the SSG 69 is typical of that of modern sniper rifles. At 100 yards a competent shot can group all five shots in less than 15 mm (0.6 in) when firing commercially manufactured ammunition.

The Steyr SSG 69 rifle uses a Kahles ZF69 telescopic sight graduated up to 800 m (875 yards) – this example is not fitted with the usual 'iron' sights. The SSG 69 uses an unusual five-round rotary magazine, but can also be fitted with a 10-round box magazine.

The Steyr SSG 69 rifle is the standard Austrian army sniper's rifle, and is used by mountain troops as it is possible for a single sniper to virtually seal a mountain pass against advancing troops for long periods. The SSG 69 is robust enough to survive in such conditions and retain its accuracy.

SPECIFICATION	
SSG 69	(10.14 lb)
Calibre: 7.62-mm (0.3-in)	**Muzzle velocity:** 860 m
Length overall:1140 mm (44.9 in),	(2,821 ft) per second
Length of barrell: 650 mm (25.6 in)	**Magazine capacity:** 5-round rotary or
Weight: empty, with sight 4.6 kg	10-round box

FN Model 30-11 Sniper rifle

The **Fabrique Nationale Model 30** is an entirely conventional Mauser-action rifle used by the Belgian army and many other military forces and law enforcement agencies as a sniper rifle.

The connection between Mauser and FN dates back to 1891, when FN began to manufacture Mauser rifles under licence for the Belgian army. Subsequent production for export was eventually agreed with Mauser after the Belgian company cheerfully sold thousands of rifles to China and South America too, an action contrary to the spirit, if not the letter, of its agreement with Mauser. From 1897 to 1940 over half a million Mauser-action rifles were made in Belgium for delivery to armies all over the world. Manufacture was interrupted by the German occupation during World War II, and when it resumed in 1946, the vast quantities of war-surplus weapons then available made it difficult to sell new bolt-action weapons except to specialist markets, hence the company's production of sports/sniper rifles.

Elderly but capable

The Model 30 was originally produced in 1930 and was itself derived from a Mauser type of 1898, slightly modified to become the Model 24.

Above: The FN Model 30-11 can be fitted with a wide range of accessories. The large sight seen here is a standard NATO infra-red night vision sight, and the bipod fitted is that used on the FN MAG machine gun.

The Belgian FN Model 30-11 rifle was originally produced for police and paramilitary use, but many are in military hands. The example seen here is fitted with target sights. The odd butt shape results from the provisions made for a wide degree of individual adjustment that can be incorporated.

Production of the Model 30 resumed in 1950. The sniper rifle version is essentially a standard Gewehr 98 type of rifle made to a much higher standard than an issue weapon. The military sniper rifle is chambered for 7.62-mm (0.3-in) x 51-mm NATO ammunition and is intended to shoot the highest quality commercial rounds. Most of the rifles are sold with the five-round internal magazine, but a detachable 10-round box magazine is also made.

The **Model 30-11** features a heavy barrel and the Mauser forward-locking bolt action. This is considered by some shooters to be inherently the safest and most accurate action. The Model 30-11 has an adjustable stock with spacers so that the weapon can be tailored to the size of the shooter. The standard sighting system is Fabrique Nationale's 28-mm telescope with x4 magnification plus aperture sights. Accessories include a bipod (the same as that of the world famous FN MAG 7.62-mm machine gun), additional butt spacer plates, a sling and a carrying case. The scope mounts will accept NATO standard kit including IR night sights.

SPECIFICATION	
Model 30-11	**Weight empty:** 4.85 kg (10.69 lb)
Calibre: 7.62-mm (0.3-in)	**Muzzle velocity:** 850 m (2,788 ft) per second
Length overall: 1117 mm (44 in)	
Length of barrel: 502 mm (19.8 in)	**Feed:** 5-round box

MAS FR-F1 & F2 Sniper rifles

MAS (Manufacture d'Armes, St Etienne) is now part of the GIAT (Groupement Industrial des Armaments Terrestres) conglomerate. The MAS company has produced most of the French army's small arms from the 1920s, and its current sniper rifle is a development of

the standard service rifle of the French army during World War II. The French army today issues sniper rifles much more widely than most Western armies. Instead of issuing a few sniper rifles to each infantry battalion, the French (like the former Soviet armies) have a dedicated sniper

in each rifle section (or squad, in US terminology). A section

comprises eight men armed with 5.56-mm (0.219-in) FA-MAS

SPECIFICATION	
FR-F1	**Weight:** empty 5.42 kg (11.95 lb)
Calibre: 7.5-mm (0.295-in) or 7.62-mm (0.3-in)	**Muzzle velocity:** 852 m (2,795 ft) per second
Length overall: 1138 mm (44.8 in)	**Feed:** 10-round box
Length of barrel: 552 mm (21.73 in)	

assault rifles, one AA-52 light machine gun, and a sniper (FR-F1 or FR-F2).

Well-proved concept

The **Fusil à Répétition F1** was developed in 1964 by the MAS bureau in general and designer Jean Fournier in particular, and manufacture began in 1966. Like the MAS 36 service rifle on which it is based, the F1 is chambered for the French army's standard 7.5-mm (0.295-in) x 54 cartridge, but is also available in 7.62-mm (0.3-in) x 51 NATO calibre. The F1 or **Tireur d'élite** has a free-floating barrel projecting from a half-length wooden stock and a distinctive pistol grip behind the trigger. A muzzle brake and bipod are fitted as standard. Wooden spacers can be used to adjust the length of the butt and cheek pieces can be

added. The Model 1953 L.806 telescopic sight is the service issue scope, but its x3.8 magnification has been criticised as insufficiently powerful for sniping. On the other hand, some units in the French army, most notably the Foreign Legion, devote enormous effort to rifle shooting and their standard of accuracy is commendable. FR-F1s used by French law enforcement agencies use more powerful scopes such as the variable (x1.5 to x6) Zeiss Diavari and others.

The **FR-F2** was introduced in 1984 and is available only in 7.62-mm NATO, thus giving a French rifle section three types of non-interchangeable ammunition for their weapons The F2 features a stronger bipod mounted on a yoke ahead of the barrel. The barrel is encased in a plastic

In this photograph the French sniper is using the telescopic sight of his FR-F1 as an observation aid, resting the barrel on a tree branch. He would never fire the weapon from such a stance, for accuracy would be minimal.

sleeve intended to reduce the 'mirage' effect generated by the heat of the barrel after repeated firing.

The F1 is also available to sports shooters in the **Tir Sportif**

or **Type B** version, which is distinguishable by the absence of the bipod and an aperture sight positioned above the receiver on a bar mounting – this is for target shooting.

Sako TRG Finnish bolt-action sniping rifles

Finnish sniping rifles have long been designed and manufactured by Sako of Riihimaki, a concern now owned by Beretta of Italy but still marketing under its own name. Their current sniping rifle is the **TRG**.

The Sako TRG is a conventional bolt-action repeating rifle, Sako being of the opinion that for first-round effectiveness and accuracy the bolt action cannot be bettered. Two specialist sniping versions are available, the **TRG 22** firing 0.308 Winchester (7.62 x 51-mm NATO) cartridges, and the **TRG 42**, firing 0.338 (8.6 x 71-mm) Lapua Magnum cartridges. The TRG 42 is also available chambered for 0.300 Winchester Magnum ammunition. The TRG 22 and TRG 42 are improved models of the earlier 7.62-mm calibre **TRG 21** and 0.338-in calibre (Lapua Magnum) **TRG**

41, with various design enhancements, including features such as an improved stock adjustment, a revised muzzle brake and an improved bipod. The receiver is machined from solid steel. It incorporates three locking lugs for maximum strength, while the bolt lift angle of 60° provides minimum bolt movement. An oversize bolt handle is provided for fast and easy operation. All models of the TRG are normally delivered without 'iron' sights as they are intended for use with either optical or electronic day/night sights, as selected by the user.

Cartridges are fed from a double-stack detachable box magazine. The TRG 22 holds 10

The Sako TRG seen on its bipod. The receiver is made from forged steel, while the heavy barrel is also cold-forged and has a combined muzzle brake and flash hider. An aluminium skeleton frame is used.

rounds, the TRG 42 five, the 0.300 Winchester Magnum TRG 42 version holds seven rounds.

Adjustable stock

The multiple-adjustment butt-stock is made from polyurethane and is reinforced through the use of an aluminium skeleton. Spacers allow the cheek-piece to be adjustable in height and infinitely adjustable in windage and pitch. The butt-plate is adjustable both for distance and angle through the use of spacers and is also adjustable in height and pitch, all factors that enable users to virtually 'customise' their

own rifle. Stocks are available for right- and left-handed users and may be olive-green or black.

The double-stage trigger pull is adjustable from 1-2.5 kg (2.2-5.5 lb). It is adjustable in length and horizontal or vertical pitch. If necessary, the entire trigger assembly, including the trigger guard, can be removed without disturbing the rest of the rifle. The safety catch, which is silent in operation, is located inside the trigger guard, in front of the trigger. The safety locks the trigger and the bolt in a closed position with the firing pin blocked from the primer cap.

SPECIFICATION	
TRG 22	
Calibre: 7.62 mm (0.3 in)	**Weight:** empty, without spacers, 4.7 kg (10.36 lb)
Length overall: without butt-plate spacers, 1150 mm (45.28 in)	**Muzzle velocity:** 900 m (2,953 ft) per second
Length of barrel: 660 mm (26 in)	**Feed:** 10-round box magazine

Hecate II French 12.7-mm bolt-action anti-materiel rifle

The **Hecate II** 12.7-mm (0.5-in) calibre sniping rifle can be considered really more of an anti-materiel rifle for use against high-value systems targets rather than individual personnel.

A conventional bolt-action repeating rifle, the Hecate II was originally designed and manufactured by PGM Precision of Poisy, France, a well-known manufacturer of sporting and police rifles. PGM Precision expanded into the field of sniping rifles during the late 1980s, with a range of designs adopted by French and other European police forces. The 12.7-mm Hecate II entered production in 1988. A marketing agreement was subsequently drawn up between PGM Precision and FN Herstal of Belgium who now market the Hecate II rifle under their own name.

Intervention origins

The Hecate II 12.7-mm sniping rifle is based on the smaller-calibre PGM Precision Intervention sniping rifle, but for the Hecate II the overall scale was enlarged significantly to accommodate the new 12.7 x 99-mm calibre (0.5-in Browning) cartridge. Using this cartridge the Hecate II is claimed to be highly effective at combat ranges up to 1500 m

The Hecate II is seen here with an optical sight. The gun is primarily designed as an anti-materiel weapon rather than a straightforward anti-personnel rifle.

(1,640 yards), although performance will depend on the particular type of ammunition involved. The magazine capacity is seven rounds and the stock assembly can be rapidly removed for transport.

The match-grade heavy barrel, which is 700 mm (27.56 in) long, is fluted for both rigidity and cooling reasons and is fitted with a large single-baffle muzzle brake assembly which is claimed to be so efficient that the recoil forces imposed on the firer are no greater than those produced by a 7.62-mm (0.3-in) rifle.

However, the side blast from the brake ports is considerable when experienced by nearby personnel. The weapon's receiver is made from high-quality aircraft-grade aluminum.

To assist in carrying the Hecate II a collapsible carrying handle is provided; the wooden butt-stock, itself fitted with a cheek piece, is also removable without the need of any specialist tools.

Once the weapon is in the firing position an optional and adjustable stock support can be added under the stock assembly both to provide a measure of steadiness while aiming and to assume the overall weight when the Hecate II rifle is in the 'sentry' or target observation position.

Early Hecate II models employed an M60-pattern folding bipod, although this was changed to other fully adjustable types on later models. The bipod is attached to the receiver fore-end. A monopod can also be fitted to the rear of the weapon, attached to a point beneath the butt, which helps to reduce the strain on the user's upper body if they are using the rifle for long periods.

Other features for the firer include a bolt handle that can be removed instantly for security or other reasons, while the sear safety is moved to the right of the receiver.

Suppressed version

The **Hecate II Suppressed** model is provided with an oversized sound suppressor secured in place over the barrel once the muzzle brake has been removed. The weight, without an optical sight, is increased to approximately 17.24 kg (38 lb). The Hecate II is known to be in service with the French army and may also be in service with others. It has been marketed in the US, primarily for use by police and internal security (IS) organisations.

SPECIFICATION	
Hecate II	**Length of barrel:** 700 mm (27.6 in)
Calibre: 12.7 mm (0.5 in) Browning	**Weight:** around 13.5 kg (29.76 lb), according to configuration
Length overall: 1380 mm (54.33 in); with stock disassembled, 1110 mm (43.3 in)	**Feed:** seven-round magazine

Gepard Hungarian sniping and anti-materiel rifles

There are three basic models in the Hungarian Gepard (cheetah) sniping rifle family, their main differences being found in the type of action or the calibre.

The 12.7-mm (0.5-in) **Gepard M1** and **M1A1** sniping rifles are single-shot weapons. The barrel is carried within a tubular cradle, which also mounts the bipod. A padded butt-plate is attached to the barrel extension. The pistol grip acts as the bolt handle and is attached to a multiple-lug breech block. To load, the pistol grip is partly rotated to unlock the breech block and then withdrawn, exposing the chamber. The cartridge is inserted and the breech block replaced, the hammer is cocked and then the trigger pressed. There is a grip for the disengaged hand on the butt and a cheek pad. There is an adjustable bipod, and a high-efficiency muzzle brake is fitted. The usual aiming system is a 12x60 telescopic sight; night sights can also be employed.

Back-pack frame

The Gepard M1A1 is basically similar to the Gepard M1 but is mounted on a back-pack frame that can double as an aiming mount for use on soft ground or snow. The bipod remains attached to the tubular cradle but it is folded up when the gun is mounted on its back-pack frame for carriage. The Gepard M1 and M1A1 rifles are both chambered for the Soviet 12.7 x 107-mm cartridge. Maximum effective aimed range at a vehicle-sized target is approximately 2000 m (2,187 yards).

Anti-materiel rifles

Although based on the Gepard M1 sniping rifle, the **Gepard M2** and **M2A1** are intended for use as anti-materiel rifles and differ mainly in having a semi-

shortened version of the M2 intended for airborne and special forces use. The size of the weapon is also said to make it ideal for operations in urban areas, where space to use a larger or longer sniping rifle may be greatly limited. The M2A1 employs a 6x42 scope but has

Above: The Gepard M1 has the ability to penetrate light concrete and brick walls. The barrel is carried in a distinctive tubular cradle and the weapon can be mounted on a Russian PKM machine gun mount.

Left: The 12.7-mm (0.5-in) Gepard M2 self-loading rifle is effective at destroying lightly armoured vehicles and helicopters at a range of up to 800 m (875 yards). A 5- or 10-round magazine is carried.

automatic action. Using a positively locked long recoil system, the Gepard M2 and M2A1 can feed Soviet 12.7 x 107-mm rounds from a five- or 10-round box magazine located next to the pistol grip and the trigger assembly.

All other aspects of the Gepard M2 are otherwise similar to the Gepard M1 and they fire the same ammunition, although the M2's effective aimed range is reduced to between 1000 and 1200 m (1,094 and 1,312 yards).

The Gepard M2A1 is a

no provision for a night sight. The 14.5-mm (0.57-in) calibre **Gepard M3** is a self-loading bipod-mounted weapon designed to provide accurate heavy-calibre fire against lightly armoured vehicles, helicopters and field defences at longer ranges. Effectively an enlarged version of the M2, the M3 is chambered for the 14.5 x 114-mm Soviet cartridge and is recoil-operated, incorporating a hydraulic buffer and a more effective muzzle brake so that the felt recoil from the firing

SPECIFICATION	
Gepard M1 **Calibre:** 12.7 mm (0.5 in) **Length overall:** 1570 mm (61.8 in) **Weight:** 19 kg (41.89 lb) **Muzzle velocity:** 842 m (2,762 ft) per second **Feed:** manual, single shot **Gepard M2A1** **Calibre:** 12.7 mm (0.5 in) **Length overall:** 1260 mm (49.6 in) **Weight:** 10 kg (22 lb) **Muzzle velocity:** 838 m (2,749 ft) per	second **Feed:** 5- or 10-round box magazine **Gepard M3** **Calibre:** 14.5 mm (0.57 in) **Length overall:** 1880 mm (74 in) **Weight:** 20 kg (44.1 lb) **Muzzle velocity:** 1002 m (3,287 ft) per second **Feed:** 5- or 10-round box magazine

shock is about the same level as that found on a heavy game rifle. Using AP ammunition, the

Gepard M3 can penetrate 30 mm (1.18 in) of homogeneous armour at 100 m (109 yards) and 25 mm (0.98 in) at 600 m (656 yards). The M3's maximum effective range is in excess of 1000 m (1,094 yards).

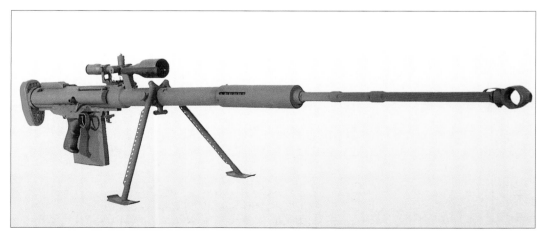

The Gepard M2A1 is fitted with a shorter barrel than the standard M2 sniping rifle and is intended for use by paratroopers and special forces. Note the position of the magazine opposite the trigger assembly.

Mauser SP 66 and SP 86 Sniper rifles

This version of the SP 66, known as the Model 86 SR, is equipped with a set of target sights and a bipod for super-accurate competition shooting; the service version is basically the same weapon fitted with a telescopic sight but lacking the forward-located bipod.

The Mauser-Werke at Oberndorf in West Germany can lay claim to a long and distinguished background and history in the design and production of manually operated (or bolt-action) rifles that are now known under the blanket name of Mauser.

The company's forward-locking bolt action is still widely used by designers, and Mauser-Werke has even introduced its own variations to the action, one of them being the relocation of the bolt handle from the rear of the bolt to the front. On most rifles this would be of little significance, but on a rifle for the highly specialised task of sniping it means that the firer can work the bolt action without having to move his head out of the way as the bolt itself can be made relatively short; it also means the barrel can be made correspondingly longer for

enhanced accuracy. This has been done on a custom-built Mauser-Werke sniper's rifle known as the **SP 66**. The revised bolt action is just a single example of the level of care lavished on this weapon: others include a heavy barrel, a buttstock with a carefully contoured thumb aperture, provision for adjustable cheek and butt pads, and a special muzzle attachment. This last is so designed that, on firing, the great bulk of the resultant flash is directed away from the firer's line of sight, and the device also serves as a muzzle brake to reduce the recoil forces transmitted through the weapon to the firer. Both of these factors are important in allowing the firer to get off further shots more accurately.

Superb finish

The standard of finish throughout the production of

the SP 66 is very high. Even such details as roughening all surfaces likely to be handled to prevent slipping have been carried out with meticulous care, and the trigger is extra wide to facilitate use with a gloved finger.

The sights have been selected with equal attention. There are no fixed sights and the standard telescopic sight is a Zeiss-Divari ZA with zoom capability from x1.5 to x6. Night sights can be fitted, though it is recommended that the manufacturer selects and calibrates them to an exact match for the rifle on which they are used. As is usual with such rifles the ammunition fired from the SP 66 is taken from

carefully chosen batches of 7.62-mm (0.3-in) NATO rounds produced for sniper use.

The SP 66 has been a considerable success even though it is manufactured virtually to order only. It is in service with the West German armed forces and more have been sold to a further 12 or so nations, most of which are unwilling to divulge their names for security reasons.

The **SP 86** is a less expensive version of the SP 66 mainly for police use. The weapon has a new bolt, cold-forged barrel, nine-round magazine, combined flash suppresser and muzzle brake, and furniture of laminated wood with ventilation to eliminate warping.

SPECIFICATION	
SP 66	
Calibre: 7.62-mm (0.3-in)	**Weight:** 6.25 kg (13.8 lb)
Length overall: 1120 mm (44.1 in)	**Muzzle velocity:** about 860 m (2,821 ft) per second
Length of barrel: 680 mm (26.8 in)	**Magazine:** 9-round box

This Mauser SP 86 is fitted with a night vision device. It is recommended that the manufacturer selects and calibrates the sights of each individual weapon.

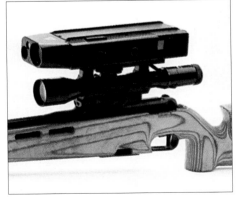

Long-range accuracy depends on good ammunition, which Mauser selects from batches of NATO 7.62-mm cartridges. This Mauser is fitted with a laser rangefinder.

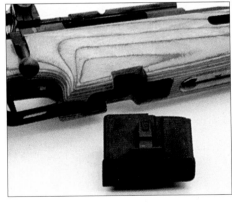

A close-up of the double-row, detachable nine-round magazine of the Mauser SP 86, one of the improvements incorporated into this development of the SP 66.

Walther WA2000 Sniper rifle

Supplied with a Schmidt & Bender telescopic sight, the remarkable Walther WA2000 fires the 0.30-in Winchester magnum cartridge.

With the **WA2000** from the Walther company of Germany, it would appear that small arms design is already in the 'Star Wars' era, for this weapon has a unique appearance more redolent of film concepts than standard small arms design. The rifle was created specifically for sniping, and the Walther approach was to put aside all known small arms design precepts, and thus to start from scratch after it had fully analysed the requirements.

The most important part of any rifle design is the barrel.

Walther decided to clamp the barrel at the front and rear to ensure that the torque imparted by a bullet passing through the bore would not lift the barrel away from the intended point of aim. The barrel is also fluted longitudinally over its entire length. This not only provides more cooling area but also reduces the vibrations imparted on firing, vibrations that can also cause a bullet to stray. The design team also opted for a gas-operated mechanism to reduce the need for bolt manipulation between shots

and, to reduce recoil, the barrel is in direct line with the shoulder so that the muzzle is not thrown upward after every shot.

Thus the strange outline of the WA2000 begins to make sense, but there is more to come for the WA2000 is a 'bullpup' design with the gas-operated bolt mechanism behind the trigger group. This arrangement makes for a shorter and therefore more easily handled design without any need for reducing the barrel length. This does mean that the ejection port is close to the firer, so there are special left- and right-handed versions. The overall standard of finish of the WA2000

is all that one would expect. The butt pad and cheek rests are adjustable, and there is a carefully-shaped pistol grip for added aiming stability. The normal telescopic sight is a Schmidt and Bender x2.5 to x10 zoom, but other types can be fitted.

Walther has decided that the best round for the sniping role is now the .300 (7.62-mm) Winchester Magnum cartridge, but while the WA2000 is chambered for this round others such as the 7.62-mm NATO or much favoured 7.5-mm (0.295-in) Swiss cartridge can be accommodated with alterations to the bolt and rifling.

SPECIFICATION	
WA2000	**Weight loaded:** 8.31 kg (18.32 lb)
Calibre: various	**Muzzle velocity:** not available
Length overall: 905 mm (35.63 in)	**Magazine:** 6-round box
Length of barrel: 650 mm (25.59 in)	

The WA2000 was created as a single-purpose rifle with a design that focused on nothing but accuracy and the ability of the firer to use the weapon effectively.

Heckler & Koch Sniper rifles

The range of Heckler & Koch rifles has now become so large that a weapon suitable for just about any application can apparently be selected from the array. Sniper's rifles have not been neglected, but in general most of the company's

weapons for this highly specialised task are little more than standard designs. Such weapons are produced with a little extra care, the addition of a few accessories and the incorporation of a mounting for the telescopic sight that is an

essential aid for accurate shooting at long range. This does not detract from the serviceability or efficiency of these weapons, and indeed many of them are altogether more suitable for typical field conditions than other designs

that have been produced with emphasis on supreme accuracy rather than a practical serviceability.

Typical of these Heckler & Koch sniper weapons are the 7.62-mm (0.3-in) **G3 A3ZF** and **G3 SG/1**, both of which were

The MSG90 is a cheaper version of the PSG1, and notable features are the lighter barrel and buttstock, and the folding bipod arrangement under the forward end of the forestock.

produced for the West German police, the latter model with a light bipod. Good as these weapons are, there can be no dispute of the fact that they are basically only 'breathed on' versions of standard weapons originally designed with mass production rather than specialisation in mind.

Accordingly Heckler & Koch turned its attention in the mid-1980s to the design and production of a special design known as the **PSG1**. It is believed that before it embarked on the design of this weapon, the company solicited the input of potential special forces operators such as the GSG9 unit

of Germany's border police, the Special Air Service Regiment of the UK and a number of Israeli counter-terrorist units.

The PSG1 is still based on the standard Heckler & Koch rotary lock mechanism, but in this instance combined with a semi-automatic operating system and a precision heavy barrel with bore characterised by polygonal rifling. The influence of the G3 can still be seen in the outlines of the receiver and also in the 5- or 20-round magazine housing (it is also possible to load single rounds manually), but the rest is entirely new. Forward of the magazine housing is a new

forestock and the long barrel, while the buttstock has been reconfigured to the widely used all-adjustable form so that the weapon can be configured for the use of a specific firer.

Precision aiming

The PSG1 was originally produced with a Hensoldt x6 telescopic sight adjustable in six settings for ranges between 100 m (110 yards) up to 600 m (655 yards), but later examples have claw fittings allowing them to accept a wide range of telescopic sight units. It has been stated that the weapon is extremely accurate, but for obvious reasons these claims are difficult to confirm independently.

For special purposes there has been mention of a precision-aiming tripod for this 7.62-mm round weapon, but its form (if any) is still unclear. It may well emerge that this tripod is an

adaptation of one of the Heckler & Koch's machine gun mountings (the butt used on the PSG1 is a much-modified HK-21 machine gun component). The PSG1 is one of the most expensive of current sniper rifles, with a price in the order of $9,000 or more.

In 1990 there appeared the latest of Heckler & Koch's sniper rifles, the **MSG90**, a designation in which the letter prefixed stands for Militärisch Scharfshützen Gewehr (military marksman rifle) and the number suffix for the year of introduction. This was created as a cheaper derivative of the PSG1 in an effort to drum up greater sales, and is therefore based ultimately on the G3. The MSG90 has the trigger group of the PSG1 in combination with a lighter barrel and a smaller buttstock. This reduces the overall length to 1165 mm (45.87 in) and the weight to 6.4 kg (14.1lb).

SPECIFICATION	
PSG1	**Muzzle velocity:** about 860 m (2,821 ft) per second
Calibre: 7.62-mm (0.3-in)	
Length overall: 1208 mm (47.56 in)	**Magazine:** 5- or 20-round straight box
Length of barrel: 650 mm (25.6 in)	
Weight empty: 8.1 kg (17.85 lb)	

Galil Sniping Rifle Combat sniping rifle

Ever since Israel was formed in 1948, the role of the sniper within the Israeli armed forces has been an important one, and over the years snipers have usually been equipped with an array of weapons from all around the world. At one point attempts were made to produce sniper rifles locally, so for a period Israeli army snipers used an indigenous 7.62-mm (0.3-in) design known as the M26. This was virtually a hand-

made weapon using design features from both the Soviet AKM and Belgian FAL rifles. However, for various reasons the M26 was deemed not fully satisfactory and work began on a sniping rifle based on the Israel Military Industries 7.62-mm Galil assault rifle, the standard Israeli service rifle.

The resultant **Galil Sniping Rifle** bears a resemblance to the original weapon, but it is virtually a new weapon. Almost

The design of the Galil sniper rifle was shaped by the IDF's extensive battlefield experience, and it is perhaps not surprising that the gun is built more for reliability in combat than exceptional accuracy in ideal conditions.

every component has been redesigned and manufactured to very close tolerances. A new heavy barrel is fitted, as is an

adjustable bipod. The solid butt (which can be folded forward to reduce carrying and stowage bulk) has an adjustable butt pad

SPECIFICATION	
Galil Sniping Rifle	**Weights:** 6.4 kg (14.1 lb) including bipod and sling
Calibre: 7.62 mm (0.3 in)	
Length overall: 1115 mm (44 in);	**Muzzle velocity:** 815 m (2,674 ft) per second
Length of barrel: 508 mm (20 in)	
	Magazine capacity: 20 rounds

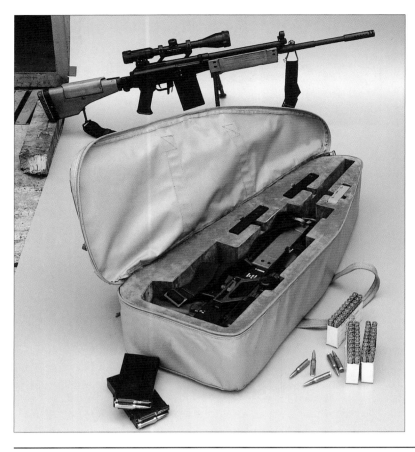

When not in use the Galil Sniping Rifle is kept in a special case together with the telescopic sight, optical filters to reduce sun glare when using optical sights, a carrying and firing sling, two magazines and the all important cleaning kit for maintenance.

and cheek rest, while a Nimrod x6 telescopic sight is mounted on a bracket offset to the left of the receiver.

New mechanism

The mechanism is now single-shot only, the original Galil 20-round magazine being retained. The barrel is fitted with a muzzle brake/ compensator to reduce recoil and barrel jump on firing. A silencer can be fitted to the muzzle, but subsonic ammunition must then be used. As would be expected, various night sights can be fitted. The Sniping Rifle also retains its 'iron' combat sights.

The Galil Sniping Rifle is a very serviceable weapon that is far more suitable for the rigours of military life than many of the current crop of super-accurate models, which are often easily damaged. Despite its basic design approach, it can still place group of rounds of less than 300-mm (11.8-in) diameter at a range of 600 m (1,969 ft), with the use of an integral bipod, which is more than adequate for most sniping purposes.

Beretta Sniper Combat sniping rifle

When the market for high-precision sniper rifles expanded in the 1970s, virtually every major small-arms manufacturer started to design weapons that they thought would meet international requirements. Some of these designs have fared better than others on the market, but one that does appear to have been overlooked by many is the **Beretta Sniper** 7.62-mm (0.3-in) sniping rifle. This design appears to have been given no numerical designation. In addition to its military applications, the weapon is likely to be in use with some Italian paramilitary police units for specialist internal security duties.

Orthodox design

Compared with many of the latest 'space-age' sniper rifle designs, the Beretta offering is almost completely orthodox but well up to Beretta's usual high standards of design and finish.

The Sniper uses a manual rotary bolt action allied to the usual heavy barrel, and one of its most prominent features is the large and unusually-shaped hole carved into the high-quality wooden stock that forms a prominent pistol grip for the trigger.

Advanced features

Despite the overall conventional design there are one or two advanced features on the Sniper.

The wooden forestock conceals a forward-pointing counterweight, under the free-floating barrel, that acts as a damper to reduce the normal barrel vibrations produced on firing. At the front end of the forestock is a location point for securing a light adjustable bipod to assist the sniper in keeping the rifle steady. The underside of the forestock contains a slot for an adjustable forward hand stop for the firer, and this forestop can also be used as the attachment point for a firing sling if one is required. The butt and cheek pads are adjustable and the muzzle has a flash hider as standard.

Unlike many of its modern counterparts, the Beretta Sniper is fully provided with a set of

A largely conventional design, the Beretta Sniper actually incorporates some advanced features, which help to make it both accurate and reliable.

all-adjustable precision match sights, even though these would not normally be used for the sniping role. Over the receiver is a standard NATO optical or night sight mounting attachment, to

accommodate virtually any military optical or electro-optical sighting system. The normal telescopic sight as recommended by Beretta is the widely-used Zeiss Diavari-Z x1.5 to x6.

SPECIFICATION	
Beretta Sniper	complete with sight and bipod
Calibre: 7.62 mm (0.3 in)	7.20 kg (15.87 lb)
Length overall: 1165 mm (46 in);	**Muzzle velocity:** about 865 m (2,838
Length of barrel: 586 mm (23 in)	ft) per second
Weights: 5.55 kg (12.23 lb);	**Magazine capacity:** 5 rounds

SVD Dragunov Combat sniping rifle

The Soviets always gave snipers a great deal of prominence in the field and always provided them with good weapons. The SVD Dragunov was very much a weapon of the Cold War, but is likely to remain in Russian army service in some numbers. Although long and bulky, it is a reliable weapon, although not as accurate as the L42 for example. It uses a modified AK-47 gas-operated, semi-automatic action, allied to a large magazine.

Anyone familiar with accounts of the Great Patriotic War cannot but help note the emphasis given to sniping by the Soviet army. Post-war, that emphasis remained undiminished, and to carry out the sniping role the Soviets developed what is widely regarded as one of the best contemporary sniper rifles. This is the **SVD**, sometimes known as the **Dragunov**.

Prized weapon

The SVD (**Samozariy-adnyia Vintokvka Dragunova**) first appeared in 1963, and ever since has been one of the most prized of infantry trophies. It is a semi-automatic weapon that uses the

same operating principles as the AK-47 assault rifle, but allied to a revised gas-operated system. Unlike the AK-47, which uses the short 7.62-mm (0.3-in) x39 cartridge, the SVD fires the older 7.62-mm x54R rimmed cartridge, originally introduced during the 1890s for the Mosin-Nagant rifles. This remains a good round for the sniping role, and as it is still used on some Russian machine guns, availability is no problem.

The SVD has a long barrel, but the weapon is so balanced that it handles well and recoil is not excessive. The weapon is normally fired using a sling rather than the bipod favoured elsewhere, and to assist aiming, a PSO-1 telescopic sight is provided. This is secured to the left-hand side of the receiver and has a magnification of x4. The PSO-1 has an unusual feature in that it incorporates an infra-red detector element to enable it to be used as a passive night sight, although it

is normally used in conjunction with an independent infra-red target-illumination source. Basic combat sights are fitted for use if the optical sight does become defective.

Perhaps the oddest feature for a sniper rifle is that the SVD is provided with a bayonet, the rationale for this remaining uncertain. A 10-round box magazine is also fitted.

Long-range accuracy

Tests have demonstrated that the SVD can fire accurately to ranges of well over 800 m (2,625 ft). It is a pleasant weapon to handle and fire, despite the lengthy barrel. SVDs were provided to many Warsaw Pact and other nations and the weapon was used in Afghanistan, some ending up in the hands of the Mujahideen. It seems reasonable to assume that te SVD remains in use in Russia and with other former client states of the USSR. The Chinese produce a direct copy of the SVD and offer this version for export, quoting an effective range of 1000 m (621 ft).

The Dragunov uses a bolt system similar to that of the AK-47 and its derivatives, but it is modified to suit the different characteristics of the rimmed 7.62-mm X 54R cartridge. The mechanisms of the SVD and AK-47 are not interchangeable.

SPECIFICATION	
SVD	**Weight:** complete, unloaded
Calibre: 7.62 mm (0.3 in)	4.39 kg (9.67 lb)
Length overall: less bayonet	**Muzzle velocity:** 830 m (2,723 ft) per
Length of barrell: 1225 mm (48.2 in);	second
barrel 547 mm (21.5 in)	**Magazine capacity:** 10 rounds

If the long barrel of the Dragunov is not a decisive recognition point, then the distinctive cut-away butt certainly is. The SVD retains the AK-47's ability to withstand harsh treatment during combat operations in the field.

VS 94 PS 7.62-mm (0.3-in) sniping rifle

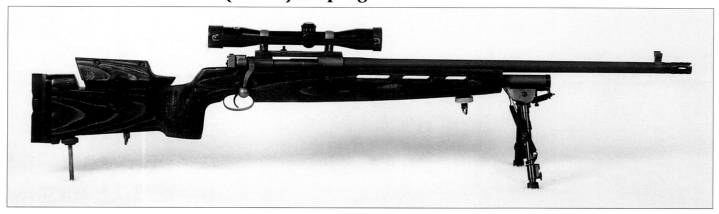

The Norwegian **VS 94 PS** 7.62-mm (0.3-in) sniping rifle employs a modified version of the widely used Mauser Gewehr 98 bolt action which is essentially similar to that employed by the 7.62-mm **NM 149S** rifle in service with the Norwegian armed forces. The rifles are basically the same weapon and follow the conventional lines employed by many other high-precision rifles. The VS 94 was developed in co-operation with the Norwegian police forces, however, primarily for employment by specialist police marksmen, although it could have many other military and para-military applications.

One aspect of the VS 94 that differs is that its weight, with an optical sight installed, is 1 kg (2.2 lb) greater than that of its military counterpart.

Both the NM 149S and the VS 94 are manufactured by Vapensmia A/S at Dokka, and share an exceptionally heavy barrel. The VS 94 is primarily intended to deliver highly accurate fire out to a range of 800 m (875 yards), and for this role it is fitted with a Schmidt & Bender 3-12 x 50 PM II telescopic sight, which may be mounted and removed from a rail over the receiver without altering the rifle's zero aiming point. Adjustable 'iron' sights are

A conventional bolt-action, single-shot 7.62-mm (0.3-in) sniping rifle, the Vapensmia VS 94 PS is essentially a police derivative of the same company's NM 149S rifle, which is in service with the Norwegian army. This VS 94 PS has been fitted with a cheek-piece.

also fitted, and the telescopic sight can be replaced by a Simrad KN250 image-intensifying sight for use at night or under poor light conditions.

Finnish ammunition

To ensure that accuracy is as high as possible, only 7.62-mm x 51 NATO match-grade ammunition is fired, the ammunition coming from Nammo Lapua of Finland. The ammunition is carried in a five-round box magazine. A fully loaded magazine can be inserted directly into the rifle or rounds can be manually fed into the weapon once the bolt has been withdrawn. A muzzle attachment serves both as a muzzle-brake

and as a firing flash suppressor. The VS 94's stock is of impregnated and laminated beech veneer and may be adjusted for length by the use of butt-plate spacers; it also has an adjustable cheek-piece. The rifle has a match trigger, adjusted to a pull of 1.5 kg (3.3 lb).

The VS 94 can be fitted with a fully adjustable bipod, which is mounted on a post located at the front of the fore-stock, the latter being ventilated by three slots on each side. A small post can be lowered onto a firm surface from under the butt-stock to enhance aiming accuracy, or to take the weight of the rifle. A sound suppressor can also be employed if required.

SPECIFICATION	
VS 94	**Weight:** empty, with telescope,
Calibre: 7.62 mm (0.3 in)	7 kg (15.4 lb)
Overall length: 1160 mm (45.7 in)	**Magazine:** five-round box
Length of barrel: 600 mm (23.6 in)	

Harris M87R and M93 0.5-in (12.7-mm) sniping rifles

Originally manufactured by the McMillan Gun Works, the **M87R** sniping rifle was subsequently brought into production by Harris in Phoenix, Arizona, which acquired the original company in 1995 and retained the weapon's initial designation.

The M87R rifle is based on the **M87**, an earlier single-shot weapon using a conventional bolt-action firing mechanism, to which was added a magazine with a capacity of five rounds. The M87R rifle is chambered for the Browning 0.5-in (12.7-mm)

cartridge, which lends the weapon a high degree of anti-materiel capability as well allowing anti-personnel sniping at extended ranges.

A very heavy barrel is fitted to the M87R, and the fore-end mounts a distinctive 'pepper pot' perforated muzzle brake. The M87R is half-stocked, although the stock is not fully hollowed

out in order to form a pistol grip, as can be found on certain weapons in this class, such as the French Hecate II 12.7-mm sniping rifle. An alternative stock can be fitted, this being made of synthetic material and allowing

The Harris (formerly McMillan) M87R 0.5-in (12.7-mm) sniping rifle is equipped with a notably heavy barrel and does not have any form of 'iron' sights.

Both the M87R and the M93 (seen here) can accept a bipod, which is attached to the front end of the stock. The M93 can be used in the explosive ordnance disposal role.

the firer to make personal adjustments to length and rake. The M87R weapon is not provided with conventional 'iron' sights and so some form of telescopic sight is essential: this is attached on a specially provided mount.

A derivative of the M87R, the **M93** differs in its 10- or 20-round magazine and in a hinged butt-stock which makes

the weapon easier to transport and put in storage.

Ordnance disposal

The M93 is optimised for the counter-sniper role but can also be used for explosive ordnance disposal. For the latter role, the weapon is fired at hazardous targets from a safe range, with the aim of detonating the suspect device. If the explosives

SPECIFICATION	
M93	(39 in)
Calibre: 0.5 in (12.7 mm)	**Length of barrel:** 737 mm (29 in)
Length overall: butt extended, 1346 mm (53 in); butt folded 991 mm	**Weight:** 9.52 kg (21 lb)
	Magazine: 10- or 20-round box

fail to detonate, the impact of the 0.5-in round will likely have disabled the detonating mechanism, making it safer to deal with the ordnance by conventional means. The M93

has been adopted by a number of US law enforcement agencies, and the M93 and M87R are used by the French army. The weapon has reportedly seen use in Bosnia and Somalia.

The Harris M87R and M93 are provided with a manual safety lever located alongside the bolt-action cocking piece. The M93 lacks the 'pepper pot' muzzle brake of the M87R rifle.

SIG-Sauer SSG 3000 7.62-mm (0.3-in) sniping rifle

The **SIG-Sauer SSG 3000** 7.62-mm (0.3-in) sniping rifle is a high-precision bolt-action repeating rifle incorporating state-of-the-art firearms technology and developed from the design basis of the successful Sauer 200 STR target rifle. Design of the SSG 3000 was a joint project undertaken by SIG Arms of Neuhausen, Switzerland and J. P. Sauer und Sohn of Eckernförde, Germany. The SSG 3000 was developed primarily for military and also special police users, who demand a very high probability of a first-round hit at very challenging ranges.

The SSG 3000 rifle is based around a modular system in which the barrel and receiver are joined by screw clamps. The trigger system and five-round box magazine form a single unit that fits into the receiver, and the basic stock used is made of a non-warping wood laminate. The stock is also ventilated to limit the warping effect of heat on the heavy barrel.

One-piece receiver

The receiver housing for the bolt action is machined from a single high-grade steel billet. Locking, achieved with six lugs, is provided by a mechanism

SPECIFICATION	
SSG 3000	without sight, 5.4 kg (11.9 lb); with
Calibre: 7.62 mm (0.3 in)	empty magazine and with sight,
Length overall: about 1180 mm	6.2 kg (13.7 lb)
(46.5 in), depending upon stock	**Muzzle velocity:** 750 m (2,461 ft) per
adjustment	second, depending on ammunition
Length of barrel: excluding flash	type
suppressor, 610 mm (24 in)	**Magazine:** 5-round box
Weight: with empty magazine and	

between the bolt and barrel. This ensures that the stresses normally imposed on the bolt when the weapon is fired are not transmitted to the receiver. A lightweight firing pin and short striking distance endow the rifle with an exceptionally short lock time. The cartridge used is the 7.62-mm x 51 NATO-standard

type. The SSG 3000's barrel is heavy, cold-hammered and fitted with a combined muzzle-brake and flash suppressor. The barrel's rifling has four grooves, with one right-hand turn in each 305 mm (12 in).

Two precision trigger actions, adjustable both for length of pull and take-up weight, are available,

The SSG 3000 is a particularly good example of the modern precision-made, bolt-action, magazine-fed sniping rifle. The modular design uses removable barrel/receiver and trigger/magazine groups.

these being of single-stage or double-stage pattern. The sliding safety catch, located above the trigger, locks the trigger, firing pin and bolt. A signal pin at the end of the striker head indicates whether the rifle is cocked.

To obtain the best accuracy performance from the SSG 3000 rifle only high-standard match-grade 7.62-mm x 51 (0.308-in

Winchester) ammunition should be fired. A sliding safety catch is located directly above the trigger, within the trigger guard.

User adjustments

The stock, which can be fitted with an adjustable cheek-piece, is ergonomically designed, allowing the weapon to be held in the aiming position for

extended periods without inducing user fatigue. The butt-plate can be adjusted for height, length, offset and rake and the entire system – stock, bolt and receiver – is also available as a completely left-handed version. A rail integrated into the fore-end accepts the adjustable bipod and a carrying or firing sling.

There are no emergency 'iron' sights offered as a 'back up', the rifle being intended solely for use with a telescopic sight. The normal mount is designed to operate with the

recommended sight, the Hensoldt 1.5-6 x 42 mm BL, which is specifically manufactured for the SSG 3000 rifle, but a NATO-standard sight base is available if preferred.

Training version

For low-cost training and practice purposes a 0.22-in LR conversion kit is available. The SSG 3000 entered production in 1991, and the basic SSG 3000 service weapon has found favour among police forces in both Europe and the US. The SIG-Sauer company later became part of SIG Arms AG that, in turn, was later renamed as SAN Swiss Arms.More recent versions of the SSG 3000 sniping rifle and those that are produced for the US market replace the original laminated wood stock with a polymer-based stock.

Rifle L42 Sniper rifle

Changes to the old No. 4 Lee-Enfield rifle for the 7.62-mm (0.3-in) sniping role involved a new heavy barrel, a new 10-round box magazine and cutting back the forestock over the barrel. A cheek rest was added to the butt and the rifle was virtually rebuilt. Changes were made to the trigger and a mounting for a telescopic sight was added.

The Lee-Enfield rifle had a long career with the British army reaching back to the 1890s, and throughout that time the basic Lee-Enfield manual bolt mechanism remained little changed. The weapon remained in service as the **Rifle L42A1** recently supplanted by the

Accuracy International L96 in the same 7.62-mm (0.3-in) calibre. These L42A1 weapons were used only for sniping, and were conversions of 0.303-in (7.7-mm) No. 4 Mk 1(T) or Mk 1*(T) rifles, as used during World War II. The conversion – or rebuilding – process involved the

addition of a new barrel and magazine, some changes to the trigger mechanism and fixed sights, and alterations to the forestock. The World War II No. 32 Mk 3 telescopic sight (renamed the L1A1) and its

mounting over the receiver were retained, and the result was a rugged and serviceable sniping rifle, used not only by the army but also by the Royal Marines.

In more modern terms the L42A1 was very much the

The L42A1 rifle was a 7.62-mm (0.3-in) conversion of an earlier 7.7-mm (0.303-in) Lee-Enfield rifle, and served the British army well over the years. It was used by the army and the Royal Marines during the Falklands War, usually in the form shown here with the weapon covered in camouflage scrim netting.

product of a previous generation, but it could still give excellent first-shot results at ranges over 800 m (875 yards), although this depends very much on the skill of the firer and the type of ammunition used. The ammunition was normally selected from special 'Green Spot' high-accuracy ammunition produced at the Royal Ordnance facility at Radway Green.

The rifle itself was also the subject of a great deal of care, calibration and attention. When not in use it was stowed and transported in a special chest containing not only the rifle but the optical sight, cleaning gear, firing sling and perhaps a few spares such as extra magazines: the L42A1 retained the 10-round magazine of the 0.303-in version but with a revised outline to accommodate the new rimless ammunition. The often- overlooked weapon record books were also kept in the chest.

The L42A1 was not the only 7.62-mm Lee-Enfield rifle still around. A special match-shooting version known as the **L39A1** was used for competitive use, and there are two other models, the **Envoy** and the **Enforcer.** The former model may be regarded as a civilian match version of the L39A1, while the Enforcer is a custom-built L42A1 variant with a heavier barrel and revised butt outline. This latter weapon was produced specifically for police use, meeting the demands of accuracy in hostage situations.

SPECIFICATION	
L42A1	
Calibre: 7.62-mm (0.3-in)	**Muzzle velocity:** 838 m (2,750 ft) per second
Length overall: 1181 mm (46.5 in)	**Magazine:** 10-round box
Length of barrel: 699 mm (27.5 in)	
Weight: 4.43 kg (9.76 lb)	

Rifle L96

After many years of faithful and effective service, the L42A1 sniper rifle, based on the Lee-Enfield bolt-action service rifle dating from the last decade of the 19th century and steadily upgraded in the half century following that time, has been replaced as the British army's standard sniping rifle by a purpose-designed weapon, the **Rifle L96A1** designed and manufactured by Accuracy International.

The Model PM's Counter-Terrorist version has at its muzzle a spiral device not fitted to the Infantry model, which has a 10-round box magazine, 'iron' sights and sling swivels.

Unlike its predecessor, the new weapon is not a conversion of a tried and trusted battle rifle, but is more akin to the special target weapons used in sporting events such as the Olympic Games and therefore optimised for great accuracy at longer ranges than would characterise modern battlefield combat.

In its No. 4 Mk 1(T) and L42A1 forms, the Lee-Enfield No. 4 rifle gave British snipers sterling service over the years, but these two weapons were originally straightforward conversions of standard rifles with few innovations for the sniper role. The L42A1 was a good weapon in terms of accuracy, but time had marched on and technological advances meant that something better could be provided. For some time the British army was denied the opportunity to procure replacement weapons by budgetary restrictions, but that changed in 1984 and the army could specify to all concerned what it wanted.

Orthodox concept

It is interesting to note that of the three weapons finally selected for final trials none were of the super-accuracy 'space-age' type. All three were conventional designs, brought up to date by the use of modern materials and design niceties. The weapons were the Parker-Hale Model 85, a design from Interarms, and the Accuracy International Model PM designed by Malcolm Cooper, an Olympic gold medallist. All three of these weapons were subjected to extensive trials by the staff of the Small Arms School Corps at Warminster in Wiltshire, and although there was apparently little to choose between the three, in the end the Model PM was selected for service. In this decision the evaluation team was probably influenced to some extent by experience gained from use of the Model PM by the SAS, which had already obtained a few of the type.

Although the Model PM appears to be an entirely

The art of sniping includes the ability of the firer to merge into his background and avoid the type of movement that will betray his presence. This sniper and his rifle are artfully draped to break up their outlines.

orthodox design, in this case the appearances are deceptive. The Model PM is in effect little more than a heavy stainless steel 7.62-mm (0.3-in) barrel secured to a bolted aluminium chassis. The entire weapon consists of a bipod, stock, action and butt-stock, all enclosed in plastic furniture provided for little reason other than to hold everything together and give it an acceptable appearance. Although the fore-stock appears to enclose the barrel, in fact it doesn't touch the free-floating barrel at any point.

Forward-locking bolt

The Model PM uses a Tasco telescopic sight and has a forward-locking manual bolt action designed so that on withdrawal the bolt does not touch the firer's face. The light alloy bipod can be allied with a retractable monopod 'spike' under the butt that can be used to act as a holding platform for prolonged periods of use (i.e. the firer can aim the rifle at a selected area with the weight taken on the bipod and spike). An integral box magazine holds five rounds and the trigger assembly can be removed entirely for adjustment.

There are at least four versions of the Model PM. Two are the so-called **Counter-Terrorist** weapon already in army use, and the **Infantry** of which the first of 1,212 were delivered from 1986. The latter has a 6x42 non-zoom scope and match sights effective at ranges up to 900 m (985 yards). The other two variants are the **Moderated** with an integral sight and the single-shot **Long-Range** chambered for the 7-mm (0.275-in) Remington Magnum or 7.62-mm Winchester Magnum.

SPECIFICATION	
L96A1	
Calibre: 7.62-mm (0.3-in)	**Weight:** 6.5 kg (14.33 lb)
Length overall: 1124 mm (44.25 in)	**Muzzle velocity:** not available
Length of barrel: 654 mm (25.75 in)	**Magazine:** 10-round box

Parker-Hale Model 82 Sniper rifle

In service with the armed forces of Australia, Canada and New Zealand, the Parker-Hale Model 82 is intended to hit point targets at up to 400 m (440 yards) in good light, or up to the maximum range of any sights fitted.

Parker-Hale Limited of Birmingham has for many years been manufacturing match rifles and their associated sights, and has also been long employed in the equally specialist task of designing and manufacturing sniping rifles. The company's best-known product to date is the 7.62-mm (0.3-in) **Parker-Hale Model 82**, also known as the **Parker-Hale 1200TX**. The Model 82 has been accepted for military and police service by several nations.

In appearance and design terms the Model 82 is an entirely conventional sniping weapon. It uses a manual bolt action very similar to that used on the classic Mauser Gewehr 98 rifle, allied to a heavy free-floating barrel; the barrel weighs 1.98 kg (4.365 lb) and is manu-factured as a cold-forged unit of chrome molybdenum steel. An integral four-round magazine is provided. The trigger mechanism is an entirely self-contained unit that can be adjusted as required.

The Model 82 is available in a number of forms to suit any particular customer requirements. Thus an adjustable cheek pad may be provided if wanted and the butt lengths can be altered by adding or taking away butt pads of various thicknesses. The sights too are subject to several variations, but the Model 82 is one weapon that is normally supplied with 'iron' match-type sights. If an optical (telescopic) sight unit is fitted, the rear sight has to be removed to allow the same mounting block to be used. The forward mounting block is machined into the receiver. Various types of 'iron' foresight or optical night sights can be fitted.

Military service

The Australian army uses the Model 82 fitted with a Kahles Helia ZF 69 telescopic sight. The Canadian army uses a version of the Model 82/1200TX altered to meet local requirements; this service knows the Model 82 as the **Rifle C3**. New Zealand also uses the Model 82.

Parker-Hale produces a special training version of the Model 82 known as the **Model 83**. This single-shot rifle is fitted with match sights only and there is no provision for a telescopic sight. The weapon was accepted by the British Ministry of Defence as

The Parker-Hale Model 82 was selected by the Canadian Armed Forces as their sniper rifle, and is seen here in winter camouflage. It uses a Mauser-type bolt action and is fitted with a four-round box magazine.

the **Cadet Training Rifle L81A1** in a form with a shortened butt-stock and a shortened fore end. The Model 82 was later updated to the **Model 85**. This introduced a butt outline that was revised by comparison with that of the Model 82, a 10-round box magazine and a bipod (optional on the Model 82) was fitted as standard.

Weighing 5.7 kg (12.57 lb), this Model 85 weapon was one of the rifles that was competitively tested by the British army to find its new sniper rifle, a competition won by Parker-Hale rival Accuracy International.

Parker-Hale then ceased the manufacture of rifles and in 1990 it sold its rifle business (which also included the rights to its wide range of designs) to the Gibbs Rifle Company of the USA, which then placed the Model 85 in production under the Parker-Hale name.

SPECIFICATION	
Model 82	**Weight empty:** 4.8 kg (10.58 lb)
Calibre: 7.62-mm (0.3 in)	**Muzzle velocity:** about 840 m (2,756
Length overall: 1162 mm (45.7-in)	ft) per second
Length of barrel: 660 mm (25.98 in)	**Magazine:** 4-round box

Rifle M21 Sniper rifle

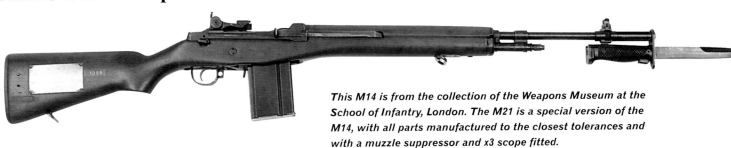

This M14 is from the collection of the Weapons Museum at the School of Infantry, London. The M21 is a special version of the M14, with all parts manufactured to the closest tolerances and with a muzzle suppressor and x3 scope fitted.

When the US armed forces made the move from the 7.62-mm (0.3-in) NATO cartridge to the smaller 5.56-mm (0.223-in) round during the late 1960s, they not surprisingly decided to retain the larger calibre for the sniping role. This was for the simple reason that the smaller round had been designed from the outset to impart its best performance at ranges much shorter than the usual sniping distances. This meant the retention of the current sniping rifle, at the time known as the **Rifle 7.62-mm M14 National Match (Accurized)**, but now known as the **Rifle M21**.

The M21 is a special version of the 7.62-mm M14. It retains the basic appearance and mechanism of the original, but some changes were introduced at the manufacturing stage.

Attention to detail

For a start the barrels were selected so that only those with the closest manufacturing tolerances were used. These barrels were left without their usual chromium plating inside the bore, again to reduce the possibility of manufacturing inaccuracies. A new muzzle suppressor was fitted and reamed to the barrel to ensure correct alignment. The trigger mechanism was assembled by hand and adjusted to provide a crisp release action at a trigger pull of between 2 and 2.15 kg (4.41 and 4.74 lb), and a new walnut stock was fitted, this latter being impregnated with an epoxy resin and individually fitted to the stock using a fibreglass compound. The gas-operated mechanism was also the subject of attention such as hand polishing and hand fitting to ensure an operation that was as smooth as possible.

The fully automatic fire mode is retained on the M21, but the weapon is normally fired only in the semi- automatic (single-shot) mode.

The main change on assembly was the fitting of a x3 magnification telescopic sight. As well as the usual aiming cross-hairs, this uses a system of graticules that allows the user to judge accurately the range of a man-sized target and automatically set the angle of elevation. Using this sight the M21 can place 10 rounds within a 152-mm (6-in) circle at 300 m (330 yards).

One unusual piece of equipment that can be fitted to the M21 is a sound suppressor. This is not a silencer in the usually accepted sense of the word, but a series of baffles. The bullet suffers no penalty in velocity, helping to ensure a trajectory as flat as possible, but the baffles reduce the velocity of the gases produced on firing to a figure below the speed of sound. This produces a muffled report with none of the usual firing signatures, and its use makes the source of the sound more difficult to detect.

SPECIFICATION	
Rifle M21	**Weight loaded:** 5.55 kg (12.24 lb)
Calibre: 7.62-mm (0.3-in)	**Muzzle velocity:** 853 m (2,798 ft) per
Length overall: 1120 mm (44.1 in)	second
Length of barrel: 559 mm (22 in)	**Feed:** 20-round box magazine

Although many Israeli snipers use the Galil sniping rifle, some still retain the American M21, the 'accurized' version of the M14 rifle. They were observed in use during the early stages of the invasion of Lebanon, and many were used against the PLO in Beirut in August 1982.

Barrett M82 & M95 Sniper rifles

One of the first sniper rifles based on the M33 ball round developed for the Browning M2 heavy machine gun was the Iver Johnson Model 500, a development of the multi-calibre Model 300.

In 1981, 26-year old Ronnie Barrett designed and made a 0.5-in (12.7-mm) semi-automatic rifle based on the Browning short-recoil operating system and firing the M33 round of the Browning M2 heavy machine gun.

The prototype offered long range and considerable accuracy in conjunction with mild recoil forces, and caught the attention of the US military, which was looking for a weapon to penetrate thin-skinned vehicles following its losses to terrorist attacks in Beirut, Lebanon. Some NATO armies also showed interest and the **M82A1** went into production as a military weapon.

During Operation 'Desert Storm' in 1991 the M82A1 won considerable approval when US ground troops used it successfully against APCs and high-value personnel. The US Marine Corps is a strong advocate of the M82A1 and has collaborated with Barrett on a programme of improvements. The latest refinements to the weapon include a removable carrying handle, improved bipod, lightened components and provision for the new day and night optics that the corps will soon be fielding.

Ammunition

The standard armour-piercing incendiary ammunition is now complemented by the new Raufoss Mk 211 round with a zirconium penetrator to ignite flammable material after impact and explosion at the target.

The two primary variants of the M82 are the M82A1 manufactured between 1983 and 1992, and the **M82A2** that entered production in 1990 as a less cumbersome 'bullpup' development of the M82A1 with the action and magazine located to the rear of the trigger group to reduce overall length to 1409 mm (55.5 in) and weight to 12.24 kg (27 lb).

The latest variant of the Barrett 0.5-in sniper rifle, intended like its predecessors for the whole range of long-range roles including explosive ordnance disposal, is the **M95**. This is basically a bolt-action derivative of the M82A2 with an overall length of 1143 mm (45 in), weight of 11.2 kg (24.7 lb), five-round box magazine and the standard x10 telescopic sight for an effective range of 1830 m (2,000 yards).

SPECIFICATION	
Barrett 'Light 50' M82A1	
Calibre: 0.5-in (12.7-mm)	**Weight:** 12.9 kg (28.4 lb)
Length overall: 1448 mm (57 in)	**Muzzle velocity:** 854 m (2,800 ft) per second
Length of barrel: 737 mm (29 in)	**Feed:** 11-round box magazine

Rifle M40 Sniper rifle

The US Marine Corps has always been allowed its own equipment procurement system, for it has long been accepted by the American authorities that the corps' particular role in the prosecution of amphibious warfare requires the adoption and use of the specialised equipment to match. Therefore when the selection of a new sniping rifle to replace the M1C and M1D weapons, both based on the M1 Garand rifle, came to be appreciated, the USMC went its own way with a weapon tailored to its own very exacting requirement.

Sniper emphasis

For the US Marines Corps the sniper has always had a special role, often operating in advance of other ground units to gain information as well as acting as a long-range killer of commanders and other high-value troops. So when, in the course of the Vietnam War, the US Marine Corps contemplated weapons such as the US Army's M14 and M21 sniper rifles, it decided that its men needed something better than these adapted service rifles. The US Marine Corps could not find exactly what it wanted on the open market, but found that the design coming the

The US Marine Corps adopted the Remington Model 700 in 1966 and had the weapon modified to meet its particular requirements. The M40A1 rifle differs from the M40 in having a heavier but shorter stainless steel barrel, a fibreglass stock and a powerful telescopic sight.

closest to meeting its requirement was a commercial rifle, as the **Remington Model 700**. This was produced to custom order by Remington as the target-tuned Model 700 weapon with a heavy barrel and the Model 40XB target rifle action. The US Marine Corps decided to standardise this weapon, which therefore became the **Rifle M40** in 1966. The original order for 800 such rifles was later increased to 995 weapons based on the Model 700BDL commercial rifle with a one-piece wooden buttstock.

The M40 has a Mauser-type manual bolt action and a heavy barrel. It is normally fitted with a Redfield telescopic sight with a zoom magnification of from x3 to x9. A five-round magazine is fitted, and the M40 is an entirely conventional but high-quality design.

On the battlefield

In service with the US Marines the M40 proved to be perfectly satisfactory, but battlefield experience gained with the basic design showed the Marines that something better could be produced. The US Marine Corps accordingly asked the Remington Arms Company to introduce a number of modifications. These included the replacement of the original barrel by a new stainless steel component, the replacement of the wooden furniture by fibreglass furniture (supplied by McMillan Brothers) and the introduction of a new sight. This Unertl telescopic sight was produced entirely to demanding US

Marine Corps specification with a fixed x10 magnification. No 'iron' sights were fitted for use as an alternative to the telescopic sight.

With all these changes embodied the M40 became the **M40A1**, and this was produced only for the US Marine Corps at its workshops at Quantico, Virginia, on the basis of parts delivered by Remington (action), Winchester (magazine floorplate), McMillan Brothers and other civil contractors.

By all accounts the M40A1 is one of the most accurate 'conventional' sniping rifles ever produced, although exact figures are not available to confirm this assertion. The main reasons for this excellence are the combination provided by the heavy stainless steel barrel and the superb optical sight. The magnification of this sight is much more than usual on such devices, but despite this fact, and the possibility of the distortion that might have resulted, the sight produces a notably bright and clearer image for the firer. All the usual adjustments can be introduced to the sight.

Magnificent accuracy

As always, the degree of accuracy is dependent on the performance of the ammunition selected and also, of course, on the skill of the firer. However, the US Marine Corps has traditionally spent a great deal of time and effort on the training of its snipers. But by all accounts the M40A1 is the rifle that 'everyone else wants'.

When the US Marine Corps decided to select its own sniping rifle it ordered numbers of commercial Remington Model 700 rifles, some still with 'iron' sights, as seen here. These became the M40 sniping rifle and many remained in use despite the introduction of the later M40A1. The weapon is used only by the US Marine Corps.

SPECIFICATION	
Rifle M40A1	**Weight:** 6.57 kg (14.48 lb)
Calibre: 7.62-mm (0.3-in)	**Muzzle velocity:** 777 m (2,549 ft) per
Length overall: 1117 mm (44 in)	second
Length of barrel: 610 mm (24 in)	**Feed:** 5-round box magazine

FN F2000 Modular system

FN Herstal offered a succession of 5.56-mm assault rifles to replace the magnificent 7.62-mm FN FAL (known to the British Army as the SLR – Self Loading Rifle) that made the company's post-war reputation. None of them achieved great success: in a crowded market, most armies either bought American (the M16) or developed their own (the French FA MAS, the Italian Berettas, the quixotic British SA 80). So Belgian equivalents like the 5.56-mm FNC had limited impact. Whether the **FN F2000** will achieve major export sales is too early to tell, but it is an interesting design from a company with an eye for innovation – its P90 personal weapon certainly caught the world's attention when touted in the late 1980s. One look at the FN F2000 suggests that the ergonomic lessons of the P90 have not been forgotten. The FN F2000 is a very easy weapon to learn to shoot, and its construction lends itself to a quick and simple field-strip.

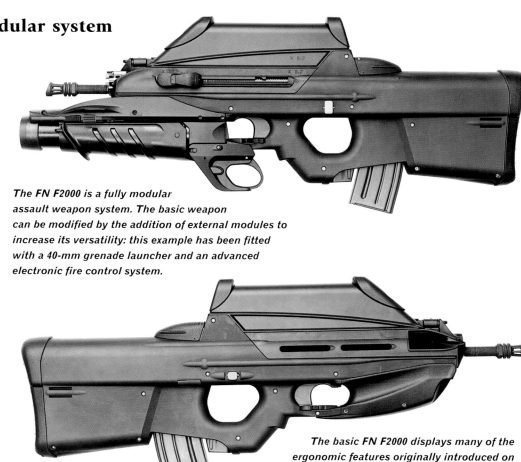

The FN F2000 is a fully modular assault weapon system. The basic weapon can be modified by the addition of external modules to increase its versatility: this example has been fitted with a 40-mm grenade launcher and an advanced electronic fire control system.

The basic FN F2000 displays many of the ergonomic features originally introduced on the advanced FN P90 sub-machine gun. Manufactured from smoothly-moulded polymers, it can be fired from either shoulder.

The mounting rail on top of the FN F2000 can accept a variety of sighting equipment. The standard x1.6 optical sight seen here can be replaced by night sights or the grenade FCS.

Weapon design

The FN F2000 is a 'bullpup' design – the magazine is located behind the trigger group to reduce the overall length of the gun to under 700 mm. This is useful for troops who will go to war in armoured personnel carriers who, when they dismount for battle, will

To allow for ambidextrous fire, spent cases are not ejected sideways as on a more conventional weapon: they are projected forwards from a port just behind and to the right of the muzzle.

often find themselves fighting in built-up areas.

The FN F2000 addresses one of the most serious drawbacks of the British bullpup rifle, the SA 80. The latter can only be fired from the right shoulder: if you try to fire it from the left, the spent cases will fly straight into your face. Since one in 20 soldiers are left-handed, this is not terribly helpful. More critically, when fighting in built-up areas, soldiers often need to be able to shoot around a left hand corner. To do so with an SA 80 forces you to expose far more of your body to return fire than is necessary.

The FN F2000 has a unique ejection system that funnels the ejected case along a tunnel, sending it forwards rather than sideways. A soldier can shoot left-handed without the risk of cases, gas or other debris striking the face. In addition, the fire selector, safety catch and magazine release are all positioned so they can be operated without difficulty with either hand.

Chambered for 5.56-mm x 45 NATO rounds, the FN F2000 is a conventional gas-operated, rotating bolt design. The high cyclic rate (over 800 rpm) produces accurate short bursts. The weapon is of modular construction. This enables users to quickly and easily modify the weapon for specific require-ments. (In truth, this is more relevant to law enforcement usage than the military, but with the growth of 'peacekeeping' missions, there is increasing cross-over between the two.) The stock is a tough polymer and the sighting rail can be fitted with whatever sighting system the user prefers (or army can afford). The standard option is a x1.6 optical sight: enough to

make an aimed shot easier but not so strong that both eyes need to be closed to aim. There is a mounting point ahead of the trigger guard so it can carry a grenade launcher, torch or other useful 'add on'.

Unlike traditional rifle designs, the FN F2000 has a pistol grip designed from the beginning to be equally comfortable when firing either rifle rounds or grenades. With a nod to developments across the Atlantic, FN do offer a comput-erised fire control module with laser rangefinder to calculate the point of aim and set the sights for the 40-mm grenade launcher. All such devices are open to the criticism that they are not truly 'soldier proof' i.e. robust enough for hard service in the field, as opposed to demonstration shoots for visiting media. They

also require power sources – batteries – that do not last long and the whole thing adds up to yet more weight for troops to carry. The fate of the famous SAS patrol 'Bravo Two Zero' should stand as a warning to even the fittest troops who attempt to go into action carrying extremely heavy loads.

Grenade launcher

The grenade launcher is a pump action, rotary locking weapon. It fires a wide range of 40-mm munitions: the basic high explosive round is fired with a muzzle velocity of 76 metres per second (249 ft/sec). The grenade launcher barrel is 230 mm (9.05 in) long and it increases the overall length of the weapon to 727 mm (28.6 in). This is still handy enough, especially compared to the older

SPECIFICATION	
FN 2000	**Length of barrell:** 400 mm (15.74 in)
Calibre: 5.56 (0.219 in) x 45 mm (1.77 in) NATO	**Magazine capacity:** 30 rounds
Length overall: 694 mm (27.3 in)	**Weight:** 3.6 kg (7.9 lb); 4.6 kg (10.1 lb) 40 mm (1.57 in) with grenade launcher

generation of 7.62-mm rifles that exceeded a metre in length.

Future prospects

Like all of today's advanced infantry weapons, the FN F2000's prospects depend on the willingness of Western governments to invest large sums of money in their infantry units. Whether any defence ministry will conclude the FN F2000 offers such a significant advantage over the M16 (or similar) that it can persuade its political masters to supply the necessary funds remains to be seen. The other stone in the road ahead is the continued commitment to 5.56-mm calibre: both the 1991 Gulf War and recent operations in Afghanistan have highlighted its limitations in a combat environment where long-range fire-fights are the rule rather than the exception. Some soldiers would like a return to 7.62-mm weapons; many armies have increased the number of 5.56-mm machine guns in their infantry units.

FABRIQUE NATIONALE: A BRIEF HISTORY

Fabrique Nationale d'Armes de Guerre has a long history of producing high quality military firearms. Established in 1889 to manufacture 150,000 Mauser rifles ordered by the Belgian government, the company entered into a significant relationship with John Moses Browning, probably the most innovative firearms designer in history.

In the 1930s, under the design leadership of Dieudonne Saive, the company began the development of a series of self-loading rifles which would provide the foundation of the company's post-war success.

The FN Model 49 was followed by the superb FN FAL, a classic battle rifle designed to make use of the new NATO standard 7.62-mm round. One of the most successful weapons of all time, the FAL was sold to more than 90 countries.

With the introduction of smaller calibre weapons in the 1960s and 1970s, FN introduced a derivative of the FAL which was redesigned to take the new NATO 5.56-mm round. The FNC was a fine weapon, being both accurate and reliable, but it did not achieve the export success of its famous progenitor.

Above: A version of the FN FAL was the standard British battle rifle for three decades.

The FN Model 49 was the company's first auto rifle.

The FNC is a light assault rifle based on the FN FAL.

FAMAS FELIN 5.56-mm assault rifle

This artwork suggests the possible appearance of French infantrymen of the next generation debussing from their VBCI infantry fighting vehicle with FAMAS FELIN rifles and PAPOP personal kit.

France introduced a bullpup rifle in 5.56-mm (0.219-in) calibre as the **FAMAS** in the course of the early 1980s after being formally adopted in 1978 following a development programme launched in 1972. The weapon's designation stands for Fusil d'Assaut de la Manufacture d'Armes de St Etienne (assault rifle from MAS), this last being a division of the state-owned GIAT Industries armaments organisation.

Successful weapon

Dubbed *le clairon* (the bugle) by the troops because of its unusual appearance, the FAMAS has gained a considerable measure of popular and operational success. This is in

marked and dramatic contrast to the dismal reputation of the British SA80 (more formally the L85), which has somehow contrived to be as heavy as the 0.3-in (7.62-mm) semi-automatic rifle it replaced.

Unlike the SA80, the FAMAS can easily be switched to fire from either shoulder (the cheek-

piece and ejector mechanism being switchable from one side to the other), and its integral folding bipod makes a long-range shot a rather more practical

The PAPOP concept is designed to produce a more capable type of French infantryman with considerably greater quantities of information available to him or her for both tactical and targeting purposes.

proposition. It is recommended that the change from left- to right-hand use, or vice versa, should not be attempted in the field as the process requires the

removal and later the reinstallation of several small components that could well be lost and thereby render the weapon inoperative.

The latest version of this useful French weapon, which operates on the delayed blow-back principle not commonly used for assault rifles and the like, is the **FAMAS G2**. This features a number of incremental improvements over the original FAMAS F1 and FAMAS F2 standards. Similar to the original FAMAS, the FAMAS G2 is designed with single-shot, three-round burst (for one pull of the trigger) and fully automatic firing capabilities controlled by a combined safety switch and selector inside the trigger guard with safe, single-shot and automatic positions. The selection between three-round burst and fully automatic fire modes is controlled by an automatic fire mode selector located beyond the magazine housing on the stock.

Other changes incorporated in this weapon include the replacement of the folding bipod (which can be reattached) by sling swivels, the omission of the inbuilt grenade launcher, the extension of the trigger guard to cover the whole of the grip, the modification of the magazine housing to accept NATO standard 30-round M16-type box magazines as well as the FAMAS's own particular 25-round magazine, and provision for the installation under the barrel of the M203 40-mm (1.57-in) grenade launcher. The FAMAS G2 can still be used to launch the 400-g (14.1-oz) rifle grenade, a type of weapon for which the French have shown great enthusiasm since World War I. The weapon's cyclic rate of fire is also adjustable in the range between 1,000 to 1,100 rounds per minute.

Recent developments

The **FAMAS FELIN** is a modified FAMAS F1 currently undergoing trials as part of France's future infantryman programme. The programme is known by the acronym PAPOP (Polyarme Polyprojectiles) and the system itself is similar in concept to the US Army's Land Warrior, the Australian Army's LAND 125 System and Britain's FIST.

The French programme involves GIAT Industries, Thomson-CSF Texen and six other companies. It also follows the basic requirements laid down in NATO Document AC225. This involves the development of the infantryman into a virtual 'weapon system' that must be able to operate at night with considerably greater efficiency and capability than are currently accepted for the infantryman; makes extensive and effective use of a wide range of visual aids for the assimilation and exploitation of tactical information; and provides a considerably superior capability in the engagement of targets behind cover than the current generation of conventional infantry armed with current in-service weapons of the rifle, machine-gun and grenade-launcher types.

Day and night firing

The FAMAS FELIN rifle thus carries equipment to facilitate day and night firing, offset firing using data received from another member of the team, rangefinding, instinctive aiming and firing and combat identification friend or foe. The weapon also carries the controls for the infantryman's communications system (radio,

*The **FAMAS FELIN** rifle adds a mass of targeting equipment and a small grenade launcher to the current **FAMAS** weapon, transforming the ability of the infantryman to fight with maximum effect by day and night.*

data and image). This combination of attributes is designed to provide a daylight 90 per cent hit probability on a standing and stationary man at 300 m (330 yards), declining to 50 per cent at 500 m (545 yards), and by night the same hit probabilities against the same type of target at 200 and 400 m (220 and 440 yards) respectively.

Ultimately this 'weapon system' concept will require a specialised and dedicated weapon that combines rifle and grenade-launcher capabilities of an advanced order. The intention is to develop and manufacture a weapon that provides its firer with significantly enhanced reach and a much higher level of lethality than the current range of personal weapons. Another feature that is required is

improved NBC protection providing full levels of protection against the effects of nuclear, biological and chemical weapons together with far greater user 'friendliness' than is provided by today's protective outfits. This is designed to ensure that the wearer has greater mobility (through reduced weight and greater flexibility, among other features) without any sacrifice in levels of protection. It is hoped that this integrated system will begin to enter service with the troops of the French army by the beginning of 2010, but this may be an overly optimistic date given the complexity of the tasks facing designers.

Weapon configuration

The current PAPOP combines a rifle, firing the now-standard

The French army is currently at a high level of operational capability, but the high command wants to transform these capabilities with more effective and versatile weapons operated by better informed troops.

5.56-mm x 45 cartridge, with a grenade-launcher that fires a grenade with a diameter of 35-mm (1.38-in) rather than 40-mm as featured in current American weapons as well as on the OICW. The reduction in calibre reduces weight and thereby improves portability and range, but care is being taken to ensure that the reductions in diameter and weight do not compromise operational capability.

Like the OICW, the French weapon has a digital 'support system'. This is designed to provide the facility for the detection of targets, by night as well as day, at ranges of up to 300 m (330 yards) and, importantly, for the discrimination between 'friendly' and 'hostile' troops. The French weapon utilises a remote sighting system to fire from cover, and can designate targets for other weapons. Video data are

transmitted to a head-up display on the soldier's visor in a fashion similar to that employed by modern warplanes. This provides the pilot with tactically important information in a readily assimilated fashion that does not require the user's eyes to be taken off the target or terrain ahead of him or her. In the land-based system, the data can be transmitted so that commanders can literally 'see' what their men are seeing.

Grenade

The French 35-mm grenade can be programmed at the moment of firing to optimise its fragmentation pattern for maximum effect on a specific target; in a fashion analogous to the adjustment of the choke of a shotgun, the fragmentation pattern of the grenade can be concentrated or dispersed. The 35-mm grenade weighs only 200 g (7 oz).

SPECIFICATION	
FAMAS G2	round magazine
Calibre: 5.56-mm (0.219in)	**Muzzle velocity:** 925 m (3,035 ft) per
Length overall: 757 mm (29.8 in)	second
Length of barrel: 488 mm (19.2 in)	**Rate of fire, cyclic:** 1,100 rpm
Weights: empty 3.8 kg (8.4 lb);	**Feed:** 30-round M16-type box magazine
4.17 kg (9.2 lb) loaded with 30-	

FN MAG Medium machine gun

The Belgian FN MAG is one of the most widely used of the post-World War II general-purpose machine guns. Well made from what are usually solid metal billets machined to specification, the MAG is a very sturdy but heavy weapon that is still in world-wide production.

World War II established the general-purpose machine gun (GPMG) as an essential weapon offering the provision for being fired from a light bipod in the assault role and from a heavy tripod in the defensive or sustained-fire roles. After 1945 many designers tried to produce their own version of the GPMG concept, and one of the best was produced in Belgium during the early 1950s. The company concerned was Fabrique Nationale (FN) based at Herstal, and its design became known as the **FN** **Mitrailleuse d'Appui Général** or **MAG**. It was not long before the MAG was adopted by many nations, and today it is one of the most widely used of all modern machine guns.

The MAG fires the standard NATO 7.62-mm (0.3-in) cartridge and is based on a conventional gas-operated mechanism in which gases, tapped off from the barrel, are used to drive the breech block and other components to the rear once a round has been fired. Where the FN MAG scores over many comparable designs is that the tapping-off point under the barrel incorporates a regulator device that allows the firer to control the amount of gas used and thus vary the fire rate to suit the ammunition and other

SPECIFICATION	
FN MAG	
Calibre: 7.62-mm (0.3-in)	**Muzzle velocity:** 840 m (2,756 ft) per second
Length overall: 1260 mm (49.6 in)	**Rate of fire, cyclic:** 600–1000 rpm
Length of barrel: 545 mm (21.46 in)	**Feed:** 50-round metal-link belt
Weights: gun 10.1 kg (22.27 lb); tripod 10.5 kg (23.15 lb); barrel 3 kg (6.6 lb)	

During the Falkland Islands campaign of 1982 the L7A1 was hastily pressed into use on improvised anti-aircraft mountings to provide some measure of defence against Argentine air attacks on the shipping in San Carlos harbour.

*The **FN MAG** is fitted to turrets of the **G**erman tanks in service with the **D**utch army. Pictured here in **S**eptember 1984 on **E**xercise 'Lionheart', the **MAG** has been fitted with a blank-firing adaptor.*

variables. For the sustained-fire role the barrel can be changed easily and quickly.

High-grade weapon

In construction the MAG is very sturdy. Some use is made of steel pressings riveted together, but many components are machined from solid metal, making the weapon somewhat heavy for easy transport. But this structural strength enables the weapon to absorb all manner of rough use, and it can be used for long periods without maintenance other than changing the barrels when they get too hot. The ammunition is belt-fed, which can be awkward when the weapon has to be carried with lengths of ammunition belt left hanging from the feed and snagging on just about everything.

When used as an LMG the MAG uses a butt and simple bipod, but as a sustained-fire weapon (with the butt usually

removed) is placed on a heavy tripod, usually with some form of buffering to absorb part of the recoil. However, the MAG can be adapted to a number of other mountings, and is often used as a co-axial weapon on armoured vehicles or as a vehicle defence weapon in a ball mounting, and as an anti-aircraft weapon on a tripod or vehicle-hatch mounting. It is also used on many light naval vessels.

British model

The MAG has been widely produced under licence. One of the better-known nations is the UK, where the MAG is known as the **L7A2**. The British introduced some modifications and have produced the weapon for export, and there is no sign of it being replaced in the foreseeable future as far as the British armed forces are concerned. Other nations that produce the MAG for their own use include Israel, South Africa, Singapore and Argentina, and there are others.

Even longer is the list of MAG users: a brief summary includes Sweden, Ireland, Greece, Canada, New Zealand, the Netherlands and so on. There is little chance of the MAG falling out of fashion.

*Right: The **FN MAG** is licence-produced in Israel by Israel Military Industries and is used by all branches of the Israeli armed forces.*

GPMG in operation
Sustained fire

The General-Purpose Machine Gun (GPMG) used by the British army is a development of the Belgian FN MAG, the most successful machine gun of the period after World War II.

Above: The GPMG provided most of the firepower of a British army infantry section. Here, the gunner concentrates on firing short bursts on the target, while his assistant ensures that the belt is feeding into the gun properly.

More than 200,000 GPMGs have been made and about 75 different armies have adopted the weapon. It is a tough, straightforward weapon, light enough to be carried by one man, but it can be tripod-mounted and used to deliver sustained fire.

When it was introduced into British service it replaced two weapons: the water-cooled Vickers heavy machine gun that had been in use since before World War I and the famous Bren light machine-gun that British troops found so effective in World War II.

For the last 50 years, infantry tactics have been built around the firepower of the individual section, varying between eight and 13 men in strength, depending upon the army. There are usually two or three men in the gun group, with the rest making up the rifle group or groups. The gun group lays down covering fire with a light machine gun on a bipod, to keep the enemies' heads down while the riflemen advance. The rifle group then lays down fire so that the gun group can advance; in this manner the section leapfrogs forward to assault the enemy. This technique was used very successfully by British troops in the Falklands.

Enemy suppression

The other main role undertaken by the machine gun is the delivery of continuous fire to suppress enemy positions or dominate areas of ground with a hail of bullets. This SF (Sustained Fire) role was traditionally left to heavy, tripod-mounted weapons, which were usually cooled by a continuous flow of water in a casing around the barrel.

During World War II, the Germans developed the MG 42 machine gun that was able to fulfil both roles. When mounted on a bipod it was excellent in the light role; and thanks to clever design and an easy-to-change barrel, it could be mounted on a tripod, fitted with special sights and successfully used in the SF role. The general-purpose machine gun had been born.

The idea of a GPMG was very attractive. Soldiers needed to learn the workings of only one weapon, and just one set of spares had to be produced. After World War II many rival designs appeared: the FN, forerunner of the GPMG, was the best.

SBS assault

In the Falklands War the Royal Marines Special Boat Squadron relied heavily on the GPMG, especially during the landings at San Carlos Water. 'S' section and some attached commandos, about 40 men in total, attacked an Argentine position on Fanning Head with 16 GPMGs between

them. They fired predominantly tracer rounds to give the impression that a unit of at least battalion strength was assaulting the position and bluffed the enemy into submission!

Firing from the hip

In close-quarter battle a belt of only 50 rounds was normally used and often the gunner employed an old 1944 pattern water-bottle pouch as a feedbag to the right of the GPMG field tray. As he advanced with a sling across his back and shoulders, he could fire the weapon from the hip at any target that presented itself.

This method was used on 19 July 1972 during the Battle of Mirbat in Oman when a force of 80 members of 'G' squadron, 22 SAS, rushed to the rescue of an eight-man SAS training team that had been attacked by 250 Arab communist guerrillas. Nearly every third man in the relief force carried a GPMG. For employment in the SF role,

the GPMG was mounted on a tripod. This was a spring-buffered assembly, and the gun was simply dropped into its cradle and held there by two pins, so that once locked in place it could recoil for a short distance, the tripod mounting's spring buffers absorbing the shock.

In British army service the GPMGs were grouped and used in the SF role, rather like the Vickers machine guns they had replaced. The use of several machine guns together allowed a large area of ground to be swept with bullets, making it impossible for enemy infantry to move across it. Placed on the flanks of a defensive position, GPMGs were used to cover the ground in front of British trenches.

Multi-purpose

Moreover, the GPMG was a multi-purpose weapon. Main battle tanks use a modified version, in which the belt can be loaded without lifting

The GPMG's integral bipod makes it very accurate indeed, especially when used from the prone position.

the top cover, an action that would be awkward in the cramped interior of a tank turret. This version also vents all gases through the barrel and thus outside the vehicle, rather than from the gas regulator; otherwise the tank would quickly fill with fumes.

The GPMG was replaced in British army infantry service by the L86 Light Support Weapon (LSW). Each section has one L86, three L85 Individual Weapons and eight SA 80 rifles.

GPMGs in the Gulf

The GPMG and its twin brother, the FN MAG, went to war in a big way in the Gulf during Operation Desert Storm in 1991. The GPMG was used by the British 1st Armoured Division, and the FN MAG equipped Coalition troops from Egypt, Pakistan, Morocco, Oman, the United Arab Emirates, Qatar and Kuwait.

The same basic machine gun has also been employed by elements of the US Army as a co-axially or trainably mounted machine gun for vehicle applications. The GPMG has performed well, sustaining its reputation as the world's best general-purpose machine gun.

THE BASIC BELGIAN: THE GENERAL-PURPOSE MACHINE GUN

Light in weight and easy to carry, strongly and simply constructed, easy to strip and maintain, and firing the potent 7.62-mm (0.3-in) NATO round, the General-Purpose Machine Gun was for many years the British Army's first-line automatic support weapon, although it has now been largely superseded by the L86 LSW in infantry service.

Gas regulator
In action, the rate of fire of the GPMG can be regulated by varying the amount of gas that acts on the piston.

Carrying handle
The main carrying handle is attached to the barrel so that it can be removed even when hot.

Breech block
The gas from every round fired acts on the piston, causing the breech block to be driven back to pick up the next round.

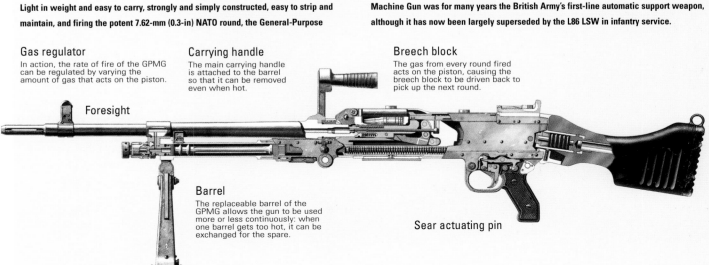

Foresight

Barrel
The replaceable barrel of the GPMG allows the gun to be used more or less continuously: when one barrel gets too hot, it can be exchanged for the spare.

Sear actuating pin

FN Minimi Light machine gun

The FN Minimi has been adopted by the US Army for the Squad Automatic Weapon (SAW) role as the M249. It entered service first with the airborne divisions of what was at the time the Rapid Deployment Joint Task Force.

With the switch from the heavy 7.62-mm (0.3-in) cartridge toward the lighter 5.56-mm (0.219-in) round for use by the standard rifles of most of the NATO nations and many others, there emerged the need for a light machine gun in the smaller calibre. FN accordingly designed a new weapon that eventually became known as the **FN Minimi** and was first shown in 1974.

The Minimi is intended for use only as a squad support weapon as there is no way that the 5.56-mm cartridge can be used effectively for the heavy support or sustained-fire role as its round is ineffective at ranges over 400 m (437 yards). Thus

Above: The ammunition belt for the Minimi is tucked neatly into a box under the weapon's body in a fashion that offers no encumbrance to the firer in tactical operations, even when firing in the prone position.

The Minimi is light, and also comfortable to carry and use. The handle above the weapon doubles for carrying the weapon and also changing the barrel.

The Minimi is fitted as standard with a folding bipod, all that is necessary to stabilize the weapon for support fire at short and medium ranges.

Into US service

The association with the M16 has benefited FN, for the Minimi has been adopted as the squad fire-support weapon of the US Army, to whom the Minimi is known as the **M249 Squad Automatic Weapon**. This fires the new standard NATO SS109 cartridge rather than the earlier M193 cartridge. The SS109 has a longer and heavier bullet than the earlier cartridge and uses a different rifling in the barrel, but is otherwise similar to the US cartridge.

Two possible variants of the Minimi are a 'para' version with a shorter barrel and a sliding butt, and a butt-less model for AFV mountings. The Minimi itself has many ingenious detail points: the trigger guard may be removed to allow convenient operation by a man wearing winter or NBC warfare gloves, the front hand-guard contains a cleaning kit, the ammunition feed box has a simple indicator to show how many rounds are left (something that can be life-saving in a combat situation), and so on.

SPECIFICATION	
FN Minimi	**Muzzle velocity:** (SS109) 915 m
Calibre: 5.56-mm (0.219-in)	(3,002 ft) per second
Length overall: 1050 mm (41.3 in)	**Rate of fire, cyclic:** 750–1000 rpm
Length of barrel: 465 mm (18.3 in)	**Type of feed:** 100- or 200-round belt
Weights: with bipod 6.5 kg	or 30-round box magazine
(14.33 lb); with 200 rounds 9.7 kg	
(21.38 lb)	

heavier-calibre weapons such as the FN MAG are retained for this longer-range role.

Mix of old and new

The Minimi uses some design features from the earlier FN MAG, including the quick-change barrel and the gas regulator, but a new rotary locking device is used for the breech block, which is guided inside the receiver by two guide rails to ensure a smooth transport. These changes have made the Minimi a remarkably reliable weapon, and further reliability was introduced in the ammunition feed. This is one of the Minimi's major contributions to modern light machine gun design as it does away with the long and

awkward flapping ammunition belts typical of many other designs. The Minimi uses a simple box (fitted under the gun body) to carry the neatly folded belt. When the weapon is fired from a bipod, the box is so

arranged that it will not interfere with normal use, and on the move the box is out of the way of the carrier. But the Minimi goes one step further: if required, the belt feed can be replaced by a magazine feed.

FN shrewdly decided that the American M16 rifle would quickly become the standard weapon in its class, and thus made provision for the Minimi to use the M16's 30-round magazine. This can clip into the receiver just under the belt feed guides.

Modern weapons have to be tolerant of effective and reliable use in any and every part of the world under the most adverse of conditions.

Chinese machine guns

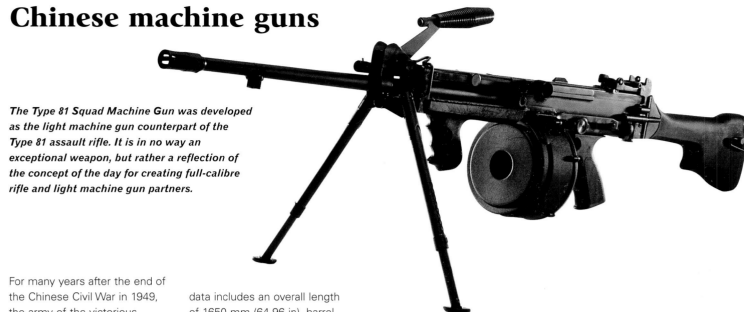

The Type 81 Squad Machine Gun was developed as the light machine gun counterpart of the Type 81 assault rifle. It is in no way an exceptional weapon, but rather a reflection of the concept of the day for creating full-calibre rifle and light machine gun partners.

For many years after the end of the Chinese Civil War in 1949, the army of the victorious communists used old weapons bought by the defeated nationalist regime and newer designs of Soviet origin but manufactured in China.

The first machine gun of Chinese design was the gas-operated **Type 67**, a 7.62-mm (0.3-in) light machine gun that drew its inspiration from a number of weapons, including the Soviet DPM, RPD and SGM for its trigger mechanism, gas regulator and barrel-change arrangement, as well as features of the feed mechanism and the bolt and piston from the MG 08 and vz 26 respectively. The Type 67 was standardised in 1967 to replace the Type 53 and Type 57 in the battalion-level heavy machine gun role on a tripod mounting, and the Type 58 in the company-level medium machine gun role on its folding bipod mounting. The Type 67 weighs 24 kg (52.9 lb), and its other data includes an overall length of 1650 mm (64.96 in), barrel length of 605 mm (23.82 in), cyclic rate of fire of 700 rounds per minute and feed from a metal-link belt carrying 250 7.62-mm x 54 cartridges fired with a velocity of 840 m (2,756 ft) per second.

Improved models

Development of the basic weapon, standardised in 1978 and 1982 respectively, are the **Type 67-1** and **Type 67-2** with their overall length reduced to 1345 mm (52.95 in). The Type 67-1 weighs 25 kg (55.1 lb) and is a modestly improved version of the Type 67, while the Type 67-2 was introduced to replace both the Type 67 and Type 67-1. The Type 67-2 makes use of composite materials to reduce weight and uses a 25-round segmented feed arrangement.

In the mid-1980s the Chinese introduced another 7.62-mm machine gun, the **Type 80** that had been standardised in 1980 as the Chinese version of the Soviet PKMS. The Type 80 is lighter than the Type 67 models, and possesses better performance.

Light machine gun

The **Type 81 Squad Machine gun** was the light machine gun counterpart of the 7.62-mm Type 81 assault rifle, and can fire from its own 75-round drum magazine or the rifle's 30-round box magazine. The machine gun has an inbuilt bipod, loaded weight of 5.15 kg (11.35 lb) and cyclic rate of fire of 700 rpm. China's new standard calibre is 8.5-mm (0.335-in), and the machine gun designed to fire the Type 87 cartridge in this calibre is the **QJY-88**. This is intended as successor to the older 12.7-mm (0.5-in) and 7.62-mm machine guns in Chinese service. The QJY-88 is a gas-operated and air-cooled weapon that can be mounted on a tripod or its inbuilt folding bipod, and weighs 11.8 kg (26 lb).

The **Type 95 Squad Machine Gun** counterpart of the new Type 95 lightweight assault rifle. This is a bullpup design with a folding bipod and feed from a prominent 75-round drum magazine.

SPECIFICATION	
Type 67-2	tripod 5 kg (11 lb)
Calibre: 7.62-mm (0.3-in)	**Muzzle velocity:** 840 m (2,756 ft) per second
Length overall: 1345 mm (52.95 in)	**Rate of fire, cyclic:** 650 rpm
Length of barrel: 606 mm (23.86 in)	**Feed:** 25-round belt segments
Weights: gun 15.5 kg (34.17 kg);	

Lehky Kulomet vz 59 Machine gun

Czechoslovak machine gun designers can trace their progeny back to the range of highly successful machine guns started with the vz (*vzor*, or model) 26 in 1926 and which led to the famous Bren gun. As successor to these designs the Czechoslovaks produced a new model during the early 1950s as the Lehky Kulomet vz 52, essentially the old design updated to use an ammunition belt-feed system. This was not the success of the earlier weapons, and is now rarely encountered other than in the hands of 'freedom fighters' and the like, and was therefore superseded by the **Lehky Kulomet vz 59**. This is much simpler than the vz 52 but follows the same general lines in appearance and operation. In fact many of the operating principles of the vz 52 were carried over to the new weapon, these including the gas-operated mechanism. The ammunition feed system was also a carry-over from the vz 52, in which it was regarded by many as being the only successful feature. In this feed system the belt is carried into the receiver by guides where a cam system takes over and pushes the cartridge forward through the belt link into the weapon. This system was copied on the Soviet PK series, but on the vz 59 the belts are fed from metal boxes. Another change in the vz 59 was the adoption of the more

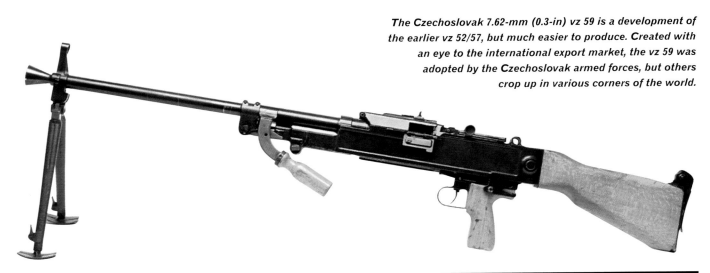

The Czechoslovak 7.62-mm (0.3-in) vz 59 is a development of the earlier vz 52/57, but much easier to produce. Created with an eye to the international export market, the vz 59 was adopted by the Czechoslovak armed forces, but others crop up in various corners of the world.

powerful Soviet 7.62-mm (0.3-in) x 54 cartridge in place of the shorter cartridge of the same notional calibre that was used in the vz 52 series.

For the light machine gun role with a light barrel and designation **vz 59L**, one of these boxes can be hung from the right-hand side of the gun in a rather unbalanced fashion. The weapon can be operated in the light machine gun role on bipod and tripod mountings.

Heavy barrel

For the sustained-fire role the vz 59 is fitted with a heavy barrel. In this form the weapon is known merely as the vz 59, but fitted with a solenoid for

installation in AFVs in a co-axial or similar mount it is the **vz 59T**. This did not exhaust the variations of the vz 59 series for, with an eye to sales outside Czechoslovakia, there is a version that fires standard NATO 7.62-mm (0.3-in) ammunition and is known as the **vz 59N** or, later, as the **Universalny Kulomet vz 68**, which is still in production by Zbrojovka Vsetin.

Telescopic sight

One rather unusual feature of the vz 59 is the x4 telescopic sight, which can be used with the bipod and the tripod. This sight may be illuminated internally for use at night and is also used for anti-aircraft fire, for which role the

SPECIFICATION	
Lehky Kulomet vz 59	8.67 kg (19.1 lb); with tripod and
Calibre: 7.62-mm (0.3-in)	heavy barrel 19.24 kg (42.42 lb)
Length overall: light barrel 1116 mm	**Muzzle velocity:** with light barrel 810
(43.94 in); heavy barrel 1215 mm	m (2,657 ft) per second; heavy
(47.84 in)	barrel 830 m (2,723 ft) per second
Length of barrel: light 593 mm (23.35	**Rate of fire, cyclic:** 700–800 rpm
in); heavy 693 mm (27.28 in)	**Feed:** 50- or 250-round metal-link belt
Weights: with bipod and light barrel	

vz 59 is placed on top of a tubular extension to the normal tripod.

In the past Czechoslovak weapons have appeared wherever there was a market for small arms, and are still popular

with many purchasers. Czechoslovak weapons have therefore been encountered in the Middle East, and especially in Lebanon during the 1970s and 1980s.

The vz 59 is a useful machine gun that can be operated in the light role with a short, light barrel and a boxed belt, or in the sustained-fire role with a long, heavy barrel and belted ammunition. The weapon is cocked by movement of the pistol grip.

Universal Machine Gun 7.62 mm

MAS AAT 52 Machine gun

The French AAT 52 uses a delayed blowback mechanism with a fluted chamber to ease extraction. A 7.62-mm (0.3-in) version – known as the AAT F1 – may also be encountered, but neither model is now in production. Bipod and tripod versions are in use, as are vehicle-mounted models.

The machine gun now known as the **MAS AAT 52** was developed as a direct result of the Indo-China campaigns of the early 1950s. At that time the French army was equipped with a wide array of American, British and ex-German weapons, and the furnishing of support and spares for this array was too much for the army, which decided to adopt one general-purpose machine gun. The result was the 7.5-mm (0.295-in) AAT 52, a weapon designed from the outset for ease of production, and thus incorporating many stamped and welded components.

Delayed blowback

The AAT 52 is unusual among modem machine guns in

The French Foreign Legion uses exactly the same weapons as the rest of the French army and so the AAT 52 machine gun, seen here in its light machine gun form, is a familiar sight wherever the legion operates.

relying on a form of delayed-blowback operation, in which the force of the cartridge firing is employed to drive back the breech block to the starting position, and also to power the feed mechanism. This system works very well with pistol cartridges in sub-machine guns, but the use of rifle cartridges in machine guns demands something more positive if safety is to be assured. On the AAT 52 a two-part block is used: a lever device is so arranged that it holds the forward part of the block in position while the rear half starts to move to the rear; only when the lever has moved a predetermined distance does it allow the forward part of the block to move back. In order to make the spent cartridge easier to extract the chamber has grooves that allow gas to enter between the chamber wall and the fired cartridge to prevent 'sticking', and a cartridge fired in an AAT 52 can always be recognised by the fluted grooves around the case neck.

Bipod and tripod

The AAT 52 can be fired from a bipod or a tripod, but when a tripod is used for the sustained fire role a heavy barrel is fitted to the weapon. When used in the light machine gun role the AAT 52 is a rather clumsy weapon to carry, especially if a

50-round ammunition box is carried on the left-hand side. For this reason the box is often left off and the ammunition belt allowed to hang free. An unusual feature of the AA 52 is that for the light machine gun role a monopod is fitted under the butt. This can be awkward, as can be the barrel-change feature: the barrel can be removed readily enough, but the bipod is permanently attached to the barrel and in the light machine gun role this can make barrel-changing very difficult, especially as the AAT 52 barrels have no plating to reduce its temperature.

The AAT 52 was originally intended to fire a 7.5-mm cartridge first developed for use by the mle 1929 light machine gun. This cartridge is powerful enough, but the switch to the NATO 7.62-mm (0.3-in) cartridge left the French army using a non-standard cartridge, and export prospects for the AAT 52 were thus reduced. The basic design was therefore adapted to fire the NATO cartridge in a version known as the **AAT F1**. Some of these were issued to French army units, but exports did not materialise.

Overall the AA 52 is an adequate machine gun, but it has many features that are at best undesirable and, in the eyes of some, inherently unsafe. The weapon is no longer in production.

SPECIFICATION	
MAS AAT 52	**Weights:** with bipod and light barrel
Calibre: 7.5-mm (0.295-in)	9.97 kg (21.98 lb); with bipod and
Length overall: with butt extended	heavy barrel 11.37 kg (25.07 lb);
(light barrel) 1145 mm (45.08 in) or	tripod 10.6 kg (23.37 lb)
(heavy barrel) 1245 mm (49.02 in)	**Muzzle velocity:** 840 m (2,756 ft)
Length of barrel: light 500 mm	per second
(19.69 in); heavy 600 mm	**Rate of fire, cyclic:** 700 rpm
(23.62 in)	**Feed:** 50-round metal-link belt

Heckler & Koch Machine guns

The German small arms designer and manufacturer Heckler & Koch, based at Oberndorf-Neckar and now owned by BAE Systems of the UK, is among the most prolific of all modern small arms design organisations, and in addition to its successful range of assault rifles and sub-machine guns, also produces a wide variety of air-cooled machine guns.

It may be an over-simplification to describe them thus, but Heckler & Koch machine guns are basically modified versions of the company's G3 and associated assault rifles. They all use the same delay-roller mechanism on their two-part breech blocks, and some of the light machine guns could be described as little more than assault rifles with heavier barrels and a bipod mounting.

To confuse the issue, Heckler & Koch produces virtually every one of its models in both belt- and magazine-fed versions, and some are produced in 7.62-mm (0.3-in) or 5.56-mm (0.219-in) calibres, with the added variation in the latter for the new SS109 cartridge or the older American M193 cartridge. A feature of several of the magazine-fed weapons is that the standard type of 20- or 30-round box magazine can be replaced by an 80-round double-drum plastic magazine.

Basic model

One of the 'base' models in the range is the 7.62-mm **HK-21A1**, a development of the original **HK-21** which entered production in 1970 but is no longer in production. The HK-21A1 uses only the belt-feed system, and can be operated as a light machine gun on a bipod or in the medium machine gun (otherwise sustained-fire) role when installed on a tripod mounting. For the sustained-fire role, a barrel-change capability is built into the weapon so that an overheating barrel can quickly be replaced.

The HK-21A1 is now made under licence only in Greece and Portugal. Even in this version of

The Heckler & Koch HK-11 is the box magazine feed variant of the HK-21 and is a 7.62-mm (0.3-in) weapon.

The Heckler & Koch HK-13 is produced in several versions. This model accommodates a 40-round box magazine.

The Heckler & Koch HK-13E has a three-round burst capability as well as full automatic fire.

The Heckler & Koch HK-21 is no longer produced in Germany, but is still in use with nations such as Portugal.

The HK-21A1 is a development of the earlier HK-21. It uses a belt feed only, and the belt can be contained in a box slung under the receiver.

the Heckler & Koch range the outline of the G3 rifle is apparent, and this is carried over to the current version of the HK-21, the **HK-21E**, which has a longer sight radius and a three-round burst selection feature. The barrel is longer, and changes have been made to the ammunition feed. There is also a 5.56-mm counterpart to this variant, the **HK-23E**.

All the variants mentioned above are belt-fed weapons. There is also a magazine-fed version for every one of them: the **HK-11A1** is the magazine counterpart of the HK 21A1, while the **HK-11E** and **HK-13E** are the magazine-fed counterparts of the HK-21E and HK-23E. The weapons of the **HK-13** series entered production in 1972, and

were designed to complement the HK-33 series of assault rifles in 5.56-mm calibre. Like the assault rifle, they found their initial market largely in South-East Asia where the small size, light weight and modest recoil forces of weapons associated with the 5.56-mm round first received universal approval during the first part of the 1970s.

Great flexibility

All this may sound rather confusing, but the basic factor that emerges from this diversity of calibres, ammunition feed systems and mountings is the ability of Heckler & Koch to produce a machine gun suited to virtually any and every tactical requirement. The belt-fed versions may be regarded as

general-purpose machine guns, although the 5.56-mm versions may really be too light for the sustained-fire role, and the magazine-fed versions may be seen as true light machine guns. The weapons of this important series offer a surprising amount of interchangeability of spare parts, and the magazines are usually the same as those used on their equivalent assault rifles, facilitating the use of the automatic as a squad support weapon.

Heckler & Koch's latest light

machine gun offering is the **MG 36** in 5.56-mm calibre. This is a state-of-the-art weapon with an overall length of 998 mm (39.3 in), barrel length of 480 mm (18.9 in) and weight of 3.57 kg (7.87 lb) with a bipod mount but without a magazine. The MG 36 reflects modern assault rifle design in its compact design, extensive use of composite materials, carrying handle with an inbuilt sight arrangement and feed from a 30-round box magazine or a 100-round dual-drum magazine.

SPECIFICATION	
HK-21A1	**Muzzle velocity:** 800 m (2,625 ft) per second
Calibre: 7.62-mm (0.3-in)	**Rate of fire, cyclic:** 900 rounds per minute
Length overall: 1030 mm (40.55 in)	
Length of barrel: 450 mm (17.72 in)	**Feed:** 100-round metal-link belt
Weight: 8.3 kg (18.3 lb) with bipod	

MG3 Machine gun

The MG3 is the modern version of the MG 42 of World War II fame, and is currently rated as one of the best machine guns of its type used by NATO. It has a high rate of fire and an easy and rapid barrel-change capability, and can be fired from the bipod shown or from a heavy tripod for the sustained fire-support role.

One of the outstanding machine gun designs of World War II was the MG 42. This German air-cooled weapon introduced the advantages of mass production to an area of weapon design that had for long clung to traditional methods of construction using large numbers of time-consuming and expensive machining operations to create

high-quality components from solid metal. With the MG 42, the new era of construction through the use of steel pressings and welded components was allied to an excellent design that attracted widespread respect and attention.

Old for new

When the Federal Republic of Germany became a member of

NATO and was once more allowed a measure of weapon production for the equipment of the new armed forces, the MG 42 was one of the first designs to be resurrected.

The original MG 42 had been designed to fire Germany's standard 7.92-mm (0.312-in) ammunition of the period up to the end of World War II. But with the adoption of the standard NATO small arms ammunition in 7.62-mm (0.3-in) calibre, the original design was reworked to accommodate the new type of ammunition. At first stockpiled MG 42 machine guns were simply modified to this calibre with the designation **MG2**, but

in parallel with this activity a production programme was launched by Rheinmetall for the manufacture of new weapons in the 7.62-mm calibre. There were several variants of this production version, all having the designation **MG1**, although there were some minor changes to suit ammunition feed and so on.

Current model

The current production version is the **MG3**, which is still manufactured in Germany by Rheinmetall.

In appearance, the war-time MG 42 and the MG3 are identical apart from some

SPECIFICATION	
MG3	**Muzzle velocity:** 820 m (2,690 ft) per second
Calibre: 7.62-mm (0.3-in)	
Length overall: 1225 mm (48.23 in) with butt	**Rate of fire, cyclic:** 700–1,300 rounds per minute
Length of barrel: 531 mm (20.91 in)	**Feed:** 50-round metal-link belt
Weight: basic gun 10.5 kg (23.15 lb); bipod 0.55 kg (1.213 lb)	

The overall tactical flexibility of the German MG3 machine gun is enhanced by the weapon's long pedigree of reliability and the availability of several types of mounting.

minor details, few of which can be detected by the untrained eye, and there are more changes between the MG1 and MG3. Overall, however, the modern MG3 retains all the attributes of the original, and many of the mountings used with the MG3 are just adaptations or simple modifications of the World War

II originals. Thus the MG3 can be used on a tripod that is virtually identical to the original, and the twin mounting for anti-aircraft use could still accommodate the MG 42 without trouble. There are now available many mountings for the MG3.

As noted above, the original MG 42 was designed for ease of mass production, and this same feature makes the MG3 very suitable for manufacture in some of the world's less industrialized nations. The MG3 has proved to be relatively easy for such facilities and it is now or has been licence-

produced in nations such as Chile, Pakistan, Spain and Turkey; some of these nations, it should be noted, fabricate versions of the MG1 rather than the MG3 proper. Yugoslavia also produces a version of this weapon, but the Yugoslav model is a direct copy of the MG 42, still in 7.92-mm calibre and designated **SARAC M1953**.

Widespread service

Within NATO the MG3, or one or other of its variants, is used by the German and Italian armed forces, and also by the forces of nations such as Denmark and Norway. Portugal

makes the MG3 for use by the Portuguese armed forces, and has also offered the type for export. Thus from many sources the old MG 42 design soldiers on, for the basic design of the MG3 is still as sound as it ever was, and any attempt to improve or modify the original appears to many to be a pointless exercise.

The MG3, seen here on its bipod mount, is operated by a two-man crew comprising the gunner and his loader, who feeds the metallic-link belts of ammunition from man-portable boxes.

PK Machine gun

One very noticeable feature in Soviet small-arms design is the strange mixture of innovation and conservatism that seems typical of every generation of weapons. Despite the impact made by the then-novel 7.62-mm (0.3-in) x 39 cartridge used in the AK-47 assault rifle family, Soviet machine guns continued to use the more powerful 7.62-mm x 54R cartridge with a rimmed base. This rim was originally used for extraction from the Mosin-Nagant rifle series, and the cartridge was also adopted for the **PK** general-purpose machine guns.

There are several members of the PK family. The PK is the basic gun with a heavy barrel marked by flutes along its exterior. This was first seen in 1946, and after that the **IKM** arrived on the scene as an improved version of the PK with

The Soviet 7.62-mm (0.3-in) PK machine gun is seen here in its PKM light machine gun form. It is a simple and sturdy weapon with few moving parts, and has been widely used by Warsaw Pact and other armed forces around the world.

features to lighten it and simplify its construction. The **PKS** is a PK mounted on a tripod for use in the anti-aircraft as well as ground fire roles. The **PKT** is for use in AFVs, while the **PKM** is the PK with a bipod. When the PKM is mounted on a tripod it becomes the **PKMS**. The **PKB** has the usual butt and trigger mechanism replaced by spade grips and a 'butterfly' trigger.

The PK appears to be all things to all men, and as far as

When mounted on a tripod for the sustained-fire role, the PKM becomes the PKMS, the bipod legs being folded back under the barrel.

the Red Army is concerned it was a true multi-role type that was used in roles ranging from infantry squad support to AFV use in special mountings.

The PK machine guns operate on the same principle, based on the Kalashnikov rotary-bolt system. The interior of the PK is populated by surprisingly few parts: the bolt/breech block, a piston, a few springs, the ammunition feed's few more parts, and that is about it. Thus the PK has few parts to break or jam. When used in the light machine gun role, the weapon generally has its ammunition in a metal box slung under the gun. For tripod operation variable-length belts are used. In the sustained-fire role the barrel has to be changed at regular

intervals even though it is chromium-plated to reduce wear and promote heat dissipation.

The latest development of the PKM is the **Pecheneg**, which has an 80% commonality of parts but introduces a new, fixed barrel with a forced-draught cooling system allowing the gun to fire about 1,000 rounds per hour or 600 rounds in 40/50-round bursts.

The PK weapons must rank among the most numerous of all modern machine guns, being used not only by the Soviet and Warsaw Pact armies and their successors, but also by a large number of export customers including the Chinese, who use the type in the form of their **Type 80** copy made within China.

SPECIFICATION	
PK	**Muzzle velocity:** 825 m (2,707 ft) per second
Calibre: 7.62-mm (0.3-in)	**Rate of fire, cyclic:** 690–720 rpm
Length overall: 1160 mm (45.7 in)	**Feed:** 100-, 200- and 250-round metal-link belts
Length of barrel: 658 mm (25.9 in)	
Weights: gun empty 9 kg (19.84 lb); tripod 7.5 kg (16.53 lb); 100-round belt 2.44 kg (5.38 lb)	

RPK Machine gun

Though the PK series was developed for the general-purpose machine gun role, the 7.62-mm (0.3-in) **RPK** was created for the light machine gun or squad support task. The RPK was first noted in 1966 and may be regarded as an enlarged version of the AKM assault rifle. It has a longer and heavier barrel and a light bipod, but is otherwise the same weapon as the AKM.

The Soviet RPK was the standard Warsaw Pact squad fire support weapon. It does not have an interchangeable barrel and thus is not capable of sustained fire. The design may be regarded as a development of the AKM assault rifle, and it fires the same 7.62-mm (0.3-in) ammunition. A Chinese version is known as the Type 74.

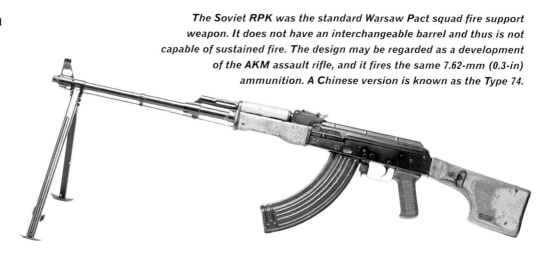

This commonality of weapons makes a great deal of sense. The AKM fires the same 7.62-mm x 39 ammunition as the assault rifle, but the commonality goes further as some spare parts can be interchanged, and any soldier who can use the AKM can pick up and fire the RPK with equal facility. In the absence of its special 75-round drum magazine, the RPK can be fitted with an AKM box magazine. However, the RPK has no bayonet-mounting lug.

Fixed barrel

Given that the weapon was intended as a light machine gun, it is surprising that the RPK does not have provision for changing the barrel when it gets hot. In order to ensure the barrel does not overheat, recruits are trained to limit burst-firing to about 80 shots per minute. For most tactical purposes this is more than adequate, but there must be times when this fire rate has its disadvantages. Apart from the 75-round drum already mentioned, there are curved box magazines holding 30 or 40 rounds. Some RPKs have been seen with infra-red night sights, and a copy produced by the Chinese is the **Type 74**.

In the early 1970s the Red Army changed its standard rifle cartridge to the 5.45-mm (0.215-in) x 18 type, and to fire this cartridge the AK-47 was developed into the AK-74. It was clear that a new version of the RPK would follow, and this materialised as the **RPK-74**. Apart from scaling down some parts to suit the smaller calibre, the RPK-74 is identical to the RPK.

Popular weapon

The RPK was a popular weapon with the Soviet and many Warsaw Pact nations to which it was delivered. The type appears to have been produced in East Germany, and as far as can be determined the RPK is still in production in what are now the countries of the CIS. The weapon was delivered to a number of countries sympathetic to the Soviet way of thinking, and needless to say the RPK has also found its way into the hands of many 'freedom fighters'. The RPK was seen in action during the Lebanese civil war of the 1970s and 1980s, and the type also saw considerable action in Angola both against the Portuguese and then in the following civil war. Despite its rate-of-fire limitations, the RPK will no doubt be around for many years to come, and the Russian army and its allies of the CIS retain huge numbers.

SPECIFICATION	
RPK	**Muzzle velocity:** 732 m (2,402 ft) per second
Calibre: 7.62-mm (0.3-in)	**Rate of fire, cyclic:** 660 rpm
Length overall: 1035 mm (40.75 in)	**Feed:** 75-round drum, or 30- and 40-round box magazines
Length of barrel: 591 mm (23.3 in)	
Weights: gun 5 kg (11.02 lb); 75-round drum 2.1 kg (4.63 lb)	

Russian heavy machine guns

The world's most powerful machine gun in large-scale service is the **KPV (Krasnoy Pulemet Vladimorova)**, a weapon designed in the USSR from 1944 to use the Soviet 14.5-mm (0.57-in) x 115 cartridge, whose API and HEIT bullets have twice as much energy as a 12.7-mm (0.5-in) projectile.

The KPV entered service in the later 1940s, and is generally associated with wheeled mountings towed by light vehicles. The standard mountings are the ZPU-1, -2 and -4 carrying one, two or four such weapons, which have also been used on a number of AFVs. Weighing 49.1 kg (108.25 lb), increasing to 161.5 kg (356 lb) in its ZPU-1 form, the KPV is air-cooled with a chromed barrel, and operated on the short-recoil system with gas assistance.

Below: On a towed four-wheel carriage, the ZPU-4 offers considerable firepower in the light anti-aircraft role, but lacks power operation and anything but a simple on-carriage sighting system.

Above: Soviet armoured fighting vehicles are fitted with an assortment of machine guns as their secondary armament, this turret-mounted weapon for the anti-aircraft and local defence role being a 12.7-mm (0.5-in) DShK-38/46.

The bolt is of the rotary type, and the weapon is fed from the left- or right-hand sides by a 40-round belt for a cyclic rate of 600 rounds per minute and a muzzle velocity of 3,281 ft (1000 m) per second. The KPV is sighted to 2000 m (2,185 yards) and is 2006 mm (78.98 in) long with a 1346-mm (53-in) changeable barrel.

One calibre down

Next down the calibre ladder is 12.7-mm, in which the DShK is complemented by the **NSV**, so named for the design team of Nikitin, Volkhov and Sokolov. This is an air-cooled and belt-fed

Fitted with a shoulder yoke and telescopic sight, and mounted on the 6T7 tripod, the NSV heavy machine gun offers devastating firepower against personnel and vehicles in the surface-to-surface role.

weapon firing a projectile capable of penetrating 16 mm (0.63 in) of armour at 500 m (545 yards). The weapon is gas operated and locked by a tilting block arrangement, and has a recoil buffer inside the receiver to smooth the action. The standard NSV, issued with an SPP x3 to x6 telescopic sight, is

complemented by the **NSVT**, which is the AFV variant.

Both NSV weapons are to be replaced early in the 21st century by the 25.5-kg (56.22-lb) **Kord** in the same calibre. This has a different locking system and is a gas-operated weapon, but again has a chromed barrel and is claimed to offer far

greater accuracy than the NSV, especially with optional telescopic or night sights. There are no dimensional data for the Kord, which weighs 41.5 kg (91.5 lb) on its tripod with a full 50-round belt, but the weapon's other data includes a muzzle velocity of 820-860 m (2,690-2,822 ft) per second.

SPECIFICATION	
NSV	ammunition 41 kg (90.4 kg)
Calibre: 12.7-mm (0.5-in)	**Muzzle velocity:** 845 m (2,772 ft) per second
Length overall: 1560 mm (61.42 in)	
Length of barrel: not available	**Rate of fire, cyclic:** 700–800 rounds per minute
Weights: gun 25 kg (55.1 lb); complete weapon with tripod mounting and 50 rounds of	**Feed:** 50-round metal-link belt

IMI Negev Machine gun

The **IMI Negev** machine gun, one of the standard light automatic weapons of the Israel Defence Forces, seems very similar to a Belgian weapon of the same class, the FN Minimi. This similarity extends further than just the appearance of the two weapons, however, for the Belgian and Israeli machine guns have about the same performance and share a high degree of accuracy, reliability and light overall weight.

Replacement weapon

Just as the Minimi has partially replaced the FN MAG in many armies, Israel plans that the Negev should supplant its MAG 58 weapons not only in the troop-carried role but also in

armoured fighting vehicle and helicopter installations. The Negev will also replace the Minimi, which was supplied in small numbers but proved unpopular, and also captured Soviet weapons such as the PK and RPD machine guns. The final trials of the Negev were completed in 1996, and large-scale manufacture of the new machine gun began in the following year.

The Negev is a gas-operated weapon of modern concept and

construction, and is produced in two variants as the Negev standard light machine gun and the shorter and lighter **Negev Commando** with an overall length of 890 mm (35.04 in) with the butt extended and 680 mm (26.77 in) with the butt folded, barrel length of 330 mm (12.99 in) and weight of 6.95 kg (15.32 lb).

The Negev Commando also lacks the rail adapter used in the standard model to carry an ITL

In its standard form, the Negev light machine gun is fitted with a bipod and fed with ammunition by means of a disintegrating metal-link belt.

AIM1/D laser pointer, and is generally fitted with a forward assault handle rather than the standard weapon's bipod. A feature of both variants is a soft ammunition drum carrying 150 rounds; the Negev can also use rifle magazines.

SPECIFICATION	
IMI Negev	but without ammunition
Calibre: 5.56-mm (0.219-in)	**Muzzle velocity:** not available
Length overall: 1020 mm (40.16 in) with the buttstock extended and 780 mm (30.71 in) with the buttstock folded	**Rate of fire, cyclic:** selectable between 700–850 or 850–1,000 rounds per minute
Length of barrel: 460 mm (18.11 in)	**Feed:** 150-round metal-link belt, or M16 or Galil assault rifle magazines
Weight: 7.6 kg (16.75 lb) with bipod	

CIS Ultimax 100 Machine gun

The relatively small nation of Singapore has in recent years become a major member of the international defence matériel market. Starting from virtually nothing, Singapore has rapidly built up a defence manufacturing industry and among recent products has been a light machine gun called the **CIS Ultimax 100** or **3U-100**.

The Ultimax 100 can trace its origins back to 1978. To provide a framework in which to work, the newly-formed Chartered Industries of Singapore (now ST Kinetics) had obtained a licence to produce the 5.56-mm (0.219-in) AR-18 and M16A1 rifles. CIS then decided to build in some ideas of its own, and the result was the Ultimax 100. After some early development problems, the Ultimax 100 is now one of the best weapons in its class.

Ammunition

The Ultimax 100 fires the 5.56-mm M193 cartridge, but could be converted to fire the new SS109. It is a light machine gun that is really light, for the company was understandably keen to produce

a weapon suited to the relatively light physiques of Asian personnel.

The result is that the Ultimax 100 handles very like an assault rifle. CIS has taken great pains to reduce recoil forces to a minimum, and has even introduced a feature it calls 'constant recoil'. With this feature the breech block does not use the back-plate of the receiver as a buffer, as is normal in many similar designs, but instead a system of springs that absorb the forces to the extent that the weapon can be handled with ease and smoothness. The Ultimax 100 can be fired from the shoulder with no problems at all.

The likeness to an assault rifle is carried over to the ammunition feed. The Ultimax 100 uses a 100-round drum magazine under the body that can be changed with the same facility as a conventional box magazine. The drum magazines can be carried in a special webbing carrier. For firing on the move a forward grip is provided, and to make the weapon even handier the butt may be removed. For more

accurate firing a bipod is a fixture and the barrel change is rapid and easy. If required normal M16A1 20- or 30-round box magazines can be used in place of the drum.

Already accessories for the Ultimax 100 abound. Perhaps the most unusual of them is a silencer which is used in conjunction with a special barrel. More orthodox items include a special twin mounting in which two weapons are secured on their sides with the drum magazines pointing outward. One very unusual extra is a bayonet, a feature which few similar weapons possess. Rifle grenades can be fired from the muzzle without preparation.

The Ultimax 100 Mk 3 light machine gun is a small weapon that is ideally suited to many Southeast Asian armed forces. It is light and easy to handle, and after its development difficulties is now a reliable and efficient weapon that is in full-scale production in Singapore.

To date the Ultimax 100 is available in two versions: the **Ultimax 100 Mk 2** with a fixed barrel and the **Ultimax 100 Mk 3** with a quick-change barrel. More versions are certain, for the Ultimax 100 has a most promising future. It is already in service with the Singapore armed forces and many more nations are showing interest.

SPECIFICATION	
Ultimax 100	**Muzzle velocity:** 990 m (3,248 ft) per second
Calibre: 5.56-mm (0.219-in)	**Rate of fire, cyclic:** 400–600 rpm
Length overall: 1030 mm (40.55 in)	**Feed:** 100-round drum, or 20- or 30-round curved box
Length of barrel: 508 mm (20 in)	
Weight loaded: 6.5 kg (14.33 lb) with 100-round drum	

Santa Barbara (CETME) Ameli Machine gun

Although it possesses striking visual similarity to the MG 42 of World War II and its MG3 modern-day development, the **CETME Ameli** machine gun is in fact an entirely new weapon. It uses the same type of roller-delayed blowback action (with a semi-rigid bolt) as the Heckler & Koch assault rifles and machine guns, and also the Model L assault rifle created by CETME, which is now controlled by the

Empresa Nacional Santa Barbara de Industrias Militares, itself owned by General Dynamics of the USA. The relationship between the Ameli and Model L is sufficiently close that there is a modicum of interchangeability between the two weapons' parts.

Quick-change barrel

The Ameli fires from an open bolt, and has a quick-change

barrel to enhance its utility for the sustained-fire role in which barrel overheating would otherwise be a major problem. The tactical versatility of the weapon is also magnified by its provision with a bipod for use

when the weapon is used in the light machine gun role, but in the sustained-fire role the weapon is generally mounted on a tripod. The Ameli fires NATO standard 5.56-mm (0.219-in) ammunition carried in

SPECIFICATION	
Ameli	**Weight empty:** 5.3 kg (11.68 lb)
Calibre: 5.56-mm (0.219-in)	**Muzzle velocity:** not available
Length overall: 900 mm (35.43 in)	**Rate of fire, cyclic:** 800–900, or 1200rpm
Length of barrel: 400 mm (15.75 in)	**Feed:** 100- or 200-round belt

The Ameli is an effective machine gun that can be operated in the light and sustained-fire roles. On the left-hand side of the weapon's body is the disposable plastic box carrying the weapon's ammunition belt.

Ameli is clearly an effective battlefield weapon. However, it has run into a considerable measure of political antipathy as it is a type favoured by terrorist and guerrilla forces. The reason for this is the fact that the Ameli can be broken down into comparatively small sections that can then be carried in a suitcase-like container. This offers the possibility of the weapon being moved around civilian areas without being seen. For this reason, the Ameli has been banned in several countries.

The Ameli incorporates a number of features to ensure that the weapon can be assembled in only the correct fashion.

belts in disposable plastic boxes holding 100 or 200 rounds, and provision is made for two rates of fire: the use of a heavy bolt results in a rate of fire of between 850 and 900 rounds per minute, while the installation of the light bolt leads to an increase in the rate of fire to some 1,200 rounds per minute.

Without doubt one of the best light/sustained-fire machine guns of the 5.56-mm calibre currently on offer, the

SIG 710-3 Machine gun

The 7.62-mm (0.3-in) SIG 710-3 general-purpose machine gun was based on German design experience in World War II and should have emerged as one of the finest machine gun designs ever, but in the event only small numbers were produced.

The Swiss 7.62-mm (0.3-in) **SIG 710-3** machine gun is a weapon that on paper appears to be one of the finest of its class. The overall design, construction and reliability of the SIG design are such that it would appear to be a world leader. In fact nothing of the kind has occurred, for this most promising of machine gun designs has now been taken out of production and can be found in service

only with nations such as Bolivia, Brunei and Chile.

Superlative weapon
The reason for this strange state of affairs can perhaps be seen in the fact that when the Swiss produce any weapon design they do so in a manner that can only attract superlatives. The Swiss produce weapons with a magnificent degree of care and attention to

finish, but while people may be willing to pay heavily for similarly engineered Swiss watches, they are not willing to pay on the same scale for machine guns, especially when such weapons can be produced on simple machine tools and metal stamping jigs.

The SIG 710-3 is the third in a series of machine guns, the first of which were produced soon after World War II. In

simple terms the first SIG 710s were machine gun versions of the Swiss Sturmgewehr Modell 57 (assault rifle model 1957), and the machine gun employs the same delayed roller and block locking system as the CETME and Heckler & Koch rifles. On the SIG 710 the system is a form of delayed blowback with the chamber fluted to prevent spent cases 'sticking'. The first SIG 710s were virtually hand-made weapons that attracted much attention but few orders, so an increasing number of production expedients was incorporated to the point where the SIG 710-3 makes use of some stampings.

The Swiss were very influenced by the MG 42, and in the years after the war produced several designs based on features of the model. The SIG 710- 3 trigger mechanism is the same as that of the MG 42, and so is the ammunition feed, which is so efficient that it accommodates both American and German belt linkings without trouble. The locking system is identical to that employed on the Sturmgewehr 45, which failed to reach service with the German army before the surrender of May 1945.

However, the SIG 710-3 does have many original Swiss features, not the least of which is the type of rapid barrel change. Many extras were developed for these machine guns, including a buffered tripod for sustained fire. Special features such as dial sights and telescopic sights were also produced, and in the end the SIG 710-3 could be regarded as one of the most advanced machine guns available anywhere. However, it was all for nothing as far as SIG was concerned – high development and production costs (combined with the strict rules of the Swiss government regarding arms sales) led to an early exit from production.

SPECIFICATION	
SIG 710-3	light barrel 2.04 kg (4.5 lb)
Calibre: 7.62-mm (0.3-in)	**Muzzle velocity:** 790 m (2,592 ft) per
Length overall: 1143 mm (45 in)	second
Length of barrel: 559 mm (22 in)	**Rate of fire, cyclic:** 800–950 rounds
Weights: gun 9.25 kg (20.39 lb);	per minute
heavy barrel 2.5 kg (5.51 lb);	**Feed:** belt

Vektor SS77 7.62-mm general-purpose machine gun

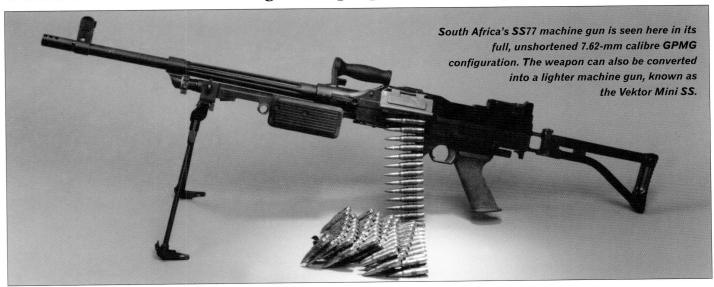

South Africa's SS77 machine gun is seen here in its full, unshortened 7.62-mm calibre GPMG configuration. The weapon can also be converted into a lighter machine gun, known as the Vektor Mini SS.

Development of the South African 7.62-mm (0.3-in) calibre **Vektor SS77** (**L9**) machine gun began in 1977 and it entered service in 1986, the time lapse being caused by a development suspension lasting several years when other local defence equipment priorities became more urgent.

The gun takes its name from its designers, Smith and Soregi. It is of conventional type, gas operated, with a quick-change barrel, bipod and folding butt, the latter having undergone several design and strengthening changes since the early models appeared. In design terms the SS77 is an amalgamation of operating features taken from several other automatic weapons including the British Bren and the Soviet RGM Goryunov, among others.

Firing mechanism
Rounds are fed into the SS77 in 100- or 200-round steel-link belts. Bolt locking is performed by swinging the rear end of the bolt sideways into a recess in the receiver wall, creating a very positive lock at the instant of firing. A gas piston beneath the barrel drives the bolt carrier back after firing. The SS77's gas

The gas-operated SS77 utilises a sideways-swinging breech block that locks into a recess in the receiver wall, this being influenced by the Soviet Goryunov system.

The SS77 machine gun is manufactured by Denel, South Africa's large arms production enterprise. The weapon has been exported to Kuwait.

regulation system allows easy maintenance. A post on the carrier, engaging in a cam path on the rectangular bolt, swings the bolt out of engagement with its locking recess and then withdraws it, extracting and ejecting the spent case downwards and forwards. A post on the top rear of the carrier engages in a belt feed lever in the top cover of the receiver. Because of the shape of this lever it is turned around a pivot so that the forward end, carrying the feed pawls, moves the incoming round half a step towards the feed position. On the return stroke the feed lever moves the round the remaining distance, the bolt loads it into the chamber and as the bolt comes to rest, the carrier continues and the post, engaged in the bolt cam path, swings the rear of the bolt into the locking recess. The post then strikes the firing pin and the round is fired.

The barrel can be rapidly removed by depressing a locking lever and rotating the barrel to disengage its interrupted lugs from the receiver. The barrel itself is fluted on the external surfaces, which both reduces weight and improves cooling. If required, the quick-release foldable butt can be removed and replaced by spade grips or a remote-control firing device. Various mountings, apart from the integral folding bipod, can be employed. These include a tripod

mounting allowing the SS77 to act as a true general-purpose machine gun, and vehicle mountings, including a truck cab roof flexible installation with two SS77 guns side by side.

Robust construction

Having been made from the finest possible raw materials and carefully manufactured, the SS77 has proved to be remarkably robust and reliable, even when operating under the extremes of the South African environment. Thousands of rounds have been fired without problems, other than changing the barrel occasionally. In addition to the bipod, a carrying handle is provided.

The SS77 is in service with the South African Defence Force (SADF) and with Kuwait. It is

widely believed to be one of the finest machine guns of its type ever built.

One unusual feature of the SS77 is that with the aid of a kit the 7.62-mm calibre weapon can be converted into the **Vektor Mini SS** 5.56-mm (0.219-in) calibre light machine gun. The kit includes a new and lighter barrel, feed cover, breech assembly, a revised locking shoulder and new gas piston. The converted weapon fires 5.56 x 45 mm ammunition fed in 100-round belts. The resultant 5.56-mm weapon is somewhat lighter, at 8.26 kg (18.2 lb) when it is empty. Once an SS77 GPMG has been converted to 5.56-mm calibre it is rarely converted back to the heavier version, especially among units who have to carry their weapons over long distances. The 5.56-mm weapons can also be manufactured from new in this configuration.

SPECIFICATION	
SS77	(21.2 lb); complete barrel, 2.5 kg (5.5 lb)
Calibre: 7.62 mm (0.3 in)	
Length overall: butt folded, 940 mm (37 in); butt extended, 1155 mm (45.47 in)	**Rate of fire, cyclic:** 600–900 rpm
	Muzzle velocity: around 840 m (2,756 ft) per second
Length of barrel: without flash hider, 550 mm (21.6 in)	**Feed:** disintegrating or non-disintegrating metal-link belt
Weight: unloaded gun, 9.6 kg	

Ruggedly designed for operations in South Africa's unforgiving bush country, the SS77 has been ranked alongside the world's best machine guns. The gun can also be safely fired from enclosed spaces, such as fighting vehicle interiors or bunkers, as the result of an adjustable gas regulator which features a position that closes the exhaust, minimising gas emissions.

ST Kinetics 50MG 0.5-in heavy machine gun

Considering that there was a need for a weapon to bridge the gap between 7.62-mm (0.3-in) machine guns and 20-mm cannon, Chartered Industries of Singapore (now Singapore Technologies Kinetics – ST Kinetics) began designing a new 12.7-mm (0.5-in) calibre machine gun in 1983. The objective was a simpler and lighter weapon than the Browning M2HB in order to improve portability and to ease the problems of field maintenance. The ability to fire locally-produced saboted light armour penetrator (SLAP) ammunition was another prime objective.

The design of the **ST Kinetics 50MG** is simple and modular in construction, allowing ease of assembly and maintenance. As a result, there are only 210 components comprising the entire gun and the weapon consists of five basic assemblies, which are as follows:

First there is the pressed-steel receiver body, this includes two tubes at the front end to house the pistons and recoil rods.

Secondly, the feed mechanism is located on top of the receiver body and uses a single sprocket. It is designed to facilitate either left- or right-hand feed of standard M15A2 link ammunition belts.

Thirdly, the trigger module houses the trigger and sear mechanisms, with provision for a safety lock. The trigger module is available in two versions, the 'semi' version with semi- and fully automatic fire modes, and the 'auto' version providing fully automatic fire only.

Barrel change can be accomplished within seconds, without any headspace problem. The gun has a fixed headspace, unlike the Browning M2HB. The gas regulator has two positions to allow setting for normal and adverse environmental conditions.

Finally, the bolt carrier group consists of a pair of pistons and recoil rods attached to the bolt carrier body by two quick-release catches. The bolt is prevented from accidental firing out of battery by a sleeve lock device between the bolt and bolt carrier body.

Gas operation

The 50MG is gas operated and fires from the open bolt position. The bolt carrier group is held back behind the feed area and the bolt carrier is engaged by a sear. Pressing the trigger releases the bolt carrier and, as the bolt moves forward, it strips the round centred on the feed tray from the ammunition belt, feeding in from the left or the right side of the gun. When chambering is complete, the combined forward movement of the bolt carrier rotates the bolt by means of a cam and locks it to the barrel. Forward momentum of the bolt carrier assembly drives the firing pin forward to fire the cartridge.

On firing, propellant gas is tapped off into a gas cylinder. The bolt carrier is driven back by the gas pistons, causing the bolt to rotate, unlock and extract the empty case from the chamber. As the bolt carrier continues to move rearward, the empty case is ejected via an ejection port at the bottom of the receiver. When the return springs are almost fully compressed, the bolt carrier begins to move forward and, if the pressure on the trigger is maintained, the bolt will then chamber the next round and fire it. If the trigger is released the bolt carrier assembly will be engaged by the sear. When the ammunition belt is exhausted the bolt carrier group will remain in the forward closed position.

The 50MG can be mounted on tripods, pintle or ring mounts and on the 40/50 Cupola Weapon Station. Optional accessories include a chromed barrel, tripod adaptor, M3 tripod, pintle mount, ammunition box bracket, blank firing attachment and an optical scope adaptor.

SPECIFICATION	
50MG	
Calibre: 12.7 mm (0.5 in)	second; with SLAP ammunition 1185 m (3,887 ft) per second
Length overall: 1778 mm (70 in)	**Maximum range:** with M8 ammunition 6800 m (7,437 yards); with SLAP ammunition 7600 m (8,311 yards); effective range 1830 m (2,001 yards)
Length of barrel: 1143 mm (45 in)	
Weight: unloaded gun 30 kg (66.1 lb); complete barrel 9 kg (19.8 lb)	
Rate of fire, cyclic: 400–600 rpm	**Feed:** dual disintegrating M15A2 link belt
Muzzle velocity: with M8 ammunition 887 m (2,910 ft) per	

Above: As well as being useful for ground forces and for vehicle use, the 12.7-mm 50MG can be used for naval applications, and is seen here on a deck mounting.

The 50MG on its tripod. Feed is provided by two belts, entering on each side of the receiver, either of which can be selected by the operator.

L4 Bren Machine gun

The latest version of the venerable Bren gun of World War II vintage is the L4A4 firing the NATO 7.62-mm (0.3-in) round. It has a new barrel, breech block and vertical 30-round box magazine, and has now been retired from British service.

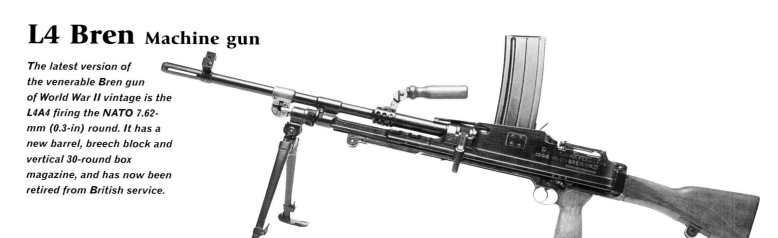

When considering modern machine guns, it seems something of a surprise that a weapon as old as the **Bren Gun** should be included, especially as the origins of this classic weapon can be traced back to a time as early as the first part of the 1930s. But the original Bren machine guns were chambered for the 0.303-in (7.7-mm) rimmed cartridge that was the standard rifle and machine gun round of the British army at that time. Moreover, when the decision was made in the 1950s to convert to the new standard NATO 7.62-mm (0.3-in) cartridge, the British armed forces still had large stockpiles of the Bren machine gun to hand. In these circumstances, therefore, it made very good financial sense to convert these elderly but still effective weapons to use the new-calibre ammunition, and such a programme was soon put into effect at the Royal Small Arms Factory at Enfield Lock in Middlesex.

Simple evolution

The conversion to the new calibre entailed a complete overhaul, but the task was made easier by the fact that during World War II a Canadian company produced numbers of Bren machine guns in 7.92-mm (0.312-in) calibre for China. As this round was rimless, it was found that the breech blocks intended for the 'China contract' were equally suitable for the new 7.62-mm cartridge, and these were used in place of the original breech blocks. A new barrel was produced with a chromium-plated interior: this not only diminished wear on the barrel, but also reduced the need for the frequent barrel changes required on World War II versions. Thus the new gun was issued with only the one barrel.

The last version of the Bren machine gun used by the British army before its switch to the L7 British version of the Belgian FN MAG general-purpose machine gun was the **L4A4**. This was produced as a conversion of Bren Mk III weapons, and was not used as a front-line infantry weapon, but instead issued to the many other arms of the service which had need of a machine gun. Thus the L4A4 was used by the Royal Artillery for the anti-aircraft and ground-defence of its batteries, by the Royal Signals for the defence of its installations in the field, by units assigned for home defence, and so on. The L4A4 was also used by the Royal Air Force.

A version known as the **L4A5**, produced by conversion of Bren Mk II weapons, was used by the Royal Navy, and this was issued with two steel barrels rather than one barrel with a chromium-plated bore.

Lesser variants

There was also a version known as the **L4A3** that was never encountered in any substantial numbers as it was a conversion of the old Bren Mk II gun. Other seldom-seen variants were the **L4A1** (originally **X10E1**) for

SPECIFICATION	
L4A4	
Calibre: 7.62-mm (0.3-in)	**Muzzle velocity:** 823 m (2,700 ft) per second
Length overall: 1133 mm (44.6 in)	**Rate of fire, cyclic:** 500 rounds per minute
Length of barrel: 536 mm (21.1 in)	
Weight empty: 9.53 kg (21 lb)	**Feed:** 30-round straight box

Although the Bren Gun had seen extensive and sometimes effective use as a light anti-aircraft weapon in World War II, no manner of later updating could retain this utility in the face of faster attack aircraft and their helicopter brethren.

development of the L4 series and produced as conversions from Bren Mk III standard with a pair of steel barrels; the **L4A2** (otherwise **X10E2**) development model produced as conversions from Bren Mk III standard with two steel barrels and a bipod; and the **L4A6** conversion from L4A1 standard with one chromium-plated barrel. The **L4A7** was developed to the drawings stage to meet the requirements of the Indian army, which needed a more modern weapon produced by conversions from Bren Mk I standard with a chromium-plated barrel.

In all these L4 versions the gas-operated mechanism of the original 0.303-in Bren machine gun remained unchanged. So few were the modifications involved in the change of calibre that the only points of note were that the 7.62-mm versions used a nearly vertical straight magazine in place of the curved magazine of the 0.303-in weapons, and a muzzle without the pronounced cone shape of the weapons comprising the original series.

For the anti-aircraft role the L4A4 was provided with some fairly sophisticated sighting arrangements. The L4A4 was not mounted on a tripod, as had been the old Bren machine guns, but instead was designed for installation on the roof hatches of self-propelled guns and howitzers as well as on other armoured fighting vehicles.

So the Bren gun soldiered on in its new form, and there seems to be no sign of its passing completely from use in the foreseeable future. Several commonwealth nations still use the Bren, some in its original 0.303-in form, so although the original design may be old, the weapon is still regarded as an effective one and in its L4A4 form the weapon is as good as many far more modern designs.

Even after its relegation from first-line service, the L4 series went on to enjoy a lengthy second-line career in the hands of gunners and other specialist troops unlikely to become directly embroiled in battlefield fighting.

L86 Machine gun

The L86A1 Light Support Weapon shares many components with the 5.56-mm L85 rifle; obvious differences are the heavier barrel, the bipod and the rear grip. The LSW uses the same magazine as the Individual Weapon.

For many years the standard squad light machine gun for the British army has been a version of the FN MAG fitted with a bipod and known as the L7A2. While this is a fine weapon, it is rather a cumbersome load for the infantryman and fires a cartridge that is now generally considered too powerful for the squad support role. With the imminent arrival of the Enfield Weapon System (or Small Arms 80, otherwise SA80 and L85), the L7A2 became due for replacement in the squad support role by a new weapon known in its development phase as the **XL73E2 Light Support Weapon** or **LSW**. It was decided that the L7A2 would be retained for the sustained-fire function for some years to come.

Entering service as the **L86A1**, the LSW is half of the Enfield Weapon System with the L85A1 standard assault rifle. The two weapons have many things in common and can be easily

SPECIFICATION	
L86A1	**Muzzle velocity:** 970 m (3,182 ft) per second
Calibre: 5.56-mm (0.219-in)	
Length overall: 900 mm (35.43 in)	**Rate of fire, cyclic:** 700–850 rounds per minute
Length of barrel: 646 mm (25.43 in)	
Weight loaded: 6.88 kg (15.17 lb)	**Feed:** 30-round curved box

*Seen here in front of the **GPMG** is the 4.85-mm (0.19-in) original development version of the **L**ight **S**upport **W**eapon, produced to complement the proposed 4.85-mm rifle. When **NATO** adopted the Belgian 5.56-mm (0.219-in) round, the 4.85-mm designs were changed despite their superior capabilities.*

recognised as coming from the same stable, but the LSW has a heavier barrel and a light bipod mounted well forward under the barrel. There is also a rear grip under what might be regarded as the butt to provide the firer with a better hold for sustained firing.

The term butt is rather misleading as the LSW is based on a 'bullpup' layout in which the trigger group is placed forward of the magazine. This arrangement makes the LSW more compact than a conventional weapon. Much of the LSW is steel, but the fore grip and pistol grip for the trigger are tough nylonite. The LSW uses the same magazine as the IW, namely a standard M16A1 30-round box.

Calibre change

The LSW has undergone several changes of calibre since it was first mooted. Originally it was calibred for the British experimental 4.85-mm (0.19-in) cartridge, but this was overruled in favour of the American 5.56-mm (0.219-in) M193 cartridge, which in turn was

superseded yet again in favour of the NATO standard 5.56-mm SS109. The first production versions were chambered for the SS109 round, and also had an optical sight known as the Sight Unit Small Arms Trilux, or SUSAT, mounted on a bracket over the receiver. It is possible to change this sight for a night sight.

Planned accessories

Various accessories were planned for the LSW once it had entered service as the L86A1 after the start of production in 1985. A training adapter firing low-powered ammunition was created as one of these options, and another was a blank-firing attachment. A multi-purpose tool is in use for stripping and first-line repairs, and it is possible to fit a sling for carrying. The muzzle attachment is so arranged that it is feasible for rifle grenades to be fired from the muzzle, although it is not envisaged that the LSW will be used extensively for this purpose.

The LSW underwent a protracted development period, some of the period being elongated by the change of NATO standard calibre and other considerations. By the time it reached the hands of the troops, the LSW should have been an excellent weapon with no bugs left to iron out, but in fact the weapon suffered from the same type of problems as encountered by the L85A1 rifle.

*With the **L1A1** rifle replaced by the 5.56-mm (0.219-in) **L85**, the **B**ritish Army adopted a squad support weapon of the same calibre to replace the **L7** general-purpose machine gun, which has been retained for the sustained-fire role.*

Browning M2HB
Heavy machine gun

The oldest machine gun design still in production and large-scale service, the **Browning M2** was designed by John Browning as an aircraft gun, but entered service as the **Model 1921** ground weapon. It was upgraded to M2 standard in 1932 and then reached its definitive form as the **M2HB** for the sustained-fire role with a heavy barrel offering increases in the practical rate of fire and number of rounds that could be fired between barrel changes. The changing of a barrel entailed the time-consuming head space and timing adjustments. This drawback was accepted with relatively good grace for a long period by operators delighted by the performance and reliability of the M2HB, but in more recent years the weapon's current US manufacturer, Ramo Defense, has introduced a QCB (Quick Change Barrel) kit applicable to all M2 variants to create the **M2HB-QCB** or **M2HQB**.

Another limitation to the tactical employment of the M2 has for long been its comparatively high weight, and Ramo Defence therefore introduced the **M2 Lightweight Machine Gun**. This is still based on the recoil-based operating system of the M2 and retains a 75% commonality of parts with that weapon, but is 11 kg (24.25 lb) lighter at a mere 27 kg (59.5 lb). The opportunity was also taken to upgrade the weapon with an adjustable buffer to allow the weapon's rate of fire to be adjusted between 550 and 750 rounds per minute, a quick-change lightweight barrel with a

Stellite-lined chromed bore with a flash suppressor, the Max Safe charging system, and a trigger safety switch.

Ammunition range

The M2 machine gun has remained in production and service for a long time not only as a result of its reliability and long-range accuracy, but also for the excellence of the ammunition designed for it. The standard range includes the M2 AP, FN 169 APEI, M8 API, M20 API-T, M2 and M33 Ball, M1 and M23 Incendiary, and M10, M17 and M21 Tracer. Each of these has a complete cartridge length of 138.4 mm (5.45 in) and weight of 120 g (4.23 oz), and fires a projectile of between 39.7 and 46.8 g (1.4 and 1.65 oz) at a muzzle velocity of between 850 and 920 m (2,789 and 3,018 ft) per second out to a maximum effective range of some 3000 m (3,280 yards).

Additional capability is offered by more modern ammunition types, of which perhaps the best is that offered by the

Despite the age of its basic design, the M2 remains the classic heavy machine gun of the Western world, and offers excellent capabilities against personnel and lighter materiel up to AFVs and helicopters.

Norwegian company Nammo, which took over Raufoss, the originator of the range. The object of the new ammunition range was to exploit the capabilities offered by the machine gun on its new 'soft mount' that improves accuracy to a marked extent at the penalty of an additional 18 kg (40 lb) of mount weight, and it is claimed that the ammunition provided capabilities not markedly inferior to those of 20-mm cannon ammunition.

Matched rounds

All three cartridges have the same dimensions, and fire projectiles of between 43 and 47 g (1.52 and 1.66 oz) at a muzzle velocity of

SPECIFICATION	
Browning M2HB	tripod 20 kg (44 lb)
Calibre: 0.5-in (12.7-mm)	**Muzzle velocity:** 930 m (3,051 ft) per
Length overall: 1650 mm (65 in)	second
Length of barrel: 1143 mm (45 in)	**Rate of fire, cyclic:** 450–600 rpm
Weights: gun 38 kg (83.8 lb); M3	**Feed:** 100-round metal-link belt

The M2HB mounted on a vehicle provides a high level of offensive and defensive capability in mobile operations. In this instance, sand bags are piled round the weapon to create a 'pit' offering good protection against machine gun fire.

915 m (3,002 ft) per second. The MP NM140 will penetrate 11mm (0.43 in) of armour at 45 degrees at 1000 m (1,095 yards) and generally breaks into some 20 effective fragments after striking 2 mm (0.08 in) of Dural. The MP-T NM160 is the slightly less accurate tracer variant. The AP-S NM173 round has the accuracy of the MP NM140 round and can pierce 11 mm of armour at 30 degrees at a range of 1500 m (1,640 yards).

Seen here on the turret mounting of an experimental AFV, the lightweight version of the M2 offers all the capabilities of the original weapon as well as less weight and greater flexibility of operation in firing rate.

M60 Medium machine gun

The **M60** is an American general-purpose machine gun that can trace its origins back to the latter period of World War II, when it was known as the **T44**. The design was greatly influenced by the superb German machine guns of the day: the ammunition feed is a direct lift from the MG 42, and the piston and bolt assembly was copied from the revolutionary 7.92-mm (0.312-in) Fallschirmjägergewehr 42 (FG 42). The T44 and its production version, the M60, made extensive use of steel stampings and plastics, and the first examples were issued for service with the US Army in the late 1950s. These first examples were not successful. They

handled badly and some of the detail design was so poor that changing a barrel, for example, involved taking half the weapon apart. The early difficulties were gradually eliminated, and the M60 is now as efficient a weapon as any, but many serving soldiers still profess not to like the weapon for its generally awkward handling properties. But the M60 is the US Army's first general-purpose machine gun, and it now serves in many roles.

Several roles

In its basic form as a squad support weapon, the M60 is fitted with a stamped steel bipod mounted just behind the muzzle.

Once located on its bipod or tripod, the M60 is an excellent and reliable machine gun whose primary limitation is the laborious process of changing the barrel. This dictates that the air-cooled M60 should not be used to fire long bursts without adequate cooling periods.

SPECIFICATION	
M60	barrel 3.74 kg (8.245 lb)
Calibre: 7.62-mm (0.3-in)	**Muzzle velocity:** 855 m (2,805 ft) per second
Length overall: 1105 mm (43.5 in)	
Length of barrel: 559 mm (22 in)	**Rate of fire, cyclic:** 550 rpm
Weights: gun 10.51 kg (23.17 lb);	**Feed:** 50-round metal link belt

The M60 is a rather bulky and heavy weapon that is awkward to handle. First produced in the late 1940s, it underwent a protracted development programme before it entered service in the late 1950s, and has been widely used ever since. It is now a reliable and efficient weapon used by several armies.

In this role it is carried by a small handle which is rather flimsy for the loads placed on it; moreover the point of balance of the handle is entirely wrong. Many soldiers prefer to use a sling, and the weapon is often fired on the move while being steadied by the sling. For the light machine gun role the M60 is a bit hefty, but it is being replaced in US Army service by the 5.56-mm (0.219-in) M249 Minimi. For heavier use the M60 can be mounted on a tripod or on a vehicle pedestal mount.

Special-role guns

Some special versions of the M60 have also been produced. The **M60C** is a remotely fired version for external mounting on helicopters. The **M60D** is a pintle-mounted buttless version for mounting in helicopter gun-ships and some vehicles. The **M60E2** is a much-altered variant for use as a co-axial gun on armoured vehicles. Throughout much of its production life the

Being a full-calibre weapon firing the NATO standard 7.62-mm (0.3-in) cartridge, the M60 is well suited to the long-range fire-support role. In this capacity the weapon is mounted on a sturdy tripod to provide a stable firing base, the light bipod legs attached near the muzzle being folded back alongside the gas cylinder.

M60 has been manufactured by the Saco Defense Systems Division of the Maremount Corporation, which was always aware of the shortcomings of the M60's design, especially in the light machine gun role.

The company therefore developed what it calls the **Maremount Lightweight Machine Gun**, which is essentially the M60 much modified to reduce weight and improve handling. The bipod has been moved back under the receiver and a foregrip has been added. The gas-operated mechanism has been simplified, and there is now provision for a winter trigger. The result is a much lighter and handier weapon than the original, although it can now be used only for the light machine gun role. The revised weapon was evaluated by several armies.

The M60 is now in service with several armies other than the US Army. Taiwan not only uses the M60 but produces it as well. South Korea is another operator, as is the Australian army.

Light mortars

The light mortar is generally regarded as a weapon with a calibre up to a maximum of 60-mm (2.36-in) and a weight (when broken down into main assemblies) light enough to permit a high level of man-portability.

The Austrian company Südsteirische Metallindustrie has made a considerable impact though its ability to design, develop and manufacture weapons of remarkable performance using the resources of its associated metal producing facilities. Mortars are in fact just one of SMI's weapons activities, and the company produces some very advanced types within this category.

On exercise in South Korea, a US Army infantryman shoulders the weight of the tripod for the M29 mortar, an 81-mm (3.2-in) weapon that the service decided was too heavy for modern battlefield requirements. This led to the M224 mortar in 60-mm (2.36-in) calibre.

SPECIFICATION	
M6/314	HE bomb 0.92 kg (2.03 lb);
Calibre: 60-mm (2.36-in)	illuminating bomb 0.8 kg (1.76 lb);
Length: 1.082 m (42.6 in)	smoke bomb 0.9 kg (1.98 lb)
Weights: mortar 18.3 kg (40.34 lb);	**Maximum range:** 800 m (875 yards)
bomb 1.6 kg (3.527 lb)	
Maximum range: 4200 m (4,595 yards)	**Lyran**
	Calibre: 71-mm (2.795-in)
	Weights: barrel pack 9 kg (19.84 lb);
51-mm Mortar	ammunition pack 8 kg (17.64 lb)
Calibre: 51-mm (2-in)	**Maximum range:** 800 m (875 yards)
Length: 0.75 m (29.53 in)	
Weights: mortar 6.28 kg (13.84 lb);	

Three subvariants

The smallest of these weapons in calibre terms is the 60-mm (2.36-in) **M6** range encompassing three weapons, namely the **M6/214 Standard**, the **M6/314 Long Range** and the **M6/530 Light**. Of these three the M6/214 is the most orthodox in concept, while the M6/314 is much longer in the barrel. The M6/530 Light, also known as the **M6/350 Commando**, uses a lightweight barrel with no bipod and only a small baseplate as it is intended for one-man use and may be fitted with a trigger mechanism. All three mortars can fire virtually any 60-mm mortar bomb, but SMI produces its own bomb, the HE-80 weighing 1.6 kg (3.527 lb) and capable of ranging out to a very respectable 4200 m (4,595 yards) when fired from the M6/314 Long Range.

Advanced weapon

The British **51-mm Mortar** was developed as successor to the 51-mm (2-in) mortar designed before World War II. Work on the new weapon started in the early 1970s mainly by the RARDE (Royal Armament Research and Development Establishment) at Fort Halstead in Kent. For much of its early development life the new

This is the US Army's M224 Lightweight Company Mortar in its simplest form with the auxiliary baseplate and no bipod. The M224's most useful capabilities derive from its use of ammunition with an advanced fuse system.

mortar had a monopod supporting leg, but this was eventually discarded as being unnecessary.

The 51-mm is used by the British army at platoon level. In its production form the weapon outwardly resembles one of the many commando-type mortars in use elsewhere, but it is more complex. It consists mainly of a barrel and baseplate, but the design detail is quite involved. The mortar uses a lanyard-operated trigger mechanism, and aiming is assisted by a complex sight with an inbuilt Trilux illuminating source for use at night. The mortar was designed for really close-range operations at ranges as close as 50 m (55 yards), and this is achieved by the use of a short-range insert (SRI) normally carried inside the barrel fitted to the muzzle cap. In use the SRI is inserted in the base of the barrel to serve as a firing pin extension while at the same time allowing propellant gases to expand around the SRI to

This Swedish soldier is seen with a complete Lyran system: in his right hand the barrel and two bombs, and in his left hand four bombs, all in two plastic containers. The Lyran system is used only for nocturnal target illumination.

produce lower barrel pressures and thus decrease muzzle velocity and range.

The normal minimum range is 150 m (165 yards), while the maximum is 800 m (875 yards). The mortar can be carried by one man using a webbing sling, and in action a webbing gaiter around the barrel is gripped to aim and steady the barrel. Ammunition is carried in a canvas satchel and a webbing satchel, and a webbing wallet is used to carry cleaning rods and a few ancillary equipment items.

The ammunition range includes HE, illuminating and smoke bombs. The HE bomb contains a wall liner of pre-notched wire for anti-personnel use. One detail design point is that the bombs cannot be double-loaded in the heat of

action: if they are the second bomb protrudes from the muzzle. The HE bomb is stated to be capable of producing a lethal area five times the size of that produced by the old 2-in mortar bombs, as a result mainly of the pre-notched wire fragments.

One of the primary uses of the 51-mm mortar in British service is to provide illumination for Milan antitank missile teams for nocturnal operations. The smoke bomb provides screening for all manner of infantry operations, while the HE bombs are used in the time-honoured manner.

The basic man-carried satchel contains five bombs, and one man can carry the mortar and a satchel without impeding his normal combat load-carrying

ability to any marked extent. A product of Sweden's small but advanced armaments industry, the **Lyran** is a special form of infantry support weapon for it fires only an illuminating round. The use of infantry support weapons to fire illuminating rounds is not new, but it has become increasingly important with a host of applications. Mortars have long been used to fire special bombs that eject a small parachute at the apogee of their trajectory and then descend as high-power flares spreading their light on the ground below. This light can be used to illuminate an attacking enemy or to reveal an armoured target for missile teams to tackle, and these are only two applications.

Man-portability

The Lyran was designed, developed and produced by Bofors, and in its infantry version (there is also a variant designed for use on combat vehicles) is based on two polyethylene packs: one contains the barrel and two flare shells, and the other four flare shells. For use the barrel is taken out of its pack and screwed into a housing on the pack itself. The firer actually sits on the pack and uses a spirit level to set the barrel at an angle of 47 degrees. A flare shell is then taken and its simple nose fuse set to operate at a range of 400 or 800 m (440 or 875 yards). The shell is then allowed to fall to the base of the barrel and is fired in the normal manner, rising to a height of 200 to 300 m (655

and 985 ft) before the parachute emerges to give the flare a burn time of about 25 seconds. At a height of 160 m (525 ft) the flare illuminates an area about 630 m (689 yards) in diameter.

For many years the US Army used the 81-mm (3.2-in) Mortar M29 as its standard weapon of this class, and although this weapon was successful it was latterly seen as lacking adequate range and, by the standards that emerged in the Vietnam War, as also being too heavy. The US Army therefore decided to revert to the 60-mm calibre as used in World War II but now updated for additional range. This led to a lengthy and involved programme of development to create the **60-mm M224 Lightweight Company Mortar**. This has been issued to infantry, airborne and air-mobile infantry units, and is a long-barrelled weapon that can be fitted with either a conventional bipod or a simple baseplate for use in the 'commando' configuration. Much use is made of aluminium alloys for components such as the large baseplate, and the entire weapon can be broken down into two loads for manpack transport. It is also possible to mount the weapon on some vehicles.

The main elements of the M224 are the 6.53 kg (14.4 lb) M225 cannon assembly, 6.9 kg (15.2 lb) M170 bipod assembly, 6.53 lb (14.4 lb) M14 baseplate assembly, and 1.63 kg (3.6 lb) M8 auxiliary baseplate, to which must be added to items

SPECIFICATION	
M224 Lightweight Company Mortar **Calibre:** 60-mm (2.36-in) **Length:** 1.106 m (40 in) **Weight:** 21.11kg (46.5 lb) **Maximum range:** 3475 m (3,800 yards)	**Maximum range:** 2000 m (2,185 yards) **60-mm Soltam Mortar** **Calibre:** 60.75-mm (2.39-in) **Length:** barrel and breech 0.74 m (29.13 in)
Hotchkiss-Brandt 60-mm Light Mortar **Calibre:** 60-mm (2.36-in) **Length:** barrel and breech 0.724 m (28.5 in) **Weights:** overall 14.8 kg (32.63 lb); 1.65 kg (3.64 lb)	**Weights:** complete with bipod 14.3 kg (31.53 kg) in firing position; bomb 1.59 kg (3.51 lb) **Maximum range:** 2555 m (2,975 yards)

such as the M64 sight unit. The M224 has a maximum rate of fire of 30 rounds per minute and a sustained rate of fire of 20 rounds per minute.

Advanced fuse

Perhaps the most important design feature of the M224 is the ammunition it fires, and especially the multi-option fuse involved. The M224 fires HE illuminating, smoke and practice rounds, and the multi-option fuse is known as the M734. This is an electronic unit, and was among the first of its type to reach service. The M734 has four detonating options: high air-burst, low air-burst, point detonation and delay. The fuse has inbuilt redundancy, in that if the chosen option does not operate the fuse automatically activates the next option. For instance, if low air-burst has been selected and does not operate, the fuse detonates on point contact i.e. when it strikes the ground; if that fails it switches itself to delay. Power to operate the microcircuits is generated inside the fuse by air passing through a miniature turbine in the nose. The ability to select high or low air-burst combines with a reasonable certainty that the fuse will operate as selected to enhance the destructive effect of the bomb. Moreover, the number of fragments spread over a wide area comes close to the destructive and anti-personnel effects of 81-mm bombs.

Laser aid

To go with the M224 and its electronically fused bombs, the US Army uses a laser rangefinder to determine target ranges with great accuracy and so allow the first bombs to arrive right on target for maximum effect. Thus the M224 lightweight company mortar has elevated the mortar from its original stage of being a humble weapon to the level at which it can be regarded as virtually a weapon system.

There are, of course, a number of other light mortars. Typical of these are the Chinese 60-mm Type 31 and Type 63 mortars, three French 60-mm Hotchkiss-Brandt mortars, Israeli Soltam 52- and 60-mm mortars, two Spanish ECIA 60-mm mortars, sundry Soviet (now Russian) 50-mm mortars and the Yugoslav 50-mm M8 mortar.

Above: A British infantryman prepares to load a bomb into the muzzle of his 51-mm (2-in) mortar. Issued at squad level, the weapon fires smoke and illuminating bombs as well as the more overtly offensive HE bomb.

The Lyran system in assembled form reveals the essentially simple nature of this useful illuminating system with the launcher attached to the carrying case that also contains two flare bombs. The other case carries four bombs.

Medium mortars

The medium mortar is generally defined as having a calibre in the range between 60- and 102-mm (2.36- and 4-in), resulting in a weapon weighing between 35 and 70 kg (77 and 154 lb) and firing a 3.5- to 7-kg (7.7- to 15.4-lb) bomb out to a range in the order of 1850 to 5500 m (2,025 to 6,015 yards).

While the light mortar provides small units, up to company size, with an organic weapon for the generation of their own tactical fire support, the medium mortar is a more ambitious weapon. It is generally allocated at battalion or regimental level, at which there is the possibility of vehicular transport, and offers a more effective blend of lethality and range. The medium mortar designed, developed and

M8/222 Long Range, the latter with a longer barrel and greater weight. As with the company's light mortars, it is intended that best results should come from the use of a special bomb, in this case the HE-70 that can be fired to a range of 6500 m (7,110 yards) by the M8/222. The mortars were developed to replace the British 81-mm weapons in service with the Austrian army, and SMI also offers the series on the export market, and also in 82-mm (3.23-in) calibre to use ammunition developed in the former Warsaw Pact.

Excellent British type

The **Mortar L16** has been one of the major British success stories of the era after World War II, for it is used not only by

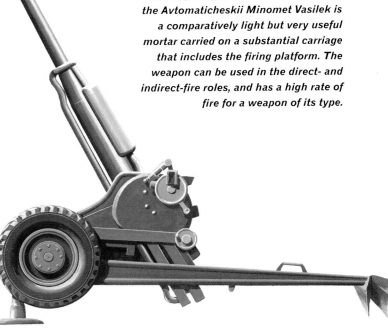

Developed by the Soviets in the 1960s, the Avtomaticheskii Minomet Vasilek is a comparatively light but very useful mortar carried on a substantial carriage that includes the firing platform. The weapon can be used in the direct- and indirect-fire roles, and has a high rate of fire for a weapon of its type.

The barrel of the L16 is much thicker than normal and equipped with cooling fins around its lower portion. These allow the L16 to fire the really hot charges that provide the weapon with remarkable range

capability: some types of bomb can be delivered to 6000 m (6,560 yards) or more. This capability is counterbalanced by disadvantages such as an uncomfortable level of muzzle blast.

Advanced features

Other features of the L16 are no less advanced than the barrel. The mounting is of a type known as a 'K' mount from its shape, and this allows rapid and easy levelling and elevation. The baseplate and sight are of Canadian design, the former made by a special process in which the aluminium alloy is blown into its mould by a controlled explosion. The baseplate provides 360-degree traverse without any need to uproot and then re-bed the base plate.

The ammunition used by the L16 can be quite varied, for the

This American mortar team was caught on camera during the Vietnam War. Medium mortars provided excellent fire support in this conflict, which nonetheless revealed the need for lighter weapons.

manufactured by the Austrian SMI organisation is the 81.4-mm (3.2-in) **M8**. The design of this weapon was influenced by that of a British mortar, but much use is made of aluminium alloy for the baseplate and high-quality steel for the barrel. As with SMI's M6 light mortar, the M8 is produced in subvariants, the **M8/122 Standard** and the

the British army but also by many other nations including the USA, where it is operated by the US Army as the **Mortar M252**. One of the main reasons for the success of the 81.4-mm (3.2-in) L16 has been its ability to fire bombs using powerful propellant charges that would normally make the barrel too hot for sustained use.

SPECIFICATION	
Mortar L16 **Calibre:** 81.4-mm (3.2-in) **Length:** barrel 1.28 m (50.4 in) **Weights:** mortar 37.85 kg (83.45 lb); HE bomb 4.2 kg (9.26 lb) **Maximum range:** 5650 m (6,180 yards) **Brandt Mortier MO 82-61 L** **Calibre:** 81.4-mm (3.2-in) **Length:** barrel 1.45 m (57.09 in) **Weights:** mortar 41.5 kg (91.5 lb);	HE bomb 4.325 kg (9.53 lb) **Maximum range:** 5000 m (5,470 yards) **82-PM 41** **Calibre:** 82-mm (3.23-in) **Length:** barrel 1.22 m (48.03 in) **Weight:** mortar 52 kg (114.6 lb) **Maximum range:** 2550 m (2,790 yards)

weapon is capable of firing any 81-mm bomb in service with NATO. As always, the best results are obtained with matching ammunition, and the latest HE fragmentation bomb is the 4.2-kg (9.2-lb) L36A2 with a maximum range of 5650 m (6,180 yards). Other bombs include smoke, short-range practice and Brandt illuminating types.

The L16 has seen combat during the Falklands and Gulf wars. In the Falklands campaign it was so effective that some Argentine reports suggested that the L16's bombs were fitted with heat-seeking guidance packages able to make the bomb home in on soldiers.

A special mounting allowing the L16's use on APCs such as the FV432 and M113 series has been developed, but for normal infantry use the L16 is broken down into a number of loads that can be manpacked into action.

Classic design

The name Brandt has been associated with the design, development and manufacture of mortars since World War I. Much of the detail development work carried out between the two world wars was undertaken by Stokes Brandt, a French company which became part of Brandt Armements. Today the range of mortar types produced by the company is prodigious in the light, medium and heavy mortar categories. Brandt medium mortars are of the 81-mm calibre and are available in several models, ranging from the basic **Mortier MO 81-61 C** to special models with long barrels, such as the **Mortier MO 81-61 L**, to obtain the maximum possible range.

Sturdy and effective

In design terms all of them are fairly orthodox, and all have been sold to many land forces around the world. To go with them, Brandt also produces a wide range of bombs and

Above: The men of an American mortar team cover their ears to provide at least a measure of protection against the damage that can be caused by the high-pressure wave spreading from the muzzle as the mortar is fired. Ear protectors are now commonly worn.

associated propellant charges. The bomb types include HE, HE fragmentation, smoke, illuminating and target-marking bombs, the last for indicating targets to aircraft.

The army of the USSR, now fragmented into the Russian Federation and a number of smaller states combined under the aegis of the Commonwealth of Independent States, controlled the development of a large number of mortar types over the years, and the surprising thing is that many of them dating from before World War II remain in large-scale service. These mortars are of the light, medium and heavy types in standard calibres such as 50-mm (1.97-in), 82-mm (3.23-in), 107-mm (4.21-in), 120-mm (4.73-in) and 160-mm (6.3-in).

Although it was the heavy mortar type, starting with a

calibre of 107-mm (4.22-in), on which they later concentrated, the Soviets did make use of medium mortars. The first of these was the **82-PM 36**, which was introduced in 1936 as a copy of a Brandt muzzle-loaded and smooth-bore weapon. The following **82-PM 37** differed mainly in its use of a round rather than square baseplate, and in the introduction of recoil springs between the barrel and the bipod. The **82-PM 41** was intended to improve the basic weapon's battlefield mobility, and instead of the standard bipod had a stub axle arrangement with two

An American mortar team is seen in action during the Korean War of the early 1950s. The often static fighting of this conflict made it sensible to construct fire positions protected by piled sandbags or natural features.

pressed-steel wheels and, in its centre, the elevating rod. The **82-PM 43** differed from the 82-PM-41 only in having fixed wheels rather than detachable wheels. Finally there appeared the **82-PM New 37** based on the 82-PM 37 but with a lighter baseplate and tripod to improve battlefield mobility.

The threat of nuclear, biological and chemical agents has long been present in battle conditions, and this L16 mortar crew is seen under training conditions wearing their NBC 'noddy' suits.

Decided oddity

An oddity among these Soviet mortars is the weapon known as the **Avtomaticheskii Minomet Vasilek** (Little Vasili automatic mortar). Introduced in 1971, this weapon is otherwise known as the **2B9** and is an 82-mm type mounted on a mountain gun carriage that can be towed by a light vehicle. Once emplaced it can be used either in the direct-fire role as a conventional gun or in the high-angle mortar role. In action the carriage's wheels are raised off the ground and the weapon rests on a firing baseplate. The weapon is fed manually at the muzzle or automatically through the breech by four-round clip. The HE bomb weighs 3.23 kg (7.12 lb), and can be fired to a maximum range of 4750 m (5,195 yards).

There are several variants of the Vasilek for installation on light armoured vehicles, usually in some form of turret. Each infantry battalion of the Soviet (and now CIS) army should incorporate a battery of six Vasilek equipments, but in fact it is probably only the motorised and mechanised battalions of first-line divisions that are fully equipped.

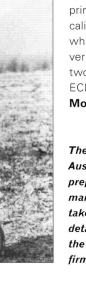

The 81-mm mortar is used by the armies of most countries as it is affordable yet provides good firepower for its weight. It is also worth noting that several countries other than those detailed above have also manufactured and fielded weapons of this type. The Chinese **Type 53**, for instance, is a copy of the 82-PM 37. The Finnish company Tampella has produced two weapons, the **M-38** and **M-56**. Like Tampella, Israel's Soltam has branched into the mortar market, its primary offering in the medium calibre being the 81-mm **M-64**, which has been developed in versions with short, long and two-piece barrels. In Spain, ECIA offer the **Model L-N** and **Model L-L** 81-mm mortars.

The British L16 mortar is seen in two of its standard applications as a ground-based weapon (above left) and vehicle-carried type (left). The vehicle is the FV432 armoured personnel carrier.

The two-man crew of an Austrian 81-mm (3.2-in) mortar prepare their weapon. While one man levels the weapon and takes preliminary sighting details, the other ensures that the spiked feet of the bipod are firmly fixed.

Heavy mortars

Heavy mortars are weapons with a calibre greater than 102-mm (4-in) and firing a bomb heavier than 7 kg (15.4 lb) to a range of more than 6000 m (6,560 yards). Such weapons hit hard at long battlefield ranges and yet are comparatively mobile in the tactical sense.

In Austria, the SMI organisation produces a large assortment of mortars in all sizes, and the largest of these is the 120-mm (4.72-in) **M12** designed for the Austrian army but also offered for export. Like many other weapons of this calibre, the design is based on that of the Soviet 120-HM 38, but much use is made of special metals both to lighten the weight and to enable larger charges to be fired for increased range.

The M12 is relatively easy to use in action as a result of a special bipod design with recoil absorbers. Once again a special bomb is produced: this the HE-78, which weighs 14.5 kg (31.97 lb) including 2.2 kg (4.85 lb) of explosive payload and can be fired to a range of 8500 m (9,295 yards).

French lead

In France, the Brandt company produces conventional light and

The Soltam 120-mm (4.72-in) Standard Mortar is a heavy mortar, and is depicted here in its form ready for towing with an eye secured at the muzzle. The carriage also carries tools, spare parts and other equipment items. The IMI illuminating round is shown with six propelling charges.

medium mortars in 60- and 81.4-mm calibres, but as an organisation it is best known for its 120-mm heavy mortars. It is in this calibre that the mortar can become a highly versatile adjunct to conventional artillery, and many armies use 120-mm mortars in place of artillery. The smooth-bore models in this range are conventional mortars that can be used in exactly the same way as smaller-calibre models, but the rifled mortars are much more complex and in many ways resemble conventional high-angle guns. The rifled weapons fire pre-rifled projectiles whose range can be enhanced by the use of an auxiliary rocket unit that cuts in

The great weight of the Soltam 160-mm (6.3-in) mortar inevitably suggested vehicles installations such as that seen here in the forward part of a converted M4 Sherman tank chassis of World War II vintage.

only when the bomb is at the top of its trajectory. A typical range with this rocket assistance is 13000 m (14,215 yards) for an HE bomb weighing 18.7 kg (41.23 lb). Despite their

size and weight, the Brandt rifled mortars can thus have a very useful performance, and key weapons on the series include the **Mortier MO-120-60** light mortar, **Mortier MO-120-**

A Brandt 120-mm (4.72-in) rifled mortar with its breech resting on the baseplate and the central part of the barrel on the wheeled carriage. The muzzle-loaded bombs weigh up to 18.7 kg (41.23 lb).

SPECIFICATION	
M12	HE bomb 18.7 kg (41.23 lb)
Calibre: 120-mm (4.72-in)	**Maximum range:** 13000 m (14,215
Length: barrel 2.015 m (79.33 in)	yards) with rocket-assisted bomb
Weights: mortar 305 kg (672.4 lb);	
HE bomb 14.5 kg (31.97 lb)	**Mortar M30**
Maximum range: 8500 m (9,295	**Calibre:** 107.7-mm (4.2-in)
yards)	**Length:** barrel 1.524 m (60 in)
	Weight: mortar 305 kg (672.4 lb);
Brandt Mortier MO-120-RT-61	HE bomb 12.2 kg (26.9 lb); smoke
Calibre: 120-mm (4.72-in)	bomb 11.32 kg (24.95 lb)
Length: barrel 2.08 m (81.9 in)	**Maximum range:** 6800 m (7,435
Weights: mortar 582 kg (1,283 lb);	yards)

Above: Mortars do not change their elevation to increase or decrease range: instead, the crew increases or decreases the propellant charge. This American 4.2-in mortar has the relevant charges and ranges inscribed permanently on the barrel.

Below: This Brandt mortar, of 120-mm (4.72-in) calibre, is typical of the more modern type of heavier mortar. The size and weight of the weapon mean that battlefield mobility can be provided only by the use of a wheeled carriage.

Below: The Soviet 160-mm Model 1943 mortar is a large weapon of elderly design, yet offers good fire-support capabilities for battlefield purposes. Often used in place of more conventional artillery, the weapon fires an HE/fragmentation bomb weighing 40.8-kg (89.5-lb).

M65 strengthened mortar, **Mortier MO-120-AM 50** heavy mortar, **Mortier MO-120-LT** mortar and **Mortier MO-120-RT-61** rifled mortar.

The American 106.7-mm (4.2-in) mortars have been around for a long time as they were first developed to fire smoke bombs before World War II. Since then they have been the subject of many improvement programmes and general updating of weapon and ammunition to the point where the present-day version is no longer known as a 4.2-in mortar (except to the soldiers who use them), but instead as the 107-mm **Mortar M30**. This is a rifled mortar that fires a spin-stabilised projectile. In its present form the M30 uses not the original rectangular baseplate but rather a heavy circular unit with the barrel supported on a single column. The barrel can rotate on the baseplate and it is fitted with a recoil system to absorb what can be quite considerable firing forces. All this adds up to a considerable degree so that the complete weapon weighs no less than 305 kg (672 lb). This is quite a lot to get in and out of action in a hurry, so the size of the mortar crew and its carrying vehicle are correspondingly large. Many M30s are in fact not ground-mounted at all but are carried on special mountings inside M113 APCs to fire through roof hatches.

Capable bomb

The ammunition used on the M30 more closely resembles an artillery round than a mortar bomb. It is of the type known as semi-fixed, for components of the charge can be added or removed as required. The range of projectile types has gradually been increased over the years and there are now no less than three HE, two smoke, one illuminating and two chemical rounds.

In Israel, Soltam produces a full range of mortars but it is with its heavy mortars that the company has made its name. Soltam produces two 120-mm models and one of a massive 160-mm (6.3-in) calibre. All these are large enough to warrant their own wheeled travelling carriages, although of the 120-mm mortars one is described as the **Light Mortar** and the other as the **M-65 Standard Mortar**.

The light model is designed for infantry use, is carried into action on its wheeled carriage and can be towed by manpower alone. The standard model is much more substantial and is towed into action. In range terms there is little to choose between the two Soltam 120-mm models, although the standard model has a slight edge. They both fire the same bombs and both can be mounted in APCs if required. The Soltam 120-mm bomb weighs 12.9 kg (28.44 lb), of which 2.3 kg (5.07 lb) is the HE payload.

Super-heavy mortar

With the Soltam 160-mm **M-66** weapon, mortars cross the line from infantry support to artillery. Each M-66 has a crew of six to eight men, and as the barrel is too long for muzzle loading a breech-loading system has to be used. The M-66 fires a 40 kg (88.18 lb) bomb to a range of 9300 m (10,170 yards), and the 1700-kg (3,748-lb) overall weight means that it is often carried by a converted tank.

The Soviet army and its successors have made extensive use of heavy mortars, including the 107-mm **107-PBHM 38**, 120-mm **120-HM 38** and **120-mm Model 43**, and **160-mm Model 1943** dating from before or during World War II. The large 160-mm weapon is used by divisional support batteries instead of conventional artillery. It is a breech-loaded weapon of great length and weight, and the latest model is known as the **M-160**.

The 240-mm (9.45-in) **M-240** is a genuinely formidable weapon that was first revealed in public during 1953. In travelling configuration, the M-240 is 6.51 m (21 ft 4 in) long, and is towed on a two-wheeled carriage. The M-240 is in many respects similar to the 160-mm M-160. Thus the M-240 is a breech-loaded weapon, the barrel being hinged around its support point so that the muzzle can be lowered and thereby reveal the breech into which the bomb and its propellant charges are inserted before the muzzle is raised and the breech closed before being locked.

The M-240 is a massive item of equipment with a barrel that is 5.34 m (210.24 in) long, and in firing position the M-240 turns the scales at 3610 kg (7,959 lb). Such size and mass are reflected in the M-240 capabilities, which including the firing of a 100-kg (220.46-lb) HE bomb out to a maximum range of 9700 m (10,610 yards after leaving the muzzle at a velocity of 362 m per second).

This behemoth of a battlefield weapon is operated by a crew of nine men, and its maximum rate of fire is one round per minute.

Other countries that have produced heavy mortars include Finland, whose Tampella company created the **120-mm M-40** and **160-mm M-58**; Spain, whose ECIA organisation developed the **105-mm (4.13-in) Model L**, **120-mm Model L** and **Model SL**; Sweden, in which Bofors made the **120-mm M/41C**; and Switzerland, where the Waffenfabrikk manufactured the **120-mm Model 64** and **Model 74**.

SPECIFICATION	
Soltam 120-mm Standard **Calibre:** 120-mm (4.72-in) **Length:** barrel 2.154 m (84.8 in) **Weights:** mortar 245 kg (540 lb) in action; HE bomb 12.9 kg (28.44 lb) **Maximum range:** 8500 m (9,295 yards) **Soltam M-66** **Calibre:** 160-mm (6.3-in) **Length:** barrel 3.066 m (120.7 in) **Weights:** mortar 1700 kg (3,748 lb)	in action; HE bomb 40 kg (88.18 lb) **Maximum range:** 9600 m (10,500 yards) **120-mm Model 1943** **Calibre:** 120-mm (4.72-in) **Length:** barrel 1.854 m (73 in) **Weight:** mortar 275 kg (606.3 lb) in action; HE fragmentation bomb 16 kg (35.27 lb) **Maximum range:** 5700 m (6,235 yards)

Gun-mortars

With its gun-mortars the French Brandt company introduced a class of ordnance that has no real counterpart anywhere else in the world. This results from the fact that Brandt combined into a single weapon the attributes of the high-angle mortar and the conventional gun. The object was the creation of a versatile close-support weapon. The concept is simple: a breech- as well as muzzle-loaded mortar is disposed in the fashion that allows the mortar bombs to be loaded into the barrel from the breech for low-trajectory firing and from the muzzle for high-angle fire.

This type of weapon was initially developed for mounting on light AFVs, but the gun-mortar has proved so attractive an option that several other applications have been evolved. The gun-mortar cannot be used from a bipod or other ground mounting, however.

Two weapon types

There are two calibres in Brandt's range of gun-mortars, namely 60-mm (2.36-in) and 81.4-mm (3.2-in). The 60-mm weapon is the one more likely to

The Brandt 60-mm Model LR gun-mortar is a gun/smooth-bore mortar hybrid. It can be loaded at the muzzle, or alternatively can be breech-loaded from within the confines of a vehicle. This long-range weapon fires a special bomb to 5000 m (5,470 yards).

Right: This is a Brandt 60-mm (2.36-in) gun-mortar on a Zodiac inflatable craft to highlight the low trunnion loadings of this weapon type. The gun-mortar can be breech- or muzzle-loaded, only the former being possible in this application.

be used for infantry support, while the 81-mm weapon is generally installed in large armoured cars and APCs. (The 60-mm versions are also used as turret weapons on light armoured vehicles, and some have been mounted on light patrol craft, including inflatable Zodiac-type boats.) These turret-mountings are designed for the close support of infantry operations.

The smooth-bore barrel is mounted so that a spring around the barrel absorbs most of the recoil forces and thus reduces the trunnion forces to a great degree. Conventional mortar projectiles can be fired, but for direct-fire use special canister rounds or hollow-charge armour-

*This **SIBMAS** 6x6 APC features a turret carrying a 60-mm (2.36-in) Brandt gun-mortar of the long-barrel type for additional range. In this type of application, the weapon is normally breech-loaded and fired using a percussion trigger.*

piercing projectiles can be fired. When fired in the low-trajectory mode, the standard 60-mm gun-mortar has a range of about 500 m (547 yards), increasing to 2050 m (2,240 yards) in the conventional mode. When the weapon is employed in the mortar role, the bombs are muzzle-loaded to fall and strike a fixed firing pin, but in the low-trajectory role they are loaded via the breech mechanism. Brandt also produced a special long-range version of the 60-mm gun-mortar with direct- and indirect-fire ranges of 500 m and 5000 m (5,470 yards) respectively, the latter with a special bomb.

Greater capability

The 81-mm weapon is more complicated. This is intended as the primary weapon for armoured vehicles, and is therefore fitted with a recoil mechanism and is

proportionally much heavier than the 60-mm models. However, the larger gun-mortar can fire the entire range of 81-mm projectiles, and even has one that is unique to its type. This is an armour-piercing 'arrow' projectile fired, with a special charge, only in the direct-fire role. It is capable of piercing up to 50 mm (1.97 in) of armour at 1000 m (1,095 yards).

Development of both gun-mortar types continues, and both weapons are in widespread service.

SPECIFICATION	
Brandt 60-mm gun-mortar (standard model)	**Brandt 81-mm gun-mortar (standard model)**
Calibre: 60-mm (2.36-in)	**Calibre:** 81.4-mm (3.2-in)
Length: 1.21 m (47.64 in)	**Length:** barrel 2.3 m (90.55 in)
Weights: gun-mortar 42 kg (92.6 lb); HE bomb 1.72 kg (3.79 lb)	**Weights:** gun-mortar 500 kg (1,102 lb); HE bomb 4.45 kg (9.8 lb)
Maximum range: 500 m (547 yards in the direct-fire mode and 2050 m (2,240 yards) in the indirect-fire mode	**Maximum range:** 1000 m (1,095 yards) in the direct-fire model and 8000 m (8,750 yards) in the indirect-fire mode

*A gun-mortar in a turret can provide light vehicles with a potent armament capability for the shorter-range direct and longer-range indirect fire roles. On this **SIBMAS** APC the 60-mm gun-mortar replaces a 20-mm cannon.*

Grenade launchers

The rifle-launched grenade is still used, but is not a fashionable weapon for several reasons. Two of these are that the firing of a rifle grenade can often cause sufficient recoil to damage the rifle, and that accurate aiming is difficult. In recent years the use of special propellant cartridges has been partially replaced by bullet traps in the tails of grenades to absorb the forces of a fired bullet and use them to propel the grenade.

In Italy this has led to the development of a special infantry support weapon known as the **AP/AV700**. In effect this is a trio of rifle-grenade launchers set side by side on a common baseplate or launcher. The finned rifle grenades fit over spigots, and are launched by standard ball cartridges loaded into the breech mechanism at the base of each spigot. The bullets are fired directly into the grenades' tails, the flash of their ignition being used to light a delay unit that in turn ignites a small rocket motor to increase range to 700 m (765 yards). Moreover, it is possible to aim fairly accurately and consistently, for in flight the grenades are stabilized by their fins and also

The Italian AP/AV700 anti-personnel and anti-vehicle weapon is an unusual grenade launcher designed to fire between one and three rifle grenades to a range of up to 700 m (765 yards). The type can be used in the ground role on the stand illustrated, or be carried by a land, sea or air vehicle.

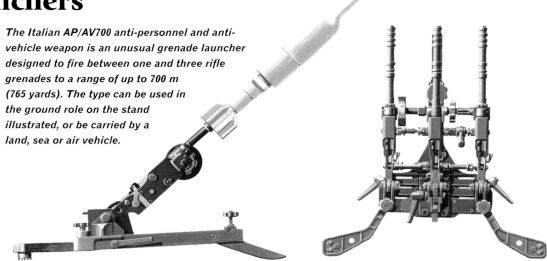

by gases vented from the rocket to add further spin.

It is possible to fire the grenades using either the standard NATO 7.62-mm (0.3-in) or 5.56-mm (0.219-in) ball cartridges, but the spigot will accept only one or the other. The grenades can also be fired from conventional rifle launchers.

The grenades have hollow-charge warheads able to penetrate up to 120 mm (4.72 in) of armour, but they also have a considerable blast and anti-personnel effect. The three-spigot launcher can fire the grenades one at a time or in one salvo, and it is perfectly

possible to fire six or seven salvoes per minute.

Multiple roles

Possible applications include its use in place of orthodox light mortars by infantry units, and its mounting on light armoured or soft-skinned vehicles. It could also be used on light patrol or landing craft, and applications at outlying or guard blockhouses can be foreseen. The launcher can be carried on a special backpack, with another carrying the grenades.

The 30-mm **AGS-17 Plamya** (flame) is an automatic grenade-launcher that first appeared in

the USSR in 1975, and is now widely employed down to company level (two weapons) on the forces of what is now the Commonwealth of Independent States. When it first appeared, the AGS-17 caused a stir in Western weapon design circles, for then there was no Western equivalent, although one has appeared since.

The AGS-17 fires small HE grenades at a rate of just one per second. The grenades are fed into the weapon from a 29-round belt, usually from a belt drum attached prominently on the right-hand side of the weapon. For firing, the AGS-17 is mounted on

Left: The AGS-17 operates on the blowback principle, the propellant forcing the bolt back and working the reloading cycle as well as driving the grenade up the barrel.

Right: The AGS-17 Plamya is not light, but turns the scales at less than a heavy machine gun and can provide a very considerable volume of fire support, albeit with less pinpoint accuracy than the heavy machine gun but with greater area saturation.

a tripod, and can be aimed with the aid of a dial sight at the rear of the weapon body. The weapon works on the simple blowback system, part of the action operating a pawl mechanism to move the ammunition belt. Firing can be of the direct or indirect types, the latter providing more range.

Afghan service

The AGS-17 was used in action in Afghanistan, and has been

seen not only on a tripod mounting but also on special helicopter mounts. In Afghanistan the AGS-17 was used widely for fire suppression. However, the weapon's aspect which has impressed Western observers most is its range, which can be up to 1750 m (1,915 yards) although operationally it is not often used at ranges greater than 1200 m (1,315 yards). This means that the weapon has a

much higher potential for fire response than a mortar, and its automatic rate of fire can quickly compensate for the small projectile payload. The main drawback of the AGS-17

seems to be its weight, for the launcher and tripod together weigh more than 53 kg (117 lb), which means it has to have a crew of at least two men to carry weapon and ammunition.

SPECIFICATION	
AP/AV700	**AGS-17 Plamya**
Length: spigot 300 mm (11.81 in)	**Calibre:** 30 mm
Weights: launcher 11 kg (24.25 lb); grenade 0.93 kg (2.05 m); grenade warhead 0.46 kg (1.01 lb)	**Length:** 840 mm (33 in)
	Weights: launcher about 18 kg (39.7 lb); tripod about 35 kg (77.2 lb); grenade 0.35 m (0.77 lb)
Maximum range: 700 m (765 yards)	**Maximum range:** 1750 m (1,915 yards)

Rifle grenades and launchers

The rifle grenade was developed as a means of bridging the range and firepower gap between the hand-thrown grenade and the light mortar. Moreover, the low velocity of the rifle grenade combined with its high trajectory to suggest the weapon's use in the anti-tank role: the steeply falling final trajectory opened the possibility of attacks on the thinner armour of any tank's upper surfaces with a small yet effective hollow-charge warhead. From these simple beginnings, and despite the major problems of having it land with any real accuracy, the rifle grenade gained a modest level of endorsement as a simple and cheap method of boosting the firepower of the infantryman.

Above: Grenade launchers like the M203 give the infantry rifleman the ability to provide his own fire support, independent of mortars and artillery.

Right: A US Army recruit receives instruction on the use of the 40-mm (1.57-in) M203 grenade launcher attached to an M16A1 rifle. The grenade launcher sights can be seen, as can the method of attaching the launcher to the rifle's fore stock.

SPECIFICATION	
Mk 19	**Length:** overall 737 mm (29 in)
Calibre: 40-mm (1.57-in)	**Weight:** launcher 2.72 kg (6 lb)
Length: overall 1.028 m (40.5 in)	**Maximum range:** 350 m (385 yards)
Weight: launcher 35 kg (77.2 lb)	
Rate of fire: 375 rounds per minute	**M203**
Maximum range: 1600 m (1,750 yards)	**Calibre:** 40-mm (1.57-in)
	Length: overall 389 mm (15.3 in)
	Weight: launcher 1.36 kg (3 lb)
M79	**Maximum range:** 350 m (385 yards)
Calibre: 40-mm (1.57-in)	

The American 40-mm (1.575-in) grenade family was originally the **M406** series, and there are dozens of different types in this series. The grenade looks like a squat rifle round of large calibre. The firing system is such that the propellant gases are allowed to flow through a series of vent holes into a

chamber in which they are allowed to expand at a relatively low pressure, thus allowing quite light weapons to fire the grenades.

Special launcher

The M406 was designed to be fired from a dedicated launcher rather than a rifle, and the first

Above: The single-shot M203, a pump-action launcher attached to an M16 series assault rifle, represents a great advance over the M79 dedicated launcher as it leaves the firer with a usable rifle already in his hands.

Right: The Mk 19 automatic grenade launcher, seen here with a belt of 40-mm (1.57-in) armour-piercing grenades, has a rate of 375 rounds per minute and offers the possibility of saturating a large area with any of several types of round.

launcher was the notably simple **M79**. To all intents and purposes this is a special single-round shotgun into which a grenade is hand-loaded after the action has been broken. The weapon is then fired from the shoulder in the normal way The main limits of the M79, which is fairly widely used (and was indeed employed by the Royal Marines in the Falklands Islands campaign of 1982), are that its single-role purpose and bulk means that it has to be carried and operated by a soldier who cannot use his rifle at the same time.

This led to the design, development and introduction of the **M203** launcher. This is again a single-shot launcher, but in this instance attached under the fore grip of an M16A1 or M16A2 rifle. The M203 was selected for service during the late 1960s, and has been in service ever since. The M203 clips under the rifle in a fashion that ensures that the launcher interferes in no way with the rifle's normal function, and the weight of the M203 is a comparatively modest 1.63 kg (3.59 lb) loaded. Almost every US Army section has at least one man (and often more) with an M203 launcher fitted to his rifle. The grenades fired are usually the HE type of the M406 series, but also available are smoke, marker smoke, flare, CS riot control and others.

Modest accuracy

The M203 offers levels of accuracy that make it feasible to engage point targets at ranges up to about 150 m (165 yards) and area targets beyond this distance up to the weapon's maximum range of between 350 and 400 m (385 and 435 yards), depending on the type of grenade fired. At these ranges the performance of the grenades (especially those of the HE type) is limited by the amount of volume required for the impact fuse, whose requirements each fit into the space available for the explosive payload proper. The fuse has to be relatively large to be fully effective and reliable, so the reduction in the explosive payload

has to be offset by an increase in the number of grenades fired at any particular target.

Automatic launcher

This requires the use of multiple rounds, and as the M79 and M203 are both single-shot weapons, a great deal of design and development effort was begun on automatic weapons to fire the 40-mm grenades.

One early effort in this field was the **XM174**, which was not taken into service as there became available the **M384** grenade, a development of the M406 with a heavier explosive payload and a more powerful propellant. To fire this improved grenade the Americans adopted an automatic launcher known as the **Mk 19**. The mechanism of this launcher is based loosely on that of the 0.5-in (12.7-mm) Browning M2 heavy machine-gun in combination with a very short barrel. A belt-feed mechanism is employed to feed the grenades into the Mk 19's mechanism, and a rate of fire as high as 375 rounds per minute can be achieved. For tactical use the Mk 19 can be mounted on a tripod, or alternatively on a pedestal mount carried by a vehicle or light vessel. Another advantage, other than the rate of fire, offered by the Mk 19 over the M79 and M204, is a considerably longer range.

Reverting to the basic concept of the rifle grenade, it is worth noting that the low cost and simplicity of the weapon, in combination with the universal availability of the rifle as the means to launch these weapons, has made it feasible for any country with even the most limited facilities for the manufacture of small arms ammunition and other light ordnance to undertake the design and manufacture of rifle grenades. Some of these grenades, especially those carrying the type of hollow-charge warhead providing a capability against armoured fighting vehicles, bunkers and light vessels, are purpose-designed for the task. Others, intended for use against troops in the open, are straightforward adaptations of standard hand-thrown HE fragmentation grenades with a finned body carrying the grenade as its warhead.

Grenade adaptation

Typical of the adapted standard hand grenade is the **GME-FMK2-MO** grenade designed and made in Argentina. This is an orthodox hand grenade with a pre-fragmented steel body weighing 165 g (5.8 oz) and carrying 75.8 g (2.67 oz) of explosive triggered by the charge in a fuse mechanism, whose body weighs 44.79 g (1.44 oz), after a delay that varies between 3.4 and 4.5 seconds. On the detonation of its HE charge, the grenade body shatters into a large number of fragments each weighing between 3 and 5 g (0.11 and 0.18 oz) and providing a useful effect against any person within 5 m (16.4 ft). For use as a rifle grenade, the weapon is seated on top of its launcher, which comes complete with the special propellant cartridge, and these two elements are located on to the barrel and into the breech of the rifle respectively. After the grenade's safety pin has been removed, the firer aims and discharges his rifle, propelling the grenade into a trajectory offering a maximum range of some 350 to 400 m (385 to 435 yards) and the possibility of an air or ground burst.

Special grenade

Typical of the purpose-designed rifle grenade is a Belgian offering, the **ARP-RFL-40 BT**, designed and made by the MECAR organisation in variants to be fired from standard 7.62- and 5.56-mm (0.3- and 0.219-in) rifles. The weapon has a maximum diameter of 40 mm and an overall length of 243 mm (9.57 in), and weighs 264 g (9.31 oz). The launching method is of the bullet trap rather than gas propellant type: at the muzzle the standard ball projectile fired by the rifle is caught by a ladder of five discs of metal inside the rear of the rifle grenade, its energy thereby being transferred to the grenade for a trajectory out to a maximum range of 275 m (300 yards) but a practical range of 100 m (110 yards) at a launch elevation of +45 degrees.

The grenade is armed 8 m (26.25 ft) after leaving the rifle at a nominal velocity of 60 m (197 ft) per second, and the penetrative capabilities of its warhead include 125 mm (4.92 in) of steel armour or 400 mm (15.75 in) of concrete after a descent at an angle of 70 degrees.

The first launcher made specifically to fire spin-stabilised grenades was the M79. This is a single-shot dedicated launcher that can fire its grenade to a maximum range of 400 m (435 yards). Its main limitation was that the firer had no rifle.

SPECIFICATION	
Heckler & Koch HK 69A1 (Germany)	**Grenade Discharger L1A1 (UK)**
Type: single-shot grenade launcher	**Type:** single-shot grenade launcher
Calibre: 40-mm (1.57-in)	**Calibre:** 66-mm (2.6-in)
Length: overall 610 mm (24 in) with the stock extended	**Length:** overall 695 mm (27.4 in)
Weight: launcher 1.8 kg (3.97 lb)	**Weight:** 2.7 kg (6 lb)
Maximum range: 300 m (330 yards)	**Maximum range:** 100 m (110 yards)

Reconnaissance specialists of the US Army, clad in distinctive 'tiger stripe' fatigues, fire M79 launchers in Vietnam, where the launcher was nicknamed the 'Blooper' gun after a children's toy of the period.

Browning Automatic Shotguns

Left: A British soldier of the 18th Independent Brigade, on patrol in the jungle during the Malayan Emergency, carries a Browning A5, which gave him formidable short-range firepower.

The Browning Automatic shotguns were not produced as dedicated military weapons, but proved tough enough for the rigours of service life. They were useful weapons in terrain which favoured the ambusher; in an emergency they could fire five rounds in three seconds.

SPECIFICATION	
Browning Automatic (standard model) **Calibre:** 12 gauge **Length:** barrel 711 mm (28 in)	**Weight:** loaded 4.1 kg (9 lb) **Feed:** 5-round tubular magazine

Any description of the **Browning Automatic** shotgun as a combat weapon is beset by the difficulty that there has never been a purpose-produced military version of any of these designs. The first Browning Automatic (actually semi-automatic or self-loading) shotgun was conceived as early as 1898, but it was left to the Belgian Fabrique Nationale (FN) to start production and many of the guns still in use are Belgian-made. They were all conceived primarily as sporting weapons, but it was not long before substantial numbers were in military hands, often as security guard weapons or for similar duties. John M. Browning also negotiated a production licence with the American Remington concern and many Remington guns used by the US Army and others during World War II were in fact Browning Automatics, typical weapons being the **Remington Model 11A** and **Remington Model 12**.

Good jungle weapon

After World War II Browning sporting guns were widely used as military weapons in regions such as Central and South America, but it took the Malayan Emergency of 1948–1960 to make the Browning Automatic an established military weapon. The British army used Greener GP guns and Browning Automatics throughout that long campaign, often (but not always) with the long sporting barrel cut back to as short a length as possible. Most guns used by the British were 12-gauge weapons with five-round magazines, and fired commercial heavy shot cartridges.

It was not long before the British relearned the old lesson that the automatic shotgun is an almost perfect weapon for the close-quarter combat of jungle warfare. As an ambush or counter-ambush gun the Browning Automatic was ideal as it could be used to get off five rounds in as few as three seconds. At the time little publicity was given to the combat use of these shotguns (the **Remington Model 870R** was also employed) but many soldiers who served in Malaya during the Emergency probably carried a Browning Automatic at some time or another.

After 1960 the British army set aside the Browning for more conventional weapons, but doubtless some are still retained for 'special purposes'. Despite the type's Malayan popularity, soldiers found that the weapon was slow to reload and took considerable care, especially when shortened barrels imposed excessive firing loads on the self-loading components.

Brownings popped up again during the Rhodesian anti-guerrilla/freedom fighter campaigns, and the gun is still a widely used 'small campaign' weapon. But there is still no sign of a combat version of the Browning Automatic.

FN Riot Shotgun

SPECIFICATION	
FN Riot Shotgun **Calibre:** 12 gauge **Weight:** 2.95 kg (6.5 lb)	**Lengths:** overall 970 mm (38.19 in); barrel 500 mm (19.7 in) **Feed:** 5-round tubular magazine

As its name implies, the **Fabrique Nationale Riot Shotgun** is primarily a police and para-military weapon. In design terms it is relatively unremarkable as a manually operated pump-action shotgun with a tubular magazine holding five rounds. FN is no stranger to shotgun design, for it was among the first to produce the many John M. Browning Automatic shotgun designs in the 1920s, and since that time the company has been among the world leaders in the manufacture of these weapons. Many of FN's designs are intended for sporting purposes, but it takes little to transform a sporting shotgun into a law enforcement weapon and FN has never been slow to commit itself to any such undertaking.

The Riot Shotgun first appeared in 1970 and was based on the widely used FN automatic sporting gun of the period. It was at one time available with three

Pump-action shotguns like the FN are used by police forces all over the world. They are reliable weapons with high short-range hit probability, and do not produce stray bullets which can be lethal to bystanders hundreds of yards away.

interchangeable barrel lengths. The first models had rear and fore sights, but on later production models these have been removed and the standard barrel length is now 500 mm (19.7 in). Rubber butt pads and sling swivels are standard.

Rugged design

The main difference between the Riot Shotgun and the FN sporting models is that the riot version is much more rugged than the civilian shotguns. There is, for instance, a bolt that runs right through the butt-stock to strengthen that component, and all metalwork has been 'beefed up' to withstand the rigours of hard use. The metal surfaces have also been specially plated so that they require only the

minimum of care and maintenance.

For reasons of maintaining an overall high standard of reliability, FN even decided to retain the original five-round tubular magazine and has thus never introduced the extension magazines used on many other contemporary paramilitary shotguns. FN instead decided to retain the simple manual

Shotgun ammunition comes in a bewildering variety of forms, which different countries unhelpfully divide into different categories. On the left is a conventional birdshot round for the FN shotgun; in the centre a flechette round; and on the right a brenecke rifled slug.

action in which each 'pump' motion ejects a spent case and loads a fresh round. FN once tried to create an automatic version of the Riot Shotgun, but this was made only as a prototype with a six-round magazine.

FN has produced its Riot Shotgun in a form suitable for firing full-calibre slugs, but the majority of guns in regular service are used to fire 12-gauge shot only: in fact there has never been a Riot Shotgun in any other calibre. The type is used by the Belgian police and some para-military units, and it has been sold to some overseas police forces. It is a very rugged weapon and is more than adequate for its paramilitary role.

Beretta RS200 and RS202P Shotguns

A company based firmly in Italy but with outlets all over the world, Armi Beretta SpA is without doubt one of the most respected names in small-arms design and manufacture, and is also no stranger to the manufacture of shotguns. Although the company's first such weapons were directed

The RS202-MI is the folding-stock version of the successful RS202P 12-gauge shotgun. Loading is marginally easier than on the original weapon, and the bolt mechanism has been altered.

mainly toward the civil market as sporting guns, Beretta soon

followed the tendency toward the manufacture of more robust shotguns intended for police and paramilitary purposes. The first result of this process was the introduction of the 12-gauge **Beretta RS200 (Police Model)**

as a manually operated pump-action shotgun.

Excellent finish

As with all other firearms from the Beretta company, this RS200 (Police Model) is a well designed and superbly finished weapon

SPECIFICATION	
RS200 (Police Model)	**Weight:** about 3 kg (6.6 lb)
Calibre: 12 gauge	**Feed:** 5/6-round tubular magazine
Lengths: overall 1030 mm (40.55 in); barrel 520 mm (20.47 in)	

notable for the degree to which it has been strengthened for the type of rough handling it can expect to receive in police and paramilitary hands.

Beretta introduced no innovations with the RS200 other than a special safety sliding-block breech locking device that prevents the possibility of the weapon being discharged before the breech locking process has been completed. The hammer also has a special safety lug feature,

and there is a bolt catch that enables a cartridge to be safely removed from the chamber without having to fire it. Another interesting feature of the RS200 for police and paramilitary use is the fact that it can be used to fire small tear gas cartridges, to a maximum range of about 100 m (110 yards), as well as the usual shot or slug loadings.

Advanced design

Although now out of production, the RS200 is used by

many police and other forces. It was replaced in manufacture by the **RS202P**, which differs from its predecessor mainly in its loading procedure, which by comparison with that of the RS200 (Police Model) was made much easier, and in slight variations to the bolt mechanism. With the introduction of the RS202P came two variants. The first was schemed to reduce the overall length of the weapon as a means of facilitating its

stowage and handling: this **RS202-MI** variant has a skeleton-type folding buttstock that can be stowed along the left-hand side of the body. The second of the variants carries over this folding buttstock, but in addition has a variable choke device over the muzzle to allow the alteration of the spread of shot, and also a perforated barrel jacket to make handling easier, as it is is impossible to hold the barrel once it has become hot after the firing of several rounds. To assist the firer in rapid aiming, special sights have been fitted to this second variant, which is known as the **RS202P-M2**.

The RS202P shotguns have followed the overall acceptance of the RS200, but the rate of sales has not been remarkable, mainly because the Beretta shotguns seem to lack the aesthetic, or perhaps futuristic, visual appeal of some of the more modern designs that have entered the market. The RS202P is now apparently being produced to order only. For all this it is a reliable and well-made gun.

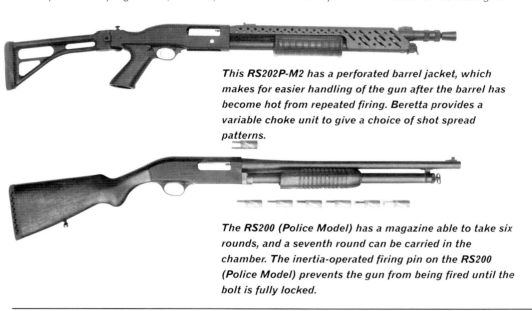

This RS202P-M2 has a perforated barrel jacket, which makes for easier handling of the gun after the barrel has become hot from repeated firing. Beretta provides a variable choke unit to give a choice of shot spread patterns.

The RS200 (Police Model) has a magazine able to take six rounds, and a seventh round can be carried in the chamber. The inertia-operated firing pin on the RS200 (Police Model) prevents the gun from being fired until the bolt is fully locked.

SPAS Model 12 Shotgun

The **SPAS Model 12** (SPAS standing for Special-Purpose Automatic Shotgun or, in civilian hands, Sporting Purpose Automatic Shotgun) is one of the most interesting and influential combat shotgun designs to have appeared for a long time. The new type was designed and has since been produced by Luigi Franchi SpA, an Italian firm which had specialised in the creation of sporting shotguns for many years. When the demand for a shot-firing combat weapon became apparent in the early 1970s, the Franchi team decided to design a new weapon using a novel approach: it opted to create a true combat weapon, not a conversion of an existing sporting model, and the result is the **SPAS Model 11**. This is optimised for the combat role in

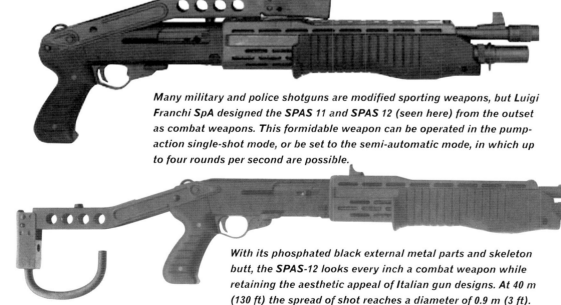

Many military and police shotguns are modified sporting weapons, but Luigi Franchi SpA designed the SPAS 11 and SPAS 12 (seen here) from the outset as combat weapons. This formidable weapon can be operated in the pump-action single-shot mode, or be set to the semi-automatic mode, in which up to four rounds per second are possible.

With its phosphated black external metal parts and skeleton butt, the SPAS-12 looks every inch a combat weapon while retaining the aesthetic appeal of Italian gun designs. At 40 m (130 ft) the spread of shot reaches a diameter of 0.9 m (3 ft).

a number of its features as detailed below, but was also made as short as possible,

optimised for reliability and low maintenance, and purposely made as 'pointable' as possible

so that the firer, after only brief training, had a good chance of securing a first-round hit.

Heavy and strong

Like its Model 12 development, the Model 11 is a heavy weapon that is so robust it can be used as a club. It has a distinctive appearance: there is no orthodox butt, but rather a fixed skeleton metal butt on the Model 11 or a folding stock on the Model 12. The mechanism at first sight appears to be a bulky manual pump action, but is in fact a combination of semi-automatic and pump-action features, the change between semi-automatic and pump-action operation being controlled by pressure on a button in the fore end and then movement of this fore end backward for pump action or forward for semi-automatic. In the semi-automatic mode, gas tapped from the barrel impinges on an annular piston round the under-barrel magazine. To work the action, which includes a vertically tilting locking lug that engages in the barrel extension to lock the bolt. The receiver is made of light alloy, while the barrel and gas piston are manufactured of steel hard-chromed to reduce the chances of corrosion. All the exterior surfaces are sand-blasted and phosphated black, and the pistol grip and fore end are of plastic.

Tubular magazine

The tubular magazine under the short barrel can accommodate up to seven rounds. These

A key feature of the SPAS-12 is the provision of a hook under the rear of the butt to hold the forearm of the firer, which allows the weapon to be fired with just one hand. However, control is distinctly limited.

rounds can vary from light bird shot to heavy metal slugs that can penetrate steel plate.

The rest of the SPAS is well provided with novel features. The variant most likely to be encountered is the Model 12, which has a bulky front hand-guard and a folding stock. The stock has a piece of curved metal under the 'butt plate' that loops around the forearm and allows the weapon to be held and fired with one hand, although anyone firing the weapon in such a way will soon learn what a handful the Model 12 can be. There is a pistol grip,

the muzzle can be fitted with a shotspreading choke device and another muzzle attachment is a grenade launcher. Small tear gas and CS projectiles can also be fired out to a range of 150 m (165 yards). Sights are provided but the spread of shot from a normal 12-gauge cartridge is such that at 40 m (45 yards) the shot pellets cover a circle with a diameter of 900 mm (35.4 in), so accuracy of aim is not vastly important at this type of typical combat range.

The SPAS is a true combat shotgun and in the hands of a fully trained operative can be a formidable weapon. The Model 12 has been sold to several military and paramilitary armed forces, and some have appeared on the civilian market. Many of these have been snapped up by shotgun enthusiasts, but in many countries the short barrel breaks legal regulations.

SPECIFICATION	
SPAS-12	**Length of barrel:** 460 mm (18.11 in)
Calibre: 12-gauge	**Weight:** 4.2 kg (9.26 lb)
Length overall: 1041 mm (40.98 in) with butt extended and 710 mm (27.95 in) with butt folded	**Feed:** 7-round tubular magazine

SPAS-15 Shotgun

The **SPAS-15** shotgun is a further development of the SPAS-12 shotgun, and is intended as police and military weapon offering considerable firepower through the use of a gas-operated semi-automatic action and a detachable single-stack box magazine. Thus multiple shots can be fired in quick succession from a magazine that is more quickly changed than refilling a tubular magazine. Versatility is offered by the provision of a manually selected single-shot pump action to complement the semi-automatic action, this allowing the weapon to fire low-pressure non-lethal ammunition such as tear gas and rubber slug projectiles. The firing modes are chosen in the fashion of the SPAS-12.

The SPAS-15 is based on an action with a rotary bolt and a short piston stroke, the latter located above the barrel. The bolt group is mounted on dual guide rods together with the recoil springs, and can be removed as a single unit.

The cocking handle is located on top of the receiver under the carrying handle, and can be operated with either hand. The SPAS-15 has a manual safety located inside the trigger guard to lock the trigger, and

The SPAS-15 offers the utmost in tactical flexibility among combat shotguns, for in addition to its butt options, selectable firing modes and detachable magazines, it has the Variochoke system to change the weapon's choke.

an automatic grip safety on the pistol grip under the trigger guard.

The SPAS-15 has open adjustable sights, and can be fitted with additional sighting devices such as red dot sights or laser pointers. The receiver of SPAS-15 is made from aluminum alloy and its furniture from polymer plastics. Earlier models had a fixed plastic or folding metal skeleton butt, but recent models have a side-folding, solid plastic butt. The magazine is plastic.

SPECIFICATION	
SPAS-15	**Length of barrel:** 450 mm (17.72 in)
Calibre: 12-gauge	**Weight:** empty 3.9 kg (8.6 lb)
Length overall: 1000 mm (39.37 in) with butt extended and 750 mm (29.53 in) with butt folded	**Feed:** 6-round detachable box magazine

Striker Shotgun

Developed by the South African company Armsel, the **Striker** is a semi-automatic 12-gauge shotgun that appeared on the market in the mid-1980s. The Striker is an indigenous South African design that is now being manufactured by Reunert Technology Systems near Johannesburg, although initial production was by Armsel; the weapon is also made under licence in the USA, where the Striker has been adopted by many law enforcement agencies for use by their weapons teams, and also been developed into other forms. The Striker was designed for a wide range of operational roles ranging from civilian self-protection to full military combat applications.

With its short overall length and seemingly massive rotary magazine, holding a very useful 12 rounds of 12-gauge ammunition, the Striker is a weapon of impressive appearance. It is also highly capable and could be a decisive short-range weapon.

Rotary magazine

The Striker's most important single feature is its 12-round rotary magazine. This is loaded with cartridges through a trap on the right rear of the drum, which is rotated by a spring tensioned by a key at the front of the magazine. Once the weapon is loaded, one pull of the trigger fires a round and rotates the next round into line with the firing pin, it being impossible to fire the weapon until the firing pin is exactly in line with the next cartridge. The recoil is claimed to be less than that of a normal shotgun, although exactly why this should be is not clear for the barrel is certainly shorter than those of most other similar weapons. It is possible that the recoil is masked by the fact that the Striker has a fore-grip under the barrel and a pistol grip; there is also a metal stock that can be folded up and over the barrel. The barrel has a perforated metal sleeve to dissipate heat and to prevent the hot barrel being touched by the firer's hand, for the rapid firing of the full 12 rounds would certainly produce a very hot barrel.

Gas ejection

Other features of the Striker are a double-action trigger and a gas ejection system to remove a spent cartridges from the system as the next round is fired.

The Striker can fire a wide range of 12-gauge ammunition ranging from bird shot (often used in old regime South Africa for the dispersal of crowds) to heavy metal slugs. The weapon can be fired with the butt folded, although the discharge of heavier loads without use of the butt could prove somewhat too lively for comfort.

Short-range use

The sights are very simple, for the Striker is obviously not meant as anything other than a very short-range weapon for clearing crowds or perhaps in close-quarter combat in built-up areas. It could also prove to be very useful in bush warfare where infantry engagements and ambushes are often at very close ranges as a consequence of the overall lack of visibility resulting from the prevalent short scrub vegetation. As well as its widespread service with US law enforcement bodies, the Striker has been adopted by the South African army and police, and has also found an operational niche with the Israeli armed forces and police.

It would have been surprising if a nation in arms such as South Africa in its apartheid days had not come up with some interesting small arms developments. The semi-automatic Armsel Striker is a case in point, its 12-shot rotary magazine giving considerably more firepower than conventional guns.

Mossberg 500 Shotguns

O.F. Mossberg and Sons Inc. is a relative newcomer to combat as opposed to sporting shotguns, for its first such weapon, the **Mossberg Model 500**, appeared in 1961. After a while Mossberg made its market breakthrough and the Model 500 remains the company's 'base' product.

The Model 500 is a manual slide-action 12-gauge weapon. The receiver body is forged from high-grade aluminium and the steel bolt locks into a barrel extension to take the firing loads off the receiver. Most components such as the extractors and action slides are 'doubled' to produce strength and reliability, and this makes the Model 500 a very robust weapon despite its low overall price. These points have made the Model 500 and its variants

Although produced by a company much younger than many of its competitors, the Mossberg Model 500 series soon found success. Later models appear very different, but the gun mechanism itself is hardly altered.

widely used police weapons, but Mossberg has also produced combat versions.

One is the **Model ATP-8SP**. This is basically a police Model 500 with a non-reflective finish and extra attention given to the protective finish of every component. A bayonet mount is provided, and there is even provision for mounting a telescopic sight for use when firing slugs, although this feature would appear to be little used. A perforated handguard may be fitted over the barrel and, as

with most of the Model 500 range, an up-and-over folding metal buttstock may be used in place of the normal hardwood fixed component. The Model 500 ATP-8SP has sold well but has been replaced by an updated combat model.

Bullpup design

This is the **Model 500 Bullpup 12**. As its name implies, this is a bullpup design with a pistol grip assembly placed forward of the receiver. This makes the weapon considerably shorter than its conventional equivalent, and thus much easier to handle and stow in confined spaces, a considerable selling point for many police and military authorities. On the Bullpup

12 the receiver and much of the weapon body are entirely enclosed in a strong thermo-plastic material so there are few components to catch on clothing or anything else This is partly negated by the all-inline bullpup layout that dictates that the rear and fore sights have to stick up on posts, but these can be folded down when not required.

The Bullpup 12 can be manufactured 'from new', but Mossberg produces a kit to convert existing Model 500 weapons to the revised configuration. Another Mossberg shotgun with a definite military potential is the **Model 590** which was developed in the 1970s and features a strengthened structure.

SPECIFICATION	
Mossberg Model 500 Bullpup 12	**Weight:** 3.85 kg (8.49 lb)
Calibre: 12 gauge	**Feed:** 6- or 8-round tubular
Lengths: overall 784 mm (30.87 in); barrel 508 mm (20 in)	magazine

---

Ithaca 37 M and P Shotguns

In the USA the shotgun is a well established police and prison service weapon, to the extent that many shotgun manufactur-ers find it well worth their while to produce weapons tailored to individual police department specifications. Some of these weapons come very close to military specifications, and such is the **Ithaca Model LAPD** shotgun, a weapon based on the **Ithaca Model DS** (DeerSlayer, from the company's trademark). In its turn the Model DS was based on a very well established design known as the **Ithaca Model 37 M and P**, very robust and well-made weapons produced for policing requirements.

Long pedigree

The Model 37 series has been around for some time: during World War II it was one of the

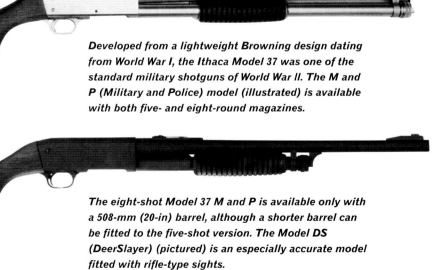

Developed from a lightweight Browning design dating from World War I, the Ithaca Model 37 was one of the standard military shotguns of World War II. The M and P (Military and Police) model (illustrated) is available with both five- and eight-round magazines.

The eight-shot Model 37 M and P is available only with a 508-mm (20-in) barrel, although a shorter barrel can be fitted to the five-shot version. The Model DS (DeerSlayer) (pictured) is an especially accurate model fitted with rifle-type sights.

shotguns selected by the US Army for military use. It was used during that period for general shotgun purposes, including riot control and guard duties, and was then available in three barrel lengths. The

current Model M and P models are not significantly dissimilar from the World War II versions, but are now made that much more rugged. The current shotguns are produced in several forms and with a range

of options available. Two important variants are the **Model 37 Homeland Security** for self-defence and police use, and the **Model 37 Stakeout** compact weapon with a shorter barrel and a pistol grip in place of the conventional stock. Model 37 weapons may be fitted with a five- or eight-round tubular magazine, and the two barrel lengths are 470 mm (18.5 in) and 508 mm (20 in). Both are used to fire the usual range of 12-gauge shot cartridges using a cylinder choke barrel whereas the Model DS has a precision-bored cylindrical barrel that can be used to fire heavy slugs. The Model DS has only the 508-mm barrel, and sights are provided. The option of a five- or eight-round magazine is carried over.

The Model LAPD for the Los Angeles Police Department is the Model DS with a rubber butt pad, special sights, sling swivels and a carrying strap. It has a 470-mm barrel, a five-round tubular magazine and, like all the other models in the Model 37 range, a robust slide pump action. Some of these weapons are used by the special forces of several nations.

All the weapons in the Model 37 M and P range have Parkerized finishes to reduce wear and the need for constant cleaning.

SPECIFICATION	
Model P and M	**Weight:** 2.94 kg (6.48 lb) or 3.06 kg (6.745 lb) depending on barrel length
Calibre: 12 gauge	
Lengths: overall 1016 mm (40 in) with the 508-mm barrel; barrel 470 or 508 mm (18.5 or 20 in)	**Feed:** 5- or 8-round tubular magazine

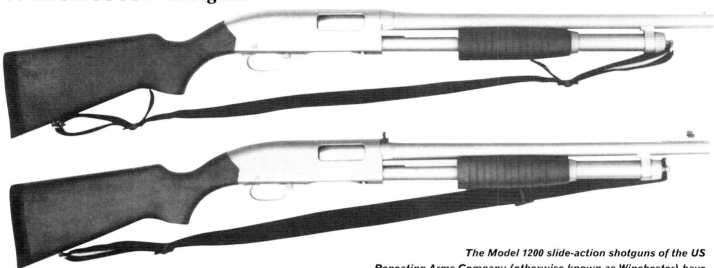

The more highly finished appearance of this Ithaca Model 37DS Police Special attests to its original role as a civilian hunting weapon. Nevertheless, its light weight, accuracy and reliable action make it effective as a para-military and law enforcement weapon.

Winchester Shotguns

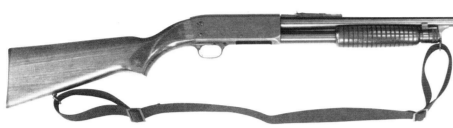

The Model 1200 slide-action shotguns of the US Repeating Arms Company (otherwise known as Winchester) have 457-mm (18-in) barrels and are finished in a satinised chrome which minimises reflected light and resists corrosion.

The US Repeating Arms Company, usually known as Winchester, is best known for its rifles, but also produces shotguns for the sporting market and for police and para-military use. In the past Winchester shotguns were produced in a wide variety of models, including the classic Model 12 used during World War II and some of the few box-magazine combat shotguns ever produced, but current models are limited to a few manual slide-action models.

The basic Winchester shotgun model is a 12-gauge design known as the **Winchester Defender**. This was specifically created, developed and manufactured for use by conventional police forces, but the weapon has also found its way into the hands of several purely military forces. In overall terms, the Defender is of conventional design, but the action is notably compact and, as is always the case with Winchester, the standard to which the weapons are manufactured is very good.

Rotary bolt action

Operating the slide action opens and closes a rotary bolt of the type that provides a very positive and safe lock, and the unlocking is recoil-assisted to speed the action considerably, placing the weapon almost into the semi-automatic class. The tubular magazine extends to just under the muzzle and can hold six or seven cartridges, depending on whether they are normal shot cartridges or the longer heavy slug type. The finish is usually blued or Parkerized, but there is a version produced specially for police use, all the metalwork being stainless steel. This version may be fitted with rifle-type sights for firing slugs, and the magazine is slightly shorter than that of the standard Defender. Sling swivels are provided.

SPECIFICATION	
Winchester Defender	(6.99 lb)
Calibre: 12 gauge	**Feed:** 6- or 7-round tubular magazine or (stainless steel models) 5- or 6-round tubular magazine
Length: barrel 457 mm (18 in)	
Weight: 3.06 kg (6.74 lb) or (stainless steel models) 3.17 kg	

British police increasingly follow this Winchester- armed American model, with fireproof overalls, bulletproof vest and visored helmet. Shotgun-armed policemen are now seen on the streets of London when the Metropolitan Police's specialist weapons officers are on duty.

Winchester has produced the Defender in three related versions, all available in butted or pistol grip form. From top to bottom, these are the Pistol Grip Defender, Pistol Grip Stainless Marine, and Pistol Grip Stainless Police. The last has a smaller magazine.

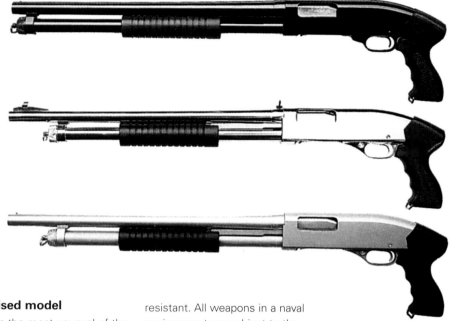

Navalised model

Perhaps the most unusual of the current Winchester shotguns is the **Model 1300 Marines** produced specially for use by naval and marine forces. This is based on the Defender but is more akin to the stainless steel police model for it has been designed to be corrosion-resistant. All weapons in a naval environment are subject to the effects of corrosive salts, and stainless steel is proof against many of them. To ensure virtually complete protection the 'marine' Winchester also has all its external metal parts chrome-plated. The result is a weapon of notably striking appearance, but one which would also seem to have some eye-catching drawbacks in combat situations. However, this model has been sold, usually to paramilitary forces such as coast guards who feel the need for a shotgun for their boarding parties.

Pancor Jackhammer Shotgun

The **Pancor Jackhammer** is a recent arrival on the combat shotgun scene, but uses an operating mechanism that has been around for some time. The weapon was designed by John Andersen, who began to seek patent protection for his design in 1984, and has many original features, not the least its ability to fire on full automatic and its use of a pre-loaded 10-round rotary magazine.

The Jackhammer is a gas-operated weapon, has an unusual appearance and is based on a 'bullpup' configuration with the rotary magazine

The unusual-looking Pancor Jackhammer is a gas-operated weapon.

therefore located behind the trigger group. The plastic magazine holds 10 rounds and is clipped into the weapon before the fore-end of the stock is moved to and fro to cock the weapon. On firing, the barrel moves forward. As it does so, a gas-operated stud moves in an angled groove on the magazine to start the rotation to the next round. Once it has reached the forward limit of its movement, the barrel is pushed back by a

SPECIFICATION	
Jackhammer	**Weight:** loaded 4.57 kg (10.1 lb)
Calibre: 12-gauge	**Rate of fire, cyclic:** 240 rounds per
Length overall: 762 mm (30 in)	minute
Length of barrel: 457 mm (18 in)	**Feed:** 10-round rotary magazine

spring and the magazine rotation is completed. (This system was used in a British weapon of World War I, the Webley-Fosbery revolver.) Once the barrel has returned, the weapon is ready for the next shot. Firing in fully automatic mode the weapon has a cyclic rate of fire of 240 rounds per minute, and barrel jump is

partially offset by a downward-angled muzzle compensator that doubles as a flash eliminator.

Little metal

The Jackhammer makes use of tough plastics in its construction. In fact only the barrel, return spring magazine rotation mechanism and muzzle flash

eliminator are steel. The magazines, known as 'ammo cassettes', are delivered pre-loaded and sealed in plastic film (removed before loading) colour-coded to indicate the type of cartridge enclosed. It is not possible to load single cartridges, but single-round fire can be selected.

The sights are contained in a

channel on the long assembly that acts as a carrying handle. Firing the Jackhammer is not a problem for left-handed firers as no spent cartridge cases are ejected: these remain in the rotary magazine discarded once all the rounds have been fired. When the magazine is empty, a retaining catch opens and allows the component to fall free.

Remington Model 870 Mk 1 Shotgun

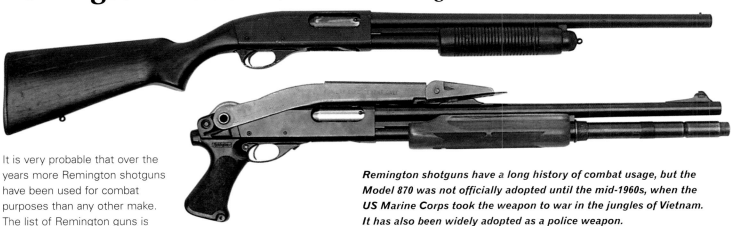

It is very probable that over the years more Remington shotguns have been used for combat purposes than any other make. The list of Remington guns is such that even a listing would probably cover a page, so only one combat model will be considered. This is the **Remington Model 870** modified for use by the US Marines Corps and known formally as the **Shotgun, 12-gauge, Remington, Model 870, Mk 1**.

Such is the utility of the shotgun in the jungle that the British army made extensive use of the weapon in counter-terrorist operations in Malaya, both against Communists and during the Indonesian confrontation. The fully stocked Model 870 is one used in the Far East; the other is a folding stocked riot gun with extended magazine.

The Model 870 has been one of the most widely-used of all shotguns for some time. It has been produced in basic models such as the **Model 870R** (Riot) and **Model 870P** (Police), but there have been many other types and an equally large number of conversions and adaptations. The Model 870 is a slide-action weapon, and when the US Marine Corps conducted prospective combat shotgun trials during 1966 it decided that, for reasons of reliability in combat, such a weapon would be preferable to one of the many semi-automatic actions available, and the Model 870 thus became the US

Remington shotguns have a long history of combat usage, but the Model 870 was not officially adopted until the mid-1960s, when the US Marine Corps took the weapon to war in the jungles of Vietnam. It has also been widely adopted as a police weapon.

Marine Corps' main choice. After a few modifications had been effected to make the weapon an exact fit to the service's requirements, the Model 870 Mk 1 was placed in production and has remained in USMC service ever since. These modifications included a longer magazine, a heatshield round the barrel to prevent the firer from burning his hands, and a protective non-glare finish that also protects the weapon from the inroads of corrosive rust.

Orthodox action

The Model 870 Mk 1 is a pump-action weapon with dual action bars and a tilting breech block that locks directly onto the barrel extension, and has a seven-round tubular magazine below the barrel. The barrel can be changed in a matter of minutes, and the weapon is used to fire a wide range of ammunition types ranging from light shot to flechettes. The gun has many 'extras', such as sling swivels, to meet the requirements of the

US Marine Corps, and the holding bracket for the magazine extension (added to increase the magazine's capacity) has a lug to mount a bayonet, which is exactly the same as that used on the M16 assault rifle. The ventilated hand-guard over the barrel and the rubber butt pads found on many civilian Model 870s are not fitted to the Model 870 Mk 1 as they were deemed unnecessary for a shotgun used in the combat role.

The US Marine Corps has used its Model 870 Mk 1 shotguns quite frequently since they were introduced. The weapon is not one that is usually carried during large-scale amphibious operations, but the US Marines Corps has many other combat tasks including the creation and despatch of boarding parties during actions such as that carried out during the 'Mayaguez incident' of May 1975, when an American merchant ship was in effect 'cut out' of an anchorage near the Cambodian port of Sihanoukville after being detained illegally. The guns were used widely during the Vietnam War (often by SEAL teams) and are still in gainful service.

At one point there was a project to convert the Model 870 Mk 1 to accommodate a 10- or 20-round box magazine, with obvious tactical advantages, but the end of the Vietnam War terminated the scheme at the advanced development stage.

The Model 870 has also found favour with police, security and para-military organisations, who generally opt for a model with its magazine lengthened to take eight rounds, fixed or folding stocks with or without a pistol grip, a 551- or 709-mm (22- or 28-in) barrel with cylinder or improved cylinder chokes, rifle-type or ghost ring (peep) sights, tactical flashlight, laser aiming spit and provision for firing a number of non-lethal special-purpose rounds (including tear gas grenades and rubber bullets).

SPECIFICATION	
Model 870 Mk 1	**Weight:** 3.6 kg (7.94 lb)
Calibre: 12-gauge	**Feed:** 7-round tubular magazine
Length overall: 1060 mm (41.73 in)	
Length of barrel: 533 mm (21 in)	

Advanced combat shotguns

Designed by Maxwell G. Atchisson in 1972, the **Atchisson Assault Shotgun** gas-assisted recoil-operated prototype paved the way for a new type of weapon, the assault (as opposed to combat) shotgun. Based on M16 rifle components, the Atchisson had about the same dimensions and configuration as the M16 rifle but was designed to fire buckshot or solid slug ammunition. Of simple design, its barrel screwed into a long, tubular receiver which housed the bolt and the recoil spring. A BAR M1918 trigger mechanism combined with the pistol grip of the Thompson sub-machine gun constituted the trigger assembly. The weapon was capable of semi-automatic and automatic fire, and fired from a five-round box or 20-round drum magazine.

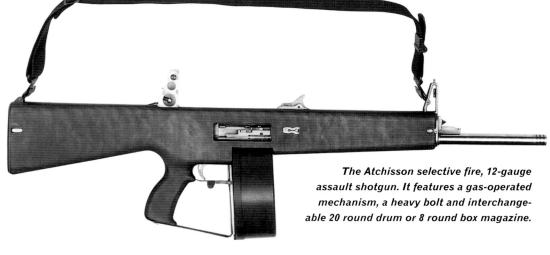

The Atchisson selective fire, 12-gauge assault shotgun. It features a gas-operated mechanism, a heavy bolt and interchangeable 20 round drum or 8 round box magazine.

Long and short variants of the Heckler & Koch/ Winchester CAW. The operation was short recoil with a cyclic full-automatic rate of 240 rounds per minute.

With the concept proved, Atchisson spent the period between 1973 and 1979 creating an improved version. The most obvious change was the enclosure of the entire mechanism in two clamshell stock halves. Production was undertaken in modest numbers from 1981 in the US and Korea, and in 1984 the standard was revised to include a bayonet mounting, and the non-slip patterning was omitted from the fore end of the clamshell. All the Atchisson weapons could fire NATO standard rifle grenades, and the magazine options were a seven-round single-row box magazine and a 20-round drum magazine.

New generation
In the early 1980s the USA began the CAWS (Close Assault Weapon System) programme to develop a weapon able to fire high-impulse multiple projectiles to an effective range of 100-150 m (110-165 yards). One of the teams was Heckler & Koch and Winchester/Olin, the former responsible for the weapon and the latter for the ammunition. The **Heckler & Koch CAW** emerged as a selective-fire smooth-bore weapon using high-pressure ammunition to fire tungsten shot and flechettes. The CAW was based on a gas-assisted recoil-operated action with a moving barrel, and in appearance was similar to the G11 assault rifle in its bullpup layout with an integral carrying handle. The cocking handle was located under the carrying handle, over the receiver, and was ambidextrous, and the safety/fire-selector's three positions were safe, semi-automatic and three-round burst. The CAW was tested in the US, but then the whole programme was closed.

SPECIFICATION	
Atchisson Assault Shotgun	**Heckler & Koch CAW**
Calibre: 12-gauge	**Calibre:** 12-gauge
Length overall: 991 mm (39 in)	**Length overall:** 988 or 762 mm (38.9 or 30 in)
Length of barrel: not available	**Length of barrel:** 686 or 457 mm (27 or 18 in)
Weight: 5.45 kg (12 lb)	**Weight:** 3.86 kg (8.5 lb)
Rate of fire, cyclic: 360 rpm	**Feed:** 10-round box magazine
Feed: 7-round tubular magazine	

Post-War Artillery

Modern artillery firepower has more than doubled since World War II while the effect of artillery ammunition has increased fourfold. Advanced metals have made guns lighter and stronger, enabling them to fire more powerful and aerodynamically sophisticated shells to greater distances.

Computerised fire control systems can direct many guns simultaneously, ranging a blizzard of shells on target in only 15 seconds. Rates of fire have increased dramatically and modern guns can fire bursts of five or more rounds in 20 seconds. Rocket artillery, used extensively in primitive form during World War II, has become accurate and even more lethal.

A single Russian artillery battalion firing 18 multiple launchers can place 35 tons of explosive rockets on a target 17 miles (27.4 km) away in just 30 seconds. The American Multiple Launch Rocket System (MLRS) can deliver 8,000 grenade-sized submunitions onto a target the size of six football fields in less than 45 seconds.

Left: Gunners of the 1st Marine Division prepare to open fire on North Vietnamese troops approaching their firebase in 1970. Their 106-mm (6.3-in) recoilless rifle was designed as an anti-tank weapon, but was more often used in the anti-personnel role in Vietnam.

Modèle 50 155-mm howitzer

The **modèle 50** 155-mm (6.1-in) howitzer was the standard towed howitzer of the French army from the early 1950s, and has also been made under licence by Bofors of Sweden for the Swedish army under the designation **15.5-cm Field Howitzer Fr**. In the French army it has been largely replaced by the 155-mm TR towed gun, which has an integral auxiliary power unit and a much longer range, while in the Swedish army it has been replaced by the Bofors 155-mm FH-77A. The modèle 50 howitzer, which is also called the **OB-156-50 BF** by the French army, was also exported to Israel, Lebanon (where some were captured from the PLO by Israel during the fighting of summer 1982), Morocco and Switzerland.

The barrel of the modèle 50 is 4.41 m (14 ft 5.6 in) long, and has an unusual multi-baffle muzzle brake, a hydro-pneumatic recoil system that varies with elevation, and a screw breech mechanism. The carriage is of the split-trail type with two rubber-tyred road wheels located on each side of

the forward part of the carriage. When being towed by a truck the ordnance is locked to the trails by a locking device which is situated in the rear part of the cradle. To enable the equipment to be towed at high speeds on roads, the modèle 50 has a brake system operated by compressed air from the towing vehicle.

When in the firing position, the forward part of the carriage is supported by a circular pivot plate underneath and by the ends of each trail.

The modèle 50 is operated by an 11-man crew, and in French service is normally towed by a Berliet GBU 15 6x6 truck, which also carries the crew and ammunition. The ammunition is of the separate-loading type, the HE projectile weighing 43 kg (94.8 lb) and having a maximum muzzle velocity of 650 m (2,135 ft) per second to give a range of 18000 m (19,685 yards). Illuminating and smoke projectiles can also be fired. Subsequently Brandt developed a rocket-assisted HE projectile with a maximum range of 23300 m (25,480 yards). The maximum

rate of fire is between three and four rounds per minute.

To meet the requirements of the Israeli army, the French Etablissement d'Etudes et Fabrications d'Armement de Bourges fitted the modèle 50 howitzer to a much modified Sherman chassis, and this entered service with the Israeli army in 1963 as the 155-mm self-propelled howitzer **Model 50** (or **M-50**). This equipment is now used only by reserve units, and will shortly be retired completely. The modifications to the chassis were extensive, and

In firing position, the modèle 50 howitzer has the weight of the ordnance and carriage supported by a turntable and the rear of the opened trails.

included moving the engine to the front of the vehicle on the right-hand side with the driver to its left. The 155-mm howitzer is mounted at the rear of the hull in an open-topped compartment, over which a tarpaulin cover can be fitted in wet weather. Stowage boxes are provided externally above the tracks. When the vehicle is in the firing position the rear of the hull folds down and doors open on each side to reveal ammunition stowage. The loaded weight of the M-50 is 31 tonnes, and the crew consists of eight men. Several of these systems were captured by the Egyptians in the heavy fighting around Suez in the 1973 Middle East War.

An interesting feature of the modèle 50 is its multi-baffle muzzle brake to reduce the forces imposed on the equipment's recoil system.

SPECIFICATION	
modèle 50	**Elevation:** -4° to +69°
Calibre: 155 mm (6.1 in)	**Traverse:** total 80°
Weight: travelling 9000 kg (19,841 lb), firing 8100 kg (17,857 lb)	**Maximum range:** 18000 m (19,685 yards) with standard round and 23300 m (25,480 yards) with rocket-assisted projectile
Dimensions: length, travelling 7.8 m (25 ft 7 in); width, travelling 2.75 m (9 ft); height, travelling 2.5 m (8 ft 2.4 in)	

OTO-Melara modello 56 105-mm pack howitzer

The mountainous terrain of northern Italy is defended by specialist Alpine brigades, and these and the sole Italian airborne brigade required a 105-mm (4.13-in) howitzer that could be disassembled for easy movement across the mountains and, in assembled form, still be light enough to be airdropped or carried slung underneath a helicopter. To meet this requirement the Italian armaments manufacturer OTO-Melara (now Otobreda) at La Spezia designed a weapon that became known as the **modello 56** 105-mm pack howitzer. This entered production in 1957, and was soon adopted by more than 30 countries all over the world. By a time early in the 21st century more than 2,500 of the weapons had been delivered, and the type has seen combat use in many areas. The British used it in the South Yemen and during the Borneo confrontation, while the Argentines used it in the Falklands campaign of 1982. By today's standards the modello 56 howitzer has a short range, and in British service the Royal Artillery has replaced it with the Royal Ordnance 105-mm Light Gun, which has a maximum range of 17000 m (18,590 yards) compared with only 10575 m (11,565 yards) for the modello 56 which, however, is a much lighter equipment.

Muzzle brake

The modello 56 has a very short barrel with a multi-baffle muzzle brake, a hydraulic buffer and helical recuperator, and a vertical sliding-wedge breech block. The carriage is of the split-trail type and fitted with rubber tyres for high-speed towing. An unusual feature of the modello 56 is that its wheels can be fitted in two different positions: in the normal field position the wheels are overslung, the weapon then having an elevation of +65° and a depression of -5°, and a total traverse of 36° (18° left and right); but for the anti-tank role the wheels are underslung and the weapon has an elevation of +25° and a depression of -5°, total traverse remaining 36°. The main advantage of having the

A Royal Artillery unit attached to the Royal Marine Commandos carry 105-mm pack howitzers in Norway. The normal towing vehicle for the pack howitzer in British Army service was the Swedish Bv 202, which was successfully used in the Falklands towing the more modern 105-mm Light Gun.

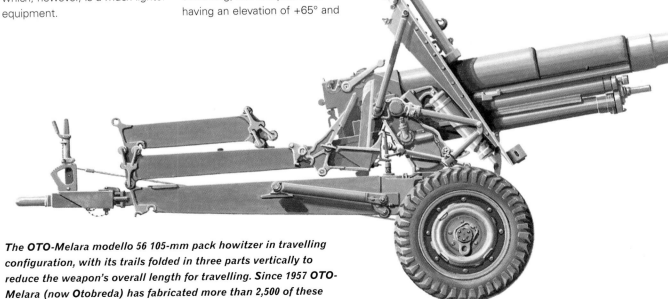

The OTO-Melara modello 56 105-mm pack howitzer in travelling configuration, with its trails folded in three parts vertically to reduce the weapon's overall length for travelling. Since 1957 OTO-Melara (now Otobreda) has fabricated more than 2,500 of these weapons for export to almost every corner of the world.

SPECIFICATION	
modello 56	**Elevation:** -5° to +65°
Calibre: 105 mm (4.13 in)	**Traverse:** total 36°
Weight: travelling 1290 kg (2,844 lb)	**Maximum range:** 10575 m (11,565 yards)
Dimensions: length, travelling 3.65 m (11 ft 11.7 in); width, travelling 1.5 m (4 ft 11 in); height, travelling 1.93 m (6 ft 4 in)	

The light weight and excellent portability of the OTO-Breda modello 56 105-mm howitzer commended the type to units faced with operations in difficult terrain. The weapon is here seen in service with the Italian army, the shield removed in order to reduce its weight further.

wheels underslung is that the height is reduced from 1.93 m to 1.55 m (6 ft 4 in to 5 ft 1 in), so making the weapon much easier to conceal, a valuable asset in the anti-tank role.

The modello 56 can be dismantled into 11 sections for transport across rough country, and in peacetime the shield is often removed to save weight. The weapon is manned by a seven-man crew, and can be towed by a long-wheelbase Land Rover or similar vehicle. It can also be carried slung under

a UH-1 or similar helicopter. Another advantage of the modello 56 is that it fires the same ammunition as the American M101 and M102 105-mm towed guns, and this ammunition is manufactured all over the world. Types of ammunition fired include a 21.06-kg (46.4-lb) HE projectile with a muzzle velocity of 472 m (1,550 ft) per second, as well as smoke, illuminating and HEAT, the last weighing 16.7 kg (36.8 lb) and capable of penetrating 102 mm (4 in) of armour.

5.5-in Gun Medium field gun

After 1945 the 100-lb (45.4-kg) projectile for the **5.5-in Gun**, a 140-mm medium weapon went out of fashion and was replaced for all fire missions by an 80-lb (36.3-kg) HE projectile with a longer maximum range of 16460 m (18,000 yards) using a five-part propellant charge system. This gun/projectile combination proved so versatile that it remained in service with many armed forces for decades after 1945. Post-war alliances and arrangements resulted in 5.5-in Guns surplus to British requirements being distributed to many nations, including

The British World War II-era 5.5-in Gun was known as the G2 in South African service and an example is pictured here undertaking a night-firing exercise.

Burma, Greece, New Zealand, Pakistan and Portugal, while the gun remained as a front-line equipment with the British Army until the last was retired in 1978. Even then a few were retained at the Royal School of Artillery at Larkhill to fire off remaining ammunition stocks for artillery burst-spotting purposes.

The last of these training veterans was not retired until the mid-1990s. A project of the 1950s to produce a self-

propelled combination of the 5.5-inch Gun and a Centurion tank chassis was unsatisfactory.

One of the most involved post-1945 users of the 5.5-in Gun was the South African army, which knew the type as the **140-mm G2**. By the late 1970s, with troubles on South

Royal Artillery gunners manhandle one of a 5.5-in Gun's spade-equipped trails. The gun was introduced into service in 1942 to fire separate-loading ammunition, and in addition to its two HE projectiles could also fire smoke and illuminating rounds.

Africa's northern borders and UN arms sanctions in place, it was discovered that the old G2 was outranged by opposing Soviet-supplied artillery. As a short-term measure, a local concern (Naschem) developed a new high-fragmentation projectile with a base-bleed unit to extend the maximum range

to 21000 m (22,965 yards), but this was little used after the new 155-mm (6.1-in) G5 and G6 indigenous artillery equipments became available. Naschem also developed an updated smoke projectile with a maximum range of 15400 m (16,840 yards).

The 10-crew 5.5-in Gun has been withdrawn from service by

all countries but Myanmar (Burma), although until recent

years it remained a reserve weapon in Pakistan.

SPECIFICATION	
5.5-in Gun	(8 ft 7 in)
Calibre: 5.5 in (140 mm)	**Elevation:** -5° to +45°
Weight: 5851 kg (12,900 lb) in	**Traverse:** total 60°
travelling and firing orders	**Maximum range:** 16460 m
Dimensions: length, travelling 7.52 m	(18,000 yards) with the 80-lb
(24 ft 8 in); width, travelling 2.54 m	(36.3-kg) HE projectile
(8 ft 4 in); height, travelling 2.62 m	

M101 105-mm howitzer

The **M101** 105-mm (4.13-in) howitzer is one of the most successful guns ever produced. Between 1940 and 1953,

production totalled 10,202 for delivery to large numbers of armies, of which 60 still field the type at the start of the 21st

century. Development of a weapon known as the **M1** started as early as 1920, but only trial numbers were

Above: In many ways obsolete, especially in terms of its projectiles' ranges, the M101 is still in widespread service as it is rugged and reliable, and was readily available from stocks of US surplus weapons.

completed, and in 1934 there appeared the **M2** development able to fire a fixed shrapnel round. This was standardised as the **M2A1** in March 1940 on the two-wheel Carriage M2. After World War II the M2 and M2A1 were reclassified as the

The M101 can be fitted with a shield, but is seldom seen with this type of crew protection. The maximum rate of fire is 10 rounds per minute, declining to three rounds per minute for sustained firing.

M101 and **M101A1** respectively. The barrel is short, which contributes to the howitzer's modest range, but it has a life of 20,000 rounds. A horizontal sliding breech block is used with a percussion firing mechanism. The hydro-pneumatic recoil system, mounted over and under the barrel, is of the constant recoil length type.

The M1 ammunition system was designed for this howitzer and later became a standard NATO ammunition usable by a number of later equipments. The M101 series fires semi-fixed ammunition, and the HE projectiles included the unitary M1 and the M444 with 18 M39 grenades. There was also a HESH round able to penetrate 102 mm (4 in) of armour at a range of 1500 m (1,640 yards). Among experimental rounds were CS, anti-personnel and HEAT. Two rocket-assisted projectiles were developed, one being standardised as the 17.46-kg (38.5-lb) M548 with a range of 14600 m (15,965 yards) by comparison with the 11270 m (12,325 yards) of the standard 21.06-kg (46.5-lb) M1 HE round. Various impact and time fuses were also developed.

The layout of the carriage is simple. The box-section, split-trail legs are straight and carry recoil stresses to inbuilt spades. The gun fires off its road wheels, above which the elevating mass is mounted at its centre of gravity. The crew is eight.

Modified weapons have included the **M3** for South-East Asian use with a shorter barrel and a 75-mm (2.95-in) field howitzer carriage, the **HM 2** French M101A1 fitted with the barrel of the AMX-105/50 or AMX-105B SP howitzer, the Canadian **C1** with a new auto-frettaged monobloc barrel, and the German **FH 105(L)** with a single-baffle muzzle brake and a longer barrel.

SPECIFICATION	
M101A1	
Calibre: 105 mm (4.13 in)	**Elevation:** -5° to +66°
Weight: (travelling and firing) 2258 kg (4,978 lb)	**Traverse:** 46°
Dimensions: (travelling) length 5.99 m (19 ft 9 in); width 2.16 m (7 ft 1 in); height 1.574 m (5 ft 2 in)	**Maximum range:** with M1 projectile 11270 m (12,325 yards) or with M548 projectile 14600 m (15,965 yards)
	Rate of fire: 10 rounds per minute

M102 105-mm howitzer

For many years the standard 105-mm (4.13-in) howitzer of the US Army was the M2, which was standardised in 1940 as an improved version of the original M1. A total of 10,202 such weapons had been built by the time production ended in 1953. After World War II the M2 became the M101, which is still in large-scale service all over the world. The main drawbacks of the M101 series are its weight of 2030 to 2258 kg (4,475 to 4,978 lb) depending on the model, and its lack of all-round traverse capability.

In 1955 a requirement was issued for a new 105-mm howitzer which would fire the same range of ammunition and yet be lighter than the M101. The Rock Island Arsenal designed a new weapon with the prototype designation **XM102**, of which the first was completed in 1962. Following trials, the weapon was classified as standard during the following year with the service designation **M102**. The first production examples of the M102 were completed in January 1964, and only a few months later the weapon was deployed to South Vietnam, where a major build-up of US armed strength was beginning to aid the South Vietnamese against local insurgents and North Vietnamese regular forces.

After so short a development period, technical and reliability problems were inevitably encountered with early M102 howitzers, but these were

An M102 of the US 82nd Airborne Division is seen in action during the 1983 invasion of Grenada. Note the gun's unusual carriage configuration.

soon rectified. The M102 was issued on the scale of 18 howitzers per battalion, each of the battalion's three batteries having six weapons. Now in reserve, the M102 was latterly allocated primarily to airborne and air-mobile divisions, for whom low weight rather than great range was the most important factor. The M102 is also used in modest numbers by Brazil, El Salvador, Guatemala, Honduras, Jordan, Lebanon, Malaysia (reserve), Philippines, Saudi Arabia (national guard), Thailand and Uruguay.

The M102 comprises four main components, namely the M137 cannon, the M37 recoil system, the M31 carriage, and the fire-control equipment. The M137 cannon has a vertical sliding- wedge breech mechanism but is not fitted with a muzzle brake. The recoil

system is of the hydro-pneumatic type and variable, so eliminating the need for a recoil pit. The most unusual feature of the M102 is the two-wheel box-type carriage, which is constructed of aluminium for the minimum possible weight. When the weapon is deployed in the firing position, a circular baseplate is lowered to the ground from its stowed position under the forward part of the base, and then the two rubber-tyred road wheels are lifted clear of the ground to ensure the highest possible

level of firing stability. A roller located at the rear of the trail assembly allows the complete carriage to be traversed through 360° on the baseplate. This facility proved to be of considerable importance in South Vietnam, where M102 howitzers had to engage

targets in different directions at only a moment's notice.

As a result of its longer barrel, the M102 fires the same ammunition as the M101 at a higher muzzle velocity and therefore to greater range: the M1 HE projectile reaches 11500 m (12,575 yards)..

SPECIFICATION	
M102	**Elevation:** -5° to +75°
Calibre: 105 mm (4.13 in)	**Traverse:** 360°
Weight: (firing and travelling) 1496 kg (3,300 lb)	**Maximum range:** with M1 projectile 11500 m (12,575 yards) or with
Dimensions: (travelling) length 5.182 m (17 ft); width 1.962 m (6 ft 5.2 in); height 1.59 m (5 ft 2.6 in)	M548 projectile 15100 m (16,515 yards)
	Rate of fire: 10 rounds per minute

M114 155-mm howitzer

The 155-mm (6.1-in) howitzer now known as the **M114** was developed in the US before World War II, standardised in May 1941 and first issued in 1942 as the **M1** successor to the 155-mm M1918 howitzer, the US-made counterpart of the French-made M1917. The origins of the M1 can be traced to 1934, when work started on the design and development of a

new split-trail carriage for the M1918. It was then decided that rather than seek to improve an existing ordnance, it would make better long-term sense to create an entirely new equipment, whose design was entrusted to the Rock Island Arsenal.

Different carriage

It was also decided that the new howitzer would use the carriage

The howitzers of the M114 series saw large-scale service with the US and allied forces in the Vietnam War. Such equipments were often sited in strategically located fire bases where they could be supplied by road or, failing that, by air in their efforts to interdict communist supply routes.

designed for a new heavy gun, in the process offering reduced design, development and manufacturing costs as well as opening the way for the US Army to field a pair of artillery

equipments that were well matched in tactical terms. The gun had originally been schemed as a 4.7-in (119-mm) weapon, but was then finalised as a 114-mm (4.5-in) weapon so that it could fire the same range of ammunition as the British 4.5-in gun.

Meanwhile, production of the M1 howitzer exceeded 6,000 units, and after World War II the weapon was redesignated as the M114 or, on a slightly modified carriage, **M114A1**.

Operated by an 11-man crew, the M114 comprises the M1 or M1A1 cannon, the M6 series recoil mechanism, and the M1A1 or M1A2 carriage. The differences are that the M1A1 cannon is built of stronger steel than the M1, and the M1A1 carriage has a rack-and-pinion firing jack while the M1A2 carriage has a screw-type firing jack. The breech block is of the stepped thread/interrupted screw type, and the recoil mechanism is of the hydro-pneumatic variable type. The carriage has split trails, and there is provision for a small shield on each side of the barrel, the top of the left-hand unit folding down in the firing position.

In the firing position the equipment is balanced on three points (the firing jack and both trails). For travelling the jack is forward of the shield, and the trails (with rear spades for enhanced firing stability) are locked together before attachment to the prime mover.

There is also an **M114A2** model with a revised and lengthened barrel incorporating a 1/20 rather than 1/12 rifling twist to promote range.

Ammunition variants

There have been seven types of projectile (including two smoke, one practice and the Copperhead laser-guided types), but the most important of these types of separate-loading rounds, fired with a muzzle velocity of 564 m (1,850 ft) per second, are the 42.9-kg (94.6-lb) M107 High Explosive and the 43.09-kg (95-lb) M449 carrying 60 anti-personnel grenades. There have also been several upgraded models created for European, Israeli and South Korean markets. Early in the 21st century the M114 howitzer family is still in service with a total of 37 countries, some of which are still using large numbers of these obsolescent but reliable and effective weapons.

SPECIFICATION	
M114	**Maximum range:** with M107 or
Calibre: 155 mm (6.1 in)	M449 projectile 14600 m
Weight: (travelling) 5800 kg (12,787	(15,965 yards)
lb) and (firing) 5760 kg (12,698 lb)	**Rate of fire:** 2 rounds in the first 30
Dimensions: (travelling) length 7.315	seconds, 8 rounds in the first 2
m (24 ft); width 2.44 m (8 ft); height	minutes, 16 rounds in the first 60
1.803 m (5 ft 11 in)	minutes, and 40 rounds per hour in
Elevation: -2° to +63°	the sustained-fire role
Traverse: 24° left and 25° right	

M-46 130-mm field gun

The M-46 130-mm (5.12-in) field gun has a distinctively long barrel with a muzzle brake of the pepperpot type. It has been in service for 50 years, but has a long range that was only recently matched by Western artillery weapons firing RAPs (rocket-assisted projectiles).

The M-46 130-mm (5.12-in) guns of a Soviet battery are camouflaged during training. When travelling, the gun has its barrel withdrawn out of battery to the rear to reduce overall length, and a two-wheel limber is used to support the closed ends aof the trails.

Rugged, reliable and possessed of excellent range with a high level of accuracy, the M-46 is still a capable and effective weapon despite the fact that it was designed in the immediate aftermath of World War II.

The **M-46** 130-mm (5.1-in) field gun is believed to have been developed from a naval weapon, and was first seen in public during the 1954 May Day parade. For this reason the M-46 is sometimes designated **M1954**. Despite its age, the gun remains an effective weapon with exceptional range, and has been used in combat in the Middle East and Vietnam. In the latter only the US M107 175-mm (6.9-in) self-propelled gun, with a range of 32700 m (35,760 yards), could outrange the M-46.

Foreign operators

In addition to being used by the USSR, the M-46 has been operated by more than 50 countries. The Indians took the weapon off its normal carriage and installed it on the chassis of the Vickers Mk 1 MBT, which was built as the Vijayanta self-propelled gun. In the Soviet army the M-46 was deployed at the army-level artillery regiment, which included two battalions each with 18 M-46s (three batteries each with six weapons). The regiment also had an HQ and service battery, a target-acquisition battery and a battalion of 18 D-20 152-mm (6-in) gun/howitzers. The artillery division, allocated at front (army group) level, included two regiments each with 54 M-46s, each regiment having three battalions of 18 weapons. The Chinese have made a different model of the M-46 field gun called the **Type 59-1**, and the gun was also manufactured in Egypt.

'Pepperpot' muzzle

The M-46 has a barrel 7.6 m (24 ft 11.2 in) long and fitted with a very distinctive 'pepperpot' muzzle brake and a horizontal sliding-wedge breech

mechanism. The recoil system consists of a hydraulic buffer and a hydro-pneumatic recuperator below and above the barrel. To reduce travelling length, the barrel is withdrawn out of battery to the rear and locked in position between the spades. The carriage is of the split-trail type and is provided with a two-wheel limber at the rear. For travelling the two spades are removed and carried on the tops of the trails. The M-46 has a nine-man crew, takes four minutes to bring into action, and can be towed by a variety of vehicles including the AT-S, ATS-59 and M1972 unarmoured artillery tractors as well as the AT-P tracked armoured artillery tractor.

The ammunition fired by the M-46 is of the separate-loading type and includes HE-FRAG (HE fragmentation) and APC-T (armour-piercing capped tracer). The former weighs 33.4 kg (73.63 lb) with a 4.63-kg (10.2-lb) bursting charge, and the maximum muzzle velocity is 1050 m (3,445 ft) per second.

The 33.6-kg (74.07-lb) APC-T projectile, with a 0.127-kg (0.26-lb) bursting charge, has the same muzzle velocity and can penetrate 230 mm (9.05 in) of armour at a range of 1000 m (1,095 yards). Other types of projectile available include illuminating and smoke, and a rocket-assisted projectile was introduced in the late 1960s. This last was first used by Syria during the 1973 Middle East war. In Iranian service the M-46 uses a locally developed base-bleed round, which increases the range to 37000 m (40,465 yards). Norinco in China also manufactures cargo rounds and an ERFB BB (extended-range full-bore base-bleed) projectile extending the range to 38000 m (41,555 yards). Further ammunition types for the M-46 are manufactured in at least 12 countries, including Finland and South Africa.

Although no longer manufactured in Russia, the M-46 remains in widespread service and has seen extensive action: in the Iran-Iraq War of the 1980s the gun was deployed by each side.

The M-46 has also been subject to various upgrades including a 155-mm (6.1-in) L/45 barrel. Such efforts have been made by China (**GM-45**),

India, Israel, the Netherlands and Yugoslavia. The Indian project is at the prototype stage, but is intended to upgrade around 750 M-46 pieces that remain in Indian service.

SPECIFICATION	
M-46	(8 ft 0.5 in); height 2.55 m (8 ft 4.4
Calibre: 130 mm (5.12 in)	in)
Weight: travelling 8450 kg (18,629 lb)	**Elevation:** +45°/-2.5°
and firing 7700 kg (16,975 lb)	**Traverse:** 50°
Dimensions: (travelling) length	**Maximum range:** 27150 m
11.73 m (38 ft 5.8 in); width 2.45 m	(29,690 yards)

S-23 180-mm gun

For most of the Cold War this weapon was able to outrange virtually all NATO towed and self-propelled artillery weapons. It was first seen in public during a 1955 Moscow parade, and for many years was thought to be a 203-mm (8-in) weapon that was known in the West as the **M1955** gun/howitzer. This is believed to have entered service several years before 1955 and to have been a development of a naval weapon. During the Middle East War of 1973 a number of these weapons were captured and then taken back to Israel for detailed evaluation by intelligence personnel. It was

then discovered that the weapon's actual calibre is 180 mm (7.09 in) and that its correct Soviet designation is **S-23**.

In the Soviet army the S-23 was issued on the scale of 12 weapons in the heavy artillery brigade of every artillery division. Subsequently, the Soviet artillery division no longer had S-23s and instead consisted of an HQ, an anti-tank regiment with 36 T-12/MT-12 towed anti-tank guns, an MRL brigade with four battalions of BM-27s (total of 72 launchers), a target-acquisition battalion, a signal company, a motor transport

An S-23 180-mm gun in travelling configuration with the dolly attached to the rear. For many years this was thought to be a 203-mm (8-in) weapon, but examination of weapons captured by Israel in 1973 showed that it was in fact of 180-mm (7.09-in) calibre.

battalion, two regiments of 130-mm (5.1-in) M-46 field guns (total of 108 equipments) and two regiments of 152-mm (6-in) D-20 gun/howitzers or M1973 self-propelled gun/howitzers (total of 108 equipments).

Export operators

The S-23 has seen service with a number of other countries including Egypt, India, Iraq and Syria, and other likely operators also include Cuba, Ethiopia, North Korea, Libya, Mongolia and Somalia. The weapon was normally towed by an AT-T heavy tracked artillery tractor, which also carried the 16-man crew and a small quantity of ready-use ammunition. The S-23 has a barrel some 8.8 m (28

ft 10.46 in) long with a pepperpot muzzle brake and a screw breech mechanism, and the recoil system is under the barrel. To reduce overall length for travelling, the barrel can be withdrawn out of battery to the rear and linked to the trails. The carriage is of the split-trail type, with two twin rubber-tyred road wheel units at the front and a two-wheel dolly at the rear.

The S-23 fires a bag-type variable-charge separate-loading 84.09-kg (185.4-lb) OF-43 High Explosive projectile with a maximum muzzle velocity of 790 m (2,590 ft per second). as well as the 97.7-kg (215.4-lb) G-572 concrete-piercing projectile, and could formerly also fire

SPECIFICATION	
S-23	**Elevation:** +50°/-2°
Calibre: 180 mm (7.09 in)	**Traverse:** 44°
Weight: in action 21450 kg	**Maximum range:** 30400 m (33,245
(47,288 lb)	yards) with the HE projectile and
Dimensions: (travelling) length	43800 m (47,900 yards) with the
10.485 m (34 ft 4.8 in); width	rocket-assisted projectile
2.996 m (9 ft 10 in); height	
2.621 m (8 ft 7.2 in)	

a 0.2-kT tactical battlefield nuclear projectile.

RAP

After the weapon had been in service for some time an HE rocket-assisted projectile (RAP) was introduced: with a muzzle velocity of 850 m (2,790 ft) per second, this has a maximum range of 43800 m (47,900 yards) compared with 30400 m (33,245 yards) for the original projectile. Because of the shell's heavy weight, the S-23 has a relatively slow rate of fire (one round per minute), dropping to one round every two minutes in the sustained-fire role.

D-20 152-mm gun/howitzer

Although it was designed shortly after the 'Great Patriotic War' of 1941–45, the **D-20** 152-mm (6-in) gun/howitzer was not seen in public until 1955, and as a result was long known in the West as the **M1955**. In accord with standard Soviet artillery design practice, the ordnance of the D-20 was placed on the carriage of an existing design, in this case the D-74 122-mm (4.8-in) field gun. Also in accord with Soviet practice, the D-20 proved to be a sound and rugged design with good all-round performance. Despite its age, the Russian armed forces are reported as still fielding more than 1,000 D-20s as front-line equipment.

Chinese variant

Although it is no longer manufactured in what was the USSR, the D-20 is still available from Norinco of the People's Republic of China, where it is known as the **Type 66**. The gun can thus be encountered all over the world.

The barrel of the D-20 is 5.195 m (17 ft 0.5 in) long and features a double-baffle muzzle brake and a semi-automatic vertical sliding wedge breech. Protection for the breech end of the barrel and the recoil mechanisms is provided by an optional shield, while the split-trail carriage can be placed on a firing pedestal lowered from under the cradle. The firing pedestal permits a full 360° traverse. For short moves each trail leg has a castor wheel. At one time the D-20 was towed by a special AT-S tracked medium tractor, although the more usual prime mover is now a Ural-375 6x6 heavy truck.

The main projectile fired by the D-20 is a TNT-filled HE-fragmentation (HE-FRAG) shell weighing 43.51 lb (95.92 lb). This can be fired to a range of 17410 m (19,040 yards), while the special RAP can reach 24000 m (26,245 yards). The latter is now little used due to its variable accuracy. Several types of HE-FRAG projectile are available, as are concrete-piercing, smoke and illuminating. Variable bagged propellant charges are employed. For an anti-armour capability the D-20 can fire either solid AP-T (with a unitary propellant charge) or a hollow-charge projectile. One unusual projectile contains flechettes for use against massed personnel while another contains several anti-tank mines scattered as the projectile is still in flight. A similar projectile containing anti-personnel mines has been withdrawn. It is understood that the D-20 can also fire the Krasnopol laser-guided projectile. The ordnance used on the 152-mm 2S3 self-propelled gun/howitzer is a development of the D-20.

The D-20 was distributed wherever Soviet influence extended, so it is likely to be encountered as far afield as the former Congo and Finland. It saw considerable action during the Iran-Iraq conflict and is still held by Syria. The Chinese Type 66 has also been widely exported to nations such as North Korea and Bolivia.

The Chinese Type 66 differs from the D-20 in a few respects. Once the former Yugoslavia designed and manufactured a variant of the D-20 with an L/39 barrel as the **M-84**, although it is no longer available for export.

SPECIFICATION	
D-20	in); height 2.52 m (8 ft 3.5 in)
Calibre: 152 mm (6 in)	**Elevation:** +65°/-5
Weight: travelling 5700 kg	**Traverse:** 58° on carriage
(12,566 lb) and in action 5650 kg	**Maximum range:** 17410 m (19,040
(12,456 lb)	yards) with the HE-FRAG projectile
Dimensions: (travelling) length 8.1 m	and 24000 m (26,245 yards) with
(26 ft 7 in); width 2.35 m (7 ft 8.5	the rocket-assisted projectile

The D-20 can fire a 48.78-kg (107.54-kg) AP projectile with a muzzle velocity of 600 m (1,969 ft) per second to penetrate 124 mm (4.88 in) of armour at 0° at a range of 1000 m (1,095 yards).

CITEFA Model 77 155-mm howitzer

During the late 1970s, Argentina purchased a number of members of the AMX-13 family of light tracked vehicles from France as well as undertaking the assembly of a quantity of vehicles. These included the AMX-13 light tank armed with a 90-mm (3.54-in) gun, the AMX VCI armoured personnel carrier, and the 155-mm (6.1-in) Mk F3 self-propelled gun.

The CITEFA Model 77 155-mm (6.1-in) howitzer in travelling configuration with trails together. Under the rear part of the trails can be seen one of the small rubber-tyred road wheels that assist the crew in bringing the weapon into action.

M114 replacement

At that time the standard 155-mm towed howitzer of the Argentine army was the American M114, which dated back to World War II and had a maximum range of 14600 m (15,967 yards). To replace the M114 the Instituto de Investigaciones Cientificas y Tecnicas de las Fuerzas Armadas (CITEFA) designed a new bottom carriage that would take the complete top carriage (barrel, cradle, recoil system and equilibriators) of the Mk F3 self-propelled gun.

Following trials, this new weapon was accepted for service with the Argentine army under the designation **155-mm Howitzer L33 X1415 CITEFA Model 77**, L33

referring to the length of the ordnance in calibres and Model 77 to the year of acceptance. A later version, the **Model 81**, differs in minor details and also has a barrel of Argentine rather than French manufacture.

Falklands combat

Together with the OTO Melara 105-mm (4.13-in) Model 56 pack howitzer, the Model 77 was deployed to the Falklands where all of these equipments were subsequently captured by the British, some of them being shipped to the UK for trial and display purposes.

The barrel of the Model 77 is 5.115 m (16 ft 9.4 in) long, and is provided with a double-baffle muzzle brake and a screw breech mechanism. The top carriage is of welded steel construction and contains the traverse mechanism and

elevating brackets. The former is mounted inside the lower part and forms the connection with the cradle trunnion attachment and the bottom carriage. The bottom carriage is of the split-trail type, and is also of welded construction. Each trail leg is provided with a small rubber-tyred road wheel, and at the end of each trail is a spade. When the equipment is in the firing position the carriage wheels are raised clear of the ground, support then being provided by a circular steel base attached to the carriage by a ball socket. When the equipment is being towed, the support is raised, giving ground clearance of 0.3 m (12 in). Maximum rate of fire is four rounds per minute, with a sustained rate of fire of one round per minute.

A circular steel base plate fixed to the underside of the carriage supports the gun in the firing position; this helps to compensate for the effects of rough ground by dissipating the recoil shock waves over a wider area of ground.

Ammunition types

The equipment fires an HE projectile weighing 43 kg (94.8 lb) with a maximum muzzle velocity of 765 m (2,510 ft) per second to a maximum range of 22000 m (24,059 yards); there are also illuminating and smoke projectiles.

A rocket-assisted projectile is available, but as far as is known such a projectile was not used in the Falklands campaign.

In order to assist the crew in bringing the Model 77 into and out of action, an additional road wheel is mounted on each leg of the split-trail carriage.

SPECIFICATION	
Model 77	**Elevation:** +67°
Calibre: 155 mm (6.1 in)	**Traverse:** total 70°
Weight: travelling 8000 kg (17,637 lb)	**Maximum range:** with normal
Dimensions: (travelling) length 10.15 m (33 ft 3.6 in); width 2.67 m (8 ft 9 in); height 2.2 m (7 ft 2.6 in)	ammunition 22000 m (24,059 yards) and with rocket-assisted projectile 23300 m (25,481 yards)

GHN-45 155-mm gun/howitzer

In the 1970s PRB of Belgium, a well-known manufacturer of ammunition, and Space Research Corporation of Canada jointly established a company called SRC International with its headquarters in Brussels.

This company developed a gun/howitzer called the **GC-45**, of which 12 were subsequently ordered by the Royal Thai Marines, as well as a conversion kit for the 155-mm (6.1-in) M114 howitzer. The first two GC-45s were built in Canada while the remaining 10 were built in Canada but assembled in Austria by Voest-Alpine.

Austrian development

Further development by Voest-Alpine resulted in the **GHN-45** 155-mm (6.1-in) gun/howitzer,

of which 200 were ordered by Jordan. Production of these weapons started in 1981, the first examples being delivered during the following year. Some of these weapons were transferred from Jordan to Iraq and used against Iran during the Gulf War in the 1980s. The original weapons supplied to Thailand were used in action on the Thai border against Kampuchea.

Basic version

The basic version of the GHN-45 is normally towed by a standard 10-tonne 6x6 truck if required. A model fitted with an auxiliary power unit on the front of the carriage was also developed. This enables the weapon to propel itself on roads at a maximum speed of 35 km/h

(22 mph), and the 80-litre (17.6-Imp gal) fuel tank provides a range of 150 km (93 miles). In normal practice the system is moved from one firing position to another by a truck with the ordnance traversed over the trails and locked in position to reduce its overall length, the APU then being used for final positioning and for bringing the weapon into and out of action.

The GHN-45 has a standard L/45 barrel fitted with a triple-baffle muzzle brake, and can fire a standard US M107 high-explosive projectile to a maximum range of 17800 m (19,466 yards) or an M101 projectile to a maximum range of 24000 m (26,247 yards). With the extended-range full-bore (ERFB) projectile manufactured by PRB, a range of 30000 m (32,808 yards) can be achieved, while the ERFB projectile with base bleed goes out to 39000 m (42,651 yards). With such long ranges, however, target acquisition and projectile dispersion are major problems.

A Voest-Alpine GHN-45 155-mm (6.1-in) gun/howitzer in the travelling position with ordnance locked over the trails. This Austrian-produced weapon first saw service with the Jordanian army and was used with notable success by Iraq during its combat with Iran.

Projectile options

The ERFB projectile, developed from the earlier extended-range sub-bore and extended-range sub-calibre projectiles, is longer and more streamlined than a conventional projectile, and therefore has reduced aerodynamic drag and thus increased range. The ERFB base-bleed is the basic projectile with a different 'boat' tail containing the base-bleed unit, which reduces drag at the rear of the projectile, which thus decelerates more slowly, so increasing range. The basic HE ERFB projectile weighs 45.54 kg (100.4 lb), of which 8.62 kg (19 lb) is the explosive. Other projectiles include smoke and illuminating.

SPECIFICATION	
GHN-45	
Calibre: 155 mm (6.1 in)	**Traverse:** total 70°
Weight: 8900 kg (19,621 lb)	**Maximum range:** with ERFB ammunition 30000 m (32,808 yards) and with ERFB base-bleed ammunition 39000 m (42,651 yards)
Dimensions: (travelling) length 9.068 m (29 ft 9 in); width 2.48 m (8 ft 1.6 in); height 2.089 m (6 ft 10.2 in)	
Elevation: +72°/-5°	

Modern Chinese towed artillery Types 85, 59-1, 83, 66, and 89

For many years almost all of the towed artillery pieces used by China's People's Liberation Army (PLA) were copies of Soviet equipment: the 122-mm (4.8-in) **Type 85** towed howitzer was derived from the Soviet D-30 (M1963), while the 130-mm (5.12-in) **Type 59-1** field gun is a direct copy of the Soviet M-46 but mounted on a lightened carriage.

Using existing Soviet designs as a basis, China then developed more modern towed artillery. More recent types include the 152-mm (6-in) L/52 **Type 83** gun developed in the early 1980s and deployed in small numbers. The widely used 152-mm **Type 66** gun/ howitzer is essentially a copy of the Soviet D-20, with a modified carriage and a much longer barrel.

Until recently, most of the PLA artillery was standardised around the established Soviet-standard calibres of 122 mm, 130 mm and 152 mm, but in recent years a move has been made to the widely deployed 155-mm (6.1-in) calibre.

To meet the requirements of the PLA and potential export customers, the 155-mm L/45 **Type 89** towed gun/howitzer was developed, and was based on Western rather than Soviet technology.

This weapon is similar in appearance to the Austrian GHN-45 (technology relating to the European weapon was passed from Austria to China in the early 1980s) and the South African G5 155-mm L/45 systems. The Type 89 is marketed in the standard towed version or fitted with an auxiliary power unit that assists in bringing the weapon into action more quickly; the latter weapon is designated WAC-021. The GM-45 uses the same armament combined with the two-wheeled carriage of the Type 59-1.

The Type 89's carriage is of the conventional split-trail type, and when deployed in the firing position the weapon is supported on its spades and a firing plate under the carriage.

A flick rammer is provided to increase the rate of fire and reduce fatigue to the gun crew, and a sustained rate of fire of two rounds per minute can be achieved by a well-trained crew. All types of 155-mm ammunition can be fired, including base-bleed rounds. A typical Type 89 company within the PLA comprises six gun/howitzers and one command and control vehicle.

The Type 89 155-mm (6.1-in) gun/howitzer reflects a gradual move within the PLA from Soviet- to Western-standard calibres. The WAC-021 version illustrated is fitted with an APU to provide limited self-propelled mobility.

SPECIFICATION	
Type 89	
Calibre: 155 mm (6.1 in)	**Maximum range:** with HE ammunition 24000 m (26,247 yards) and with ERFB base-bleed ammunition 39000 m (42,651 yards)
Weight: 9700 kg (21,384 lb)	
Dimensions: (travelling) length 13.512 m (44 ft 4 in); width 2.69 m (8 ft 10 in); height 3.048 m (10 ft)	

TR 155-mm towed gun

While the UK, Italy and West Germany elected to develop a 155-mm (6.1-in) towed howitzer first (FH-70) and then a self-propelled model (SP-70), France decided to do the reverse. The 155-mm GCT self-propelled gun on an AMX-30 MBT chassis entered production for Saudi Arabia in 1977, first production vehicles being completed during the following year, but the type was not formally adopted by the French army until 1979. It was subsequently also ordered by Iraq. The prototype of the **TR** 155-mm towed gun was revealed for the first time in 1979 and, following trials with eight prototypes, production started in 1989. The French army bought an initial batch of 105 systems to replace the older towed 155-mm modèle 50 howitzer.

The TR 155-mm gun has an auxiliary power unit on the front of the carriage. This not only provides the power required to propel the weapon around on its own, but also to bring the weapon into and out of action as well as running the projectile loading mechanism.

A TR 155-mm gun in the firing position during Desert Storm. The French army took delivery of its TR systems to replace the 155-mm Modèle 50 howitzer, which had been in service for 30 years.

Weapon design

The TR 155-mm towed gun has a barrel 6.2 m (20 ft 4 in) long, a double-baffle muzzle brake, a hydro-pneumatic recoil system and a horizontal-wedge breech mechanism. The carriage is of the split-trail type, with an auxiliary power unit located on the forward part. The 29-kW (39-hp) engine drives three hydraulic pumps, one for each of the main road wheels and the third to provide power for elevation, traverse, and raising the suspension, trail wheel jacks and projectile-loading mechanism. The APU enables the weapon to propel itself around the battery position or on the road at a maximum speed of 8 km/h (5 mph).

When being towed or travelling under its own power, the TR 155-mm gun has its barrel traversed 180° and locked in position over the closed trails. The projectile-loading system makes possible firing rates of three rounds in the first 18 seconds, six rounds per minute for the first two minutes and 120 rounds per hour thereafter. In the event of breakdown of the loading system manual loading is possible. In any Cold War European battlefield scenario such a weapon would have had to be redeployed in a very short time as its position would be quickly determined by the enemy.

Ammunition types

The TR 155-mm towed gun was designed to be able to use any standard NATO or French 155-mm round, and has been used to fire several types of ammunition: the older model 56/59 HE projectile to a range of 19250 m (21,050 yards), the more recent Cr TA 68 HE projectile weighing 43.2 kg (95.25 lb) to a range of 24000 m (26,245 yards), the 155-mm illuminating projectile (providing a blinding 800,000 candelas of light) to a range of 21500 m (22,515 yards), a smoke incendiary projectile to a range of 21300 m (23,295 yards), and a Brandt rocket-assisted projectile to a range of 30500 m (33,355 yards). Other ammunition types fired include several cargo rounds, variously able to dispense six anti-tank mines or 63 anti-personnel bomblets. Most recently the weapon has been used to fire the Franco-Swedish BONUS round, jointly developed by GIAT and Bofors, which has entered service with the French and Swedish armies. BONUS carries a pair of anti-armour sensor-fused submunitions. These destroy hard and semi-hard targets by a 'top attack' on the target roof where the armour is thinnest.

The TR 155-mm gun has an eight-man crew, and it is towed by the TRM 10000 (6x6) truck, which also carries a battle-ready load of 48 projectiles, charges and fuses and is equipped with a crane for handling artillery pallets. The TR can also be towed by various other prime movers.

SPECIFICATION	
TR	1.65 m (5 ft 5 in)
Calibre: 155 mm (6.1 in)	**Elevation:** +65°/-5°
Weight: travelling and firing 10650 kg (23,479 lb)	**Traverse:** total 65°
Dimensions: length, travelling 8.25 m (27 ft 0.8 in); width, travelling 3.09 m (10 ft 1.7 in); height, firing	**Maximum range:** with standard projectile 24000 m (26,245 yards) and with rocket-assisted projectile 30500 m (33,355 yards)

Soltam M-68 and M-71 155-mm gun/howitzers

The only manufacturer of towed artillery in Israel is Soltam. The **M-68** 155-mm (6.1-in) gun/howitzer was developed as a private venture in the late 1960s, the first prototype being completed in 1968 and the first production models following two years later. As far as is known, the towed model is used only by Singapore and the Thai Marines, although the Soltam L-33 self-propelled gun/howitzer uses the ordnance, elevation and traverse system of the M-68. The L-33 entered service with the Israeli army in time to take part in the 1973 Middle East campaign.

The ordnance of the M-68 is 5.18 m (17 ft) long and is fitted with a single-baffle muzzle brake, fume extractor and a horizontal breech mechanism. The recoil system is below the barrel and the counter-recoil system above, the pneumatic equilibriators being located on the sides of the barrel. When travelling, the top carriage is traversed to the rear so that the ordnance is over the closed trails. The carriage is of the split-trail type. Two rubber-tyred road wheels are mounted on each side; each wheel is fitted with a hydraulic brake, and a maximum towing speed of 100 km/h (62 mph) is thus possible. When in the firing position the carriage is supported by a screw-type firing jack. Four spades are carried, one of these being attached to the end of each trail for firing when the weapon is brought into action. The other two are carried to

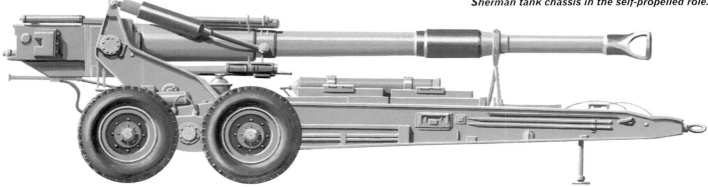

The Soltam M-68 155-mm gun/howitzer in the travelling position with ordnance traversed to the rear and locked in position over the trails. The Israeli army has used this weapon mounted on a rebuilt Sherman tank chassis in the self-propelled role.

enable the eight-man crew to change direction and open fire again without taking out the original spades.

Projectiles

The M-68 fires a standard NATO HE projectile weighing 43.7 kg (96.3 lb) to a maximum range of 21000 m (22,965 yards), as well as smoke and illuminating projectiles. The weapon can also fire Soltam-designed projectiles with a higher muzzle velocity (820 m/ 2,690 ft per second compared with 725 m/2,380 ft per second) to a maximum range of 23500 m (25,700 yards).

The Soltam M-68 is no longer in volume production, although it could be placed back in production if sufficient numbers were ordered. It was followed by the **M-71** howitzer, which uses the same carriage, breech and recoil system as the M-68 but is fitted with a longer L/39 barrel. Mounted on the right trail of the M-71 is a rammer powered by a compressed air cylinder, enabling the weapon to be loaded at all angles of elevation and so making possible a short-period fire rate of four rounds per minute.

The M-71 is known to be service with the Israeli army, and fires an HE projectile to a maximum range of 23500 m (25,700 yards).

For trials purposes one M-71 has been fitted with an auxiliary power unit on the left trail and an ammunition handling crane on the right trail. The APU enables this weapon, called the **Model 839P**, to travel on roads at a maximum speed of 17 km/h (10.6 mph). The product-improved **Model 945** has in turn been superceded by the new 155-mm **TIG** gun/ howitzer, which is air-transportable in the C-130 and has barrels of 39, 45 or 52 calibres. These can easily be replaced in the field.

Above: The 155-mm M-68 gun/howitzer in the firing position with trails firmly staked into the ground. The split-trail carriage was unusual for its time, having four rubber-tyred road wheels, each of which has a hydraulic brake operated from the towing vehicle.

SPECIFICATION	
Soltam M-68	2 m (6 ft 6.7 in)
Calibre: 155 mm (6.1 in)	**Elevation:** +52°/-5°
Weight: travelling 9500 kg	**Traverse:** total 90°
(20,944 lb) and firing 8500 kg	**Maximum range:** standard HE
(18,739 lb)	projectile 21000 m (22,965 yards)
Dimensions: length, travelling 7.2 m	
(23 ft 7.5 in); width, travelling 2.58	
m (8 ft 5.6 in); height, travelling	

The Soltam M-68 155-mm gun/howitzer in travelling configuration, being towed by a truck. Over the last 30 years, the M-68 has provided the basis for several generations of improved guns.

FH2000 155-mm gun/howitzer artillery system

The 155-mm (6.1-in) **FH2000** towed gun/howitzer was developed in Singapore from the earlier 155-mm FH-88 howitzer, the first example appearing during early 1990. The FH2000 differs from the the earlier weapon in that the barrel of the FH-88 is 39 calibres long, while that of the FH2000 is 52 calibres long to provide greater range. FH2000 development lasted until late 1992 and by mid-1995 the Singapore defence forces had 18 examples in service. This was a remarkable performance by a small city state, for those FH2000s were the first 52-calibre artillery equipments, towed or self-propelled, to enter service anywhere in the world. As far as is known the FH2000 has not yet been exported.

In most other respects, the FH-88 and FH2000 are similar overall, although the FH2000 has been elevated in status to an artillery system with items such as matched projectiles being manufactured locally. The system is manufactured by Singapore Technologies Kinetics (STK) who also manufacture the ammunition.

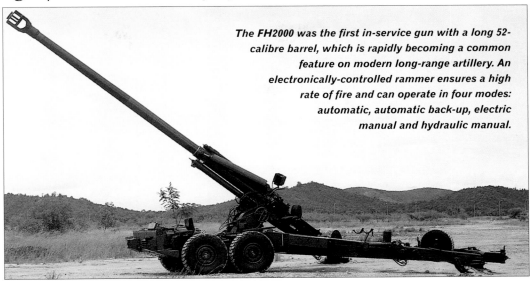

The FH2000 was the first in-service gun with a long 52-calibre barrel, which is rapidly becoming a common feature on modern long-range artillery. An electronically-controlled rammer ensures a high rate of fire and can operate in four modes: automatic, automatic back-up, electric manual and hydraulic manual.

The L/52 barrel provides a maximum possible range of 40000 m (131,234 ft) using an advanced Extended Range, Full Bore, Base Bleed (ERFB-BB) projectile. The range using a standard M107 HE projectile is 19000 m (62,336 ft). The ERFB-BB projectile weighs approximately 46.7 kg (103 lb) and contains a nominal 8 kg (17.63 lb) of TNT, the high-quality steel body providing enhanced fragmentation effects. Also available, apart from similar smoke and incendiary projectiles, is an ERFB-BB cargo round carrying 64 dual-purpose bomblets. The cargo projectile and its contents were designed in Singapore and it has entered service.

The FH2000 carriage includes a 53-kW (71-hp) auxiliary power unit (APU) which provides the artillery system with a degree of self-propulsion around the immediate firing area as well as providing hydraulic power for lowering the firing platform and for opening and closing the split-trail legs.

SPECIFICATION	
FH2000	(with display unit) 2.55 m (8 ft 4.4 in)
Calibre: 155 mm (6.1 in)	**Elevation:** +70°/-3°
Weight: travelling 13500 kg (29,762 lb)	**Traverse:** 30° each side
Dimensions: length, travelling 10.95 m (35 ft 9 in); width, travelling 2.80 m (9 ft 5 in); height,	**Maximum range:** ERFB-BB projectile 40000 m (131,234 ft)

FH-70 155-mm Towed howitzer

This FH-70 155-mm howitzer is illustrated as it would appear in firing position. The weapon fires a standard high-explosive projectile out to a maximum range of 24 km (15 miles).

In 1968 a Memorandum of Understanding (MoU) was signed between the UK and West Germany for the joint development of a 155-mm (6.1-in) howitzer which would replace the British 5.5-in gun and the American-supplied M114 155-mm howitzer.

The main requirements the new weapon had to meet included a high rate of fire with a burst fire capability, increased range and lethality together with a new family of ammunition, high mobility and a minimum of effort for deployment.

The UK was team leader for this weapon, which became known as the FH-70, while West Germany became team leader for the abortive self-propelled equivalent, the SP-70.

Italian partner

Nineteen prototypes of the FH-70 were built, and in 1970 Italy joined the project as a full partner. In 1976 the FH-70 was accepted for service, the first production weapons being completed in 1978. Production lines were established in all three countries. The UK ordered 71 equipments, West Germany 216 and Italy 164. The weapon entered service with Saudi Arabia, and has been manufactured under licence in Japan for the Ground Self Defence Force.

The 6.02-m (19-ft 9-in) long barrel of the FH-70 has a double-baffle muzzle brake and a semi-automatic wedge-type breech mechanism. The carriage of the FH-70 is of the split-trail type, with an auxiliary power unit mounted on the forward part. This enables the FH-70 to propel itself on roads and across country at a maximum speed of 16 km/h (10 mph). In addition the APU provides power for steering, and for raising and lowering the main and trail wheels. When travelling, the ordnance is traversed to the rear and locked in position over the closed trails. To achieve the requirement for burst-fire a semi-automatic loading system is fitted, and this operates at all angles of elevation. The loading system includes a loading tray that presents the projectile to the chamber. A burst rate of three rounds in 13 seconds can be achieved, while the normal sustained rate of fire is six rounds per minute.

Ammunition

The FH-70 has been cleared to fire most NATO standard 155-mm ammunition, including guided and extended-range

rocket-assisted, but generally is limited to three main types: HE with a weight of 43.50 kg (96 lb) smoke (base ejection), and illuminating. The last provides one million candelas for one minute.

In addition to its original developers in Britain (illustrated), Germany and Italy, the FH-70 is used by the Saudi Arabian army and the Japanese GSDF.

SPECIFICATION	
FH-70 field howitzer	height, travelling 2.56 m (8 ft 4.8 in)
Calibre: 155 mm (6.1 in)	**Elevation:** +70°/-3°
Weight: travelling and firing 9300 kg (20,503 lb)	**Traverse:** total 56°
Dimensions: length, travelling 9.80 m (32 ft 1.8 in); width, travelling 2.20 m (7 ft 4.6 in);	**Maximum range:** with standard round 24 km (15 miles) and with rocket-assisted projectile 30000 m (32,810 yards)

Bofors FH-77 155-mm Towed howitzer

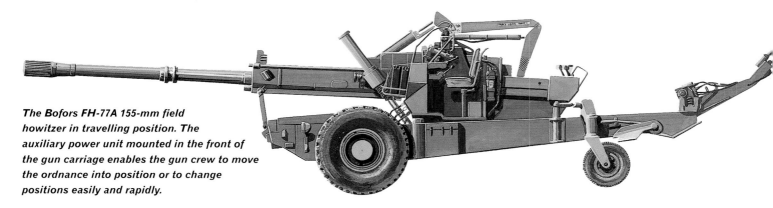

The Bofors FH-77A 155-mm field howitzer in travelling position. The auxiliary power unit mounted in the front of the gun carriage enables the gun crew to move the ordnance into position or to change positions easily and rapidly.

In the late 1960s the Swedish army carried out a series of studies to determine its future artillery requirements. It decided to develop a new 155-mm (6.1-in) towed weapon that would have superior cross-country performance, a high rate of fire, and a good range with more effective ammunition.

At that time Bofors was building the 155-mm (6.1-in) Bandkanon 1A self-propelled gun, which is fully armoured and has a high rate of fire as it

is fitted with an automatic loader for 16 rounds of ready-use ammunition. Its main drawback, however, was, and is, its size and weight (53 tonnes), which limit its movement in certain parts of Sweden as well as making it difficult to conceal.

Bofors was awarded the development contract for the new towed weapon, which subsequently became known as the **FH-77A 155-mm field howitzer**, for which the first orders were placed by the

Swedish army in 1975. The FH-77A has a barrel 5.89 m (19 ft 4 in) long, fitted with a pepperpot muzzle brake and a vertical sliding breech mechanism. The split-trail carriage has an auxiliary power unit mounted on the front, enabling the FH-77A to propel itself on roads and across country. The equipment is normally towed by a Saab-Scania (6x6) truck, which also carries ammunition in pallets and the six man crew consisting of commander,

gunner, two ammunition handlers, loader and a crane handler.

Cross-country

When the truck and the FH-77A encounter very rough country the main wheels of the howitzer can be engaged from the cab of the truck, so giving an 8x8 combination at a maximum speed of 8 km/h (5 mph). When this speed is exceeded the main wheels of the FH-77A are disengaged automatically. Elevation and traverse of the FH-77A is hydraulic, though manual controls are provided for emergency use. Mounted on the right side of the FH-77A is the loading tray, on which clips of three projectiles can be placed.

A typical firing sequence is that the cartridge case is placed on the loading tray followed by the projectile, which is fed from the loading table. When the projectile has slipped down into the neck of the cartridge case the projectile and charge are

rammed, the breech is closed and the weapon is fired. Three rounds can be fired in six to eight seconds, though normal sustained fire is six rounds fired every other minute for 20 minutes.

The Bofors-developed NY77 projectile weighs 42.40 kg (93.28 lb), has a muzzle velocity of 774 m (2,540 ft) per second and goes out to a maximum range of 22 km (14 miles). It is believed that Bofors is currently developing a base-bleed projectile which will have a

maximum range of between 27 and 30 km (17 and 19 miles).

Export guns

Bofors developed the **FH-77B** for export, with a longer barrel, increased elevation of +70°, mechanised loading system and

other major improvements. The FH-77B has been supplied to Nigeria, India and others. For the Swedish coastal artillery, Bofors has developed the **CD80**, essentially the carriage of the FH-77A fitted with a 120-mm (4.72-in) ordnance.

SPECIFICATION	
Bofors FH-77A field howitzer	**Dimensions:** length, travelling 11.60 m (38 ft 0.7 in); width, travelling 2.64 m (8 ft 8 in); height, travelling 2.75 m (9 ft 0.3 in)
Calibre: 155 mm (6.1 in)	
Weight:: travelling 11500 kg (25,353 lb)	
	Elevation: +50°/+3°
	Traverse: total 50°
	Maximum range: 20 km (14 miles)

Armscor G5 155-mm Towed gun/howitzer

Inspired by the eccentric but supremely capable artillery designer Gerald Bull, the G5 incorporated features from several different artillery pieces. The result outperformed all of its progenitors, proving to be one of the longest-ranged and most accurate 155-mm weapons ever built and sent into action.

For many years after World War II, the mainstays of South African field artillery units were the British 5.5-in (140-mm) medium gun with a maximum range of 16.46 km (10 miles) and the 25-pdr (88-mm) field gun with a maximum range of 12.25 km (8 miles).

Outranged

During operations in Angola the South Africans found themselves outranged by Soviet-supplied artillery and rockets. This led to the urgent development of two indigenous systems, since at that time no Western country would supply South Africa with the arms it required.

The **G5 155-mm gun/ howitzer** and the 127-mm (5-in) 24-round multiple rocket system were developed and put into

production in time to have seen combat during raids into Angola.

The G5 owes much to the Canadian Space Research Corporation GC 45 155-mm (6.1-in) weapon. However, so many additional features have been incorporated into the G5 that it is in essence a completely new weapon.

The G5 has a 45-calibre barrel fitted with a single- baffle muzzle brake and an interrupted-thread breech mechanism. To the rear of the breech is a pneumatically operated rammer to ram projectiles into the chamber at all angles of elevation; this is powered by an air bottle

which is mounted on the right trail. The bagged charges are loaded by hand.

On the forward part of the split trail carriage is the auxiliary power unit, which consists of a 51-kW (68-hp) diesel engine. In addition to providing power to the main driving wheels, the APU also supplies power for raising and lowering the circular firing platform under the carriage, for opening and closing the trails, and for raising and lowering the trail wheels. To reduce the overall length of the G5 for travelling, the ordnance is normally traversed through 180° and locked in position over the trails.

Rate of fire

The ordnance has a total traverse of 84° below 15° of elevation, and 65° above that. Maximum rate of fire over a 15-minute period is three rounds

per minute, with two rounds per minute possible in the sustained fire role. The G5 is operated by an eight-person crew.

The G5 can fire five types of ammunition, also manufactured in South Africa. The standard HE projectile weighs 45.50 kg (100 lb), and is of the Extended-Range Full Bore (ERFB) type. The HE base-bleed (HE BB) type is slightly heavier because of the base-bleed attachment, but has a range of 37000 m (40,465 yards) at sea level, though greater ranges are attained when the G5 is fired at altitude. The other three projectiles are illuminating, smoke and white phosphorus.

To operate with the G5, South Africa developed a complete fire-control system including a muzzle-velocity measuring device, AS 80 artillery fire-control system with a 16-bit minicomputer, S700

SPECIFICATION	
G5 gun/howitzer	travelling 2.30 m (7 ft 6.6 in)
Calibre: 155 mm (6 in)	**Elevation:** +73°/-3°
Weight: travelling 13500 kg (29,762 lb)	**Traverse:** total 84° (but see text)
	Maximum range: with standard ammunition over 30000 m (32,810 yards) and with base-bleed projectile 37000 m (40,465 yards)
Dimensions: length, travelling 9.10 m (29 ft 10.3 in); width, travelling 2.50 m (8 ft 2.4 in); height,	

meteorological ground station and a complete range of communications equipment. South Africa has also developed a 155-mm (6.1-in) self-propelled 6x6 howitzer called the **G6**, which has an ordnance based on the G5 weapon and uses the same ammunition.

In addition to South Africa, the G5 has been sold to at least four other armies. Saddam Hussein's Iraq used the type during the occupation of Kuwait in 1990, but most were destroyed in the Gulf War which followed.

Right: The G5 was designed to be towed into action behind a SAMIL 100 6x6 10-tonne truck. The vehicle also carries the gun crew and the ammunition.

Below: G5s open fire with their barrels at a flat elevation. At full range the G5 can shoot to a distance of 37 km (23 miles).

105-mm Light Gun
Lightweight fire support

The 105-mm Light Gun is ideally suited for the support of mobile forces operating in many types of third-world conditions: rugged and reliable, it can provide modest fire support over tactically useful ranges.

Though its projectiles lack the range and explosive effect of the shells fired by larger-calibre weapons, the British 105-mm (4.13-in) L118A1 Light Gun is a very useful weapon for forces operating in adverse conditions (especially soft terrain of any sort) and without the support of heavier vehicles, including both trucks and helicopters, for the movement of the guns and their ammunition.

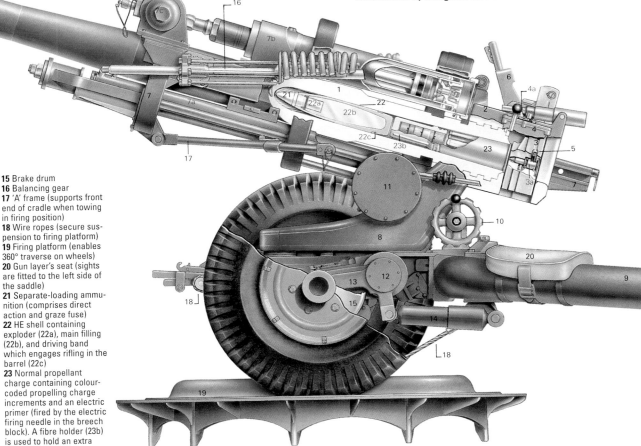

L118A1 Light Gun

1 Barrel
2 Breech ring
3 Breech block: an electric firing needle assembly (3a) within the breech block completes a contact when the breech is closed
4 Firing mechanism: actuated by the firing lever (4a)
5 Electric contact in breech block
6 Breech mechanism lever lowers and raises the breech block as required. Opening breech breaks mechanical lock, retracts electrical firing needle, lowers breech block, engages extractor levers (not shown) and pulls spent case from breech
7 Cradle, in which barrel assembly slides, providing anchorage for the recoil system. This consists of hydraulic recoil buffer (7a) and compensating cylinders, and a hydro-pneumatic recuperator (7b) with its air reservoir (7c), which returns the barrel to its starting point after firing
8 Saddle-pintle mounted allowing 5° traverse left and right
9 Trail assembly
10 Traversing wheel
11 Elevating gears
12 Torsion-bar suspension
13 Suspension arm
14 Damper

15 Brake drum
16 Balancing gear
17 'A' frame (supports front end of cradle when towing in firing position)
18 Wire ropes (secure suspension to firing platform)
19 Firing platform (enables 360° traverse on wheels)
20 Gun layer's seat (sights are fitted to the left side of the saddle)
21 Separate-loading ammunition (comprises direct action and graze fuse)
22 HE shell containing exploder (22a), main filling (22b), and driving band which engages rifling in the barrel (22c)
23 Normal propellant charge containing colour-coded propelling charge increments and an electric primer (fired by the electric firing needle in the breech block). A fibre holder (23b) is used to hold an extra increment of charge

Left: Designed by the Royal Armament Research and Development Establishment at Fort Halstead in Kent, the Light Gun was manufactured by Royal Ordnance Nottingham, later taken over by British Aerospace (now BAe Systems). Deliveries for British use totalled 168 guns including a number of reserve and training weapons; total production amounts to over 400 for the home and export markets. The weapon is pictured in the firing position: the 105-mm Light Gun has among the longest range of any weapon of its type.

Above: A 105-mm (4.13-in) L118A1 Light Gun of the British Army is caught by the camera during an exercise in Norway. Part of the UK's NATO commitment is to the defence of northern Norway, where light and mobile artillery is a major asset.

Above: The Light Gun fires at its maximum elevation of 70° during demonstrations at the Royal School of Artillery at Larkhill in Wiltshire. The 105-mm Light Gun has a seven-charge firing system allowing the delivery of its projectile to any range between 2500 and 17200 m (2,735 and 18,810 yards). The 105-mm shared the same highly lethal range of ammunition as the Abbot 105-mm self-propelled gun formerly in use with the British Army.

Right: A key feature of the Light Gun, created to provide superiority to the OTO-Melara Pack Howitzer in terms of range, firing stability, reliability, and high-speed towing, is the trail. Fabricated from corrosion-resistant steel, this is shaped to allow the breech operator and loader to remain within the trail at all angles of elevation. The latest model of the 105-mm Light Gun, as built by BAe Systems, is illustrated.

A 1-tonne Land Rover moves off towing an L118A1 Light Gun, in this instance with its elevating mass in the firing position rather than rotated through 180° back over the trail. With the gun crew and some ready-use ammunition carried in the Land Rover, the combination is well optimised for 'shoot and scoot' tactics.

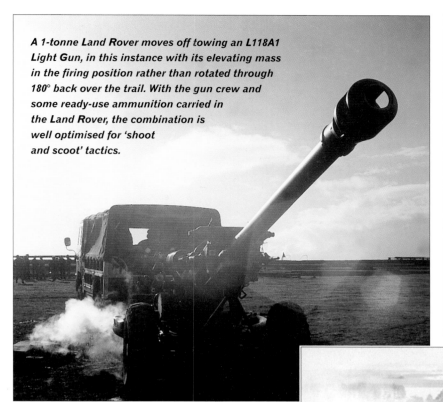

SPECIFICATION

105-mm L118 Light Gun

Barrel

Calibre: 105 mm (4.13 in)
Length: 3.175 m (10 ft 5 in)

Muzzle brake

Double baffle

Recoil system

Hydro-pneumatic type
Recoil length: 1.07 m (42.125 in) at 0° and 0.33 m (13 in) at 70°

Breech

Vertical sliding type

Weights

In travelling and firing orders: 1860 kg (4,100 lb)
Elevating mass: 1066 kg (2,350 lb)

Dimensions

Length travelling with gun forward: 6.629 m (21 ft 9 in)
Length travelling with gun over trail: 4.876 m (16 ft)
Length firing with ordnance at 0°: 7.01 m (23 ft)

Width: 1.778 m (5 ft 10 in)
Height travelling with gun forward: 2.63 m (8 ft 2 in)
Height travelling with gun over trail: 1.371 m (4 ft 6 in)
Ground clearance: 0.5 m (19.75 in)
Track: 1.4 m (4 ft 7 in)

Elevation

-5.5° to +70°

Traverse

Total on carriage: 11°
Total of platform: 360°

Rate of fire

12 rounds per minute for 1 minute
6 rounds per minute for 3 minutes
3 rounds per minute sustained

Range

Minimum: 2500 m (2,735 yards)
Maximum: 17200 m (18,810 yards)

Projectile types

16.1-kg (35.5-lb) L31 HE, 10.49-kg (23.125-lb) L42 HESH, 15.88-kg (35-lb) L37, L38 and L45 Smoke, and L43 Illuminating

Right: Royal Artillery 105-mm Light Guns in action at the Royal School of Artillery, Larkhill, Wiltshire. In addition to being used by the Royal Artillery, the Light Gun has also seen service with many overseas countries, including Australia (where it has been built under licence), Brunei, Ireland, Kenya, Malawi, Oman and the United Arab Emirates.

Below: A Light Gun in action. With weight reduction paramount in the design of this weapon, features such as a gun shield were omitted even though this leaves the crew somewhat vulnerable to shell splinters. The Light Gun has a limited but adequate number of projectile types, and adequate minimum and maximum ranges.

M198 155-mm towed howitzer

The M198 155-mm (6.1-in) howitzer is seen in one of its two travelling configurations. This is now the standard 155-mm howitzer of the US Army and Marines, and replaced the old 155-mm M114. The gun has been the subject of a Product Improvement Program to ensure its viability into the twenty-first century.

Below: This M198 howitzer is in firing position with its firing crew in attendance. A crew of nine is required to fire the weapon. The M198 has been used operationally in both Lebanon and the Middle East.

For many years the standard 155-mm (6.1-in) towed howitzer of the US Army was the respected M114. This had been developed in the 1930s and, by the end of World War II, an impressive total of 6,000 had been built.

Like the 105-mm (4.13-in) M101 towed howitzer, the M114 suffered the major drawback of having limited range and also traverse capabilities. Following the issue of a formal requirement for a new 155-mm howitzer, Rock Island Arsenal started design work in 1968, its first development prototype being completed two years later.

Prototype weapons

A total of 10 prototypes were built under the designation **XM198** and, after trials and the usual modifications, the new howitzer was adopted for service as the **M198**. Production started at Rock Island Arsenal in 1978, with the first battalion of 18 M198 howitzers forming at Fort Bragg in the following year. Each battalion has three batteries each with six M198s. In addition to being used by the US Army and US Marine Corps, the M198 was also ordered by Australia (an initial batch of 36 to replace the British 5.5-in gun) and a number of other countries, notably in the Middle East.

Air mobility

In the US Army and US Marine Corps the M198 is towed by a 5-ton 6x6 truck which also carries the ammunition and nine-man crew, although the weapon can be towed by a variety of other tracked and wheeled vehicles. It is air portable, and can be carried slung underneath US Army CH-47C Chinook and US Marine Corps CH-53E Super Stallion helicopters. The M198 is normally issued to US infantry,

A laser-guided projectile departs the barrel of an M198 howitzer during a firing exercise at the White Sands Missile Range in New Mexico. These shells are designed to hit either stationary or moving targets with a single round.

airborne and air assault divisions, while mechanised infantry and armoured divisions have the 155-mm M109 self-propelled howitzer. The M198 was first used operationally by the US Marines in Lebanon in 1983.

Principal parts

The main components of the M198 are the carriage, recoil system, fire-control equipment and cannon (or ordnance, as the British prefer to call it). The carriage is of the split-trail type and fitted with a two-position rigid suspension. When the weapon is in the firing position, a firing platform is lowered to the ground under the forward part of the carriage and the wheels are raised clear of the ground. The cradle has the elevation and traverse system, while the top carriage has the assembly cradle, equilibrators and recoil guides. The recoil mechanism is of the hydro-pneumatic type with a variable recoil length. The M199 cannon has a double-baffle muzzle brake, thermal warning device and a screw-type breech mechanism. The fire-control equipment includes an M137 panoramic telescope, two elevation quadrants, and an M138 elbow telescope.

Travelling position

When in the travelling position the ordnance is normally traversed to the rear and locked in position over the trails. Unlike most modern European 155-mm towed guns (including the multi-national FH-70, the French TR and the Swedish FH-77), the M198 does not have an auxiliary power unit to enable it to be moved under its own

power. The M198 can fire all types of current US/NATO 155-mm separate-loading ammunition, including anti-tank (carrying mines), Copperhead laser-guided, high explosive, high explosive with various grenades, rocket-assisted, illuminating and smoke projectiles and tactical nuclear.

SPECIFICATION	
M198	**Elevation:** -5° to +72°
Calibre: 155 mm (6.1 in)	**Traverse:** total 45°
Weight: travelling and firing 7163 kg (15,790 lb)	**Maximum range:** with M107 projectile 18150 m (19,850 yards) and with M549A1 rocket-assisted projectile 30000 m (32,810 yards)
Dimensions: (travelling) length 12.34 m (40 ft 6 in); width 2.794 m (9 ft 2 in); height 2.9 m (9 ft 6 in)	

This M198 is seen in the static fire position, with sand bags providing a measure of protection. The weapon has been sold to a number of other operators including Australia and some Middle Eastern armies.

Modern US towed artillery M777 and M119A1 howitzers

Three separate trends can be detected on the current US towed artillery scene, although one of them is not, in fact, towed. Two of the trends can be seen in the introduction into service of the 155-mm (6.1-in) **M777 Joint Lightweight Howitzer** and the retention of the 105-mm (4.13-in) **M119A1 Lightweight Towed Howitzer**, which was at one time scheduled to be phased out of service. The third trend is associated with the M777, as it is the adoption of a lightweight artillery system to augment the fire of the M777. This system is known as the High Mobility Artillery Rocket System (HIMARS), and is in essence one six-rocket pod in place of the two normally used by the Multiple Launch Rocket System (MLRS). To reduce weight for air transport, the HIMARS is carried on a 6x6 truck chassis.

Upgrade programme

At one time it was scheduled that the US Army's M119A1 (which is a US version of the British Royal Ordnance 105-mm Light Gun design) would be

US Army troops are seen on exercise somewhere in Europe with their 105-mm (4.13-in) M119A1 Lightweight Towed Howitzer. This weapon has been reprieved from retirement and is to receive a series of new extended-range projectiles.

phased out of service in favour of new equipments such as the M777. However, the greater importance of high-mobility operations and special forces applications, coupled with range-enhancing ammunition developments, now makes the 105-mm weapon more attractive than before. Various updating options are being studied to enhance the M119A1, which

fires the standard suite of US/NATO ammunition such as the M1 HE round. For the most part these enhancements are concentrated on more streamlined projectiles with rocket assistance that can

extend the existing M119A1 range of about 11500 m (12,575 yards) to more than 17100 m (18,700 yards).

These improvements are still pending, with other equipments being investigated, the most

SPECIFICATION

M777
Calibre: 155 mm (6.1 in)
Weight: 3745 kg (8,256 lb)
Dimensions: (travelling) length 9.275 m (30 ft 3 in); width 2.77 m (9 ft 1 in); height 2.26 m (7 ft 5 in)

Elevation: -5° to +70°
Traverse: total 45°
Maximum range: with standard projectile 24690 m (27,000 yards) and with rocket-assisted projectile 30000 m (32,808 yards)

intriguing being the South African 105-mm Lightweight Experimental Ordnance (LEO) with its standard range of 24000 m (26,245 yards) or 30000 m (32,808 yards) with base-bleed ammunition, combined with a high-fragmentation projectile which, when air burst, has a lethal radius performance similar to standard 155-mm projectiles. In the meantime, the M119A1 seems destined for retention.

Future projects

The M777 Joint Lightweight Howitzer will replace all US Marine Corps cannon systems and become that service's primary direct-support weapon. The US Army will use the weapon for the general support of light forces and as a direct-support weapon for the Light Cavalry Regiment, replacing all M198 towed howitzers. The M777's L/39 cannon is similar to that used by the the M109A6 Paladin. The M777 is only now entering service, but is already scheduled for a whole raft of improvements mainly connected with fire control and ergonomic handling. Yet the replacement

for the M777 is already being investigated under the heading of Future Combat Systems (FCS) Non Line Of Sight Cannon (NLOS-C). A technology demonstrator has already been test-fired using an M777 barrel. One planned version will also have a band track for improving mobility. The British army has a similar re-equipment programme to the US NLOS-C known as the Lightweight Mobile Artillery Weapon System or LIMAWS (G). Both the M777 and the HIMARS are candidates for this particular project.

Above: The British Ministry of Defence is contemplating the M777 towed howitzer as a solution to its requirement for a Lightweight Mobile Artillery Weapon System. Several systems are being evaluated.

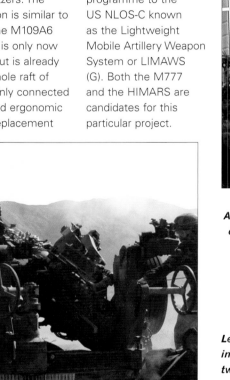

Left: The M777's lightweight carriage includes two forward stabilisers, and two split trails fitted with self-digging spades and dampers. The standard crew is seven.

D-30 122-mm towed howitzer

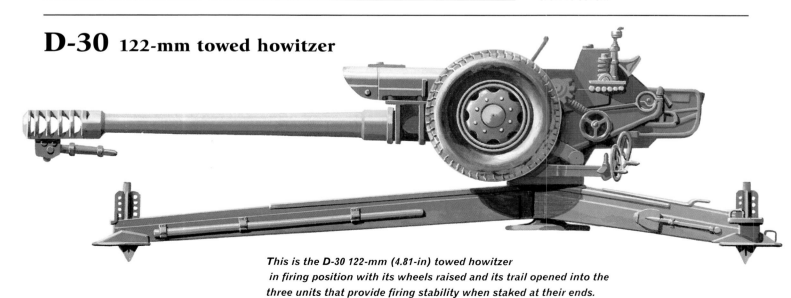

This is the D-30 122-mm (4.81-in) towed howitzer in firing position with its wheels raised and its trail opened into the three units that provide firing stability when staked at their ends.

The **D-30** 122-mm (4.81-in) howitzer was designed by the F.F. Petrov Design Bureau at Artillery Plant No. 9 at Sverdlovsk to replace the 122-mm M1938 (M-30) howitzer, introduced into Soviet service shortly before World War II. The D-30 entered service in the early 1960s and offered several significant advantages, including a range of 15400 rather than 11800 m (16,840 rather than 12,905 yards) and traverse of 360° rather than 49°. The weapon is still in service with 65 countries, and the 2S1 Gvozdika self-propelled howitzer has an ordnance based on the D-30. Other SP versions of the D-30 were developed in Syria and for Egypt.

Soviet issue

In Soviet service the D-30 was issued on the scale of 36 per tank division (one regiment of two 18-weapon battalions each of three six-gun batteries), and 72 per motor rifle division (each motorised rifle regiment having a battalion of 18 D-30s and the artillery regiment two 18-gun battalions). The Soviet forces later increased the battery from six to eight guns: each battalion thus had 24 rather than 18 D-30s.

The D-30 has a 4.875-m (16-ft) barrel with a multi-baffle muzzle brake and a semi-automatic vertical sliding wedge breech mechanism, the recoil system being mounted over the ordnance. The weapon is towed muzzle first, the three trails being clamped in position under the ordnance. On arrival at the firing position, the crew first unlock the barrel travel lock, which then folds back onto the central trail. The firing jack under the carriage is then lowered to the ground, so raising the wheels, and the outer trails are each spread through 120°. The firing jack is raised until the trail ends are on the ground to provide a stable firing platform after they have been staked to the ground. The D-30 has a small shield, and is normally towed by a ZIL-157 or Ural-375D 6x6 truck, or an MT-LB tracked vehicle.

The D-30 fires case-type separate-loading ammunition including FRAG-HE, HEAT-FS (able to penetrate 460 mm/ 18.1 in of armour), smoke, chemical, illuminating and, later, a rocket-assisted projectile for a range of up to 21000 m (22,965 yards).

The **D-30M** has a revised double-baffle muzzle brake and a square rather than round baseplate. The **D-30A** has other improvements including a new cradle and a modified recoil system.

Left and below left: The D-30 122-mm (4.81-in) howitzer was produced in very large numbers in the USSR, and was also made in China, Croatia, Egypt, Iran, Iraq and Yugoslavia. Substantial numbers are still in service.

Right: Three Soviet D-30 122-mm (4.81-in) howitzers in firing position. For many years the Soviet D-30 was the backbone of Soviet artillery regiments, but was succeeded by the 2S1 Gvozdika SP equipment.

SPECIFICATION	
D-30	**Elevation:** -7° to + 70°
Calibre: 121.92 mm (4.8 in)	**Traverse:** 360°
Weight: travelling 3210 kg (7,077 lb) and firing 3150 kg (6,944 lb)	**Maximum range:** 15400 m (16,840 yards) with HE projectile
Dimensions: (travelling) length 5.4 m (17 ft 8.6 in); width 1.95 m (6 ft 4.8 in); height 1.66 m (5 ft 5.6 in)	and 21000 m (22,965 yards) with rocket-assisted HE projectile

2A36 152-mm towed gun

The **2A36** 152-mm (6-in) towed long-range gun was originally developed during the 1970s at the Perm Machine Works as successor to the old (and heavy) M-46 130-mm (5.12-in) gun. When it first appeared it was known in the West as the **M1976** although the Soviet armed forces named it the **Giatsint-B** (hyacinth-B). The Giatsint-S self-propelled equivalent did not proceed past the prototype stage.

Production

The 2A36 was not shown in public until 1985, but production is understood to have started in 1976. Production continued into the late 1980s, although marketing for potential export continued until the late 1990s. Production totalled about 1,500, the only confirmed export orders from outside the former USSR being for Finland (24) and Iraq (an undetermined quantity).

The 2A36 has a multi-baffle muzzle brake and a semi-automatic horizontal sliding breech mechanism. The carriage allows high-speed cross-country towing.

Characterised by useful range and accuracy with an HE-FRAG shell that can be pre-set for maximum blast or high fragmentation, the 2A36 is used mainly in the counter-battery role.

The L/49 barrel of the 2A36 is 8.187 m (26 ft 10.5 in) long and the weapon's primary projectile is an HE-FRAG type whose effect (high blast or high fragmentation) is set by adjustment of the fuse before firing. This projectile weighs 46 kg (101.4 lb) and can be fired to 27000 m (29,530 yards). A special rocket-assisted projectile can reach 40000 m (43,745 yards). An armour-piercing (AP-T) projectile is available for direct fire against armoured targets. With the latter the muzzle velocity is about 800 m (2,625 ft) per second. At one time a special 2A36 nuclear projectile was reported, but this has long been withdrawn from service. Other projectiles available include smoke, concrete-piercing and incendiary.

Deployment

The guns are usually deployed in batteries of six or eight weapons, so marketing material has emphasised that a single battery

can place more than 1 tonne of projectiles on a target in one minute.

References have been made to an improved version of the 2A36 Giatsint-B having an L/53.8 barrel, but it appears this project did not progress far as it was the later 2A65 152-mm (6-in) gun that was selected for service.

The 2A36 has a crew of eight, some of them partially protected by a shield. The loading of the gun is greatly assisted by a loading tray that aligns with the horizontally opening breech

when the latter is opened. The projectile is then hydraulically rammed and a fixed charge in a cartridge case is then inserted. Using this system the maximum rate of fire can be as high as five or six rounds per minute for short periods. Each gun is intended to be taken into action with 60 ready-use rounds.

The 2A36 is normally towed by a KrAZ-260 9-tonne 6x6 truck, although vehicles of similar capacity, including tracked prime movers, can be used. When on tow the gun carriage is

supported by a four-wheel (two wheels on each side) walking beam suspension, permitting the gun to be towed over rough terrain at speeds of up to 30 km/h (18.6 mph). In firing position the trail legs are split and the gun rests on a circular

jack under the forward part of the carriage. This arrangement allows a traverse of 25° to left and right. Several types of trail spade are available to suit the season, the 'summer' spades being larger for the use of the gun in softer ground.

SPECIFICATION	
2A36	
Calibre: 152.4 mm (6 in)	**Elevation:** -2.5° to +57°
Weights: travelling 9800 kg (21,605 lb) and firing 9760 kg (21,517 lb)	**Traverse:** 25° left and right
	Maximum range: 27000 m (29,530 yards) or, with RAP, 40000 m (43,745 yards)
Dimensions: length (travelling) 12.92 m (42 ft 4.7 in); width 2.788 m (9 ft 1.8 in); height 2.76 m (9 ft 0.7 in)	

Russian anti-tank guns T-12/MT-12 and 2A45M Sprut-B

While many armed forces have come to rely on guided missiles for anti-armour warfare, Russia has always retained specialised anti-tank guns, considering them reliable and more versatile than the 'one-shot' guided missile. While any Russian artillery piece can be regarded as a potential anti-tank weapon, the Russian armoury still contains two main types of dedicated-to-role towed anti-tank gun.

The oldest of this pair dates from 1961 and is the 100-mm (3.9-in) **T-12** (otherwise known as the **2A19**) and the related **MT-12** (**2A29**). The main difference between the two is that the more numerous MT-12 has a modified carriage to reduce the chances of the carriage overturning while on tow. Most of these guns now likely to be encountered are MT-12s.

Smooth-bore barrel

The 100-mm barrel is smooth-bored to enhance the muzzle velocity and thus the kinetic energy of the armour-piercing, fin stabilised, discarding sabot (APFSDS) projectile. This weighs 4.55 kg (10.03 lb) and is fired at a muzzle velocity of 1548 m (5,079 ft) per second. The projectile has a maximum operational range of about 3000 m (3,281 yards) and it can penetrate 215 mm (8.47 in) of armour at 1000 m (1,094 yards). Another specialised anti-armour round is the 9M117

Kastet (knuckleduster) laser-guided missile. The latest model of this missile is the 9M117M with a tandem shaped-charge warhead capable of penetrating 550 mm (21.7 in) of armour at any direct-fire range. Both the T-12 and MT-12 can also fire conventional shaped-charge (HEAT) projectiles. Increasing their versatility, the guns are provided with indirect-fire sights and HE projectiles to enable their deployment as field guns.

It has been estimated that the Russian armed forces maintain over 6,000 of these guns. Although no longer in production in the former USSR, the gun is available from Norinco of China as the **Type 73**. Norinco have exported their product, so the T-12 and MT-12 are likely to be encountered almost anywhere.

The second Russian gun model is the 125-mm (4.92-in) **2A45M Sprut-B** (octopus). First seen during the late 1990s, the 2A45M combines the main attributes of the 125-mm D-81 tank gun and cradle, normally mounted on tanks such as the T-72, and the triple-trail 360° traverse carriage of the 122-mm (4.8-in) D-30 towed field howitzer. It was originally designed as the long-term replacement for the 100-mm T-12/MT-12 series but up to the time of writing production has been confined to trial batches.

APFDS projectile

The 125-mm 2A45M has an L/51 smoothbore barrel with a double-baffle muzzle brake and fires the same ammunition as the D-81. This includes an

Crew and combat equipment for the T-12/MT-12 and 2A45M anti-tank guns are transported by the MT-LB tracked prime mover or Ural-4320 6x6 truck. Here East German army MT-LB vehicles tow 100-mm (3.9-in) T-12 guns.

APFSDS projectile weighing 7.05 kg (15.54 lb) and fired at a muzzle velocity of 1700 m (5,577 ft) per second to a maximum effective range of about 2100 m (2,297 yards). At that range it can penetrate almost 250 mm (9.84 in) of armour. The 2A45M can also fire the laser-guided 9M119M Svir (sabre) projectile that can penetrate 700 mm (27.56 in) of armour at any direct-fire range up to 5000 m (5,468 yards) by

SPECIFICATION	
MT-12	**2A45M Sprut-B**
Calibre: 100 mm (3.9 in)	**Calibre:** 125 mm (4.92 in)
Weight: in action 2750 kg (6,063 lb)	**Weight:** in action 6575 kg (14,495 lb)
Dimensions: length, travelling 9.48 m (31 ft 1.2 in)	**Dimensions:** length, travelling 7.12 m (23 ft 4.3 in)
Elevation: -6°/+20°	**Elevation:** -6/+25°
Traverse: total 54°	**Traverse:** 360°
Maximum range: 3000 m (3,281 yards)	**Maximum range:** 2100 m (2,297 yards)

employing a shaped-charge warhead. As with other Russian anti-tank guns, the 2A45M can also fire conventional HEAT and HE projectiles.

One of the main reasons why the 2A45M has yet to enter full-scale production is its weight, 6575 kg (14,495 lb) in the firing position. To assist short moves the carriage is provided with an APU that drives the carriage wheels. In this mode the maximum speed is limited to 14 km/h (8.7 mph) for short distances only. Longer-distance moves are made with the gun towed by a heavy 6x6 truck or another type of tracked prime mover.

Krasnopol-M Cannon-launched guided projectile

Perhaps the most significant of all recent Russian artillery developments has been the introduction of standard NATO-calibre 155-mm (6.1-in) models to render existing Russian-derived 152-mm (6-in) artillery ammunition more attractive to overseas markets. The 152-mm calibre has few adherents outside the former Warsaw Pact bloc (and China) so any move towards 155-mm ammunition could be important.

Westernised CLGP

One of the most attractive types of ammunition already modified to 155-mm calibre is the **Krasnopol-M** cannon-launched guided projectile (CLGP). This differs from the standard 152-mm **9K25 Krasnopol** CLGP in being entirely re-engineered to fit into NATO-pattern stowage racks and handling equipment, but the guidance techniques remain the same. These techniques rely on laser target indication from a forward position within visual range of the intended target. The gun firing the projectile is laid towards the approximate direction of the target and the barrel elevation set as usual. Once the Krasnopol-M has been fired the target is subjected to laser energy from a ground-based, tripod-mounted target

Above: In Russian service, the 152-mm Krasnopol CLGP is associated with the D-30 towed howitzer. A forward observer illuminates the target for the Krasnopol using a tripod-mounted 1D22 laser target designator with an integral rangefinder.

Right: The semi-active laser-guided Krasnopol-M in 155-mm calibre can be fired from Western systems such as the M109 and G6 self-propelled guns. The projectile makes a top attack on its target's upper armour, striking at an angle between +35° and +45°.

designator system. Some of this energy is reflected from the target and detected by a sensor mounted in the projectile nose. The appropriate trajectory corrections can then be made using an on-board electronic computer that introduces changes to the tailfin surfaces – the tailfins spring out into position only after the projectile has left the gun muzzle. In this way the projectile homes onto the target at a steep angle, the target often being as small as a tank.

Each Krasnopol-M is 955-mm (37.6-in) long overall and weighs 45 kg (99.2 lb) complete. Of this, 20 kg (44.09 lb) is formed by the high-explosive fragmentation (HE-FRAG) warhead containing 6 kg (13.23 lb) of explosive. The maximum range is in the order of 22000 m (24,059 yards), while the maximum range of the laser target designator is about 7000 m (7,655 yards) for static targets (less for moving targets).

Export success

The 155-mm Krasnopol-M has reportedly been sold to India and it has been tested by France and South Africa, primarily to expand their suites of 155-mm projectiles already on offer. Norinco of China is understood to be producing the type under licence.

Other recent types of Russian projectile have included a cargo projectile that dispenses radio jammer bodies. Regarding Russian sub-munitions, their cargo projectile offerings contain much heavier sub-munitions than in the West. For instance, one Russian 152-mm projectile contains eight dual purpose sub-munitions, each weighing 1.4 kg (3.09 lb). The standard NATO M864 contains 72 'bomblets', each weighing about 210 g (7.41 oz).

SPECIFICATION	
Krasnopol-M	**Range:** around 22000 m (24,059 yards)
Type: cannon-launched guided projectile	**Warhead:** 20-kg (44.09-lb) high-explosive fragmentation (HE-FRAG) containing 6 kg (13.23lb) explosive
Calibre: 155 mm (6.1 in)	
Weight: 45 kg (99.21 lb)	
Length: 955 mm (37.6 in)	

M-56 105-mm howitzer

With the German surrender in Yugoslavia at the end of World War II, large quantities of German artillery were abandoned and much of this was taken over by the Yugoslav army. Some 40 years later, numbers of German 88-mm (3.46-in) guns were still in service in the coastal-defence role, while the 105-mm (4.13-in) towed M18, M18M and M18/40 howitzers continued to be used by reserve units. In the immediate post-war period the United States supplied Yugoslavia with considerable amounts of towed artillery, including 155-mm (6.1-in) M114 and 105-mm (4.13-in) M101 howitzers, and 155-mm (6.1-in) M59 'Long Tom' guns. Some of these remained in service until the disintegration of the Yugoslav state in the early 1990s, together with a copy of the M114 called the M-65. Yugoslavia also designed and built two weapons to meet its own requirements, these being the 105-mm (4.13-in) howitzer **M-56** and the 76-mm (3-in) mountain gun M-46, the latter developed to meet the specific requirements of Yugoslav mountain units.

Above: A Yugoslav M-56 105-mm howitzer in its travelling configuration. This particular model has wheels with solid rubber tyres similar to those fitted to German 105-mm howitzers also used by the Yugoslav army following World War II.

M-56 carriage

The M-56 has a barrel 3.48 m (11 ft 5 in) long with a multi-baffle muzzle brake, a hydraulic recoil buffer and hydro-pneumatic recuperator above and below the barrel, and a horizontal sliding-wedge breech mechanism. The carriage is of the split-trail type, with a spade attached to each end of the pole-type trail. The M-56 has a split shield that slopes to the rear and sides. Some carriages have been observed with American-type road wheels and tyres similar to that fitted to the M101, which allows the weapon to be towed up to 70 km/h (43.5 mph), while others have wheels with solid tyres similar to those fitted to the German 105-mm (4.13-in) howitzers of World War II. When the latter are fitted the weapon cannot be towed at high speed. Fire-control equipment consists of a panoramic telescope with a magnification of x4, a direct-fire anti-tank telescope with a magnification of x2, and a gunner's quadrant.

Projectile types

Ammunition is of the semi-fixed type (e.g. projectile and a cartridge case containing the bagged charge). The following projectiles can be fired at a maximum rate of 16 rounds per minute for a short period: HE projectile weighing 15 kg (33.1 lb) with a muzzle velocity of 570 m (1,870 ft) per second, smoke projectile weighing 15.8 kg (34.8 lb), armour-piercing tracer, and high-explosive squash head tracer (HESH-T). The HESH-T projectile weighs 10 kg (22.05 lb), and when it hits an armoured vehicle the 2.2 kg (4.85 lb) of explosive flattens itself against the armour before exploding, when it can penetrate up to 100 mm (3.9 in) of armour plate at an angle of 30°.

An unusual feature of the M-56 is that in an emergency it can be fired before the trails are spread, although in this case total traverse is limited to 16° and elevation to +16°. The M-56 has a crew of 11 men and is normally towed by a TAM 1500 (4x4) truck. It was initially thought to be in service only with the Yugoslav army and its antecedents, but some have been observed in El Salvador, in this instance towed by American 2½-ton (6x6) trucks, and also in Cyprus. Further examples of the M-56 were exported to Iraq, these weapons seeing action during the 1990 Iraqi invasion of Kuwait and the ensuing Operation Desert Storm. The M-56 howitzer was also widely

Seen in service with El Salvador, the M-56 105-mm howitzer bears a strong resemblance to the US 105-mm M101 howitzer that was supplied to Yugoslavia in the years after World War II. The M56, however, is fitted with a larger shield and has a multi-baffle muzzle brake.

used by various warring parties during the Yugoslavian civil wars of the 1990s, for example in the three-month bombardment of the Croatian city of Dubrovnik by Yugoslavian army forces in 1991, and also during the bloody siege of Sarajevo that ran between 1992 and 1996.

SPECIFICATION	
M-56	m (7 ft 0.6 in); height, travelling
Calibre: 105 mm (4.13 in)	1.56 m (5 ft 1.4 in)
Weight: travelling 2100 kg (4,630 lb)	**Elevation:** +68°/-12°
and firing 2060 kg (4,541 lb)	**Traverse:** total 52°
Dimensions: length, travelling 6.17	**Maximum range:** 13000 m (14,215
m (20 ft 3 in); width, travelling 2.15	yards)

Mk 61 105-mm self-propelled howitzer

The development of the AMX-13 light tank by the Atelier de Construction d'Issy-les-Moulineaux during the late 1940s laid the basis for one of the largest families of tracked vehicles ever developed. At an early stage the French army issued a requirement for a 105-mm (4.13-mm) self-propelled howitzer, and it was decided to base this **Mk 61** equipment on a modified AMX-13 tank chassis. After trials with prototype vehicles, the equipment was placed in production at the Atelier de Construction Roanne in the late 1950s under the designation **Obusier de 105 Modèle 50 sur Affût Automoteur** for the French army. The type was later supported by Creusot-Loire (now GIAT) after this company had taken over responsibility for the AMX-13 and its derivatives.

In addition to being used by the French army, the Mk 61 was also purchased by Israel, Morocco and the Netherlands, the equipments for the last having a longer L/30 barrel. The first to phase the type out of service was Israel, where the Mk 61 was replaced by the 155-mm (6.1-in) M109A1; in the French army it was replaced by the 155-mm GCT self-propelled weapon.

The vehicle was of all-welded steel construction providing the crew with protection from small arms fire and shell splinters. The engine and transmission were at the front, the driver on the left side and the fully enclosed gun compartment at the rear. Access hatches were provided in the roof and rear, and the

commander had a cupola with periscopes for all-round observation. The suspension was of the well-proven torsion-bar type, and on each side comprised five rubber-tyred road wheels and three track-return rollers, together with the drive sprocket at the front and the idler at the rear. Hydraulic shock absorbers were fitted at the first and last road wheel stations. The tracks were steel, but could be fitted with rubber pads to reduce damage to the road surface.

Ordnance details
The 105-mm howitzer had a double-baffle muzzle-brake, and could be elevated between -4° 30' and +66°, while traverse was 20° left and right; elevation and traverse were both manual. Various types of separate-loading ammunition could be fired, including an HE projectile weighing 16 kg (35.3 lb) to a maximum range of 15000 m (16,405 yards) and a HEAT projectile which could

penetrate 350 mm (13.8 in) of armour at an incidence of 0°, or 105 mm (4.13 in) of armour at 65°. A total of 56 rounds of ammunition was carried, and of these six were normally HEAT rounds. A 7.62- or 7.5-mm (0.3- or 0.295-in) machine-gun was mounted externally on the roof for AA defence; a similar weapon was carried inside the vehicle for use in the ground role; 2,000 rounds of ammunition were carried for these weapons.

The Mk 61 did not have an NBC system, and lacked any amphibious capability. Another drawback was the limited traverse of the Mk 61's ordnance. There appeared prototypes,

The Mk 61 was based on the AMX-13 light tank chassis. The lack of a true turret and fitting of a medium-calibre gun soon rendered the type obsolete.

some of them purchased by Switzerland, of a similar vehicle with a turret that could be traversed through 360°. By the time the turret version was ready most countries had decided to replace their 105-mm equipments with more effective 155-mm weapons. The Mk 61's chassis was also used for prototype trials with the Roland SAM system and also as a motorised minelayer.

SPECIFICATION	
Mk 61	(250 hp)
Crew: 5	**Performance:** speed 60 km/h
Weight: 16500 kg (36,375 lb)	(37 mph); range 350 km (217
Dimensions: length 5.7 m (18 ft 8.4	miles)
in); width 2.65 m (8 ft 8.3 in);	**Gradient:** 60 per cent
height 2.7 m (8 ft 10.3 in)	**Vertical obstacle:** 0.65 (2 ft 2 in)
Powerplant: one SOFAM 8Gxb	**Trench:** 1.6 m (5 ft 3 in)
petrol engine delivering 186 kW	

Mk F3 155-mm self-propelled gun

In the period immediately after World War II the standard self-propelled howitzer of the French army was the US 155-mm (6.1-in) M41 Howitzer Motor Carriage, essentially the M24 Chaffee light tank chassis fitted

with a slightly modified version of the standard M114 towed howitzer. This was replaced in the 1960s by the 155-mm **Mk F3** self-propelled gun, which is basically a shortened AMX-13 light tank chassis with a

155-mm gun, based on the Modèle 50 towed weapon, mounted at the rear of the hull. In addition to deliveries to the French army, which knew the type as the **Canon de 155 mm Modèle F3 Automoteur** and

replaced it with the 155-mm GCT in the 1980s, the Mk F3 was also sold to Argentina, Chile, Cyprus, Ecuador, Kuwait, Morocco, Peru, Qatar, Sudan, the United Arab Emirates and Venezuela.

The Mk F3 155-mm self-propelled gun in the firing position with the two rear-mounted spades lowered to stabilise the system. The total lack of gun and crew protection is self evident.

Production of the Mk F3, along with other members of the AMX-13 light tank family, was originally undertaken at the Atelier de Construction Roanne, a French government facility. As this plant tooled up for production of the AMX-30 family of MBTs and other vehicles and also of the AMX-10P family, however, production of the whole AMX-13 family, including the Mk F3, was transferred to Creusot-Loire at Châlon-sur-Saône, now part of GIAT, which still supports the series.

Gun elevation

The 155-mm ordnance is mounted at the very rear of the manual. When travelling, the ordnance is held in a travel lock and traversed 8° to the right. The L/33 barrel has a double-baffle muzzle-brake and a screw breech mechanism.

The ammunition is of the separate-loading type, and the following can be fired: HE with a maximum range of just over 20000 m (21,875 yards), illuminating and smoke to a range of 17750 m (19,410 yards) and a rocket-assisted projectile to range of 25330 m (27,670 yards). The rate of fire for the first few minutes is three rounds per minute, but when the Mk F3 is used in the sustained-fire role the rate is one round a minute.

A major disadvantage of the Mk F3, in addition to the total lack of protection for the gun and its crew, is that only the driver and commander can be carried in the actual vehicle. The other members of the gun crew are carried in an AMX VCA (Véhicule Chenillé d'Accompagnement, or tracked support vehicle) or a 6x6 truck which also carries 25 projectiles, charges and associated fuses. The VCA can also tow a 2-tonne F2 ammunition trailer carrying an additional 30 projectiles and charges.

The Mk F3 can ford to a depth of 1 m (3 ft 3 in) but has no NBC system; active or passive night-vision equipment can be installed and all vehicles have direct and indirect sights, and a loudspeaker and cable. The basic vehicle is powered by a petrol engine, but in many examples has been replaced by a General Motors Detroit Diesel 6V-53T delivering 209 kW (280 hp). This produces a slightly higher road speed and an increase in operational range from 300 to 400 km (185 to 250 miles).

Left: In 2003, the Mk F3 remained in service with 11 nations, the most recent deliveries being made from French stocks to the largest operator, Morocco, in 1997.

chassis and can be elevated from 0° to +67°, with a traverse of 20° left and right up to an elevation of +50° and of 16° left and 30° right from +57° upward. Elevation and traverse are both

Before firing commences two spades are manually released at the rear of the hull and the vehicle then reversed backward onto them to create a more stable firing platform.

SPECIFICATION	
Mk F3	**Powerplant:** one 186-kW (250-hp)
Crew: 2	SOFAM 8Gxb petrol engine
Weight: 17400 kg (38,360 lb)	**Performance:** speed 60 km/h
Dimensions: length (gun forward)	(37 mph); range 300 km (185
6.22 m (20 ft 5 in); width 2.72 m	miles)
(8 ft 11 in); height 2.085 m (6 ft	**Gradient:** 40 per cent
10 in)	**Vertical obstacle:** 0.6 m (2 ft)
	Trench: 1.5 m (4 ft 11 in)

Developed in the 1950s, the Mk F3 can fire a range of ammunition, including the Mk 56 HE projectile, smoke and illuminating shells and the M107 round.

Israeli self-propelled artillery M-50, L33, Romach and Doher

In the 1950s Israel used many types of towed artillery weapons to support their mechanised units, but found that such weapons could not keep up with these highly mobile forces when they deployed to the desert, where roads were non-existent. Despite the fact that they felt, as did most members of NATO at that time, that the 155-mm (6.1-in) projectile was much more effective than the 105-mm (4.13-in) shell because of the former's greater HE payload, Israel bought quantities of the US World War II Priest and French Mk 61 105-mm self-propelled howitzers.

Service

The first self-propelled weapon of 155-mm calibre to enter service with the Israeli army was the **M-50** developed in France by the Etablissement d'Etudes et Fabrications d'Armement de Bourges for a service debut in 1963. This system was essentially a Sherman tank chassis rebuilt with the engine moved forward to the right of the driver to make it possible for a French Modèle 50 howitzer, already used by Israel in its towed form, to be mounted in an open-topped compartment at the rear of the hull.

When the vehicle was deployed in action, the two doors opened to each side of the hull rear revealing horizontal ammunition racks, and a tailgate folded down to provide space for the crew to operate the howitzer. Additional ammunition storage space was provided under the mount, and external stowage compartments were provided in each side of the hull. The howitzer fired a 43-kg (95-lb) HE projectile to a maximum range of 17600 m (19,250 yards). The howitzer's maximum elevation was +69°, but the traverse was very limited. The M-50 had a crew of eight and weighed 31000 kg (68,340 lb) fully loaded. The main drawback of the system, which was used for the first time in the 1967 Six-Day War, was the lack of any overhead protection for the crew.

The M-50 was followed in Israeli service by the **L33** (named after the length of the ordnance in calibres), which was developed in Israel by Soltam, and this saw action for the first time in the 1973 Yom Kippur War. This is based on the M4A3E8 Sherman chassis, which has HVSS (Horizontal Volute Spring Suspension) rather than the VVSS (Vertical Volute Spring Suspension) of the M-50 and gives a much improved ride across country. The original petrol engine has since been replaced by a Cummins diesel which

The crew of a 155-mm (6.1-in) L33 man their vehicle during an exercise. Based on the M4A3 tank chassis, the L33 was extensively used in combat during the 1973 Arab-Israeli War and incorporates the armament of the M-68 towed gun/howitzer system.

SPECIFICATION	
Soltam L33	**Powerplant:** one Cummins VT
Crew: 8	8-460-Bi liquid-cooled diesel
Weight: 41500 kg (91,490 lb)	delivering 343 kW (460 hp)
Dimensions: length (gun forward)	**Performance:** maximum road speed
8.47 m (27 ft 9.5 in) and (hull)	36.8 km/h (23 mph); maximum
6.47 m (21 ft 2.7 in); width 3.5 m	range 260 km (162 miles)
(11 ft 6 in); height 3.45 m (11 ft	**Gradient:** 60 per cent
3.8 in)	**Vertical obstacle:** 0.91 m (3 ft)
	Trench: 2.3 m (7 ft 6.6 in)

offers a much increased operational range.

Proven ordnance

The 155-mm M-68 gun/howitzer is almost identical to the standard towed weapon, and is mounted in the forward part of the superstructure with an elevation arc between -3° and +52°, and traverse 30° left and right. Weapon elevation and traverse are manual. The ordnance has a single-baffle muzzle-brake, a fume extractor, a barrel travel lock and a horizontal sliding semi-automatic breech block.

Powered rammer

To assist in maintaining a high rate of fire and in loading the ordnance at any angle of elevation, a pneumatic rammer is installed. The weapon fires the 43-kg HE projectile to a range of 21000m (22,965 yards) at maximum charge; smoke and illuminating projectiles can also

The first 155-mm (6.1-in) self-propelled gun to enter service with the IDF was the M-50. This entered service in 1963 and first saw action in the Six-Day War of 1967.

be fired. A total of 60 projectiles and charges is carried, 16 of which are for ready use. A 7.62-mm (0.3-in) machine gun is roof-mounted for local and anti-aircraft defence.

The hull is of all-welded steel construction and protects the crew from small arms fire and shell splinters. Entry doors are provided on each side of the

hull, and ammunition resupply doors are fitted in the hull rear; ammunition can be loaded via these doors when the weapon is still firing. The driver is seated at the front on the left with the commander to his rear, and the machine-gunner is in a similar position on the opposite side: each of these crew members is provided with a roof hatch and

bulletproof windows to their front and side for observation.

Unlike the earlier M-50 conversion, which entailed moving the engine forward, the L33 has its engine at the rear, power being transmitted to the transmission at the front by a two-part propeller shaft.

Israel also operates two US self-propelled artillery systems,

the 175-mm (6.9-in) M107 gun and 155-mm M109 howitzer, and has upgraded many of these equipments to the **Romach** and **Doher** standards, respectively. The former fires a locally-designed Extended Range Sub Calibre Mk 7 Mod 7 projectile to a range of 40 km (24.9 miles) and carries an extra 7.62-mm machine gun.

ASU-57 Airborne self-propelled anti-tank gun

An ASU-57 airborne self-propelled anti-tank gun, armed with a 57-mm (2.24-in) Ch-51M gun with a double-baffle muzzle brake. For many years this was the main self-propelled anti-tank gun of the Soviet airborne divisions but it was replaced by the ASU-85, which had a bigger gun and much improved armour protection.

The **ASU-57** (ASU being the Soviet designation for airborne assault gun and 57 for the calibre of the gun) was developed in the 1950s specifically for use by the Soviet airborne divisions and was seen in public for the first time during a parade held in Red Square, Moscow, during 1957. The gun itself was a development of the World War II ZIS-2 (M1943) anti-tank gun while the engine was from the Pobeda civilian car.

Limited protection

The hull of the ASU-57 was of welded aluminium construction with a uniform thickness of only 6 mm (0.24 in), making it very

vulnerable. The engine was at the front on the right with the cooling system on the left and transmission at the very front. The open-topped crew compartment was at the rear with the driver and loader on the right, and the commander, who also acted as the gunner, on the left. Forward of the driver and commander was an armoured flap which contained two vision blocks; when the vehicle was not in the combat area this flap could be folded forwards to provide improved vision. The top of the ASU-57 could be covered by a tarpaulin cover, and an unditching beam was often carried at the rear, the latter

being a common feature on Soviet armoured vehicles.

The torsion-bar suspension consisted of four single rubber-tyred road wheels with the drive sprocket at the front and the fourth road wheel acting as the idler; there were two track-return rollers. The ASU-57 could ford to a depth of 0.7 m (28 in), but had no NBC protection system.

The vehicle was armed with a Ch-51 or Ch-51M rifled gun offset slightly from the vehicle's centreline. The Ch-51 was the first model to enter service and had a long barrel with a multi-slotted muzzle brake. This was followed by the Ch-51M, which had a shorter barrel fitted with a

double-baffle muzzle brake. Both weapons had a vertical sliding breech-block and hydro-spring recoil system, and fired the following types of fixed ammunition: HE fragmentation (muzzle velocity 695 m/2,280 ft per second), AP-T (muzzle velocity 980 m/3,215 ft per second and capable of penetrating 85 mm/3.35 in of armour at 0° at a range of 1000 m/1,094 yards), and HVAP (capable of penetrating 100 mm/3.94 in of armour at 0° at a similar range). A total of 30 rounds of ammunition was carried, and it was estimated that a well-trained crew could fire a maximum of 10 rounds per minute. The gun

An ASU-57 advances across the snow while in the background an 85-mm (3.35-in) auxiliary propelled anti-tank gun is positioned. Note the unditching beam carried on the left side of the hull of the ASU-57, and the driver's head in an exposed position.

had manual elevation and traverse, the former being from -5° to +12°, and the latter 8° left and 8° right. The vehicle was often used to carry four paratroops, and a 7.62-mm (0.3-in) machine gun was carried. This could be dismounted for use in the ground role.

Deployment

Each Soviet airborne division had three rifle regiments, and each of these had one battalion each with three six-gun batteries with

ASU-57s, giving the division a total of 54 such weapons. In the USSR the ASU-57 was used for training after it has been replaced in front-line use by the ASU-85, which not only had a more powerful gun but also much improved armour protection.

It is interesting to note that the ASU-57 was developed at roughly the same time as the American M56 self-propelled anti-tank gun with its 90-mm (3.54-in) gun.

SPECIFICATION	
ASU-57 (with Ch-51M gun)	**Powerplant:** one 41-kW (55-hp) M-20E 4-cylinder petrol engine
Crew: 3	**Performance:** maximum road speed
Weight: 3.35 tonnes	45 km/h (28 mph); maximum road
Dimensions: overall length 4.995 m	range 250 km (155 miles)
(16 ft 4.7 in); hull length 3.48 m (11	**Gradient:** 60 per cent
ft 5 in); width 2.086 m (6 ft 10 in);	**Vertical obstacle:** 0.5 m (20 in)
height 1.18 m (3 ft 10.5 in)	**Trench:** 1.4 m (4 ft 7 in)

When introduced, the ASU-57 was packed in a special container and two of these could be carried under a Tupolev Tu-4 transport, one under each wing. On the Antonov An-12

introduced in the late 1950s, two ASU-57s could be carried nternally on individual pallets. The pallets were provided with parachutes and a retro-rocket system to soften the landing.

ASU-85 Airborne self-propelled anti-tank gun

Soviet ASU-85s parade through Moscow. The ASU-85 was not widely exported, but saw action during the 1968 occupation of Czechoslovakia.

For many years the standard self-propelled anti-tank gun of the Soviet airborne division was the ASU-57. This weighed only 3.35 tonnes and was armed with a long-barrel 57-mm (2.24-in) gun. In addition to the lack of penetration provided by the 57-mm ammunition, the ASU-57 had very thin armour protection and the crew compartment was not provided with any serious overhead protection.

ASU-57 successor

In the late 1950s the more capable **ASU-85** self-propelled anti-tank gun was developed and this entered service with the Soviet airborne divisions in 1960 and also saw service with Poland. Compared to the older ASU-57, the ASU-85 had improved armour, firepower and mobility. The 85-mm (3.35-in) SD-44 gun was mounted in a well-sloped glacis plate with a total traverse of 12° and with

elevation from -4° to +15°; traverse and elevation were manual. The gun fired fixed-type ammunition including HE armour-piercing and HVAP; a total of 40 rounds of ammunition was carried. A 7.62-mm (0.3-in) PKT machine gun was mounted co-axially. Some vehicles were also fitted with a roof-mounted 12.7-mm (0.5-in) DShKM machine gun for air defence purposes.

The hull of the ASU-85 was of all-welded steel armour with the highest level of protection over the frontal arc. The vehicle could be carried inside a tactical transport aircraft such as the An-12, and could be

A column of ASU-85 self-propelled guns is seen on the move while on exercise, with local air defence provided by 14.5-mm (0.57-in) ZPU-1 anti-aircraft guns.

dropped by parachute. Standard equipment included night-vision devices, and additional fuel drums were normally mounted on the hull rear to extend the operational range of the vehicle. The ASU-85 was phased out of Soviet military service without

a direct replacement, and the airborne units' long-range anti-tank warfare capability was subsequently entrusted to anti-tank guided missile systems and the gun- and missile-armed BMD series of vehicles.

SPECIFICATION	
ASU-85	developing 179 kW (240 hp)
Crew: 4	**Performance:** maximum road speed
Weight: 15.6 tonnes	45 km/h (28 mph); maximum road
Dimensions: overall length 8.49 m	range 260 km (162 miles)
(27 ft 10.2 in); hull length 6 m (19 ft	**Fording:** 1.1 m (3 ft 7 in)
8 in); width 2.8 m (9 ft 2.2 in);	**Gradient:** 70 per cent
height 2.1 m (6 ft 10.7 in)	**Vertical obstacle:** 1.1 m (3 ft 7 in)
Powerplant: one V-6 diesel engine	**Trench:** 2.6 m (8 ft 6 in)

SU-100 Tank destroyer

During World War II, the Soviets developed a number of tank destroyers based on tank chassis. These included the SU-85 and **SU-100** based on the T-34, and the SU-152 based on the KV heavy tank chassis. These were quicker and easier to produce than tanks and were built in large numbers.

The SU-85 and SU-100 were very similar in appearance with the main difference being in the calibre of the weapon: 85 mm (3.35 in) for the SU-85 and 100 mm (3.94 in) for the SU-100. The SU-100's fighting compartment was at the front of the vehicle with the main D-10S armament carried in a ball-type mount in the front of the well-sloped hull and with limited manual traverse and elevation.

The SU-100 carried a total of 34 rounds of main-gun ammunition, with the HE armour-piercing projectile capable of penetrating over

180 mm (0.7 in) of armour at a range of 1000 m (1,904 yards). Other types of ammunition that could be fired included OF-412 HE fragmentation projectiles.

Wartime use

Used in combat for the first time in Hungary in January 1945, the prime role of the

The SU-100 was similar in configuration to the T-34, sharing almost 75 per cent of its components. Although based on a common hull, the frontal armour of the SU-100 was increased from 45 mm (1.77 in) to 75 mm (2.95 in) compared to the earlier SU-85.

SU-100 was to engage enemy tanks but it could also be used in the direct fire support role which proved very useful in urban fighting towards the end of World War II.

By the end of the war some 3,037 SU-100 tank destroyers had been built and in the post-war period large numbers of these weapons were exported, especially to the Middle East where some of these saw action with Egypt and Syria. The SU-100 remained in service

within the armies of most of the members of the Warsaw Pact for many years after the end of the war and was also manufactured in Czechoslovakia during the 1950s. In mid-2004, SU-100s remained in service in a few countries.

When eventually withdrawn from front-line service with the Soviet army, many SU-85 and SU-100 assault guns were converted into armoured recovery vehicles. Some SU-100s were also used in the command post role for which they were fitted with additional communications equipment.

SPECIFICATION	
SU-100	**Performance:** maximum road speed
Crew: 4	55 km/h (34 mph); maximum road
Weight: 31.6 tonnes	range 300 km (186 miles)
Dimensions: overall length 9.45 m	**Fording:** 1.3 m (4 ft 3 in)
(31 ft); hull length 6.19 m (20 ft	**Gradient:** 60 per cent
3.7 in); width 3.05 m (10 ft); height	**Vertical obstacle:** 0.73 m (29 in)
2.245 m (7 ft 4.4 in)	**Trench:** 2.5 m (8 ft 2 in)
Powerplant: one V-2-34M diesel	
developing 388 kW (520 hp)	

The SU-100 tank destroyer began to enter service in December 1944 and remained in Warsaw Pact use until the late 1970s. Meanwhile, the type also saw action during wars in the Middle East and Angola.

M50 Ontos Tank destroyer

In the early 1950s the US Marine Corps issued a requirement for a highly mobile tank destroyer, and in October 1951 authorisation was given for the building of no less than five prototype vehicles, all of which had various numbers of recoilless rifles as their main armament. These were built and tested, and in February 1953 approval was given for the procurement of 24 examples of the **T165**, which was armed with six 106-mm (4.2-in) recoilless rifles. Trials with the

Below: The M50's six recoilless rifles had a maximum effective range of around 1095 m (1,200 yards) but could reach targets at a distance of up to 6860 m (7,500 yards).

Above: The M50 Ontos tank destroyer as used by the US Marine Corps. Note the 0.5-in (12.7-mm) spotting rifles above the top four 106-mm (4.2-in) recoilless rifles. The crew had to leave the vehicle to reload the latter.

first of these vehicles showed that some work was required with the mounting, fire-control system and suspension. The remaining vehicles were built to a slightly modified design and designated the **T165E2**. Following trials with the latter vehicles, and more modifications, the vehicle was finally accepted for service with the US Marine Corps and in 1955 was standardised as the **Rifle, Multiple, 106-mm Self-Propelled, M50** or, as it was normally called, the **Ontos** (Greek for 'the thing'). In August 1955 Allis Chalmers was awarded a production contract for 297 vehicles, all of which had been completed by November 1957. At a later date it was decided to replace the original General Motors petrol engine with a Chrysler petrol engine developing 134 kW (180 hp) and subsequently, in June 1963, the original manufacturer was awarded a contract to rebuild 294 M50 vehicles to this new configuration, known as the **M50A1**; at the same time a number of other minor improvements were made to the vehicle.

Ontos in combat

The M50 was used in South Vietnam and in the Dominican Republic, but it was retired from service with the US Marine Corps without a direct replacement, although ground- and vehicle-launched TOW ATGWs carry out a similar function. The vehicle was armed with six M40A1C recoilless rifles

mounted on a common mount at the rear of the hull. These had a traverse of 40° left and right with an elevation of +20° and a depression of –10°, elevation and traverse all being manual. The top four recoilless rifles were fitted with a 0.5-in (12.7-mm) M8C spotting rifle: the weapons were first lined up with the optical sight and the spotting rifle was then fired, a hit on the target being indicated by a puff of smoke, whereupon the gunner knew that the recoilless rife was correctly aligned with the target. One or more of the recoilless rifles could be fired, the maximum effective range being about 1095 m (1,200 yards), although maximum range

was more than 6860 m (7,500 yards). The ammunition was of the fixed type and included HEAT and HEP-T (high explosive plastic tracer), the latter type being known as HESH in British service. Totals of 18 rounds of 106-mm and 80 rounds of spotting ammunition were carried. In addition a 0.3-in (7.62-mm) M1919A4 machine-gun was fitted above the mount for local protection.

The driver was seated at the front of the hull on the left, with the engine to his right and the very cramped crew compart-ment at the rear; entry to the last was effected via two doors

An M50 Ontos is seen here in action in South Vietnam, providing a good view of the vehicle's potent arrangement of 106-mm recoilless rifles.

in the hull rear. The engine was coupled to a General Motors Corporation (Allison Division) XT-90-2 cross drive transmission that delivered power to the drive sprockets at the front of the hull.

The M50's chassis was also used for a number of experimental vehicles but none of these, including several armoured/infantry carriers, entered production or service.

SPECIFICATION	
M50 Ontos	**Performance:** maximum road speed
Crew: 3	48 km/h (30 mph); maximum range
Weight: 8640 kg (19,050 lb)	240 km (150 miles)
Dimensions: length 3.82 m (12 ft 6	**Gradient:** 60 per cent
in); width 2.6 m (8 ft 6 in); height	**Vertical obstacle:** 0.762 m (30 in)
2.13 m (6 ft 11 in)	**Trench:** 1.42 m (4 ft 8 in)
Powerplant: one 108-kW (145-hp)	
GMC Model 302 petrol engine	

M56 Scorpion 90-mm airborne self-propelled anti-tank gun

The M56 90-mm (3.54-in) self-propelled anti-tank gun, or Scorpion, was created specifically for the US 82nd and 101st Airborne Divisions. Its main drawback was the lack of armour protection, apart from the small shield, for the gun crew.

Apart from hand-held weapons, the most important anti-tank weapon used by US airborne forces in World War II was the Jeep-towed 57-mm (2.24-in) M1 anti-tank gun, which was essentially the British 6-pdr made in the United States. After the war a requirement was issued for a highly mobile self-propelled anti-tank gun that could be air-dropped by

parachute during the initial phases of any airborne opera-tion and have a firepower similar to that of a tank. Two prototypes of a vehicle called the **T101** were built by the Cadillac Motor Car Division of the General Motors Corporation. Further develop-ment resulted in the improved **T101E1** which was eventually standardised as the **Gun, Anti-**

tank, Self-Propelled, 90-mm M56, or more commonly the **Scorpion**. Production was undertaken by the Cadillac Motor Car Division between 1953 and 1959. In the US Army the M56 was issued only to the 82nd and 101st Airborne Divisions, but was replaced in the 1960s by the M551 Sheridan Armored Reconnaissance/Airborne

Assault Vehicle. A few M56s were supplied to Spain and Morocco, and some were also deployed by the US Army to Vietnam, where they were used mainly in the fire-support role.

The hull of the M56 was of welded and riveted aluminium construction, with the engine and transmission at the front, gun in the centre and the crew

One of the T101 prototypes for the M56 is seen shortly after the 90-mm gun has fired, showing the gun recoiling to the rear and the forward part of the chassis lifting clear of the ground. The dust often obscured the gunner's line of sight for the next shot.

area at the rear. The engine was coupled to a General Motors Corporation (Allison Division) transmission with one reverse and two forward ranges which in turn supplied power to the final drives on each side. The suspension was of the torsion-bar type with four rubber-tyred road wheels, the idler at the rear and the drive sprocket at the front; there were no track-return rollers. The track consisted of a steel-reinforced endless rubber band.

Muzzle brake

The main armament was a 90-mm (3.54-in) M54 gun fitted with a muzzle brake and a vertical sliding breech block. Manually controlled, the gun had an elevation of +15° and depression of -10°, and a traverse of 30° left and right. A total of 29 rounds of fixed ammunition was carried under and to the rear of the gun; AP-T, APC-T, HE-T, HEAT, HEAT-T, HEP-T, WP, TP-T, HVAP-T and HVTP-T rounds could be fired. The main drawback of the M56, which had much better

firepower than the M41 light tank with its 76-mm (3-in) gun, was that the chassis was too light and when the 90-mm gun was fired the vehicle often moved several feet and the target was obscured by dust from the muzzle blast.

Another drawback was the complete lack of armour protection for the crew, apart from the very small shield. The driver, who was equipped with a steering wheel, was seated to the left of the gun with the gunner to the rear; the latter was provided with a sight with a magnification of x4.1 or x8. A box on the left-hand side of the driver's station held the vehicle's radio. The commander sat on top of the radio. The other two and unluckier members of the crew were positioned on the right-hand side of the vehicle, near the exhaust pipe which was situated opposite their station.

The chassis of the M56 was also used as the basis for a number of other vehicles including an armoured personnel carrier with a much higher superstructure incorporating a rear troop compartment, 81-mm (3.2-in) and 107-mm (4.2-in) self-propelled mortar carriers, a 106-mm (4.17-in) M40 recoilless anti-tank gun carrier, a missile launcher and an anti-aircraft vehicle fitted with four 0.5-in (12.7-mm) M2HB machine-guns; none of these entered production.

SPECIFICATION	
M56 Scorpion	149 kW (200 bhp)
Crew: 4	**Performance:** maximum road speed
Weight: 7030 kg (15,500 lb)	45 km/h (28 mph); maximum road
Dimensions: length (including gun)	range 225 km (140 miles)
5.841 m (19 ft 2 in) and (hull)	**Gradient:** 60 per cent
4.555 m (14 ft 1 in); width 2.577 m	**Vertical obstacle:** 0.762 m (30 in)
(8 ft 5 in); height 2.067 m (6 ft 9 in)	**Trench:** 1.524 m (5 ft)
Powerplant: one Continental	
6-cylinder petrol engine developing	

M107 175-mm self-propelled gun

In the 1950s the standard 203-mm (8-in) self-propelled howitzer of the US Army was the M55, which had the chassis and turret of the M53 155-mm (6.1-in) self-propelled gun. The main drawbacks of both these weapons were that at a weight of about 45 tons they were too heavy for air transport and their petrol engines gave them an operating range of only 260 km (160 miles). In the mid-1950s a

decision was taken to design a new family of self-propelled artillery that would share a common chassis and mount, be air-portable, and come into and be taken out of action quickly. Prototypes were built by the Pacific Car and Foundry Company as the **T235** 175-mm (6.89-in) self-propelled gun, T236 203-mm self-propelled howitzer, and T245 155-mm self-propelled gun. Further development,

including the replacement of the petrol engines by diesels for increased operational range, resulted in the T235 being

standardised as the **M107** and the T236 as the M110. The chassis of the family was also used as the basis for a number

SPECIFICATION	
M107	**Powerplant:** one 302-kW (405-hp)
Crew: 5+8	Detroit Diesel Model 8V-71T diesel
Weight: 28168 kg (57,690 lb)	**Performance:** maximum road speed
Dimensions: length (gun forward)	56 km/h (35 mph); maximum range
11.256 m (36 ft 7 in) and (hull)	725 km (450 miles)
5.72 m (18 ft 9 in); width 3.149 m	**Gradient:** 60 per cent
(10 ft 4 in); height 3.679 m (12 ft)	**Vertical obstacle:** 1.016 m (3 ft 4 in)
	Trench: 2.326 m (7 ft 9 in)

A US Army M107 in travelling order. All of these vehicles were subsequently converted to the M110A2 configuration by replacing the 175-mm (6.89-in) main gun.

of armoured recovery vehicles (ARVs), but only the T120E1 was placed in production as the M578 light ARV; this has served with many countries including the United States.

Production of the M107 was undertaken initially by the Pacific Car and Foundry Company; the first vehicles were completed in 1962, with the first battalion forming at Fort Sill (home of the US Field Artillery) in early 1963. At a later date production was also undertaken by FMC, and between 1965 and 1980 by Bowen-McLaughlin-York.

The US Army deployed the 175-mm M107 in 12-gun battalions at corps level but all of these weapons were later converted to the 203-mm M110A2 configuration as this could fire the somewhat heavier 203-mm HERA (HE rocket assisted) round to a range only slightly reduced to just over 29000 m (31,715 yards). The M107 was exported to Greece, Iran, Israel, Italy, South Korea, the Nether-lands, Spain, Turkey, the UK and West Germany; many of these countries also converted their M107s to the M110A2 configuration.

The chassis of the M107 is fully described in the entry for the M110. The 175-mm gun had an elevation of +65° and a depression of -2°, and the traverse was 30° left and right. Traverse and elevation were powered, with manual controls provided for emergency use. Only one round was ever standardised for US Army use – the M437A1 or M437A2 HE type which, with a charge three propellant, had a maximum range of 32700 m (35,760 yards), although a special round was used by Israel with a range of some 40000 m (43,745 yards). To assist the crew in loading the 66.78-kg (147-lb) projectile, a rammer and loader assembly was mounted at the rear of the chassis. This lifted the projectile from the ground and then rammed it into the chamber. The charge was loaded and the ordnance fired. Only two projectiles and charges were carried on the M107, which had a crew of 13, of whom five (driver, commander and three gunners) travelled on the M107. The remainder were carried in the M548 tracked cargo carrier that carried the bulk of the ammunition. Some countries used 6x6 trucks to support the M107, but often these offered poor cross-country mobility.

An M107. This weapon was deployed throughout the NATO area, and fired a 66.78-kg (147-lb) HE shell at a muzzle velocity of 914 m (2,998 ft) per second. The M107 was also used to provide long-range fire support from up to 30 km (18.6 miles) during the Vietnam War.

2S1 Gvozdika (M1974) 122-mm self-propelled howitzer

In the period after World War II the Soviet Union placed its main emphasis on the continuing development of towed artillery whereas NATO emphasised self-propelled weapons. Although the latter are much more expensive to build, maintain and operate they do have many advantages over their towed counterparts, including increased cross-country mobility, full armour protection for the crew and ammunition, the possibility of an NBC system, and a reduction in the time necessary for the equipment to be brought into and taken out of action. The Soviet Union did continue to develop specialised tank destroyers, but it was not until 1974 that the first 122-mm (4.8-in) self-propelled howitzer made its appearance during a parade in Poland, although it had entered service with the Soviet Union and Poland in 1972. NATO calls this 122-mm (4.8-in) self-propelled howitzer the **M1974**, this being the year when it was first seen, while the Soviet designation is **2S1**. The system has also been used by Algeria, Angola, Bulgaria, Cuba, Czechoslovakia, Ethiopia, East Germany, Finland, Hungary, Iran, Iraq, Libya, Romania, Syria, Toga, Uruguay, Yemen and Yugoslavia and its antecedents. Licensed production took place in Bulgaria and Poland and the type is used by most former Soviet states. In the Soviet army the M1974 was employed on the scale of 36 per motorised rifle division and 72 per tank division.

Configuration

The layout of the M1974 is similar to that of the M109 with the engine, transmission and driver at the front and the fully enclosed turret at the rear. The suspension is adjustable, and consists of seven road wheels with the drive sprocket at the front and the idler at the rear; there are no track-return rollers. When operating in the snow or swampy areas the normal 400-mm (15.75-in) wide tracks can be replaced with 670-mm (26.4-in) wide tracks to reduce the vehicle's ground pressure. Standard equipment includes an NBC system and a full suite of night-vision equipment for the driver and commander. The M1974 is fully amphibious, being propelled in the water by its tracks at a speed of 4.5 km/h (2.8 mph).

The turret is fitted with a modified version of the standard 122-mm D-30 towed howitzer, which has an elevation of +70° and depression of -3°; turret traverse is 360°. Turret traverse and weapon elevation are electric, with manual control for emergency use. The ordnance has a double-baffle muzzle brake, a fume extractor and a semi-automatic vertical sliding breech block; an ordnance travel lock is mounted on top of the hull. The howitzer fires an HE projectile weighing 21.72 kg (47.9 lb) to a maximum range of 15300 m (16,730 yards), and can also fire chemical, illuminating, smoke and HEAT-FS projectiles.

The M1974 received the Soviet designation 2S1 Gvozdika (carnation) and is fully amphibious, unlike the 2S3 Akatsiya. The chassis is also used for the MT-LBus (or Artillery Command and Reconnaissance Vehicle in NATO circles), the MTK-2 mineclearing vehicle, and for the RKhM chemical warfare reconnaissance vehicle. This is a Finnish 2S1.

The last is used to engage tanks and will penetrate 460 mm (18.1 in) of armour at an incidence of 0° at a range of 1000 m (1,095 yards). An HE/RAP round is available, and this has a maximum range of 21900 m (23,950 yards). The 2S1 can also fire the Kitolov-2 laser-guided artillery projectile with a 12000-m (13,123-yard) range. A normal ammunition load consists of 40 projectiles: 32 HE, six smoke and two HEAT-FS. It is believed that a power rammer is fitted to permit a higher rate of fire (five rounds per minute) and also to enable the ordnance to be loaded at any angle of elevation.

The chassis of the M1974 is also used for a large number of armoured command and reconnaissance vehicles (ACRVs) fitted with the artillery/mortar-locating radar, a chemical reconnaissance vehicle and a mine-clearing vehicle.

SPECIFICATION	
2S1 Gvozdika	diesel developing 224 kW (300 hp)
Crew: 4	**Performance:** maximum road speed
Weight: 15700 kg (34,612 lb)	61.5 km/h (38 mph); maximum
Dimensions: length 7.3 m (23 ft 11.4	range 500 km (311 miles)
in); width 2.85 m (9 ft 4 in); height	**Gradient:** 77 per cent
2.4 m (7 ft 10.5 in)	**Vertical obstacle:** 0.7 m (2 ft 3 in)
Powerplant: one YaMZ-238N V-8	**Trench:** 3 m (9 ft 10 in)

2S19 152-mm self-propelled artillery system

The 152-mm (6-in) **2S19** (**MSTA-S**) self-propelled gun was designed to combine the assets of the 2S3 152-mm howitzer and the 2S5 gun into a single self-propelled equipment. The 2S19 therefore combines the long 152-mm ordnance of the 2S5 self-propelled gun with a new hull employing both T-72 and T-80 tank components, with the gun fully enclosed within a large,

steel armour turret mounted over the centre of the hull, the turret having a full 360° traverse.

Under the codename of Ferma (farm) work on the 2S19 began during 1985 at the same Uraltransmash facility at Ekaterinburg that manufactured the 2S5 gun. Initial 2S19 production began at Uraltransmash during 1988 before the production line was

transferred to the Sterlitamak Machine Construction Factory (STEMA) at Bashkiriya. The Soviet army accepted their first examples during 1989 but subsequent production was slow by the usual Soviet standards, with only about 650 having been manufactured by 2002. Belarus and Ukraine also operate the type.

As the 152-mm 2A64 ordnance is the same as that for the 2S5

the ballistic performance remains as before. The maximum range is 24700 m (27,012 yards) with standard 152-mm HE-FRAG projectiles and 28900 m (31,605 yards) with base-bleed HE projectiles. Each standard HE projectile weighs 43.56 kg (96 lb) and the 2S19 can also fire the 50-kg (110-lb) 9K25 Krasnopol laser-guided projectile with a range of 15000 m (16,404 yards).

An advanced onboard land navigation and fire-control system enables each 2S19 to operate as an independent unit should the need arise.

The 2S19 has a crew of five; commander, driver, gunner and two loaders. A further two personnel from a reload vehicle are required when ammunition is fed to the gun from an external source (as is carried out whenever possible to keep the onboard load ready for future use). A hydraulic crane arm is provided to assist this operation and also to reload the turret. All the ammunition stowage and semi-automatic handling systems for 50 projectiles and propellant charges are located within the turret. The ammunition handling capacity is efficient enough to permit burst fire rates of up to eight rounds each minute. For local and air defence a 12.7-mm (0.5-in) heavy machine gun is carried on the turret roof.

High performance

Compared to many earlier self-propelled artillery equipments the 2S19 has excellent performance,

mainly due to the provision of a V-12 diesel power pack capable of delivering 626 kW (840 hp) for a maximum road speed of 60 km/h (37 mph).

From 1993 onwards the Uraltransmash marketing forces made considerable sales efforts to sell the 2S19 for export sales, with no results. Development work is therefore being directed towards a 155-mm (6.1-in) version initially developed for a Russian army requirement but now firing NATO standard projectiles and charges for export operators. Known as the **2S19M1** or **MSTA-S-155**, this export model has a 52-calibre barrel providing a range of 30000 m (32,808 yards) using NATO-standard L15A1 155-mm HE projectiles. Enhanced-range base-bleed projectiles can be expected to achieve 41000 m (44,838 yards) and smart

The 2S19 was developed as a replacement for the 152-mm 2S3 Akatsiya and the 155-mm 2S5 Giatsint artillery and is normally deployed in six-gun batteries.

projectiles including the BONUS can also be fired. It is understood that by early 2003 prototypes

of the 2S19M1 had been completed but had yet to be officially demonstrated.

SPECIFICATION	
2S19	**Performance:** maximum road speed 60
Crew: 5	km/h (37 mph); road range 500 km
Weight: 42000 kg (92,592 lb)	(311 miles)
Dimensions: length 11.9 m (39 ft);	**Fording:** 1.2 m (3 ft 11 in) without
width over skirts 3.58 m (11 ft 9	preparation
in); height 2.985 m (9 ft 9.5 in)	**Gradient:** 47 per cent
Powerplant: One V-84A V-12 diesel	**Vertical obstacle:** 0.5 m (1 ft 7 in)
developing 626 kW (840 hp)	**Trench:** 2.8 m (9 ft 6 in)

2S3 Akatsiya (M1973) 152-mm self-propelled gun/howitzer

Known as the 2S3 Akatsiya (acacia) in Soviet army service, this vehicle forms the basis for a standard chassis design used for other purposes, including the 'Ganef' launcher and the GMZ minelayer.

The **M1973** 152-mm (6-in) self-propelled gun/howitzer was known as the **2S3** in the Soviet Union, and was issued on the scale of 18 per tank division and a similar number per motorised rifle division. The equipment has also been operated by Algeria, Angola, Bulgaria, Cuba, East Germany,

Iraq, Libya, Syria, Vietnam and former Soviet states. Its chassis is a shortened version of that used for the Krug (SA-4 'Ganef') surface-to-air

missile system and GMZ armoured minelayer.

The M1973 has three compartments, that for the driver at the front, that for the engine to its right and that for the turret at the rear, the last being slightly forward of the very rear as it has

such a large overhang. The torsion-bar suspension consists of six road wheels, with a distinct gap between the first and second and the third and fourth road wheels; the drive sprocket is at the front with the idler at the rear, and there are

SPECIFICATION	
2S3 Akatsiya	**Powerplant:** one V-59 V-12 diesel
Crew: 4	developing 388 kW (520 hp)
Weight: 27500 kg (60,626 lb)	**Performance:** maximum road speed
Dimensions: length (gun forward)	60 km/h (37 mph); maximum range
8.4 m (27 ft 6.7 in); length (hull)	500 km (311 miles)
7.8 m (25 ft 7 in); width 3.2 m (10 ft	**Gradient:** 60 per cent
6 in); height 2.8 m (9 ft 2.2 in)	**Vertical obstacle:** 0.7 m (3 ft 7 in)
	Trench: 3 m (9 ft 10 in)

four track-return rollers. The commander's cupola is on the roof of the turret, on the left side, and this is fitted with a 7.62-mm (0.3-in) machine-gun for local and anti-aircraft defence. This is the only hatch in the roof, but there is also a hatch in the right side of the turret. In the hull rear is a large hatch that opens downwards and on each side of this is one circular hatch. These, and the two square openings in the turret rear, are used for the rapid loading of projectiles and fuses.

The ordnance is based on the 152-mm D-20 gun/howitzer but with a bore evacuator, which helps stop fumes from entering the crew compartment when the breech is opened, to the rear of

the double-baffle muzzle-brake. The ordnance fires an HE-FRAG projectile weighing 43.5 kg (95.9 lb) to a maximum range of 18500 m (20,230 yards). Other projectiles that can be fired include HEAT-FS, AP-T, HE-RAP (Rocket-Assisted Projectile with a range of 24000 m/26,245 yards), illuminating, smoke, incendiary, flechette, scatterable anti-tank or anti-personnel mines, the Krasnopol laser-guided projectile and 2-kT tactical nuclear. A total of 45 projectiles and charges is carried, and maximum rate of fire is four rounds per minute. The ordnance has an elevation of +60° and a depression of -4°; turret traverse is 360°.

Unlike the 122-mm (4.8-in) M1974 self-propelled howitzer,

the M1973 does not have amphibious capability, although it can ford to a depth of 1.5 m

(4 ft 11 in). The M1973 is fitted with an NBC system, and with infra-red night-vision equipment.

The 2A33 152-mm gun adopted by the 2S3 is ballistically identical to that used on the D-20 towed artillery piece and shares ammunition commonality.

2S5 Giatsint 152-mm self-propelled gun

The self-propelled gun that was to become the **2S5 Giatsint** (hyacinth) had its design origins during the late 1960s, the prototypes appearing during 1972. Production preparations at what is now the Uraltransmash facility at Ekaterinburg began during 1976, the first examples being delivered to the Soviet army during 1980. The intention was to produce a long-range gun to partner the 2S3 152-mm (6-in) self-propelled gun/howitzer, both sharing the same hull and suspension design. However, the gun installation of the 2S5 was left completely open with no protection for the limited traverse gun and crew. It was probably felt that the long-range capabilities of the gun enabled them to be fired from well to the rear. The maximum range is 28400 m (31,059 yards) with standard 152-mm projectiles and 37000 m (40,464 yards) with HE

projectiles of an advanced aerodynamic form.

The steel hull armour is 15 mm (0.59 in) thick to provide some measure of protection against shell splinters and small arms fire when travelling. For travelling the driver and gun commander are located under armour at the hull front, the commander behind the driver as the 388 kW (520-hp) diesel engine is located to the right of the driver. The other three members of the crew of five travel under armour in a separate compartment at the hull rear.

Into action

Time into and out of action is about three minutes. To bring the gun into action a stabiliser spade is lowered from the hull rear. Some examples have been seen with a front-mounted dozer blade to clear battlefield obstacles or for digging in without specialised engineering support. When

travelling, the long barrel of the 2A37 gun, which is provided with a multi-baffle muzzle brake, is secured in a clamp which has to be released when preparing for firing.

The 2S5 can carry 30 projectiles and charges ready for use, the separate-loading rounds being delivered from a vertical stowage, carousel type magazine to the breech using a conveyor system. Loading and ramming the rounds into the breech are semi-automatic and powered. These arrangements enable up to six rounds to be fired in one minute, the vertical sliding breech opening and ejecting the spent case automatically after each firing. It is claimed that a six-gun 2S5 battery can have 40 projectiles in the air before the first of them impacts on the target area. Each 2S5 artillery battalion has three batteries.

Each standard HE-FRAG projectile weighs 46 kg (101 lb), the propellant charge and case weighing a maximum of 34 kg (75 lb). The 2S5 is one of the equipments that can fire the 9K25 Krasnopol laser-guided projectile.

The 2S5 can be supplied with ammunition either from onboard the rear of the vehicle or from the ground. A total of 30 projectiles and charges are carried in the vehicle.

Production of the 2S5 ceased after just over 2,000 had been manufactured. Sales were made to Finland (18) in 1994 but that was the only export success, the rest of the output being delivered to various states within the old Soviet Union. The 152-mm 2S19 self-propelled gun is now replacing many of those examples remaining in Russian service. However, the 2S5 production line is still in existence as efforts have been made to market it on the open defence market. Further operators of the 2S5 comprise Belarus, Georgia, Ukraine and Uzbekistan.

SPECIFICATION	
2S5 Giatsint	388 kW (520 hp)
Crew: 5	**Performance:** maximum road speed
Weight: 28200 kg (62,170 lb)	63 km/h (39 mph); maximum road
Dimensions: length 8.33 m (27 ft	range 500 km (311 miles)
3.9 in); width 3.25 m (10 ft 8 in);	**Fording:** 1.05 m (3 ft 5 in)
height 2.76 m (9 ft)	**Gradient:** 58 per cent
Powerplant: one V-59 V-12	**Vertical obstacle:** 0.7 m (3 ft 7 in)
supercharged diesel developing	**Trench:** 2.5 m (8 ft 2 in)

Abbot 105-mm self-propelled gun

Used in the Field Regiments of the Royal Artillery, the Abbot was supported by the amphibious 6x6 Alvis Stalwart High Mobility Load Carrier with pre-packed ammunition pallets, and was capable of operating in an NBC environment.

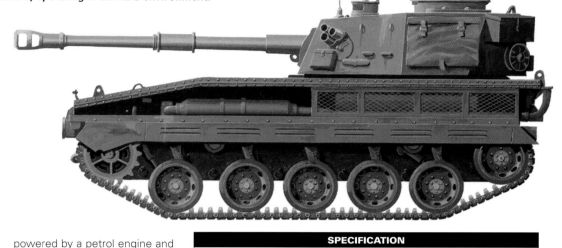

After the end of World War II the standard self-propelled gun of the British Royal Artillery was the 25-pounder Sexton, which was designed and built in Canada. Prototypes of various self-propelled guns were built on a modified Centurion tank chassis, including one with a 25-pounder gun and the other with a 5.5-in (140-mm) gun. By the 1950s these calibres were not standard within NATO, which was standardising on 105-mm (4.13-in) and 155-mm (6.1-in) rounds. To meet the Royal Artillery's immediate requirements for SP weapons of the latter calibre, quantities of American M44 self-propelled howitzers were supplied while development in England concentrated on a 105-mm self-propelled gun which used the engine, transmission and suspension of the FV432 series of APC.

New contract

Vickers of Elswick was awarded a contract to build 12 prototypes, of which six were

Originally planned for replacement in the late 1980s by the abortive SP-70 155-mm (6.1-in) gun, the Abbot was not fitted with the flotation screen during the latter part of its career.

powered by a petrol engine and six by a diesel engine. Following trials with these prototypes the company was awarded a production contract, series ehicles being built between 1964 and 1967. In the British Army the **FV433 Abbot** 105-mm self-propelled gun was used by the Royal Artillery in regiments of three batteries, each battery having eight Abbots. The Abbot was deployed in West Germany with the British Army of the Rhine, while a few served with the Royal School of Artillery at Larkhill, Wiltshire, and at the British Army Training Area in Suffield, Canada. The **Value Engineered Abbot**, which was the basic vehicle without such luxuries as flotation screen, powered traverse, NBC system and night-vision equipment, was produced for India although the British Army also adopted a few.

Armour protection

The hull and turret of the Abbot were of all-welded steel, providing the four-man crew with complete protection from small arms fire and shell splinters. The driver was seated at the front on the left, with the engine to his right. The turret was mounted at the very rear of the hull, with the commander and gunner on the right and the loader on the left. In addition to the commander's cupola and loader's roof hatches a large door was provided in the hull rear which was also used for ammunition supply. The Abbot was fitted with an NBC system, infrared driving lights and, when originally introduced into the British Army, with a flotation screen; the last was later removed.

Main armament consisted of a 105-mm gun manufactured by the Royal Ordnance Factory Nottingham, a 0.3-in (7.62-mm) Bren light machine gun at the

SPECIFICATION	
Abbot	**Powerplant:** one Rolls-Royce
Crew: 4	6-cylinder diesel developing
Weight: 16556 kg (36,500 lb)	179 kW (240 hp)
Dimensions: length (gun forward)	**Performance:** maximum road speed
5.84 m (19 ft 2 in); length (hull)	47.5 km/h (30 mph); maximum
5.709 m (18 ft 8.8 in); width	range 390 km (240 miles)
2.641 m (8 ft 8 in); height (without	**Gradient:** 6 per cent
armament) 2.489 m (8 ft 2 in)	**Vertical obstacle:** 0.609 m (2 ft)
	Trench: 2.057 m (6 ft 9 in)

commander's station for use in the anti-aircraft role, and one bank of three electrically-operated smoke dischargers on each side of the turret. The 105-mm gun had a double-baffle muzzle brake, a fume extractor and a semi-automatic breech. Traverse was powered through 360°, while elevation was manual from -5° to +70°. The gun had a maximum range of 17000 m (18,600 yards) and fired the following types of separate-loading ammunition: HE, HESH, practice, smoke (three types) and illuminating. A total of 40 projectiles was carried.

The ammunition of the Abbot is also used in the Royal Ordnance Factory Nottingham (now BAE Systems) 105-mm Light Gun, whose ordnance was developed from the L13A1 gun of the Abbot.

Replacement of the Abbot by the 155-mm M109A2 started in the early 1980s, but the Abbot was not retired from the Royal Artillery until the early 1990s, when it was replaced by the AS90 and MLRS.

AS90 155-mm self-propelled gun/howitzer

The fully-tracked 155-mm (6.1-in) **AS90** self-propelled gun/howitzer started life as a Vickers Shipbuilding and Engineering private venture that gained acceptance by the British Army after the intended international 155-mm SP-70 programme was terminated during 1986. Changing what was essentially then a simple-to-use equipment intended for a Third World market into the advanced artillery system demanded by the Royal Artillery took some years, the first deliveries of an ordered batch of 179 being made during 1993.

AS90 has undergone several significant changes since 1993, some of which are still in progress. Perhaps the most significant change has been the replacement of the original 155-mm L/39 barrel by a completely new barrel with a length of 52 calibres. This considerably enhances the maximum range, originally 24700 m (27,012 yards) but now 30000 m (32,808 yards) with a slightly modified L15 pattern high-explosive projectile as fired from the old FH-70. Using enhanced-range ammunition, the re-barrelled AS90 can reach over 40000 m (43,744 yards). Both long and short barrels can fire all existing NATO standard projectiles. At present only 96 of the British Army's equipments are scheduled to carry the new L/52 barrel, although others may follow.

To make the best use of this range performance, numerous computer-based systems have been added to the AS90, covering all manner of operations from electrical barrel and turret drives to land navigation and communications. Also involved is a new ammunition handling system to operate with the modular propellant charges of South African origin employed in place of the original bagged charges.

Sufficient on-platform data processing and fire-control equipment is provided to make each individual AS90 an independent combat unit, although the equipments are normally deployed in batteries of eight. Each gun can fire bursts of three rounds in 10 seconds, or a steadier rate of 18 rounds in three minutes. Ammunition stowage is provided for 48 rounds.

Two AS90 variants have been developed for the export market,

The AS90 was initially fitted with an L/39 barrel, but a conversion programme has introduced an L/52 barrel. This modification offers greater range and improved ballistic performance. Barrel-laying is fully electrical.

both containing the systems and long barrels developed for the British Army's AS90. One is for general sales and is named **Braveheart**, while the **Desert AS90** is intended for operations under extreme conditions as it features extra cooling arrange-ments and similar modifications to suit desert environments. The turret and L/52 barrel intended for the Braveheart have been selected by Poland for mounting on a tracked chassis.

SPECIFICATION	
AS90	diesel developing 492 kW (660 hp)
Crew: 5	**Performance:** maximum road speed
Weight: 45000 kg (99,208 lb)	55 km/h (34 mph); maximum road
Dimensions: length 9.9 m (32 ft	range 370 km (229 miles)
5 in); width 3.4 m (11 ft 1 in);	**Gradient:** 60 per cent
height 3 m (9 ft 9 in)	**Vertical obstacle:** 0.88 m (2 ft 9 in)
Powerplant: one Cummins V-8	**Trench:** 2.8 m (9 ft 2 in)

Although its onboard systems are arguably as advanced as those of the German PzH 2000, the AS90 has met with little export success, sales being limited to the British Army.

PzH 2000 155-mm self-propelled howitzer

Following the termination of the trilateral SP-70 program in 1986, the **Panzerhaubitze 2000** 155-mm (6.1-in) self-propelled howitzer was developed for the German army by Krauss-Maffei Wegmann (KMW), with Rheinmetall Landsysteme as the main sub-contractor. By the end of 2002, the **PzH 2000** had been ordered by Germany (185 systems delivered), Greece (24), Italy (70) and the Netherlands (57).

Main armament

The PzH 2000 is armed with a newly developed Rheinmetall L/52 main armament that is compatible with all current NATO shells and charges. This offers an effective range of 30000 m (32,808 yards) using conventional L15A2 ammunition, or up to 41000 m (44,838 yards) using various assisted rounds. Typical of these is the Rheinmetall RH 40 base-bleed ammunition, fired with a modular charge system.

Electrically controlled, the gun can be automatically elevated between -2.5° and +65° and is capable of 360° traverse. In order to lay the gun barrel precisely and at high speed,

the PzH 2000 is equipped with a GPS navigation system. An onboard ballistic computer with a radio datalink to an external fire-control command post enables missions to be undertaken autonomously, using unprepared firing positions, after having received target position and ammunition data. The position of the gun is checked after each round fired and if necessary it is relayed

automatically using fire-control data provided by the ballistic computer. The gun is capable of multiple-round simultaneous impact (MRSI) firing and has demonstrated a five-round MRSI on a target at a range of 17000 m (18,600 yards).

The fully automatic ammunition loading system includes different semi-automatic and manual back-up modes, and allows a rate of fire of 10 rounds per minute (increased to 12 during tests with an improved autoloader). A sustained rate of fire of three rounds per minute can be maintained until the ammunition is spent. The vehicle carries a total of 60 projectiles in the centre of the chassis and 288 modular charges (or equivalent bagged charges). Complete

The total German army requirement for the PzH 200 is expected to be around 450 units, and the type has also been ordered by the Italian, Dutch and Greek armies, making it something of a European standard for self-propelled artillery.

replenishment by two crewmembers takes under 12 minutes. A crew of five is normally maintained, although only three are required for normal operations. A 7.62-mm (0.3-in) machine-gun is carried to provide a measure of local and AA defence. The PzH 2000 has recently undergone trials in Sweden for use as a coastal artillery system, and successfully engaged moving targets at sea.

SPECIFICATION	
PzH 2000	**Powerplant:** one MTU MT881 Ka-500 diesel V-8 diesel developing 736 kW (987 hp)
Crew: 3 + 2	
Weight: 55330 kg (121,981 lb)	**Performance:** maximum road speed 61 km/h (37 mph); cruising range 420 km (260 miles)
Dimensions: length (gun forward) 11.669 m (38 ft 3 in); length (hull) 7.92 m (25 ft 1 in); width 3.58 m (11 ft 8 in); height (to turret roof) 3.06 m (10 ft 0 in)	
	Gradient: 50 per cent
	Vertical obstacle: 1 m (3 ft 3 in)
	Trench: 3 m (9 ft 9 in)

Bandkanon 1A 155-mm self-propelled gun

Bofors has long been known for its expertise in the design, development and production of guns (and their associated ammunition systems) for both land and sea applications. This work was put to good use in the development of the **Bofors Bandkanon 1A** 155-mm (6.1-in) self-propelled gun for the

Swedish army. The first prototype was completed in 1960, and after extensive trials and some modifications the equipment was manufactured between 1966 and 1968. The Bandkanon 1A has the distinction of being the first fully automatic self-propelled gun to have entered service. It is also the heaviest and slowest, which

makes the equipment very difficult to conceal and of limited tactical mobility.

The hull and turret are of all-welded steel construction between 10 and 20 mm (0.4 and 0.8 in) thick. The vehicle uses many automotive components of the Bofors S-tank, including the powerpack and suspension.

The engine and transmission are at the front of the hull, with the driver seated to the immediate front of the turret. The suspension is of the hydro-pneumatic type and consists on each side of six road wheels, with the drive sprocket at the front and the last road wheel acting as the idler. To provide a more stable firing platform the suspension can be locked.

Turret mounting

The turret is mounted at the rear of the hull, and is a two-part assembly with the 155-mm ordnance mounted between the parts. In the left part are the commander, gun layer and radio operator, while in the right part are the loader and 7.62-mm (0.3-in) AA machine-gunner. Turret traverse is manual, 15° left and right with the ordnance above 0° in elevation, reducing to 15° left and 4° right with the ordnance below 0°. Elevation is electric from +2° to +38° and manual from -3° to +40°. The 155-mm ordnance has a

pepperpot muzzle-brake, no fume extractor and a semi-automatic wedge breech block that opens downward. An unusual feature of the ordnance is that it has a replaceable liner. When travelling, the ordnance is held in position by a lock pivoted at the front of the hull. The ammunition is fed from a 14-round clip carried externally in an armoured magazine at the rear of the hull. This clip consists of seven compartments, each of which contain two rounds of ammunition, these being fed to the breech by a loading tray before being rammed into the breech by a rammer. The loading tray and rammer are operated by springs that are cocked by the

Operated only by Sweden, the Bandkanon 1A is heavy and slow, but its L/50 ordnance fires a comparatively heavy shell to a tactically useful range.

run-out of the gun. The first round has to be manually loaded but after this the sequence is fully automatic and the gunner can select single shots or fully automatic. The empty cartridge cases are ejected rearward from the breech. Once the clip of ammunition has been expended a fresh clip is brought up by truck, the ordnance is elevated to +38°, covers on the magazine

are opened vertically, a hoist on the upper part of the turret slides along the slide bar before picking up the clip and placing it in the magazine, the doors are then closed and the hoist is returned to travelling position. This sequence takes two minutes.

The standard HE projectile weighs 48 kg (105.8 lb) and has a range of 25600 m (28,000 yards).

SPECIFICATION	
Bandkanon 1A	**Powerplant:** one Rolls-Royce diesel
Crew: 5	developing 179 kW (240 hp) and
Weight: 53000 kg (116,845 lb)	one Boeing gas turbine developing
Dimensions: length (gun forward) 11	224 kW (300 shp)
m (36 ft 1 in); length (hull) 6.55 m	**Performance:** maximum road speed
(21 ft 6 in); width 3.37 m (11 ft 0.7	28 km/h (17.4 mph); maximum
in); height (including AA MG) 3.85	range 230 km (143 miles)
m (12 ft 7.6 in)	**Vertical obstacle:** 0.95 m (3 ft 1.4 in)
	Trench: 2 m (6 ft 6.7 in)

Palmaria 155-mm self-propelled howitzer

Specifically developed for export, the Palmaria has now been bought by Libya and Nigeria, while 20 turrets were delivered to Argentina for local installation on the chassis of the TAM tank. Palmaria is based on the chassis of the OF-40 MBT.

The **Otobreda Palmaria** 155-mm (6.1-in) self-propelled howitzer was developed by what was then OTO-Melara for the export market, and shares many components with the OF-40 MBT, which is in service with Dubai. The first Palmaria prototype was completed in 1981, and production vehicles were completed in the following year. The type has so far been ordered by Argentina (20 turrets), Libya (210) and Nigeria (25 or possibly 50).

The layout of the Palmaria (named after an Italian island) is similar to that of a tank, with the driver at the front of the hull, the turret in the centre, and the engine and transmission at the rear. The major difference between the chassis of the Palmaria and that of the OF-40 MBT is that the former has thinner armour and is powered by a V-8 diesel developing 559 kW (750 hp) whereas the OF-40 has a V-10 diesel developing 619 kW (830 hp).

The 155-mm (6.1-in) L/41 barrel is fitted with a fume extractor and a multi-baffle muzzle-brake. The turret has 360° traverse and the ordnance can be elevated from -4° to +70° hydraulically, with manual controls for emergency use. An unusual feature of the Palmaria is the installation of an auxiliary power unit to provide turret power, thus conserving fuel for the main engine. The Palmaria is available with a normal manual loading system or a semi-automatic loading system. With

the latter, a three-round burst can be fired in 30 seconds and then one round every 15 seconds can be maintained until the 23 ready-use projectiles have been fired; a further seven projectiles are stowed elsewhere in the hull. Once the ordnance has fired, it automatically returns to an elevation of +2°, the breech opens, the projectile is loaded with power assistance, the charge is loaded manually, the breech is closed and the ordnance can be fired. A complete range of ammunition has been developed for the Palmaria by Simmel: the range consists of five rounds, each weighing 43.5 kg (95.9 lb). The standard HE, smoke and illuminating projectiles have a range of 24700m (27,010 yards), the HE LT projectile 27500 m (30,075 yards), and the HE rocket-assisted projectile 30000 m (32,810 yards). The extra

range of the RAP has a penalty, however, in as much as it is achieved only at the expense of HE content, which is 8 kg (17.6 lb) compared with 11.7 kg (25.8 lb) in the standard and LT projectiles. A 7.62-mm (0.3-in) machine-gun is mounted at the commander's station on the right side of the turret roof, and four electrically operated smoke dischargers can be fitted on each side of the turret.

Much optional equipment can be fitted, including passive night vision equipment and an NBC system, and the vehicle's

standard equipment includes a hull escape hatch, bilge pumps and also a fire-extinguishing system.

SPECIFICATION	
Palmaria	**Powerplant:** one V-8 diesel
Crew: 5	developing 559 kW (750 hp)
Weight: 46000 kg (101,410 lb)	**Performance:** maximum road speed
Dimensions: length (gun forward)	60 km/h (37 mph); maximum range
11.47 m (37 ft 7.6 in); length (hull)	400 km (250 miles)
7.4 m (24 ft 3.3 in); width 2.35 m	**Gradient:** 60 per cent
(7 ft 8.5 in); height (without MG)	**Vertical obstacle:** 1 m (3 ft 3 in)
2.87 m (9 ft 5 in)	**Trench:** 3 m (9 ft 10 in)

ZTS vz 77 Dana 152-mm self-propelled gun/howitzer

The Czechoslovak (now Czech and Slovak) **ZTS vz 77 Dana** was the first wheeled self-propelled howitzer to enter modern service. Self-propelled artillery of the wheeled type has several advantages over its more common tracked counterpart: it is cheaper and easier to manufacture and to maintain, and has much greater strategic mobility as almost without exception wheeled armoured vehicles are much faster than their tracked counterparts and have a greater operational range.

The Dana, which entered service in 1981, is based on the Tatra T815 8x8 truck, which probably has the best off-road performance of any truck in existence. The crew compartment is at the front, the fully enclosed two-part turret in the centre, and the engine compartment at the rear. The armour is of all-welded steel and provides the crew with complete protection from small arms fire and shell splinters. The crew normally travel in the front compartment, entering the turret only for action.

The engine is coupled to a manual gearbox with 10 forward and two reverse gears, which in turn transmits power to a two-

speed transfer box, so giving a total of 20 forward and four reverse gears. Steering is power-assisted on the front four wheels, and a central tyre pressure-regulation system allows the driver to adjust the pressure to suit the ground being crossed.

Before firing can begin, three hydraulically operated stabilisers (one at the rear of the hull under the engine compartment and one on each side between the second and third axles) are lowered to the ground to provide stability. The turret can be traversed 225° left and right, and the 152-mm (6-in) ordnance (with a muzzle brake but without a fume extractor as the ordnance is carried between the two sealed turret halves) fires Czechoslovak and Russian ammunition, and can be elevated from -4° to +70°.

The ordnance is supplied by a hydraulically powered automatic loading system, and the gunner can select single-shot or fully automatic fire from the maximum 60 but more normal

The vz 77 Dana is based on the Tatra T815 8x8 truck chassis, and its centrally mounted turret carries the ordnance between two sealed outer halves.

40 separate-loading rounds carried in the system. The maximum rate is five rounds per minute, while the sustained rate is 30 rounds in seven minutes. The ordnance can fire two types of HE round, each weighing 43.56 kg (96 lb), the standard type to 18700 m (20,450 yards) and the base-bleed type to

20080 m (21,960 yards). There is also the EKK dispenser round carrying 42 anti-tank bomblets. Equipment includes NBC and air-conditioning systems, and on the right side of the turret a 12.7-mm (0.5-in) NSV machine-gun. Built in the Slovak Republic, the Dana has sold to Libya, Poland and to both its parent countries.

SPECIFICATION	
vz 77 Dana	**Powerplant:** one Tatra V-12 diesel
Crew: 5	developing 257 kW (345 hp)
Weight: 29250 kg (64,484 lb)	**Performance:** maximum road speed
Dimensions: length (gun forward)	80 km/h (50 mph); maximum range
11.156 m (36 ft 7.2 in); width 3 m	740 km (460 miles)
(9 ft 10 in); height (turret roof)	**Vertical obstacle:** 0.6 m (24 in)
2.85 m (9 ft 4.2 in)	**Trench:** 2 m (6 ft 7 in)

By early 1994 over 750 units of the Dana had been produced but more recent development has focused on the 155-mm ZTS Zuzana on a similar chassis.

G6 155-mm self-propelled gun/howitzer

Ever since its appearance in prototype form during 1981, the 155-mm (6.1-in) self-propelled gun/howitzer created by Denel, but now known as the **LIW G6**, has been the subject of a seemingly endless series of enhancements and updates. These have covered just about every aspect of the G6 system, only the basic 6x6 automotive platform having remained essentially without change over the years.

When the G6 first appeared it had an L/45 barrel, the same as that employed on the G5 towed howitzer. Using the ammunition then available, the maximum range was just under 40000 m (43,745 yards). In its latest developmental form, using an L/52 barrel firing enhanced-range ammunition, this range can be increased to more than 53000 m (57,960 yards). Work in progress is expected to result in a range of over 70000 m (76,555 yards), the

projectile incorporating ramjet propulsion. A trajectory-correction system will be included to maintain accuracy at extreme ranges.

Together with these range enhancements, the fire-control system has undergone numerous changes, while the turret interior has been revised to include improved turret-drive and gun-laying systems. Improved communication suites have been installed as well as a land navigation system, the commander being provided with a gun management system that displays data relating to command, fire orders, communications, navigation and general ballistic information dealing with the gun.

Despite all these changes the crew of the G6 remains at six, and the number of projectiles carried is still 45. The original bagged charges have now been replaced by easier to handle

modular charges. The projectiles are of a type known as ERFB (Extended-Range Full Bore) with the option of attaching a BB (Base Bleed) motor to break up the drag-inducing eddies behind the projectile base. The HE projectile weighs 45.3 kg (99.9 lb), increased to 47.7 kg (105.2 lb) with the BB motor in place. Other projectiles include Smoke, Illuminating, Incendiary, Leaflet and Radar Echo. The enhanced-range HE projectile is the Velocity-enhanced Long-Range Artillery Projectile (VLAP). As this projectile combines both BB and rocket assistance to extend the range to more than 53000 m the HE payload is less than the usual 8.7 kg (19.2 lb). The G6 can be

The G6 offers an attractive combination of capability and low cost. South Africa took 43 vehicles, and Oman and the UAE received 24 and 78 respectively.

fired from its wheels, but stability is better if the four outrigger legs are lowered. During firing the barrel can be traversed under power control through 90° to each side, and elevation is -5° to -75°.

The standard rate of fire is four rounds per minute for 15 minutes, though three rounds in 25 seconds is possible with a semi-automatic rammer assisting the loading processes. The G6 is operated by Oman and the UAE in addition to South Africa.

The most remarkable aspect of the G6's capabilities is the exceptional range offered by its ordnance in either its original L/45 or more recent L/52 forms.

SPECIFICATION	
LIW G6	**Powerplant:** one air-cooled diesel
Crew: 6	developing 386 kW (518 hp)
Weight: 47000 kg (103,616 lb)	**Performance:** maximum road speed
Dimensions: length (gun forward)	90 km/h (56 mph); maximum range
10.34 m (33 ft 11 in); length (hull)	700 km (435 miles)
9.2 m (30 ft 2.2 in); width 3.4 m	**Fording:** 1 m (3 ft 3 in)
(11 ft 2 in); height (turret top) 1.9 m	**Vertical obstacle:** 0.5 m (20 in)
(6 ft 3 in)	**Trench:** 1 m (3 ft 3 in)

GCT 155-mm self-propelled gun

To replace the 155-mm (6.1-in) Mk F3 and 105-mm (4.13-in) Mk

61 in French service, during the late 1960s a new self-propelled

gun was developed as the **GCT** (*Grande Cadence de Tir*, or great weight of fire) on a slightly modified AMX-30 MBT chassis. The first prototype was completed in 1972, and after trials with a pre-production batch of 10 vehicles, production got under-way in 1977. For a number of reasons Saudi Arabia was the first country to deploy the GCT,

ordering an eventual 63 systems plus a complete fire-control system. The French army designates the GCT as the **155 AUF1**, and deploys most of its 273 systems in regiments of 20 weapons (four five-gun batteries). Later orders were placed by Iraq and Kuwait for 86 and 18 systems respectively. The GCT is manufactured by Giat Industries.

SPECIFICATION	
155 AUF1	110 water-cooled V-12 multi-fuel
Crew: 4	engine developing 537 kW (720 hp)
Weight: 42000 kg (92,595 lb)	**Performance:** maximum road speed
Dimensions: length (gun forward)	60 km/h (37 mph); maximum range
10.25 m (33 ft 7.5 in); width 3.15 m	450 km (280 miles)
(10 ft 4 in); height 3.25 m (10 ft 8	**Gradient:** 60 per cent
in)	**Vertical obstacle:** 0.93 m (37 in)
Powerplant: one Hispano-Suiza HS	**Trench:** 1.9 m (6 ft 3 in)

The GCT's equipment includes night vision and ventilation equipment, while options include an NBC system and muzzle velocity measuring gear.

the turret rear. The ammunition mix depends on the tactical situation, but can consist of 36 (six racks of six) HE and six (one rack of six) smoke projectiles.

Reloading

Access to the ammunition racks for reloading purposes is via two large doors in the turret rear. The crew can reload the GCT in 15 minutes. The auto-loader enables a rate of eight rounds per minute, and the gunner can

select single shots or six-round bursts, the latter taking just 45 seconds. The GCT can fire HE (four types including a base-bleed type with a range of 29000 m/31,715 yards), illuminating, smoke and carrier projectiles. A 7.62- or 12.7-mm (0.3- or 0.5-in) machine-gun is mounted on the roof.

The later **155 AUF1 T** had a number of improvements, and 174 French systems are being upgraded to **155 AUF2** standard with an L/52 ordnance able to fire the base-bleed projectile to 40000 m (43,745 yards), and a Mack E9 diesel engine. The L/52 turret is also available for use on other 40-tonne class MBT chassis.

The all-welded turret is fitted with a 155-mm L/40 barrel fitted with a multi-baffle muzzle brake and a vertical sliding-wedge breech block. Elevation is from -4° to +66°, and traverse 360°. Turret traverse and gun elevation are hydraulic, with manual controls for emergency use. The major feature of the GCT is the automatic loading system for 42 projectiles and a similar number of cartridges carried in racks in

Although developed as a successor to the Mk F3 and Mk 61 SP guns in French army service, the GCT was first deployed by Saudi Arabia, since when it has also been adopted by Iraq and Kuwait. The auto-loader enables the 155-mm GCT to fire at a rate of up to eight rounds per minute.

Slammer 155-mm self-propelled howitzer

The **Slammer** 155-mm (6.1-in) self-propelled howitzer was developed to meet an Israeli army requirement and was first revealed during 1990, although the first of the two prototypes completed to date was ready during mid-1983. However, no orders for the Slammer (known locally as the **Sholef**) have been announced, although it is

marketed for possible export as being ready for production.

To assist Israeli armed forces logistics, the Slammer consists of a 155-mm howitzer and turret on a chassis derived from that of the Merkava MBT. The fully traversing welded steel turret and its L/52 howitzer were developed and manufactured locally by Soltam Systems. The

howitzer has an elevation arc of -3° to +75° and, firing enhanced-range 155-mm projectiles, has a maximum range of over 40000 m (43,745 yards). Combined with the howitzer is a computer-controlled Loader Control System (LCS) that permits nine rounds to be loaded automatically and fired in one minute. Bursts of three rounds

in 10 seconds are possible. The LCS also selects and sets the projectile fuses and inserts the propellant charge primer. Using the LCS only two ammunition handlers are needed in the turret, the commander controlling and monitoring all processes from a control panel. The remaining member of the four-man crew is the driver.

Full NBC protection is provided, while night driving systems are standard.

For normal self-propelled fire missions the Slammer carries 60 projectiles and propellant charges, all readily accessible by the LCS. A further 15 projectiles are carried at various stowage points around the interior. For more static fire missions, ammunition can be fed into the system from an external stockpile, projectiles being passed into the turret via an elevator. In an emergency the LCS can be replaced by manual operation, although the fire rate is reduced. The LCS, including the complete ordnance, can be retrofitted into existing SP systems, the M109 being mentioned in marketing material as a likely recipient. Various auto-nomous fire control and land navigation systems can be installed according to choice.

Modified ordnance

The Slammer's 155-mm ordnance is a modified version of that proposed for a towed model, the TIG 2000. The same ordnance has been proposed for the ATMOS 2000 on a modified Tatra 6x6 truck chassis. For travelling, the barrel is firmly held in a remotely controlled external clamp. It is provided with a double-baffle muzzle brake and a fume evacuator.

Though based on that of the Merkava, the Slammer chassis has some role-specific modifications, but has the same diesel powerpack coupled to an automatic transmission. Though lighter than the Merkava (the exact weights have not been released), the Slammer thus has a road range of about 400 km (248 miles) and a speed of 46 km/h (28.5 mph). It is anticipated that any production Slammers would be manufactured to the latest Merkava standard and thus have better all-round automotive and battlefield performance.

The Slammer has a number of very advanced features as well as a capable ordnance that can fire projectiles to a considerable range, but it has not been ordered.

SPECIFICATION	
Slammer	(900 hp)
Crew: 4	**Performance:** maximum road speed
Weight: not released	46 km/h (28.5 mph; maximum
Dimensions: length (gun forward) 11	range 400 km (248 miles)
m (36 ft 1 in); width 3.7 m (12 ft	**Fording:** 1.3 m (4 ft 3 in)
1.7 in); height 3.4 m (11 ft 2 in)	**Gradient:** not released
Powerplant: one General Dynamics	**Vertical obstacle:** not released
AVDS-1790-6A liquid-cooled V-12	**Trench:** not released
diesel engine developing 671 kW	

Type 75 155-mm self-propelled howitzer

When the Japanese Ground Self-Defence Force was formed in the 1950s, all of its artillery was of the towed type and supplied by the US. With increased mechanisation taking place in the 1960s, the US also supplied 30 105-mm (4.13-in) M52 and 10 155-mm (6.1-in) M44 self-propelled howitzers. In the later 1960s development of indigenous 105-mm and 155-mm self-propelled howitzers started in Japan, the former eventually being standardised as the Type 74 and the latter as the **Type 75**.

Only 20 of the Type 74 were built as a decision was taken to concentrate on the more effective 155-mm Type 75 system. Production lasted into the later 1980s and amounted to 201 systems: Mitsubishi Heavy Industries was responsible for the hull and final assembly, and Japan Iron Works/Nihon Seiko for the gun and turret.

M109 similarities

In many respects the Type 75 is similar to the M109 operated by the US Army and a large number of other forces, with the engine and transmission at the front and the fully enclosed turret at the rear. The six-man crew consists of the commander, layer, two loaders and radio operator in the turret, and the driver in the front of the hull. The hull and turret are constructed of all-welded aluminium to a thickness that provides the crew with complete protection from small arms fire and shell splinters. The suspension is of the torsion-bar type, and on each side comprises six road wheels, of which the rear unit serves as the idler; the drive sprocket is at the front, and there are no track-return rollers.

The L/30 barrel has a breech block of the interrupted screw type, a fume extractor and a double-baffle muzzle brake. When the Type 75 is travelling the barrel is normally held in a travel lock mounted on the glacis plate. The ordnance has an elevation of +65° and a depression of -5°, and the turret can be traversed through 360°. The elevation of the weapon

The Type 75 self-propelled howitzer is essentially a Japanese-designed and Japanese-built counterpart to the ubiquitous M109 SP howitzer of US origin.

and the traverse of the turret are both hydraulically powered, with manual controls provided for emergency use. Before fire is opened, two spades are manually lowered to the ground at the rear of the hull to provide a more stable firing platform.

The Type 75 can fire 18 rounds in three minutes, such a rate being achieved by the use of two drum-type magazines (one on each side of the turret and containing nine projectiles

each), a two-part extending loading tray and a hydraulic rammer. Once the gun has been fired, it returns automatically to an elevation angle of +6° for

reloading, the breech is opened, the extending loading tray is positioned, the projectile and charge are then loaded with the aid of the hydraulic rammer, the breech is closed, the loading tray is returned to the normal position, and the weapon is ready to be fired once more. The drum magazines are rotated electrically or manually, and can be reloaded from outside the vehicle via two doors/hatches in the turret rear.

In action the Type 75 would probably fire 12 or 18 rounds before moving off to a new fire position before the enemy could return fire. In addition to the 18 projectiles in the two magazines, a further 10 projectiles are carried internally, as are 56 fuses and 28 bagged charges. Mounted externally at the commander's station, for anti-aircraft and local defence purposes, is a standard 0.5-in (12.7-mm) M2HB machine-gun.

SPECIFICATION	
Type 75	cooled 6-cylinder diesel developing
Crew: 6	336 kW (450 hp)
Weight: 25300 kg (55,775 lb)	**Performance:** maximum road speed
Dimensions: length (gun forward)	47 km/h (29 mph); maximum range
7.79 m (25 ft 6.7 in); width 3.09 m	300 km (185 miles)
(10 ft 1.7 in); height (without MG)	**Gradient:** 60 per cent
2.545 m (8 ft 4 in)	**Vertical obstacle:** 0.7 m (27 in)
Powerplant: one Mitsubishi water-	**Trench:** 2.5 m (8 ft 2 in)

Chinese self-propelled artillery PLZ45 and Types 54-1, 83 and 85

Over the years the Chinese defence industry, centred on Norinco, has developed several types of self-propelled artillery for export and domestic use. One recent export success has been the 155-mm (6.1-in) **PLZ45** sold to Kuwait, which took 27 systems. The PLZ45 is thoroughly modern with an L/45 barrel firing ERFB (extended-range full-bore) projectiles, with or without base-bleed units, the latter weighing 47.6 kg (104.9 lb) and reaching 39000 m (42,650 yards) after being fired with a muzzle velocity of 903 m (2,963 ft) per second. The PLZ45 resembles the US M109, but

The Type 83 is based on a new fully tracked chassis and carries heavy ordnance in the form of a derivative of the 152-mm (6-in) Type 66 towed howitzer.

there are numerous differences. The PLZ45 was first displayed publicly in 1988, and is also in service with the Chinese army.

Basic weapon

Another export success was made by the **Type 54-1**, a basic and elderly equipment with the Soviet 122-mm (4.8-in) howitzer of 1938 in a limited-traverse, forward-firing mounting on a modified YW531 APC. Despite the limited ballistic performance of its short-barrel howitzer (maximum range of 11800 m/ 12,905 yards with a 21.76-kg/ 48-lb projectile), the Type 54-1 was bought by Bolivia (18), and large numbers remain in Chinese service. The Type 54-1 is a sturdy and reliable equipment, but is no longer in production.

Another low-cost and basic equipment also based on the YW531 is the **Type 85** with the 122-mm Soviet-designed D-30 howitzer mounted in a semi-open limited-traverse mounting firing forward. Its standard 21.76-kg projectile reaches 15300 m (16,770 yards) and an enhanced-range projectile 21000 m (22,965 yards); the enhanced-range projectile includes some cargo-carrier types. As far as is known, no Type 85 equipments have been exported. It is no longer in production, although marketing continues.

Returning to a larger calibre, Norinco also continues to market the **Type 83**, a design with close affinities to the Soviet 2S3 and mounting an almost identical 152-mm (6-in) gun/howitzer manufactured in China as the Type 66. As with the PLZ45, the immediate visual similarities are misleading as the Type 83 employs an entirely new tracked chassis design which has also been adapted for other vehicles, including a trench digger. The Type 83 can fire a Type 66 HE projectile, weighing 43.56 kg (96 lb), to a range of 17230 m (18,845 yards) at a steady rate of four rounds per minute. Although extensively marketed by Norinco, the Type 83 is in service only with China. A 130-mm (5.12-in) gun is offered as an alternative to the 152-mm ordnance, while one variant, the PTZ89 deployed as a tank destroyer, carries a 120-mm (4.72-in) high-velocity gun. Production of the Type 83 is complete.

SPECIFICATION	
PLZ45	L413FC air-cooled diesel engine developing 391 kW (525 hp)
Crew: 5	
Weight: 33000 kg (72,751 lb)	**Performance:** maximum road speed 56 km/h (35 mph); maximum range 336 km (450 miles)
Dimensions: length (gun forward) 10.15 m (33 ft 3.6 in); width 3.236 m (10 ft 7.4 in); height 3.502 m (11 ft 6 in)	**Gradient:** 58°
	Vertical obstacle: 0.7 m (27 in)
Powerplant: one Deutz BF12	**Trench:** 2.7 m (8 ft 10 in)

M109 155-mm self-propelled howitzer

The basic M109 self-propelled howitzer mounted the short-barrel M126 weapon. The M109 series is the most widely used of all self-propelled weapons and has seen extensive combat service throughout the world, as well as seeing constant adaptation and updating.

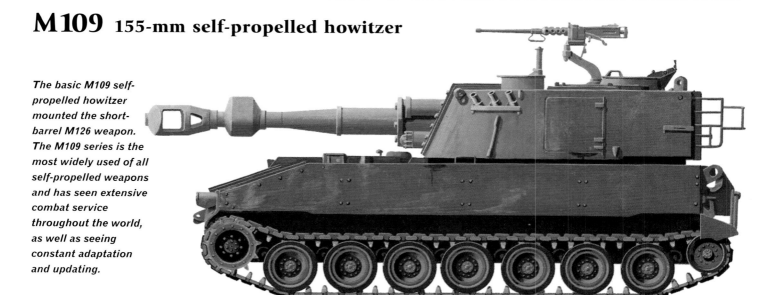

The **M109** 155-mm (6.1-in) self-propelled howitzer is the most widely used weapon of its type in the world. Its development can be traced to 1952, when a requirement was issued for a new SP howitzer to replace the 155-mm (6.1-in) M44. At that time the 110-mm (4.33-in) T195 self-propelled howitzer was already being designed, and it was decided to use its hull and turret as the basis for the new weapon, which would be armed with a 156-mm (6.14-in) howitzer. But in 1956 it was decided to stick to a 155-mm (6.1-in) calibre for commonality within NATO, and in 1959 the first prototype was completed under the designation **T196**. There were numerous problems, and much redesign work had to be carried out to improve its reliability.

Diesel power

At the same time a decision was taken that all future US armoured vehicles would be powered by diesel engines for greater operating range, so the vehicle was redesignated T196E1 with such a powerplant. In 1961 this was accepted for service as the M109 SP howitzer, and the first production vehicles were completed late in 1962 at the Cleveland Army Tank Plant, this facility being run by the Cadillac Motor Car Division but later run by Chrysler. In the 1970s all production of the M109 series was taken over by Bowen-McLaughlin-York (now United Defense).

In the US Army the M109 is issued on the scale of 54 per armoured and mechanised division (three battalions each of 18 vehicles, each battalion having three batteries of six M109s). In addition to the US

SPECIFICATION	
M109A6 Paladin	Model 8V-71T liquid-cooled diesel developing 328 kW (440 hp)
Crew: 4	
Weight: 28849 kg (63,600 lb)	**Performance:** maximum road speed 64.5 km/h (40 mph); maximum range 344 km (215 miles)
Dimensions: length overall (gun forward) 9.677 m (31 ft 8 in); width 3.922 m (12 ft 10.4 in); height 3.62 m (11 ft 10.5 in)	**Gradient:** 60 per cent
	Vertical obstacle: 0.53 m (21 in)
Powerplant: one Detroit Diesel	**Trench:** 1.83 m (6 ft)

Army and US Marine Corps, the M109 is still used by 29 other countries, and a few countries have given it up in recent years. The weapon has been used in action in conflicts in the Middle East and the Far East.

Layout

The hull and turret of the M109 are of all-welded aluminium construction. The driver is seated at the front on the left, with the engine compartment to his right, and the turret is at the rear. The suspension is of the well-tried torsion-bar type, and on each side consists of seven road wheels with the drive sprocket at the front and the idler at the rear; there are no track-return rollers. Standard equipment includes IR driving lights and an amphibious kit enabling the vehicle to propel itself across slow-flowing rivers with its tracks.

The M109 has a 155-mm M126 howitzer with an elevation arc of -5° to +75° in

Steady development has kept the M109 series fully capable of effective use in modern operations, the adoption of longer ordnances increasing projectile ranges most usefully.

a 360° traverse turret. Both gun elevation and turret traverse are powered, with manual controls available for emergency use. The ordnance has a large fume extractor, large muzzle brake and a Welin-step thread breech block. Normal rate of fire is one round per minute, but for short periods three rounds per minute can be attained. The weapon has been qualified to fire a wide range of projectiles including HE (maximum range 14320 m/15,660 yards), illuminating, tactical nuclear, smoke, tactical CS and Agents VX or GB; 28 projectiles and charges are carried. A 0.5-in (12.7-mm) M2HB machine-gun, for which 500 rounds are provided, is mounted on the commander's cupola for local defence.

One of the reasons that the M109 has been in production for so long is that its basic chassis has proved capable of constant updating and of accepting longer-barrelled ordnance that fires projectiles to a greater distance.

The main variants have been the M109 baseline model, **M109A1** with the longer M185 ordnance, **M109A2** with a redesigned rammer and 22 more rounds, upgraded **M110A3**, **M109A4** conversion of two earlier variants with NBC protection, **M109A5** upgraded M109A4, and **M109A6 Paladin**. The last is the production model in the first part of the 21st century (957 ordered for the US Army), and incorporates a host of tactical and reliability improvements.

M110 203-mm self-propelled howitzer

The **M110** 203-mm (8-in) self-propelled howitzer uses the same chassis and mount as the 175-mm (6.9-in) M107 self-propelled gun. The M110 was one of a complete family of self-propelled weapons developed by Pacific Car and

Foundry for trials as the T235 175-mm (6.9-in) gun, **T236** 203-mm howitzer and T245 155-mm (6.1-in) gun.

The M110 entered service with the US Army Field Artillery in 1963, and was issued on the scale of one battery of four

M110s per infantry division and one battalion of 12 for each armoured and mechanised division. Production was originally completed in the late 1960s, but was resumed in the 1970s by Bowen-McLaughlin-York, which later merged with FMC to create United Defense. In addition to being used by the US Army and US Marines, the M110 has been or still is operated by the armies of Bahrain, Belgium, Germany, Greece, Iran, Israel, Italy, Japan, Jordan, Morocco, the Netherlands, Pakistan, Saudi

Arabia, South Korea, Spain, Taiwan, Turkey and the UK. In many cases, and especially in Europe, the M110s were upgraded with the aid of US-supplied kits.

The chassis of the M110 is of all-welded steel construction with the driver seated under armour at the front on the left, with the engine compartment to his right and the howitzer on its mount on top of the chassis at the rear. The suspension is of the torsion-bar type and consists on each side of five large road wheels with the rearmost acting as the idler; the

SPECIFICATION	
M110A2	Model 8V-71T liquid-cooled diesel developing 302 kW (405 bhp)
Crew: 5 + 8	**Performance:** maximum road speed 54.7 km/h (34 mph); maximum range 523 km (325 miles)
Weight: 28350 kg (62,500 lb)	
Dimensions: length (gun forward) 10.73 m (35 ft 2.4 in); width 3.15 m (10 ft 4 in); height 3.14 m (10 ft 3.6 in)	**Gradient:** 60 per cent
	Vertical obstacle: 1.016 m (40 in)
Powerplant: one Detroit Diesel	**Trench:** 2.36 m (7 ft 9 in)

five large road wheels with the rearmost acting as the idler; the drive sprocket is at the front and there are no track-return rollers. When the M110 is in firing position, the suspension can be locked to provide a more stable firing platform.

The 203-mm M2A2 howitzer was developed well before World War II and is located on the M158 mount, this allowing an elevation arc between -2° and +65°; the traverse arc of 30° left and right. Elevation and traverse are hydraulically powered, with manual controls for emergency use. The M2A2 has no muzzle brake or fume extractor, and has an interrupted screw breech block. At the rear of the chassis

is a loader and rammer assembly to lift the projectile from the ground, position it and ram it into the chamber. The following projectiles can be fired: 92.53-kg (204-lb) HE to a maximum range of 16800 m (18,375 yards), HE carrying 104 or 195 grenades, Agents GB or VX, and tactical nuclear. Only two projectiles and charges are carried on the M110, others being provided from the M548 carrier that also transports the remainder of the crew. The complete crew of the M110 consists of 13 men, of whom five (commander, driver and three gunners) are on the M110.

One of the main drawbacks of the M110 is the complete lack of

any protection for the gun crew from shell splinters, small arms fire and NBC agents. A protection kit was developed but not fielded.

All US M110s were upgraded to **M110A1** or **M110A2** standards. The M110A1 has a longer M201 ordnance firing the M106 HE projectile to a maximum of 22860 m (25,000 yards) or the M650 HE rocket-assisted projectile to 29990 m (32,800 yards); other rounds were the M404 Improved

Conventional Munition carrying 104 anti-personnel grenades, the M509A1 ICM carrying 180 anti-personnel/materiel grenades, Agents GB or VX, Binary or tactical nuclear.

The M110A2 is almost identical to the M110A1 but has a muzzle-brake which enables it to fire charge nine of the M118A1 propelling charge, whereas the M110A1 can go only up to charge eight and thus offers a reduced maximum range capability.

An M110A2 of the US Army. This differs from previous M110 versions in having a long, muzzle-braked barrel. All of the M110 series equipments in the US Army were to have been fitted with a crew shelter and NBC system, but in the end were not so fitted.

Crusader 155-mm self-propelled howitzer

Although the **Crusader** 155-mm (6.1-in) self-propelled artillery project is no more, the programme suffering final

cancellation in 2002, it still provides an indication of the state-of-the art for future field artillery. The Crusader was

innovative in many ways, not the least being that it was a two-part system, comprising the howitzer unit itself plus an ammunition carrier/reload system.

The howitzer component was the **XM1001 Self-Propelled Howitzer** (SPH), and the other component was the **XM1002 Resupply Vehicle** (RSV). The two vehicles were to operate on a one-to-one basis, the two being

virtually joined together for the ammunition and fuel resupply operation. Throughout the system computer-controlled automation was employed. For instance all ammunition and fuse selection, handling and loading on the SPH was mechanical, the crew of three not even seeing the processes involved. The crew of three on the RSV could transfer fresh rounds within

SPECIFICATION	
XM1001 Crusader	**Powerplant:** one Honeywell/General Electric LV-100-5 gas turbine developing 1118 kW (1,500 shp)
Crew: 3	
Weight: 43630 kg (96,186 lb)	
Dimensions: length (gun forward) 7.01 m (23 ft); width 3.33 m (10 ft 11 in); height 2.92 m (9 ft 7 in)	**Performance:** maximum road speed 67 km/h (41.5 mph)

seconds, again without human intervention other than monitoring. The SPH could carry 48 rounds and charges, with another 100 on the RSV.

Liquid cooling

The 155-mm XM297E2 howitzer barrel was an L/56 unit, enabling a maximum range with suitable projectiles of over 40000 m (43,745 yards) or 50000 m (54,680 yards) or more with enhanced-range projectiles such as the XM982. It was planned that the barrel would be able to fire at a rate of up to 10 rounds per minute so the barrel featured liquid cooling. Time in and out of action was planned as about 30 seconds, with high-speed moves powered by a Honeywell/ General Electric gas turbine engine driving via an Allison automatic transmission.

Development reached the test turret and chassis stage before changing priorities led to cancellation as, with each vehicle exceeding 45 tonnes, the

system was becoming too heavy. Some Crusader technology may be used in future but lighter projects. Pending another system, the US Army is continuing to field the 155-mm M109A6 Paladin system.

Above: In firing trials, the Crusader SPH confirmed that it could start firing within 40 seconds of coming to a halt, and that burst rates of 10–12 rounds per minute were possible. The powerplant was originally to have been based on a Perkins CV-12 diesel engine from the UK, but in 2000 it was decided to standardise the gas turbine of the M1A2 Abrams MBT.

Left: The Crusader was based on a hydro-pneumatic suspension system, there being six dual rubber-tyred road wheels on each side, together with a front idler, rear drive sprocket and unspecified number of track-return rollers.

ASTROS II Artillery Saturation Rocket System

Based on its experience in the design, development and production of a variety of ground- and air-launched unguided rockets for the Brazilian armed forces, the Brazilian company of AVIBRAS subsequently developed a much more effective artillery rocket system called **ASTROS II** (Artillery Saturation Rocket System). Development of this was completed in the early 1980s with the first production systems being completed in the 1983 and since then large numbers have been produced for the home and export markets, especially the Middle East (Iraq, Qatar and Saudi Arabia) and more recently Asia (Malaysia). Iraq manufactured a version of the ASTROS II named **Sajeel**.

ASTROS II consists of two key elements, both of which are based on the same 6x6 cross-country truck chassis: these are the actual launcher and the ammunition resupply vehicle which is fitted with a crane for loading new rockets. Both of these are provided with fully armoured forward control cabs. There is also an optional command centre/fire-control system based on a similar or more compact 4x4 chassis.

The launcher for the unguided surface-to-surface rockets is mounted at the rear and can be fitted with various pods of different calibre rockets with the larger the calibre the greater the operational range.

The shortest rocket is the SS-30 with each launcher having 32 tubes with a stated maximum range of 30 km (18.6 miles). The next model is the SS-40 with a range of 35 km (21.7 miles) and 16 tubes. The largest rocket currently in production is the SS-60 with a maximum stated range of 60 km (37.3 miles) and four tubes. Development of the SS-80 is complete and this has a maximum range of 90 km (55.9 miles).

A Saudi Arabian ASTROS II system in a dug-in firing position during the 1990-91 Gulf War, in which both Iraqi and Saudi Arabian systems saw extensive use.

Warhead types

To meet different operational requirements, various types of warhead can be fitted including bomblet type to attack the vulnerable upper surfaces of armoured vehicles, mines or anti-airfield, for example. More recently it has been revealed that a winged version has been developed with a longer range. The latter is known as the ASTROS TM (Tactical Missile) and is understood to have a range of 150 km (93.2 miles) but has yet to enter production.

The rockets can be launched by the operator seated in the safety of the cab either singly or in ripples. The standard rockets are unguided and have solid propellant with wrap-around fins that unfold at the rear.

Although originally developed for surface-to-surface applications, the ASTROS II is now being marketed for coastal defence applications with the first customer being the Brazilian army. This system is used in conjunction with a vehicle-mounted radar system to detect surface craft before they are engaged by the ASTROS II rockets.

More recently it has been revealed that AVIBRAS is working on an **ASTROS III** system which will be based on a much larger 8x8 truck which in addition to carrying and launching the standard series of SS-30, SS-40, SS-60 and SS-80 rockets will also launch a new generation of rockets including the SS-150.

SPECIFICATION	
ASTROS II (SS-30 rocket)	**No. of launch tubes:** 32
Crew: 3	**Rocket length:** 3.9 m (12 ft 10 in)
Chassis: 10000-kg (22,046-lb)	**Rocket weight:** 68 kg (149.9 lb)
Tectran AV-VBA 6x6 truck	**Maximum range:** 30 km (18.6 miles)
Calibre: 127 mm (5 in)	**Warhead types:** HE

WS-1B Four-round artillery rocket system

NORINCO (China North Industries Corporation) have developed almost all of the surface-to-surface rocket systems used by the Peoples Liberation Army (PLA). In the past some of these have been very simple systems and as well as being procured by the PLA have also been exported in some quantities, especially to Middle East armies.

Some of the more recent sophisticated surface-to-surface rocket systems have bee developed by the China Precision Machinery Import and Export Corporation (CPMIEC) with one of the latest being the 302-mm (11.89-in) **WS-1B** (four-round) system. There was also an earlier 320-mm (12.59-in) system known as the **WS-1** but this is no longer marketed. WS-1B is based on a locally manufactured Mercedes-Benz forward-control (6x6) truck chassis and to the rear of the cab there is a small pod for additional crew members.

Mounted at the very rear of the chassis is a launcher with four tubes each of which carries and launches one unguided rocket. To provide a more stable firing platform, four hydraulic stabilisers are lowered to the

SPECIFICATION	
WS-1B	**Warhead types:** ZDB-2 blast-type HE
Chassis: Mercedes-Benz 6x6 truck	or SZB-1 submunition; effective
Calibre: 302 mm (11.89 in)	lethal radius (ZDB-2) 70 m
No. of launch tubes: 4	(76 yards)
Rocket length: 6.182 m (20 ft 4 in)	**Warhead weights:** warhead 150 kg
Rocket weight: 708 kg (1,561 lb)	(331 lb); propellant 370 kg (816 lb);
	rocket motor 538 kg (1,186 lb)

ground. Two of these are at the rear and the other two are located on each side to the rear of the cab.

Battery components

A typical WS-1B battery would consist of one command truck, six to nine rocket launcher trucks designated **HF-4** and a similar number of transport and loading trucks designated QY-88B. All of these are based on the same 6x6 chassis for logistical and training reasons.

Target information is relayed to the battery command truck which in turn provides this information to each launcher. The turntable mounted launcher pod has a traverse of 30° left and right with elevation limits from 0° to +60°.

The rockets have a solid propellant motor and can be fitted with two different types of warhead to suit the type of target being engaged. One warhead is of the high explosive type which is claimed to have an effective radius of at least 70 m

(76 yards). The second warhead carries over 450 sub-munitions to attack the vulnerable upper surfaces of armoured vehicles. Each sub-munition is fitted with a high explosive anti-tank (HEAT) type warhead which will penetrate up to 70 mm (2.75 in) of conventional steel armour. It is also highly effective against soft-skinned vehicles and troops in the open.

Once the rockets have been launched the HF-4 launchers would normally rapidly move to avoid counter battery fire. In a safe and probably camouflaged area they would be reloaded by the QY-88B transport and loading truck using its onboard crane.

In recent years surface-to-surface rockets have been deployed by an increasing number of countries but they supplement rather than replace conventional towed and self-propelled tube artillery. Surface-to-surface rocket systems such as the WS-1B are very much area weapons.

The WS-1B system is a further development of the WS-1 that is understood to be in service with the PLA and also based on a Mercedes 6x6 truck chassis.

LARS Light Artillery Rocket System

The 110-mm (4.33-in) **Light Artillery Rocket System (LARS)** was developed by Wegmann (later Krauss-Maffei Wegmann) in the mid-1960s and accepted into West German army service in 1969. Designated **Artillerie Raketenwerfer 110 SF2** by the West German army, the type was issued on the scale of one battery of eight launchers per army division, each battery also having two 4x4 truck-mounted Swiss Contraves Fieldguard fire-control systems on 4x4 truck chassis and a resupply vehicle with 144 rockets.

Following upgrading to the **LARS II** standard, each launcher is now mounted on the rear of a 7000-kg (15,432-lb) MAN 6x6 truck chassis and consists of two

side-by-side banks of 18 launcher tubes. The fin-stabilised solid propellant rockets can all be fired within 17.5 seconds, manual reloading taking approximately 15 minutes. The minimum and maximum ranges are 6 km (3.7 miles) and 14 km (8.7 miles) respectively. There are seven major types of warhead that can be fitted to the rocket, these including the DM-711 mine dispenser with five

Above: The German army's Light Artillery Rocket System was upgraded from LARS to LARS II standard. The programme included a new fire-control system, additional rocket types and an increase in mobility by fitting the launcher to the MAN 6x6 chassis, the standard German army cross-country truck.

Left: Mounted on the cab of the MAN 6x6 truck of the LARS II system is a 7.62-mm (0.3-in) MG3 machine gun with 360° traverse and elevation of +9° to +50°. The crew of three all sit in the unarmoured cab.

parachute-retarded AT2 anti-tank mines, the DM-21 HE-fragmentation (proximity fuze), and the DM-701 mine dispenser with eight AT1 anti-tank mines. Diehl and DM-28 training and practice warheads, DM-11 fragmentation (impact fuze), DM-39 radar target and DM-15 smoke warheads are further options.

By the mid-1980s, a total of 209 LARS II launchers was in service with the West German army, and these were relegated to reserve units as the longer-range MLRS was phased into service during the late 1980s and early 1990s. At the beginning of the 21st century, LARS II was no longer in front-line German service, although units may be passed on to another NATO member.

SPECIFICATION	
LARS II	**Rocket length:** 2.263 m (7 ft 5 in)
Combat weight: 17480 kg (38,537 lb)	**Rocket weight:** 35 kg (77 lb)
Crew: 3	**Warhead types:** HE fragmentation,
Chassis: 7000-kg (15,432-lb) MAN 6x6 truck	submunition, smoke, practice, radar target
Calibre: 110 mm (4.33 in)	**Warhead weights:** 17.3 kg (38 lb)
No. of launcher tubes: 36	

Valkiri Mk 1 Multiple artillery rocket system

Development of the 127-mm (5-in) **Valkiri Mk 1** started in 1977 as a counter to the Soviet 122-mm (4.8-in) BM-21 MRL and other long-range artillery pieces in service with neighbouring African countries. The first systems entered service in late 1981 with the South African army, and were deployed with artillery regiments in batteries of eight launchers that were tasked either to work on their own or with more conventional tube artillery to attack area targets such as guerrilla camps, troop or artillery concentrations, and soft-skinned vehicle convoys. The system consists of a 24-round launcher mounted on the rear hull of a 4x4 SAMIL truck chassis with overhead canopy rails so as to

make it appear to be just a normal truck when travelling. The highly mobile Valkiri was ideally suited to mechanised cross-border raids against SWAPO guerrilla bases and Angolan army units deep within Angola. A second 5-ton truck with 48 reload rounds is assigned to each Valkiri Mk 1. The full load of 24 rounds can be fired in 24 seconds, reloading taking about 10 minutes. The solid-propellant rocket is fitted with an HE fragmentation warhead filled with some 3,500 steel balls to give a lethal area of some 1500 m² (16,146 sq ft). The range can be varied from a minimum of 8 km (5 miles) to a maximum of 22 km (13.7 miles) depending upon which spoiler rings are fitted.

Above: Overhead canopy rails are fitted to the Valkiri Mk 1 launcher in order to camouflage the vehicle to appear as a normal South African army SAMIL 20 4x4 light truck. With the canopy down it is almost impossible to tell the difference.

SPECIFICATION	
Valkiri Mk 1	**Rocket length:** 2.68 m (8 ft 10 in)
Combat weight: 6440 kg (14,198 lb)	**Rocket weight:** 53 kg (117 lb)
Crew: 2	**Warhead type:** HE fragmentation
Chassis: 2200-kg (4,850-lb) SAMIL 20 4x4 truck	with contact of proximity fuze; lethal area 1500 m² (16,146 sq ft)
Calibre: 127 mm (5 in)	**Maximum range:** 22 km (13.7 miles)
No. of launcher tubes: 24	

The launch signature of the Valkiri is minimal. This helped the system avoid counter-battery fire from the long-range Soviet-supplied artillery pieces of surrounding African states and guerrilla forces.

NORINCO WM-80 273-mm (10.75-in) multiple rocket system

Since the early 1970s the China North Industries Corporation (NORINCO) has developed numerous multiple rocket systems for the home and export markets. One of the more recent systems is the **NORINCO WM-80** 273-mm (10.75-in) MRS, which is based on a new 8x8 all-terrain chassis

with a forward control cab and, mounted at the rear, the turntable carrying the eight-round launcher. This is aimed and fired with the crew inside the cab, which contains all of the fire-control and associated laying equipment. In addition to being launched from within the cab, the rockets can be launched by

remote control. When the rockets are about to be launched, shutters are closed over the cab windows to prevent them being

SPECIFICATION	
NORINCO WM-80	**Powerplant:** one air-cooled diesel developing 390 kW (523 hp)
Calibre: 273 mm (10.75 in)	**Performance:** max. speed 70 km/h (43.5 mph); range 400 km (249 miles)
Crew: 5	
Weight: 34000 kg (74,956 lb)	**Fording:** 1 m (3 ft 3 in)
Dimensions:	**Gradient:** 35 per cent

damaged from the blast. The launcher can be traversed 20° left and right with elevation limits from +20° to +60°.

The system takes between three and five minutes to come into action and once the solid-propellant rockets have been launched the vehicle normally shifts to another position, where its launcher is reloaded in five to eight minutes by the resupply vehicle, which is fitted with a hydraulic crane. To provide a more stable firing platform, four stabilisers are lowered to

This NORINCO WM-80 MRS is seen with its eight-round launcher partly elevated, but still trained to the front.

the ground by remote control before the rockets are launched.

The rockets have a launch weight of 505 kg (1,113 lb) and can be fitted with various types of conventional warhead, including cargo and 150-kg (331-lb) HE. The former carries some 380 anti-tank/anti-personnel submunitions that are dispensed over the target. The rockets can be fired one at a time or in salvoes depending on the type of target.

According to NORINCO, the system has a maximum range of more than 80 km (49.7 miles), with a minimum range of 34 km (21.1 miles).

The WM-80 launcher is normally marketed as a

complete system, a typical battery having six launchers, six resupply vehicles on a similar chassis, command post vehicle and associated logistics vehicles. These can be combined in battalion/regiment establishment together with forward observer vehicles.

In addition to NORINCO, the China Precision Machinery Import and Export Corporation (CPMIEC) is now involved in the development of MRSs. These include the 320-mm (12.6-in) four-round WS-1, 302-mm (11.89-in) four-round WS-1B and latest 300-mm (11.81-in) 10-round A100. The last is based on the Russian Spav BM 9A52 12-round Smerch system which was developed some years ago and built in significant quantities for the home and export markets.

The NORINCO WM-80 MRS launches one of its eight rockets. A small inbuilt motor is used to impart rotation and thus enhance both stability and accuracy.

The Chinese version has 10 rather than 12 rocket tubes, is based on a different 8x8 all-terrain chassis, and fires rockets with a maximum range of 100 km (62.1 miles).

Above: The NORINCO WM-80 MRS is seen in travelling configuration with the shutters open.

NORINCO Type 83 273-mm (10.75-in) multiple rocket system

NORINCO has developed a complete series of MRSs (multiple-rocket systems) including the **NORINCO Type 83** 273-mm (10.75-in) four-round system based on the Type 59 series fully tracked carrier used by the Chinese army for a wide range of missions. These include towing field and anti-aircraft guns as well carrying troops and cargo. The chassis has been modified for this more

specialised role and armoured shutters can be lowered over the two-part windscreen to prevent blast damage when the rockets are launched. The standard Type 59 can be fitted

This is the NORINCO Type 83 rocket launcher deployed in the firing position and with its four rocket pack of launcher tubes in the elevated position.

SPECIFICATION	
NORINCO Type 83	**Powerplant:** one Model 12150L V-12
Calibre: 273 mm (10.75 in)	diesel developing 225 kW (302 hp)
Crew: 5	**Performance:** maximum road speed
Weight: 17542 kg (38,474 lb)	45 km/h (28 mph)
Dimensions: (travelling) length 6.19	**Fording:** 1 m (3 ft 3 in)
m (20 ft 4 in); width 2.6 m (8 ft 6	**Gradient:** 60 per cent
in); height 3.18 m (10 ft 5 in)	

with a power-operated winch for self-recovery operations or the recovery of other vehicles.

The enclosed two-door cab is at the front, and at the very rear is a turntable on which is mounted a side-by-side bank of four tubes for the 273-mm rockets. Elevation is powered and there are also manual back-up controls. Traverse is 10° left and right, and elevation between +5° and +56°. The system takes one minute to prepare and launch its four

rockets. To avoid counter-battery fire, the Type 83 then moves to another position to be reloaded from a resupply vehicle.

The Type 83 MRS is an area-saturation rather than precision attack weapon as rockets tend to be less accurate than conventional tubed artillery. Tube artillery and MRSs are complementary, the former being able to engage targets at a much shorter range than the latter.

Typical roles for the Type

83 include destroying troop concentrations, artillery batteries, command posts, air-defence systems and other high-value targets. The unguided rockets have launch and maximum velocities of 30 and 810 m (98 and 3,657 ft) per second respectively for a maximum range of 40 km (24.85 miles). All the rockets are launched in just a matter of four seconds. The HE warhead is believed to be activated either by an impact or possibly by a proximity fuse.

It is possible that other warheads may well have been developed to provide greater operational flexibility.

As far as is known, the Type 83 MRS was not exported and is no longer marketed. NORINCO now places its main export thrust on other MRSs such as the more recent WM-80 whose advantages include enhanced strategic mobility as it is mounted on an 8x8 wheeled chassis, and fires rockets of greater range and effectiveness.

NORINCO 130-mm (5.12-in) multiple rocket systems

NORINCO's complete family of unguided surface-to-surface 130-mm (5.12-in) MRSs (multiple rocket systems) includes types on tracked and wheeled chassis.

The first-generation MRSs were the **Type 63** and **Type 70** 19-round systems. The Type 63 was based on an unarmoured 4x4 truck chassis while the Type 70 was based on the YW 531 fully tracked APC used in large numbers by the Chinese army. Both systems are fitted with a turntable- mounted launcher carrying 19 rocket tubes in two layers. The launcher can fire a complete family of unguided rockets fitted with various types of warhead. These include HE, HE fragmentation and HE incendiary, all with a maximum range of just over 10 km (6.2 miles). There is also an extended -range HE rocket with a maximum range of 15 km (9.3 miles).

These two systems were replaced in production by the

Type 82 and **Type 85** 30-round systems firing the same rockets to the same ranges. These are similar in concept to the earlier systems but have more modern chassis and a new launcher with its 30 tubes disposed in three layers. The Type 82 is mounted on a 6x6 forward control chassis and has greater cross- country mobility than the earlier 4x4 model. In addition, it has sufficient space for the crew and

Above: Being based on the Type 65 tracked APC with armour providing protection against small arms fire and shell fragments, the Type 85 MRS is well suited to the battlefield role. The Type 70 was based on the older YW 531 APC.

a complete reload of 30 rockets.

The Type 85 is based on the more recent Type 85 fully tracked APC developed for a wide range of specialised roles. It is fully amphibious, being propelled in the water by its tracks at 6 km/h (3.7 mph).

In addition to these tracked and wheeled self-propelled MRSs there is also a special

single-round version which was designed for use by light forces or guerrilla units. This weighs about 25 kg (55 lb) without a rocket.

In recent years NORINCO has concentrated its export marketing on a variety of 122-mm (4.8-in) MRSs firing the same rockets as their Russian counterparts.

Turning the scales at 14000 kg (30,864 lb) with all of its 19 launcher tubes loaded, the Type 70 is based on the YW 531 tracked APC used by the Chinese army as the Type 63.

SPECIFICATION	
Type 82	**Type 85**
Calibre: 130 mm (5.12 in)	**Calibre:** 130 mm (5.12 in)
Crew: 7	**Crew:** 6
Weight: 9100 kg (20,062 lb)	**Weight:** 14500 kg (31,966 lb)
Dimensions: length 6.5 m (21 ft 4 in); width 2.25 m (7 ft 4.5 in); height 2.52 m (8 ft 3 in)	**Dimensions:** 6.13 m (20 ft 1.33 in); width 3.06 m (10 ft); height 3.02 m (9 ft 11 in)
Powerplant: one diesel	**Powerplant:** one diesel
Performance: maximum road speed 80 km/h (50 mph)	**Performance:** maximum road speed 60 km/h (37 mph)
Fording: 0.85 m (2 ft 9 in)	**Fording:** amphibious
Gradient: 60 per cent	**Gradient:** 60 per cent

BM-21 (Polish upgrade) 122-mm (4.8-in) multiple rocket system

The Russian Splav BM-21 122-mm (4.8-in) 40-round MRS is the most widely used MRS in the world, and is currently in front-line service with more than 50 countries. It has been manufactured or copied by many countries, and has seen widespread combat use in Africa, Middle East and Asia.

Although the basic design of the BM-21 was created in the mid-1950s, it is still a highly effective system and many countries intend to keep it in service well into the 21st century. Its main drawback is considered to be its rocket's modest range.

Poland, once a member of the Warsaw pact but now a member of NATO, has operated the BM-21 for many years, and is now engaged in a major upgrade to extend the system's life by another 20 years. The **BM-21**

(Polish upgrade) is extensive. The 40-round launcher has been removed from its Russian Ural-375D series 6x6 chassis and installed on a new locally manufactured Star 1466 6x6 truck, for which logistic support is much easier. This chassis has a new four-door cab (with seats for up to six people) that can be tilted forward to provide access to the powerpack for routine maintenance purposes. The cab has also been designed with provision for applique armour to provide protection from small arms fire and shell splinters.

Improved mobility

For improved cross-country mobility the chassis is fitted with a central tyre pressure-regulation system that allows the driver to adjust the tyre pressure to suit the terrain being crossed.

When crossing sand, for example, the tyres can be deflated to increase the surface areas of the tyres in contact with the ground. When running on roads, the tyre pressure can be increased.

The launcher has powered elevation and traverse with manual back-up. For improved firing accuracy it is envisaged that production systems would be used in conjunction with the new Polish fire-control system, which will also be used with the Polish army's 122-mm 2S1 self-propelled howitzers, its new 155-mm (6.1-in) L/52 Krab self-propelled guns and its 98-mm (3.86-in) mortars.

The standard Russian 122-mm rockets had a maximum range of just over 20 km (12.4 miles), but a new family of rockets has been developed for the upgraded system by French and Polish industry. The rockets of this new generation enable targets to be engaged at extended ranges, and so reduce

The Polish upgrade of the BM-21 40-round MRS is based on a locally manufactured Star 1466 6x6 truck chassis and offers several improvements.

the threat of counter-battery fire. The baseline new-generation rocket is fitted with an HE warhead and has a maximum range of 41 km (25.5 miles). The other two rockets are cargo and anti-tank mine types, and each has a maximum range of 35 km (21.75 miles). The cargo rocket carries 42 locally developed and comparatively small HEAT (HE anti-tank) submunitions, while the other projectile carries five larger anti-tank mines.

SPECIFICATION	
BM-21 (Polish upgrade) **Calibre:** 122 mm (4.8 in) **Crew:** typically 3 **Weight:** 14000 kg (30,864 lb) **Dimensions:** length 7.4 m (24 ft 3 in); width 2.5 m (8 ft 2 in); height 3 m (9 ft 10 in)	**Powerplant:** one MAN 6-cylinder diesel developing 121 kW (162 hp) **Performance:** maximum road speed 85 km/h (53 mph); range 700 km (435 miles) **Fording:** 1.2 m (3 ft 11 in) **Gradient:** 60 per cent

Chinese 122-mm rocket launchers Types 81, 83, 89, and 90

The 122-mm (4.8-in) **Type 81** is the most widespread rocket launcher in the Chinese People's Liberation Army (PLA). The system is based on the Soviet-designed BM-21 multiple rocket launcher (MRL). At least 48 countries possess the BM-21 system, and at least 15 countries produce warheads for the rockets.

Typical warheads include high explosive (HE), HE/fragmentation, incendiary, and improved onventional munitions (ICM) sub-munitions. However, a wide variety of other warhead types are available worldwide. Diverse warhead types include smoke, illumination, anti-tank mines, anti-personnel mines, chemical, and radio frequency (RF) jammers.

The Chinese Type 83 rocket launcher is mounted towards the rear of a 6x6 cross-country vehicle chassis. The vehicle has an enlarged cab for the crew.

The Type 81 rocket system and its derivatives are common on several different tracked and wheeled PLA platforms. A common type of chassis is the Yanan SX250 6x6 truck. The system is also fitted aboard some naval ships. The launcher consists of four rows of 10 launch tubes and all 40 rockets can be launched in 20 seconds. A seven-man crew can reload the rockets in eight minutes.Although the 122-mm Type 81 is smaller in calibre than

the PLA's 130-mm (5.12-in) rockets, the warheads are equally effective and the rockets have increased range. The smaller calibre allows more rockets to be fired from PLA vehicles. However, the

rockets have a large circular error probability (CEP) and are best suited against area targets.

Area denial

The 122-mm **Type 83** MRL system is primarily used for

firing FASCAM area-denial rockets, but is also used for delivering conventional warheads. It uses a smaller 24-round rocket pack on a CA-30 type truck chassis. The vehicle is modified with a larger cab for the crew. The MRL takes up the entire cargo area except for a small space for the spare tyre and vehicle tools.

The **Type 89** MRL is a fully armoured version of the Type 81 wheeled MRL. The system is mounted on a Type 321 tracked utility chassis. The system performance is comparable to the Type 81, but its combat ability is enhanced by a computerised fire-control system. The vehicle is also fitted with an NBC protection system. The Type 89 can carry a total of 80 rockets. The 40-round launcher is mounted at the rear of the vehicle, with the reload pack in front of it. After launch, the five-man crew can reload the Type 89 in three minutes.

The 122-mm **Type 90** MRL is also based on the Type 81. The system has an enhanced fire-control system compared to the Type 81. The Type 90's 40-round launcher is mounted on a Tiema SC2030 6x6 flatbed truck. Similar to the Type 89 MRL, the launcher is at the rear of the vehicle, with the reload pack in front of it. The vehicle features a convertible canvas cover which conceals its cargo, and makes the Type 90 appear as a normal truck. The onboard fire-control computer can handle all the fire control and reloading.

A Type 90 rocket system fires a single projectile. The system is mounted on a Tiema SC2030 truck. Note the rolled-back canvas cover.

SPECIFICATION	
Type 81 rocket	**Weight:** 66.8 kg (147 lb)
Calibre: 122 mm (4.8 in)	**Range:** 20-30 km (12.4-18.6 miles)
Length: 2.87 m (9 ft 5 in)	**Warhead:** HE or enhanced frag

Chinese 107-mm rocket launchers Type 63 and Type 81

The 107-mm (4.21-in) **Type 63** and **Type 81** are two related multiple rocket launchers (MRLs) in service with the Chinese People's Liberation Army (PLA).

The Type 63 was developed in 1963. When new, each PLA infantry regiment had a Type 63 MRL company consisting of six units in its artillery battalion. The system was subsequently reduced in importance with the introduction of the PLA's 130-mm (5.12-in) MRL. The Type 63 MRL remains in service, but is now primarily found in light infantry, airborne, and mountain units. Due to its simplicity and low cost, the system has been widely exported, and can be found widely in Third World countries.

The Type 63 MRL is mounted on a split-pole trailer with rubber tyres. Almost any vehicle with a towing capability can transport the launcher. The **Type 63-I** variant is a packed model for airborne and mountain units. There is also a single launcher tube mounted on a man-portable tripod for use by special forces units.

The Type 63 MRL has 12 tubes arranged in three rows of four tubes each. All the tubes are mounted co-axially on a cradle. The ammunition for the Type 63 consists of a single-piece rocket, with the warhead attached to the rocket motor. A fixed amount of propellant is contained in the rocket motor. The rockets are stabilised by the canted exhaust nozzles, which impart a slow spin.

The Type 63's rocket is an electrically initiated projectile incorporating a high-explosive/ fragmentation (HE/frag) warhead. The spin-stabilised incendiary rocket variant is made of metal, and contains white phosphorous in its warhead. The 107-mm **Type 63-2** rocket is made of metal, weighs 18.8 kg (41 lb) and contains a main charge of TNT explosive weighing 1.3 kg (2.9 lb). These rockets are normally fired from a trailer- or truck-mounted multiple launcher, but may also be fired from single-tube launchers mounted on small vessels.

The loaded weight for the Type 63 MRL is 613 kg (1,351 lb). The rockets have a typical range of 8.5 km (5.3 miles), and all 12 rockets can be fired in nine seconds. A five-man crew usually operates the Type 63, and can reload the launcher in three minutes. The launcher is not accurate, and has a high circular error probability (CEP).

Mobile variant

The Type 81 MRL is a self-propelled version of the Type 63 mounted on a 4x4 truck chassis. The 4x4 truck can carry 12 rocket reloads, and has an enlarged cab to accommodate the four-man crew. The Type 81 system has an overall weight of 3454 kg (7,615 lb), and has a maximum road speed of 100 km/h (62 mph). The entire launcher can be removed from the chassis and placed on a trailer for transportation. When firing, the vehicle suspension is locked to enhance stability. The launcher unit can be fired from the cab, or from a remote position away from the rocket back-blast. The CEP for the Type 81 is similar to that of the Type 63.

The Type 63 multiple rocket launcher is seen here mounted on its usual split-pole trailer. This system replaced the earlier 102-mm (4.02-in) Type 50.

SPECIFICATION	
Type 63-2 rocket	**Range:** 8.5 km (5.3 miles)
Calibre: 107 mm (4.21 in)	**Warhead:** 1.3-kg (2.9-lb) TNT
Weight: 18.8 kg (41 lb)	

LOV RAK 24/128 and M96 Tajfun Multiple rocket launchers

The Croatian Lako Oklopno Vozilo (LOV) which translates as light armoured vehicle, forms the chassis of the **LOV RAK 24/128** self-propelled multiple rocket launcher (MRL). The LOV RAK 24/128 is in service with the Croatian military.

Torpedo of Croatia builds the LOV armoured personnel carrier (APC). Developed in 1992, the LOV was first seen in public in 1995. The base chassis for the LOV was the wheeled Torpedo HV 4x4 TK-130 T-7. An armoured body is built onto the chassis with welded steel plates. These plates afford the LOV APC protection from 5.56-mm (0.219-in) and 7.62-mm (0.3-in) rounds. The armour plating also protects against artillery shell fragments and anti-personnel mines.

The LOV driver sits in the front left of the vehicle, and is provided with small bulletproof windows. To the driver's right is the commander's position. The commander is equipped with a 360° periscope. The LOV troop compartment is at the rear, and soldiers can enter and leave through two rear doors, mid-body doors on each side of the vehicle, or through three roof hatches. There are also firing ports on each side of the troop compartment. The LOV APC has no amphibious capability.

In the LOV RAK 24/128 configuration, the primary mission is multiple rocket launch. Secondary support tasks can also be carried out if required. A multiple rocket launch turret replaces the troop compartment in the LOV RAK 24/128. The enclosed space in front of the turret accommodates the firing crew, fire-control equipment and 24 additional rocket rounds. The LOV RAK has a total of 24 rocket tubes, with 12 tubes located on each side of the turret mechanism. The turret can rotate

Mounted on a Tatra 8x8 cross-country truck chassis, the M96 Tajfun multiple rocket launcher (MRL) system includes 32 launch tubes for the 122-mm (4.8-in) rockets as well as a similar number of reloads.

through 360°, and has an elevation range between -5° and +45°.

The LOV RAK 24/128 is armed with the 128-mm (5.04-in) M91 rocket, which has a range of 8500 m (9,296 yards). The 128-mm M93 rocket can also be fired, and has a range of 13500 m (14,764 yards). Firing the rockets can be controlled from on board the vehicle or by a hand-held computer connected to the vehicle via a 50-m (55-yard) cable. This distance allows the operator to be situated well away from the rockets' back-blast. The LOV RAK has a maximum speed of 100 km/h (62 mph) and a maximum range of 700 km (435 miles).

M96 Tajfun

The **M96 Tajfun** (typhoon) is another Croatian multiple rocket launch vehicle, that fires 122-mm (4.8-in) rockets. The 23500-kg (51,808-lb) system is mounted on the Czech-built Tatra 813 8x8 heavy truck chassis. This is probably the finest cross-country vehicle of its type and thus affords the M96 Tajfun excellent mobility over rough ground. A fire-control computer controls the 32-round rocket launcher, and a land navigation computer featuring a global positioning system (GPS) receiver aids in this task. When preparing to fire, four stabilisers are lowered at the corners of the load area. The entire load area is taken up by the turntable-mounted MRL, an extra reload pack containing a full load of 32 rockets, and the associated fire-control computer.

Based on an existing APC chassis, the LOV RAK 24/128 MRL features a central tyre-pressure regulation system and offers armour protection.

LAROM Multiple launch rocket system

The **LAROM** is a multiple launch rocket system (MLRS) developed cooperatively by Aerostar SA of Bacau in Romania, Israel Military Industries (IMI), the Romanian Ministry of Defence, and Romtechnica RA. Aerostar SA is the launcher contractor that is responsible for producing and also upgrading the LAROM launchers.

The LAROM MLRS is an upgraded system based on the existing wheeled APRA-40 FMC multiple rocket launcher fire-unit, which can fire 40 122-mm (4.8-in) rockets. The APRA-40 is mounted on the Romanian-built DAC 665 truck chassis. Approximately 160 APRA-40 fire-units are currently in Romanian military service. The upgraded LAROM MLRS is

deployed and operated by a five-man crew of soldiers.

The LAROM MLRS is designed to be a dual-calibre rocket launcher. Substantial upgrades to the APRA-40's hydraulic, stabilisation and fire-control systems are embodied in the LAROM. The LAROM MLRS has added the capability of launching both the original 122-mm rockets and IMI's 160-mm (6.3-in) Light

Artillery Rocket (LAR) family of weapons. A future weapon for the LAROM is IMI's ACCULAR trajectory-corrected rocket.

LAROM upgrades

Aerostar SA can upgrade any APRA-40 MLRS system to LAROM configuration. The upgrades that result in the new LAROM system encompass various parameters. These include an assessment of the vehicle chassis and the artillery system to be upgraded, a reduction of overall system weight to compensate for the added weight of the upgraded LAROM launcher pod, and new variants of ammunition. Additionally, the launchers' hydraulic and electric systems receive modernisation, as do the command and fire-control systems through the use of tactical computers that allow for automatic data processing. The stabilisation system is also improved, increasing accuracy.

LAROM is fitted with 26 launch tubes in two tactical launch pod containers. The launcher can fire single shots, or automatically in partial or complete salvos at variable firing rates in four settings between 0.5 and 1.8 seconds.

A LAROM launcher can fire 40 Grad rockets in 20 seconds, or 26 LAR Mk IV rockets in 45 seconds. Each LAR disperses 104 bomblets in a 200-m (219-yard) diameter circular footprint. The LAR Mk IV has a range of 45 km (28 miles), and can have a cluster payload of IMI's dual-effect anti-personnel or anti-material bomblets. The LAR uses a composite solid-propellant motor and is fitted with wrap-around stabilising fins that deploy when the rocket leaves the launch tube. Superficially similar to the earlier LAR Mk II, the Mk IV uses a modified propellant to increase its range.

Fire control

The system's fire-control unit is operated either from the vehicle cabin or from a shelter via a 50-m (55-yard) control cable. The LAROM's tactical computer has an advanced man/machine interface that allows for quick actuation of aiming and sighting controls, as well as weapon actuation. The fire-control system also incorporates an advanced artillery command and control system (ACCS). This system supports all artillery units and types of ammunition.

During training or fire accuracy adjustment, practice LARs can be used. These rockets do not contain cluster sub-munitions, however they are fitted with a smoke charge for observers to identify impact points. This allows for realistic firing procedures. A training pod with identical weight and 13 inert rockets is also available. This pod has simulated electronics for all LAROM system operating modes. All the LAR pods are expendable launch pod containers (LPCs) which need minimal maintenance.

The LAROM rocket system is the product of a joint collaboration between Israel Military Industries and an assortment of Romanian defence companies.

IMI rocket systems MAR 290, LAR 160 and LAR 350

In the mid-1960s the Rocket Systems Division of Israel Military Industries (IMI) started development work on unguided surface-to-surface artillery rocket systems. The first such system to be developed was a 290-mm (11.41-in) weapon that was designated **MAR-290** and was mounted on an obsolete Sherman medium tank chassis. This system had four rockets in the ready-to-launch position with the rockets capable of achieving a maximum range of 25 km (15.5miles).

Since the introduction of the MAR-290 a number of additional systems have been developed with emphasis being placed on systems for the export market. The two principal systems are the **Light Artillery Rocket 160** (also known as the **LAR 160**) and the larger-calibre **Medium Artillery Rocket 350** (or **LAR 350**). The LAR 160 consists of pods of factory-sealed rockets that contain a total of 13 or 18 rockets. These pods are mounted on a power-operated turntable that can be fitted to a wide range of chassis. Argentina, for example, uses a modified TAM tank chassis. This can carry two pods of 18 160-mm (6.29-in) LAR 160 rockets or one rack of four 350-mm (13.78-in) LAR 350 rockets. Once expended, new pods of rockets are loaded from

New 18-round pods of LAR 160 rockets are loaded onto an AMX-13 series fully tracked chassis. The LAR series of rocket launchers, available in 160-mm and 350-mm calibre, can be mounted on a wide range of armoured vehicles with minor modification.

These Israeli LAR 160 rockets are mounted on a modified Argentine TAM tank chassis. The rocket can carry a variety of different warheads and the pods are pre-sealed by the manufacturer to enable rapid replacement after a full salvo has been expended.

a 6x6 supply truck fitted with a crane. There is also a trailer-based version which is normally towed by a truck.

The first 160-mm rocket was the **Mk I** which had a minimum range of 12 km (7.5 miles) and a

Left: A pod of 18 160-mm **LAR 160** rockets is seen being loaded onto a **TAM**-based launcher chassis in service with the Argentine army. Reloading of the rocket pods requires a truck equipped with a crane.

Below: As well as tracked and armoured vehicle applications, the Israeli **LAR** series of rockets can be mounted on flat-bed trucks and towed trailers. Here a trailer version of the **LAR 160** launches a 160-mm rocket.

maximum range of 30 km (18.6 miles). The latest **Mk IV** rocket uses a new propellant to give a minimum range of 12 km (7.5 miles) and a maximum range of 45 km (27.9 miles).

The rockets can be fitted with various types of warhead such as high explosive, or carrier-type with anti-tank bomblets fitted with a self-destruct fuze. These have a HEAT warhead to attack the vulnerable upper surfaces of armoured fighting vehicles.

The larger-calibre 350-mm rocket has a minimum range of 30 km (18.6 miles) and a maximum range of 100 km (62.1 miles) with all four rockets being launched within 30 seconds.

SPECIFICATION	
LAR 160 on TAM chassis	height 3.05 m (10 ft 0 in)
Crew: 3	**Performance:** maximum road speed
Weight: 33700 kg (74,295 lb)	75 km/h (46 mph); road range 590
Powerplant: one MTU V-6 diesel	km (366 miles)
developing 537 kW (720 hp)	**Fording:** 1.5 m (4 ft 11 in)
Dimensions: length 6.75 m (22 ft	
1 in); width 3.12 m (10 ft 2 in);	

Egyptian multiple rocket launchers SAKR-18/-30 and VAP

The Egyptian arms industry produced copies of the Soviet 132-mm (5.2-in) rocket for the army's elderly BM-13-16 Soviet systems and 122-mm (4.8-in) rockets for its BM-21 systems. It also reverse-engineered the latter to produce a new 30-round launcher mounted on a Japanese 2500-kg (5,512-lb) Isuzu 6x6 truck chassis, as well as the more usual 40-round

version on a Soviet 3500-kg (7,716-lb) ZIL truck. The former is similar in appearance to the North Korean BM-11 variant of the BM-21, which is mounted on the same chassis.

In addition to the reverse-engineered models, two indigenous systems were also designed and built for the Egyptian army. These are the 122-mm calibre **SAKR-18** and

the 122-mm calibre **SAKR-30** MRLs. The former has a range of 18 km (11.2 miles) and has been built in 21-round, 30-round and 40-round versions mounted on lorry chassis types. It utilises a 3.25-m (10.66-ft) long, 67-kg (141.7-lb) weight rocket fitted with a 21-kg (46.3-lb) sub-munition warhead containing either 28 anti-personnel or 21 anti-tank bomblets.

The SAKR-30 has a range of 30 km (18.6 miles) and fires three types of rocket which vary in length from 2.5 m (8.2 ft) to 3.16 m (10.37 ft). The longest weighs 63 kg (138 lb) and carries a 24.5-kg (54-lb) warhead which delivers five anti-tank mines. The medium-length round measures

3.1 m (10.17 ft) in length, weighs 61.5 kg (135.6 lb) and carries a sub-munition-dispensing 23-kg (50.7-lb) warhead with either 28 anti-tank or 35 anti-personnel bomblets as its payload. The anti-tank bomblet is the same as that used in the SAKR-18, and can pierce over 80 mm (3.15 in) of armour, while the anti-personnel bomblets of both systems are lethal to a radius of 15 m (49.2 ft) from the point of detonation. The smallest round weighs 56.5 kg (124.6 lb) and has a basic 17.5-kg (38.6-lb) HE-fragmentation warhead. The increased range over the BM-21 and SAKR-18 systems was achieved by using an improved lightweight rocket motor and

An Egyptian army 80-mm (3.15-in) rocket launcher system mounted on a **VAP-80** light vehicle with the 12-round launcher elevated to the firing position. The 12-kg (26.5-lb) rocket has a range of 8 km (5 miles).

case coupled with a new composite-bonded stargrain propellant instead of the standard Soviet double-base grained propellant used in the shorter-range systems.

Lightweight rocket

For infantry and anti-guerrilla use, the 12-round 80-mm (3.15-in) **VAP** light vehicle-mounted MRL was produced. This is mounted on a pedestal which is fitted in the rear of a 4x4 Jeep-type vehicle and is fired by remote control. The 1.49-m (4.92-ft) long 12-kg (26.5-lb) fin-stabilised rocket

The Egyptians have made use of locally-made 12-round rocket launchers on the rear of Walid 4x4 APCs to fire 80-mm (3.15-in) D-3000 smoke screen rockets to hide major troop and armour attacks.

can be fitted with either an HE-fragmentation or an illuminating warhead. The maximum range is 8 km (5 miles).

Smoke screen

There is also a specialised system for laying down smoke screens. This has been seen either as a 12-round rectangular frame launcher in the rear of a Walid 4x4 wheeled APC or as quadruple box-like launchers mounted on each side of a T-62 main battle tank turret.

The rocket fired in both cases is the 80-mm (3.15-in) calibre 1.51-m (4.95-ft) long **D-3000** which can form a smoke screen that lasts up to 15 minutes. A full 12-round salvo from a Walid can form a 1000-m (3,281-ft) long smoke screen.

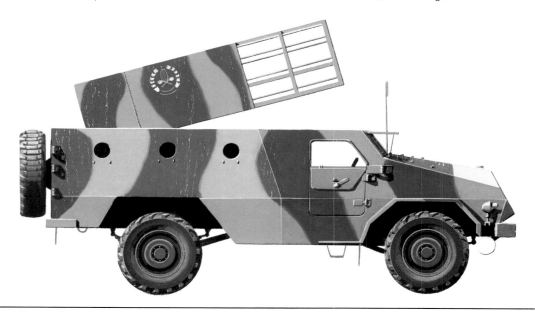

Type 75 130-mm multiple rocket system

To supplement its towed and self-propelled artillery systems the Japanese Ground Self Defence Force (JGSDF) awarded a joint contract for the development of a 130-mm (5.1-in) self-propelled rocket system.

The Komatsu company was responsible for the chassis as it had considerable experience in the development of fully tracked vehicles. Development of the unguided surface-to-surface rocket was entrusted to the Aerospace Division of the Nissan Motor Company that is today known as the IHI AeroSpace Company.

The first prototypes were completed in 1973 and following extensive trials it was type-classified as the **Type 75** multiple rocket system. A total of 66 production systems was built.

In recent years this system has been supplemented by the US 227-mm (8.94-in) 12-round Multiple Launch Rocket System (MLRS). The systems integrator for this system in Japan is IHI AeroSpace. The MLRS has a much longer range than the Type

The Type 75 multiple rocket launcher is seen with its 30-round launcher in the elevated position for firing. Noteworthy is the 12.7-mm (0.5-in) Browning machine gun mounted seen directly below the front of the launcher installation.

75 and is also more accurate. The Type 75 multiple rocket launcher is based on a fully tracked armoured chassis that uses some components from the Type 73 tracked armoured personnel carrier. The fully enclosed crew compartment is at the front and mounted above this is a 12.7-mm (0.5-in) M2 machine gun for self-defence purposes.

Mounted towards the rear of the hull is a power-operated turntable on which is located the launcher which contains a total of 30 rockets that have an actual diameter of 131.5 mm (5.17 in). The rockets have a solid-propellant motor which gives a maximum range of 14500 m (15,857 yards) which is rather short by modern standards. The rockets can be launched one at a time or a full salvo in 12 seconds.

The vehicle is fitted with night-driving aids but is not amphibious as this was not a requirement of the JGSDF.

To provide higher accuracy, the 130-mm Type 75 multiple rocket launcher is normally used in conjunction with a Type 75 self-propelled wind-measuring unit. This is based on the Mitsubishi Type 73 APC and has a mast which is extended to enable accurate wind measurements.

SPECIFICATION	
Type 75	in); width 2.8 m (9 ft 1 in); height
Crew: 3	2.7 m (8 ft 10 in)
Weight: 16500 kg (36,376 lb)	**Performance:** maximum road speed
Powerplant: one 537-kW (720-hp)	50 km/h (31mph); road range 300
Mitsubishi V4 water-cooled diesel	km (186 miles)
Dimensions: length 5.78 m (18 ft 11	**Fording:** 1 m (3 ft 2 in)

BM-21 Grad Multiple-launch rocket system

Above: The BM-21 was the standard MLRS used by Warsaw Pact countries. Production exceeded 2,000 units, and several countries, including China, Croatia, Egypt, India, Iran, Iraq, North Korea, Pakistan, Slovakia and Romania, have copied the system.

With its good cross-country mobility and rugged reliability, the BM-21 is ideally suited to operations such as Afghanistan, where its high-trajectory fire allows the rockets to penetrate deep valleys.

As prime contractor for all Soviet and Russian multiple-launch rocket systems (MRLSs), the Splav Scientici Production Concern (now the Splav State Unitary Enterprise) designed the **BM-21 Grad** (hail) MLRS as a divisional-level *reaktivaya sistema zalpovogo ognya* (salvo fire rocket system) in the mid-1950s. Develop-ment was completed in 1958, and the weapon entered service in 1963. Each division's artillery component has a battalion of BM-21 equipments, its peacetime establishment of 12 systems increasing to 18 in time of war. The system is also found at army and front

(army group) levels, where the unit is the regiment of three battalions each with 12 (18 in war) systems.

Principal roles

The primary divisional-level task of the BM-21 is support fire for the suppression of anti-tank missile, mortar and artillery positions, destruction of strongpoints and elimination of any centres of resistance.

The BM-21 is based on the Ural-375D or, in its latest **BM-21-1 Grad** form, Ural-4360 6x6 truck with the launcher (four 10-tube

Top: Reloading of the BM-21 takes seven minutes as the rockets have to be slipped into the 40 tubes manually.

Above: The multiple-launch rocket system first found favour with the USSR, which devoted much of its land warfare design capability to the development of weapons such as the BM-21.

Right: In northern Lebanon, a BM-21 of the Tawheed Islami is readied for movement as Syrian troops collect heavy arms belonging to leftist militias and Muslim fundamentalists after bloody fighting.

banks) over the two rear axles in a position allowing 180° traverse (60° left and 120° right) and 55° elevation (0° to +55°). The vehicle is stabilised in firing position by the lowering of two stabilisers, and the rockets are fired individually or in rippled or full salvoes from a firing position in the cab or at the end of a 60-m (65-yard) cable. The discharge of 40 rockets takes 20 seconds, the launcher being reloaded in 7 minutes.

Each BM-21 comprises one BM-21 MLRS and one 9F37 resupply vehicle to bring up the required numbers of the M-21-OF rocket, which has the manufacturing designation 9M22U. The basic rocket is roll-stabilised in flight by four

Based on a truck with 6x6 drive and a useful ground clearance figure, the BM-21 is admirably suited to European and Middle Eastern conditions.

spring-out tail fins, and has a diameter of 122 mm (4.8 in) and a length of 3.226 m (10 ft 7 in). The complete round weighs 77.5 kg (170.9 lb) and can carry HE fragmentation, smoke, incendiary and chemical warheads: the first and last weigh 19.4 and 19.3 kg (42.77 and 42.55 lb) respectively. At a burn-out velocity of 690 m (2,264 ft) per second the rocket attains a maximum range of 20380 m (22,290 yards). Other rockets include the

66-kg (145.5-lb) 9M22M that is 2.87 m (9 ft 5 in) long and carries an 18.4-kg (40.56-lb) HE fragmentation warhead to 20000 m (21,875 yards), and the 48.5-kg (106.9-lb) 9M28 that is 1.905 m (6 ft 3 in) long and carries the standard warhead types to 10800 m (11,810 yards).

In 1976 the Soviets introduced the 36-tube **BM-21 Grad-1** based on the MT-LB tracked chassis, for the six-launcher MLRS batteries of some tank and motorised rifle regiments. The system uses an updated rocket with a warhead of the HE fragmentation (pre-formed) or incendiary types.

The 6000-kg (13,123-lb) **BM-21 Grad-V** is a lightweight system for parachute delivery, and comprises 12 tubes on the back of a GAZ-66B 4x4 truck. The rockets can be fired singly or in a rippled salvo, and reloading takes five minutes. The **BM-21-P** is a single-tube launcher. Some 54 countries have the BM-21 in active service, and the weapon is still the subject of constant improvement.

The BM-21 system's launcher unit can be elevated to 55° and traversed respectively 60° and 120° degrees to the left and right of the vehicle's centreline.

SPECIFICATION	
BM-21 **Type:** 40-tube multiple-launch rocket system **Crew:** 6 **Weight:** 13700 kg (30,203 lb) fully loaded **Chassis:** 4000-kg (8,818-lb) Ural-375D 6x6 truck **Dimensions:** (travelling) length 7.35 m (24 ft 1 in); width 2.69 m (8 ft 10 in); height 2.85 m (9 ft 4 in) **Powerplant:** one ZIL-375 water-cooled V-8 petrol engine developing 134 kW (180 hp)	coupled to a manual gearbox with five forward and one reverse gears **Performance:** maximum road speed 80 km/h (50 mph); maximum range 1000 km (621 miles) **Fording:** 1.5 m (4 ft 11 in) **Gradient:** 60 per cent **Vertical obstacle:** 0.65 m (2 ft 1.6 in) **Trench:** 0.875 m (2 ft 10.4 in) **Rocket:** 122-mm (4.8-in) type in different lengths with an option of several warheads including (9M218 rocket) 45 anti-tank submunitions

MLRS Multiple Launch Rocket System

The US Army has never been a great exponent of the multiple rocket-launcher concept. Only two such systems, adapted from air-launched weapons, have been fielded since World War II. Nevertheless, in 1976 the Army's Redstone Arsenal launched a feasibility study for a General Support Rocket System. It was considered that such a system would offer a low-cost weapon offering a high rate of fire, with the ability to be deployed effectively against troops, light equipment, air defence systems and command posts.

NATO launcher

Five initial submissions were whittled down to two before trials started in 1979, and in 1980 the **Vought Multiple Launch Rocket System** was declared the winner. By this time, the original simple concept had evolved into the considerably more advanced NATO **Multiple Launch Rocket System** or MLRS, which began to enter American service in 1982.

The MLRS is now produced by the Missiles and Fire

Control division of the Lockheed Martin Corporation.

More than 850 units have been fielded by the US Army, and as a NATO programme, the MLRS has also been exported to numerous NATO countries, including Denmark, France, Germany, Greece, Italy, the Netherlands, Norway, Turkey and the United Kingdom. Other export customers include

Bahrain, Israel, Japan and South Korea.

The Multiple Launch Rocket System is a highly mobile, automatic system that fires surface-to-surface rockets and missiles from the M270 platform. The firing unit is the **M270 Self-Propelled Launcher Loader**, which is based on the chassis of the M2/M3 Bradley fighting vehicle.

Based on the M2 Bradley Fighting Vehicle chassis, the M270 MLRS is well able to keep up with armoured and mechanised forces over the roughest of terrain.

Tracked chassis

The fully-tracked chassis carries on its rear a traversing and elevating launcher for 12 rockets in two six-round pods, which can be power-reloaded from a re-supply vehicle in 10 minutes. Missiles can be fired individually or in ripple-fired salvos of between two and 12 projectiles. The computerised fire-control system automatically realigns the launcher after each round. From inside the fully-armoured cab, the crew of three can fire all 12 MLRS rockets in under 60 seconds.

The MLRS family of munitions includes three rocket types, with an additional six variants in development.

The computerised fire-control system of the MLRS re-aligns the launcher in seconds, allowing all 12 M26 rockets to be salvoed accurately in under a minute.

The MLRS rocket is unguided, so it is not suitable for engaging precision targets at its maximum range of 32 km (20 miles). However, against dispersed targets it is lethal.

The basic **MLRS M26 Rocket**, used by all operators of the system, was developed in the early 1980s.

Submunitions

A free flight rocket with a range of 32 km (20 miles), each missile carries 644 M77 dual purpose bomblets, dispensed from the carrier round above the target. The bomblets are optimised for the destruction of personnel, as well as soft ground targets and light armoured vehicles. An anti-tank variant was also developed, carrying 28 German-developed anti-tank mines.

Developed in the early 1990s, the **Extended-Range Rocket M26A1/A2** carries a reduced load of 518 bomblets, but has a range of 45 km (28 miles). The **Reduced-Range Practice Rocket** was introduced to allow MLRS units to carry out live training at standard US Army artillery ranged. The rocket has a maximum range of

15 km (9 miles) and the warhead bay is ballasted with non-explosive material.

New rockets currently under development include the **Guided MLRS (XM30)**, an international cooperative program started in 1999 by the United States, the United Kingdom, Italy, France and Germany. GMLRS will have a global positioning system aided inertial guidance package integrated in the rocket body and small canard fins on the guided rocket nose to add manoeuverability. Maximum range is expected to be in excess of 60 km (37 miles), and accuracy will be measured in meters. **MSTAR** is a further programmme which

will incoporate Smart Loitering Munition technology into the next generation munition system.

Lockheed Martin is under contract to incorporate two new upgrades to the current MLRS system. The new **M270A1** launcher incorporates an Improved Fire Control System (IFCS) and an Improved Launcher Mechanical System (ILMS). The US Army began

converting the US MLRS fleet to M270A1 in 2002.

MLRS saw its debut in the 1991 Gulf War. More than 10,000 rockets and 32 ATACMS were fired in combat by the US and British Armies in Desert Storm, with devastating effect on exposed Iraqi troops. To those Iraqi survivors of such horrific attacks, MLRS strikes were known darkly as 'Steel Rain'.

A battery of MLRS launchers firing together can be devastating, delivering thousands of grenade-sized submunitions onto an area target simultaneously.

SPECIFICATION	
Lockheed Martin Multiple Launch Rocket System **Type:** self-propelled 9-in (227-mm) multiple-launch rocket system **Crew:** 3 crew, driver, gunner, section chief **Dimensions:** length overall 6.9 m (22 ft 7.7 in); width 2.9 m (9 ft 9 in), height 2.6 m (8 ft 7 in) **Weight:** 25191 kg (55,535 lb) **Powerplant:** turbo-diesel engine delivering 373 kW (500 hp)	**Performance:** Max road speed: 64 km/h (40 mph); road range 438 km (300 miles) **Weapons load:** two six-round 9-in (227-mm) rocket pods **Rate of fire:** 12 rockets in under 60 seconds **Time to reload:** under 10 minutes – (one-man loading possible) **Rocket range:** 32 km (20 miles) normal or 45 km (28 miles) extended

ATACMS Army Tactical Missile System

During the 1980s, the MLRS was adapted to become the platform for the **Army Tactical Missile System**, or **ATACMS**. It was designed to provide operational commanders with a long-range missile able to mount deep interdiction attacks far behind the front line. Much larger than the M26 rocket normally used by the MLRS, each ATACMS missile is packaged in a MLRS look-alike launch pod and is fired from the MLRS family of launchers.

Combat tested

The initial ATACMS was introduced in the late 1980s, and was combat-tested during Operation Desert Storm when 32 missiles were successfully fired. Each four-meter missile carries 950 M74 anti-personnel/anti-materiel submunitions, and can deliver them out to a range

*The **ATACMS** can be fired by the standard M270 launcher without alteration. One of the large missiles can take the place of six of the standard M26 227-mm (9-in) rocket projectiles.*

in excess of 160 km (99 miles). Over 1600 **Block I** missiles were produced and fielded before the improved **Block IA** missile was produced.

ATACMS Block IA missiles have an improved guidance package which incorporates Global Positioning System. It carries a reduced payload of 300 M74 submunitions, but in spite of a range increase to 300 km (186 miles), it is at least as lethal as the earlier missile thanks to its greater accuracy. The **ATACMS Block IA Unitary** is the same missile, but is armed with a single 500-lb (227-kg)

warhead. Lockheed Martin Missiles and Fire Control – Dallas is under contract to develop the 140-km (87-mile) range **ATACMS Block II Missile**, which carries 13 Brilliant Anti-Armor (BAT) submunitions. Key features of this ATACMS missile variant include a solid fuel rocket motor and a GPS/ inertial guidance unit.

Key to the effectiveness of the ATACMS is its ability to deliver hundreds of submunitions accurately.

The BAT submunitions developed by Northrop Grumman are unpowered gliders able to seek out targets independently, using acoustic and thermal sensors for target detection and terminal homing. The improved BAT P3I submunition will be able to seek out and destroy fast moving targets at very long range, providing a deep attack capability. An ATACMS Universal Dispenser is also under development. This is designed to allow differing size munitions to be fitted into the standard ATACMS Block II missile.

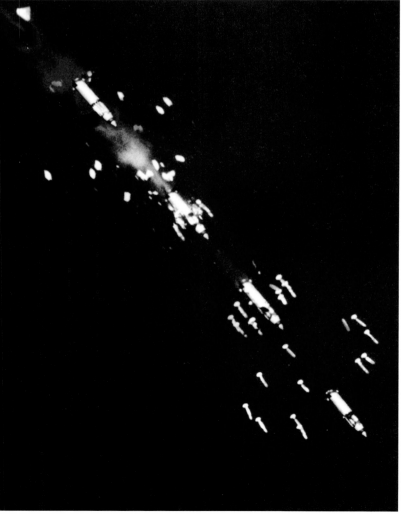

SPECIFICATION	
Army Tactical Missile System, ATACMS **Length:** approximately 4 m (13 ft) **Diameter:** approximately 61 cm (24 in) **Range:** more than 160 km/ 99 miles (ER variant more than 300 km/186 miles) **Propusion:** solid fuel rocket motor	**Guidance:** ATACMS ring laser gyroscope (Block I); inertial navigation with GPS (Block IA, II, IIA) **Warload:** anti-personnel/anti-materiel, precision anti-armour and other submunitions **Load:** two missiles per launcher – two pods with one missile each

HIMARS High-Mobility Artillery Rocket System

The **High Mobility Artillery Rocket System (HIMARS)** is the newest member of the MLRS family, offering MLRS firepower on a wheeled chassis. HIMARS carries a single six-pack of rockets or one Army Tactical Missile System (ATACMS) missile on the Army's new **FMTV** five-ton truck, compared to the two six-packs or missiles carried by the standard M270 tracked launcher.

The main benefit of HIMARS will be that it can launch the entire MLRS family of munitions, and is able to provide overwhelming fire-support for spearhead and light forces.

One handicap of the standard MLRS is its lack of strategic mobility; it is air portable, but the heavy tracked launchers can only be carried in Air Force C-5 and C-17 aircraft, which in a

major campaign will always be in short supply.

Because of its size, HIMARS is transportable, in the ubiquitous Lockheed Martin C-130 Hercules, allowing MLRS firepower to be moved rapidly into areas previously inaccessible. It also retains the self-loading and autonomous features that have made MLRS so successful.

Prototypes are currently in service with the XVIII Airborne Corps of the US Army, and, in 2000, the United States Marine Corps joined the HIMARS

The HIMARS launcher vehicle is based on a high-mobility five-ton truck, part of the US Army's new FMTV or Family of Medium Tactical Vehicles.

program. The Marine evaluation has the objective of fully incorporating HIMARS into the Corps. The first operational line units are expected to be in service by 2005.

Above: A dramatic (and dramatised) publicity shot of the launch of an ATACMS missile from the HIMARS platform shows that the wheeled launcher can fire all MLRS rounds.

RM-70 122-mm Artillery Rocket System

The RM-70 is seen here with its rocket launcher elevated and traversed. The Tatra vehicle is also available without an armoured cab.

The **RM-70** artillery rocket system dates from the early 1970s. It was designed and built in Czechoslovakia.

In 1985 an updated version was introduced and an ammunition upgrade package is now available. The system is supported by ZTS Dubnica nad Vahom of Slovakia who maintain the system on a production as required basis.

The main feature of the RM-70 is its rapid reload system. Once all 40 122-mm (4.8 in) fin stabilised rockets have been fired, the launcher barrels can be aligned with a magazine pack of a further 40 rockets that are then mechanically inserted into the empty barrels. The entire reloading process can take less than a minute, far shorter than employing the usual manual reloading methods and

Below: Despite being armoured, the outline of the cab betrays the Tatra 8x8 truck routes of the RM-70's carrying vehicle. Versions of the system are also available fitted with a dozer blade.

enabling the RM-70 to deliver two rapid, destructive salvos, each complete salvo lasting a total of between 18 to 22 seconds.

The RM-70 is carried on Tatra 8x8 trucks, originally a Tatra 813 with an armoured cab. After 1985 the improved Tatra 815 was introduced and the cab carrying the crew of four was left unarmoured. A dozer blade to clear obstacles is an optional add-on to both trucks.

The 122-mm rockets are essentially the same as those fired from the Soviet/Russian BM-21 Grad (Cherrystone) system, with a range of 20000 m (65,616 ft). By updating the rocket motors the latest versions of these rockets can extend the maximum range up to 36000 m (118,110 ft). Warhead can vary from high explosive fragmentation to enhanced warheads with pre-formed fragments. Cargo warheads can also scatter small anti-tank mines.

RM-70 systems were once used by East Germany. In 1994 150 of these were passed to Greece. Export sales were also made to Angola, Ecuador, Rwanda and Zimbabwe.

SPECIFICATION	
RM-70	**Warhead weight, each:** 18.4 kg (40.5 lb)
Crew: 4	**Max range:** 20000 m (65,616 ft) (36000 m/118,110 ft updated)
Rocket calibre: 122 mm	
Number of barrels: 40	**Dimensions:** length 8.8 m (28 ft)
Weight, complete system: 25300 kg (50, 705 lb)	width 2.55 m (8 ft 4.4 in)
Rocket weight, each: 66 kg (145 lb)	height 2.96 m (9 ft 8.5 in

Iraqi Artillery Rocket Systems

Prior to Operation Iraqi Freedom the Iraqi armed forces fielded a remarkable array of artillery rocket systems. They included imported systems such as licence-produced **Brazilian Avibras Astros** rockets of various calibres (the **Sajeel** series) and large numbers of 122-mm (4.8-in) **BM-21 Grad** systems from Egypt and the former Soviet Union. In addition to these, several systems were developed locally, some of them with technical assistance from elsewhere.

One of these was a 107-mm (4-in) 12-barrel system virtually identical to the **Chinese Norinco 107-mm Type 63** and was almost certainly produced using Chinese technical assistance. Most of these 107-mm launchers were towed while others had the launchers mounted on tracked armoured carriers. According to Iraqi sources the maximum range was 8000 m (26,246 ft) firing a 19 kg (41.8 lb) rocket.

Another locally copied system involves 122-mm rockets launched from various types of vehicle in salvos of up

to 30 rockets. The source appears to have been the Egyptian **Sakr-36** with a range of 20000 m (65,616 ft) using a 66 kg (145 lb) rocket. Again, some of these 122-mm systems were mounted on tracked armoured carriers.

Abadeel

At one stage the former Yugoslavia used Iraqi funds to co-develop a 262-mm (10.3-in) system known in Iraq as the **Ababeel 50**, the Yugoslav version being known as the **M-87 Orkan**.

The system involved 12 launcher barrels carried on a heavy track, each rocket having a weight of about 389 kg (850 lb) and a maximum range of 50000 m (164,041 ft). It appears that few of these systems were manufactured in Iraq and were used against Iran.

Frog

Another rather rare system was known as the **Ababeel 100** and appears to have been locally developed. This involved four truck-mounted launch tubes.

A long way from its cold Russian home: An Iraqi Frog-7 system is seen here following the end of Operation Desert Storm. Saddam Hussein's army used several foreign-artillery systems.

Few details are available although the range has been quoted as 100000 m (328,083 ft). Also available was the **Laith 90**, a 550-mm (21.6-in) calibre copy of the Soviet **Frog-7** series with a maximum range of 90000 m (295,275 ft). Several of these systems will have been destroyed during Operation Desert Storm and later during Operation Enduring Freedom.

SPECIFICATION	
Frog-7	**Warhead weight, each:** 550 kg (1212 lb)
Crew: 4	**Max range:** 70000 m (229,658 ft)
Weight, complete system: 25705 kg (56, 669 lb)	**Dimensions:** length 10.7 m (35 ft)
Rocket weight, each: 2300 kg (2 tons 590 lb)	width 2.8 m (9.3 ft)
Warhead: high explosive, chemical, nuclear-capable	height 3.5 m (11 ft 5 in)

Roketsan Artillery Rocket System

Formed in 1988, Roketsan of Turkey manufacture rocket and missile technology for the Turkish armed forces. Among other products, Roketsan build the launch and flight motors for Stinger missiles under licence from Raytheon in the United States. Roketsan includes the companies MKEK, Aselsan, Kalekalip, STFA, Kutlutas and TSKGV.

Grad

Roketsan also build two artillery rocket systems, both of them based on designs originally produced elsewhere. A 107-mm (4.2-in) towed system is based on a Chinese design: the 107-mm **Type 63** while a 122-mm (4.8in) truck-carried system is based on the Soviet/Russian 122-mm **Grad** (Cherrystone) system.

The Roketsan 107-mm towed system has 12 barrels and is known as the **T-107**. A complete salvo can be launched in from seven to nine seconds, each salvo delivering about 100 kg (220 lb) of explosive. The rockets involved are spin stabilised with warheads that can be either high explosive or with 2,800 steel balls packed around the explosive content to increase the lethal radius of each rocket to about 25 m (82 ft). The maximum range using standard rockets is 8500 m (27,887-ft), although an extended range rocket known as the **TR-107** can extend the range to 13000 m (42,650 ft).

The Roketsan 122-mm system is known as the **T-122** and is normally carried on a locally-produced MAN 6x6 tactical truck chassis.

Rapid-fire

Rockets are launched from two elevating and traversing arrays of barrels at the rear of the vehicle, each array containing 2.03 m

Roketsan rocket artillery system can be truck mounted on a MAN 6x6 chassis, although this 107-mm (4.2-in) system is based on a Chinese design and is seen here fitted onto a trailer.

(6 ft 6 in) long barrels. All 40 rockets can be fired within 80 seconds. A completely loaded system, with the truck, weighs 22200 kg (48,941 lb).

Balls of steel

The standard 122-mm rockets fired are essentially the same as those for the Russian Grad system, the maximum range being 20000 m (65,616 ft). Locally developed rockets can have warheads with up to 5,500 steel balls added to the explosive content. Also locally developed is the **TRB-122** rocket with a range of 40000 m (131,233 ft) and the **TRK-122** capable of scattering 56 bomblets over 30000 m (98,425 ft).

SPECIFICATION	
T-107	**T-122**
Rocket calibre: 107 mm (4.21-in)	**Rocket calibre:** 122 mm (4.8-in)
Number of barrels: 12	**Number of barrels:** 2 x 20
Weight, complete system: 620 kg (1,366 lb)	**Weight, complete system:** 22200 kg (48,941 lb)
Rocket weight, each: 19.5 kg (43 lb)	**Rocket weight, each:** 66.6 kg (146.8 lb)
Warhead weight, each: 8.4 kg (18.5 lb)	**Warhead weight, each:** 18.4 kg (40.5 lb)
Max range: 8500 m (27,887 ft)	**Max range:** 20000 m (65,616 ft)
Barrel length: 880 mm (34 in)	**Barrel length:** 3 m (9 ft 10.1 in)

Valkiri Mk II 127-mm multiple artillery rocket system

When South Africa invaded Angola in 1984 it deployed old British-supplied 25-pdr field guns and 5.5-in medium guns. These were outgunned by the Soviet artillery systems supplied to Angola that included 122-mm (4.8-in) D-30 towed howitzers and 122-mm BM-21 multiple rocket launchers (MRLs).

To counter these threats, South Africa started an extensive artillery programme that included the development of the 155-mm (6.1-in) G5/45 towed artillery system and the 127-mm (5-in) Valkiri Mk I MRL. The latter was developed by Somehem and used an unarmoured Mercedes-Benz Unimog 4x4 truck chassis that was operated in large numbers by the South African army. On the rear of this was mounted a 24-round launcher for 127-mm unguided surface-to-surface rockets. The rockets had a minimum range of 8000 m (8,749 yards) and a maximum range of 22000 m (24,059 yards).

The Valkiri Mk I system was subsequently replaced in front-line service by the much improved 127-mm 40-round **Valkiri Mk II** multiple artillery rocket system (MARS) which is also referred to as the **Bateleur**.

This offers a significant increase in firepower as well as having greater cross-country mobility as it is mounted on a 6x6 rather than a 4x4 chassis.

The Valkiri Mk II is mounted on a locally built SAMIL 100 chassis which is fitted with a fully armour-protected cab for its crew. Not only does this cab provide the occupants with protection from small-arms fire and shell splinters, but the lower half has a V-shape to provide protection against anti-tank mines which have been a major problem in southern Africa.

Mounted at the rear of the chassis, the powered launcher contains 40 unguided 127-mm rockets. The rockets can be supplied with various warhead

A Valkiri Mk II multiple artillery rocket system (MARS) launches a single 127-mm rocket. This system replaced the previous Valkiri Mk I in South African service.

types including a high-explosive pre-fragmented type activated by a proximity fuze for maximum destructive effect on the target.

The rockets can be fired in single rounds or in salvoes, with the complete load of 40 rockets being fired in 20 seconds. When deployed in the firing position, two hydraulically operated

stabilisers are lowered to the ground to provide a more stable firing platform.

The solid-propellant rockets used by the Valkiri Mk II have a minimum range of 8000 m

(8,860 yards) and a maximum range of 36000m (39,370 yards), which is much greater than that of the BM-21 40-round MRL which the South African army encountered in Angola.

SPECIFICATION	
Valkiri Mk II	**Performance:** maximum road speed over 90 km/h (56 mph); range 800 km (497 miles)
Crew: 3-4	
Dimensions: length 9.3 m (30 ft 6 in); width 2.35 m (7 ft 8.5 in); height 3.4 m (11 ft 2 in)	**Fording:** 1.2 m (3 ft 11 in)
	Gradient: 50 per cent
Weight: 21500 kg (47,399 lb)	**Vertical obstacle:** 0.5 m (1 ft 8 in)
Powerplant: one ADE V-10 diesel developing 234.9 kW (315 hp)	**Weapons load:** 40 127-mm (5-in) rockets

The Valkiri Mk II is based on an armour-protected SAMIL 100 6x6 cross-country truck chassis.

Teruel 140-mm multiple rocket launcher

For some years the Spanish army deployed a number of multiple rocket launchers (MRLs) including the locally developed D-10 (10-round) and E-21 (21-round) systems mounted on the rear of locally produced 6x6 cross-country truck chassis.

These older MRLs have since been replaced by the 140-mm (5.51-in) 40-round **Teruel** MRL built by Santa Barbara Sistemas (now owned by General Dynamics Land Systems of the US). Teruel was developed by the Spanish government-owned Council for Rocket Research and Development.

Teruel is based on a Spanish-built Pegaso 3055 6x6 cross-country truck chassis. This is used by the Spanish army in large quantities for a wide range of missions which range from towing 105-mm (4.13-in) and

The Teruel MRL deployed in the firing position. Covers are drawn up around the cab to protect the crew from rocket blast when firing.

155-mm (6.1-in) artillery systems to carrying cargo.

For the Teruel application the forward-control cab has been armoured to avoid damage to the cab or crew when the 140-mm rockets are launched. The front and side windows are protected by armour and there is also a roof hatch which can be fitted with a 7.62-mm (0.3-in) machine gun for local and air defence purposes.

To provide a more stable firing platform when the rockets are launched, four stabilisers are lowered to the ground by remote control. Two of these are to the rear of the front axle, with the other two at the very rear of the chassis.

The launcher has powered elevation from 0 to +55° and can be traversed through 240°. The unguided rockets have a minimum range of 6000 m (6,562 yards) and a maximum range of 28000 m (30,621 yards).

The rockets have been produced with various types of warhead including high-explosive/fragmentation and sub-munition. The sub-munition type has 42 anti-personnel bomblets or 28 larger bomblets with a HEAT warhead. The latter is designed to attack the vulnerable upper surfaces of tanks and other armoured

A rear view of the Teruel's 40-round rocket battery. Remote-controlled legs at the rear of the vehicle provide stability when the rockets are fired. In the future Spain may supplement or replace the Teruel with the MLRS, which offers both greater range and a wider variety of rocket types.

vehicles and according to the manufacturer will penetrate over 100 mm (3.9 in) of conventional armour plate. There are also special cargo rockets carrying anti-tank mines or smoke grenades.

Rapid resupply

Once the rockets have been launched the Teruel system will normally rapidly move to a resupply area where new rockets would be reloaded manually in about five minutes with a well-trained crew.

The first customer for the Teruel MRL was the Spanish army which took delivery of a total of 14 systems. The Teruel was also offered on the international export market, but as far as it is known the only export customer was Gabon, which took delivery of eight systems.

SPECIFICATION	
Teruel	**Performance:** maximum road
Crew: 3	80 km/h (50 mph); range 550 km
Dimensions: 7 m (22 ft 11.6 in);	(342 miles)
2.2 m (7 ft 2.6 in); 2.9 m (9 ft 6 in)	**Fording:** 1.1 m (3 ft 7 in)
Weight: 19000 kg (41,887 lb)	**Gradient:** 55 per cent
Powerplant: one Pegaso 6-cylinder	**Weapons load:** 40 140-mm (5.51-in)
diesel developing 149.1 kW (200	rockets
hp)	

RT 2000 and Kung Feng AMLRS and MRL series

Left: The RT 2000 AMLRS launches a projectile. Note the stabilising legs extended from the body of the HEMTT truck upon which the system is mounted.

Below: The Kung Feng IV multiple rocket launcher (MRL) is normally mounted on the roof of the M113 series of armoured personnel carrier.

To replace older multiple rocket launcher (MRL) systems that lacked mobility, range and firepower, the Missiles and Rocket Systems Research Division of the Taiwanese Chung-Shan Institute of Science and Technology developed the **RT 2000** artillery multiple launch rocket system (AMLRS).

Production

The RT 2000 was first revealed in 2000 and the system is in quantity production for the Republic of China (ROC) Army and has also been offered on the export market. The system has been developed not only to engage conventional land-based targets, but also to engage landing craft off-shore in the event of an invasion of Taiwan by the Chinese People's Liberation Army (PLA).

The latest RT 2000 AMLRS is installed on the US-supplied Oshkosh M977 Heavy Expanded Mobility Tactical Truck (HEMTT) which has been in service with the ROC Army for some years. The M977 has a high level of cross-country mobility, and for this application the chassis is fitted with four hydraulically operated stabilisers which are extended when deployed in the firing position. Mounted on the rear of the 8x8 HEMTT is the power-operated launcher which can be fitted with three different pods of rockets, each of which has a different calibre and range.

The smallest rocket is the MK 15, with the pod containing 20 rockets with a calibre of 117 mm (4.61 in) and a maximum range of 15000 m (16,404 yards). The MK 30 rocket pod contains nine rockets with a calibre of 180 mm (7.09 in) and a maximum range of 30000 m (32,808 yards). The MK 45 rocket pod contains six

230-mm (9.05-in) calibre rockets with a maximum range of 45000 m (49,213 yards).

Dual facility

These solid-propellant rockets can be fitted with two types of warhead, conventional high-explosive or carrying a large number of anti-personnel/anti-armour bomblets. When the rockets have been fired, new pods of rockets are loaded onto the launcher using an onboard crane mounted to the rear of the cab.

The new RT 2000 supplements older **Kung Feng** MRL systems which have been in service with the ROC for many years. The 126-mm (4.96-in) 40-round Kung Feng system has been deployed in a number of configurations.

The two-axle trailer system is the **Kung Feng III**, while the more widely deployed M113-based system is the **Kung Feng IV**. The solid-propellant rockets have a useful maximum tactical range of 10500 m (11,483 yards) and weigh 24.4 kg (53.8 lb) at the moment of launch. Some examples have also been installed on Taiwanese Marine Corps LVTP5 series armoured amphibious assault vehicles (AAVs). These were followed by the 117-mm (4.61-in) 45-round **Kung Feng VI** MRL based on a US-supplied 6x6 truck chassis. The rocket launcher is mounted at the rear and the rockets have a maximum range of 15000 m (16,404 yards) with the rockets weighing 42.64 kg (94 lb) at launch.

M-87 Orkan and M-77 Oganj 262-mm and 128-mm MRS

The former Yugoslavia has considerable experience in the design, development and production of towed and self-propelled multiple rocket systems (MRS).

In the 1980s Yugoslavia began development of the 262-mm (10.31-in) 12-round **M-87** MRS that has also been referred to as the **Orkan**. Iraq subsequently joined the programme and its version is the **Ababeel 50**, which is almost identical in appearance.

The M-87 Orkan system is based on a locally built FAP 3235 8x8 heavy truck chassis which is fitted with a two-door fully enclosed cab that can be tilted forwards to allow access to the powerpack for maintenance purposes. Mounted at the very rear of the chassis is the launcher that has powered elevation and traverse. To provide a more stable firing platform, hydraulic stabilisers are lowered to the ground before the rockets are launched.

The solid-propellant rocket motors give the rockets a maximum range of 50000 m (54,681 yards). The rockets can be delivered with various types of warhead including high explosive as well as a variety of

sub-munitions of the anti-tank and anti-personnel types.

Limited production
No details of quantities of M-87 Orkan systems produced have ever been released, but it is understood that the system was not produced in large numbers owing to the civil war in Yugoslavia in the 1990s.

In the 1970s Yugoslavia produced the 128-mm (5.04-in) 32-round **M-77 Oganj** MRS which is based on the locally produced FAP 2026 series 6x6

cross-country chassis. This has a two-door cab with a reload pack of 32 128-mm rockets in the centre and the 32-round rocket launcher at the rear.

When travelling, the launcher and its associated rocket resupply system can be rapidly covered by bows and a tarpaulin cover which make the launcher vehicle very difficult to distinguish from a standard truck. This feature was subsequently adopted by Yugoslavia for the larger 262-mm M-87 Orkan MRS.

The 128-mm rockets used within the M-77 Oganj system have a maximum range of 20600 m (22,528 yards) and all of the rockets can be fired in under 30 seconds from within the cab or by remote control. The rockets are fitted with a high-explosive/fragmentation

The 262-mm (10.31-in) M-87 Orkan multiple rocket system is seen in the firing position. Crewed by five troops, the system also features a roof-mounted machine gun for self-defence. Note the bows for the tarpaulin cover.

warhead. Once the full load of 32 rockets has been expended, the system can be rapidly reloaded using the pod of rockets located to the immediate rear of the cab.

Like the larger 262-mm M-87 Orkan system, the chassis of the 128-mm M-77 Oganj system is fitted with a central tyre-pressure regulation system. This allows the driver to adjust the truck's tyre pressure to suit the terrain being crossed.

Glossary

AA Anti-aircraft.

AFV Armoured fighting vehicle.

AP Armour piercing.

APCR Armoured piercing cored round, ammunition with a hard core (usually tungsten).

APDS Armoured piercing discarding sabot.

Battery Descriptive term for when a cartridge is in place and the gun is ready for firing.

Bolt The part of a firearm which usually contains the firing pin or striker and which closes the breech ready for firing.

Blowback Operating system in which the bolt is not locked to the breech, thus it is consequently pushed back by breech pressure on firing and cycles the gun.

Breech The closed end of the barrel (also used to measure its length.

Breech-block Another method of closing the breech which generally involves a substantial rectangular block rather than a cylindrical bolt.

Bullpup Term for when the receiver of a gun is actually set in the butt behind the trigger group, thus allowing for a full length barrel.

Carbine A shortened rifle for specific assault roles.

Calibre The inside diameter of the barrel (also used to measure its length).

Chamber The section at the end of the barrel which receives and seats the cartridge ready for firing.

Closed Bolt A mechanical system in which the bolt is closed up to the cartridge before the trigger is pulled. This allows greater stability through reducing the forward motion of parts on firing.

Compensator A muzzle attachment which controls the direction of gas expanding from the weapon and thus resists muzzle climb or swing during automatic fire.

Delayed Blowback A delay mechanically imposed on a blowback system to allow pressures in the breech to drop to safe levels before breech opening.

Double action Relates to pistols which can be fired both by cocking the hammer and then pulling the trigger, and by a single long pull on the trigger which performs both cocking and firing actions.

Effective Ceiling The highest altitide (of an approaching aircraft) to which a AA gun can fire for 30 seconds before it reaches maximum elevation.

Effective Range The furthest distance a weapon can be accurately aimed.

Elevation The amount a gun can be moved vertically.

Flash Suppressor A device that minimises the visible flash from the gun when fired.

Flechette An bolt-like projectile which is smaller than the gun's calibre and requires a sabot to fit it to the barrel. Achieves very high velocities.

Gas Operation Operating system in which a gun is cycled by gas being bled off from the barrel and used against a piston or the bolt to drive the bolt backwards and cycle the gun for the next round.

GPMG General Purpose Machine Gun.

HE High exlposive.

HESH High explosive shaped head, ammunition with a shaped charge warhead.

LMG Light Machine Gun.

Locking The various methods by which the bolt or breech block is locked behind the chamber ready for firing.

Long Recoil A method of recoil operation where the barrel and bolt recoil for a length greater than that of the entire cartridge, during which extraction and loading are performed.

MG Machine gun.

Muzzle The front, open end of the barrel

Muzzle Brake A muzzle attachment which diverts muzzle blast sideways and thus reduces overall recoil.

Open Bolt A mechanical system in which the bolt is kept at a distance from the cartridge before the trigger is pulled. This allows for better cooling of the weapon between shots.

PDW Personal Defence Weapon. A compact firearm, smaller than a regular assault rifle but more powerful than a pistol, intended as a defensive weapon for personnel whose duties do not normally include small arms combat.

Penetration (of armour) Given in the form AA/BBB/C, where AA is the thickness of armour penetrated in millimetres; BBB is the range at which it occurred; and C is the slope of the armour. Thus, 75/1000/30 degrees means that the shot penetrated 75mm (2.95-in) of armour at 1000 metres range, striking at an angle of 30 degrees to the target face.

Receiver The body of the weapon which contains the gun's main operating parts.

Recoil The rearward force generated by the explosive power of a projectile being fired.

Recoil Operated Operating system in which the gun is cycled by the recoil-propelled force of both barrel and bolt when the weapon is fired. Both components recoil together for a certain distance before the barrel stops and the bolt continues backwards to perform reloading and rechambering.

Rifled (barrel) A barrel with spiral grooves that make the shell spin, for greater accuracy.

Sabot A protective sleeve that fits round a (usually finned) shell fired from a smoothbore gun.

SAW Squad Automatic Weapon.

Self-loading Operating system in which one pull of the trigger allows the gun to fires and reload in a single action.

Shaped (charge) Explosive that is shaped or becomes shaped on impact in a way that gives it maximum destructive value when it burns.

Short Recoil A compressed version of recoil operation in which the barrel and bolt move back less than the length of the cartridge before the bolt detaches.

Shrapnel Ammunition that, when it explodes, spreads small pieces of hot metal in all directions, most effective against infantry.

Smoothbore A barrel that does not have rifled grooves.

Traverse The amount a barrel can be moved horizontally.

Index Page numbers in *italics* refer to illustrations